Fernand Braudel

CIVILIZATION AND CAPITALISM
15th-18th Century

VOLUME III

THE PERSPECTIVE
OF THE WORLD

Translation from the French
by Siân Reynolds

PERENNIAL LIBRARY

Harper & Row, Publishers
New York, Cambridge, Philadelphia, San Francisco
London, Mexico City, São Paulo, Singapore, Sydney

First PERENNIAL LIBRARY edition published 1986.

Library of Congress Cataloging in Publication Data

(Revised for volume 3)

Braudel, Fernand.
    Civilization and Capitalism, 15th–18th century.

    Translation of: Civilisation matérielle, économie et capitalisme: XVe–XVIIIe siècle.
    Vol. 1: Translation from the French revised by Siân Reynolds, v. 2–3: Translation from the French by Siân Reynolds.
    Vol. 2 has imprint: London : Collins.
    Includes bibliographical references and indexes.
    Contents: v. 1. The structures of everyday life : the limits of the possible—v. 2. The wheels of commerce—v. 3. The perspective of the world.
    1. Economic history.   2. Social history—Modern, 1500–   3. Civilization, Modern—History.   I. Title.
HC51.B67413   1982   909.08   81-47653
ISBN 0-06-014845-4 (v. 1)
ISBN 0-06-091294-4 (pbk.)
ISBN 0-06-015091-2 (v. 2)
ISBN 0-06-091295-2 (pbk.)
ISBN 0-06-015317-2 (v. 3)
ISBN 0-06-091296-0 (pbk.)

86   87   88   89   90   MPC   10   9   8   7   6   5   4   3   2   1

THE PERSPECTIVE OF THE WORLD

Books by Fernand Braudel

CIVILIZATION AND CAPITALISM, 15TH–18TH CENTURY
THE STRUCTURES OF EVERYDAY LIFE (VOLUME I)
THE WHEELS OF COMMERCE (VOLUME II)
THE PERSPECTIVE OF THE WORLD (VOLUME III)

THE MEDITERRANEAN AND THE MEDITERRANEAN
WORLD IN THE AGE OF PHILIP II (VOLUMES I AND II)

To Clemens Heller

Contents

BY WAY OF CONCLUSION:
PAST AND PRESENT

Maps and Graphs

Illustrations

Foreword

My third and last volume proceeds from a gamble and a presumption: together they have given it its direction. The gamble lies in the trust I have placed in drawing as widely as possible on history, which is now seen as unfolding in chronological order, with its different time-scales; I have in other words abandoned myself to the march of time, with its ups and downs and its own logic, thereby submitting to the ultimate test which will confirm or invalidate the research contained in the previous two volumes. And the gamble, as the reader will realize, incorporates a sizeable presumption – that is that history can offer itself both as explanation (one of the more convincing ones) and as a means of verification(the only kind indeed to be sought outside our abstract deductions, our *a priori* reasoning and even the traps that common sense is always laying for us). Perhaps it is an even greater presumption to try to present a valid outline of world history using data at once terribly incomplete and yet too abundant to be fully encompassed?

Such at any rate is the purpose of this volume. The reader will find in it plenty of descriptions, narratives, images, developments, regular patterns and breaks in those patterns – but from start to finish I have tried to refrain from the urge to describe everything, for the mere pleasure of drawing a picture, underlining a point or directing attention to a telling detail. I have simply tried to see things and to present them in such a way as to understand, that is to verify. But I have done so with some insistence, suspecting that only here, in the front line as it were of the endeavour, could my own research, and indeed the trade of historian itself, be justified.

Attempting to write the entire history of the world might nevertheless be thought sufficiently daunting an enterprise to discourage the most intrepid and even the most naive. It is like trying to chart a river with no banks, no source and no mouth – and even this comparison is inadequate, for history is not one river but several. Fortunately, historians are accustomed to facing its abundant flow. They simplify matters by dividing history into sectors (and call them political, economic, social and cultural history). Above all, they have learned from economists that time may be divided into different time-scales and thus made more manageable. One can look at the long or the very long-term; the various rates of medium-term change (which will be known in this book as the *conjuncture*); and the rapid movement of very short-term developments – the shortest usually being the easiest to detect. The means available then for simplifying and organizing the history of the world are by no means negligible. And we can distinguish a type of time experienced on a world scale: *world time*,[1] which is not however, and never can be the sum total of human history. This exceptional time-scale governs certain areas of the world and certain realities depending on period and place. Other areas and other realities will always escape it and lie outside it.

To illustrate what I mean, consider the great subcontinent of India: draw four lines – along the coast of Coromandel, the Malabar coast, from Surat to Delhi and from Delhi to the delta of the Ganges. You have now enclosed India in a quadrilateral.[2] Only the edges of this quadrilateral can really be said to have lived at the same pace as the outside world, keeping up with the trades and rhythms of the globe – and even then not without a measure of difficulty and time-lag. *World time* applied primarily to such axes of activity. Did it ever penetrate inside the quadrilateral? Here and there perhaps. But on the whole it was absent from this area. And what was true of India could be said of every populated area of the globe – even of the British Isles during the industrial revolution. There are always some areas world history does not reach, zones of silence and undisturbed ignorance. 'There are regions in our kingdom [of Naples], wrote the economist Antonio Genovesi (1712–69) 'compared to which the Samoyeds seem cultivated and civilized.'[3] At first sight then, our task looked overwhelming: now we have reduced the map of the world to manageable proportions, since it is scattered with innumerable blank spaces from which no sound comes at all – often the very regions, on the margin of official history, with which we were most concerned in the first volume of this book.

World time then might be said to concentrate above all on a kind of super-structure of world history: it represents a crowning achievement, created and supported by forces at work underneath it, although in turn its weight has an effect upon the base. Depending on place and time, this two-way exchange, from the bottom upwards and from the top down, has varied in importance. But even in advanced countries, socially and economically speaking, world time has never accounted for the whole of human existence.

*   *   *

In theory, this volume will give most prominence to one sector of history – the material and economic. My aim in this third and last volume is primarily to encompass the *economic* history of the world between the fifteenth and eighteenth centuries. This simplifies, or ought to simplify my task. There already exist dozens of excellent, general economic histories, some remarkable for their conciseness,[4] others for their extensive documentation. I have used, since their publication in 1928–9, the two volumes of Josef Kulischer's *Allgemeine Wirtschaftsgeschichte*,[5] still today the best of guides and the most reliable of reference works. I have made equal use of Werner Sombart's monumental *Der moderne Kapitalismus* (1928 edition), a fantastic combination of erudition and analysis. But all these general works are invariably confined to the European context. And I am convinced that history would benefit immeasurably from comparisons made on the only valid scale – that of the world. Novalis (1772–1801) wrote: 'All history must necessarily be world history'.[6] And it is indeed easier to make sense of the economic history of the world than of the economic history of Europe alone. But can it be described as simpler?

The problem is all the greater since economists over the last thirty years[7] (and historians since even earlier) have stopped thinking of economics as a self-contained discipline and of economic history as a neatly-defined territory which one could study in isolation from the outside world. Unanimity on this point is now quite clear. As Witold Kula puts it, 'the theory of the autonomous economy in advanced capitalism [and I would add in early capitalism too] is now regarded as no more than an academic convention'.[8] For José Gentil da Silva, 'in history, everything is connected; and economic activity in particular cannot be isolated either from the politics and values which surround it, or from the possibilities and constraints which situate it'.[9] To the question 'Is man in society fundamentally *homo economicus*?', W. W. Rostow gives an emphatic no.[10] G. Lukacs considered it ludicrous to think that the subject matter of economics 'could really be isolated from all the other social, ideological and political problems'.[11] All human actions, according to Raymond Firth, 'have an economic aspect, a social aspect and a cultural aspect' – and no doubt a political aspect as well.[12] For Joseph Schumpeter, economic history 'cannot be purely economic'[13] and for the ethnologist Jean Poirier, 'the economic phenomenon cannot be properly grasped by the economist unless he goes beyond the economy'.[14] One contemporary economist even argues that 'being cut off from the other social sciences ... is unacceptable in political economy'[15] – as Jean-Baptiste Say was already saying in 1828: 'Political economy, which appeared to concern only material goods, has turned out to embrace the social system as a whole; [it] is related to everything in society'.[16]

So the economic history of the world is the entire history of the world, but seen from a certain vantage-point – that of the economy. To choose this vantage-point and no other is of course to favour from the start a one-sided form of explanation (one that is therefore, I realize, dangerous and from which I am aware that it will be difficult entirely to escape). One cannot with impunity give precedence to the series of phenomena known as 'economic'. However carefully one seeks to control them, to keep them in order and above all to look beyond them, can one ever avoid an insidious form of 'economism' and the problem of historical materialism? We shall be walking over quicksands indeed.

So as is often the case, I have tried with what I hope are good arguments, to exorcise the difficulties that lie ahead along the route. But as we proceed, the difficulties will inexorably come crowding in again from the very start. After all, if there were no such difficulties, no one would ever take history seriously.

*   *   *

The reader will see in the following pages how I have tried to overcome these problems.

The first thing to do was to light the way ahead. So the first chapter – *Divisions of Space and Time* – is theoretical and seeks to locate the economy in time and space, alongside, beneath or above those other aspects of life with which it has to share such time and space: politics, culture and society.

The next five chapters are an attempt to master time – from now on my principal indeed my only adversary. Once more, I have favoured the *long-term*;[17] this means once more putting on seven-league boots and passing over certain short-term realities and episodes. In the following pages, the reader will find no biography of Jacques Coeur, no portrait of Jakob Fugger nor an *nth* explanation of Law's System. These are omissions, I admit – but how else could I logically limit the size of the book? That said, I have followed venerable and normal practice in dividing *world time* up into long periods which reflect above all the successive ages of Europe. Two chapters (Chapter Two on Venice, and Chapter Three on Amsterdam) are about *The City-Centred Economies of the European Past*. Chapter Four, *National Markets*, studies the blossoming of the national economies in the eighteenth centuries – particularly those of France and Britain. Chapter Five – *The World For and Against Europe* – makes a tour of the world in the Age of Enlightenment. Chapter Six, the last long chapter, *The Industrial Revolution and Growth*, looks at the great divide that created the world we are still living in today. And my conclusion is a final short chapter in itself.

I hope that the analyses of the preceding volume will be borne out by these different historical experiences observed at some length and at close quarters. Joseph Schumpeter, in the work which historians consider his masterpiece – the *History of Economic Analysis*, 1954 – said that there are three ways to approach economics:[18] by way of history, economic theory and statistics, but that if he were to have his time over again, he would be a historian. I should be happy if other social scientists could, like him, see history as an exceptional means of discovery and research. Is not the present after all in large measure the prisoner of a past that obstinately survives, and the past with its rules, its differences and its similarities, the indispensable key to any serious understanding of the present?*

---

* Notes to the text will be found on pp. 633–78.

Divisions of Space and Time
in Europe

AS ITS TITLE SUGGESTS, this chapter, which has a theoretical function, falls into two parts: it seeks first to divide up space, then to divide up time – the problem facing us being to define economic realities, and their concomitant social realities, according first to location and then to duration. The processes of definition, particularly the first, which is essential for the better comprehension of the second, will require some time. But both are, I believe, useful: they will both map out and justify the path to follow and will provide us with a convenient vocabulary. As in all serious debates, definition of terms is crucial.

Economies in space: the world-economies

Geographical space as a source of explanation affects all historical realities, all spatially-defined phenomena: states, societies, cultures and economies. Depending which of these 'sets'[1] we choose, the significance and role of space will be modified accordingly – though not unrecognizably so.

I should like first to single out the economies of the world. Then I shall try to define the area and influence of the other 'sets'. To begin by looking at the economy is not only appropriate to the plan of the book: of all the ways of apprehending space, the economic is the easiest to locate and the widest-ranging, as we shall see. And its significance is not confined to the material aspects of world time: all the other social realities, whether favourable to it or not, are concerned in the working of the economy, constantly intervening and being in turn influenced by it – to put it mildly.

World-economies

To open the discussion, I should elucidate two expressions which might lead to confusion: *the world economy* and *a world-economy*.

The world economy is an expression applied to the whole world. It corresponds, as Sismondi puts it, to 'the market of the universe',[2] to 'the human race, or that part of the human race which is engaged in trade, and which today in a sense makes up a single market'.[3]

A *world-economy* (an expression which I have used in the past as a particular meaning of the German term *Weltwirtschaft*)[4] only concerns a fragment of the world, an economically autonomous section of the planet able to provide for most of its own needs, a section to which its internal links and exchanges give a certain organic unity.[5]

I have in the past, for instance, studied the Mediterranean in the sixteenth century as a *Welttheater* or *Weltwirtschaft*[6] – a world-theatre or world-economy – meaning by this not merely the sea itself but the whole area stimulated by its trading activities, whether near its shores or far away. I have treated it in short as a world in itself. The Mediterranean region, although divided politically, culturally and indeed socially, can effectively be said to have had a certain economic unity, one imposed upon it from above on the initiative of the dominant cities of northern Italy, Venice foremost among them, but also Milan, Genoa and Florence.[7] This Mediterranean economy did not however represent the *whole* of the economic life of the sea and its surrounding regions. It was so to speak the highest plane of the economy, whose activity, more or less intensive depending on place, was to be found along all the coastlines and sometimes deep inland. Such activity ignored the frontiers of empires – whether the Spanish Empire completed by Charles V (1519-1555) or the Turkish Empire which had begun its expansion well before the capture of Constantinople (1453). It also ignored the well-marked and strongly-felt boundaries between the civilizations which divided up the Mediterranean: Greek civilization lying humiliated and in disarray under the increasingly heavy Turkish yoke; Muslim civilization centred on Istanbul; Christian civilization with its twin poles of Florence and Rome (the Renaissance and the Counter-Reformation). Islam and Christendom faced each other along the north–south divide between the Levant and the western Mediterranean, a line running from the shores of the Adriatic to Sicily and then on to the coast of present-day Tunisia. All the great battles between Christians and Infidels were fought on this line. But merchant vessels sailed across it every day.

For it was precisely a characteristic of this singular world-economy – that of the sixteenth-century Mediterranean – that it bestrode the political and cultural frontiers which each in its own way quartered and differentiated the Mediterranean world. So in 1500, Christian merchants would have been found in Syria, Egypt, Istanbul and North Africa; while Levantine, Turkish and Armenian merchants later reached the Adriatic. The economy, all-invading, mingling together currencies and commodities, tended to promote unity of a kind in a world where everything else seemed to be conspiring to create clearly-distinguished blocs. Even society in the Mediterranean can roughly be divided into two types: Christian society with a predominantly hereditary seigniorial system; and Muslim society where the system of livings predominated, that is life-holdings bestowed as rewards for men who distinguished themselves in battle. On the

Venice, the ancient centre of the fifteenth-century European world economy, was still, in the late seventeenth and early eighteenth century, a cosmopolitan city where easterners could feel at home. Luca Carlevaris, *La Piazzetta* (detail), Oxford, Ashmolean Museum.

death of the holder, the living or title reverted to the state and was reallocated.

In short, from studying a particular case, we may deduce that a world-economy is a sum of individualized areas, economic and non-economic, which it brings together; that it generally represents a very large surface area (in theory the largest coherent zone at a given period, in a given part of the globe); and that it usually goes beyond the boundaries of other great historical divisions.

There have always been world-economies

There have been world-economies if not always, at least for a very long time – just as there have been societies, civilizations, states and even empires. If we take

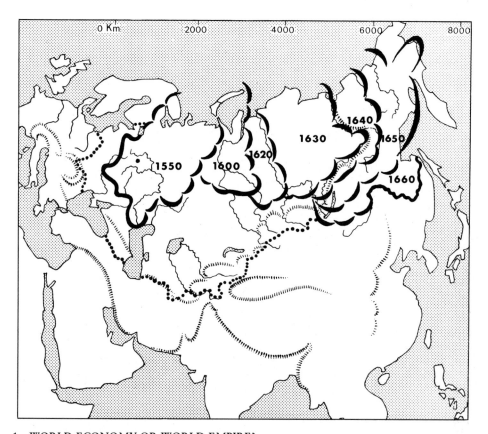

1 WORLD-ECONOMY OR WORLD-EMPIRE?
Russia expanded into Siberia in the space of a hundred years, taking over first the flood plains of western Siberia, then the plateau of central Siberia and the mountains of the east, where progress was difficult especially since she clashed with China in the south. Was this a world-economy or a world-empire – a question discussed by Immanuel Wallerstein? Let us concede to him that Siberia was conquered by force and that the economy – the supply side – merely followed. The dotted line shows the present day frontier of the USSR.

giant steps back through history, we could say of ancient Phœnicia that it was an early version of a world-economy, surrounded by great empires. So too was Carthage in its heyday; or the Hellenic world; or even Rome; so too was Islam after its lightning triumphs. In the ninth century, the Norman venture on the outer margins of western Europe laid down the lines of a short-lived and fragile world-economy which others would inherit. From the eleventh century, Europe began developing what was to be its first world-economy, afterwards succeeded by others down to the present day. Muscovy, connected to the East, India, China, Central Asia and Siberia, was another self-contained world-economy, at least until the eighteenth century. So was China, which from earliest times took over and harnessed to her own destiny such neighbouring areas as Korea, Japan, the East Indies, Vietnam, Yunan, Tibet and Mongolia – a garland of dependent countries. Even before this, India had turned the Indian Ocean into a sort of private sea, from the east coast of Africa to the islands of the East Indies.

Might it not in short be said that here was a process of constant renewal as each configuration gave way almost spontaneously to another, leaving plentiful traces behind – even in a case, at first sight unpromising, like the Roman Empire? The Roman economy did in fact extend beyond the imperial frontier running along the prosperous line between Rhine and Danube, or eastwards to the Red Sea and the Indian Ocean. According to Pliny the Elder, Rome had a deficit of 100 million sesterces in its trade with the Far East every year. And ancient Roman coins are still being dug up in India today.[8]

Some ground rules

The past offers us a series of examples of world-economies then – not very many but enough to make some comparisons possible. Moreover since each world-economy lasted a very long time, it changed and developed within its own boundaries, so that its successive ages and different states also suggest some comparisons. The data available is thus sufficiently plentiful to allow us to construct a *typology* of world-economies and at the very least to formulate a set of rules or tendencies[9] which will clarify and even define their relations with geographical space.

Our first concern, in seeking to explain any world-economy, is to identify the area it occupies. Its boundaries are usually easy to discover since they are slow to change. The zone it covers is effectively the first condition of its existence. There is no such thing as a world-economy without its own area, one that is significant in several respects:
– it has boundaries, and the line that defines it gives it an identity, just as coastlines do a sea;
– it invariably has a centre, with a city and an already-dominant type of *capitalism*, whatever form this takes. A profusion of such centres represents either immaturity or on the contrary some kind of decline or mutation. In the

face of pressures both internal and external, there may be shifts of the centre of gravity: cities with international destinies – *world-cities* – are in perpetual rivalry with one another and may take each other's place;

– it is marked by a hierarchy: the area is always a sum of individual economies, some poor, some modest, with a comparatively rich one in the centre. As a result, there are inequalities, differences of voltage which make possible the functioning of the whole. Hence that 'international division of labour', of which as P.M. Sweezy points out, Marx did not foresee that it 'might harden into a pattern of development and under-development which would split mankind into haves and have-nots on a scale far wider and deeper than the bourgeois-proletarian split in the advanced countries themselves'.[10] All the same, this is not in fact a 'new' division, but an ancient and no doubt an incurable divide, one that existed long before Marx's time.

So there are three sets of conditions, each with general implications.

Rule One: the boundaries change only slowly

The limits on one world-economy can be thought of as lying where those of another similar one begin: they mark a line, or rather a zone which it is only worth crossing, economically speaking, *in exceptional circumstances*. For the bulk of traffic in either direction, 'the loss in exchange would outweigh the gain'.[11] So *as a general rule*, the frontiers of a world-economy are quiet zones, the scene of little activity. They are like thick shells, hard to penetrate; they are often natural barriers, no-man's lands – or no-man's-seas. The Sahara, despite its caravans, would have been one such, separating Black Africa from White Africa. The Atlantic was another, an empty expanse to the south and west of Africa, and for long centuries a barrier compared to the Indian Ocean, which was from early days the scene of much trade, at least in the north. Equally formidable was the Pacific, which European explorers had only half-opened to traffic: Magellan's voyage only unlocked one way into the southern seas, not a gateway for return journeys. To get back to Europe, the expedition had to take the Portuguese route round the Cape of Good Hope. Even the first voyages of the Manila galleon in 1572 did not really overcome the awe-inspiring obstacle posed by the South Sea.

Equally daunting obstacles were the barriers between Christian Europe and the Turkish Balkans, between Russia and China, between Europe and Muscovy. In the seventeenth century, the eastern boundary of the European world-economy ran east of Poland, excluding all of Muscovy. The latter, to a European, represented the ends of the earth. A traveller to Persia[12] entering Russian territory at Smolensk in 1602, found Muscovy a 'great and vast' country, 'wild, deserted, marshy and covered in scrub' and forests, 'interspersed with swamps which one crosses by paths made of fallen tree-trunks' (he noted 'over 600 crossings of this type' between Smolensk and Moscow 'often in very poor condition'); a country like nowhere else on earth, empty ('one can go for twenty or thirty miles without coming across a single town or village'), with appalling roads, difficult even in summer, a country in short 'so resistant to access that it is impossible to enter or leave it discreetly, without permission or a safe-conduct from the Grand-Duke'. It was an impenetrable country, thought a Spanish traveller remembering a journey from Vilna to Moscow by Smolensk in about 1680: 'all Muscovy is one continuous forest' he says; there is no countryside except where it has been cleared with the axe.[13] Even in mid-eighteenth century, the traveller who went beyond Mittau, the capital of Courland (Kurland) could find no other shelter than 'flea-bitten hospices' kept by Jewish innkeepers, 'where one had to sleep in with the cows, pigs, hens, ducks and a nest of Israelites, where the odours all combined with the excessive heat of the stove'.[14]

It is worth taking the measure once again of these hostile expanses. For it was within the limits imposed by such difficulties that world-economies became established, grew, survived and developed. They had to overcome distance to prevail, and distance was forever taking its revenge, obliging them to redouble their efforts. Europe miraculously extended her frontiers at a stroke, or very nearly so, with the great discoveries at the end of the fifteenth century. But once this space had been opened up, it had to be controlled, whether the waters of the Atlantic or the wastes of America. Controlling the empty expanse of the Atlantic and the near-empty expanse of America was not easy. But neither was it easy to open a passage into another world-economy, to send out a high-tension cable as it were. How many conditions had to be fulfilled in order to keep the door open to trade in the Levant, for centuries on end, under the baleful gaze of two hostile camps! The triumph of the route round the Cape would have been unthinkable without this previous long-standing achievement. And even then how much effort, how many favourable conditions it demanded: the pioneer of the route, Portugal, literally wore herself out trying to operate it. And the victory of the camel-trains across the deserts of Islam was a similar exploit, one achieved by the slow creation of a network of oases and watering-places.

Rule Two: a dominant capitalist city always lies at the centre

A world-economy always has an urban centre of gravity, a city, as the logistic heart of its activity. News, merchandise, capital, credit, people, instructions, correspondence all flow into and out of the city. Its powerful merchants lay down the law, sometimes becoming extraordinarily wealthy.

At varying and respectful distances around the centre, will be found other towns, sometimes playing the role of associate or accomplice, but more usually resigned to their second-class role. Their activities are governed by those of the metropolis: they stand guard around it, direct the flow of business toward it, redistribute or pass on the goods it sends them, live off its credit or suffer its rule. Venice was never isolated; nor was Antwerp; nor, later, was Amsterdam. These

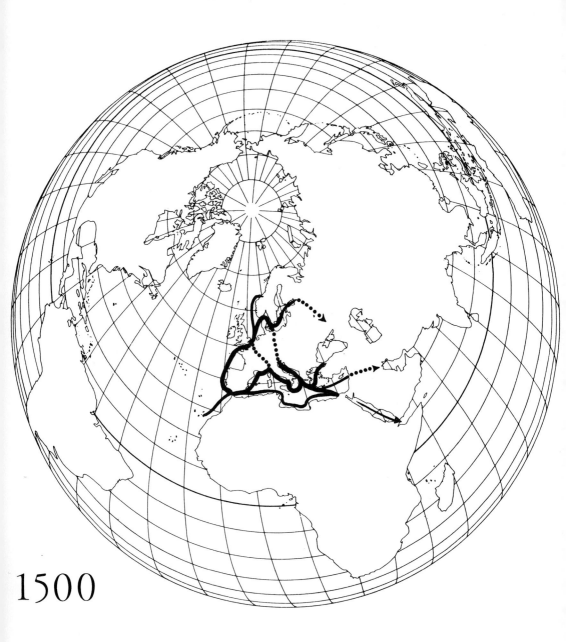

1500

2 and 3   EUROPEAN WORLD-ECONOMIES ON A GLOBAL SCALE
The expanding European economy, represented by its major commodity trades on a world scale.
In 1500, the world-economy with Venice at its centre was directly operating in the
Mediterranean (see Fig. 15 for the system of the *galere da mercato*) and western Europe; by way
of intermediaries, the network reached the Baltic, Norway and, through the Levant ports, the
Indian Ocean.

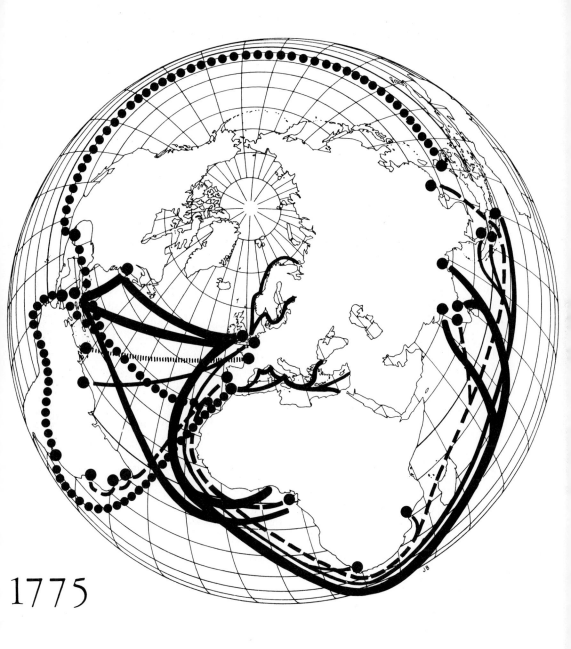

1775

In 1775, the octopus grip of European trade had extended to cover the whole world: this map shows English, Dutch, Spanish, Portuguese and French trade networks, identifiable by their point of origin. (The last-named must be imagined as operating in combination with other European trades in Africa and Asia.) The important point is the predominance of the British trade network which is difficult to represent. London had become the centre of the world. The routes shown in the Mediterranean and the Baltic simply indicate the major itineraries taken by all the ships of the various trading nations.

metropolises came accompanied by a train of subordinates; Richard Häpke coined
the expression 'an archipelago of towns', an evocative image. Stendhal was
under the illusion that the great cities of Italy had treated the lesser cities kindly
out of generosity.[15] But how could they have destroyed them? They certainly
subjugated them, but no more, since they needed their services. A world-city
could not reach and maintain its high standard of living without some sacrifices,
willingly or unwillingly made by other large towns, which it resembled – a city
is a city is a city after all – but from which it stood out: the metropolis was a
super-city. And the first sign by which it could be recognized was precisely its
retinue of assistants and subordinates.

Exceptional and enigmatic, this handful of extraordinary cities dazzled observers. Venice, said Philippe de Commynes in 1495, was 'the most triumphant
city I have ever seen'.[16] Amsterdam was, in Descartes' view, a sort of 'inventory
of the possible'. 'What place on earth could one choose', he wrote to Guez de
Balzac on 5 May 1631, 'where all the commodities and all the curiosities one
could wish for were as easy to find as in this city?'[17] But these splendid cities
were disconcerting too; the visitor was bewildered by them. Every visiting
foreigner, particularly if he was French in the age of Voltaire and Montesquieu,
made desperate efforts to understand and make sense of London. The journey to
England, that literary genre, was a voyage of discovery which always came up
against the supercilious originality of London. Perhaps the visitor feels the same
about New York today.

Any town of any importance, particularly if it was a seaport, was a 'Noah's
Ark', 'a fair of masks', a 'Tower of Babel', as Président de Brosses described
Livorno.[18] How much more so were the real metropolises! They were the scene
of fantastic mixtures, whether London or Istanbul, Isfahan or Malacca, Surat or
Calcutta (the latter from the time of its very earliest successes). Under the pillars
of the Amsterdam Bourse – which was a microcosm of the world of trade – one
could hear every dialect in the world. In Venice, 'if you are curious to see men
from every part of the earth, each dressed in his own different way, go to St
Mark's Square or the Rialto and you will find all manner of persons'.

This colourful cosmopolitan population had to coexist and work in peace.
The rule in Noah's Ark was live and let live. Of the Venetian state, Villamont[19]
thought in 1590 'that there is nowhere in all Italy where one may live in greater
liberty ... firstly because the Signoria rarely condemns a man to death, secondly
arms are not forbidden,[20] thirdly there is no inquisition in matters of faith, lastly
everyone lives as he pleases in freedom of conscience, which is the reason why
several libertine[21] Frenchmen reside there so as not to be pursued and controlled
and so as to live wholly without constraint'. I imagine that Venice's innate
toleration helps to explain her 'notorious anticlericalism'[22] or as I would prefer
to call it her vigilant opposition to Roman intransigence. But the miracle of
toleration was to be found wherever the community of trade convened.
Amsterdam kept open house, not without some merit after the religious

violence between the Arminians and the Gomarists (1619–1620). In London, every religion under the sun was practised. 'There are', said a French visitor in 1725,[23] 'Jews, Protestants from Germany, Holland, Sweden, Denmark and France; Lutherans, Anabaptists, millenarians, Brownists, independents or Puritans; and Tremblers or Quakers.' To these might be added the Anglicans, Presbyterians and the Catholics who, whether English or not, were in the habit of attending mass in the chapels of the French, Spanish or Portuguese embassies. Each sect or faith had its own churches and meeting-places. And each one was identifiable to the outside world. 'The Quakers can be recognized a mile off by their dress: a flat hat, a small cravat, a coat buttoned up to the neck and their eyes shut most of the time.'[24]

Perhaps the most distinctive characteristic of all of these super-cities was their precocious and pronounced social diversification. They all had a proletariat, a bourgeoisie, and a patriciate, the latter controlling all wealth and power and so self-confident that before long it did not even bother, as it had in Venice or Genoa in the old days, to take the title of *nobili*.[25] Patriciate and proletariat indeed grew further apart, as the rich became richer and the poor even poorer, since the besetting sin of these pulsating capitalist cities was their high cost of living, not to mention the constant inflation resulting from the intrinsic nature of the higher urban functions whose destiny it was to dominate adjacent economies. Economic life flowed spontaneously towards their high prices. But caught in this high-tension system, the city and the economy concentrated upon it ran the risk of being burned. In London and Amsterdam, the cost of living sometimes reached well-nigh intolerable levels, just as New York today is losing its firms and businesses, as they leave to escape the huge cost of local rates and taxes.

And yet these great urban centres appealed too strongly to interest and imagination not to be heard, as if individuals hoped to be able to take part in the spectacle, the luxury and the high life of the town and to forget the problems of everyday living. These world-cities put all their delights on display. Seen through a reminiscent glow, the image reaches absurd proportions. A guide for travellers written in 1643[26] describes Antwerp in the preceding century: a city of 200,000 inhabitants, 'both nationals and foreigners', capable of taking 'at one time in the port 2500 ships [which would wait] a month lying at anchor without being able to unload'; a town of great wealth, which had paid Charles V 300 tons of gold, and into which there flowed every year '500 million in silver, 130 million in gold', 'not counting exchange currency which comes and goes like the tide'. Such a picture is completely unrealistic – but there was something behind the hyperbole. In 1587, Alonso Morgado's *Historia de Sevilla* claimed that 'with the treasure imported into the city, every street could have been paved with gold and silver!'[27]

Rule Two (continued): cities take it in turns to lead

Dominant cities did not dominate for ever; they replaced each other. This was as true at the summit as it was at every level of the urban hierarchy. Such shifts, wherever they occurred (at the top or half-way down), whatever their causes (economic or otherwise) are always significant; they interrupt the calm flow of history and open up perspectives that are the more precious for being so rare. When Amsterdam replaced Antwerp, when London took over from Amsterdam, or when in about 1929, New York overtook London, it always meant a massive historical shift of forces, revealing the precariousness of the previous equilibrium and the strengths of the one which was replacing it. The whole circle of the world-economy was affected by such changes and the repercussions were never exclusively economic, as the reader will probably already suspect.

When in 1421 the Ming rulers of China changed their capital city – leaving Nanking, and moving to Peking, in order to face the dangers of the Manchu and Mongol frontier – the massive world-economy of China swung round for good, turning its back on a form of economic activity based on ease of access to sea-borne trade. A new landlocked metropolis was now established deep in the interior and began to draw everything towards it. Whether conscious or unconscious, this choice was decisive. In the race for world dominion, this was the moment when China lost her position in a contest she had entered without fully realizing it, when she had launched the first maritime expeditions from Nanking in the early fifteenth century.

Philip II made an equally momentous decision in 1582. At the height of Spain's *political* domination of Europe, Philip II conquered Portugal in 1580, and elected residence, with his government, in Lisbon for a period of almost three years. Lisbon thus gained immeasurably. Looking out over the ocean, this was an ideal place from which to rule the world. Backed up by the king and the presence of the government, the Iberian fleet drove the French out of the Azores in 1583, hanging all prisoners from the yard-arms of the ships. So to leave Lisbon in 1582 meant leaving a position from which the empire's entire economy could be controlled, and imprisoning the might of Spain in Madrid, the landlocked heart of Castile – a fateful mistake! The Invincible Armada, after years of preparation, sailed to its disaster in 1588. Spain's action suffered from this retreat inland, as contemporaries fully realized. In the reign of Philip IV, there were still some advisers who urged the Catholic king[28] to fulfil the 'old Portuguese dream' and transfer the capital from Madrid to Lisbon. 'Sea power is more important to the ruler of Spain than to any other prince' wrote one of these men, 'for it is only by sea power that a single community can be created out of so many provinces so far apart.'[29] Taking up the same idea in 1638, a military writer anticipated the views of Admiral Mahan: 'The might most suited to the arms of Spain is that which is placed on the seas, but this matter of state is so well known that I should not discuss it, even if I thought it opportune to do so'.[30]

The triumph of English naval power: the defeat of the Spanish Armada. Detail from an anonymous painting in the National Maritime Museum in Greenwich. (Photo by the museum.)

Discoursing on what might have happened is frivolous. The only thing of which we can be sure is that if Lisbon, encouraged by the presence of the king of Spain, had triumphed, there would have been no Amsterdam, or at any rate not so soon. For there is only room for one centre at a time in a world-economy. The success of one sooner or later means the eclipse of another. During the reign of Augustus, in the Roman Mediterranean, Alexandria challenged Rome, which emerged triumphant. In the Middle Ages, in the race to capture the exploitable riches of the East, either Genoa or Venice had to come out on top. The victory remained for a long while in the balance until the end of the Chioggia War (1378–1381) which saw the sudden triumph of Venice. The city-states of Italy waged their power-struggle with a ferocity that would not be surpassed by their successors, the states and nations of modern times.

Such movements towards success or failure brought major upheavals. If the capital city of a world-economy fell, it sent ripples throughout the system to the periphery. And it is indeed in these marginal regions, true or pseudo-colonial territories, that one can often best observe what is happening. When Venice began her decline, she lost her empire: Negropont in 1540, Cyprus (the jewel in the crown) in 1572, Candia (Crete) in 1669. When Amsterdam began her climb to eminence, Portugal lost her empire in the Far East and very nearly lost Brazil as well. France lost the first serious round of her duel with Britain in 1762: she gave up Canada and practically all hopes of a future in India. When in 1815, London was reaching her apogee, Spain was losing, or was about to lose Latin America. Similarly after 1929, the world which had been centred on London shortly before, began to shift towards New York – and after 1945, the colonial empires of the European countries were all blown away by the wind of change: the British, the French, the Dutch, the Belgian, the Spanish (or what remained of it) and more recently, the Portuguese. The string of colonial losses was no accident: a number of chains of dependence were being snapped. And it is not hard to imagine the repercussions that would be felt world-wide at the present time if American hegemony were to come to an end.

Rule Two (continued): the power and influence of cities may vary

The reference to dominant cities should not lead us to think that the successes and strengths of these urban centres were always of the same type: in the course of their history, these cities were sometimes better or worse equipped for their task, and their differences or comparative failings, when looked at closely, oblige one to make some fairly fine distinctions of interpretation.

If we take the classic sequence of dominant cities of western Europe – Venice, Antwerp, Genoa, Amsterdam, London – which we shall presently be considering at length – it will be observed that the three first-named did not possess the complete arsenal of economic domination. Venice at the end of the fourteenth century was a booming merchant city; but possessed no more than the beginnings of an industrial sector; and while she did have financial and banking institutions, this credit system operated inside the Venetian economy, as an internal mechanism only. Antwerp, which possessed very little shipping of her own, provided a haven for Europe's merchant capitalism: operating as a sort of bring and buy centre for trade and business, to which everything came from outside. When Genoa's turn came, it was really only because of her banking supremacy, similar to that of Florence in the thirteenth and fourteenth centuries; if she played a leading role, it was firstly because her chief customer was the king of Spain, controller of the flow of bullion, and secondly because no one was quite sure where the centre of gravity really lay between the sixteenth and seventeenth centuries: Antwerp fulfilled this role no longer and Amsterdam was not yet ready: the Genoese supremacy was no more than an interlude. By the time Amsterdam and London took the stage, the world-cities possessed the whole panoply of means of economic power: they controlled everything, from shipping to commercial and industrial expansion, as well as the whole range of credit.

Another factor which could vary from one dominant city to another was the machinery of political power. From this point of view, Venice had been a strong and independent state: early in the fifteenth century, she had taken over the *Terraferma*, a large protective zone close at hand; since 1204 she had possessed a colonial empire. Antwerp by contrast had virtually no political power at her disposal. Genoa was a mere territorial skeleton: she had given up all claim to political independence, staking everything on that alternative form of domination, money. Amsterdam laid claim in some sense to the United Provinces, whether they agreed or not. But her 'kingdom' represented little more than the *Terraferma* of Venice. With London, we move into a completely different context: this great city had at its command the English national market and later that of the entire British Isles, until the day when the world changed and this mighty combination dwindled to the dimensions of a minor power when compared to a giant like the United States.

In short, the outline of the history of these successive dominant cities in Europe since the fourteenth century provides the clue to the development of their underlying world-economies: these might be more or less firmly controlled, as they oscillated between strong and weak centres of gravity. This sequence also incidentally tells us something about the variable value of the weapons of domination: shipping, trade, industry, credit, and political power or violence.

Rule Three: there is always a hierarchy of zones within a world-economy

The different zones within a world-economy all face towards one point in the centre: thus 'polarized', they combine to form a whole with many relationships. As the Marseille Chamber of Commerce put it in 1763, 'All trades are linked and join hands so to speak'.[31] A hundred years earlier in Amsterdam, an observer was already concluding from the Dutch example 'that there was such a close connection between all the parts of commerce in the universe that to be ignorant of one was to be ill-informed of the others'.[32]

And once such connections were established, they lasted.

Early enthusiasm made me study the history of the Mediterranean in the second half of the sixteenth century. I navigated mentally through these fifty years, putting in to port, bartering and trading. Then I moved on to the history of the Mediterranean in the seventeenth and eighteenth centuries, thinking that I would feel lost, that this would be a strange world in which I would have to serve my apprenticeship all over again. But I quickly discovered that I was on familiar territory, in 1660 or 1670, or even in 1750. The basic distances, routes, delays, production, merchandise and stopping-places – everything or almost every-thing had remained the same. There were a few changes here and there, but they nearly all had to do with the superstructure – which is at once important and almost nothing, even though this 'almost nothing' – money, capital, credit, increased or diminished demand for a given product – may govern ordinary, 'natural', day-to-day living. But the latter is carried on without people being entirely aware that their real masters are no longer those of yesterday – or caring greatly about it either way. The olive oil of Apulia was, by the eighteenth century, being exported to northern Europe through Trieste, Ancona, Naples and Ferrara, and much less was going to Venice;[33] this was a significant change, but did it matter very much to the peasants in their olive-groves?

It is on the basis of this experience that I interpret the construction of world-economies and of the mechanisms through which capitalism and the market economy can coexist and interpenetrate one another without always merging entirely. At ground level and sea level so to speak, the networks of local and regional markets were built up over century after century. It was the destiny of this local economy, with its self-contained routines, to be from time to time absorbed and made part of a 'rational' order in the interest of a dominant city or zone, for perhaps one or two centuries, until another 'organizing centre' emerged; as if the *centralization* and *concentration* of wealth and resources[34] necessarily favoured certain chosen sites of *accumulation*.

A significant example, to remain within this context, is the domestication of the Adriatic by Venice, for her own purposes. Having controlled this sea since at least 1383 and the capture of Corfu, regarding it as a sort of *national market*, Venice called the Adriatic 'her gulf' and claimed to have won it with her own blood. Only during the severest storms of winter did the gilded prows of the galleys interrupt their coming and going. But Venice had not invented the Adriatic: she had not created the cities along its shores, but had found its coastal goods, trade and sea-faring peoples already in existence when she came on the scene. All she had to do was to bring together, like so many threads, the trades operating before her arrival: olive oil from Apulia, wood for shipbuilding from the forests of the Monte Gargano, stone from Istria, the salt in demand on both shores for men and livestock, wines, grain. She also brought together travelling merchants and hundreds and thousands of boats and sailing ships, reorganized all this shipping to suit her own needs, and integrated it into her own economy. This takeover is the typical model for the construction process of any world-economy, with its inbuilt monopolies. Venice insisted that *all* Adriatic trade ought to pass through her port and under her control, whatever its destination. She devoted herself to this claim tirelessly, fighting Segna and Fiume, two centres of piracy, as well as Trieste, Ragusa and Ancona, her commercial rivals.[35]

Roundships putting in at Venice. V. Carpaccio, *The Legend of Saint Ursula*, detail of the departure of the betrothed couple. (Photo Anderson-Giraudon.)

The pattern of domination exerted by Venice can be found elsewhere as well. Essentially it rests upon a dialectic between a market economy developing almost unaided and spontaneously, and an over-arching economy which seizes these humble activities from above, redirects them and holds them at its mercy. I mentioned the olive oil of Apulia, which Venice long monopolized. In order to do so, Venice had, in the oil-producing region in 1580, no less than 500 Bergamask merchants,[36] Venetian subjects, occupied in collecting, storing and organizing exports. The dominant economy thus embraced all production, and directed it towards appropriate outlets. Any means that worked were used, in particular the granting of judicious credit: this was how the English gained supremacy over Portugal after Lord Methuen's treaty of 1703, and it was also the method by which the Americans drove the British out of South America after World War Two.

Rule Three (continued): Von Thünen's zones

One explanation (though not *the* explanation) may be sought in the work of Johann Heinrich von Thünen (1780-1851) who ranks alongside Marx as the greatest German economist of the nineteenth century.[37] It is certainly the case that every world-economy obeys the rules laid down in his book *Der isolierte Staat* (1826). 'Imagine', he writes, 'a great city in the midst of a fertile plain, where there is no navigable river or canal. The said plain is constituted of the same kind of soil throughout and is uniformly cultivable. Some distance from the city, the plain ends on the edge of a wild and uncultivated zone which completely cuts off our state from the rest of the world. The plain contains no other town besides the great city.'[38] (Let us salute *en passant* the need economists always feel to depart from the real world, the better to understand it.)[39]

This unique city and its unique plain then, react upon each other as if in a bell-jar. Since all activities are determined by distance (for there are no differences in the soil to encourage the growing of different crops), a number of concentric rings around the city will take shape: the first circle will be made up of market gardens (close to the city and perhaps even inside it) as well as dairy production; in the second and third circles will be found cereals and livestock. This picture is a microcosm, a model which can be applied to other cities: G. Niemeier has applied it to Seville and Andalusia;[40] and I have mentioned it in connection with the regions supplying London or Paris;[41] indeed it can be applied to any great city. The theory can be accommodated to real life insofar as the model proposed is empty of detail: one can provide the contents oneself.

I would not criticize the Von Thünen model for failing to recognize the appearance and development of industry (which existed well before the industrial revolution of eighteenth-century England) nor for describing an abstract countryside in which distance is the only criterion for the definition of the circles of activity, one in which there are no villages and small towns, none of the human realities, that is, of the actual market. One can easily fill in these missing elements when one applies this simplified model to a real-life case. But what I would criticize is the absence from this schema of the very important concept of inequality. The inequality between the different zones described is patent, but it is stated without comment. The 'great city' dominates the countryside, full stop. But why does it do so? The town-country exchange which creates the elementary circulation of the economic body is a good example, *pace* Adam Smith,[42] of unequal exchange. And this inequality has its origins and its genesis.[43] Economists are inclined to overlook historical evolution in this context: it has clearly been a force to be reckoned with from early on.

Rule Three (continued): the spatial arrangement of the world-economy

Every world-economy is a sort of jigsaw puzzle, a juxtaposition of zones interconnected, but *at different levels*. On the ground, *at least* three different areas or categories can be distinguished: a narrow *core*, a fairly developed middle zone and a vast *periphery*. The qualities and characteristics of the type of society, economy, technology, culture and political order necessarily alter as one moves from one zone to another. This is an explanation of very wide application, one on which Immanuel Wallerstein has based his book *The Modern World-System* (1974).

The centre or *core* contains everything that is most advanced and diversified. The next zone possesses only some of these benefits, although it has some share in them: it is the 'runner-up' zone. The huge periphery, with its scattered population, represents on the contrary backwardness, archaism, and exploitation by others. This discrimatory geography is even today both an explanation and a pitfall in the writing of world history – although the latter often creates the pitfalls itself by its connivence.

The central zone holds no mysteries: when Amsterdam was the 'warehouse of the world', the United Provinces (or at any rate the most active among them) formed the central zone; when London imposed its supremacy, England (if not the whole of the British Isles) formed the surrounding area. When Antwerp found itself in the sixteenth century the centre of European trade, the Netherlands, as Henri Pirenne said, became 'the suburb of Antwerp'[44] and the rest of the world its periphery. The 'suction and force of attraction of these poles of growth'[45] were clear to see.

Detailed identification is more difficult though when it comes to the regions outside this central zone, which may border on it, are inferior to it but perhaps only slightly so: seeking to join it, they put pressure on it from all directions, and there is more movement here than anywhere else. It is not always easy to spot the differences: Paul Bairoch has argued[46] that differences in levels between economic zones were much less pronounced in the past than they are today; Hermann Kellenbenz has even queried whether they were real at all.[47] But these differences did exist, whether marked or not, as we can tell by the criteria of prices, wages, living standards, national product, per capita income, and trade balances – that is when the figures are available.

The simplest, if not the best criterion, the most immediately accessible one at any rate, is the presence or otherwise, in a given region, of colonies of *foreign* merchants. If he rules the roost in a given city or region, the foreign merchant is a sign of the inferiority of that city or region, compared with the economy of which he is the representative or emissary. There is no shortage of examples of such superiority: the Genoese merchant bankers in Madrid in the days of Philip II; the Dutch merchants in Leipzig in the seventeenth century; the English merchants in Lisbon in the eighteenth century; or above all the Italians, in Bruges, Antwerp, Lyon or Paris (until the age of Mazarin). In about 1780, 'in Lisbon and Cadiz, all the trading-houses are branches of foreign firms', *alle Häuser fremde Comptoirs sind*.[48] And the same was true or nearly so in Venice in the eighteenth century.[49]

Any uncertainty evaporates on the other hand as soon as one enters the regions of the periphery. Here no confusion is possible: these are poor, backward countries where the predominant social status is often serfdom or even slavery (the only free or quasi-free peasants were to be found in the heart of the West); countries barely touched by the money economy; countries where the division of labour has hardly begun; where the peasant has to be a jack of all trades; where money prices, if they exist at all, are laughable. A low cost of living is indeed in itself a sign of under-development. The Hungarian preacher Martino Szepsi Combor, returning to his native country in 1618, 'noted the high price of foodstuffs in Holland and England; the situation began to change in France, then in Germany, Poland and Bohemia, and the price of bread went on falling all the way until he reached Hungary'.[50] Hungary was very nearly the bottom rung of the ladder; but one could go even lower: at Tobolsk in Siberia, 'the necessities of life are so cheap that a common man can live quite well on ten roubles a year'.[51]

The backward regions on the fringes of Europe afford many examples of these marginal economies: 'feudal' Sicily in the eighteenth century; Sardinia, in any period at all; the Turkish Balkans; Mecklemburg, Poland, Lithuania – huge expanses drained for the benefit of the western markets, doomed to adapt their production less to local needs than to the demands of foreign markets; Siberia, exploited by the Russian world-economy; but equally, the Venetian islands in the Levant, where external demand for raisins and strong wines, to be consumed as far away as England, had already by the fifteenth century imposed an intrusive monoculture, destructive of local balance.

There were *peripheries* in every quarter of the world of course. Both before and after Vasco da Gama, the black gold-diggers and hunters of the primitive countries of Monomotapa, on the east coast of Africa, were exchanging their gold and ivory for Indian cottons. China was always extending her frontiers and trespassing on to the 'barbaric' lands as the Chinese texts call them – for the Chinese view of these peoples was the same as that of the classical Greeks of

A 'raw barbarian': Chinese drawing representing
a half-naked Cambodian holding a seashell.
Engraving from the Che Kong Tu.
(B.N., Paris.)

non-Greek-speaking populations: the inhabitants of Vietnam and the East Indies
were 'barbarians'. In Vietnam however, the Chinese made a distinction between
those barbarians who had been touched by Chinese civilization and those who
had not. According to a Chinese historian of the sixteenth century, his compatriots called 'those who maintained their independence and their primitive customs "*raw*" barbarians, and those who had more or less accepted Chinese ways
and submitted to the empire "*cooked*" barbarians'. Here politics, culture, economy and social model contributed jointly to the distinction. The *raw* and the
cooked in this semantic code, explains Jacques Dourbes, also signifies the contrast between culture and nature: rawness is exemplified above all by nakedness.
'When the Pötao ['kings' of the mountains] come to pay tribute to the Annamite
court [which was Chinesified] it will cover them with clothes.'[52]

Similar dependent relationships were also to be found on the large island of
Hainan, off the south coast of China. The centre of the island was mountainous
and self-contained, inhabited by non-Chinese primitive people, while the lowlands with their rice-fields were already in the hands of Chinese peasants. The
mountain-dwellers, who made a living out of raiding the lowlands, but were also
sometimes hunted down like wild beasts, were willing to barter hardwoods
('eagle-wood' and *calamba*) and gold dust in a sort of wordless exchange: the
Chinese merchants would 'first leave their fabrics and articles of drapery up in
the mountains'.[53] Except that it was transacted in silence, this barter is not unlike
the exchanges on the Atlantic coast of the Sahara in the time of Henry the

Navigator, when cloth, cottons and blankets from Portugal were beginning to be bartered for the gold dust and black slaves brought to the coast by Berber nomads.

Rule Three (continued): do neutral zones exist?

However, the backward zones are not to be found exclusively in the really peripheral areas. They punctuate the central regions too, with local pockets of backwardness, a district or 'pays', an isolated mountain valley or an area cut off from the main communication routes. *All* advanced economies have their 'black holes' outside *world time*: the historian seeking to discover an almost always inaccessible past feels like a deep-sea diver. In recent years, I have made strenuous efforts – even more than the first two volumes of this work might suggest – to find out more about these primitive destinies, this unique historical fabric which takes us underneath or to the margins of the market, since the trading economy completely bypassed these worlds apart – worlds that were in human terms neither more fortunate nor more unfortunate than any other, as I have often had cause to point out.

But such underwater expeditions are rarely rewarded: there are few documents and the details one gleans are more picturesque than useful. What we really need is enough data to able to gauge the extent and the character of economic life at this very low level. And of course that is asking a great deal. There can be no doubt however of the existence of such 'neutral' zones, almost outside commercial exchange and contact. In eighteenth-century France, these backward islands were as likely to be found in the terrifying interior of Brittany as in the Alpine massif of the Oisans[54] or the Morzine valley,[55] above the Montets col, or in the high valley of Chamonix, which was quite cut off from the outside world until mountain-climbing became popular. One French historian, Colette Baudouy,[56] has had the good fortune to find a peasant community, Cervières, in the mountains of the Briançonnais, 'still living at the same pace as its ancestors, with the mental attitudes of the past, producing food according to ancient techniques, surviving ... amid the general collapse of its neighbours' – and she has made the most of it.

If 'islands' like this could still exist in France in 1970, we should not be surprised that in England, even on the eve of the industrial revolution, the traveller or investigator was always coming across backward districts. David Hume[57] (1711-1776) noted in mid-eighteenth century that there were many regions in Great Britain and Ireland where the cost of living was as low as in France – a roundabout way of referring to regions we should today call 'under-developed', where traditional life carried on, where the peasants had access to plenty of game, and to the salmon and trout that abounded in the rivers. And the people were near-savages. In the Fens, for instance, near the Wash, in the early seventeenth century, when large-scale drainage on Dutch lines was begun, the

Two world-economies meet: a western merchant sees spices being produced. Illustration from the *Book of Marvels*, Marco Polo, fifteenth century. B.N., Paris, Ms. fr. 2810. (Photo B.N.)

irrigation works produced a capitalist land pattern where previously there had only been free-living men, catching fish and game. These simple people fought desperately to defend their way of life, attacking the engineers and navvies, breaking the dykes, murdering the hated workmen.[58] And similar conflicts between old and new, archaism and modernization, are going on before our own eyes, in the interior of Campania in Italy for instance and in many other parts of the world.[59] Nowadays however, such violence is *comparatively* rare. In general, 'civilization' has many means of winning people over when it wants to and of penetrating regions long left to themselves. But is the result so very different?

Rule Three (conclusion): envelope and infrastructure

A world-economy is like an enormous envelope. One would expect *a priori*, that given the poor communications of the past, it would have to unite considerable resources in order to function properly. And yet the world-economies of the past did incontestably function, although the necessary density, concentration, strength and accompaniments only effectively existed in the core region and the area immediately surrounding it; and even the latter, whether one looks at the hinterland of Venice, Amsterdam or London, might include areas of reduced economic activity, only poorly linked to the centres of decision. Even today, the United States has pockets of under-development within its own frontiers.

So whether one considers a world-economy in terms of its area on the face of the globe, or in terms of its depth at the centre, one's astonishment is the same: the machine seems to work and yet (especially if one thinks of the earliest outstanding cities in European history) it seems to have such a modest power supply. How was such success possible? The question will keep cropping up throughout this book, and we shall never be able to give a categorical answer: Dutch trade successfully penetrated the hostile France of Louis XIV; England gained control of an immense country like India, and these are indeed achievements bordering on the incomprehensible.

But perhaps I may be allowed to suggest one explanation, by the artificial device of an image.

Think of a huge block of marble, chosen by Michelangelo or one of his contemporaries from the quarries of Carrara,[60] an immensely heavy weight which was nevertheless cut out by primitive means and moved with very modest energy sources: a little gunpowder (which had already been used for some time in quarries and mines), two or three levers, perhaps a dozen men if that, ropes, a haulage team, wooden rollers if it was to be taken any distance, an inclined plane – and there it was. The whole thing was possible because the giant slab was helpless on the ground with its own weight: it represented a huge force, but one inert and neutralized. Cannot this analogy be applied to the great mass of elementary economic activities which was also trapped, imprisoned, unable to move from the ground, and therefore more easily manoeuvrable *from above?* The devices and levers that made the achievement possible in this case consisted of a little ready money, the silver coin that arrived at Danzig or Messina, the tempting offer of credit, a little 'artificial' money or a rare and coveted product; or even the market system itself. The high prices at the far end of a trading chain were a continual lure: the word got round and the whole chain went into motion. One might add to the list the force of habit: pepper and spices had been coming for centuries to the gates of the Levant to meet the much sought-after silver.

There were violent means of persuasion too: Portuguese or Dutch squadrons were backing up commercial operations long before the 'age of gunboat diplomacy'. But it was more often the case that apparently modest means were insidiously used to manipulate dependent economies, and this goes, on the whole, for all the mechanisms of the world-economy, whether in the relations between core and periphery or within the core itself. For the centre of a world-economy was itself divided and subject to hierarchy – as indeed were the peripheries. 'It is notorious', wrote a Russian consul, 'that in Palermo almost any article costs 50% more than in Naples.'[61] But he omits to define what he means by 'article' or how many exceptions his 'almost' admits. We have to imagine for ourselves the reactions and movements that such price differences might create between the capitals of the two kingdoms making up the under-privileged *Mezzogiorno* of Italy.

The world-economy: an order among other orders

However plentiful the evidence of economic subordination, and whatever its consequences, it would be a mistake to imagine that the order of the world-economy governed the whole of society, determining the shape of other orders of society. For other orders existed. An economy never exists in isolation. Its territory and expanse are also occupied by other spheres of activity – culture, society, politics – which are constantly reacting with the economy, either to help or as often to hinder its development. It is all the more difficult to distinguish these orders one from the other since what is visible to the naked eye – the reality of experience or the 'really real' as François Perroux[62] calls it – is a *totality* which we have already described as society *par excellence*, 'the set of sets'.[63] Each set[64] we have singled out for the purposes of exposition is in real life inextricably mingled with the others. I cannot for a moment agree with T.S. Willan[65] that there is a no-man's land between economic history and social history. One could formulate the following equations in any order: the economy equals politics, culture and society; culture equals the economy, politics and society, etc. Or one could say that in a given society, politics governs the economy and vice versa; that the economy benefits or discourages culture and vice versa; or even as Pierre Brunel[66] has said that 'everything human is political, therefore all literature (even the hermetic poetry of Mallarmé) is political'. For if one of the specific characters of the economy is that it extends beyond its own area, can the same not equally be said of the other social 'sets'? They all nibble at frontiers, seek to extend their territory and create their own Von Thünen circles.

A state may for instance appear to be divided into three zones: capital, provinces and colonies. This pattern applies to Venice in the fifteenth century: the city and its immediate surroundings – the *Dogado*;[67] the towns and districts of the *Terraferma*; and the colonies – known as the *Mar*. In the case of Florence, there was the city, the *Contado* and the *Stato*.[68] Would it be true to say of the latter, conquered at the expense of Siena and Pisa, that it comes into the category of pseudo-colonies? One need hardly go on to mention the triple

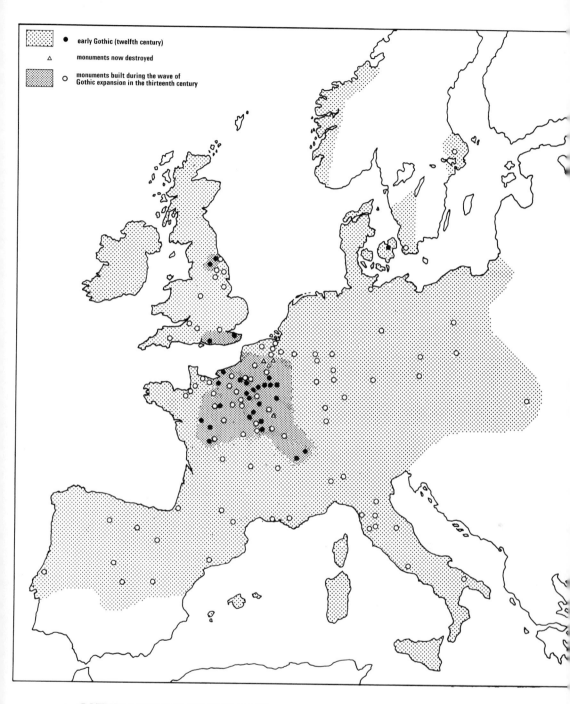

early Gothic (twelfth century)

monuments now destroyed

monuments built during the wave of Gothic expansion in the thirteenth century

4 GOTHIC MONUMENTS IN EUROPE
(From the *Atlas historique* edited by Georges Duby, Larousse, 1978.)

division of France in the seventeenth, eighteenth, nineteenth and twentieth centuries, or that of Britain or Holland. But on a European-wide scale, was not the *European balance of power*[69] which historians have so eagerly studied, a sort of political response by the world-economy? Its aim was to create and maintain peripheries and semi-peripheries where mutual tensions would not always cancel each other out so that the central power should not be threatened. For politics too had its 'core', a narrow zone from which an eye could be kept on developments close at hand or far away, on the 'wait and see' principle.

Social forms too had their differential geography. How far for instance did slavery, serfdom or feudal society actually extend in area? Over distance, society could completely change. When Dupont de Nemours agreed to be tutor to the son of Prince Czartoryski, he discovered in Poland to his stupefaction what serfdom was like, and that there could be peasants who were ignorant of the state and knew only their overlord, or princes who remained like peasants in their everyday lives; Prince Radziwill, who 'ruled 'over a domain greater than Lorraine', slept on an earthen floor.[70]

Similarly culture divided up geographical space into concentric circles: in the age of the Renaissance, there was Florence, Italy and the rest of Europe. And these circles corresponded of course to cultural conquests over space. Consider how 'French' Gothic church architecture spread from the area round the Seine and Loire all over Europe; or how the baroque, the creation of the Counter-Reformation, conquered the whole continent from Rome and Madrid, even contaminating Protestant England; how in the eighteenth century, French became the *lingua franca* of all cultivated Europeans; how Islamic art and architecture spread from Delhi throughout both Muslim and Hindu India, and even reached the East Indies, which had been converted to Islam by Indian merchants.

It would no doubt be possible to map the way in which these different 'orders' of society existed in space, to locate their poles, central zones and lines of force. Each has its own history and its own domain; and each influences and is influenced by the others. None can ever assert itself for good over the others. Their ranking order, if ranking order there is, is forever changing, slowly it is true, but changing all the same.

The economic order and the international division of labour

With modern times, nevertheless, the primacy of economics became more and more overwhelming: it directed, disturbed and influenced the other orders. Exaggerating inequalities, it imprisoned the various partners in the world-economy either in poverty or in wealth, assigning to each a role it was apparently destined to hold for a very long time. One economist[71] has quite seriously expressed this as 'a poor country is poor because it is poor'; and a historian has written 'growth breeds more growth'[72] – in other words, 'a country becomes rich because it is already rich'.

These deliberately simple-minded tautologies make more sense to my mind than the so-called 'irrefutable' pseudo-theorem[73] of David Ricardo (1817), whose terms are well known: that the relations between two given countries depend on the 'comparative costs' obtaining in them at the point of production; all foreign trade tends towards a mutual balance and can only be profitable to both sides (or at worst can benefit one of them only slightly more than the other) since it:

> binds together, by one common tie of interest and intercourse, the universal society of nations throughout the civilised world. It is this principle which determines that wine shall be made in France and Portugal, that corn shall be grown in America and Poland, and that hardware and other goods shall be manufactured in England.[74]

The picture is rather too reassuring. For there is an unasked question here: when did the division of tasks (which Ricardo assumed in 1817 to be part of the natural order) begin and why?

It was certainly not the result of 'natural' and spontaneous tendencies, but rather an inheritance, the consolidation, historically achieved over time, of a situation dating from some earlier period. The division of labour on a world scale (or on world-economy-scale) cannot be described as a concerted agreement made between equal parties and always open to review. It became established progressively as a chain of subordinations, each conditioning the others. Unequal exchange, the origin of the inequality in the world, and, by the same token, the inequality of the world, the invariable generator of trade, are longstanding realities. In the economic poker game, some people have always held better cards than others, not to say aces up their sleeves. Certain activities have yielded more profits than others: it was more profitable to grow vines than wheat (that is if someone else grew the wheat for you), more profitable to be in the secondary sector than in the primary and in the tertiary sector than in the secondary. If trade between England and Portugal in Ricardo's time was such that the former was selling cloth and other industrial products and the latter wine, then Portugal was in the primary and therefore inferior sector. For centuries before this England had left off exporting raw materials such as wool, even before the reign of Elizabeth, in order to advance her industry and trade; and for centuries Portugal, once a rich country, had been moving in the other direction, or had been pushed towards it. For the Portuguese government in the time of the Duke of Erceira had used the weapons of mercantilism to defend herself and encouraged the development of her indigenous industry. But two years after the death of the duke (1690), all such efforts were abandoned; and ten years or so later, she was signing the treaty with Lord Methuen. Who could possibly claim that Anglo-Portuguese relations were dictated by 'common ties of interest' between friendly communities, rather than by power politics developing in an irreversible direction?

Power relations between nations sometimes date back to very ancient states of affairs. An economy, society, civilization or political complex finds it very

An allegory of the trade of Danzig by Isaac van de Luck (1608) decorating the ceiling of the Hanse Hall, today the Town Hall of Gdansk. The entire activity of the town revolved round grain ferried down the Vistula and brought via a connecting canal (see Volume I, p. 128 and Volume II, p. 268) to the port and its ships, which can be seen in the background. At the bottom of the picture are Polish and western merchants, recognizable by their costume: these were the men who forged the chain of dependence linking Poland to Amsterdam. (Photo Henryk Romanowski.)

hard to live down a dependent past. The Italian *Mezzogiorno* for instance, has been a backward region for a very long time, since at least the twelfth century. A Sicilian writer says with some exaggeration, 'we have been a colony for 2500 years'.[75] Brazil has been independent since 1822, but Brazilians used to feel, and still do to some extent that they were in a 'colonial' situation, not vis-à-vis Portugal but vis-à-vis Europe and the United States. There is a saying there today, 'we are not the United States of Brazil, but the Brazil of the United States'.

Similarly, France's slow industrial takeoff which was evident by the nineteenth century, cannot be explained without going a long way back in time. According to some historians[76] France missed the chance of industrial transformation and of successfully challenging England for the leadership of Europe because of the upheavals of Revolution and Empire; it is argued that this was a major lost opportunity. It is true that under pressure of circumstances, France abandoned the entire world to Great Britain's commercial exploitation; and it is equally true that the combined effects of Trafalgar and Waterloo dealt her a crushing blow. But should one really forget the missed opportunities even before 1789? In 1713, at the end of the War of the Spanish Succession, France was deprived of free access to the silver of Latin America. In 1722, with the failure of Law's System, she was deprived until 1776 of a central bank.[77] In 1762, even before the Treaty of Paris, France had already lost Canada and for all practical purposes India as well. And going much farther back into the past, the prosperous France of the thirteenth century, boosted artificially by the *land-routes* converging on the Champagne fairs, had lost this advantage by the beginning of the fourteenth century with the establishment of a *maritime* link, via Gibraltar, between Italy and the Netherlands; she now found herself (as I shall later explain)[78] outside the essential 'capitalist' circuit of Europe. The moral of the story is that a loss is never the result of a single throw – nor indeed is a triumph. Success depends on seizing the opportunities of a given period, on doing so time and time again, and piling advantage advantage on advantage. Power is accumulated like money, which is why I favour the apparently over-obvious remarks of Nurske and Chaunu. 'A country is poor because it is poor', or to put it more clearly because it is poor to start with, caught up in 'the vicious poverty cycle', to use another of Nurske's expressions.[79] 'Growth breeds growth', a country develops because it is already developing, because it is caught up in a movement already under way which helps it. So the past always counts. The inequality of the world is the result of structural realities at once slow to take shape and slow to fade away.

The state: political power and economic power

The state is back in fashion again, even among philosophers. Any analysis which does not now grant it an important place is placing itself outside a developing trend, one which has its excesses and simplifications of course, but which has at least the advantage of making some French historians think again and pay attention to something they were ready to dismiss, or at any rate neglect, in the past.

Between the fifteenth and eighteenth centuries however, the state was far from occupying the entire social stage; it did not possess the 'diabolical' power of penetration attributed to it today; in the past, the means were simply lacking. And it had suffered a body-blow from the long crisis between 1350 and 1450. Only with the second half of the fifteenth century did its recovery begin. The city-states, which tended, before the territorial states, to play the leading role until the early eighteenth century, were at this time tools completely in the hands of their merchants. Things were far less simple in the territorial states whose power was only slowly restored. But the first territorial state to complete its transformation into a national economy or national market, England, fell under the domination of its merchants fairly soon after the 1688 revolution. It is hardly surprising then if in preindustrial Europe a certain determinism seems to have brought about the coincidence of political power and economic power. At any rate, the map of the European world-economy, with its highly-charged central zones, and its concentric rings of variation, is likely to correspond fairly closely to a political map of Europe.

At the centre of the world-economy, one always finds an exceptional state, strong, aggressive and privileged, dynamic, simultaneously feared and admired. In the fifteenth century it was Venice; in the seventeenth, Holland; in the eighteenth and still in the nineteenth, it was Britain; today it is the United States. How could these 'central' governments fail to be strong? Immanuel Wallerstein has taken some trouble to prove that this was not the case for the government of the United Provinces in the seventeenth century – which has been described as virtually non-existent by contemporaries and historians alike. But this is to overlook the inevitable: as if the central position itself could fail to create and demand effective government,[80] as if government and society could fail to form an indivisible whole, and as if money could fail to create both social discipline and an extraordinary capacity for action.

There were strong governments then, in Venice, even in Amsterdam, and in London, governments capable of asserting themselves at home, of keeping the 'common people' of the towns in order, of raising taxes when the situation required, and of guaranteeing commercial credit and freedom; capable too of asserting themselves abroad: it is to these governments, who never hesitated to employ violence, that we can readily apply, at a *very early* date and without fear of anachronism, the words *colonialism* and *imperialism*. This did not prevent – far from it – such 'central' governments from being more or less dependent on a precocious form of capitalism already sharp in tooth and claw. Power was shared between the two. Without ever being swallowed up, the state was thus drawn into the intrinsic movement of the world-economy. By serving others and serving money, it was serving its own ends as well.

The official pomp of the Venetian state: an ambassador taking his leave of the Doge. V. Carpaccio, *The Legend of Saint Ursula* (about 1500). (Photo Giraudon.)

The picture is rather different when one turns to the active but less developed zone outside the central area but still close to it, where the state had long been a combination of traditional charismatic monarchy and modern organization. Here governments were stifled by societies, economies, sometimes cultures, that were in part archaic; they had difficulty breathing a wider air. The monarchies of continental Europe were obliged willy-nilly to govern with, or against, the nobilities surrounding them. Without the latter how could the only partially-complete state (even if it was France under Louis XIV) carry out its tasks? There was of course the rising 'bourgeoisie' whose advance was fostered, but only prudently, by the state; and such processes in any case took time. At the same time, these states had before their eyes the successes of the merchant states better placed than they at the crossroads of trade; they were aware of what amounted to their inferior position, so that their chief preoccupation was to join the superior category at all costs, to move into the centre. One method was to copy the model and to appropriate the recipe for success – England's *idée fixe* in her competition with Holland. Another was to create and mobilize the resources and revenues required for foreign wars and for conspicuous luxury which was after all one way of governing. It seems to be the case that every state anywhere near the centre of a world-economy became more quarrelsome, going out to make conquests as if the proximity excited its bile.

But we should not be misled by conquests: there was a considerable difference between modern seventeenth-century Holland and majestic-looking states like France or Spain. This distance is revealed in the attitudes of governments towards an economic policy regarded at the time as a panacea and which we now call by a word invented after the event, *mercantilism*. When we made up this word, we historians assigned it a variety of meanings. But if one of those meanings was to be paramount, it would be that which implied a defence against others. For mercantilism was above all a means of self-defence. The prince or state which applied its rules was no doubt following the fashion, but at the same time admitting an inferiority which had to be tempered or made good. Holland was only mercantilist at certain very rare moments – precisely those at which she was aware of an external threat. As a rule unchallenged, she was able to practise free trade with impunity since it could only benefit her. When in the eighteenth century, England began to move away from strict mercantilism, was it, as I am inclined to think, proof that the age of Britain's power and greatness on a world scale had dawned? A century later (1846) she could embrace free trade without running any risk at all.

The scene changes yet again, if we move to the outer fringes of a world-economy. Here were the colonies, enslaved peoples deprived of the right to govern themselves: their ruler was the mother country, determined to preserve for itself all the trading profits deriving from the monopoly it always exercised, whatever form it might take. It is true that the mother country might be far away, and that the cities and local elites controlled affairs on the spot. But such power of the local administrations and interests, what was known as 'American democracy', was only an elementary form of government – something like that of the ancient Greek city-states, if that, as would become clear when the first colonies gained their independence, creating a sudden power vacuum. After the artificial colonial state had been destroyed the new one had to be built from scratch. The United States, constituted in 1787, took a long time to turn the federal state into a coherent and effective power. And the process was equally slow in other American countries.

In non-colonial peripheries, notably in eastern Europe, there were at least states in existence. But here the economy was dominated by a group with foreign connections, so that in Poland for instance the state had become merely an institution stripped of all substance. Similarly eighteenth-century Italy no longer had any real governments. 'Italy is treated', said the count Maffei in 1736, 'and the fate of her peoples decided as if they were of no more account than flocks of sheep or other common animals.'[81] Even Venice, after the battle of Passarowitz (1718) plunged with eagerness or relief into 'neutrality' – in other words she abandoned the struggle.[82]

The only way out for these losers was to resort to violence, aggression and war. Sweden under Gustavus Adolphus is a good example; or even better the Barbary corsairs in North Africa. It is true that with the Barbary Coast we are outside the European world-economy and have moved instead into the political and economic area controlled by the Turkish Empire, a world-economy in itself, of which more in a later chapter. But the state of Algiers is exemplary in its own way, lying on the divide between two world-economies, the European and the Turkish, but obeying neither, having virtually broken all its ties of vassalage with Istanbul, while the growing maritime strength of Europe prevented it benefiting from Mediterranean trade. The piracy of Algiers was the only possible way of making any impact on the European hegemony. And other things being equal, was not Sweden similarly placed, on the border between two economies, the European and the Russian, and similarly excluded from the benefits of Baltic trade? War was a form of salvation for her.

Empire and world-economy

The empire, a sort of super-state which might cover the entire area of a world-economy, presents us with a broader problem. On the whole, the world-empires, as Wallerstein calls them, were no doubt archaic formations, representing ancient triumphs of the political over the economic. But during the period covered by this book, they were still in existence outside the western world: the Mogul Empire in India, the Chinese and Persian Empires, the Ottoman Empire and the Empire of the Tsars in Muscovy. Immanuel Wallerstein has argued that wherever there was an empire, the underlying world-economy was unable to develop – that its career was stunted. It might also be argued that these were examples of the *command economy*, to use John Hicks's term, or of the *Asiatic mode of production*, in Marx's now-dated phrase.

It is true that an economy's wings could be clipped by the demands and constraints of an imperial policy without means of redress. No merchant or capitalist could ever feel completely free under an empire. Michael Cantacuzenus, who was a sort of Fugger to the Ottoman Empire, was summarily hanged on 13 March 1578, at the gates of his own luxurious palace at Anchioli in Istanbul, on the orders of the sultan.[83] In China,[84] Heshen, the ultra-rich favourite minister of the emperor K'ien Long, was executed and his fortune confiscated by the new emperor, after his master's death. In Russia,[85] Prince Gagarin, the governor of Siberia, although a master of prevarication, was beheaded in 1720. And one thinks of course of Jacques Cœur, Semblançay and Fouquet in France: in their own way, their trials (and the execution of Semblançay) tell us something of the political and economic conditions in France. Only a capitalist regime, however archaic it might be, had the stomach to swallow and digest such scandals.

All the same, I am personally inclined to think that even under the constraints of an oppressive empire with little concern for the particular interests of its different possessions, a world-economy could, even if rudely handled and closely watched, still survive and organize itself, extending significantly beyond the imperial frontiers: the Romans traded in the Red Sea and the Indian Ocean; the Armenian merchants of Julfa, the suburb of Isfahan, spread over almost the entire world; the Indian Banyans went as far as Moscow; Chinese merchants frequented all the ports of the East Indies; Muscovy established its ascendancy over the mighty periphery of Siberia in record time. I grant that Wittfogel[86] is not mistaken when he says that in these political high-pressure areas of the empires of traditional southern and eastern Asia, 'the state was much stronger than society' – stronger than society it may have been; but it was not stronger than the economy.

To return to the European example, can we not say that it escaped very soon from the stifling embrace of empire? The Roman Empire was at once more and less than Europe; the Carolingian and Ottonian Empires had little control over a Europe already in decline. The Church, while it succeeded in extending its culture over the entire surface of Europe, failed in the end to establish its political supremacy. This being so, is it wise to exaggerate the political importance of the attempts to create a *universal monarchy* made by the emperor Charles V (1519–55) or by Philip II of Spain (1555–98)? This focusing of the spotlight on the imperial preponderance of Spain, or to be more precise, the insistence with which Immanuel Wallerstein dates the approximate birth of the European world-economy from the collapse of the Habsburg dream (rather arbitrarily equated with the bankruptcy of 1557) does not seem to me to be the best way to approach the problem. To my mind, people have already made too much of the policy of the Habsburgs – a spectacular one it is true, but at the same time hesitant, a combination of strength and weakness and, above all anachronistic. Their efforts not only encountered the obstacle formed by France, a hostile mass at the centre of the communication routes of the dispersed Habsburg state, but also the hostility of the rest of Europe. And the European balance of power this represented was not a recent phenomenon, emerging, as has been suggested, only after Charles VIII's expedition to Italy in 1494; it was a longstanding combination, as W. Kienast[87] has rightly pointed out, dating back at least to the conflict between the Capets and the Plantagenets, or even earlier according to Federico Chabod. The Europe the Habsburgs thought to reduce to obedience had been bristling with protective defences, both political and economic, for centuries. Finally, and most important of all, the same Europe had already made its entry on to the world stage, invading the Mediterranean in the eleventh century, and the Atlantic with the fantastic voyages of Columbus in 1492 and Vasco da Gama in 1498. In short, Europe's destiny as a world-economy pre-dated the destiny dreamed for her by the melancholy emperor. Even supposing that Charles V had had his way (as all the celebrated humanists of his time hoped), would not capitalism which was already established in the key cities of the new Europe – Antwerp, Lisbon, Seville and Genoa – somehow have managed to escape unhurt? Would the Genoese not have dominated the transactions of the European fairs in just the same way by handling the finances of 'Emperor' Philip II, rather than those of King Philip II?

But to leave the episodic for the heart of the debate, we must ask when Europe became sufficiently active, privileged and animated by powerful trade currents for a number of different economies to take up residence there together, living alongside and in competition with each other? Some form of international coordination was initiated in Europe at a very early date, by the Middle Ages, and it would continue over the centuries; thus the complementary zones of a world-economy, a hierarchy of production and exchange, appeared here very soon, and were operative almost from the start. What Charles V, despite a lifetime of effort, failed to do, Antwerp, the centre of the renewed world-economy of the early sixteenth century, achieved effortlessly. The city on the Scheldt gained control of the whole of Europe and of those areas of the world dependent on the old continent.

Thus through all Europe's political upheavals, an economic order became established in advance, spilling out over the frontiers of the continent, drawing on its differences of voltage and current. From earliest times, the core or 'heart' of Europe was surrounded by a nearby semi-periphery and by an outer periphery. And the semi-periphery, a pericardium so to speak enclosing the heart and forcing it to beat faster – northern Italy around Venice in the fourteenth and fifteenth centuries, the Netherlands around Antwerp – was probably the essential feature of the structure of Europe. There does not seem to have been a semi-periphery around Peking or Delhi, Isfahan, Istanbul or Moscow.

I am therefore inclined to see the European world-economy as having taken shape very early on; I do not share Immanuel Wallerstein's fascination with the sixteenth century. Is the problem that perplexes him not in the end the same one that was raised by Marx? Let me quote again the famous sentence 'The life-history of capital begins in the sixteenth century'. For Wallerstein, the European world-economy was the matrix of capitalism. I do not dispute this point, since to say central zone or capitalism is to talk about the same reality. By the same token however, to argue that the world-economy built in the sixteenth century on its European site was not the first to occupy this small but extraordinary continent, amounts to saying that capitalism did not wait for the sixteenth century to make its first appearance. I am therefore in agreement with the Marx who wrote (though he later went back on this) that European capitalism – indeed he even says capitalist *production* – began in thirteenth-century Italy. This debate is anything but academic.

War and the zones of the world-economy

Historians study individual wars one after another, but the history of warfare itself, stretching back through time, rarely seems to have engaged their interest, even in as justly celebrated a book as Hans Delbrück's.[88] But war has always been present, an obstinate unwanted guest in every century of the past. War implies many things: clear-headed calculation, courage and cowardice; Werner Sombart argued that war created capitalism, but the contrary is also true: war is the balance of truth, a trial of strength between states whom it helps to identify, and a sign of that folly which is never cured. It is such an important index of all that combines and flows together in human history, that setting war in the context of the world-economy enables one to discover a new meaning to human conflicts, and it brings unexpected confirmation of Immanuel Wallerstein's proposed model.

War never has a single unchanging face. Geography colours and divides it. Several forms of war may coexist at any time, primitive and modern, just as slavery, serfdom and capitalism coexisted. Men wage war with whatever comes to hand.

Werner Sombart was not mistaken when he talked about a new kind of war, rejuvenated by technology, the midwife of modern times, hastening the establishment of capitalist systems. By the sixteenth century, advanced warfare was furiously engaging money, intelligence, the ingenuity of technicians, so that it was said that it changed its nature from year to year at the dictates of a much less innocuous fashion than that which governed changes in costume. But this kind of war, both the mother and the daughter of progress, only existed at the core of world-economies; in order to develop, it required large numbers of men and resources, and grand designs. Once one leaves this centre-stage of the world theatre, brightly illuminated by the information and historiography of the time,

FIGVRE DV CORPS
D'ARMEE CARRE': COMME IL FORME
l'ordre de bataille.

Premier ordre.

caualerie.

canon.

moufquetaires.   canon.   moufq.   canon.   moufq.   canon.

c.

bagages.   chariots & bagages.   bagage.   Front de l'armee.

moufquetaires.   moufq.   moufq.

canon.   canon,   canon.   canon.

c.   c.

5 INSTRUCTION IN THE ART OF WAR

One of the innumerable 'orders' for marching, drawing up lines and giving battle, suggested and commented on in *Les Principes de l'art militaire* by I. de Billon, seigneur de la Brugne, according to 'the rules laid down by that great and excellent captain, Prince Maurice of Nassau' (p. 44).

and turns to the poor and sometimes primitive peripheries, there is no sign of this glorious warfare: or rather here it was ridiculously out of place and, what was more, ineffective.

Diego Suárez, the soldier-chronicler of Oran, provides us with some telling evidence on this point.[89] In about 1590, the Spanish government had the rather incongruous idea of sending out to the little African fortress a *tercio* of crack troops transferred from the fighting in Flanders – the theatre *par excellence* of advanced warfare. On the first sortie by this band of neophytes (as the old hands of the Oran garrison regarded them) a few Arab horsemen appeared on the horizon. The men of the *tercio* immediately fell into battle squares. But here their military skills were useless; the enemy took care not to come within range of the resolute combatants. And the garrison laughed their useless manoeuvre to scorn.

Advanced warfare was in fact a game it took two to play, as is well demonstrated by the long war in the Brazilian *Nordeste* between 1630 and 1654, described in a recent lively book by a young Brazilian historian.[90] The scene is set, without any possible doubt, on the outer margins of 'greater Europe'. The Dutch, who had occupied Recife by force in 1630, had not managed to conquer the whole of the sugar-growing province of Pernambuco. For twenty years, they were to be virtually blockaded in their town, receiving all their rations, munitions, reinforcements, even stone and brick for buildings, by sea. In the end, unsurprisingly, the conflict was resolved in 1654 in favour of the Portuguese, or rather the Luso-Brazilians, since it was the latter – and they neither concealed nor forgot it – who liberated Recife.

Until 1640, the king of Spain had also been the ruler of Portugal, which he had conquered in 1580, over half a century before. So the troops sent to this distant theatre of war were veteran officers and soldiers from the Flanders army, both Italians and Spaniards. But there was immediate trouble between these regular troops from Europe and the army levied locally, the *soldados da terra*. The Neapolitan, Count de Bagnuolo, who commanded the expeditionary force was indeed continually cursing the local troops, fretting with indignation and it was said, drowning his sorrows in drink. What did he want? Simply to be able to run the war in Brazil like the war in Flanders, with regular sieges and defences according to the text-books. When the Dutch captured Parahyba for instance, he saw fit to write to them in the following terms: 'May the captured town be of profit to Your Lordships. I am sending five prisoners with this message'.[91] This was not only advanced warfare, it was polite warfare in the spirit of the surrender of Breda in 1625 as depicted by Velasquez in the painting known as *Las Lanzas*.

The surrender of Breda, 1625. *Las Lanzas* by Velasquez. Spinola is being presented with the keys to the city. (Photo Giraudon.)

But the war in Brazil simply could not be fought like the war in Flanders, whatever the grumbles and irrelevant boasts of the veterans. The Indians and Brazilians, past masters of the raid and ambush, turned it into a guerrilla war. And if Bagnuolo, in an effort to rally their morale before launching them on an attack in the grand manner, was foolish enough to distribute a ration of rum, they went away to sleep off the alcohol. At the slightest excuse, these strange soldiers would slip out of their ranks and melt into the woods or vast swamps of the country. The Dutch, who also wanted to make war by the European rules, were disgusted at these insubstantial enemies, who instead of giving battle properly, drawn up on an open field, ran away, hid, and laid ambushes. What cowards and poltroons! The Spanish heartily agreed. As one of their veterans put it, 'We are not monkeys, to fight in the trees!' But these old soldiers may not have been entirely ungrateful, living behind their fortified lines, for the vigilant protection afforded by their sentinels, who were of exceptional quality, or for the agility of the effective little bands of men, past masters at skirmishing and what was called at the time *la guerra do matto* (war in the woods) or even more picturesquely *guerra volante* (flying warfare).

However in 1640, Portugal rebelled against Spain, and the two crowns were separated. A war began in the Iberian peninsula between Spain and Portugal which was to last almost thirty years until 1668. In Brazil of course, there was no longer any back-up from the Spanish fleet. Consequently there were no more veterans or expensive matériel. On the Brazilian side, the war now became entirely a matter of *guerra volante* – the poor man's war – and against all the odds this finally got the better of Dutch patience in 1654, at a time, it is true when the United Provinces were engaged in their first war with England, and thus much weakened, militarily speaking. Besides, Portugal was wise enough to pay handsomely, in shipments of salt, for the peace now within her grasp.

Evaldo Cabral de Mello's book lends some credence to a well-entrenched tradition that Garibaldi, fighting as a young man in the Brazilian wars (this time in about 1838, on the occasion of the uprising of the *Faroupilhas*, 'the ragged rebels') learned there the secrets of a singular kind of warfare: the rebels would converge on one point from a number of different directions, launch their attack and then disperse as swiftly and silently as they had come, to strike again elsewhere. This was the tactic he used in Sicily in 1860, after the landing of the Thousand.[92] But *guerra do matto* was by no means confined to Brazil. Guerrilla warfare still exists today, and the reader will no doubt have been reminded of recent examples. And Garibaldi could have learned it elsewhere than in Brazil. In French Canada, at the time of the war with the English, a regular officer condemned the ambushes laid by his French Canadian compatriots, who lay in wait for the enemy as they might to trap big game: 'This is not war', he said, 'it is murder.'[93]

In Europe on the contrary, near the central zones, war was waged with much to-do, with the deployment of huge armies, undertaking sophisticated and disciplined manoeuvres. The seventeenth century was the age *par excellence* of sieges, artillery, logistics and pitched battles. It was of course, an ever-open abyss into which money poured. States of small dimensions went under, in particular city-states, however sparing they were with their arsenals of weapons and their recruitment of mercenaries. If the modern state expanded at this time, and if modern capitalism took up residence within it, war was often the instrument: *bellum omnium pater*. But this kind of war fell very short of total war: prisoners were exchanged, rich men were ransomed, campaigns were more expertly waged than bloody. The Irishman Roger Boyle, Earl of Orrery[94] declared roundly in 1677: 'We make War more like Foxes than like Lyons and you have twenty Sieges for one Battel'. War waged without mercy would only come with Frederick II of Prussia or with the French Revolutionary and Napoleonic Wars.

One vital rule of this superior form of war was that one should always take the battle on to the enemy's territory, taking advantage of the weaker or the less strong. If, by some powerful rebound, it should cross back over the sacrosanct frontier, it meant the loss of primacy. There were few exceptions to this rule: the so-called Italian Wars sealed the subordinate fate of the peninsula which had hitherto dominated Europe. Holland resisted Louis XIV in 1672 and held her ground – but she could not stand up against Pichegru's cavalry in 1795; for now she no longer lay at the heart of Europe. No power, in the nineteenth or twentieth century, succeeded in crossing the Channel or the North Sea. England waged her wars at a distance, saved by her splendid isolation and by the handsome subsidies she distributed to her allies. For a strong power could make sure war was fought somewhere else. At the moment of Napoleon's encampment at Boulogne, British money was distributed in Austria, and the *Grande Armée* wheeled round at as if at a signal to face the Danube.

Societies and the world-economy

Societies evolve very slowly – something which is helpful to historical observation. China has always had mandarins in one form or another – will she ever be rid of them? India still has her caste system, and the Mogul Empire had its *jagindars*, a near-equivalent of the Turkish *sipahis*, until the very end of its days. Even western society, although more mobile than any other, evolves only at a slow pace. English society which visitors from continental Europe found as astonishing in the eighteenth century as non-British historians still do today (and I speak from experience) began to take shape after the Wars of the Roses, three hundred years earlier. Slavery, which Europe re-created in colonial America, was only abolished in the United States in 1865, and in Brazil in 1888– a mere century ago.

I do not on the whole believe that social change happens quickly, in sudden bursts. Even revolutions are not complete breaks with the past. As for social mobility, although it is certainly accelerated in times of economic progress, the 'rise of the bourgeoisie' for instance does not mean a massive surge forward in serried ranks, since the proportion of the privileged compared to the overall population always remained small. And in hard times, the upper class puts up the barriers: it takes a clever man to slip past them then. This was what happened in France in the 1590s. Or to take a small-scale example, what happened in the tiny republic of Lucca in the years 1628 and 1629.[95] For the state, contrary to a common misconception, only intermittently favoured the rise of the bourgeoisie and then at times that suited itself. And if over the years, the tiny ruling class did not suffer a loss in numbers, then social advance was even more slow, although in France as elsewhere, 'the third estate [is] always anxious to imitate the nobility towards which it constantly seeks to raise itself, by *unbelievable efforts*'.[96] Since social advancement was difficult and long sought after, it was normal that the few who made it into the upper class should often do no more than buttress the existing order. Even in the little towns of the Roman Marches, controlled from above by the Papal State, a select nobility jealous of its prerogatives would accept only a few new recruits who never threatened the existing social order.[97]

So it is not surprising if the social material poured into the mould of the world-economy seems in the end to have taken up the same contours, to have set solid and to have become indistinguishable from it. It was never short of time to adapt to the prevailing circumstances and to adapt circumstances to its own desirable equilibrium. So moving from one zone of the world economy to another meant for several centuries passing synchronically from wage labour to serfdom and slavery. The social order steadily and monotonously reproduced itself, in accordance with basic economic necessities. Every task, once allocated in the international division of labour, created its own form of control and that control articulated and governed the form taken by society. England at the core of the world-economy at the end of the eighteenth century, was the country where wage labour was penetrating both the countryside and urban activity; soon it would have spread to every area of British life. On the continent, wage labour and the degree to which it was prevalent, was a measure of the advance of modernity, but there were still many independent artisans; sharecropping – a sort of compromise between old-style serfdom and tenant-farming – was still widespread; and there were innumerable peasant smallholders in revolutionary France. Meanwhile serfdom was alive and well and spreading through the refeudalized countryside of eastern Europe and in the Turkish Balkans, while slavery had by the sixteenth century been dramatically revived for export to the New World, as if here the clock was to be turned back to the beginning again. In every case, society was responding to a different economic obligation and found itself caught by its very adaptation, incapable of escaping quickly from these structures once they had been created. So if society took a different form here or there, it was because it represented *a* solution or perhaps *the* solution, 'which was best suited (other things being equal) to the particular types of production with which it was confronted'.[98]

Such adaptation of the social to the economic had nothing of the foregone or mechanical conclusion about it, I hardly need say: there were strong overall imperatives, but also aberrations and departures from the norm, depending on cultural conditions and sometimes on geographical circumstances. No model completely and perfectly fits real life. I have several times pointed out the exemplary value of the case of Venezuela.[99] With the arrival of the Europeans here everything began again virtually from scratch. In the middle of the sixteenth century, there were perhaps 2000 whites and 18,000 natives in this huge country. Pearl-fishing along the coast lasted only a few decades. The working of the mines, notably the Yaracuy gold-mines, led to the first episode of slavery: a few Indians captured in battle and Negroes shipped in from Africa, but the numbers were small. The first real success was stock-raising, principally on the vast *llanos* of the interior, where a few white landlords and the Indian herdsmen on horse-back combined to form a primitive society reminiscent of feudalism. Later, and particularly in the eighteenth century, the cocoa plantations in the coastal zone led once more to the use of imported black slaves. So there were two Venezuelas, one 'feudal', the other 'slave-owning', the former having developed first. But it is worth pointing out that in the eighteenth century quite a number of black slaves were also incorporated into the *haciendas* of the *llanos*. And it should also be said that Venezuelan colonial society with its burgeoning cities and institutions cannot by any means be wholly accounted for by this two-fold model.

Perhaps one should insist upon what may seem self-evident. In my view, all the divisions and 'models' analysed by sociologists and historians are to be found from very early on in the social samples we have in front of us. It is quite possible for classes, castes (that is closed groups), and 'orders', usually favoured by the state, to coexist simultaneously. The class struggle appears very soon here and there, and dies away only to break out later. For there are no societies from which conflicting forces are absent. And there are no societies without some form of hierarchy, that is in general without the reduction of the masses which compose them to labour and obedience. Slavery, serfdom and wage labour are historically and socially different solutions to a universal problem, which remains fundamentally the same. And comparisons *can* be made from one case to another, fair or unfair, superficial or far-reaching though they may be. 'The servants of a great lord of Livonia', writes Staunton in 1793, 'or the Negroes who serve in the household of a planter in Jamaica, although slaves themselves, regard themselves as greatly superior the former to peasants and the latter to Negroes who work on the land.'[100] At about the same period, Baudry des Lozìeres, in a polemic against 'blatant Negro-lovers' went so far as to claim that:

at bottom, the word *slave*, as used in the colonies, simply means the indigent class whom nature seems to have created especially for labour; [indeed] this is the class which covers the greater part of Europe. In the colonies, the slave lives by working and always finds lucrative work; in Europe, the wretched man does not always find work to do and dies in misery ... Show me one unfortu-

Domestic slavery in Brazil. (J.-B. Debret, *Voyage pittoresque...*, 1843. Photo B.N., Paris.)

nate who has died in need in the colonies, who has been obliged to fill his empty stomach with grass, or who has been driven by hunger to kill himself! In Europe, there are many cases of those who have perished of starvation ...[101]

This takes us to the heart of the problem. Social modes of exploitation may exist side by side and indeed complement one another. What may be possible at the core of a world-economy, thanks to the abundance of population, transactions and money, may no longer be possible in the same way on its various peripheries. Between one point and another of the economic 'territory' there is in effect a historical regression. But I greatly fear that the present system, *mutatis mutandis*, is still embroidering on the structural inequalities produced by historical time-lags. For a long time, the central zones siphoned off the populations of their outer margins: these were the favourite places for recruiting slaves. And where do the unskilled workers come from today, to work in the industrial areas of Europe, the United States and the Soviet Union?

Immanuel Wallerstein argues that the pattern of the world-economy and the social picture it reveals, establishes that there can be coexistence of 'modes of production' from slavery to capitalism, that the latter can only live if it is surrounded by the other modes, and indeed at their expense. Rosa Luxemburg was right.

This confirms me in an opinion which has gradually imposed itself on me: capitalism implies above all hierarchy, and it takes up a position at the top of the hierarchy, whether or not this was created by itself. Where it appears only belatedly, it merely requires a way in, a foreign but colluding social hierarchy which extends and facilitates its action: a great Polish landowner interested in the Gdansk market; an *engenho*-owner of the Brazilian *Nordeste* who has connections with the merchants of Lisbon, Oporto or Amsterdam; a Jamaican planter in touch with the London merchants – and the connection is made, the current transmitted. Such 'entry points' are quite evidently part and parcel of capitalism. Elsewhere, by means of 'forays' or 'liaisons' established from the core zone, capitalism inserts itself into the chain leading from production to wholesale trade, not seeking to take over entire responsibility for them, but to occupy the strategic points controlling the key sectors of accumulation. Is it because this chain, with its established hierarchy, is so long-drawn-out, that all social development linked to the whole is so slow? Or, and this amounts to the same thing, is it as Peter Laslett suggests, because most ordinary economic tasks are burdensome, and a heavy load on the shoulders of men,[102] and because there have always been a number of privileged persons (of various kinds) who have managed to heap on to other shoulders the wearisome tasks necessary for the life of all?

The cultural order

Cultures (or civilizations: the two words, whatever people say, are interchange-able in most contexts) are ways of ordering space just as economies are. While they may coincide with the latter (particularly since a world-economy *taken as a whole*, *tends* to share the same culture, or at least elements of the same culture, as opposed to neighbouring world-economies) they may also be distinguished from them: the cultural map and the economic map cannot simply be super-imposed without anomaly, and this is after all only logical, if only because culture dates from even further back in time than the world-economy, impressive though the lifespan of the latter may be. Culture is the oldest character in human history: economies succeed each other, political institutions crumble, societies replace each other, but civilization continues along its way. Rome fell in the fifth century AD, but the Church of Rome is still with us. When Hinduism stood up against Islam in the eighteenth century, it opened up a vacuum into which the British conquest could insinuate itself, but the struggle between the two old civilizations is still going on before our eyes, with all its consequences, whereas the British Raj ended over thirty years ago. Civilization is the grandfather, the patriarch of world history.

At the heart of every civilization, religious values are asserted: this is something that goes back to the very earliest times. If the Church, in the Middle Ages and later, fought against usury and the introduction of money, it was because the Church stood for a former age, one long pre-dating capitalism, and found these new-fangled devices intolerable. But religion alone cannot stand for a whole culture, which also represents thought, way of life in every sense of the term, literature, art, ideology, intellectual developments: a culture is made up of a multitude of goods, both material and spiritual.

And to make things even more complicated, culture is at the same time society, politics and economic expansion. What society does not succeed in doing, culture does; what the economy might do if left to itself, culture limits, and so on. And indeed no recognizable cultural boundary exists which is not living evidence of a multitude of processes. The frontier between the Rhine and the Danube was during the period covered by this book a cultural frontier *par excellence*: on one side the original Christian Europe, on the other the 'Christian periphery' conquered at a later date. When the Reformation occurred, it was along virtually the same frontier that the split in Christianity became established: Protestants on one side and Catholics on the other. And it is of course visibly the ancient *limes* or outer limit of the Roman Empire. Many examples would tell a similar story – the spread of Romanesque and Gothic architecture, for example which were both, with only a few exceptions, confined to western Europe, thus indicating the growing cultural unity of the West – a world-culture or world-civilization.

World-civilizations and world-economies of course join hands and help each other. The conquest of the New World also meant the spread of European civilization in all its forms, underpinning and guaranteeing colonial expansion. In Europe itself, cultural unity aided economic exchange and vice versa. The first appearance of Gothic architecture in Italy, in the city of Siena, was a direct import by the Sienese merchants who attended the Champagne fairs. It led to the rebuilding of all the façades in the main square of the city. Marc Bloch saw in the cultural unity of Christian Europe in the Middle Ages one of the reasons why it was so penetrable by and suited to trade, and this remained the case well after the Middle Ages.

The bill of exchange for instance, the key weapon in the armoury of merchant capitalism in the West, was still, even in the eighteenth century, circulating almost exclusively within the bounds of Christendom; it did not move outside them into Islam, Muscovy or the Far East. In the fifteenth century, there were, it is true, bills of exchange from Genoa to be found in centres in North Africa, but they would have been underwritten by a Genoese or an Italian, and received by a Christian merchant in Oran, Tlemcen or Tunis.[103] So it was still circulating among friends so to speak. Similarly, in the eighteenth century, returns made by bill of exchange from Batavia[104] or British India, or Mauritius[105] remained transactions between Europeans, who held both ends of the chain. Venetian bills of exchange on the Levant did exist, but they were usually drawn on or underwritten by the Venetian *bailo* in Constantinople.[106] Not to be doing business with one's own people, that is merchants subject to the same rules and codes of conduct, would mean taking risks beyond the bounds of common sense. But this was not simply a matter of technical obstacles; it was symptomatic of a real cultural divide – since outside the West there were plenty of effective circuits of bills of exchange on behalf of Muslim, Armenian or Indian merchants. And these circuits too stopped at the respective cultural boundaries. Tavernier explains how one could transfer money from place to place by a series of bills issued by Banyan merchants, from anywhere in India to the Levant, the *ne plus ultra*. Here world-civilizations and world-economies put up identical barriers and obstacles.

Inside any world-economy on the other hand, the cultural and economic maps might differ considerably, and even contrast with each other, as the respective centres of gravity of economic zones and cultural zones significantly demonstrate. In the thirteenth, fourteenth and fifteenth centuries, the cultural centre of Europe was neither Venice nor Genoa, the two queens of trade, which dominated western civilization, but Florence. Florence set the tone, invented the

6   IMITATIONS OF VERSAILLES IN EIGHTEENTH-CENTURY EUROPE
This map showing the many copies of Versailles, from Spain to Russia and from Sweden to Naples, is a measure of French cultural supremacy in the Europe of the Enlightenment. (From Louis Réau, *L'Europe française au Siècle des Lumières*, 1938, p. 279.)

Renaissance and sent it all over Europe, and at the same time imposed her dialect – the Tuscan tongue – on Italian literature. The lively Venetian dialect, which might *a priori* have been thought a strong rival, made no such attempt. Was this because an economically victorious city or a too-dominant state could not do everything at once? In the seventeenth century, Amsterdam ruled the world, but the baroque, which invaded Europe, this time came from Rome, or possibly from Madrid. And in the eighteenth century, cultural supremacy did not lie in London. The Abbé Le Blanc, visiting England between 1733 and 1740 was not very impressed with the architecture, remarking that Wren[107] designing St Paul's (in the seventeenth century it is true) 'had merely reduced St Peter's in Rome to two-thirds its size'. He follows this up with some unfavourable comments on English country houses, 'which are still in the Italian taste but it is not always very well applied'.[108] In fact in the eighteenth century, England was influenced not so much by Italian culture as by borrowings from France, at the time generally recognized as the cultural centre of Europe, with her supremacy in wit, art and fashion, to console her no doubt for not ruling the world. 'The English are so fond of our language as to read even Cicero in French',[109] writes our informant Le Blanc. And tired of hearing how many French servants there were in London, he retorted 'if you find so many Frenchmen to serve you in London, it is because your people have a craze for being dressed, curled and powdered like us. They are mad about our fashions and will pay well those who teach them to adorn themselves with our Follies'.[110] So even London, the centre of the world, with a brilliant culture of its own, made many concessions to and borrowings from France – not always generally appreciated, since in about 1770, there existed a Society of Anti-Gallicans, 'the first principle of which is not to use for clothing any article of French Manufacture'.[111] But what could a society do to stop fashion? England, though elevated by her economic advance did not challenge the intellectual leadership of Paris; and the whole of Europe, even as far off as Moscow, collaborated to turn French into the language of high society and the vehicle of European thought. Similarly, in the late nineteenth century and early twentieth, France, though lagging behind the rest of Europe economically, was the undisputed centre of western painting and literature; the times when Italy and Germany dominated the world of music were not times when Italy or Germany dominated Europe economically; and even today, the formidable economic lead by the United States has not made it the literary and artistic leader of the world.

Technology on the other hand (though not necessarily science) has always noticeably developed in the leading zones of the economic world. The Venetian Arsenal was still a centre of technology even in the sixteenth century. First Holland, then Britain inherited this double privilege in turn. It now lies with the United States. But technology is perhaps the body rather than the soul of a civilization. It is logical that it should be encouraged by the industrial activity and high wages of leading economic regions. Science on the other hand is not the

An example of the prestige of France and Venice in the eighteenth century: gondolas taking part in a Venetian festival at the castle of Nymphenburg, a Bavarian Versailles, in 1746. (Nymphenburg Castle, Munich, Armand Colin Coll.)

particular privilege of any single nation. Or at least it was not until recently; now I am not so sure.

The world-economy model is certainly a valid one

The model proposed by Immanuel Wallerstein in his book *The Modern World-System*, which I have presented here in general outline, has, like all controversial theses, provoked both praise and criticism since its appearance in 1974. An extraordinary number of antecedents have been sought and found. The thesis has been discovered to have multiple applications and implications: even national economies have been described as fitting the same pattern, interspersed and surrounded as they are with autarkic regions; indeed the world could be said to be full of 'peripheries', in other words under-developed zones, belts and economies. Within the reduced scale of the model as applied to specific 'national' areas, one can find examples that apparently contradict the general thesis,[112] such as Scotland, the 'periphery' of England, which in fact took off economically in the late eighteenth century. One might, in seeking to explain the failure of Charles V's imperial designs in 1557, prefer my explanation to Wallerstein's, or criticize him, as I have implicitly, for letting the lines of his model get in the way of observing realities other than the economic order. Since Wallerstein's book is to be followed by three others, the second of which will have been published by the time the English version of this one appears (I have partly read it in manuscript), and since the last two will take us up to the present day, we shall have plenty of time to consider the merits, novelties and limitations of this systematic approach – one that is a little too systematic, perhaps, but which has proved itself to be extremely stimulating.

And it is this success that deserves most emphasis. The way in which the inequality of the world accounts for the progress and establishment of capitalism, explains why the central region surpasses itself, taking the lead in every kind of progress; why the history of the world is an undivided procession, a cortège of coexisting modes of production which we are too inclined to think of as following one another in successive historical periods. In fact the different modes of production are all attached to each other. The most advanced are dependent on the most backward and vice versa: development is the reverse side of under-development.

Immanuel Wallerstein tells us that he arrived at the theory of the world-economy while looking for the largest units of measurement which would still be coherent. But of course in the battle this sociologist and expert on Africa is waging against history, his task is still unfinished. Divisions according to space must certainly be made. But one also needs a temporal frame of reference. For several world-economies have succeeded in each other in the geographical expression that is Europe. Or rather the European world-economy has changed shape several times since the thirteenth century, displacing the core, rearranging the peripheries. Should we not therefore ask ourselves what, in a given world-economy, is the longest *temporal* unit of reference which can undeniably be said, despite its length and many changes, to have coherence? Whether one is dealing with time or space, coherence is essential: without it there would be no unit of measurement at all.

The world-economy and divisions of time

Time like space, can be divided up. Our problem now is to use such divisions, at which historians excel, the better to locate chronologically and the better to understand those historical monsters, the world-economies. It is not an easy task, for in their slow historical progress they admit only approximate dates: a period of growth can be dated to somewhere between ten and twenty years and not always then; a change in centre of gravity might take more than a century: Bombay, ceded to the English by the Portuguese government in 1665, had to wait a hundred years before it supplanted the trading city of Surat around which the economic activity of the whole of western India had previously been organized.[113] So we are dealing with history in slow motion, with journeys that seem never-ending and so lacking in revealing incidents that there is a risk of inaccuracy in reconstructing their routes. These huge leviathans seem suspended in time: history takes centuries to build or destroy them.

A further difficulty is that we have to use the only services available, those of conjunctural history, the history of short- and medium-term change, and this is naturally more concerned with short-lived movements than with the slow-moving shifts and fluctuations we are looking for. Our first step must be therefore to offer a preliminary explanation to help us to look beyond these short-term movements – the ones of course which it is easiest to detect and interpret.

The rhythms of the 'conjuncture'

It was about fifty years ago that the social sciences made the discovery that human life was subject to fluctuations and swings of *periodic* movements, which carry on in endless succession. Such movements, harmonious or discordant, bring to mind the vibrating cords or sounding-boards of schoolday physics. G.H. Bousquet for instance[114] wrote in 1923; 'The different aspects of social movement [have] an undulating rhythmic profile, not one that is invariable or varies regularly, but one marked by periods when [their] intensity increases or diminishes'. 'Social movement' can be taken to refer to all the movements at work in a given society, the combination of movements which forms the *conjuncture* or rather the *conjunctures*. For there may be different conjunctural rhythms affecting the economy, political life, demography and indeed collective attitudes, preoccupations, crime, the different schools of art or literature, even fashion (although fashion in dress changes so quickly in the West that it is more a question of the day-to-day than the conjunctural). Of all these, only the economic conjuncture has been seriously studied, if not pursued to its logical conclusion. So conjunctural history is extremely complex and by no means complete, as we shall see when we have to draw some conclusions.

For the moment, let us concentrate on the economic conjuncture and in particular on prices, which have been the subject of a vast body of research. The theory of prices was worked out in about 1929–32 by economists looking at the contemporary situation. Historians followed suit and thanks to their work, it gradually became possible to go back in time, producing a series of ideas, evidence and a new language. The overall movement was divided up into particular movements, each being given its own code, period and, if possible, significance.[115]

Seasonal shifts, which can still play a role even today (one thinks of the drought in 1976 for instance) are usually obscured in the complicated economies of the present day. But they were not always so invisible, on the contrary. Poor harvests or food shortages could in a few months create inflation equivalent to the entire sixteenth-century price revolution! The poor were then obliged to live on as little as possible until the next harvest. The only good thing about this type of movement was that it was quite short-lived. After the storm, as Witold Kula puts it, the Polish peasant would, like the snail, come out of his shell.[116]

Other movements, or as they tend to be called *cycles*, imply a much longer time-span. In order to distinguish between them, they have been dubbed with the names of certain economists: thus a *Kitchin* is a short cycle of three or four years; the *Juglar*, or intra-decade cycle (that bane of the *ancien régime*) lasts from 6 to 8 years; a *Labrousse* (also known as an *intercycle* or *inter-decade* cycle) can last 10 or 12 years or more: this is the combination of the latter phase of a Juglar (three or four years) and of a whole Juglar which fails to take off and thereafter remains at a low level: a half-Juglar plus a whole Juglar in other words. The classic example of the *Labrousse* is the intercycle which brought depression and stagnation to France between 1778 and 1791 on the eve of the Revolution, which it must surely have helped to unleash. The hypercycle or *Kuznets*, a double Juglar, lasts about twenty years, while a *Kondratieff*[117] spreads over a half-century or more: one Kondratieff began in 1791, reached its peak in 1817 and then went downhill until 1851, lasting almost until the Second Empire in France (1852–1870). The longest cycle of all is the secular trend – which has been very little studied in fact, and to which I shall shortly be returning. Until the last named has been closely examined and restored to its true importance, conjunctural history, despite all the work it has so far inspired, remains terribly incomplete.

All these cycles are of course contemporaneous with each other, synchronic: they coexist, overlap and intensify or diminish by their own movements the general trend. But it is technically easy to divide the general trend into particular movements, and to eliminate one group or another, the better to study an individual movement.

The crucial initial question to be asked is whether such cycles, which have been identified by present-day economic observation, existed in the pre-industrial

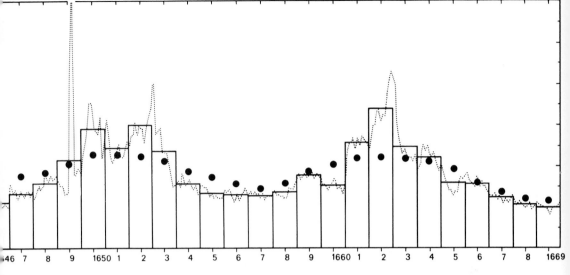

46 7 8 9 1650 1 2 3 4 5 6 7 8 9 1660 1 2 3 4 5 6 7 8 1669

7 HOW TO BREAK DOWN PRICE SERIES INTO DIFFERENT CYCLES
Three different series of price records are superimposed in this figure: they all relate to the price
of a *setier* of wheat on the Paris Halles:

— the dotted line represents monthly shifts. Fairly calm in normal years, this shoots up at times
of shortage or when there was a shortfall before the next harvest;

— the stepped blocks show the annual average calculated on the harvest-year (August to July);
bad years (1648-9 to 1652-3; the *Fronde*, 1661-2; and the accession of Louis XIV) alternate with
good years when the harvest was abundant;

— the large black dots indicate cyclical movements, calculated on sliding seven-year averages.
These movements run from 1645-6 to 1655-6, and from 1656-7 to 1668-9. Translation of the
data into these broad cycles is a way of relating price fluctuations to the secular trend.

economies of the past. Were there such things as Kondratieffs before 1791 for
instance? One historian would reply a little maliciously that if one goes looking
for any kind of cycle before the nineteenth century, one is virtually certain to
find it.[118] His warning is useful so long as it does not obscure the importance of
what is at issue. If today's cycles do in fact have some resemblance to those of
the past, that indicates that there is a certain continuity between *ancien régime*
and modern economies: rules similar to those governing our present experience
may have operated in the past. And if the range of fluctuations turns out to be
different, if they bear some other kind of relationship to each other, then it may
be possible to detect a significant evolution. I do not therefore think that the
Kitchin cycles Pierre Chaunu has detected in the trade of Seville in the sixteenth
century are a mere detail of no consequence,[119] nor that the series of Kondratieffs
in the history of cereal and bread prices in Cologne between 1368 and 1797[120]
have nothing important to tell us about this primordial question of continuity.

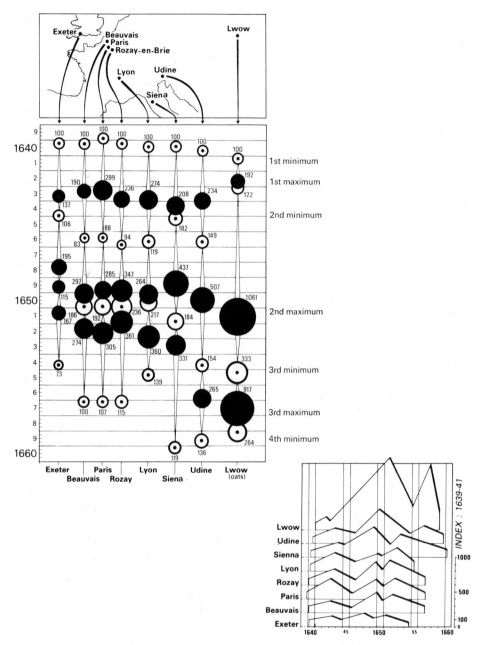

8 DO PRICE CHANGES TRAVEL IN WAVES? GRAIN CRISES IN EUROPE 1639–1660
On the left-hand graph which was devised by Frank Spooner (*Cambridge Economic History*,
1967, IV, p. 468), the black circles represent the maximum prices in four successive crises; they
swept across the whole of Europe, from the Atlantic to Poland. The index of 100 is calculated
from the last quarter of 1639 to the first quarter of 1641. The second graph (courtesy of the
Laboratory of the École des Hautes Études) represents the same waves of prices more schematically.

Fluctuations across a spatial sounding-board

Prices (and in pre-industrial societies calculations are usually based on cereal prices) are constantly fluctuating. Their variations, visible from very early on, are a sign that a network of markets was established in Europe at an early stage, the more so since such variations occur at very much the same time across a broad area. Europe in the fifteenth, sixteenth and seventeenth centuries, although far from presenting a unified picture, was already clearly obeying a general series of rhythms, an overall order.

And indeed this has been rather discouraging for the historian of prices and wages: whenever he set out to reconstruct an unknown series, he would inevitably find, when the work was complete, that it was just the same as all the others. One piece of research would simply duplicate the results of another. The map in Figure 8, taken from the *Cambridge Modern Economic History of Europe*[121] displays this unison, as if the waves of high and low prices moved across Europe with sufficient coherence to be shown on a map, like isobars in meteorology. Frank Spooner has tried to present this in visible terms and the graph he has devised indicates the problem very well if it does not resolve it. To solve it, one would have to detect the epicentre of these waves, if there was one. Is this likely? According to Pierre Chaunu, 'if there was an early version of a world-economy in the sixteenth-century ... the source of the movements in unison [seems] to be somewhere between Seville and Vera Cruz'.[122] If I had to choose one place, I would tend to see these conjunctural vibrations as emanating rather from Antwerp, if not necessarily originating there, since this city was the centre of European trade at the time. But perhaps the reality is too complicated to admit of any single centre, wherever one locates it?

At all events, these prices that rise and fall in unison provide us with the most convincing evidence of the coherence of a world-economy penetrated by monetary exchange and developing under the already directive hand of capitalism. The rapidity with which these prices spread and reached 'equilibrium' is evidence of the effectiveness of trade, subject to the speeds of the means of transport of the time. Such speeds may seem derisory to us nowadays. But special couriers were nevertheless wearing out their horses racing from one big centre to another after every international fair, bearing useful messages, quoting prices, and carrying the bundles of bills of exchange which had to travel by mail. And bad news, notably of local shortages or bankruptcies, even very distant ones, travelled fast. In September 1751, it was reported from Livorno, an active port, but by no means the hub of European economic life, that 'the large number of bankruptcies occurring in various towns has brought considerable harm to the trade here, and it has just suffered a fresh blow with news of the bankruptcy of Messrs Leake and Prescot in St Petersburg, which is said to be of the order of five hundred thousand roubles. It is feared that [trade in Livorno] will also be much affected by the decision taken by the Genoese to restore the franchise of the port of Genoa'.[123] Reports like this are surely palpable evidence of the unity (inevitably the conjunctural unity) of Europe. Everything moved at virtually the same pace.

But the really curious thing is that the rhythms of the European conjuncture transcend the strict boundaries of their own world-economy and already have a sort of power of remote-control. Prices in Muscovy, insofar as they are known to us, lined up with those of the West in the sixteenth century, probably by the intermediary of American bullion, which here as elsewhere acted as a 'transmission belt'. Similarly, Ottoman prices followed the European pattern for the same reasons. America, at least in places like New Spain and Brazil where prices fluctuated, also imitated the distant European model. Louis Dermigny has even written that 'the Atlantic-Pacific correlation demonstrated by Pierre Chaunu[124] is not confined to Manila'.[125] European prices had a knock-on effect, reaching beyond even the route of the Manila galleon, in particular to Macao. And we know from the research by Aziza Hazan, that the European inflation of the sixteenth century was echoed, with about twenty years' time-lag, in India.[126]

The interest of such evidence is clear: if the rhythm of price-changes, whether imposed or passed on, is really a sign of domination or allegiance, as I believe, then the influence of the world-economy centred in Europe must very soon have exceeded even the most ambitious frontiers ever attributed to it. This directs our attention to the 'antennae' which a conquering world-economy throws out ahead of it, high tension cables as it were, of which the best example is the Levant trade. Historians (Wallerstein included) have tended to underestimate this type of exchange, to regard it as subsidiary because it only concerns luxury products, so that it could be eliminated without in the least affecting people's daily life, which is true enough. But since it had its place at the heart of the most sophisticated capitalism, it had *consequences* which did indeed have some bearing on everyday life – on prices, but on other things too. And this directs our attention once more to money and precious metals, instruments of domination and weapons of war to a greater extent than is usually admitted.

The secular trend

The longest-lasting of all these cycles is the secular trend – and it is also perhaps the most neglected. In part this is because economists are on the whole interested in short-term developments – 'a purely economic long-term analysis is meaningless', writes André Marchal.[127] Partly it is because its slow movement conceals it. The secular trend seems like a baseline from which prices as a whole take off. If the baseline moves slightly up and down or remains steady, who is going to take much notice, when all the other price movements, those of the short term, superimpose on this base their much more erratic developments, their abrupt rises and falls? The secular trend is sometimes regarded as what is left when all the surface movements have been smoothed out by calculation. If we promote it to the status of indicator (please note that I am not yet saying 'efficient cause') shall we not be running the risk (as there was with Simiand's A and B phases, but on a different time-scale) of concealing the real problems? Indeed, does the secular trend really exist at all?

More than one economist and historian is likely to retort that it emphatically does not; or simply to act as if it did not. But what if these cautious sceptics were wrong? The appearance, in visible form in 1974, though its origins go back further than that, of a long-term, abnormal and disconcerting world crisis has suddenly concentrated the minds of specialists once more on the long-term. Léon Dupriez was the first to raise the alarm, with many warnings and observations. Michael Lutfalla has even referred to 'the return to Kondratieff'. And Rondo Cameron[128] has suggested that there might be what he calls 'logistic' cycles of between 150 and 350 years in length. But apart from the label, how do these really differ from the secular trend? The time is therefore ripe to plead the cause of the secular trend.

Barely visible in everyday life, but plodding inexorably on, always in the same direction, the trend is a *cumulative* process, building on its own achievements: almost as if it were determined gradually to raise the mass of prices and economic activities until some turning-point when, with equal obstinacy, it begins working to bring them down again, slowly and imperceptibly but over a long period. Year by year it is hardly discernible, but measured century by century, it is something of importance. So if one tried to measure the secular trend more accurately and to superimpose it systematically on to European history (as Wallerstein has superimposed on to European history the spatial model of the world-economy) some explanations might emerge of the economic currents to which we are still subject today, without our being able either to understand them very well or to find reliable remedies for them. I have neither the intention nor the means, of course, of improvising a theory of the secular trend: at best I shall simply try to present the content of the classic works by Jenny Griziotti Krestchmann[129] and Gaston Imbert[130] and to note their possible consequences. This is a way of defining the problem more clearly but not of solving it.

A secular cycle, like any other cycle, has a point of departure, a peak and a point of arrival, but because of the generally rather low profile taken by the secular trend, the location of these points is somewhat approximate. Of the peaks, one says for instance 'round about' 1350 or 1650. From data accepted at present,[131] four successive secular cycles can be identified, *as far as Europe is concerned*: 1250 [1350] 1507-1510; 1507-10 [1650] 1733-1743; 1733-1743 [1817] 1896; 1896 [1974?] … The first and last date in each case represent the beginning of an upward movement and the end of a downward one; the middle date in square brackets indicates the peak, the point at which the secular trend begins to go into decline, in other words, the moment of crisis.

Of all these chronological signposts, the first is by far the most uncertain. I would personally choose the beginning of the twelfth century rather than 1250 as a point of departure. The problem is that price records are very imperfect for these distant times and one cannot be at all certain, but the beginnings of the huge expansion in the western towns and countryside and the launching of the crusades suggest that the starting-point of European growth might be put back at least fifty years.

These preliminary remarks have a purpose: they show us that it is very difficult, with evidence of only three secular cycles – the fourth (if we are right about the 1970s as a turning-point) being only half-way through its course – to draw conclusions about the comparative length of these cycles. It does look however as if there is a tendency for these great waves rolling in from the deep to become shorter in length. Should one attribute this to a speeding up in the pace of history, a sort of snowball effect?

This is not our problem; we are concerned to find out whether this secular movement, which was imperceptible to contemporaries, is a reliable record or an aid to understanding the long-term destiny of the world-economies; whether it was the world-economies, in spite or because of their weight and duration, which contributed to create these cycles, kept them going, were subject to them and both explain and are explained by them. To find that this was precisely the case would be too good to be true. Without wishing to impose a solution, and in order to shorten the discussion, I shall restrict myself to taking the successive peaks of 1350, 1650, 1817 and 1973–4 as vantage points. In theory, these look-out years should enable us to have a view of two different and contradictory landscapes, standing as they do at a turning-point of two processes. I have not chosen them myself, but accepted them as a result of calculations made by other people. It is certainly the case that the watersheds which they record fit, probably not by chance, the periodizations of various kinds made by historians. If they also correspond to significant breaks in the history of the European world-economies, at least it will not be because I have overworked the data too far in one direction or another.

An explanatory chronology of the world-economies

The horizon revealed from these four peaks may not explain the entire history of Europe, but if these points have been judiciously identified, they ought to suggest and virtually guarantee, since they correspond to analogous situations, some useful comparisons across the whole range of experience referred to.

In 1350, the Black Death was adding its horrors to the slow but steady decline which had begun before mid-century. The European world-economy of the time embraced as well as the landmass of western and central Europe, the North Sea and the Mediterranean. It is quite clear that this Europe-Mediterranean system was undergoing a profound crisis; Christendom, losing the taste or the capacity for launching more crusades, had come up against the resistance and inertia of

Islam, to whom she had surrendered the last important outpost in the Holy Land, Acre, in 1291; by about 1300, the Champagne fairs, halfway between the Mediterranean and the North Sea, were in decline; in about 1340, equally seriously, the 'Mongol' silk route was interrupted – this had been a free channel of trade for Venice and Genoa, reaching beyond the Black Sea to India and China. The Islamic barrier, across which this route had been the only way, became a reality once more, and Christian shipping had to fall back on the traditional ports of the Levant in Syria and Egypt. In 1350 or so, Italy was also becoming the scene of industry, dyeing the unbleached cloth from the north to sell it in the east and later starting to manufacture it herself. The *Arte della Lana* was soon to dominate Florence. In short this was no longer the age of St Louis and Richard Cœur de Lion. The European system which had been balanced between the northern and the Mediterranean poles of attraction, was now swinging towards the south as the primacy of Venice showed: a shift of gravity had occurred in her favour. The world-economy centred on Venice would before long be procuring her relative prosperity, soon to reach dazzling heights in a weakened Europe now in evident recession.

Three hundred years later, in 1650, the long age of prosperity of the 'extended' sixteenth century was (after an Indian summer between 1600 and 1630–1650) drawing to a close. Was the problem in the American mining areas? Or was there a downward turn in the conjuncture? Here again, at a precise point in time, identified as the turning-point in the secular trend, a *broad* decline in the world-economy is visible. While the Mediterranean system had already collapsed, beginning with Spain and Italy, both of which were too closely tied to the bullion of America and the finances of the Habsburg Empire, the new Atlantic system in turn began to break down. This general recession became the 'crisis of the seventeenth century', a subject of much controversy and few conclusions. And this was the moment when Amsterdam, already at the centre of the world when the seventeenth century began, established herself there in triumph. From now on, the Mediterranean lay firmly outside the mainstream of history which it had almost exclusively dominated for centuries on end.

1817: the precise dating of this turning-point should not be taken literally: signs of the reversal of the secular trend had appeared in England in 1809 and 1810; in France with the crises of the last years of the Napoleonic era. And in the United States, 1812 clearly marked a new departure. Similarly the Mexican silver mines, the hope and envy of Europe, were dealt a severe blow by the 1810 revolution and if they did not immediately begin producing again afterwards, the general conjuncture is partly to blame. Europe and the world ran short of silver. What was now happening was a shift in the economic order of the whole world from China to the Americas. England lay at the heart of this world, and suffered, despite her victory, taking many years to recover. But she succeeded in taking the leading position which no other country was able to wrest from her (Holland having long since disappeared over the horizon).

What about 1973-4 then? Is this a short-term conjunctural crisis, as most economists seem to think? Or have we had the rare and unenviable privilege of seeing with our own eyes the century begin its downward turn? If so, the short-term policies admirably directed towards immediate ends, advocated by our political leaders and economic experts, may turn out to be powerless to cure a sickness of which our children's children will be very lucky to see the end. Present-day history is giving us a nod and obliging us to ask ourselves this question. But before taking heed of this warning, let me open a parenthesis.

Kondratieff cycles and the secular trend

The secular trend ferries along with it, as we have noticed, other cycles which have neither its longevity, serenity or unobtrusiveness. They shoot up and down, and are easy, indeed conspicuous, to see. Everyday life, today as in the past, is punctuated by these short-lived movements which must all be added to the trend in order to estimate them as a whole. But for present purposes, we shall restrict ourselves to discussing only the respectable-sized Kondratieffs, which are also fairly long-winded since each of them corresponds roughly to a good half-century, the length of two generations, one living through a favourable conjuncture, one through a downward trend. If we put together these two cycles, the secular trend and the Kondratieff, we shall have the score of a long conjunctural movement for two voices. This may complicate our first appraisal, but also strengthens it, since contrary to what has been said by historians, Kondratieffs made their first appearance on the European stage not in 1791 but hundreds of years earlier.

By adding to their movements to the upward or downward secular trend, the Kondratieffs either reinforce it or attenuate it. One time in two, the peak of a Kondratieff coincides with the peak of a secular trend – as in 1817. This may also be true (if my analysis is correct) of 1973-4; possibly of 1650. Between 1817 and 1971 there were two independent Kondratieff peaks: in 1873 and 1929. If our data were invulnerable to any criticism, which is far from being the case, we could say that in 1929 the crash which sparked off the worldwide depression was merely the turning-point in a simple Kondratieff, the upward phase of which had begun in 1896, continued through the last years of the nineteenth century, the first of the twentieth, the First World War and the ten grey years of the post-war period, to reach the peak of 1929. The crash of 1929-1930 was such a shock to contemporaries and specialists – particularly the latter – that a huge effort was made to understand what had happened; François Simiand's book is a good example.

In 1973-4, we saw the turning-point of another Kondratieff, one which had begun in 1945 (with an upward phase of about a quarter-century, which is about normal) but this may also have coincided, as in 1817, with a reversal of the secular trend, making it a double watershed. I am inclined to think that this is

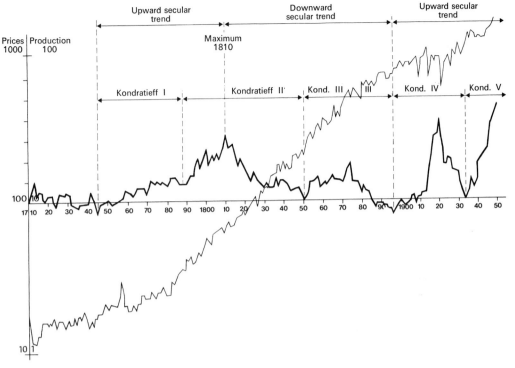

9   KONDRATIEFF CYCLES AND THE SECULAR TREND
This graph, based on prices in Britain from 1700 to 1950, shows both the Kondratieff cycles and
the secular trend. The production curve has been added: note its discordance with the price
curve. From Gaston Imbert, *Des mouvements de longue durée Kondratieff*, 1959, p. 22.

the case, although I have no evidence for it. And if this book should chance to
fall into the hands of a reader some time after the year 2000, perhaps he or she
will be able to chuckle over these lines, much as I have (with a rather guilty
conscience) chuckled at some unwise prophecy from the pen of Jean-Baptiste
Say.

Whether a double or single turning-point, the change that began in 1973-4
has certainly opened up a long recession. Those who can remember the crisis of
1929-30 have a memory of an unexpected hurricane blowing up out of a
clear sky – but which did not last very long. The present crisis which refuses to
go away is more sinister, as if it cannot manage to show its true face, or find a
label or model which would explain it and reassure us. It is not so much a
hurricane as a flood, with the water rising slowly but alarmingly, under a sky
obstinately grey and waterlogged. All the foundations of economic life and all
the lessons of experience past and present seem to be being challenged. For
paradoxically we have recession, slowdown of production and unemployment,
but prices are still going up, against all the old rules. Calling this phenomenon

stagflation brings us no nearer to an explanation of it. Is the state, which nowadays sees its role as that of provider, which had mastered short-term crises by following the teaching of Keynes, and which thought it was proof against the recurrence of a disaster like 1929, responsible for the heights reached by the crisis, by dint of its very efforts? Or is the defensive and watchful strategy of the workers' organizations the barrier that explains the obstinate rise of wages and prices in spite of everything? Léon Dupriez[132] raises these questions, without resolving them. We do not know the end of the story, nor consequently the exact meaning of these long cycles which seem to obey certain rules or trends which remain hidden from us.

Can the long-term conjuncture be explained?

Economists and historians have observed and described these movements and noted how they are superimposed, just as the tide, as François Simiand put it, carries on its back the shorter movements of the waves; the experts have also paid much attention to their many consequences, and are always surprised at their extent and their eternal regularity.

But they have never tried to explain *why* they happen, why they develop and succeed each other. The only initiative in this direction concerns Juglar cycles, which some people have tried to connect with sunspots! No one seriously believes in such a close connection. And how is one to explain other types of cycle, not only those of price history but those concerning industrial production (see Hoffmann's curves) or the Brazilian gold cycle in the eighteenth century, or the two-hundred-year Mexican silver cycle (1696–1900), or the fluctuations of the traffic in the port of Seville in the days when it commanded the entire economy of the Atlantic? Not to mention the long-term shifts in population which seem to follow the variations in the secular trend and are probably as much consequence as cause. Not to mention either the flow of precious metals so much studied by historians and economists. Here too, given the multitude of actions and inter-actions, one should beware of a simple-minded determinism: quantitative theory has a part to play but I agree with Pierre Vilar[133] that any economic takeoff can create its own money supply and credit.

To clarify (I cannot say resolve) this impossible problem, one should perhaps have recourse to the periodic vibrations we are taught about in elementary physics. Movement is the consequence of an external impact as when a string or blade is struck, and of the response of the body which is made to vibrate. The strings of a violin vibrate under the bow. One vibration can naturally lead to another; when a body of soldiers comes to a bridge it has to break step, otherwise the bridge would vibrate in time to their marching feet and might in certain circumstances shatter like glass. So let us imagine that in the complex conjuncture, one movement can have an impact on another, and then on a third and so on.

The most important impact is undoubtedly that caused by external, exogenous causes. The *ancien régime* economy as Giuseppe Palomba has said, was dominated by the calendar, which brought a host of servitudes and vibrations caused by the harvest of course, but to take one example, winter was the season *par excellence* when peasant-artisans sat down to work. And there were also phenomena beyond the control of men and their authorities, times of plenty and times of famine, market fluctuations which might spread, the vicissitudes of foreign trade and the consequences these might have on 'domestic' prices: any contact between inside and outside meant a breach or a wound.

But just as important as the external impact is the context in which it occurs: is it possible to identify a finite plane or body which, being the site of a movement, fixes its time-span? I have a distant memory (1950) of a conversation with Professor Urbain, the professor of economics at Louvain University, who was always extremely careful to relate price variations to the area or volume they concerned. According to him, only those prices which obtained in the same vibrating plane were comparable. The vibrations caused by the impact of prices are felt, in fact, in the previously established networks which in my view constitute vibrating surfaces *par excellence: price structures* (to use the term in a slightly different sense from Léon Dupriez). The reader will see what I am getting at: the world-economy is the greatest possible vibrating surface, one which not only accepts the conjuncture but, at a certain depth or level, manufactures it. It is the world-economy at all events which creates the *uniformity* of prices over a huge area, as an arterial system distributes blood throughout a living organism. It is a structure in itself. The problem still remains however whether, despite the coincidences I have pointed out, the secular trend is or is not a good indicator of this sounding-board. My view is that the secular vibration, inexplicable without this huge but finite surface of the world-economy, opens, closes and opens once again the gates of the complex flow of the conjuncture.

I am not sure that economic and historical research is being directed today towards these long-term problems. Pierre Léon[134] once wrote: 'Historians have usually remained indifferent to the long term'. Ernest Labrousse even wrote at the beginning of his thesis, 'I have abandoned any attempt at an explanation of long-term movements'.[135] Within the time-span of an intercycle, the secular trend can of course be ignored. Witold Kula[136] on the other hand is interested in the long-term movements which 'by their cumulative action provoke structural transformations', but he is almost alone in this. Michel Morineau at the other extreme,[137] has called for a history that restores 'to the experience of life its savour, its intensity and its event-studded fabric'. And Pierre Vilar[138] has pleaded that the short-term should not be lost from sight, for this would mean 'systematically drawing a veil over all conflicts and class struggles; these stand revealed, both in the *ancien régime* and under capitalism, in short-term events'. We do not have to take sides in this debate which is really a false debate, since

Wealth in the sixteenth century meant the accumulation of sacks of grain. (*Chants royaux de la conception*, B.N., Paris, French manuscripts 1537.)

the conjuncture should be studied in all its richness: it would be regrettable if historians did not seek to locate its boundaries on one side in the history of events and the short term, and on the other in the long-term and the secular trend. The short and the long-term coexist; they cannot be separated. Keynes whose theory was built on the short-term made the much-quoted remark: 'In the long run we shall all be dead' – a remark which if it were not a joke would be both banal and absurd. For we all live in both the long-term and the short-term: the language I speak, the trade I practise, my beliefs, the human landscape surrounding me are all inherited: they existed before me and will go on existing after me. Nor do I agree with Joan Robinson[139] who thinks that the 'short period' is 'not a length of time but a state of affairs'. At that rate what would the long-term be? This is to reduce time to what it contains, to the people who throng it. Is this possible? Beyssade more sensibly says that time is 'neither innocent nor anodine';[140] if it does not create its content, it acts upon it and gives it form and reality.

Past and present

To finish this chapter which is intended simply as a theoretical introduction, an attempt to define an approach to the problem, the effort ought to be made to construct, brick by brick, a typology of the secular periods, those where there is an upward trend, those with a downward trend, and the crises that mark their peaks. Neither retrospective economics nor the most audacious kind of history will support me in this endeavour. And it is also quite possible that future historical studies will simply ignore the problems I am trying to formulate.

In all three cases (upward trend, crisis, downward trend) we should have to classify and divide further, using Wallerstein's three circles, which give us nine different situations; and since we have also distinguished four social 'sets' – economics, politics, culture, and social hierarchy – this brings the number to thirty-six. It is highly probable moreover that a regular typology would fail to take account of everything: if we had the appropriate data we should also have to make distinctions to account for many particular cases. We shall have to be prudent and stay on the level of generalities, however debatable and fragile these may be.

So let us simplify without feeling too guilty about it. The preceding lines have already summarized what I think about crises: they mark the beginning of a process of destructuration: one coherent world system which has developed at a leisurely pace is going into or completing its decline, while another system is being born amid much hesitation and delay. This break with the past appears as the result of an accumulation of accidents, breakdowns and distortions. And the following chapters of this book will attempt to cast light on these transitions from one system to another.

If one looks at the upward secular trends, it is clear that the economy and the social order, culture and the state are all flourishing simultaneously. Earl J. Hamilton, in the conversations that we used to have at Simancas so long ago (1927), used to say, 'In the sixteenth century, every wound heals, every break-down can be repaired, every lapse is made good', and this was so in every field: production was on the whole good, the state had the means to act, society was allowing its small group of aristocrats to expand, culture was flourishing, the economy, supported by a rise in population, was creating ever more trade circuits; these by multiplying the division of labour encouraged prices to rise; the money supply was increasing and capital was accumulated. All upward trends are moreover conservative, safeguarding the status quo: they are favourable to *all economies*. It was during such upward turns that a multi-polarity of centres was possible: in the sixteenth century for instance, Venice, Antwerp and Genoa all had some share in the glory.

With a persistent downward trend, the scene changes: healthy economies are now found only at the centre of the world-economy. There is a general with-drawal and concentration around a single centre; states become touchy and aggressive. Frank Spooner has invented a 'law' for France, that when the econ-omy is in an upward phase, the country tends to split up and become divided against itself (as during the Wars of Religion) whereas bad times bring the different parts of the country together again in support of a strong government. But does this law work for the whole French history or for any other state? As for high society, during lean years it fought for its living, barricaded itself in and restricted its size (late marriage, emigration of the young surplus population, early use of contraceptive practices as in seventeenth-century Geneva). But culture runs strangely against the general trend; if it has a high profile, like the state, during these long downward phases, perhaps that is because one of its functions is to fill the breaches and gaps in the social fabric (is culture 'the opium of the people'?). Perhaps too it is because cultural activity is the least expensive? The Spanish Golden Age for instance flowered when Spain had already embarked upon her decline, as a concentration of culture in the capital: the Golden Age was above all the splendour of Madrid, with its court and its theatres. And under the extravagant regime of the Count Duke Olivares, how many buildings were built hastily, and one almost dares to say, cheaply. I do not know if the same explanation can be applied to the age of Louis XIV. But it does strike me that secular decline appears to encourage what seem to us today to be cultural explosions. After 1600, there was the autumn flowering of Italy in Venice, Bologna and Rome. After 1815 came romanticism to inflame an already ageing Europe.

These rather hastily-pronounced remarks do at least raise the usual problems, though not to my mind the essential problem. Without perhaps making it sufficiently clear, I have consistently been stressing progress or decline at the highest level of social life: in culture (the culture of the elite), social order (that of the most privileged at the top of the pyramid), the state (at government level), and economic production (in the sector of circulation and exchange, which in fact means only a part of production, that of the most developed areas). Like all historians and without meaning to, I have automatically been neglecting the lot of the great mass of mankind, the huge majority of living beings. What happened in broad terms to these masses during the ebbs and flow of the secular trend?

Paradoxically, things were worse for them when all the indicators of the economy were set fair, when increased production was making its effects felt, increasing the number of people, but laying a heavier burden on the various worlds of action and labour. A gap opened up, as Earl J. Hamilton[141] has shown, between prices and wages – which lagged behind. It is quite clear, if one refers to the work of Jean Fourastié, René Grandamy, Wilhelm Abel and particularly to the published research of E.H. Phelps Brown and Sheila Hopkins[142] that there was a drop in *real wages*. The progress made by the upper reaches of the economy and the increase in economic potential were paid for by the hardship of the mass of people whose numbers were increasing as fast as or faster than production. And it was perhaps when this multiplication of numbers, of trade and efforts was no longer counter-balanced by increases in productivity that something snapped, that crisis point was reached, the secular trend was reversed and the downturn began. The strange thing is that the downturn at superstructural level actually led to an improvement in living standards for the masses, since real wages began to go up again. Between 1350 and 1450, at a really black point in the graphs of European growth or lack of it, there was a sort of golden age in the daily life of ordinary people.

In the perspective of what would have been called in Charles Seignobos's time[143] 'sincere' history, the really crucial event, a long-term event with huge consequences which in fact constitutes a complete break with the past, was that the long upward trend of the nineteenth century, with the industrial revolution, did not lead to any serious deterioration of general well-being, but on the contrary to a rise in per capita income. It is not easy to say anything about this problem either. But one can suggest at least that the immense sudden rise in productivity, thanks to machines, at a stroke raised the ceiling of possibilities. It is within this new universe that an unprecedented rise in world population has for over a century been accompanied by an improvement in per capita income. Social progress has clearly changed in every form. But what will be the outcome of the recession which seems so clearly to have begun in the 1970s?

In the past, the well-being of ordinary people which went hand in hand with secular recession had always been paid for in advance by some enormous sacrifice: millions had died in 1350 with the Black Death; the seventeenth century saw serious demographic stagnation. And it was precisely the smaller size of the population and the relaxing of economic tension which brought obvious improvement for the survivors, those whom the scourges or population drop had spared. The present crisis has none of these symptoms: world population is still rising, production is falling, unemployment is becoming endemic and yet infla-

2

The City-Centred Economies of the European Past: Before and After Venice

FOR LONG PERIODS in the past, the European world-economy appears to have rested on the slender basis of a single city-state, one with perfect or near-perfect freedom of movement, but with few resources outside itself. In order to compensate for its weaknesses, such a city would frequently play off one region or community against another, taking advantage of the differences between them, and relying heavily on the few dozen towns, or states, or economies which served it; for serve it they did, either in their own interest or because they had no choice.

One cannot help wondering how such far-ranging supremacy can possibly have been established and maintained on such a narrow foundation – particularly since power inside a city-state was always being challenged from within, viewed as it was from close quarters by a strictly-governed population, often one which had been 'proletarianized'. And all this for the benefit of the handful of families (easily identifiable and thus the obvious target of resentment) who held – but might one day very well lose – the reins of power. These families moreover fought bitter feuds among themselves.[1]

It is true that the world-economy by which such cities were surrounded was itself still a fragile network – though by the same token, if its fabric was torn, the damage could be made good without too much trouble. It was merely a matter of vigilance and the judicious application of force. (Could not the same be said of British policy under Palmerston and Disraeli in a later age?) In order to control the large expanses in question, it was sufficient to hold a few strategic points (Candia, captured by Venice in 1204; Corfu, 1383; Cyprus, 1489 – or indeed Gibraltar, which the British took by surprise in 1704, and Malta, which they captured in 1800) and to establish a few convenient monopolies, which then had to be maintained in good working order – as we do machines today. Such monopolies often continued to operate out of a kind of force of inertia, although they were naturally challenged by rivals who could sometimes cause serious problems.

But perhaps historians have paid too much attention to these external ten-

Four images of the Venetian empire: Corfu (top left), the key to the Adriatic; Candia (Crete) (top right) which Venice kept until 1669; Famagusta (bottom left) in Cyprus, lost in 1571; Alexandria (bottom right) the gateway to Egypt and the spice trade. These rather fanciful landscapes are from a collection of about twenty miniatures illustrating the journeys to the Levant of a Venetian nobleman in 1570–71. (Bibliothèque Nationale, Paris.)

sions, to the events and episodes which illuminate them, and to the internal dramas, the political battles and social movements which lend such high colour to the domestic history of the city-states. The fact is that both the supremacy of these cities in foreign affairs and the supremacy within their walls of the rich and powerful, were long-lasting realities; nothing, neither the tensions, nor the struggles for wages or work, nor all the bitter feuding between political clans or parties, ever prevented the steady development necessary for the good health of capital. Even when the most bloodthirsty scenes were taking place on stage, profitable business was being carried on in the wings.

The merchant cities of the Middle Ages all strained to make profits and were shaped by the strain. Paul Grousset had them in mind when he claimed that 'contemporary capitalism has invented nothing'.[2] Armando Sapori[3] is even more explicit: 'Even today, it is impossible to find anything – income tax for instance[4] – which did not have some precedent in the genius of one of the Italian republics'. And it is true that everything seems to have been there in embryo: bills of exchange, credit, minted coins, banks, forward selling, public finance, loans, capitalism, colonialism – as well as social disturbances, a sophisticated labour force, class struggles, social oppression, political atrocities. By at least the twelfth century in Genoa and Venice, as well as in the towns of the Netherlands, extremely large payments were being made in cash.[5] But credit was quick to follow.

Modern forces, ahead of their time, the city-states took advantage of the backwardness and inferiority of others. And one could almost say that it was the combination of weaknesses surrounding them which condemned them to expand, to become domineering, to exercise a near-monopoly over the large profits of long-distance trade, in short to stand outside the normal rules. Their only potential rival, the territorial state, the modern state foreshadowed by Frederick II's achievements in southern Italy, had got off to a poor or at any rate a slow start, and was in addition to be adversely affected by the fourteenth-century recession, when a whole series of would-be territorial states were dislocated and damaged, leaving the field clear once again for the cities.

Cities and states remained potential enemies however. Which was to dominate the other? This was the burning question in medieval Europe, and the prolonged supremacy of the city is not easily explained. Jean-Baptiste Say[6] expresses quite understandable surprise that 'the Republic of Venice in the thirteenth century, although possessing not an inch of territory on the Italian mainland, [should have] become wealthy enough through trade to conquer Dalmatia, most of the Greek islands and Constantinople'. Nor is it paradoxical to think that the cities needed the space around them, the markets, the protected circulation zones – in short that they required larger states to batten on: they were obliged to prey on others to survive. Venice would have been unthinkable without first the Byzantine and later the Turkish Empire. The story is the familiar and tragic one of the enemies who cannot do without each other.

The first European world-economy

The predominance of the city-states can only be explained in the context of the first world-economy ever to take shape in Europe, between the eleventh and thirteenth centuries. It was in this period that the extensive trading-zones were established of which the cities were at once the instruments, the articulations and the beneficiaries. The birth of Europe, that monstrous shaper of world history, took place not in 1400, the starting-point of this book, but at least two hundred years earlier.

It is worthwhile therefore stepping outside the chronological boundaries of this study for a moment and going back to the beginning, to see how, in real terms, a world-economy was actually born, out of the evolving hierarchy and still-imperfect organization of the geographical areas which would make it up. The major coordinates and articulations of European history were already beginning to emerge and the huge problem of the continent's modernization (a word that begs many questions) can thus be placed in a longer and more balanced perspective. In what were emerging as the core or central zones, a proto-capitalism almost inevitably appeared; in this context, modernization appears not as a simple transition from one identifiable state to another, but as a series of stages and transitions, the earliest dating from well before what is usually known as 'the' Renaissance of the late fifteenth century.

European expansion from the eleventh century

In this long gestation process, the cities naturally played a leading part, but they were not alone. Europe as a whole carried them on its back – that is to say 'all of Europe considered collectively' as Isaac de Pinto puts it,[7] the entire political and economic area known as Europe, with its long past; an inheritance including the shape imposed upon the continent long ago by Rome, which was of some importance; including too the expansion in many directions which followed the great invasions of the fifth century, as settlement extended beyond the boundaries of the Roman Empire towards Germany and eastern Europe, Scandinavia and the only partly-Romanized British Isles. Gradually the seas surrounding the old continent – the stretch of water encompassing the Baltic, the North Sea, the English Channel and the Irish Sea – were colonized. Here too, the 'new West' went beyond what Rome had accomplished: despite her fleets based at the mouth of the Somme and at Boulogne,[8] Rome had never really ruled the northern waves. 'All the Baltic ever brought Rome was a little ambergris.'[9]

More spectacular was the reconquest of the southern waters of the Mediterranean which were reclaimed from Islam and Byzantium. What had once been the *raison d'être* and the heart of the Roman Empire in its prime, 'a pool set in a

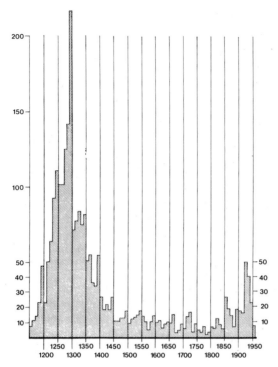

10   THE FOUNDATION OF TOWNS IN CENTRAL EUROPE
The graph shows the exceptional burst of urbanization in the thirteenth century.
(After Heins Stoob in W. Abel, *Geschichte der deutschen Landwirtschaft*, 1962, p. 46.)

garden', [10] was reoccupied by the ships and merchants of Italy, a victory culminating in the eastward surge of the Crusades. The Christian reoccupation was
resisted however in Spain, where the Reconquest marked time after making
initial progress (Las Navas de Toloso, 1212); and it was also resisted in North
Africa, from Gibraltar to Egypt; in the Levant, where the states in the Holy Land
led a precarious existence; and in the Greek Empire (but that collapsed in 1204).

Nevertheless, as Archibald Lewis rightly points out, 'the most important
frontier in European expansion was the internal frontier of forest, marsh and
heath'.[11] The uninhabited wastes were reduced in size as the European peasants
cleared the land; as people became more numerous, they harnessed the power of
wheel and windmill; communications were established between regions once
completely foreign to each other; barriers came down; countless towns sprang
up or revived wherever there was a crossroads of trade, and this was undoubtedly
the crucial factor. Europe was suddenly covered with towns – more than 3000 in
Germany alone.[12] Some of them, it is true, were little more than villages, despite
their city walls, harbouring a mere two to three hundred souls. But many of them
grew to become towns of a new and unprecedented kind. Classical antiquity had

had its free cities, the Greek city-states; but these had been open to the inhabitants of the surrounding countryside, who were free to come and go as they pleased. The west European medieval town was on the contrary a closed citadel behind its walls. 'The wall separates the townsman from the peasant', as a German proverb says. The town was a world of its own, protected by its privileges ('the city air makes men free'), an aggressive world and an active force for unequal exchange. And it was the medieval city – a more or less active ferment depending on period and place – which, like the yeast in some mighty dough, brought about the rise of Europe. Can the prominent role of the city be accounted for by its having been able to expand and develop in an already-structured rural world, rather than in a vacuum like the towns of the New World (and possibly the Greek city-states themselves)? In other words, it had material available to work on, at the expense of which it could grow. What was more, the territorial state, since it took so long to appear on the scene, offered no competition: this time, the hare easily and predictably outstripped the tortoise.

The town consolidated its future with its roads, its markets, its workshops and the money that accumulated within its walls. Its markets ensured its food supply, as peasants came to town with their daily produce: 'The markets offered an outlet for the growing surpluses of the lordly domains, and for the huge amounts of produce resulting from the payment of dues in kind'.[13] According to B.H. Slicher van Bath, after about 1150, Europe moved beyond 'direct agricultural consumption', i.e. self-sufficiency, to the stage of 'indirect agricultural consumption' created by the marketing of surplus rural production.[14] At the same time, the town attracted all the skilled crafts, creating for itself a monopoly of the manufacture and marketing of industrial products. Only later would pre-industry move back into the countryside.

In short, 'economic life ... especially after the thirteenth century, began to take precedence over the [earlier] agrarian aspects of the towns'.[15] Over a very wide area, the crucial move was made from a domestic to a market economy. In other words, the towns were beginning to tower above their rural surroundings and to look beyond their immediate horizons. This was a 'great leap forward', the first in the series that created European society and launched it on its successful career.[16] There is only one event even remotely comparable to this: the creation by the first European settlers in America of the many transit-towns, linked to each other by the road and by the requirements of commerce, command and defence.

Let me add my voice to those of Gino Luzzatto and Armando Sapori:[17] this age marked Europe's true Renaissance (for all the ambiguity of the word) two or three hundred years before the traditional Renaissance of the fifteenth century. That does not however make it any easier to explain.

True, there was demographic expansion, which may have determined everything else, but must itself be explained – notably perhaps by the wave of progress in agricultural techniques which began in the eleventh century, with the improved

Peasants bringing small quantities of produce to town. Detail from the painting by Lorenzo Lotto, *Storie de Santa Barbara*. (Photo Scala.)

design of the plough, triennial rotation and the open field system for stock farming. Lynn White[18] regards agricultural progress as of prime importance in the rise of Europe. Maurice Lombard[19] lays more stress on the progress made in trade: Italy had early links with Islam and Byzantium, and thus came into contact with the already active monetary economy of the East, which she transmitted to the rest of Europe. Towns spelled money, the essential ingredient of the so-called commercial revolution. Georges Duby,[20] and with some reservations Roberto Lopez,[21] tend to agree with Lynn White: the vital factor was agricultural over-production and the large-scale redistribution of surpluses.

The world-economy and bi-polarity

All these explanations must in the end be combined. How could there have been any growth unless everything progressed at more or less the same pace? A larger population, the perfection of agricultural techniques, the revival of trade *and* the first wave of craft industry were all essential factors if the area known as Europe was to develop an urban network, an urban superstructure, with inter-city links encompassing all underlying activities and obliging them to become part of a 'market economy'. This market economy, though still modest in size, would also lead to an energy revolution, with the widespread use of mills for industrial purposes, eventually creating a world-economy on a European scale. Federigo Melis[22] locates this first *Weltwirtschaft* within the polygon Bruges-London-Lisbon-Fez-Damascus-Azov-Venice, an area taking in the 300 or so trading cities to and from which the 153,000 letters in the archives of Francesco di Marco Datini, the merchant of Prato, were dispatched. Heinrich Bechtel[23] speaks of a quadrilateral: Lisbon-Alexandria-Novgorod-Bergen. Fritz Rörig,[24] the first his-torian to give the meaning 'world-economy' to the German word *Weltwirtschaft*, suggests that its eastern frontier was a line running from Greater Novgorod on lake Ilmen, to Byzantium. The intensity and volume of trade all contributed to the economic unity of this vast area.[25]

The only unresolved question is the date at which this *Weltwirtschaft* really. began to exist – and this is well-nigh insoluble. There could be no world economy until there was a dense enough urban network with trade of sufficient volume and regularity to breathe life into a central or core zone. But in these distant centuries, nothing can be firmly asserted, nothing established beyond reasonable doubt. The upward secular trend from the eleventh century encouraged develop-ment in general, but led to the growth of a number of different centres. Not until the rise of the Champagne fairs in the early thirteenth century did it become evident that a coherent zone existed, stretching from the Low Countries to the Mediterranean, bringing advantages not to ordinary towns, but to those with fairs, not to sea-passages but to the long overland routes. This was an original first stage or rather episode in European history, since it cannot be accounted the true beginning. For what would the Champagne fairs have been without the

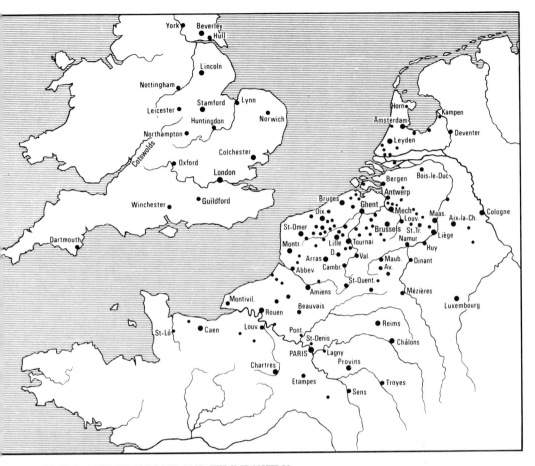

11   THE 'NORTHERN POLE' AND ITS INDUSTRY
The cluster of textile workshops, from the Zuyder Zee to the Seine valley. On the North–South system as a whole, see below, Figure 13, the map showing the influence of the Champagne fairs. (From Hektor Ammann in *Hessisches Jahrbuch für Landesgeschichte*, 8, 1958.)

pre-existing prosperity of the Low Countries and northern Italy, two areas of precocious development destined by the force of circumstance to come into contact with one another?

For the true beginning of the new Europe, we have to look at the growth of these two complexes, the North and the South, the Low Countries and Italy, the North Sea-Baltic and the Mediterranean. There was not one pole of attraction in the West but two, and this bipolarity, pulling the continent in two directions, would last in some form for several centuries. This was to be one of the major features of European history – possibly the most important of all. When we speak of medieval and modern Europe, we must speak two different languages: what was true of the North was never literally applicable to the South.

The pattern had probably become established by the ninth or tenth century: two extensive regional economies had very early taken shape, almost independently of each other, out of the still malleable material of Europe's economic activity. In the North the process was rapid: here there was little resistance from the surrounding regions which were not even emergent but simply primitive. In the Mediterranean, in regions already developed by a long history, the revival may have begun later, but it progressed more quickly, as the rise of Italy drew strength from the accelerating presence of Islam and Byzantium. As a result, the North was, other things being equal, less sophisticated than the South, more 'industrial', while the South was the greater trading centre. Poles apart, both geographically and electrically, these two worlds were bound to attract and complement one another. Their meeting was effected by the North–South overland route, of which the thirteenth-century Champagne fairs were the first obvious sign.

This contact did not end the duality, but rather reinforced it as the system reproduced itself, strengthened by the two-way traffic which gave each partner even greater vitality compared to the rest of Europe. If there were any super-cities in this first urban flowering of European civilization, they were invariably to be found in one or other of these zones, or along the axes linking them. Their location shows us the bone-structure or rather the arterial system of the European organism.

The emergence of a single centre for the European economy could only be achieved of course at the price of a struggle between these two poles. Italy was the stronger until the sixteenth century, for as long as the Mediterranean remained the heart of the Old World. But in about 1600, the balance shifted northwards. The rise of Amsterdam was certainly not a minor incident, a mere transfer of weight from Antwerp to Holland, but a much more serious turning-point: once the Mediterranean and the former glories of Italy had been eclipsed, Europe would have only one centre of gravity, in the North; and for centuries to come, right down to the present day, the patterns and circles of her profound imbalances would emanate from this pole. So before proceeding any further, it is necessary to outline the genesis of these crucial regions.

The northern complex: the heyday of Bruges

The northern economy was built up from scratch. The Low Countries were actually created *ex nihilo*: 'Most of the great cities of Italy, France, the Rhineland and the Danube predate modern times', writes Henri Pirenne. 'It was only in the early Middle Ages on the other hand that Liège, Louvain, Malines [Mechelen], Antwerp, Brussels, Ypres, Ghent and Utrecht emerged.'[26]

By making their headquarters at Aix-la-Chapelle (Aachen) the Carolingians had contributed to a first awakening of the region which was interrupted by the ravages of the Norsemen from 820-891.[27] But the return of peace and the restoration of links across the Rhine and with the regions bordering the North Sea reanimated the Low Countries, which were now no longer a 'finis terrae', the end of the earth, but an inhabited area covered with fortified castles and walled towns. Bands of hitherto vagrant merchants settled down near the towns and castles. By mid-eleventh century, the weavers of the flatlands had come to live in the urban centres. The population increased, large agricultural estates prospered, and the textile industry kept workshops busy from the banks of the Seine and Marne to the Zuyder Zee.

It was all to culminate in the dazzling fortune of Bruges. By 1200, this city, together with Ypres, Thourout and Messines,[28] was included in the circuit of the Flemish fairs. This in itself made Bruges a more important place: she was receiving foreign merchants, her industry was thriving and her trade was reaching England and Scotland where she found the wool needed both for her looms and for re-export to the cloth-making towns of Flanders. Her English contacts also served her well in the provinces of France owned by the king of England: hence her early dealings in Normandy grain and Bordeaux wines. And finally the arrival in Bruges of Hanseatic ships confirmed and developed her prosperity. She built new outer harbours, first at Damme (1180) and later at Sluys at the mouth of the Zwyn: their construction was called for not only by the gradual silting-up of the harbour in Bruges, but also by the need for deeper moorings for the heavy *Koggen* of the Hanseatic ports.[29] Negotiating on behalf of subjects of the empire, envoys from Lübeck and Hamburg obtained trade privileges from the countess of Flanders in 1252. But she refused the Lübeckers permission to set up near Damme a *Kontor* or agency on the lines of the *Stahlhof* in London, which the English had so much trouble getting rid of later.[30]

In 1277, the first Genoese ships put in to Bruges. The establishment of a regular maritime link between the Mediterranean and the North Sea ushered in a decisive invasion by the southerners – for the Genoese were but a foretaste of what was to come: the last of the newcomers, the Venetian galleys, arrived in 1314. For Bruges this could be described both as an annexation and as a new departure. It was an annexation because the southerners effectively captured a development which Bruges might conceivably have been able to manage single-handed. But it was also a new departure in the sense that the arrival of the sailors, ships and merchants of the Mediterranean brought in a wealth of goods, capital, and commercial and financial techniques. Rich Italian merchants came to live in the city, and brought with them consignments of some of the most precious commodities of the time: spices and pepper from the Levant which they exchanged for the industrial products of Flanders.

Thus Bruges came to be the centre of a huge trading area, covering no less than the Mediterranean, Portugal, France, England, the Rhineland, and the Hansa. The town grew in size: 35,000 inhabitants in 1340, and possibly 100,000 by 1500. 'In the age of Jan van Eyck (c. 1380–1440) and Memling (1435–94) it was unquestionably one of the finest cities in the world'[31] – and certainly one of

Section of the plan of Bruges by Marc Gheeraert, 1562, Paris, B.N., Gee 5746 (9). The Grand Marché, the central market, at the top of the picture near the Church of Saint Jacques (No. 32 on the plan) was in the town centre, the main square of Bruges. In the square (but off the top of this section) were the Halles and their bell-tower. Going along the Rue Saint Jacques (Sint Jacob Straete) one reaches Ezel Straete (Rue des Baudets) leading to the fortified Porte des Baudets (No. 6 on the plan, ED), Porta Asinorum. Below No. 63 is the Place de la Bourse. For the different commercial districts, see R. de Roover, *Money, Banking and Credit in Medieval Bruges*, 1948, pp. 174–5. This fragment of the plan shows how big the city was, with its streets, monasteries, convents, churches, noblemen's houses, moats, ramparts, windmills, canals with their barges. To the north of the town (at the bottom of the picture) there were extensive vacant lots inside the walls, with no buildings – a frequent rule in the sixteenth century.

the most industrious. The textile industry was not only well-established in Bruges, but had also spilled out into the towns of Flanders, bringing prosperity to Ghent and Ypres – creating an industrial region unparalleled anywhere else in Europe. And the commercial life of Bruges culminated in the creation in 1309, alongside and above the fairs, of her famous Bourse – soon to be the centre of a sophisticated money market. Francesco Datini's correspondent wrote from Bruges on 26 April 1399, '*A Genova pare sia per durare larghezza di danari e per tanto non rimettete là nostri danari o sarebbe a buon prezo piutosto a Vinegia o a Firenze o qui o a Parigi rimettete, o a Monpolier bien se lla rimesse vi paresse migliore*'. ('It appears that there is an abundance of specie in Genoa; so do not send our money to Genoa, or only if you can get a very good price for it; put it rather in Venice or Florence, or here in Bruges or in Paris or Montpellier; or wherever seems best to you.')[32]

Important though the position of Bruges was, we must not allow ourselves to be too impressed. I cannot agree with Henri Pirenne when he argues that Bruges was of *greater* international importance than Venice – this is retrospective nationalism on his part. And Pirenne himself recognized that most of the ships in the harbour 'belonged to foreign owners', that 'her inhabitants played only a minor part in active commerce. They were content to act as intermediaries for the merchants who flocked into the town from every direction'[33] – which is virtually an admission that the people of Bruges were cast in a subordinate role and that the city's trade was, to use an eighteenth-century expression, 'passive'. This was the point of departure for a celebrated article by J.A. van Houtte (1952) contrasting Bruges and Antwerp: the national port of Bruges and the 'international' port of Antwerp.[34] But perhaps this is leaning too far in the other direction. I am prepared to say of Bruges (to please Richard Häpke)[35] and of Lübeck (to please Fritz Rörig)[36] that both were already *Weltmärkte*, world-markets – but not quite world-cities, that is undisputed stars at the centre of a galaxy.

The northern complex: the rise of the Hansa[37]

Bruges was only a single point – the most important, true, but a single point all the same – in a mighty northern complex stretching from England to the Baltic. These trading waters – the Baltic, the North Sea, the English Channel and even the Irish Sea – were the scene of the sea-borne commercial triumph of the Hansa, which revealed itself in 1158 with the foundation of the town of Lübeck, close to the Baltic and surrounded by the protective marshes of the Trave and the Wakenitz.

But this was no creation *ex nihilo*. In the eighth and ninth centuries, the limits of this northern maritime empire had already been staked out and sometimes exceeded by the expeditions, invasions and piracy of the Norsemen. Their venture may have become dispersed over the broad spaces and coastlines of

Europe, but something of it remained in its place of origin. For some time afterwards, Scandinavian longboats ranged the North Sea and the Baltic – the Norwegians went to the English coast and the Irish Sea;[38] the peasants of Gotland sailed into ports and rivers as far away as Novgorod;[39] from Jutland to Finland there sprang up the Slavonic towns whose remains are now being uncovered by archaeologists;[40] Russian merchants reached Stettin, hitherto a completely Slav town.[41] But there was no truly *international* economy before the Hanseatic League. Gradually, peaceably, thanks to trading and agreements with princes, but with the occasional use of force and violence too, this double sea-space, the North Sea and the Baltic, was taken in hand and organized by the cities, merchants, soldiers and peasants of Germany.

But it should not be imagined that these cities were closely linked from the start. The word *Hansa* (= group of merchants)[42] appeared only later, and was written down officially for the first time in an English royal document dated 1267.[43] In the beginning there was simply an association of merchants plus an association of ships, from the Zuyder Zee to Finland, and from Sweden to Norway. The central axis of their trade ran from London and Bruges to Riga and Reval, which were the gateways to either Novgorod or to Vitebsk and Smolensk. Exchange took place between the still underdeveloped Baltic countries, which produced raw materials and foodstuffs, and the North Sea, where the West had already established its networks and laid down its rules. In the port of Bruges, the world-economy centred on Europe and the Mediterranean welcomed the great boats of the Hansa, the solid clinker-built *Kogge* which first appeared at the end of the thirteenth century (and were to serve as models for the roundships of the Mediterranean).[44] Later came the hooker,[45] another type of flat-bottomed merchant vessel capable of carrying heavy cargoes of salt, bulky casks of wine, wood and other forest products, or grain loaded directly into the hold. The control of the seas by the Hanseatic League was evident if far from complete: until about 1280, their ships avoided crossing the dangerous Sound, and even when the *Umlandfahrt*[46] (the circumnavigation which did use the strait) became normal practice, the *isthmus route* between Lübeck and Hamburg (along several stretches of river and one canal) although time-consuming, was still being used.[47]

The isthmus route resulted in the pre-eminence of Lübeck, since all goods travelling between the North Sea and the Baltic had to pass through the town. In 1227, Lübeck obtained the privilege of becoming an imperial city, the only one in this category east of the Elbe.[48] Another advantage was the town's proximity to the rock-salt mines of Lüneburg, which fell very early into the hands of the Lübeck merchants.[49] Beginning in 1227 (with the victory over the Danes at Bornhöved),[50] the city's success was sealed with the granting to the Hanseatic merchants of privileges in Flanders – in 1252-3[51] – a whole century before the first general Diet of the Hansa which brought together its representatives in Lübeck in 1356, *only then* creating the Hanseatic League.[52] But well before this date, 'Lübeck had been the standard-bearer of the Hanseatic League ... recognized by all as the capital of the merchant confederation ... The city's arms – the imperial eagle – became in the fifteenth century the arms of the League itself.'[53]

The products of the North and East – wood, wax, fur, rye and wheat – were only of value however when re-exported to the West. And in the other direction came the inevitable counterpart – salt, cloth and wine. The system was a simple and well-founded one, but it had its problems. And it was the overcoming of such problems which welded together the urban league of the Hansa into a unit at once fragile and solid. Its fragility resulted from the instability of a group composed of so many towns – between 70 and 170 – all at some distance from each other, and whose delegates were never all united in a single general assembly. Behind the Hansa there was no state, not even a firmly-constituted organization. It consisted simply of many towns, proud and jealous of their prerogatives, sometimes competing with each other from the protection of their stout walls, each with its merchants, its patricians, its guilds, fleet, warehouses and accumulated wealth. The solidity of the Hansa came from the community of interests it stood for, from the need to play the same economic game, from the common civilization created by trading in one of the most frequented maritime areas of Europe, between the Baltic and Lisbon, and lastly from a common language which made no small contribution to the unity of the Hansa. This language 'had as its substratum Low German (differing from the German spoken in the South) enriched according to need by borrowings from Latin, from Estonian (in Reval), Polish (in Lublin), from Italian, Czech, Ukrainian and possibly Lithuanian'.[54] It was the language of 'a power elite and a wealth elite, implying membership of a defined social and professional group'.[55] And since these patrician merchants were remarkable for their mobility, the same families – the Angermündes, Veckinghusens, Von Soests, Gieses and Von Suchtens – might be found anywhere between Reval, Gdansk, Lübeck and Bruges.[56]

All these links made for coherence, solidarity, habits in common and a shared pride. Force of circumstance did the rest. In the Mediterranean, with its comparative abundance of wealth, the different cities could all operate independently and compete with each other in fierce rivalry. In the Baltic and North Sea, such behaviour would have been difficult. The profits to be made from bulky goods, large in volume but low in price, were not great, and the risks and expenses were considerable. The profit rate was 5% at best.[57] Here more than elsewhere the merchant had to calculate, save and look ahead. One of the rules of success was to control both supply and demand – whether for exports to the West or redistribution of imports within the East. The *Kontors* (trading-posts or agencies abroad) established by the Hansa were strongholds shared by all the Hanseatic merchants, protected by privilege and defended to the utmost, whether the *Sankt Peterhof* in Novgorod, the *Deutsche Brücke* in Bergen, or the *Stahlhof* in London. As visitors to the trading-post for a season, the Germans were subject to strict discipline. In Bergen, young men 'serving an apprenticeship' might stay for ten years, learning the local languages and trading practices, and were obliged to remain single. In this branch of the Hansa, the rules were all laid down by the Council of Elders and two aldermen. Except in Bruges, where it was not materially possible, the merchant had to lodge in the *Kontor*.

The whole of the North eventually found itself trapped by a chain of supervision and dependence. In Bergen, Norwegian interests proper were continually trampled underfoot. With their insufficient agricultural production, the Norwegians[58] depended on the grain which the Lübeckers brought in from Pomerania and Brandenburg. When Norway tried to reduce the privileges of the Hansa, a grain blockade (as in 1284-5) soon brought her to heel. And inasmuch as competition from imported grain blocked the development of self-sufficiency in agriculture, the foreign merchants were able to obtain whatever they wanted from the Norwegians: salt meat, salt or dried cod from the Lofoten Islands, wood, grease, tar, furs.

In the West, where the competition was rather stiffer, the Hansa was nevertheless able to obtain privileges, in London more easily than in Bruges. In the English capital, the *Stahlhof* near London Bridge was another *Fondaco dei Tedeschi*, with its wharves and warehouses; the Hanseatic merchants were exempted from most taxes; they had their own judges and were even granted the signal honour of guarding one of the city gates.[59]

The fortunes of Lübeck and the towns associated with its career reached a peak quite late, between 1370 and 1388; in 1370, the Hansa triumphed over the king of Denmark by the Treaty of Stralsund[60] and occupied certain fortresses on the Sound; in 1388, following a quarrel with Bruges it forced the wealthy city and the government of the Netherlands to capitulate, by means of an effective blockade.[61] But these late triumphs concealed the beginnings of a decline which was soon clear for all to see.[62]

It is in any case hard to see how the Hanseatic merchants could have been spared during the great crisis which gripped the western world in the second half of the fourteenth century. It is true that despite the drop in population, the West's demand for Baltic products remained the same. The population of the Low Countries was in any case little affected by the Black Death and the growth of the navies of the West suggests that imports of wood had not fallen, indeed the reverse. But the movement of prices in the West discriminated against the Hansa. After 1370, cereal prices fell, and those of furs dropped after 1440, while the price of industrial products continued to rise. This scissors-movement operated against the trade of Lübeck and other Baltic towns.

In an associated movement, the hinterland of the Hansa now experienced a series of crises which set prince and noble, peasant and town against one another. And close on their heels followed the decline of the distant silver and gold mines of Hungary and Bohemia.[63] Finally came the challenge from new or revived territorial states: Denmark, England, the Netherlands, now reorganized under the Valois of Burgundy, Poland (which had triumphed in 1466 over the Teutonic

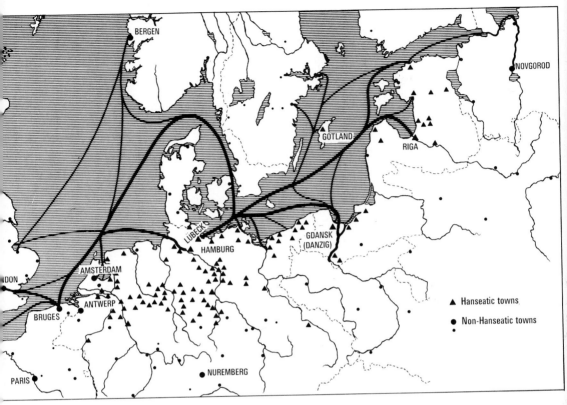

12　THE TRADE OF THE HANSEATIC LEAGUE IN ABOUT 1400
From F. W. Putzger's *Historischer Weltatlas*, 1963, p. 57.

Knights), Muscovy under Ivan the Terrible who in 1476 had put an end to the independence of Novgorod.[64] Moreover the merchants of England, Holland and Nuremberg were beginning to penetrate the heartland of the Hansa itself.[65] Certain cities defended themselves: thus Lübeck got the better of the English in 1470–74; others preferred to come to terms with the new arrivals.

German historians have explained the decline of the Hansa in terms of Germany's *political* immaturity. Eli Heckscher[66] disagrees with them though without fully explaining why. At a time when cities ruled the world, could it not be argued that a strong German state might have hindered the Hanseatic towns as much as it helped them? Their decline seems rather to have followed from the meeting between their somewhat under-developed economy and the already quite advanced economy of the West. And in any case, on a continental scale, one would hardly place Lübeck on the same level as Venice or Bruges. Between the bustling West and the rather less bustling East, the Hanseatic societies clung to an elementary kind of capitalism. Their economy hesitated between barter

The Hansa building in Antwerp. Its late date (1564) corresponds to a revival in the Hanseatic trade in Antwerp. From the water-colour by Cadliff, 1761. (Photo Giraudon.)

and money; it made little call on credit: silver coin was for a long time the only currency allowed. Such traditions were signs of inferiority, even in the context of the capitalism of the time. The very serious crisis of the late fourteenth century could not but damage economies with still shaky foundations. Only the strongest were *comparatively* untouched.

The other pole of attraction: the Italian cities

Islam did not conquer the Mediterranean at a stroke in the seventh century. And the crisis provoked by successive waves of Islamic invasion in fact emptied the sea of trade, if we are to believe E. Ashtor.[67] But in the eighth and ninth centuries, trading revived: shipping was once more seen in the Mediterranean, and all coastal dwellers benefited, rich and poor alike.

Along the coasts of Italy, small seaports began to thrive – not only Venice, which was still insignificant at this time, but ten or twenty little Venices. Prominent among them was Amalfi,[68] although there was hardly room for the harbour, houses and later the cathedral, in the little space left between the mountains and the sea. The rise of Amalfi, though not easily comprehensible at first sight, is explained by the port's early privileged contacts with Islam, as well as by the very poverty of its infertile hinterland, which drove the little town to commit itself single-mindedly to maritime ventures.[69]

For the fortune of these small ports was determined many hundreds of miles from their home waters. For them, success meant making contact with the rich regions of the Mediterranean – the cities of Islam, or Constantinople – and obtaining gold currencies,[70] the dinars of Egypt and Syria, in order to buy the fine silks of Byzantium which they resold in the West in a triangular transaction. In other words, Italy was still only a poor 'peripheral' region, intent on making her services acceptable to others as a purveyor of timber, grain, linen cloth, salt and slaves from the European interior. All this was before the Crusades and the confrontation between Christendom and Islam.

Such activity reawakened the Italian economy which had fallen into a semi-slumber after the fall of Rome. Amalfi was penetrated by a monetary economy: notarial documents show that her merchants were using gold coin to buy land as early as the ninth century.[71] Between the eleventh and the thirteenth century, the landscape of the *valle* of Amalfi was thereby transformed: chestnut trees, vines, olive-groves, citrus fruits and mills appeared everywhere. The Amalfi Tables (*Tavole Amalfitane*) became one of the great maritime codes of Christian shipping in the Mediterranean, a sign of the prosperous international dealings of the town. But Amalfi had her share of misfortunes too: in 1100, she was conquered by the Normans; twice in a row, in 1135 and in 1137, she was sacked by the Pisans; finally in 1343, the lower part of the town was destroyed by a tidal wave. Although remaining a presence in the Mediterranean, Amalfi thereafter loses her place in the mainstream of history.[72] After 1250, her trade dwindled to

Aerial view of Amalfi, demonstrating strikingly the town's narrow site between the sea and the mountains. (Publi Aerofoto.)

perhaps a third of what it had been in 950-1050; the distance covered by her shipping gradually shrank to the proportions of the coastal trade along the shores of Italy, carried out by a few dozen small boats, saëtes and brigantines.

Venice's first steps were identical. As early as 869, the worldly goods left by the doge Giustiniano Partecipazio had included 1200 *libri* of silver, a considerable sum.[73] Like Amalfi in its hollow among the mountains, Venice, scattered over sixty or so islands and islets, was a strange world, a refuge perhaps but hardly a convenient one: there was no fresh water, no food supply – only salt in abundance. Of the Venetian, it was said: '*Non arat, non seminat, non vendemiat*' – he ploughs not, he sows not, he reaps not.[74] 'Built in the sea and totally without vines and cultivated fields', was how the doge Giovanni Soranzo described his city in 1327.[75] Is this an example of the town reduced to bare essentials, stripped of everything not strictly urban, and condemned, in order to survive, to obtain everything from trade: wheat or millet, rye, meat on the hoof, cheese, vegetables, wine, oil, timber, stone – and even drinking water? Venice's entire population lived outside the 'primary' sector, usually so well represented even inside pre-industrial cities. Venice's activities all fell into the sectors which economists would nowadays describe as secondary and tertiary: industry, commerce, services – sectors where labour was more profitably employed than in rural activities. This meant leaving the less profitable tasks to others, creating that imbalance which all great cities would experience: Florence, although rich in farmland, was importing grain from Sicily by the fourteenth and fifteenth centuries and planting her nearby hills with vines and olives; Amsterdam was by the seventeenth century eating wheat and rye from the Baltic, meat from Denmark and herrings from the deep-sea catches off the Dogger Bank. But towns like Venice, Amalfi and Genoa – none of which had any real territory – were condemned to live like this from the start: they had no choice.

When in the ninth and tenth centuries Venetian foreign trade was beginning to take shape, the Mediterranean was divided between Byzantium, Islam and western Christendom. At first sight, Byzantium might seem likely to become the centre of the reviving world-economy. But burdened by her past, Byzantium showed little combative spirit.[76] Islam, expanding into the Mediterranean, extending towards the Indian Ocean and China with its caravans and convoys of ships, was gradually overtaking the old metropolis of the Greek Empire. Was Islam therefore about to inherit the mantle of leadership? Not as it turned out, since Byzantium still remained a formidable obstacle, by dint of her former wealth, her experience and authority, in a world which proved difficult to reconstruct precisely because of the great conurbation, a weight that could not easily be displaced.

So the Italian cities, Genoa, Pisa and Venice, gradually inserted themselves into the spaces between the dominant economies. Venice's good fortune may have been that she had no need to resort to force and piracy, as Genoa and Pisa did, to establish her place in the sun. Regarded as being under the hypothetical rule of the Greek Empire, Venice was able to penetrate more successfully than any other power the huge, ineffectually defended market of Byzantium, rendering many services to the empire and even contributing to its defence. In return, she obtained massive privileges.[77] She nevertheless remained, despite the rise of a certain form of 'capitalism', a modest city. For centuries, St Mark's Square was encumbered with vines, trees and temporary buildings; it was cut in two by a canal, and given over to an orchard on the northern side (hence the name the *Brolo*, the orchard, which this site kept after it had become the haunt of noblemen and the centre of political intrigue and gossip).[78] The streets were merely beaten earth, the bridges wooden like the houses, so that the growing town, for fear of fire, banished its glass-making furnaces to Murano. Signs of economic activity became more frequent it is true: the minting of silver coins, loans stipulated in hyperpers (the gold currency of Byzantium), but barter persisted, the credit rate was still very high (*de quinque sex*, that is 20%) and the draconian conditions for repayment indicate how rare cash must have been and how modest the scale of economic life.[79]

One cannot be categorical about all this however. The history of Venice before the thirteenth century is lost in an impenetrable mist. Experts are divided about it, much as the experts on antiquity are divided about the distant origins of Rome. It seems probable, for instance, that Jewish merchants who had settled in Constantinople, Negropont and on the island of Candia, were frequenting the port and the town of Venice at a very early date, though the island known as the Giudecca, despite its name, was not necessarily the place where they stayed.[80] Similarly, it is more than likely that by the time Frederick Barbarossa and Pope Alexander III met at Venice in 1177, trade links already existed between Germany and the city of Saint Mark, and that silver from the German mines was already playing an important role in Venice in competition with Byzantine gold.[81]

But before Venice could really become Venice, she would have to bring all her lagoons under control, arrange for free passage along the waterways which reach the Adriatic at this latitude, and clear the Brenner route (controlled by Verona until 1178) for her own use.[82] She would have to expand her merchant fleet and her navy, and turn her Arsenal, under construction from 1104,[83] into an unrivalled power-house, gradually making the Adriatic 'her gulf', and overcoming or by-passing competition from towns like Comacchio, Ferrara and Ancona, or from Spalato, Zara and Ragusa on the *altra sponda*, the other side of the Adriatic – not to mention the rivalry with Genoa which began at an early stage. Venice would also have to forge her own fiscal, financial, monetary, administrative and political institutions, and her rich men (the 'capitalists' as G. Gracco[84] calls them in a revolutionary book on the origins of Venice) would have to take power, following the reign of the last autocratic doge, Vitale Michiele (1172).[85] Only then would the lineaments of Venice's greatness truly emerge.

It was however beyond all question the fantastic adventure of the Crusades which really launched the trading fortunes of Christendom and of Venice. The men from the North set off for the Mediterranean, arrived in Italy complete with horses, offered to pay their passage to the Holy Land on ships from the Italian ports, and ruined themselves to pay their expenses. Giant transport ships were immediately built in the yards of Pisa, Genoa or Venice. Christian states were settled in the Holy Land, opening a gateway to the East and its precious merchandise: pepper, spices, silk and drugs.[86] The really crucial turning-point for Venice was the terrible Fourth Crusade[87] which began with the capture of the Christian stronghold Zara (1203), and ended with the sack of Constantinople in 1204. Until then, Venice had been a parasite on the Byzantine Empire, eating it from within. Now it all but became her property. But all the Italian cities benefited from the collapse of Byzantium; similarly they all benefited from the Mongol invasion which after about 1240 opened up for a century or so a continental route from the Black Sea to China and India, one that had the inestimable advantage of by-passing the Islamic barrier.[88] Rivalry between Genoa and Venice reached an ever greater pitch on the now vital waters of the Black Sea and, of course, in Constantinople.

It is true that the Crusades had run out of steam even before the death of Saint Louis in 1270, and that Islam, by recapturing Acre in 1291, took the last important Christian stronghold in the Holy Land. But the island of Cyprus, a key strategic post, continued to protect Christian merchants and sailors in the seas of the Levant.[89] And above all, the Mediterranean, having become Christian, remained so in its entirety, confirming the supremacy of the Italian cities. The minting of gold currencies[90] in Florence in 1250, in Genoa even earlier and in Venice in 1284, marked the achievement of Italian economic emancipation from the dinars of Islam: this was a sign of strength. Moreover the cities had little difficulty in manipulating the territorial states: Genoa restored the Greek Empire of the Palaeologi in 1261 and furthered the Aragonese takeover of Sicily in 1282. The Vivaldo brothers[91] sailed out of her harbour, two hundred years before Vasco da Gama, on what was essentially a search for a route round the Cape. Both Genoa and Venice possessed colonial empires, and it looked as if Genoa would reign supreme when she dealt Pisa a mortal blow at the battle of La Meliora in 1284 and destroyed the Venetian galleys off the island of Curzola (Korčula) in the Adriatic in September 1298. Marco Polo is sometimes said to have been taken prisoner in this encounter.[92] As the thirteenth century drew to a close, the odds were strongly in favour of the imminent and total victory of the city of St George.

As it happened, the favourite did not win: Venice carried off the crown. The important point however is that from now on the struggle in the Mediterranean would not be one between Christendom and Islam, but one waged within the cluster of trading and industrious cities which the sea's prosperity had helped to develop in northern Italy. The coveted prize was access to the pepper and spices of the Levant, a privilege with consequences going far beyond the Mediterranean, and indeed the major asset of the Italian merchants in the north European complex which had come into being at the same time as the revival of the western Mediterranean.

An interlude: the Champagne fairs

Thus it was that the two major economic zones – the Low Countries and Italy – slowly and simultaneously came into being. And it was between these poles, these two potential 'core-zones', that the Champagne fairs had their day. Neither North nor South triumphed (nor indeed did they consciously compete with each other) in this early form of the European world-economy. Its economic centre lay for many years midway between the two poles of attraction, as if to satisfy both, in the six fairs held annually in Champagne and Brie, changing location every two months.[93] 'First, in January, came the fair at Lagny-sur-Marne; then on the Tuesday before the middle of Lent, the fair at Bar-sur-Aube; in May fell the first Provins fair, known as the St Quiriace fair; in June, the "hot fair" at Troyes; in September, the second Provins St Ayoul fair, and finally in October, the cycle was closed by the "cold fair" at Troyes.'[94] The gathering of traders and businessmen travelled round from one town to another. The clockwork machinery in operation by the thirteenth century was not even new, since it was probably imitated from the earlier rotation of the Flanders fairs[95] and had simply taken over and reorganized a chain of pre-existing regional markets.[96]

So the six fairs of Champagne and Brie, each lasting two months, covered the entire annual cycle, forming a 'continuous market'[97] which was at the time unrivalled. What remains today of the old town of Provins gives some idea of the size of the warehouses of the past. As for their fame, the popular expression, 'not to know your Champagne fairs' meant not to know what everyone else knew.[98] They were a rendezvous for the whole of Europe, for the offerings of both North and South. The trade caravans would converge on Champagne and Brie in assembled and guarded convoys, not unlike the other caravans with their camels which crossed the great deserts of Islam on their way to the Mediterranean.

It is not beyond our means to map these journeys. As one might expect, the Champagne fairs brought prosperity to the countless family workshops making linen or woollen cloth locally, from the Seine and Marne to Brabant. And these fabrics travelled south, throughout Italy and along all the sea-routes of the Mediterranean. The transit of northern fabrics through Genoa is recorded in the notarial archives of the latter half of the twelfth century.[99] In Florence, the unbleached cloth from the North was dyed by the *Arte di Calimala*,[100] the guild uniting the richest merchants in the city. Meanwhile from Italy came pepper, spices, drugs, silk, coins and credit. From Venice and Genoa, goods travelled by sea to Aigues-Mortes, then up the long valleys of the Rhône, Saône and Seine. Land-routes crossed the Alps, like the *Via Francigena* which linked Siena and many other towns to distant France.[101] From Asti[102] in Lombardy, came carriers and a throng of small-time merchants, usurers and second-hand dealers who would soon make the name of the Lombards well-known (and disliked) in the West as pawn-brokers. This traffic was joined by goods from the different French provinces, from England, Germany and the Iberian Peninsula, the latter using the pilgrim route from Santiago de Compostela.[103]

The originality of the Champagne fairs lay less however in the super-abundance of goods on sale than in the money market and the precocious workings of credit on display there. The fair always opened with a cloth sale and the first four weeks were confined to commodity trading. But the following month, the money-changers came into their own. These were apparently modest individuals who set up shop on a fixed date 'in Provins in the upper town, on the old market-place in front of St Thibaut's church', or 'in Troyes, in the Rue Moyenne and the Spice-market near the church of St John of the Market'.[104] In fact these money-changers, usually Italians, really called the tune for the whole fair. Their equipment consisted simply of a 'table covered with a cloth', a pair of scales – and several sacks 'filled with ingots or coins'.[105] All compensatory payments balancing sales and purchases, all deferred payments between one fair and another, all loans to lords and princes, the settlement of bills of exchange which expired at the fair, as well as the making out of new ones to be sent elsewhere – passed through their hands. As a result, all the international and above all most modern aspects of the Champagne fairs were controlled, on the spot or at a distance, by Italian merchants whose firms were often huge concerns, like the *Magna Tavola* of the Buonsignori family, the thirteenth-century Rothschilds of Siena.[106]

This already foreshadowed the situation which would later occur in the Geneva and Lyon fairs: Italian credit would be able, through the gatherings at these international fairs, to exploit to its own advantage the huge market of western Europe, with its cash returns. Was it with a view to the advantage to be derived from the European market as a whole that the Champagne fairs were located not at its economic centre, which was unquestionably northern Italy, but near the customers and suppliers in the North? Or was it perhaps that they had to be held in Champagne since the centre of gravity of overland continental trade had, after the eleventh century, shifted towards the larger-scale industrial production of the North? The Champagne fairs were certainly located near the outer limit of this productive zone: Paris, Provins, Chalons and Reims were all textile centres by the twelfth century. Italy by contrast, the triumphant leader of the thirteenth century, remained above all a commercial centre, leading the world in business techniques: she had introduced to Europe minted gold money, the bill of exchange and the practice of credit, but did not really develop her industrial sector until later, after the crisis of the fourteenth century.[107] Meanwhile, northern cloth was indispensable for her trade with the Levant, the key source of her fortune.

Such constraints counted for more than the liberal policies of the counts of

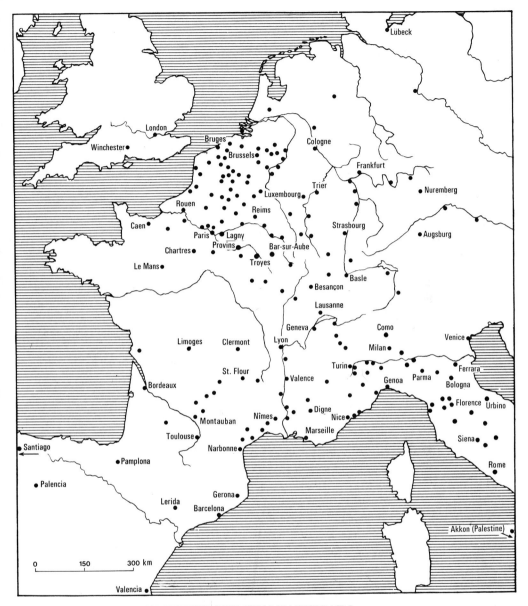

13 TOWNS IN CONTACT WITH THE CHAMPAGNE FAIRS
(TWELFTH AND THIRTEENTH CENTURIES)
This map clearly reveals the economic structure and notably the bi-polarity of thirteenth-century
Europe, centred on the Netherlands in the North and Italy in the South. (From H. Ammann, in
Hessisches Jahrbuch für Landesgeschichte, 8, 1958.)

Champagne frequently invoked by historians.[108] It is true that the merchants were always looking for liberties (that is the waiving of local regulations), something the count of Champagne certainly offered them, from his position of virtual independence, despite the nominal suzerainty of the king of France. For the same reasons, the fairs organized in the county of Flanders would be favoured by the merchants,[109] who were anxious to avoid the dangers and inconvenience usually caused by over-powerful states. All the same, can we seriously believe that it was the occupation of Champagne by Philip the Bold in 1273, and its attachment to the French crown by Philip the Fair in 1284[110] which dealt the Champagne fairs their *coup de grâce?* The fairs had been in decline for many other reasons, in the latter years of the thirteenth century, hitherto so favourable to them. The slow-down in trade hit commodities first; credit operations kept going for longer, until about 1310-20.[111] And these dates also coincide with the series of crises of varying duration and seriousness affecting the whole of Europe at the time, from Florence to London, heralding what was to become, in conjunction with the Black Death, the great recession of the fourteenth century.

These crises seriously compromised the prosperity of the fairs. But they were dealt a further blow by the inauguration, in the late thirteenth and early fourteenth centuries, of a regular sea-route, which was naturally competitive, between the Mediterranean and the North Sea, through the Straits of Gibraltar. The first regular link was established by the Genoese merchant fleet in 1277. The other Mediterranean cities followed suit, after some delay.

At about the same time, another trade route was being developed, this time overland: the western Alpine passes – the Mont-Cenis and the Simplon – were being overtaken in importance by the eastern passes, the St Gotthard and the Brenner. In 1237, the bold construction of the bridge over the Reuss opened up the St Gotthard pass[112] and the 'German isthmus' found more favour from this date. Germany and Central Europe now experienced a period of general growth with the prosperity of their silver and copper mines, the progress of their agriculture, the establishment of the fustian industry and the development of markets and fairs. The spread of the German merchants was noted throughout the West and in the Baltic, in Eastern Europe as well as at the Champagne fairs, or in Venice, where the *Fondaco dei Tedeschi* appears to have been founded in 1228.[113]

Does the possibility of sending goods over the Brenner explain why Venice waited so long (until 1314) to follow the Genoese on the shipping routes to Bruges? We know that on account of the role silver played in the Levant trade, the Italian cities were extremely interested in the German silver mines. And there was very soon a thriving network of money-changers throughout the towns of High Germany and the Rhineland, playing the same role as the merchant bankers of Bruges or Champagne.[114] So the old rendezvous in France was gradually being outflanked by the system of competitive routes on both land and sea.

It is sometimes suggested that the Champagne fairs may have suffered from the 'commercial revolution', when the merchant took to staying in his shop or *Kontor*, entrusting his affairs to representatives stationed abroad and to professional transporters, and began to conduct business from a distance, thanks to improved accounting methods and to an abundant correspondence in which he conveyed information, instructions and complaints. But the practice of doing business with one travelling partner and one partner at home was already in existence well before the Champagne fairs – and in any case, what was to prevent the new methods from being employed in Provins or Troyes?

France's lost opportunity

Who can tell how beneficial the prosperity of the Champagne fairs was to the kingdom of France and in particular to Paris?

If the French kingdom, which had been politically structured from the reign of Philip Augustus (1180–1223) had unquestionably become the most successful of European states by the age of St Louis (1226–70), this was as a result of the general advance of Europe, but also because the centre of gravity of the European world lay only one or two days' journey from the French capital. Paris became a major trading city and would remain one of importance until the fifteenth century. The city profited by the proximity of so many businessmen. At the same time, Paris was becoming the seat of the institutions of the French monarchy and building a wealth of monuments. She already possessed the outstanding university in Europe, a natural setting for the scientific revolution which followed the re-discovery of the thought of Aristotle. During this 'great century' [the thirteenth], writes Augusto Guzzo, 'all eyes were turned towards Paris. Many Italians were students and sometimes teachers there, St Bonaventura and St Thomas for example.'[115] Was this the 'age of Paris', as seems to be suggested *a contrario* by the title of a passionately-argued book by Giuseppe Toffanin, a historian of humanism, about the thirteenth century which he calls *Il Secolo senza Roma*, 'the age without Rome'?[116] Gothic architecture, the art of France, certainly travelled abroad from the Paris region, and the Sienese merchants who frequented the Champagne fairs were not the only ones to take word of it home with them. And since such things tend to go together, this was also the period when the French *communes* began to assert themselves; in Sucy-en-Brie, Boissy, Orly and other places in the Paris region, between 1236 and 1325, the emancipation of the peasants was proceeding fast with the favour of royal authority.[117] This was also the age of St Louis, when France assumed the leadership of the Crusades in the Mediterranean – in other words the highest honour in Christendom.

The fairs of Champagne were however no more than an interlude in the history of Europe and of France. This was the first and last time that the economic complex which had taken shape in Europe centred on a string of fair-towns – and ones in the heart of the continent to boot. It was also the first and last time that France saw the economic centre of the West located on her soil: this was a treasure briefly possessed then lost, without the leaders of France being aware of it.[118] Yet what was taking place under the last of the Capets was the relegation of France to a kind of backwater for many years to come. The development of north-south routes between Germany and Italy, the sea-link between the Mediterranean and the North Sea had, even before the end of the thirteenth century, established the preferred circuit of capitalism and of modernity: this encircled France at a distance, hardly touching her territory. If one excepts Marseille and Aigues-Mortes, large-scale trade and the capitalism it brought with it were carried on virtually outside French soil, which would only be partly touched by foreign trade for a period during and immediately after the hardships and shortages of the Hundred Years' War.

But was not the territorial state, quite as much as the French economy, being squeezed out, well before the recession that would coincide with the Hundred Years' War? If the French kingdom had maintained its strength and cohesion, Italian capitalism might not have been able to operate so freely. But by the same token, the new circuits of capitalism meant the creation of such a powerful monopoly to the advantage of the city-states of Italy and the Netherlands that embryo territorial states like England, France and Spain necessarily suffered the consequences.

The belated rise of Venice

France then had let slip an opportunity in Champagne. Who took it up? Neither the fairs of Flanders, nor the city of Bruges (*pace* Lamberto Incarnati[119]) in spite of the founding of the famous Bourse in 1309. The ships, businessmen, precious goods, money and credit that came to Bruges came chiefly from the South as we have seen. 'The experts on credit', as Incarnati himself points out,[120] 'were mostly Italians.' And the Netherlands trade balance favoured the southerners until the fifteenth century and perhaps later.[121]

If the centre of gravity had remained halfway between the Adriatic and the North Sea, it might have become established in Nuremberg for instance, the meeting point of about a dozen major routes, or in Cologne, the largest of the German cities. But if Bruges or some other intermediate centre equivalent to the Champagne fairs did not take over this role, perhaps it was because Italy no longer had the same need to look northwards, now that she had developed, in Florence, Milan and elsewhere, her own industrial centres, within easy reach of the merchants. Florence which had hitherto concentrated most of her craft activity on dyeing natural cloth from the North, now saw the *Arte della Lana* take over from the *Arte di Calimala*, and her industrial development was both rapid and spectacular.

Another factor was the recession which was already, years ahead, preparing the way for the apocalyptic Black Death and the shattering decline in economic life which followed. Crisis and the reversal of a trend tended, as we have seen,[122] to bring about the deterioration of existing systems, wiping out the weakest and reinforcing the comparative preponderance of the strongest, though even these might not emerge from a crisis unscathed. Italy, like other countries, was afflicted and shaken by the torment: achievements and successes became infrequent. But in her case falling back on her own resources meant falling back on the Mediterranean, still the most active of zones and the heart of the most profitable international trade. During the general recession of the West, Italy was what economists would call a 'protected zone': she had the lion's share of the best trade; her dealings in gold,[123] and her experience in handling money and credit helped to preserve her; her city-states, much lighter machines than the cumbersome territorial states, were able to manoeuvre freely in this stormy climate. Others were worse affected, notably the great territorial states which suffered and broke down. The Mediterranean and the active part of Europe were reduced more than ever to 'archipelagos' of cities.

The Lion of St Mark, 1516, Venice, Ducal Palace. (Photo Giraudon.)

It is not surprising then that in this gradual re-centring of the European economy, the only rivals left in the ring were the Italian cities – in particular Venice and Genoa, which disputed the crown in the name at once of passion and of interest. Both were equally capable of winning. So what explains Venice's triumph?

Genoa versus Venice

In 1298, Genoa had routed the Venetian fleet off Curzola. Eighty years later, in August 1379, she seized Chioggia, a little fishing port which commanded one of the gateways from the lagoon of Venice to the Adriatic.[124] The proud city of Saint Mark seemed doomed, but with a prodigious effort managed to reverse the situation: in June 1380, Vettor Pisani recaptured Chioggia and destroyed the Genoese fleet.[125] The peace treaty, signed the following year in Turin, gave no formal advantage to Venice.[126] But it spelled the beginning of the end for the Genoese – who would never be seen in the Adriatic again – and the assertion of Venetian pre-eminence which would subsequently remain undisputed.

Neither the original defeat, nor the eventual triumph are easy to understand. And in any case, Genoa was not banished from the ranks of rich cities after Chioggia. So why did this battle effectively put an end to the struggle in the Mediterranean millpond, in which the two rivals had so long been at one another's throats, sacking a coast here, capturing a convoy there, destroying the rival's galleys, calling on princely intermediaries such as the Angevins, the Hungarians, the Palaeologi or the Aragonese? Perhaps the answer is that only prolonged prosperity and a rising tide of trade had made it possible to indulge for so long in battles which were fierce but not in the end mortal, since the wounds healed quickly. If the war of Chioggia marks a break, is it because in the 1380s a long period of growth had unquestionably been brought to an end? Both major and minor wars had now become too expensive a luxury. Peaceful coexistence would have to be the rule – particularly since the interests of both Genoa and Venice, as merchant and colonial powers (and the *colonial* tells us that they had already reached an advanced stage of capitalism) discouraged them from fighting to the death of one or other: capitalist rivalries always admit a degree of complicity, even between determined adversaries.

I certainly do not believe that the rise of Venice is accounted for by the outstanding excellence of her capitalism, which has been hailed by Oliver C. Cox[127] as the appearance of an original model. For no historian could deny that Genoa was first in the field, with a uniquely modern approach to capitalism. Genoa was far more modern than Venice from this point of view; and may indeed have been somewhat vulnerable by virtue of this forward position. Perhaps it was one of Venice's advantages to be more conventional, less audacious. And her geographical situation undoubtedly favoured her. No sooner was a ship out of the lagoon than in the Adriatic, and for a Venetian this was still to be in home waters. Genoese mariners sailed straight out of port into the Tyr-rhenian, and this was a sea too large to patrol effectively, so that in practice it belonged to everyone.[128] And as long as the East was the chief source of wealth, Venice with the facilities of her route through the islands to the Levant would have the advantage. When in the 1340s, the 'Mongol route' was blocked, Venice outstripped all her rivals to be the first to knock at the gates of Syria and Egypt in 1343 – and she did not knock in vain.[129] Finally, did Venice not have better contacts than any other Italian city with Germany and Central Europe – the most reliable customers for her cotton, pepper and spice and the best source of silver coin which was the key to the Levant trade?

Venice reigns supreme

At the end of the fourteenth century, Venice's primacy was unquestioned. In 1383, she occupied Corfu, the gateway to the Adriatic. Without difficulty, though at great expense,[130] between 1405 and 1427, she occupied the towns of the *Terraferma*: Padua, Verona, Brescia, Bergamo.[131] Now she was protected from the rest of Italy by a ring of towns and territories. The occupation of this mainland zone, already penetrated by the Venetian economy, was in fact part of a significant larger movement: Milan was taking over Lombardy; Florence was asserting herself over Tuscany and in 1405 overcame her rival Pisa; Genoa succeeded in spreading her rule to the two 'rivieras', the east and the west, and filled in the harbour of her rival Savona.[132] Everywhere the leading Italian cities were gaining strength at the expense of lesser ones – a classic process.

Much earlier than this, Venice had successfully carved herself out an empire – modest in extent but of remarkable strategic and commercial importance since it was strung out along the routes to the Levant. This was a scattered empire, reminiscent, though on a very different scale, of the Portuguese and later the Dutch Empires in the Indian Ocean, a trading-post empire forming a long capitalist antenna; an empire 'on the Phoenician model', to use a more ancient parallel.

Power and wealth went hand in hand. And Venice's wealth (and consequently her power) can be put to the test by looking at the city's budgets, the *Bilanci*[133] as well as at the famous speech delivered by the elderly doge Tommaso Mocenigo, just before his death in 1423.

In that year, the receipts of the *city* of Venice alone amounted to some 750,000 ducats. If the proportions I have suggested elsewhere[134] are applicable here – i.e. if the budget was between 5 and 10% of national income – then the gross national income of the city lay somewhere between 7.5 million and 15 million ducats. Since the estimated population of Venice and the *Dogado* (the suburbs as far as Chioggia) was 150,000 at most, per capita income in the city would be between 50 and 100 ducats – very high indeed; even the lower figure is hardly credible.

We can measure this even more effectively if we try to compare it with other economies of the time. A Venetian document[135] conveniently offers us a list of European budgets in the early fifteenth century: the data is presented in Figure 14. Whereas receipts for the city of Venice alone were between 750,000 and 800,000 ducats, the entire kingdom of France (in a parlous state at the time it is true) could assemble a mere million ducats; Venice's budget was equal to that of Spain (though quite what 'Spain' means in this context is disputed), almost equal to that of England, and far exceeded those of the other Italian cities deemed to be her peers: Milan, Florence and Genoa. It is true that the figures for the budget of Genoa do not mean much, since private interest had commandeered a huge slice of public revenue for itself.

And so far, we have only been talking about Venice and the *Dogado*. To the revenue of the Signoria (750,000 ducats) we should add those of the *Terraferma* (464,000) and of the empire – the *Mar* or sea as it was called (376,000). The total (1,615,000 ducats) sets the Venetian budget in the front rank of budgets in Europe – and even this is not quite the whole story. For if the population of the entire Venetian complex (city, *Terraferma* and empire) is estimated at about one and a half million maximum, and that of France under Charles VI as fifteen million (for the purposes of a very rough and ready calculation), then the latter, with ten times as many inhabitants, ought to have had a budget ten times that of Venice – viz. 16 million ducats. The paltry size of the French budget, one million, serves to underline the overwhelming superiority of the city-states compared to the 'territorial' economies and allows one to imagine what this early concentration of capital must have signified for a single city – when all is said and done a mere handful of men. To suggest a further interesting if not conclusive comparison: the same document reveals that budgets had shrunk in the fifteenth century, but unfortunately without indicating the year in which the decline began. Compared to the former level, the English budget had apparently fallen by 65%, that of Spain (again what 'Spain'?) by 73%, but that of Venice by only 27%.

The second test we can apply is the celebrated speech of the doge Mocenigo, a combination of last will and testament, statistical survey and political invective.[136] On the point of death, the old doge made a desperate attempt to prevent the succession of Francesco Foscari, of the war party (who did in fact succeed him on 14 April 1423, and presided over Venice's destiny until his deposition on 23 October 1457). The old doge explained to his listeners the advantages of peace if the fortunes of the state and its citizens were to be preserved. If you elect Foscari, he said, 'you will soon be at war. The man who has 10,000 ducats now will be left with a thousand, he who has ten houses will have only one, he who has ten garments will hardly have one, those with ten petticoats or pairs of hose or shirts will hardly have one left and so it will be with everything'. If on the contrary, the peace is kept, 'if you follow my advice, you will find that you are the masters of the gold of Christendom'.

This is surprising language for 1423. It assumes that Venetians of this time

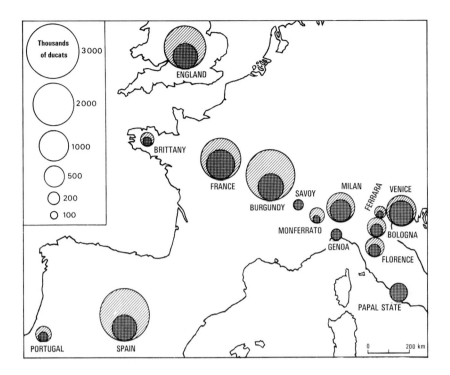

14   COMPARATIVE BUDGETS:
VENICE FARES BETTER DURING THE CRISIS THAN THE OTHER STATES
This diagrammatic representation of the Venetian figures (*Bilanci generali*, I, 1912, pp. 98–9)
shows both the respective size of European budgets and their greater or lesser decline during the
first quarter of the fifteenth century. The figures referred to in the text, which are the most
reliable, correspond to the darker circle, probably for the year 1423. The lighter circle represents
the previous size of the budgets – considerably larger.

could understand that looking after one's ducats, dwellings and doublets was
the road to true power; that it was possible to become 'masters of the gold of
Christendom', that is the entire European economy, by trade – and not by arms.
According to Mocenigo (and his figures which were once challenged have now
been accepted) the volume of capital invested annually in trade was ten million
ducats. These ten million brought investors not only two million interest on the
capital but also a trading profit of two million. We might note the distinction
made between the trading profits and the revenue from invested capital, each
reckoned at 20%. So the return on foreign trade in Venice was according to
Mocenigo 40%, a fabulous rate which explains the precocious, indeed blooming
state of Venetian capitalism. To talk of capitalism in twelfth-century Venice is
'nonsensical' according to Werner Sombart. But what other name can one give
to the world glimpsed in Mocenigo's astonishing speech in the fifteenth century?
    The four million ducats' annual revenue from trade estimated by the doge is

Giovanni Antonio Canaletto (1697-1768), *Il Campo di San Giacometto*. All the great merchants would meet under the portico of this little church off the Rialto. (Dresden Museum, photo by the museum.)

somewhere between a quarter and a half of my own estimate of the total revenue of the city. Mocenigo's speech also gives a few statistical estimates about trade and the Venetian fleet. They bear out the order of magnitude of my own calculations and these do not clash unduly with what we know of the activity of the *Zecca*, the Venetian mint (in a later period it is true, and an inflationary one corresponding to what some people have described as 'the decadence of Venice'). In the last years of the sixteenth century, the *Zecca* was coining about two million ducats' worth a year of gold and silver coins.[137] This suggests a monetary flow of up to 40 million,[138] one which merely passed through Venice, but which was renewed every year. This is not really surprising when one considers that her merchants firmly controlled all the major commodity trades in the Mediterranean – pepper, spices, Syrian cotton, grain, wine and salt. Pierre Daru, in his classic and still useful *Histoire de Venise* (1819) was already pointing out 'how much this branch of the salt trade had benefited Venice'.[139] The Signoria consequently took care to control the salt-marshes of the Adriatic and the coasts of Cyprus. Every year more than 40,000 horses came from Hungary, Croatia and even Germany to load Istrian salt alone.[140]

Further signs of Venice's wealth could be seen in the enormous concentration of might in her Arsenal, in the number of her galleys and cargo vessels, and in the system of *galere da mercato*, of which more later.[141] Equally significant was the constant embellishment of the city which gradually took on a new appearance in the fifteenth century: the streets of beaten earth were paved, the old wooden bridges and piers of the canals were replaced by stone bridges and *fondamenta* (this 'petrification' of capital investments was as much necessity as luxury), not to mention other works of town improvement – the digging of wells[142] and the cleaning of the canals where the stench was sometimes unbearable.[143]

This can all be ascribed to the politics of prestige, which may be for a city, a state or an individual, a way of ruling. The Venetian government was well aware of the need to embellish the city, '*non sparangando spexa alguna come e conveniente a la beleza sua*' – sparing no expense, as is appropriate to its beauty.[144] The restoration of the Doges' Palace may have dragged out over a long period, but it continued without interruption: on the Rialto Vecchio, the new Loggia (which functioned as a stock exchange for merchants) was put up in 1459 opposite the *Fondaco dei Tedeschi*.[145] Between 1421 and 1440, the Contarini family built the *Ca' d'Oro* on the Grand Canal where many new palaces were springing up. This building craze was no doubt common to many cities in Italy and elsewhere. But building in Venice, on top of the thousands of oak piles sunk in the sand and mud of the lagoon, meant that stone had to be brought from Istria, and required absolutely colossal sums of money.[146]

Venice's strength was also manifested with *éclat* in the political arena of course. Here Venice excelled: she very quickly had a corps of ambassadors, the *oratori*. She also had mercenary troops to service her policies: anyone who had the money could hire them and push them out as pawns on the battlefield. They were not necessarily the best of soldiers, since the *condottieri* on the whole went in for 'phoney' wars in which the two sides circled each other amicably without joining battle.[147] But the fact that Venice blocked Milan's attempts to gain hegemony; that she participated in the Peace of Lodi (1454) which created or rather stabilized the Italian balance of power; that during the second war of Ferrara (1482–83) she stoutly resisted enemies who were dreaming, as one of them said, of pushing Venice back into the sea where she belonged;[148] that in 1495 she was at the centre of the negotiations which took Commynes by surprise and sent the little French king Charles VIII back home unaccompanied by fanfares, after his excessively easy romp to Naples – all these testify to the might of an extremely rich city-state. Priuli had some cause for pride when he described in his *Diarii*[149] the extraordinary meeting of all the ambassadors of the princes of Europe, plus the representative of the Sultan, from which emerged the anti-French league of 31 March 1495. This was founded to defend poor Italy after the French invasion, that Italy of which 'the Venetians, defenders of Christendom, are the fathers'.[150]

The world-economy centred on Venice

The world-economy centred on Venice, the source of the city's greatness, is not easy to represent on a map of Europe. Its eastern frontier, clear enough where it touches Poland and Hungary, is less distinct in the Balkans, on account of the Turkish conquests which *preceded* the capture of Constantinople (1453) and extended irresistibly northwards: Adrianople had been occupied in 1361; the battle of Kossovo which destroyed the great Serbian Empire took place in 1389. Its western frontier on the other hand is no problem: the whole of Europe was in Venice's hands; so too was the Mediterranean, including Constantinople until 1453, and beyond it the Black Sea which would still be exploited by the West for a few more years. The coasts of Islamic countries not yet seized by the Turks (North Africa, Egypt and Syria) were open to Christian merchants (from Ceuta, which became Portuguese in 1415, to Beirut and Tripoli in Syria). But they kept for themselves the routes that ran far inland through their territory towards Black Africa, the Red Sea and the Persian Gulf. Spices, drugs and silks were conveyed to the Levant ports, where the western merchants waited.

Even more complicated than the external frontiers of this world-economy is the definition of the zones that made it up. The central zone is at least easily recognizable: the speech by Tommaso Mocenigo already quoted reveals the preferential relations between Venice and Milan, the towns of Lombardy, Genoa and Florence. This archipelago of towns, bounded to the south by a line running from Florence to Ancona and to the north by the Alps, was unquestionably the heart of the world-economy centred on Venice. But the string of glittering towns continued north over the Alps, like a milky way: Augsburg, Vienna, Nuremberg, Ratisbon (Regensburg), Ulm, Basle, Strasbourg, Cologne, Hamburg and even Lübeck, ending with the still-brilliant constellation of the Netherlands, with Bruges as yet its leading light, and the two English ports of London and Southampton (*Antone* as the latter was called by the southerners).

Europe was thus bisected by a Venice–Bruges–London axis running from south to north: both east and west of this line lay vast areas much less animated than the axis itself; these would always remain peripheral. The centre of gravity of the whole, defying the elementary laws which had produced the Champagne fairs, lay at the very southern tip of the axis, at the point where it met the Mediterranean axis, that east–west line representing the essential route for Europe's far-distant trade, and the major source of its profits.

Venice's responsibility

Was there perhaps another reason for the location of the centre of the whole system in Italy – namely the economic policy of Venice? The Venetians had put into practice the methods from which their own merchants had suffered when they were penned up in the *fonduks* (a street or a row of buildings) in Islamic countries.[151] Venice treated German merchants in exactly the same way, assigning them a compulsory segregated residence, the *Fondaco dei Tedeschi*,[152] opposite the Rialto, in the heart of the business quarter. Every German merchant had to deposit his merchandise here and lodge in one of the rooms provided, sell his goods under the watchful eye of the Signoria's agents and use the proceeds to buy Venetian goods. German merchants were continually complaining of this strict surveillance: it effectively excluded them from the profitable long-distance trade which Venice jealously kept for her *cittadini de intus et extra*, the citizens of the city itself and the outlying districts. If a German merchant tried to join in, his merchandise was liable to be confiscated.

On the other hand, Venice virtually forbade her own merchants to buy and sell directly in Germany.[153] As a result, the Germans were obliged to come to Venice in person to buy cloth, cotton, wool, silk, spices, pepper and gold – the opposite of what was to happen after the voyage of Vasco da Gama, when the Portuguese set up their *feitoria*[154] in Antwerp and took the pepper and spices themselves to their northern customers. The German purchasers could of course have gone to Genoa, and some of them did, since it was open to them without many restrictions. But Genoa was really the port for communications with Spain, Portugal and North Africa, and besides, the Germans could find nothing there they could not also find in Venice, which had become a sort of universal warehouse of the world as Amsterdam was to be, on a larger scale, in a later century. How could they resist the convenience and temptation of a city lying at the heart of a world-economy? The whole of Germany joined in, delivering to the merchants of Venice iron, hardware, fustians (cotton-linen mixtures) and, from mid-fifteenth-century onwards, ever-larger quantities of silver currency) some of which the Venetians took to Tunis to exchange for gold dust.[155]

That this was conscious policy on Venice's part can hardly be doubted, since she forced it upon all the cities more or less dependent upon her. All trade to and from the *Terraferma*, all exports from her islands in the Levant or cities in the Adriatic (even goods travelling to Sicily or England) were obliged to pass through the port of Venice. Thus Venice had quite deliberately ensnared all the surrounding subject economies, including the German economy, for her own profit: she drew her living from them, preventing them from acting freely and according to their own lights. If Lisbon had forced northern ships to come to get their spices and pepper from her warehouses after the great discoveries, she might have smashed or at any rate damaged the quickly-established supremacy of Antwerp. But perhaps Lisbon did not possess the necessary strength or the merchant and banking experience of the Italian cities. The strategem of the *Fondaco dei Tedeschi* may have been as much consequence as cause of Venetian supremacy.

The galere da mercato

Venice's communications with the Levant and Europe, even in her heyday, caused certain problems, in particular that of transport over the Mediterranean and in the Atlantic, since she redistributed precious goods to the whole of Europe. In prosperous times, communications took care of themselves. When the economic sky darkened, ways and means had to be devised.

The system of the *galere da mercato* was one of these interventionist measures by the Venetian state, inspired by hard times. Invented in the fourteenth century to meet a persistent crisis, as a 'method of dumping' as Gino Luzzatto has described it, this system was a combination of state enterprise and private association, the latter being a kind of consortium of export merchants[156] anxious to reduce their transport costs and to remain competitive (in practice unbeatable) as against foreign rivals. The Signoria itself, probably as early as 1314 and certainly by 1328, was having the Arsenal build the *galere da mercato*, merchant vessels (originally of 100 tons and later as much as 300) capable of carrying in their holds the equivalent of 50 cartloads of goods. On the way into or out of port, the *galere* used oars; the rest of the time they sailed like ordinary round ships. They were certainly not the largest merchantmen of their day, since the Genoese carracks of the fifteenth century reached and even exceeded 1000 tons.[157] But they were safe ships, which sailed in convoy and were defended by archers and slingsmen. Later they would have cannon hoisted aboard. Among the slingsmen (*ballestieri*) were a number of impoverished aristocrats to whom the Signoria thus offered a lifeline.

The chartering of these state vessels was adjudicated by an annual auction. The patrician who was successful at the *incanto* could in turn collect charters from other merchants, the freight charges corresponding to the volume of goods loaded. Thus the 'private' sector was able to make use of facilities built by the 'public' sector. Whether the clients travelled by pooling their resources '*ad unum denarium*', or whether they formed a company for the freighting and return of a single galley, the Signoria encouraged all such practices, which in theory offered equal opportunities to all participants. Similar 'pools' open to any merchant were commonly organized for the purchase of cotton in Syria or even pepper in Alexandria. On the other hand, the Venetian authorities stepped in to disband any cartel which appeared to be tending towards creating a monopoly for an exclusive group.

The documents preserved in the *Archivio di Stato* in Venice make it possible to reconstruct the voyages of the *galere da mercato*, year by year, to observe the expansion (and contraction) of the tentacular network which Venice maintained in the Mediterranean, with one extra long arm snaking out to Bruges (or rather

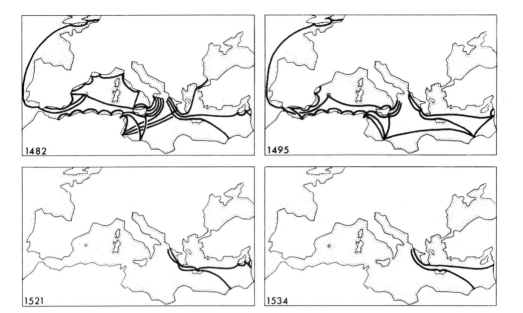

1482

1495

1521

1534

15 THE VOYAGES OF THE GALERE DA MERCATO
The four sketch maps above are taken from the long narrative by Alberto Tenenti and Corrado
Vivanti in *Annales E.S.C*, 1961, and summarize the stages by which the old system of convoys of
galere da mercato declined (they had sailed to Flanders, Aigues-Mortes, Barbary, the 'Trafego',
Alexandria, Beirut and Constantinople). All these lines were working in 1482. By 1521 and 1534,
only the profitable links with the Levant survived. To simplify the map, all routes are shown
from the entrance to the Adriatic only, not from Venice.

to the city's seaport at Sluys) after 1314, when the *galere di Fiandra* were
introduced (see Figure 15). The system was probably operating at peak capacity
in about 1460,[158] when the Venetian government introduced the *galere di trafego*,
the curious shipping line which greatly stepped up Venice's trade with North
Africa, giving access to the gold of the Sudan. In later years, the system had its
failures, and it deteriorated in the sixteenth century. But its decline interests us
less than the success which preceded it.

The Venetian model of capitalism

Oliver C. Cox[159] has argued that Venice's success was the result of her precocious
capitalist organization: in his view, capitalism was born or invented in Venice
and spread only later to other places. Was this really so? Other capitalist cities
were in existence before or at the same time as Venice. And if Venice had not so
quickly taken the lead, Genoa could no doubt have done so without difficulty.
For Venice was no isolated phenomenon, but had grown up surrounded by a
network of thriving towns, all inspired to similar responses by the age they lived

in. The real innovations often did not come from Venice at all. She was far behind the pioneer cities of Tuscany as regards banking or the formation of large firms. It was not in Venice but in Genoa that the first gold coins were minted in the early thirteenth century, with Florence following suit in 1250. (The Venetian ducat, soon to be known as the sequin or *zecchino*, was not minted until 1284.)[160] Cheques and holding-companies were invented not in Venice but in Florence.[161] Double-entry book-keeping too was first introduced in Florence, where an early example dating from the end of the thirteenth century has been preserved in the papers of the Fini and Farolfi companies.[162] The useful simplification of the procedure for maritime insurance, eliminating the need for a notary, was devised not in the seaports but in Florence.[163] And it was Florence, yet again, which developed industry to the maximum and moved unequivocally into what can be described as the manufacturing phase.[164] The first *regular* sea-link with Flanders via Gibraltar (a major innovation) was effected by Genoa in 1277. And the imaginative search for a direct route to the Indies was another Genoese initiative, that of the Vivaldo brothers in 1291. At the end of the year 1407, the Genoese went into action again, perhaps sensing the coming Portuguese voyages of discovery, and sent an expedition under Malfante in search of the gold of Tuat.[165]

In the field of capitalist technique and enterprise then, Venice was if anything rather slow off the mark. Can this be explained by her preferred (and traditional) links with the Orient, whereas the other Italian cities were more concerned with the western world, then slowly taking shape? Perhaps Venice's easily-acquired riches imprisoned the city within a set of strategies determined by ancient custom, whereas other cities, with less assured fortunes, were sooner or later obliged to become more cunning and inventive? For all that, Venice succeeded in establishing a system which from the very first raised all the problems of the relations between Capital, Labour and the State, relations which would increasingly come to be identified with the word *capitalism* in the course of its long subsequent development.

By the late twelfth or early thirteenth century, and *a fortiori* by the fourteenth, the Venetian economy was already well-equipped with institutions: it had markets, shops, warehouses, the Ascensiontide Fair (*la Sensa*), the Mint (the *Zecca*) the Doges' Palace, the Arsenal, the Dogana. Every morning, while the money-changers and bankers stationed themselves in front of the little church of San Giacometto,[166] opposite them on the Rialto would assemble all the wealthy merchants, Venetian or otherwise, some from the *Terraferma*, from Italy or from beyond the Alps. The bankers were conveniently nearby, pen and notebook in hand, to write down transfers of money from one account to another. Book-keeping (*scritta*) was the miraculous method of settling transactions between merchants on the spot, by transferring payments, without the use of cash and without having to wait for the infrequent settlement days at the fairs. The *banchi di scritta*[167] even made it possible for certain clients to have overdrafts; they sometimes issued credit notes (known as *cedole*[168]) and were already beginning to speculate with the money entrusted to them – that is when they were not lending it to the state.

The 'stock-exchange' meetings on the Rialto fixed commodity prices, and were before long fixing the interest rates on public loans (for the Signoria, which had at first been content to levy taxes, began increasingly to resort to loans).[169] They fixed the premiums for maritime insurance. The name of the *Calle delle Sicurtà*, which is still just round the corner from the Rialto, commemorates the insurance men of the fourteenth century. All major business matters were therefore handled literally in the streets surrounding the bridge. If a merchant was 'deprived of his right to go to the Rialto', this punishment signified 'as numerous appeals indicate, that he was deprived of the right to participate in big business'.[170]

A commercial hierarchy was very soon established. The first known census of Venetian taxpayers (1379-80)[171] enables us to distinguish from among those liable to tax (1211 in all) the 20 or 30 richest families, as well as to spot the new rich *popolani* (6 in all) and a few well-off shopkeepers – butchers, shoemakers, masons, soap-makers, goldsmiths and spice-merchants, the latter being the most prosperous.

The distribution of wealth in Venice was already very diversified, and the profits from trade were accumulating in a variety of repositories, modest and otherwise; such money was constantly being invested and reinvested. Venetian cargo vessels – great floating mansions as Petrarch later saw them – were almost invariably divided into 24 carats, each investor holding a certain number. So ships were capitalist enterprises virtually from the start. The goods they carried had usually been paid for with loans advanced by moneylenders. As for the cash loan or *mutuo*, this had always been available, and contrary to what one might think, was not necessarily caught in the toils of usury. The Venetians very early accepted 'the legitimacy of credit operations according to the criteria of modern businessmen'.[172] That is not to say that usury as we understand it was not also practised, and interest rates could be very high (since the normal rate, *secundum usum patriae nostrae*, was as much as 20%); and such loans might be accompanied by pledges which remained in the clutches of the lender. It was by such procedures that the Ziani family had by the twelfth century acquired most of the sites around St Mark's Square and along the *Mercerie*. But then usury was perhaps a necessary evil everywhere before the coming of modern banking. Soon after the Chioggia war, which had terribly disturbed the city, Venice resigned herself to admitting the first *condotta* (consortium) of Jewish usurers (1382-87[173]) who lent money to small borrowers and even on occasion to patricians.

But the commercial loan, the *mutuo ad negotiandum*, was another matter. This was an indispensable instrument of trade, and its interest rates, though high, were not regarded as usurious since they were more or less the same as those charged by bankers. Nine times out of ten, this kind of loan was associated with a partnership or *colleganza* agreement. These made their first appearance in at least 1072–1073[174] and were soon to be found in two versions. There was the unilateral *colleganza*, whereby one party (known as the *socius stans* or stationary partner) advanced a sum of money to the *socius procertans* (or travelling partner). At the end of the voyage when the accounts were settled, the traveller, after repaying the sum originally advanced, kept one quarter of the profits, the rest going to the 'capitalist'. Alternatively there was the bilateral *colleganza* whereby the lender put up only three-quarters of the sum required and the *socius procertans* contributed not only his work but one-quarter of the capital. In this case, the profits were split fifty-fifty. The second kind of *colleganza*, Gino Luzzatto suggests,[175] more than once served to disguise the usurious tendencies of the first kind. Despite its name, the *colleganza* is in fact exactly the same thing as the *commenda* practised in other Italian towns, and equivalent arrangements are to be found both at very early and very late dates in places like Marseille or Barcelona. Since in Venice the word *commenda*[176] meant a deposit, another word had to be found to describe the maritime loan.

Given the position outlined above, it is easy to understand the conclusion arrived at by André-E. Sayous in 1934,[177] and accepted by most subsequent historians including Marc Bloch,[178] namely that there was a divergence of interests, a split between Capital and Labour in Venice, between 1050 and 1150. Was the *socius stans* not simply the capitalist, staying at home, while his partner boarded a ship bound for Constantinople and perhaps Tana or Alexandria as well? When the ship came home, the working partner, the *socius procertans*, appeared with the money he had borrowed, plus the fruits of that money if the voyage had been a success. It looks very much as if we have Capital on one side, Labour on the other. But certain documents which have come to light since 1940[179] make it necessary to revise this simple explanation. In the first place, the *socius stans*, despite his title, was in fact perpetually on the move. In the period under consideration (before and after 1200) he is to be found in Alexandria in Egypt, Acre, Famagusta, and even more often in Constantinople (a significant detail in itself, revealing the extent to which Venice's fortune was carved out of the living heart of the Byzantine economy). As for the *socius procertans*, he was nothing like an exploited worker. Not only did he embark on every voyage with up to a dozen *colleganze* (which meant that if all went well he stood to make a great deal of money) but he was often simultaneously lending money to one enterprise while borrowing it for another.

What is more, the names of the lenders, when we have them, reveal a wide range of 'capitalists' or so-called capitalists, for some of them were men of very modest means.[180] The entire Venetian population seems to have been advancing money to the merchant venturers, thus perpetually creating and renewing a sort of commercial society embracing the whole town. This constantly available and spontaneously offered supply of credit made it possible for merchants to operate alone or in temporary associations of two or three partners, without the need for the long-term companies with capital funds which characterize the most

Venetian merchants exchanging bolts of cloth for the produce of the Orient. Marco Polo's *Book of Marvels*. (B.N., Paris, MS 2810.)

advanced commercial activity in Florence.

Perhaps it is the very perfection and convenience of this organization, the capitalist self-sufficiency of Venice, which explains the limited nature of Venetian enterprise. The city's bankers, usually outsiders, were 'entirely taken up with the activity of the Venetian market and were not at all tempted by the possible transfer of their business to the outside world and the search for foreign custom'.[181] Consequently there was nothing in Venice comparable to the ventures of Florentine capitalism in England or Genoese capitalism later on in Seville and Madrid.

Similarly the easy availability of credit and business enabled the merchant to choose one transaction after another, to operate on a deal-to-deal basis. The departure of a ship marked the opening of a partnership between several merchants; her return closed it. And the whole process began again. The Venetians did practise large-scale investment, but only in the short-term. Longer-term loans and investments did of course appear sooner or later, in long-distance maritime enterprises like the Flanders run, and more especially in industry and the other long-standing activities of the city. The loan or *mutuo*, originally a very short-term affair, gradually became subject to repeated renewals and could last for years. The bill of exchange on the other hand, which appeared in Venice rather late, in the thirteenth century, and spread only slowly,[182] remained a short-term credit instrument, limited to the duration of a return journey between two financial markets.

So the economic climate of Venice was a very special one. The intense trading activity of the city was split up into a multitude of small transactions. While the *compagnia* or durable partnership did appear here from time to time, giant concerns on the Florentine pattern never flourished in Venice. Possibly the reason was that neither the government nor the patrician elite was ever seriously challenged in Venice (as they were in Florence). The city was a haven of comparative security. Or possibly it was because commercial life had got off to an early start in Venice and was content to settle for tried and trusted methods. But the character of the transactions themselves also had something to do with it. The life-blood of Venetian trade was the Levant connection. This undoubtedly required a massive outlay of capital: almost the entire Venetian money supply was tied up in it, to such an extent that when the galleys had sailed for Syria, the city was literally drained of specie,[183] just as in later years Seville would be by the departure of the Indies fleets.[184] But the *turnover* of capital was quite rapid: six months or a year. And the comings and goings of the ships dictated the rhythm of the whole city's activity. So if Venice appears to be a special case, is it because her entire commercial activity from A to Z was dictated by the Levant? I wonder for instance whether the reason why gold ducats were not minted in Venice until the late date of 1284 was simply because until then Venice found it easier to go on using the gold currency of Byzantium. Was it the sudden devaluation of the hyperper which obliged Venice to change her policy?[185]

It could be argued then that Venice was from the start trapped by the logic of her own success. The true doge of Venice, standing opposed to all the forces of change, was the city's own past, the precedents to which reference was made as if they were the tablets of the law. And the shadow looming over Venice's greatness was that of her greatness itself. This has some truth. Could the same not be said of twentieth-century Britain? Leadership of a world-economy is an experience of power which may one day blind the victor to the march of history.

Labour in Venice

Venice was a huge city: her population was already probably over 100,000 by the fifteenth century, and had reached 140,000 to 160,000 by the sixteenth and seventeenth. But apart from a few thousand privileged persons – the *nobili*, *cittadini* and clergy – or paupers and vagabonds, this enormous population worked with its hands for a living.

Two worlds of labour rubbed shoulders here: on one hand there were the unskilled workers, men without any association to protect or organize them, and these included what Frederic C. Lane has called 'the proletariat of the sea':[186] porters, stevedores, seamen, oarsmen; on the other hand there was the world of the *Arti* or guilds the organized framework of the different trades practised in the city. Sometimes the borderline between the two worlds is indistinct and the historian does not always know how to classify the occupations he discovers. We can probably place in the first category the dockers who worked along the Grand Canal, on the *Ripa del Vin*, the *Ripa del Ferro* or the *Ripa del Carbon*; the thousands of gondoliers, most of whom were in the service of rich families; or the poor men who signed on as crews in front of the Doges' Palace – where there was literally a labour market.[187] On being hired, each man received a bonus. If he did not appear on the appointed day, he would be hunted down, arrested and sentenced to pay a fine of twice the bonus, then escorted on board ship where his wages would be confiscated to pay off his debt. Another major group of unorganized workers consisted of the men and women who carried out menial tasks for the silk and wool trades. Surprisingly however, the *aquaroli* who transported boatloads of fresh water from the Brenta, the *peateri* who steered barges, the *conzalavezi*, travelling tinkers and even the *pestrineri* who delivered milk from door to door, had their own duly-constituted guilds.

Richard Tilden Rapp[188] has attempted to calculate the relative size of these two sets of workers in order to estimate the entire labour force in the city. In spite of the deficiencies of the sources, his overall conclusions seem fairly convincing, and since they do not indicate *any major modification* during the sixteenth and seventeenth centuries, they do provide a sort of structural model of employment in Venice. In 1586, when the city had about 150,000 inhabitants, the labour force represented about 34,000 individuals, that is, allowing four people to a worker's family, it accounted for virtually the entire population, apart from the 10,000 or so people making up the tiny privileged elite. Of the 33,852 workers counted by Rapp, members of the *Arti* accounted for 22,504, and the so-called 'free', i.e. unregulated workers 11,348; that is two-thirds of the labour force were in the guilds, and the rest outside them.

The last-named group – men, women and children included – represented at least 40,000 people, a heavy burden on the labour market. This was the proletariat – or rather the sub-proletariat – demanded by every urban economy. It is not even clear that it was sufficient for Venice's needs: the poor people of the lagoons and the city did not provide enough seamen, so proletarians from abroad were very soon making up the difference – not always of their own free will. Venice went in search of crews in Dalmatia and the Greek islands, and sometimes manned her galleys with seamen from Candia or later Cyprus.

Gondoliers in Venice. Detail of *The Miracle of the Holy Cross* by Carpaccio. (Photo Anderson-Giraudon.)

By comparison, the organized 'industries' seem a privileged world. Not that life in the guilds always proceeded according to the rule-book. Regulations were one thing, practice another. The state kept a beady eye on the leather industries of the Giudecca; the glassworks of Murano; the *Arte della Seta* which was already in existence before the workers of Lucca came to swell its ranks in 1314; the *Arte della Lana*, which seems to have made a fresh start in spring 1458, according to a Senate declaration,[189] and which the state had to protect from the merchants of Venice itself – who certainly wished to manufacture 'Florentine-type cloth', but only if they could do so abroad, in Flanders or England,[190] where labour was cheap and the rules less strict. The over-watchful Venetian state imposed strict standards of quality, specifying the length of the pieces, the choice of raw materials, the density of the weave, the permitted dyestuffs and so on; in the end this made it difficult to adapt production to the ups and downs of demand, although at the same time it did establish the reputation of Venetian goods, particularly in the Levant markets.

All these trades, the old and the new, had been organized since the thirteenth century into *Arti* (guilds) or *scuole* (brotherhoods).[191] But this self-protection system guaranteed the artisan neither against the government intervention so characteristic of Venice, nor against interference by the merchants. The *Arte della Lana*, which was in its prime in the sixteenth century, reaching a peak in 1600–1610, was only able to develop and prosper within the framework of a *Verlagssystem* frequently controlled by foreign merchants, notably Genoese residents in Venice. Even the ancient ship-building industry, with its guild-masters who owned whole shipyards, was by the fifteenth century bowing to the preponderance of the merchant-ship-fitters who put up the money for wages and materials.

Had industry become Venice's major activity?

This was a world of labour controlled both by money and by the public authorities. The latter had four organs of supervision and arbitration at its disposal: the *Giustizia Vecchia*, the *Cinque Savii alla Mercanzia*, the *Provveditori di Comun* and the *Collegio alle Arti*. Is the remarkable absence of social disturbances in Venice to be explained by this high degree of supervision and tight control? Serious incidents were few and far between. The volunteer oarsmen came, but in sorrow more than in anger, to the Doges' Palace in February 1446, to claim their unpaid wages.[192] And the great Arsenal itself, which was a state enterprise employing at least 3000 workers summoned daily by the *Marangona*, the great bell of St Mark's, was very strictly run. At the least whisper of protest, one or two ringleaders were hanged, *impicati per la gola*, and no more was heard.

In no circumstances did the Venetian *Arti* have access to the government of the city – as was the case in Florence for instance. They were kept at a respectful distance. But the peacefulness of the Venetian social scene is nonetheless astonishing. It is true that even the humblest toilers fortunate enough to inhabit the heart of a world-economy might pick up scraps from the capitalists' table. Was this one of the reasons for the lack of trouble? Wages in Venice were comparatively high. And whatever their level, it was never easy to reduce them. This was one point on which the *Arti* were able to stand firm, as would become clear at the beginning of the seventeenth century, when the prosperity of the *Arte della Lana*, faced with competition from northern cloth, was compromised by the high wages which its artisans refused to forego.[193]

But by the seventeenth century, the city's industrial activity was already in decline, as it succumbed to competition both from the nearby *Terraferma* and from the distant industries of the north. It is to fifteenth- and sixteenth-century Venice – an exemplary case in so many ways – that we must turn if we want to know whether, as Richard T. Rapp suggests, her industrial activity was in fact the city's *major* economic feature. More generally, was it inevitably the case that leading cities became converted to manufacturing activity – as certainly happened in Bruges, Antwerp, Genoa, Amsterdam and London? Given the range of activities in fifteenth-century Venice, the quality of her technology and her precocious development (everything referred to in Diderot's *Encyclopédie* was already in operation in Venice two hundred years earlier), I am willing to concede that at this time Venice was probably the leading industrial centre in Europe, that this fact greatly influenced her career, and that the decline of her industrial prosperity at the end of the sixteenth century and during the first two decades of the seventeenth marked the beginning of the end. But does it actually *explain* the decline of Venice – was it the cause? That is another question. The primacy of commercial capitalism over industrial capitalism until at least the eighteenth century is not seriously challenged. It is worth noting that when, in 1421, the old doge Priuli was listing the riches of his city, he did not mention its industrial riches; and that the *Arte della Lana*, although probably in existence in the thirteenth century, seems to have been revived in 1458 after a long period of inactivity. Its real growth period did not come until between 1580 and 1620. All in all, industry seems to have contributed to Venetian prosperity only rather late in the day, as a makeweight, a compensation when the climate was unfavourable, a state of affairs very similar, as we shall see, to that in Antwerp from about 1558-9.

The Turkish peril

The progressive decline of the queen of the Adriatic was not entirely brought about from within. Even before Europe had expanded into the rest of the world with the Great Discoveries (1492-98), the territorial states had once more re-entered the fray: there was once again a dangerous king of Aragon, a king of France in a commanding position, a prince in the Netherlands prepared to wield a sword, a German emperor – if only the impecunious Maximilian of Austria – with alarming designs. The future of the city-states was once more under threat.

Of all the states now riding on the new tide, the largest, and the one most feared in Venice was the Turkish Empire under the Osmanlis. In the early days, Venice had underestimated the Turks: she considered them landlubbers, easily outwitted at sea. But before long Turkish pirates (or pirates calling themselves Turks) were appearing in the waters of the Levant, while the overland conquests of the Osmanlis were gradually casting a circle around the sea, subduing its coasts in advance of the fleet. The fall of Constantinople in 1453, which came as a bolt from the blue, took the Turks to the very heart of the Mediterranean, into a city which might have been tailor-made to dominate the sea. Drained of its substance by the Latins (including the Venetians) the city had really crumbled from within before the Turkish advance. But it was quickly replaced by a new and powerful capital, Istanbul, and its population swelled to huge proportions, partly through forced immigration.[194] The Turkish capital was soon the power-house of a maritime policy virtually forced upon the sultans, as Venice was to realize to her cost.

Could Venice have opposed the conquest of Constantinople? By the time she thought of doing so, it was too late[195] and afterwards the city quickly learned to live with the *fait accompli*, choosing to be on good terms with the sultan. As the doge explained to Bartolomeo Marcello, the Venetian *orator* (ambassador) to the sultan, on 15 January 1454, '... *dispositio nostra est habere bonam pacem et amicitiam cum domino imperatore turcorum*', it is our intention to live in peace and friendship with the Turkish emperor.[196] If business was to flourish peace was essential. As for the emperor, if he wished to trade with Europe – and his empire could not afford not to – how could he do so without going through Venice? This was a classic example of 'complementary enemies': everything separated them, but vital interests forced them to coexist, increasingly so as the Turkish conquests advanced. The capture in 1475 of Caffa in the Crimea virtually closed the Black Sea to Genoese and Venetian trade. The occupation of Syria and Egypt in 1516 and 1517 offered the Turks the possibility of closing the traditional gateways of the Levant – although in fact they refrained from doing so, since this would have interrupted a traffic from which they derived large profits.

Venetians and Turks were condemned to live together; but their forced cohabitation was punctuated by some fierce storms. The first major Turco-Venetian war (1463–79) revealed the flagrant disparity of forces of the two sides.[197] This was not, as Anglo-Russian hostilities were later to be described, a battle between the whale and the bear. The Turkish Empire was certainly a bear. But its adversary was no bigger than a wasp – a wasp of great persistence it is true. Venice was in touch with European technological progress, which was an advantage; moreover she could draw on her wealth to recruit troops from all over Europe (even from Scotland during the war of Candia 1649–69); and she was able to hold out and pester her enemy. In the end, the bear was out of breath and the wasp exhausted. Venice also had the means to act inside Istanbul, by well-informed corruption; and even when war was raging, still managed to maintain some trade through Ragusa and Ancona. She was also able to stir up other bears to tackle the Turk: Charles V's empire, Philip II's Spain, the Holy Roman Empire, Russia under Peter the Great and Catherine, Austria under Prince Eugene. She even succeeded briefly during the war of Candia, in interesting Louis XIV's France; and in an effort to attack the Turks from the rear she alerted distant Persia under the Safavids (the Shiite Persians being hostile to the Sunnite Turks, for Islam too had its wars of religion). In short, Venice put up remarkable resistance to the Turks until 1718 and the Treaty of Passarowitz (Pozharevats) which marked the end of her struggle – over two hundred and fifty years after the peace of Constantinople.

Such were the mighty shadows which the Turkish Empire cast over Venice's anxious existence, draining the city gradually of its life-force. But Venice's decline after the early decades of the sixteenth century was not simply the result of a commonplace conflict between city and state. And in any case another city, Antwerp, was on the point of becoming the centre of the world after 1500. The ancient prevailing structures of the urban economy had not yet been shattered, but the European centre of capitalist wealth and achievement had quietly shifted from Venice. To find out why, we must look at the great maritime discoveries, the opening up of the Atlantic and the unexpected rise of Portugal.

The unexpected rise of Portugal;
or from Venice to Antwerp

The rise of Portugal has received much attention from historians: it is well-known that the narrow kingdom played a major role in the cosmic upheaval generated by the geographical expansion of Europe at the end of the fifteenth century. Portugal was the detonator of an explosion which reverberated round the world. This was her finest hour.

The traditional explanation[198]

Until recent times, the traditional version of this story was accepted with little question. Perched on the western outposts of Europe, Portugal was so to speak poised for expansion; by 1253, the Portuguese had reconquered their territory from Islam and were free to look further afield; the capture in 1415 of Ceuta, south of the Gibraltar Straits, had initiated them to the secrets of long-distance trade and aroused in them the aggressive spirit of the crusades. The gateway was now open to voyages of exploration and ambitious expeditions down the African coast. And at this timely moment, a hero appeared: Henry the Navigator (1394–1460), the fifth son of John I of Portugal, and Master of the very rich Order of Christ, which had set up its headquarters in 1413 in Sagres, near Cape Saint Vincent at the southern tip of the country. Surrounding himself with scholars, map-makers and navigators, Henry was to be the enthusiastic patron of the voyages of discovery which began in 1416, a year after the capture of Ceuta.

Contrary winds, the uncompromisingly inhospitable nature of the Saharan coastline, spontaneous fear of the unknown (which the Portuguese indeed encouraged among their rivals in order to conceal the secrets of their discoveries) – the problems of financing the voyages which had little popular appeal – all these factors made the reconnaissance of the long coast of Africa a lengthy and slow undertaking: Cape Bojador, 1416; Cape Verde, 1445; the crossing of the equator, 1471; the discovery of the mouth of the Congo 1482. But the accession of John II (1481–95), an enthusiast for maritime exploration who took over the mantle of the Navigator, hastened developments towards the end of the fifteenth century. Bartholomew Diaz reached the southern tip of Africa in 1487, and baptized it the Cape of Storms, but the king re-named it the Cape of Good Hope. The way was now clear for Vasco da Gama's historic voyage, which took place, for a number of reasons, only after another ten years.

To complete the traditional explanation, I might mention the invention of the caravel, a light reconnaissance vessel with a double rig, the lateen for tacking home and the square rig to catch a following wind. Over the years, Portuguese navigators built up a formidable body of knowledge of the winds and currents of the Atlantic. 'It was almost accidental', writes Ralph Davis, 'that at the climax of Portuguese pioneering enterprise, the most crucial of all the discoveries was made by a Genoese in the service of Spain'[199] – that is of course the discovery of America by Christopher Columbus. Indeed at the time, his sensational discovery had less immediate impact than the voyage made a few years later by Vasco da Gama. Once a ship had sailed round the Cape of Good Hope, the Portuguese quickly became familiar with the trade routes of the Indian Ocean, as they were ferried, guided and instructed in the ways of these waters. Once they had made their appearance, no ship or port in the Indian Ocean was safe from the gunfire of their fleets; Arab and Indian shipping was thwarted, disrupted and dispersed. The newcomers made themselves masters and before long reigned unchallenged. Thus the Portuguese discoveries (if one discounts the exploration of the Brazilian coast by Alvarez Cabral in 1501) came to the end of their heroic period, one which culminated spectacularly in the direct shipment of pepper and spices to Lisbon, a revolution in itself.

New interpretations[200]

Over the past twenty years or so, new interpretations of the old story have been suggested by historians – particularly in Portugal itself. The standard version still stands, like a traditional tune, but it is now accompanied by a number of variations.

In the first place, the Portuguese state is no longer dismissed as having been a negligible quantity within Europe. It was after all roughly the equivalent of Venice and the *Terraferma* combined. Neither unduly small, nor unduly poor, by no means cut off from the rest of the continent, it was in fact an autonomous power, well capable of initiatives – as events were to prove – and free to take its own decisions. Above all, the Portuguese economy was neither primitive nor elementary: it had for centuries been in contact with Muslim states – like Granada, which remained independent until 1492, or the towns and states of North Africa. Such relations with advanced regions had encouraged the development within Portugal of a monetary economy sufficiently vigorous for wage-labour to have been introduced in both town and countryside. And if that countryside reduced the acreage devoted to cereals in favour of vines, olives, cork-oaks or the sugar plantations of the Algarve, no one will now claim that such specialization – recognized as a sign of economic prosperity in Tuscany for example – was a backward step in Portugal. Nor will it be argued that Portugal was handicapped by being obliged to buy grain from Morocco, since when the same situation occurs in Venice and Amsterdam it is generally considered to have been a by-product of economic superiority and advantage. Moreover, Portugal traditionally possessed a string of seaside towns and villages inhabited by a population of seafarers and fishermen. Their *barcas* were modest vessels of twenty or thirty tons, heavily overmanned and with conventional square rig, but they were nevertheless soon to be found anywhere between the African coast or the Canaries and Ireland or Flanders. So the necessary motor of Portuguese expansion was in position in good time. And in 1385, two years after Venice had occupied Corfu, a 'bourgeois' revolution brought the Aviz dynasty to power in Lisbon. The latter brought to prominence a bourgeoisie 'that lasted for some generations',[201] spelling the semi-eclipse of a landed aristocracy which nevertheless continued to lay a heavy yoke on the peasants, while at the same time being willing to provide the necessary leadership for the military command and maintenance of strongholds abroad, or the development of colonial estates; this developed into an aristocracy of service to its country (a feature which distinguishes Portuguese expansion from the purely mercantile colonization of the Dutch). It would perhaps be an exaggeration to describe Portugal at the end of the fourteenth century, after the Black Death – which the country did not escape – as a modern state; but all things considered, it was already halfway there.

Portugal suffered however, throughout its golden age, from not being at the centre of the European world-economy. Although privileged in many ways, the Portuguese economy was still peripheral to the world-economy. As early as the end of the thirteenth century, when sea links were established between the Mediterranean and the North Sea, Portugal had been drawn into and made use of by the long maritime capitalist trade circuit connecting the Italian cities to

Portuguese vessel carved and painted on a rock at the entrance to the 'Amegas' Chinese temple in Macao. (Photo Roger-Viollet.)

England, Bruges and indirectly to the Baltic.[202] And as the western Mediterranean gradually began to lose touch with the Levant traffic, where Venetian supremacy was turning into monopoly, a section of Italian business enterprise, under Genoese and Florentine influence, was looking westwards to Barcelona, and more particularly to Valencia, the Moroccan coast, Seville and Lisbon. The latter thus became an international centre: foreign communities[203] sprang up there and made a useful, though never disinterested contribution to its prosperity. The Genoese, always quick to make themselves at home, were soon handling wholesale trade there – and even retail trade which was in theory confined to Portuguese nationals.[204] Lisbon, and through Lisbon the whole of Portugal, was thus under the partial control of foreigners.

The latter inevitably played a part in Portuguese expansion. But this need not be exaggerated. It would probably be nearer the truth to say that foreign merchants followed the successful venture and took it over once it had taken place rather than initiating it. I am not sure for instance, despite what is sometimes suggested, that the Ceuta expedition (1415) was launched at the instigation of the foreign merchants. Genoese residents in the Moroccan ports were indeed openly and undisguisedly hostile to the Portuguese occupation.[205]

The picture becomes clearer after the first triumphs of Portuguese expansion, once the profitable shores of Black Africa had been occupied, from Cape Bojador to the mouth of the Congo, between 1443 and 1482. Along with the occupation of Madeira in 1420, the rediscovery of the Azores in 1430, the discovery of the Cape Verde islands in 1455, and of Fernando Po and São Tomé in 1471, this brought into being a coherent economic zone, based essentially on trade in ivory, malaguetta (a pepper substitute), gold dust (between 13,000 and 14,000 ounces a year on average) and the slave trade (a thousand or so a year in mid-fifteenth century, rising before long to 3000). Moreover, Portugal laid claim to a monopoly of trade with Black Africa, by the treaty of Alcobaça, signed with Spain in 1479. The construction in 1481 of the fort at São Jorge da Mina (for which every stone, brick and piece of timber or metal had to be shipped in from Lisbon) guaranteed and set the seal on this monopoly, which would be closely controlled thereafter. According to a contemporary account by Duarte Pacheco, *Esmaraldo de Situ Orbis*,[206] the gold trade brought profits of 'five for one or more'. As for the black slaves who ended up on the Portuguese market, they provided the households of the rich with the inevitable black servant, and made possible the establishment of large estates in the deserted Alemtejo (which had been depopulated since the end of the *Reconquista*), as well as the development of the sugar plantations in Madeira, where sugar cane had replaced wheat by 1460.

This conquest of Africa and the Atlantic islands was essentially achieved by the Portuguese. But a considerable contribution was made by the Florentines, the Genoese (and even in the case of the Azores by the Flemish). It was after all the Genoese who had first promoted the spread of sugar plantations from the eastern Mediterranean to Sicily, southern Spain, Morocco, the Portuguese Algarve and eventually to Madeira and the Cape Verde islands. Later on, and for similar reasons, sugar spread to the Canaries under Castilian occupation.

Similarly while the crowning achievement of the Portuguese discoveries, the voyage of Vasco da Gama, 'owed nothing to the Genoese', as Ralph Davis[207] is right to point out, the merchants of Italy, High Germany and the Netherlands who were either already in Lisbon or who flocked there on hearing the news, were very closely associated with the commercial exploitation of the venture. Could the Portuguese and the Merchant-King of Lisbon have financed unaided the long and expensive East Indies shipping route – a far more demanding one than the route managed by the *Carrera de Indias* between the Spanish West Indies and Seville?

Lastly, it is worth noting that their concentration on the Indian Ocean cost the Portuguese America – which could so nearly have been theirs: Christopher Columbus took his fantastic proposal to the king of Portugal and his advisers just after Bartholomew Diaz had returned to Lisbon in 1488 with news that there was definitely a sea-passage between the Atlantic and the Indian Ocean. The Portuguese preferred the scientifically attested bird in the hand to an unknown number in the bush. When eventually they too discovered America, sending their fishermen and whalers to Newfoundland in about 1497, and landing on the coast of Brazil in 1501, they were already years behind. But who could have foretold that they had made a major miscalculation, when Vasco da Gama's return in 1498 meant that the race for the pepper trade had been won and could be exploited immediately, when all the merchants of Europe were hastily sending their most energetic representatives to Lisbon; when Venice, hitherto the queen of eastern trade seemed to be staggering as if stabbed in the back? In 1504, when the Venetian galleys arrived in Alexandria in Egypt, they found not a single sack of pepper waiting for them.[208]

Antwerp: a world capital created by outside agency

But for all Lisbon's importance, it did not become the new world capital. The Portuguese city seemed to hold all the trump cards – but another city snatched victory from under its nose: Antwerp. While the dethroning of Venice is logical, the failure of Lisbon to make sure of the succession is at first sight surprising. But it becomes easier to explain if one remembers that even in the moment of triumph, Lisbon remained the captive of a certain world-economy into which the city was already integrated and in which it had a fixed place; if one remembers too that northern Europe had not ceased to weigh heavily in the balance; that the centre of gravity of the entire continent was tending – not without good cause – to shift northwards; and last but not least, that something like nine out of ten consumers of pepper and spices lived in the north.

But we should not be too quick to explain Antwerp's sudden fortune in such over-simple terms. It is sometimes said that the port on the Scheldt, having long stood at the crossroads of northern trade and exchange, was merely replacing Bruges: that this was a simple matter of an up-and-coming town replacing one in decline. Later on, when Antwerp was in turn captured by Alexander Farnese in 1585, her place was taken by Amsterdam. But this may be to take too parochial a view of what happened.

In real life, things were more complicated. Antwerp was in fact as much the successor to Venice as to Bruges. During the 'age of the Fuggers',[209] which was actually the age of Antwerp, this city was the centre of the *entire* international economy – something Bruges had never been even at its height. Antwerp was not simply taking over from her nearest rival, although like Bruges, the city was created by outside agency. When the first Genoese galleys sailed into Bruges in 1277 they promoted the little town on the Zwyn above her station. Similarly, it

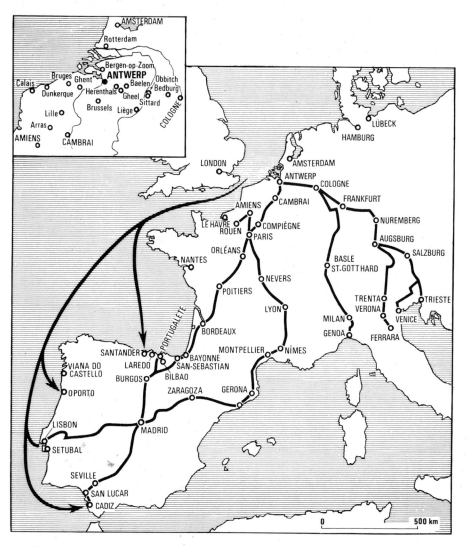

16 THE PRINCIPAL TRADE ROUTES TO AND FROM ANTWERP
In this diagram, the routes stop short at the Italian distribution points and at the major centres of Lisbon and Seville, but there were in fact extensions, not shown here, to Brazil, the Atlantic islands and the coasts of Africa. The Mediterranean was hardly touched directly at all by this traffic. (From V. Vasquez de Prada, *Lettres marchandes d'Anvers*, 1, s.d., p. 35.)

was the alteration of world trade routes and the beginnings of an Atlantic economy at the end of the fifteenth century which decided the future of Antwerp: the first sign of the new order was the arrival in the docks of the Scheldt of a Portuguese ship laden with pepper and cinnamon in 1501. Others were to follow.[210]

So the rise of Antwerp was not generated from within – how could it have been? 'Antwerp', wrote Henri Pirenne, 'did not possess a merchant fleet any more than Bruges.'[211] Nor, another disadvantage, was the city governed either in 1500 or later by her merchants. The aldermen (or the 'lords of Antwerp'[212] as the English called them) belonged to a handful of the families which composed the tiny landed aristocracy, and they retained their power for several centuries. In theory they were even forbidden to have dealings in trade – a rather curious prohibition, but one frequently repeated, no doubt because it was not always observed. Lastly, Antwerp did not have her own native merchants of inter-national standing: foreigners dominated the scene – Hanseatic traders, English, French and above all southern merchants: Portuguese, Spanish and Italian.

This picture probably needs some qualification. Antwerp did have a mer-chant fleet:[213] a hundred or so small vessels of between 80 and 100 tons apiece, but what were these beside the foreign ships that sailed up the Scheldt or anchored off the island of Walcheren: ships from Holland, Zeeland, Portugal, Spain, Italy, Ragusa, Catalonia, England and Brittany?[214] As for the lords of Antwerp, these august personages were often moneylenders, either discreetly or openly.[215] In their own way, they were serving the port's commercial interests. All the same, the city was an economic innocent: other people came knocking at the door, moved in and made her fortune for her. Antwerp did not set out to capture the world – on the contrary, a world thrown off balance by the great discoveries, and tilting towards the Atlantic, clung to Antwerp, *faute de mieux*. The city did not struggle to reach the visible pinnacle of the world, but woke up one morning to find itself there.

And it has to be said that Antwerp was not ideally suited to her role. She had not yet learned what was expected of her; and was not an *independent* city. Having been reabsorbed into the duchy of Brabant in 1406,[216] Antwerp was under the nominal rule of a prince. It is true that she could, and did, resort to subterfuge vis-à-vis her ruler, deliberately delaying the execution of inconvenient ordinances for instance. On the religious front, Antwerp even succeeded in safeguarding a policy of toleration, which was essential to her expansion.[217] Ludovico Guicciardini, who observed this at a rather late stage in 1567, was aware of her aspirations to independence: 'She rules and governs herself almost like a free city'.[218] But Antwerp was not Venice or Genoa. She suffered severely for instance from the effects of the monetary measures taken at the height of her activity by the 'government' in Brussels in 1518 and 1539.[219] And after all, when her career began, she was still an old, medieval town, as has been remarked.[220] Her experience was confined to fairs[221] that is to say, she was accustomed to welcoming foreigners and possessed certain skills in the handling of commercial transactions which required speedy conclusion. But she had little or no experi-ence of maritime enterprise, of long-distance trade, or of the modern forms of association between merchants. How could she have walked straight into the leading role now thrust upon her? But she quickly learned to adapt and improv-ise: indeed the age of Antwerp was the age of improvisation.

The old port of Antwerp. Attributed to S. Vranck, Musée Massey, Tarbes. (Photo Giraudon.)

Stages in Antwerp's career

That Antwerp's new role depended on international and in a sense external circumstances is borne out by all the evidence. Venice, after a long struggle, had managed to enjoy rather over a century of unchallenged supremacy (1378-1498). In similar circumstances, Amsterdam ruled for a century and more. Antwerp by contrast had a very up and down career between 1500 and 1569, marked by an abundance of setbacks, leaps forward and recoveries. The basis of her prosperity was always shaky, because of or in spite of the irregular lines of force which came together in her market place, bringing the many contributions but also the conflicting or ambiguous desires of a Europe in the process of seizing world control. The chief reason for Antwerp's uncertain career (I now think after re-reading Hermann Van der Wee's classic study[222]) was that the overall European economy was still, in the sixteenth century, subject to shocks and surprises, and had not yet found its cruising rhythm or its long-term equilibrium. With every change of fortune of any significance, Antwerp's prosperity seemed to alter as well, declining or alternatively recovering dramatically and expanding – to such an extent in fact that the city's career fairly faithfully reflects the fortunes of Europe as a whole.

With very little exaggeration, it can be said that three cities succeeded each other in Antwerp, similar yet different, each one developing in the course of a period of growth, followed by a number of lean years.

Of the three phases of expansion (1501-21; 1535-57; 1559-68) the first was initiated by Portugal. Pepper was the key, though as Hermann Van der Wee has shown,[223] Portugal was able to play the role to the full only thanks to the collusion between the king in Lisbon who controlled the flow of spices and the merchants of High Germany who controlled the flow of silver: the Welsers, the Hochstetters and the firm that was either greater or luckier than the others, the Fuggers. The second phase of expansion can be attributed to Spain and the silver, this time from America, which in the 1530s gave her political masters a decisive argument for an outward-looking economy. The third and last phase was the result of the return to peace after the Treaty of Cateau-Cambrésis (1559) and the breakneck growth of industry in Antwerp and the Netherlands. (Though in this period, was putting effort into industry not something of a last resort?)

Antwerp's first experience of expansion and disappointment

In 1500, Antwerp was still serving her apprenticeship. But the surrounding highly-populated regions of Flanders and Brabant were experiencing a sense of euphoria. It is true that the Hanseatic trade had been all but driven out:[224] sugar from the Atlantic had now taken the place of honey, and the luxury of silks was replacing the luxury of furs; but even in the Baltic itself, the ships of Holland and Zeeland were now challenging those of the Hansa. The English had chosen the fairs of Bergen-op-Zoom and Antwerp as the staple for their woollen cloth which was imported unbleached, dyed on the spot and then redistributed all over the continent, particularly to central Europe.[225] A further advantage of Antwerp was that the German merchants, especially those of High Germany had moved into the town en masse: according to recent research[226] it seems that they were the first to transfer their allegiance from Bruges to Antwerp which was easier of access for them. They brought in Rhine wines and the copper and silver which had made the fortune of Augsburg and its merchant bankers.

The unexpected arrival on the Antwerp scene of pepper, which was shipped in directly once the Portuguese had opened up the Indies route, entirely changed the terms of trade there. The first spice ship dropped anchor in 1501; in 1508, the king of Lisbon founded the *Feitoria de Flandres*[227], the Antwerp branch of the *Casa da India* in Lisbon. But why did the king choose Antwerp? No doubt because, as I have already mentioned, the major market for pepper and spices was northern and central Europe, a market hitherto supplied from the south, via the *Fondaco dei Tedeschi* in Venice. Because, too, Portugal had maintained ancient shipping links with Flanders. But last and most important of all, Portugal had reached the Far East by dint of strenuous efforts; she had neither the resources nor the credit with which Venice had maintained and administered her fortune, that is organized the distribution of the spices from start to finish. As it was, huge sums of money had had to be advanced for the return trips to the Indies, and after the early pillaging expeditions in the Indian Ocean, all spices and pepper had to be paid for in cash, with copper or silver coin. Handing over the distribution network to someone else meant that that someone else had the headache of handling the retail trade (as the great Indies Companies later discovered in their turn) with the attendant problem of allowing credit to retailers (delays in repayment ran to 12 or 18 months). For all these reasons, the Portuguese entrusted their business to the market place of Antwerp. Could it not do for pepper and spice what it had long been doing for English woollens? In exchange, the Portuguese picked up in Antwerp the copper and silver from the German mines which they needed for their purchases in the Far East.

Redistribution to northern Europe via Antwerp was certainly efficient. Within a few years, the Venetian monopoly had been broken or at any rate severely dented. At the same time, copper and silver were being diverted on a massive scale from Venice to Lisbon. In 1502-3, only 24% of the Hungarian copper exported by the Fuggers had gone to Antwerp; by 1508-9, 49% was going to Antwerp and only 13% to Venice.[228] As for silver, a Netherlands government document of 1508 estimates the weight of silver passing through Antwerp to Lisbon as 60,000 marks:[229] the West was being drained of its silver for the benefit of the Portuguese trade circuit. The German merchants were therefore central to the boom Antwerp was experiencing, whether the Schets of Aix-la-Chapelle (Aachen) - a centre of the copper industry[230] - or the Imhofs, Welsers and Fuggers of Augsburg. Their profits piled up: between 1488 and 1522, the Imhofs increased their capital by 8.75% every year; the Welsers' went up by 9% between 1502 and 1517; and the Fuggers' by 54.7% in all between 1511 and 1527.[231] In this rapidly-changing world, Italian firms found themselves in serious difficulties: the Frescobaldis went bankrupt in 1581; and the Gualterottis wound up their business in 1525.[232]

But Antwerp's visible prosperity did not immediately lead to the creation of a real money-market; this could only exist if contact was established with the circuit of bills of exchange, payments and credit which operated between the major financial centres of Europe (notably Lyon, Genoa and the fairs of Castile), and Antwerp inserted herself into this network only slowly. She did not for instance have any links with Lyon, at the time the leading European financial centre, until about 1510-15[233]

Then after 1523, came lean years. The wars between the Valois and the Habsburgs paralysed international trade and consequently damaged the embryonic Antwerp money market. By the 1530s, the markets for pepper and spices were declining. In the first place, Lisbon had taken back the role of distributor: the *Feitoria de Flandres* lost its *raison d'être* and was closed in 1549.[234] Perhaps this was, as V. Magalhaes Godinho[235] has suggested, because Portugal had a supply of silver, this time from America, closer to home in Seville, whereas the German mines were in decline and had virtually stopped producing after 1535.[236] But above all, Venice had begun to fight back. The pepper she imported from the Levant was dearer than that sold by Lisbon, but the quality was better:[237] and in the 1530s particularly after 1540, her shipments from the Middle East increased. By 1533-1534, Venice was accounting for 85% of pepper sales in Lyon.[238] Lisbon did not of course stop sending stocks to Antwerp where Portuguese pepper was still an important market force: between November 1539 and August 1540, 328 Portuguese vessels dropped anchor off the island of Walcheren.[239] But in these changed circumstances, pepper was no longer the unrivalled dynamo of trade. Portugal had failed to secure her monopoly. She had had to go halves with Venice and this division became established. Moreover, there is no reason to suppose that the short-term recession in mid-sixteenth century did not contribute to Antwerp's difficulties, on the contrary.

Antwerp's second boom and slump

Antwerp's second boom was launched by the increase in imports of silver from South America via Seville. By 1537, silver was so abundant in Spain that Charles V's government was forced to revalue gold: the gold/silver ratio went up from 1:10.11 to 1:10.61.[240] This influx of wealth gave Spain (or more properly Castile) a new economic and political dimension. The Habsburg dynasty, in the person of the emperor Charles V, found itself master not only of Spain but of the Netherlands, the empire and Italy which had been firmly under its control since 1535.[241] Being obliged to pay out sums of money all over Europe, the emperor had had dealings since 1519 with the merchant-moneylenders of Augsburg, whose real centre of operations was Antwerp. It was the Fuggers and the Welsers who raised and transported the money without which there would have been no imperial policy. In the circumstances, the emperor could not do without the services of the Antwerp money market which was being created between 1521 and 1535, precisely during the years when trade was in the doldrums and loans to the sovereign were the only fruitful means of employing capital – which was not uncommonly being lent at rates of over 20%.[242]

What had happened to Portugal now began to happen to Spain. Confronted with her new transatlantic task of developing and building up the Americas, she found it beyond her means, and could only fulfil her obligations with help from various parts of Europe. Spain needed the timber, beams, tar, ships, wheat and rye of the Baltic, as well as manufactured goods to send to America – linen, light woollens, household goods from the Netherlands, Germany, England and France – sometimes in very large quantities: in 1553[243] more than 50,000 pieces of linen left Antwerp for Spain and Portugal. The ships of Zeeland and Holland had taken over the Flanders–Spain run, if not by 1530 then certainly by 1540, finding the way clear since the Biscay ships had been attracted away to the *Carrera de Indias*, leaving a gap to be filled in the shipping between Bilbao and Antwerp. So we are not surprised to find that for his expeditions against Tunis in 1535 and Algiers in 1541, Charles V requisitioned literally dozens of Flemish ships for the transport of men, horses, munitions and supplies. Northern ships were sometimes even requisitioned to swell the fleets of the *Carrera* itself.[244] I cannot overstress – and shall indeed have more to say about this[245] – how important this victorious liaison between the north and the Iberian peninsula was to the history both of Spain and of the world.

In the other direction, Spain sent Antwerp wool (which was still being unloaded at Bruges,[246] but was then taken straight to Antwerp), salt, alum, wine, dried fruits, oil and overseas products such as cochineal, American dye-woods and sugar from the Canaries. But these were insufficient to balance the deficit and Spain therefore had to make up the difference by sending silver coin and ingots which were often melted down and coined at the Antwerp Mint.[247] American silver and the merchants of Spain were in fact the agents of the port's revival. The infant Antwerp of the beginning of the century, a Portuguese and German creation, was replaced by 'Spanish' Antwerp. After 1535, the trade depression which had brought unemployment to the city was dispelled. The transformation was rapidly effected and all concerned drew the consequences. The industrial town of Leyden abandoned the cloth hall it had established in Amsterdam in 1530 for the purposes of selling cloth to the Baltic, and opened another in Antwerp in 1552, aimed this time at markets in Spain, the New World and the Mediterranean.[248]

The years 1535-57 unquestionably correspond to the high point of Antwerp's career. Never had the city been so prosperous. It was constantly expanding: the

View of Antwerp in about 1540. Antwerp, National Scheepvaartmuseum.

population had been no more than 44,000 to 49,000 in 1500, in the early days; by 1568 it was probably 100,000, and the number of houses had virtually doubled, from 6800 to 13,000. The city was covered with building sites, as new squares were designed, new streets (almost 8 kilometres of them) cut across the old – in short as a new economic infrastructure with several centres was constructed.[249] Luxury, capital, industrial activity and culture all blossomed together. And of course there was the other side of the coin: rising wages and prices, with a growing gap between the rich who became richer and the poor who became poorer, as the numbers swelled of the proletariat of unskilled labourers – porters, unloaders, errand-boys. The deterioration of conditions found its way into the powerful guilds where wage-labour was gaining ground over independent craft production. The tailors' guild in 1540 included over a thousand unskilled or semi-skilled workers. Masters were now being authorized to employ eight, sixteen, even twenty-two workers – a far cry from the restrictive code of Ypres in the old days.[250] Manufactories were set up in new industries: sugar and salt refineries, soap-making, dye-works; these employed poor wretches at derisory wages, barely 60% of a skilled worker's pay. The mass of unskilled labour undoubtedly curtailed the possibility of striking, which remained the weapon of the skilled worker. But if there were few strikes, there were or would be one day explosions of anger and violent revolts.

Antwerp's second period of prosperity came to an abrupt end with the Spanish state bankruptcy of 1557, a bankruptcy which affected all the countries ruled by Spain – and in addition hit France, which was surrounded by such countries and where the Lyon money market crashed at the same time as the royal finances under Henri II in 1558. The financial circuit which had been supporting Antwerp collapsed and never really recovered again: the German bankers lost their position in Castilian finances where their place was taken by the Genoese. The age of the Fuggers was over.

Antwerp's industrial phase

The Antwerp economy did however revive, but this time – the third period of prosperity – the impetus came from quite a different direction. After the Treaty of Cateau-Cambrésis (1559) which exorcized the threat of war between Valois and Habsburgs, trade picked up again with Spain, France, Italy and the Baltic (where the Hansa seemed to be having something of a revival too – it was at this time that the magnificent Hansa building was erected in Antwerp).[251] In spite of war scares between England and France, or between Denmark, Sweden and Poland, and despite the sequestration of ships in the Channel, the North Sea and the Baltic, the flow of goods through Antwerp improved, though without ever recovering its pre-crisis level.[252] There were problems from the English quarter. The revaluation of the pound sterling at the beginning of Elizabeth's reign had thrown the island's economy into severe crisis, which explains England's bad temper towards the Hanseatic merchants and those of the Low Countries. In July 1567, after much hesitation, the English chose Hamburg as the staple for their woollen cloth, and this city, which provided easier access than Antwerp had to the German market, was soon in a position to finish and sell the un-bleached cloth shipped in from England.[253] This was a serious blow for Antwerp. What was more, Thomas Gresham, who was only too familiar with the Antwerp market, had in 1566 laid the first stone of the London Royal Exchange. This was another area in which England was anxious to assert her independence of Antwerp – almost in the spirit of a child rebelling against a parent.

It was in these circumstances that Antwerp sought and found salvation in industry.[254] Since capital was unable to find sufficient employment in trade or government loans, it turned to the workshops. There was an extraordinary wave of expansion in the cloth industry, linen and tapestry-making, in Antwerp and throughout the Netherlands. As early as 1564, an observer of the city would have felt safe predicting where its future fortune lay. And indeed, Antwerp's industrial boom was eventually destroyed not by economic factors, but by the widespread social, political and religious disturbances which devastated the Netherlands.

According to the politicians, the crisis was one of insubordination. In reality it went much deeper: a profound religious revolution had erupted against a background of economic crisis and all the social problems associated with a high cost of living.[255] This is not the place to describe and analyse the Revolution; the important thing for our purposes is that Antwerp was caught up in the tumult from the start. The outbreak of iconoclasm swept through the town for two days, on 20 and 21 August 1566, to general stupefaction.[256] Calm might have been restored as a result of the compromises and concessions made by the regent, Margaret of Parma,[257] but Philip II chose to take a hard line and almost a year to the day after the Antwerp riots, the duke of Alva arrived in Brussels at the head of an expeditionary force.[258] Order was restored, but the war which did not break out in earnest until April 1572, was already under way below the surface. In 1568,[259] the English captured some Biscayan *zabras* laden with silver and bales of wool and intended for the duke of Alva, plus the contraband silver the transporters were carrying on their own account. For all practical purposes, communication by sea between Spain and the Netherlands was cut.

This did not spell immediate death for Antwerp. For a considerable time to come, the city would remain an important centre, with its concentrated industry and its position as financial intermediary for Spanish policy; but the silver and bills of exchange needed to pay the troops fighting for Spain would in future come in from the south, via Genoa; and it was to Genoa, on account of the new route taken by Philip II's political silver, that the centre of gravity of Europe now shifted. The decline of Antwerp on a world scale was registered far away – on the sensitive indicators of the Mediterranean, as I shall shortly explain.

The originality of Antwerp

The career of Antwerp, although comparatively brief, nevertheless represents an important and in some ways original episode in the history of capitalism.

It is true that Antwerp learned a great deal from her foreign residents: she adopted double-entry book-keeping which was introduced both here and elsewhere in Europe by the Italians; for international settlements, she used, like everyone else (though with a degree of caution and even parsimony) the bill of exchange, which put her in touch with the circuits of credit and capital linking all the major financial centres. But she could also be capable of devising her own solutions.

In 1500 for instance, she had had to cope as best she could with day-to-day situations which took her by surprise and occasioned 'extreme tensions'.[260] Unlike Bruges, Antwerp did not even have a proper banking system at this time, perhaps, as Hermann Van de Wee suggests, as a result of the prohibitive measures enacted by the dukes of Burgundy in 1433, 1467, 1480, 1488 and 1499, which had literally destroyed any initiative of the kind. So in Antwerp a merchant could not, as he could 'on the Rialto', 'write down' his debt or credit in a banker's ledger, thus balancing his receipts and outgoings. Nor could he really borrow money as was common practice in most exchange centres, by selling a bill payable by a correspondent in say Florence – or even at the Antwerp or Bergen-op-Zoom fairs. And yet the supply of money in the town was inadequate for the volume of transactions – so some fictional paper money had somehow to be invented to ease the flow of business while remaining in some kind of relation with actual cash reserves.

The solution devised in Antwerp had originated in the practice at the Brabant fairs[261] and was a very simple one: settlements in both directions whether payments or receipts, were effected by the letter obligatory (*cédule obligatoire*): a merchant who underwrote one committed himself to paying a given sum within a given period and the letter was the property of its holder. If I had wanted to obtain credit for example, I could have sold to anyone who would accept it a letter obligatory signed by myself. If A owed me a sum of money, he could similarly sign one of these letters, but I could transfer it to B, to whom I owed an equivalent amount. Thus debts and credits circulated on the market, creating an extra form of currency with the advantage that it could cancel itself out in the miraculous reckoning known as the *scontro*, the clearing house or *rescontre* as it was called in Holland. The same piece of paper passed from hand to hand until it expired, as the creditor who finally received the letter as payment would himself be the original signatory.[262]

It was to guarantee the whole system of endorsements that the ancient practice of assignment was generally revived: this established the responsibility of the original debtor until a third party had satisfied the original creditor, a detail which is worth noting, for the word 'assignment' (*assignation*) eventually took over in common parlance from the term 'letter' or *cédule*. A merchant writes: 'I will pay by assignment, as is our practice among merchants', *la usanza entre mercedores*.[263]

But such guarantees for everyday practice, combined with legal penalties for defaulting were not the whole story. The beauty of this system was the great ease and efficiency with which it operated. Nothing could be easier: bills of exchange drawn into transactions at Antwerp could simply be transformed into letters obligatory, and as such circulate from hand to hand. As for efficiency, this circulation resolved, though without institutionalizing it, a persistent and ever-present problem in matters of exchange: the rate of discounting, that is the price or rent paid for time. Discounting (accepting a lower sum if a bill was paid before it fell due) as established in eighteenth-century England,[264] was in fact a revival of ancient practices. If I were to buy or sell a letter obligatory, the amount stated on it would not actually refer either to its selling price or to its purchasing price. If I were buying it for cash, I would pay less than its face value, but if I were receiving it in lieu of a debt, I would oblige the signatory to write it out for a higher sum than he owed me. Since the letter had to be worth its face value on expiry, it was naturally worth less on issue than on repayment. In short this was a flexible arrangement which ran itself and flourished outside the traditional

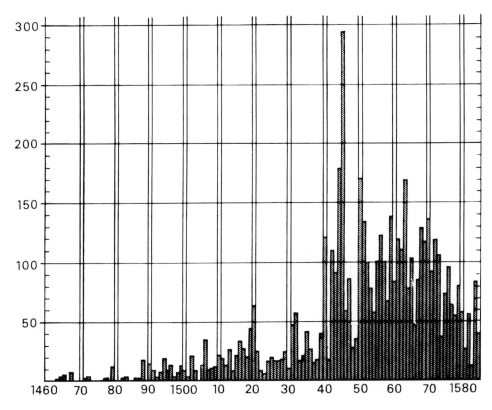

17   THE NUMBER OF FRENCH MERCHANTS REGISTERED AS LIVING IN ANTWERP
BETWEEN 1450 AND 1585
This varies according to movements which closely reflect those of trade in Antwerp in general.
(From E. Coornaert, *Les Français et le commerce international à Anvers*, II, 1961.)

circuits of bills of exchange and banking. We might note that the new system
also operated in Rouen, Lisbon and undoubtedly in London which inherited this
particular technique from Antwerp, whereas Amsterdam from the start and
throughout its career, remained faithful to the traditional workings of the bill of
exchange.

It is tempting too to give Antwerp credit for the first steps in industrial
capitalism, which was clearly developing here and in other thriving towns of the
Low Countries. This is argued persuasively and passionately by Tibor Witt-
mann[265] but I am afraid his book sacrifices too much to theoretical principles.
Did the sixteenth century really innovate very much in this area compared to the
progress made in Ghent, Bruges and Ypres – not to mention Florence, Lucca and
Milan – in previous centuries? I doubt very much whether that is the case, even
bearing in mind the large-scale building programme of Antwerp and the early
urban development there which was years ahead of other European cities, or
considering, as Hugo Soly has, the extraordinary career of the businessman

Gillebert Van Schoonbecke. When called upon in 1550 to take charge of the building of the city walls, Van Schoonbecke organized a sort of vertical trust managing about fifteen brickworks, a gigantic peat-bog, various lime-kilns, a forestry estate and a collection of workers' lodgings – which did not prevent him from calling in addition on sub-contractors for this huge undertaking. He was the biggest entrepreneur and profiteer in the colossal transformation of Antwerp which took place between 1542 and 1566. But tempting though it might be, does this really enable us to talk of industrial capitalism as another feather in Antwerp's cap?

Putting the record straight: the age of the Genoese

The age of Antwerp had been the 'age of the Fuggers'. The following century would be the 'age of the Genoese' – not quite a hundred years but seventy, from 1557 to 1627, of a rule that was so discreet and sophisticated that historians for a long time failed to notice it. Richard Ehrenberg many years ago (1896) voiced his suspicions in a book which is still unrivalled despite its great age. Felipe Ruíz Martin has now uncovered the true dimensions of the phenomenon in his study *El Siglo de los Genoveses*, still alas unpublished because of the author's scrupulousness and indefatigable pursuit of unpublished documents. But I have read this exceptional book in manuscript.

For three-quarters of a century, 'the Genoese experience' enabled the merchant-bankers of Genoa, through their handling of capital and credit, to call the tune of European payments and transactions. This is worth studying in itself, for it must surely have been the most extraordinary example of convergence and concentration the European world-economy had yet witnessed, as it re-oriented itself around an almost invisible focus. For the focal point of the whole system was not even the city of Genoa itself, but a handful of banker-financiers (today we would call them a multinational consortium). And this is only one of the paradoxes surrounding the strange city of Genoa which, though apparently so cursed by fate, tended both before and after its 'age of glory' to gravitate towards the summit of world business. To me Genoa seems always to have been, in every age, the capitalist city par excellence.

'A screen of barren mountains'

Genoa, even counting her two rivieras, east and west, was contained in a very small space. In the words of a French diplomatic report, the Genoese had 'about thirty leagues along the coast from Monaco to Massa, and seven or eight leagues of plain towards the Milanese. The rest is a screen of barren mountains'.[266] Along the coast, every creek or inlet had its port, or village or little town, with invariably a few vines, orange groves, flowers, palm trees growing in the open air, excellent wines (especially in Tabia and the *Cinque Terre*) and plenty of high-quality oil in Oneglia, in the Marro and in Diano, and in the four valleys of Ventimiglia.[267] 'There are few cereals', wrote Giovanni Botero in 1592, 'and little meat, but it is all of the best quality.'[268] For beauty and fragrance this was one of the most delightful countries in the world, a paradise garden. The traveller who arrived here from the North at the end of winter found himself in a land of sparkling waters, flowers and the joys of nature.[269] But this enchanting region was only a narrow strip along the coast; behind it the Apennines, running up to meet the Alps at Nice, reared their obstinate bulk, barren hillsides without trees, 'without grass' even; here and there were the extraordinary hilltop villages, poor and backward, where the *Nobili Vecchi* of Genoa had their feudal estates and their peasant vassals, to be called upon as strong-arm men in emergencies.[270] Like an espalier against an old wall, Genoa the modern city, had its back against the 'feudal' mountains – one of the many paradoxes surrounding it.

In the city itself, building-space was in short supply, and the palaces of the rich had no choice but to expand dizzily upwards. The streets were so narrow that only in the *Strada Nova* and the *Via Balbi* was it possible to drive a carriage;[271] elsewhere one had to travel by sedan chair or go on foot. Space was even short outside the city walls, in the neighbouring valleys, where so many country villas were built. On the San Pier d'Arena road, going out of Campo Marone, writes a traveller,[272] 'one sees the Durazzo palace, a large and magnificent dwelling which looks superb among fifty or so other fine palaces'. 'Fifty or so fine palaces' – even in the country, the Genoese had to live packed together, cheek by jowl with their neighbours. And it was hard to get out of these tiny settled valleys since they were so cut off from one another. Once the noblemen had left town for their villas, if their presence was deemed necessary in the Great Council, the only way to bring them back to Genoa was to send one of the Republic's galleys to fetch them![273] And even this was impossible if bad weather settled on the Gulf of Genoa, bringing torrential rain and rough seas which could last for days and weeks, trapping everyone at home.[274]

This was a handicapped community then, never able to relax and afflicted with congenital weaknesses. How was the city to be fed – or defended? Although the mountains might appear to be a protection, the city was in fact in danger from them. An enemy approaching from the north could arrive at a point overlooking the town: and if he brought up his artillery, all was lost. Genoa was constantly surrendering to other powers, either forcibly, voluntarily or out of prudence, as when she surrendered to the French king in 1396[275] and to the duke of Milan in 1462.[276] The foreigner was always at the gates, whereas Venice, protected by her stretches of water remained impregnable, yielding for the first time only in 1797 – and then to Bonaparte. Genoa on the other hand was captured in 30 May 1522[277] by the Spanish and their allies the *Nobili Vecchi*, and subjected to terrible pillage, eclipsed only by the sack of Rome a few years later in 1527. The same thing happened again much later, in September 1746;[278] this time the aggressors were the Sardinians and the Austrians, who forced an entry without bloodshed and then proceeded to impose a host of requisitions and indemnities on the wealthy city – the modern version of pillage. True, the rapacious victors were driven out three months later during a violent uprising by the common people of Genoa, who were energetic and easily roused.[279] But the cost was once more heavy: a city unable to defend itself paid a high price: on being liberated, Genoa lurched into a spectacular crisis; banknotes were printed, bringing uncontrolled inflation and in 1750, the *Casa di San Giorgio* which had been closed down was forced to open again. In the end things settled down, needless to say: the Republic took the situation in hand and resolved the crisis, not by the minuscule tax it placed on capital (1%) but by turning the screw once more on the indirect tax on consumption[280] – a practice typical of Genoa. Once more it was the mass of the poor who suffered.

Genoa was just as vulnerable from the sea. Her harbour gave on to a stretch of water controlled by no one, therefore abused by all.[281] Savona, on the western riviera, which had aspirations to independence, operated for a long time as the base for hostile expeditions; so, even further west, did Nice and Marseille.[282] In the sixteenth century, Barbary pirates were always appearing on the horizon, carried on the south wind towards Corsica and the Genoese coasts which had poor defences – indeed how could they be defended? Genoa had no *Mare Nostrum* as Venice had the Adriatic, no lagoon to protect her harbour entrance. In May 1684, Louis XIV had Duquesne's squadron bombard the town – an ideal target pinned out on its hillside. The terrified 'inhabitants fled to the mountains, leaving their houses still furnished and exposed to looting'. The marauders seized the opportunity with both hands.[283]

Operating by remote control

Genoa's weakness was, let me repeat, congenital. The city and its dependencies could only survive by calling on the outside world. From some it asked for fish, grain, salt and wine; from others, salt meats, firewood, charcoal and sugar; and so on. If the open boats of the Mediterranean, the *bastimenti latini con viveri* did not turn up, if the northern ships (from St Malo, England or Holland) did not arrive in time with their cargoes of *cibi quadragesimi* – salt herring and cod to be eaten during Lent – then Genoa was in difficulties. During the War of the Spanish Succession, when the seas were swarming with pirates, the state had to intervene to prevent the townspeople from starving. 'Yesterday', announces a letter from a consul, 'there arrived in the port the two boats the Republic of Genoa has armed to escort smaller vessels; they came in from Naples, Sicily and Sardinia bringing a convoy of forty or so boats, seventeen laden with wine from Naples, ten with grain from the Romagna, and the others with various foodstuffs

The port of Genoa in 1485. Painting by Cristofor Grassi, *Civico Museo navale* of Pegli, Genoa. The town forms a semi-circle round the harbour, with its tall houses, fortifications, the arsenal and the lighthouse; in the bay are galleys and some enormous carracks.

such as chestnuts from Naples, cheeses, dried figs, grapes, salt and other similar goods.'[284]

Usually, it must be said, supply problems were solved without difficulty: Genoa's money opened doors easily. Grain apparently materialized out of thin air. Criticisms have often been voiced of the *Magistrato dell'Abbondanza*, a sort of Grain Office which Genoa had instituted like many other Italian towns; but this one did not have a farthing of its own, not a '*giulio*', and 'when it had to buy up stocks, it borrowed money from the citizens, and later sold the grain at retail prices so high as to prevent any risk of loss . . . which would otherwise have fallen upon the rich. So in this way, the poor suffer all the hardship and the rich do rather well out of it'.[285] Once again, this was typical of Genoa's way of doing things. But if the *Abbondanza* had no reserves or budget, this was because the merchants could usually arrange for the town to have ample supplies of grain. In the eighteenth century, Genoa was the equal of Marseille as a redistribution port for cereals, and the equal of Venice for salt, buying her supplies from all over the Mediterranean.

A balancing act

With a population varying between 60,000 and 80,000 (over half a million counting all the dependencies) Genoa had nevertheless succeeded over the centuries in solving the nagging problem of her daily supplies (apart from some brief but painful alerts); but this was only achieved by an extraordinary balancing act.

In fact Genoa's entire existence was a sort of balancing act. She manufactured goods, for other people; sent out her shipping, for other people; invested, but in other places. Even in the eighteenth century, only half of Genoese capital remained in the city;[286] the rest, for want of local investment openings, went abroad. The constraints of geography sent it on foreign ventures. But how was its security and profitability to be protected in the outside world? This was Genoa's constant worry: she had to live forever on the *qui-vive*, obliged to take risks and at the same time to exercise great prudence. The rewards could sometimes be fabulous, but there were catastrophic failures too. The collapse of Genoese investments after 1789 (not only in France) is not an isolated example. The crises of 1557, 1575, 1596, 1607, 1627 and 1647[287] which all had Spanish origins, were so many serious blows, shaking the foundations of the city. And Genoese banks had already experienced failure as early as 1256–9.[288]

The corollary of these dangers was the development, at the heart of this eventful form of capitalism, of the Genoese businessman: remarkable for his adaptability, versatility, 'weightlessness' and that total 'absence of inertia' admired by Roberto Lopez.[289] Time after time, Genoa changed course, accepting on each occasion the need for another metamorphosis. Building up one foreign empire after another for her own use, then abandoning it once it became unworkable or uninhabitable, devising and creating another (deserting the East for the West in the late fifteenth century, pulling out of the Black Sea in favour of the Atlantic,[290] unifying Italy in the nineteenth century[291]) – such was the destiny of Genoa, a fragile creation and an ultra-sensitive seismograph, whose needle quivered whenever there were stirrings in the rest of the world. A monster of intelligence – and of hard-heartedness if necessary – was Genoa not doomed to eat or be eaten?

And this had been the guiding principle of her history. Historians have expressed surprise at her early maritime expeditions against Islam or at the number of galleys she sent to fight Pisa or Venice in the thirteenth century.[292] But the entire active male population of the city went aboard the narrow warships if the word was given; the whole city was mobilized. Similarly – like an incandescent ball of silver – Genoa diverted to her own advantage precious goods, pepper, spices, silks, gold and silver, forcing an entry to ports and trade routes – as is illustrated by the successful settlement of Genoese merchants in the Constantinople of the Palaeologi (1261), and their strenuous ventures in the Black Sea.[293] Venice followed, but at a distance. Twenty years later, in 1283, came the Sicilian Vespers[294]: Florence had taken the side of the Angevins, Genoa that of the Aragonese, and when the latter triumphed, she triumphed with them. But it would take the verve and the erudition of a Carmelo Trasselli[295] to describe the modernity and alacrity with which the Genoese moved into Sicily. That they should have driven out the other 'capitalists' – the Lucchese and Florentines – or at any rate pushed them to one side, establishing their headquarters in Palermo, not too far from the harbour and the Piazza Marina,[296] and that they should have begun lending money to the viceroys and great nobles is perhaps only to be expected. Less predictable was the way in which they took over the export trade in Sicilian grain – the grain which was indispensable to the populations of the North African coast, where famine was endemic at the time – obtaining in return gold dust from Tunis or Tripoli to which it had been brought from the depths of Black Africa. It was no accident then that the feudal estates bought up by the Doria family in Sicily were wheat-growing lands lying on the vital axis linking Palermo and Agrigento.[297] By the time the Catalan merchants attempted to dislodge the Genoese it was far too late. It was also the Genoese who organized Sicilian sugar production,[298] and the Genoese yet again who dominated the trade in silk from Sicily and Calabria via Messina.[299] There were still Genoese merchants and shopkeepers on the island in the early eighteenth century, and they still had interests[300] in the grain and silk trades. They even consented to send to Sicily (since their trade balance was in deficit) 'considerable sums of money in *genovines*, a very fine silver currency which is in great demand in Italy'. Uztáriz was wrong to be surprised: picking up more on the roundabouts than they lost on the swings came as second nature to the Genoese.

In the thirteenth and fourteenth centuries, in spite of, or sometimes because of competition from Venice, Genoa forced her way into every corner of the

European world-economy, either getting there first or elbowing others aside. Before the fourteenth century, she was using her base on Chios to exploit the alum in Phoceaea (Fokia) and was trading in the Black Sea; her carracks were sailing to Bruges and England.[301] In the fifteenth and sixteenth centuries, she gradually lost her hold in the East: the Turks took Caffa in 1475 and Chios in 1566, but from the beginning of the fifteenth century, and therefore far ahead of the field, the Genoese had settlements in North Africa,[302] Seville,[303] Lisbon,[304] and Bruges; later on they were to be found in Antwerp. It was to a Genoese, Christopher Columbus, rather than to Castile, that it fell to discover America. And until 1568, the lengthy voyages between Spain and America were financed by the Genoese merchants of Seville.[305] In 1557, the huge contract they had been eyeing, that of making loans to the government of Philip II, was offered to them.[306] They seized the opportunity, thus inaugurating a new phase in their history, the *siglo de los Genoveses*.

Genoa's discreet rule over Europe

Genoa, classed as a 'second-rank power' after her defeat in the Chioggia war, and remaining one throughout the fourteenth and fifteenth centuries, acquired front-rank status in the years 1550–70 and retained it until the 1620s.[307] It is hard to give a precise chronology of Genoa's supremacy, since in the early days Antwerp was still or seemed to be the most important economic centre, and towards the end of the period, from about 1585, Amsterdam was beginning to assert herself. But most of all it is hard to be precise because Genoa's reign remained from beginning to end extremely discreet: comparable (if I am not too mistaken in my parallel, and other things being equal) with the Bank for International Settlements at Basle.

It was not by her ships, seamen, merchants and captains of industry that Genoa ruled the world, although she had her fair share of all these and was perfectly capable, when the occasion demanded it, of building excellent ships in the yards of San Pier d'Arena, and even of selling or hiring them to others. She also hired out her galleys – strong and elegant ones which the city's patricians, who were willing to turn *condottieri* though only on the sea, placed at the service of foreign sovereigns; among their clients were the king of France and later Charles V, after 1528 and the 'treachery' of Andrea Doria – who deserted François I, abandoning the blockade of Naples, which Lautrec was besieging from the landward side, and went over to the cause of the emperor.[308]

It was in that far-off year of 1528 that Charles V, though still dependent on the merchant-bankers of Augsburg, especially the Fuggers who had hitherto provided the finances his policy required, first borrowed money from the Genoese.[309] And in 1557, when the Spanish state bankruptcy ended the reign of the German bankers, the Genoese naturally stepped into the breach with alacrity

Giant ships in fifteenth-century Genoa. Detail of the preceding plate.

and without difficulty, since they had already begun to participate in the complicated game (which they helped to complicate further) of international finance.[310] The crucial service they performed for the king of Spain was to provide him with a *regular* income, by converting the fiscal revenues and American silver imports which were both *irregular* sources of finance. The Catholic king, like all princes, paid his expenses from day to day and had to transfer large sums of money over the huge chequerboard of Europe: he received money in Seville, but had to pay out regularly in Antwerp or Milan. I need hardly dwell on this phenomenon, which is now well known to historians.[311]

As the years went by, the merchants of Genoa found that they were being drawn into a very considerable undertaking. The revenues of the Spanish king were constantly increasing, but so were his outgoings and consequently the profits of the Genoese. No doubt they were lending the king money deposited with them by the investors and savers of Spain and Italy.[312] But all their own available capital was also being sucked into the machine. Since they could not do everything, we find that in 1568[313] they ceased to take an interest in financing trade between Seville and America, and were no longer participating as much as in the past in purchases of wool from Segovia, silk from Granada or alum from Mazaron. They were moving out of trade and exclusively into finance. If one can believe what they said, they were barely scraping a living out of these visibly gigantic undertakings. The loans they advanced to the king carried an interest rate of 10% but, they argued, there were expenses, mishaps and delays in repayment – which was undeniably the case. On the other hand, according to the secretaries in the royal service, the bankers were making up to 30% on the deals.[314] Probably neither side was speaking the whole truth. But it is clear that the Genoese gamble paid off when one takes account of interest rates, of interest on the interest rates, of the sharp practice possible in exchange and re-exchange deals, of the purchase and sale of gold and silver coins, of speculation in *juros* and the extra profit of 10% paid in Genoa on sales of silver[315] – sources of income which varied and are difficult to estimate but which brought substantial profits. Moreover, given the huge size of the sums lent by the merchants (which as I have already said, far exceeded their own disposable capital) the overall profits would in any case have been enormous, even if the unitary rate of profit was modest.

And after all, the political money of Spain was only one current of finance among others which it stimulated or encouraged. The galleys laden with chests of reals or ingots which began arriving in fabulous quantities in Genoa in the 1570s, were unquestionably an instrument of domination. They made Genoa the arbiter of the fortune of the whole of Europe. Not all the Genoese ventures came off of course; not everything they touched turned to gold. But these extraordinary businessmen have to be judged and explained on the sum total of their dealings over the long run. Their wealth in the sixteenth century came not so much from gold or silver as from 'the possibility of mobilizing credit', a difficult game, which they were playing from a privileged position, as is increasingly clear from the series of documents at last becoming available to refine and improve our explanation of what went on.

Reasons for the Genoese success

How are we to explain the Genoese success? We could start with a hypothesis. Between approximately 1540 and 1560, Europe was more or less gravely affected by a crisis which cut the sixteenth century in half: Henri II's France was not the sunlit landscape ruled by François I; Elizabethan England was not the same as the kingdom of Henry VIII. Was it this crisis which put an end to the age of the Fuggers? I am inclined to say yes, without being able to prove it. Would it not be natural to assume that the financial crises of 1557 and 1558 resulted from the depression?

It is at any rate beyond doubt that these years saw the breakdown of a long-standing monetary equilibrium. Until 1550, silver, as a comparatively rare

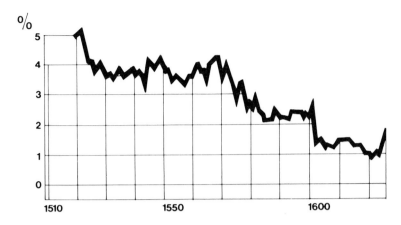

18 SURPLUS CAPITAL IN GENOA BETWEEN 1510 AND 1625
The graph shows real interest on the *luoghi* (annuities with variable interest rates issued by the *Casa di San Giorgio*) as calculated by Carlo Cipolla, 'Note sulla storia del saggio d'interesse ...' in *Economia Internazionale*, 1952. Interest rates declined so much that they were only 1.2% at the end of the seventeenth century. (For more details, see F. Braudel, *The Mediterranean* ..., English edition; II, p. 700.)

metal, had tended to increase its value relative to gold, which was by contrast comparatively plentiful; and silver was the currency used for big business, the means of preserving the value of one's wealth (and indeed the explanation of the rise of the Fuggers). But even before 1550, the value of gold, which was becoming comparatively less plentiful, had begun to move upwards. In this new context, who could fail to see the importance of the decisions made by the Genoese financiers who were the first people, according to Frank Spooner,[316] to start investing in gold on the Antwerp market? Consequently were they not better placed than anyone else, given the task of making payments in Antwerp on behalf of the Spanish king, to control the gold market, since bills of exchange had to be paid for in gold?[317] Is this the 'right' explanation?

I am not entirely convinced that it is, although I agree with those who set great store by the flair and intelligence of the Genoese. But success of this kind is by definition limited to the short-term. It could not long remain the exclusive property of the more far-sighted merchants.

In fact the game played by the Genoese was a complex one which prevailed by its very complexity. It embraced silver, gold and bills of exchange. The Genoese had not only to acquire silver by means of the *sacas de plata* (silver exports)[318] granted to them in their *asientos* (contracts) with the king, or by means of the contraband trade they arranged via Seville[319] – but they also had to sell it. There were two possible customers: either the Portuguese or the Italian cities with dealings in the Levant trade, such as Venice and Florence. The latter were the major clients and this explains how the Levant trade underwent a renaissance, how spices and pepper once more poured into Aleppo and Cairo, and how silk became extremely important as a transit commodity in the trade of the ports in Turkey and Asia Minor. Venice and Florence purchased this silver in return for bills of exchange on northern countries where they had positive trade balances.[320] It was in this way that the Genoese were able to arrange transfers of money to Antwerp, which even after its great days remained the centre for paying the Spanish troops, a place of corruption (rather like Saigon with its traffic in piastres during the Indo-China war). And since bills of exchange could only be paid for in gold after Charles V's ordinance of 1537,[321] the silver sold by the Genoese to the Italian cities was converted into gold currency payable in the Netherlands. Gold indeed remained the most effective instrument the Genoese had for controlling their three-way system. When in 1575, the king of Spain quarrelled with them and decided to do without their services, they succeeded in blocking the circulation of gold. The unpaid Spanish troops mutinied and sacked Antwerp in November 1576.[322] And the king was eventually obliged to give in.

When all this evidence is laid end to end, only one conclusion is possible: Genoa's fortune depended on the American treasure of Spain and the wealth of Italy itself, which was a major source of benefit. By means of the dominant system of the Piacenza fairs,[323] the capital of the Italian cities was all drained towards Genoa. And a multitude of small investors, Genoese and others, entrusted their savings to the bankers for modest returns. There was thus a permanent link between the finances of Spain and the economy of the Italian peninsula – hence the upsets which regularly followed the bankruptcies in Madrid; the 1595 bankruptcy[324] was passed on and did much damage to the savers and investors of Venice.[325] At the same time in Venice itself, the Genoese, since they controlled the supply of silver which they delivered in vast quantities to the *Zecca*,[326] had acquired control of currency exchange and maritime insurance.[327] Detailed research into the economy of other Italian cities would probably turn up similar results. In short, the Genoese undertaking was possible, and I dare say even easy, so long as Italy continued to thrive economically. Just as the peninsula had willy-nilly supported the fortune of Venice in the fourteenth and fifteenth centuries, so it supported that of Genoa in the sixteenth. Should the economy of Italy falter, it would be goodbye to the cosy meetings and banquets almost behind closed doors at the Piacenza fairs.

Behind the success of the bankers, there was, we should not forget, the city of Genoa itself. When one begins to unravel the extraordinary mechanism which the Genoese had established, it is easy to confuse Genoa with her great bankers, many of whom were living in Madrid, appearing at court and handling tremendous contracts, acting as advisers and collaborators of the king and living in their own expatriate world, a hotbed of resentment and repressed feuds, intermarrying, and rising as a single man every time the Spanish king threatened them or their associates in Genoa (who bore the brunt of any mistakes) expressed alarm. The discovery, by Franco Borlandi and his pupils of the unpublished correspondence of these businessmen will, we hope, be able to shed new light on such relations. But it must be remembered that these *hombres de negocios*, as they were known in Madrid, were very few in number, twenty or thirty at most. Alongside – and underneath them – we must imagine the hundreds, perhaps thousands of Genoese merchants of various status, humble clerks, shopkeepers, go-betweens, commission agents, who peopled their own city and all the cities of Italy and Sicily. They were solidly established in Spain, at every level of the economy, in Seville as well as in Granada. To call them a 'merchant state within a state' would perhaps be too strong; but this was a system which had taken root in the fifteenth century and would long endure: at the end of the eighteenth century, the Genoese community in Cadiz was still handling a turnover comparable to that of the English, Dutch or French merchant colonies there,[328] a fact that is often overlooked.

This pattern – the takeover of an economic zone abroad – seems always to have been the condition for the success of a powerful city which had ambitions – not always consciously formulated – to dominate some large-scale system. It is repeated so often as to become a commonplace of history: Venice's takeover of the Byzantine Empire; Genoa's move into Spain; Florence's capture first of England then of France; and the parallel can be extended to Louis XIV's France and the English colonization of India.

The Genoese withdrawal

Building up an empire away from home carried risks: success was usually short-lived. Genoese control of Spanish and thereby European finances lasted little more than sixty years.

Nevertheless the Spanish bankruptcy of 1627 did not, as is sometimes suggested, bring the Genoese Empire tumbling down. To some extent, there was a voluntary disengagement on their part. They were somewhat reluctant in fact to go on bailing out the government of Madrid with the prospect of ever more bankruptcies threatening their profits – and their capital. Withdrawing their funds, as quickly as the difficult circumstances allowed, and reinvesting them in other financial enterprises, was the programme they sought to put into effect as best they could, as I have argued in a recent article based on the detailed correspondence of the Venetian consuls in Genoa.[329]

But as so often, a single explanation will not do. We need to know more about the position of the Genoese moneylenders in Spain itself, and in relation to their Portuguese rivals who were taking over the task of providing finance for the Catholic king. Were the latter propelled into this role by the decisions taken by the count duke Olivares? Were they pushed forward by the development of the Atlantic economy? It has been suspected that they were merely straw men for the Dutch capitalists – a reasonable enough assumption, but some evidence needs to be produced. And at all events, the peace signed between Spain and Charles I's government in 1630 had rather odd consequences.[330] The English negotiator Sir Francis Cottington added a subsidiary clause to the agreement, specifying no more or less than that Spanish silver should be transported to the Netherlands in English ships. One third of this silver would be minted between 1630 and 1643 in the workshops of the Tower of London. So it was through the offices of the English, and not the Genoese, that the river of Spanish silver was channelled north for years on end.

Was this the reason for the Genoese withdrawal? Not necessarily, for given the late date of the agreement, 1630, it is more likely, though again there is no evidence, that it was the breakdown of the Genoese arrangements which produced this curious solution. One thing at least is certain: Spain needed a *reliable* system for the transport of her funds. The Genoese solution, consisting of transferring funds by means of bills of exchange, an elegant arrangement but one that depended on control of an international network of payments, was succeeded by the easy solution of appointing as transporters the very people whose piracy, acts of war and attacks by sea Spain feared. After 1647 or 1648, the ultimate irony, the Spanish silver so essential for the administration and defence of the southern provinces of the Low Countries was transported not in English but in Dutch ships – possibly even before the separate peace of Munster (January 1648) had been signed by the United Provinces.[331] On this occasion, Protestants and Catholics could agree on the *non olet* principle.

Genoa survives

To return to Genoa, there was unquestionably a disengagement from the Spanish contracts. The *asentistas* appear to have saved a substantial part of their capital, in spite of the rather harsh and undoubtedly worrying conditions of the Spanish bankruptcy of 1627, and the series of difficulties that were consequently created for them in Spain, in Lombardy or in Naples. The success of the rescue operation is ascertainable I think from the volume of pieces of eight which arrived in Genoa, of which the annual record can be reconstructed.[332] They went on arriving in large, even massive quantities, after 1627. And Genoa still appeared to have access to the flow of American silver. How? Through trade in Seville and later Cadiz, almost certainly, since there were still networks of Genoese merchants in Andalusia who kept alive their communications with America. What was more, even after the appearance on the scene of other moneylenders, the Portuguese *marranos*, the Genoese *partitanti* consented to participate once more in the Spanish contracts – for example in 1630, 1647 and 1660.[333] If they agreed to join in once more, might this not have been because shipments of silver into Seville and later Cadiz were more plentiful than is claimed by the official figures?[334] Loans to Spain once more became safe bets and were even profitable – and they offered further opportunities for a share of the immense flow of

1698

1699

1700

Samples of Genoese printed fabrics (1698–1700)

contraband silver then flooding Europe. The Genoese did not let the occasion slip.

Another way of drinking at the Spanish source was to export Genoa's own manufactured goods. Indeed Genoa played a greater part than Venice in the industrial expansion of the seventeenth and eighteenth centuries, seeking to tailor her production to demand in the Cadiz and Lisbon markets, the better to obtain the gold of the latter and the silver of the former. As late as 1786, Spain was still importing a great many Genoese fabrics, 'and there are even particular manufactories catering for Spanish tastes, for instance large pieces of silk scattered with little flowers: at the one end, there is a closely embroidered border of large flowers with semi-embossed centres. ... These fabrics are used for ceremonial dress: some of them are magnificent and very expensive'.[335] Similarly, a large proportion of the production of the paper works in Voltri near Genoa 'is destined for the Indies, where it is used like tobacco [leaves] for smoking' [sic].[336] So Genoa was taking care to defend herself against competition from Milan, Vicenza, Nîmes, Marseille and Catalonia.

The policy of the Genoese merchants seems then to have been flexible, interrupted now and then, but adaptable to new circumstances – like that of any self-respecting capitalist. In the fifteenth century, they secured a place on the gold route from North Africa to Sicily; in the sixteenth, they acquired a share of the American treasure via Spain; in the seventeenth, they swelled their commerce by exporting manufactured goods. And in every age, they practised banking and finance as the circumstances allowed.

And indeed there was no lack of custom in the financial world after 1627. Although the Spanish government no longer offered the same opportunities as in the past, Genoese capital sought and found other clients: cities, princes, states and individual entrepreneurs or private citizens – as Giuseppe Felloni's recent book makes clear.[337] Even before the disengagement of 1627, Genoese capital had begun 'a radical and wholescale redistribution of [its] financial commitments'.[338] As early as 1617, the Genoese were investing in Venetian stocks. In Rome, where they had ousted the Florentine bankers even in the fifteenth century, they participated in the revival of loans to the Papacy with the creation in 1656 of the *Monte Oro*, whose first stocks were almost entirely bought up by Genoese subscribers.[339] Their first investments in France were made between 1664 and 1673.[340] In the eighteenth century, they were investing as far afield as Austria, Bavaria, Sweden, the Austrian provinces of Lombardy and in cities such as Lyon, Turin and Sedan.[341] As in Amsterdam or Geneva, and with the same tactics (using intermediaries and touting for custom) the government loans industry became part of everyday life in Genoa, as can be seen from the broadsheets and gazettes. 'Last Friday', reports a French agent in 1743, 'there were dispatched to Milan [under Austrian rule at the time] in several carriages under a strong escort, the 450,000 florins which private citizens of this town have lent the Queen of

Hungary [Maria Theresa] on the security of the precious stones I have mentioned.'[342]

And the volume of capital invested abroad grew progressively, as if the old machine was being spurred on to new speeds by the greater dynamism of the eighteenth century: in millions of *lire di banco* in round figures, it amounted to 271 in 1725; 306 in 1745; 332 in 1765; 342 in 1785, with an annual income which rose from 7.7 million in 1725 to 11.5 million in 1785. The *lira di banco*, the Genoese money of account, remained constant at 0.328 grammes of gold between 1675 and 1793. But rather than calculate in terms of gold weights, it may be more meaningful to say that the income of Genoese investors in 1785 was equivalent to over half the total income of Genoa[343] on an approximate calculation.

How curious it is that with the new expansion of investment, Genoa should have remained faithful to the geographical radius of her former splendour! Genoa's capital, unlike that of Holland or Geneva, did not go to England, but large amounts of it went to France (35 million *livres tournois* on the eve of the Revolution). Was it because in the north the Catholic bankers of Genoa found themselves up against the network of Protestant bankers? Or was it rather the consequence of clinging to old habits which acted as a straitjacket on the imagination and far-sightedness of the Genoese businessmen?[344]

Whatever the reason, it was a choice which sent Genoese capital tumbling into the abyss that swallowed up the *ancien régime*. But in the following century, Genoa re-emerged once again as the most thriving economic centre of the peninsula. In the age of steamships and the Risorgimento, she was to set up her own industry, a strong modern merchant navy, and the *Banco d'Italia* was very largely her creation. As one Italian historian[345] has put it: 'Genoa created Italian unification'; and he adds 'for her own benefit'.

Back to the world-economy

But the conversion, or rather the successive conversions of Genoese capitalism did not bring Genoa back to the heart of the world-economy. Her 'age' on the international stage had ended by 1627, or perhaps even 1622 when the Piacenza fairs ceased to function.[346] If one looks at the events of this crucial year, one has the impression that the Venetians, Milanese and Florentines dissociated themselves from the Genoese bankers. Perhaps they could not continue to collaborate with the city of St George without putting themselves at risk? Perhaps the rest of Italy was no longer able to pay the price of Genoese supremacy? But perhaps too, the European economy as a whole was no longer able to support a fiduciary circulation out of all proportion to its metallic reserves and to the volume of production? The Genoese system, too ambitious and complicated for an *ancien régime* economy, had collapsed partly under its own weight, with the European crisis of the seventeenth century, the more so since the centre of gravity of Europe was now tilting northwards, where it would stay for long years to come. It was symptomatic that when Genoa lost control of the finances of Europe and ceased to be the centre of the world-economy, that centre should have shifted to Amsterdam, a city which had made its recent fortune – another sign of the times – out of commodity trading. Amsterdam would have its moment as a financial centre too, but only later; and curiously enough the problems raised by the Genoese experience would crop up here too.

3

The City-Centred Economies of the European Past: Amsterdam

WITH AMSTERDAM[1] the age of empire-building cities came to an end. It was the last time, writes Violet Barbour,[2] that 'a veritable empire of trade and credit could be held by a city in her own right, unsustained by the forces of a modern state'. The interesting thing about this episode is therefore that it lies between two successive phases of economic hegemony: on the one hand the age of the city, on the other that of the modern territorial state and the national economy, heralded by the rise of London with the backing of the entire English economy. At the heart of a Europe swollen with success and tending, by the end of the eighteenth century, to embrace the whole world, the dominant central zone had to grow in size in order to balance the entire structure. Cities standing alone, or almost alone, by now lacked sufficient purchase on the neighbouring economies from which they drew strength; soon they would no longer measure up to the task. The territorial states would take over.

The emergence of Amsterdam, prolonging the old pattern, took place, logically enough, according to the old rules: the cities of Antwerp and Genoa were succeeded by another city, Amsterdam. But in the process, the North was re-asserting itself over the South – this time for good. So Amsterdam was taking over not only from Antwerp, as is often claimed, but also from the Mediterranean, which had still been preponderant during the Genoese episode.[3] The ultra-rich southern sea, blessed with every gift and advantage, saw its place taken by the ocean which had long been its poor relation, which was still not being used to the full, and to which the international division of labour had so far allocated only the most arduous and least rewarding tasks. The withdrawal of Genoese capitalism and with it of Italy as a whole (now under attack from all sides) left the way clear for the victory of the mariners and merchants of the North.

The victory was not achieved overnight, however, any more than the decline of the Mediterranean and Italy was itself an overnight eclipse: it was a long-drawn-out process in which one stage slowly followed another. In the 1570s, English ships once more appeared in Mediterranean waters. In the 1590s, it was the turn of the Dutch. But the roundships, *saëtes*, *marciliane* and *caramusalis* did not vanish from the Mediterranean. Before the invasion of the northern merchantmen could bear fruit, the ports of North Africa and the Levant, the harbours of Livorno and Ancona had to open their gates to them and be won over, the rich cities of the Mediterranean had to accept the services of the newcomers and consent to freight them. The English had moreover to sign their 'capitulations' with the Grand Turk in 1579, something the Dutch did not achieve until 1612. In addition, northern cloth, linen and other industrial products had to penetrate Mediterranean markets, ousting the local goods traditionally sold there.[4] At the beginning of the seventeenth century, Venice, with her good-quality cloth, still dominated the Levant market. So Venice and the other cities had still to be overcome. And the newcomers would also have to wait for the days of Genoese credit hegemony to wane. Such were the processes of varying duration implied in the rise of Amsterdam which – unlike Antwerp – would not pass the torch back to the Mediterranean economies.

The States-General of the United Provinces meeting in Amsterdam in 1651, with all the ceremonial of a sovereign state. (Photo Rijksmuseum.)

The United Provinces: the economy begins at home

Contemporary observers saw only the illuminated surface of events. Failing as usual, to notice the long processes which had prepared the ground, they suddenly discovered Holland's greatness when it was already a dazzling *fait accompli*. They found quite incomprehensible therefore the abrupt fortune, extraordinary rise and unexpected power of this little and almost brand-new country. There was much talk of the 'Dutch miracle', the 'Dutch secret' and the 'stupendous wealth' of Holland.

A strip of land, lacking in natural wealth

The United Provinces covered a very small area – no bigger than the kingdom of Galicia, as a Spaniard observed in 1724;[5] and less than half the size of Devonshire, as Turgot later commented, quoting the English writer Tucker.[6] 'It is a very small country', one of Louis XIV's ambassadors wrote in 1699, 'taken up on the seaward side with barren sand-dunes, subject both from this quarter, and from the rivers and canals with which it is intersected to frequent flooding, and fit only for the grazing which is the country's sole wealth; the amount of wheat and other grains grown here does not suffice to feed a hundredth part of its inhabitants'.[7] It was not even enough, as Defoe ironically remarked, 'to feed its cocks and hens'.[8] 'All that Holland produces', another informant tells us in 1697, 'is butter, cheese and clay for turning into crockery'.[9] 'Half the country is under water', explains the serious Spanish economist Ustariz in 1724, 'or is land that can produce nothing, and scarcely one quarter of it is cultivated in any one year; so several writers assure us that the country's harvest barely yields a quarter of the food consumed there.'[10] A letter written in 1738 goes further: 'Holland is a barren country. It is a land floating in water, a field that is flooded for three parts of the year. This territory is so narrow and confined that it cannot feed a fifth part of its Inhabitants'.[11] Even Accarias de Sérionne (whose judgment can usually be relied upon) unhesitatingly states in 1766 that Holland (that is the United Provinces) 'has never been able to feed or clothe one quarter of its subjects'.[12] In short, this was a poor country: nothing would grow but a little poor wheat and some rye and oats; there were few sheep, no vines except occasionally against a sheltered wall in a country house or garden, and no trees except along the canals in Amsterdam or around the villages. On the other hand, there were plenty of pasture lands, 'which towards the end of October or sometimes November, begin to be covered with waters which are swollen by the winds, storms and continual rain ... So in many places there is nothing to be seen but dikes, church towers and houses which seem to be standing in a great sea'.[13] The winter rains would be drained away 'in spring, by means of windmills'.[14]

To Mediterranean eyes, this was strange to the point of absurdity 'The land is low-lying', writes the Florentine Lodovico Guicciardini in 1567, 'all the rivers and canals are enclosed by dikes, so that they do not flow at ground level, and in many places one sees with great astonishment that the water is higher than the land.'[15] Two hundred years later, in 1760, another traveller from Geneva considered that 'everything is artificial in the province of Holland, even the country itself and its natural features'.[16] A Spanish visitor, Antonio Ponz, in 1787 even pronounced it 'more imaginary and poetic than real!'[17]

Agricultural achievement

And yet the United Provinces did have soil, villages and farms. There were even, in Gelderland, poor country squires with peasants working for them, an authentic fragment of feudal Europe; in Groningen, there were gentleman farmers; and in Friesland, tenant-farmers.[18] The Leyden region could boast intensive market-gardening – sending vegetables to be sold in the streets of Amsterdam – as well as the best butter in the United Provinces,[19] and a bridge over the old Rhine known as 'the Corn Bridge, because on market days the peasants are to be found there with their grain'.[20] Here and there, one might meet rich farmers, dressed in black, without cloaks, 'but their wives [are] loaded with silver and their fingers dripping with gold rings'.[21] Every spring, 'a great quantity of lean cattle and oxen come from Denmark, Jutland and Holstein, which cattle are taken straight to the pastures. Three weeks later, they are sleek and plump'.[22] 'Towards the middle of November, [prosperous householders] buy a side of beef or a whole carcase according to the size of their family, and they salt or smoke it ... and eat it with butter or lettuce. Every Sunday, they take a big piece out of the salting-tub and cook it, making it last for several meals. The piece of cold beef comes back to table along with a few scraps of boiled meat, milk and or some vegetables.'[23]

Since land was scarce, both agriculture and animal husbandry had to stake everything on productivity. The stock was better fed here than anywhere else. Cows gave as much as three pails of milk a day.[24] Agriculture had become close to gardening and invented ingenious methods of crop rotation, achieving higher yields than elsewhere by the use of manure, including refuse from the towns. Sufficient progress had been made by 1570 for agriculture to play a role in the early stages of the country's economic takeoff, inspiring Jan de Vries[25] to write that capitalism grew out of the soil in Holland.

It is true that subsequent progress, although on a small scale, ushered in an agricultural revolution which was to spread to England, but that is another story. The important point is that through contact with the towns, the Dutch countryside became commercialized at an early stage, and indeed urbanized after a fashion, dependent, like the towns, on produce from outside. Since at least half the country's grain supply (this is nearer the true figure) had to be imported in

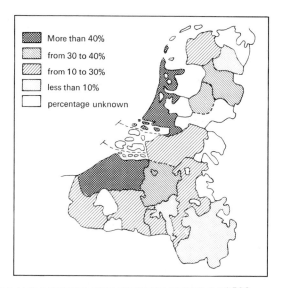

19   THE NETHERLANDS UNDER BURGUNDIAN RULE IN 1500
The proportion of the population living in towns had already reached record levels by 1500. It
was over 40% in Flanders and in the province of Holland. (From Jan de Vries, *The Dutch Rural
Economy in the Golden Age, 1500–1700,* p. 83.)

any case, Dutch farming tended to turn to cash-crops: flax, hemp, rape, hops,
tobacco and dye-plants like woad and madder, the latter introduced by refugees
from Flanders.[26] The dyestuffs were a timely arrival, since English woollens were
imported to Holland undyed, 'in the white' as it was called, to be dyed and
dressed in Holland. And fulling and dyeing alone cost twice as much as cloth
production itself (raw material, combing, spinning and weaving).[27] Hence James
I's decision in 1614 to forbid the export of 'white cloth' from England.[28] But the
outcome was a complete fiasco since, in the dyeing and dressing processes, the
English were no match for the Dutch who had the advantage of more advanced
technology and the equally great one of possessing the dyestuffs on their very
doorstep.

To the extent that they had yielded to the temptation of growing cash-crops,
Dutch peasants were necessarily dependent on the market for their food as well
as for supplies of wood or peat. Thus they were drawn out of their rural
isolation. Large villages became meeting-places, perhaps with a market or even
a fair. Merchants for their part were often able to make direct contact with
producers.[29]

Advanced rural commercialization meant rural wealth. 'It is not out of the
way to meet peasants here worth 100,000 *livres* or more.'[30] However, wages in
the countryside tended to approximate to wages in the towns,[31] as a complaint
by Pieter de la Court shows (1662): 'Our peasants are obliged to pay such high
wages to their workers and farmhands that [the latter] carry off a large share of

the profits and live more comfortably than their masters; the same inconvenience is experienced in the towns between the artisans and their servants who are more insupportable and less obliging than anywhere else in the world'.[32]

A high-voltage urban economy

Compared to the rest of Europe, the little country of the United Provinces was a highly urbanized, highly organized community, precisely because of its population density, 'proportionately the highest in Europe' as Isaac de Pinto wrote.[33] A traveller who made the journey from Brussels to Amsterdam in 1627 would 'find all the towns as full of people as those held by Spain [in Flanders] are empty ... on my way from one to the other of these towns which lie two or three leagues apart, I met such throngs of people that there are not as many carriages in the streets of Rome [which were full enough, goodness knows] as there are carts here crowded with passengers, whilst the canals which run through the country in every direction are covered with numberless vessels'.[34] Was this so surprising? Half the population of the United Provinces lived in the towns[35] – the highest figure in Europe – hence the volume of traffic, the regularity of communications, and the need to make full use of the sea routes, rivers, canals and the roads, which were frequented by peasant carters as much as in the rest of Europe.

The United Provinces was an assembly of seven minuscule states – Holland, Zeeland, Utrecht, Gelderland, Overijssel, Friesland and Groningen – each considering itself independent and priding itself on behaving accordingly. In fact each of these provinces consisted of a more or less closely-knit network of towns. In Holland, the six ancient towns with the right to vote in the States of Holland had been joined by another twelve, including Rotterdam. Each of these towns was self-governing, collected its own taxes, administered its own justice, kept a close eye on its neighbours and never ceased to defend its prerogatives, its autonomy and its fiscal rights. This was the main reason for the large number of tolls,[36] 'an immensity of tolls',[37] and obstructive customs barriers at the entrance to towns. And yet this compartmentalization of the state, this amazing degree of decentralization, did also bring a measure of individual freedom. The patrician bourgeoisie which ruled the towns had complete control of the judicial system, exacting any penalties it chose, banishing offenders for life from a town or from the entire province if it saw fit – a judgment against which there was virtually no appeal. On the other hand, it defended and protected its citizens, shielding them from higher instances of justice.[38]

Since they had to live together, the Dutch towns could not escape the need for joint action. 'Their interests', as Pieter de la Court says, 'are intertwined one with another.'[39] Quarrelsome and jealous, they were nevertheless subject to the law of the beehive, which obliged them to combine their efforts and cooperate in commercial and industrial activity. Together they formed a power bloc.

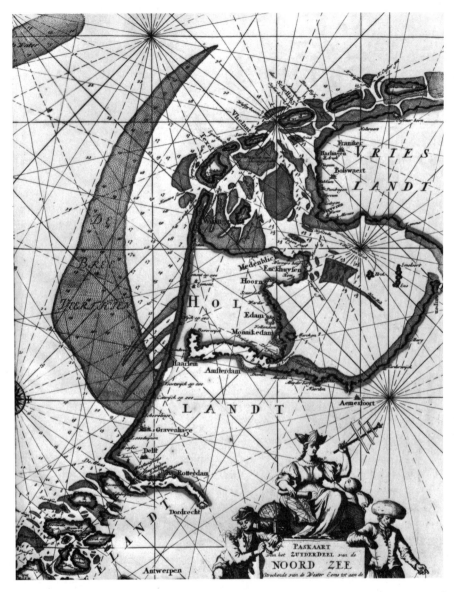

A marvellous map of the United Provinces showing how they were invaded by the waters and sands of the North Sea, the latter surrounding the coasts and islands. This map was published by Johannes Lootz in about 1707 but never distributed. This copy is in the Bibliothèque Nationale in Paris, Ge DD 172, map 52. (Photo B.N.)

Amsterdam

Linking hands then and sharing tasks among themselves, these towns formed networks and grouped themselves into a hierarchy or pyramid. The centre or summit of the whole would necessarily be occupied by a leading city, one more important and commanding than those surrounding it. To the towns of the United Provinces, Amsterdam stood in the same position as did Venice to those of the *Terraferma*. Indeed Amsterdam bore an uncanny physical resemblance to Venice, with the same water everywhere, dividing the city up into islands, islets and canals, surrounding it on all sides with marshes;[40] Amsterdam had her *vaterschepen*,[41] the little boats which ferried in fresh water, just as the boats on the Brenta did for Venice. Both cities were after all ringed round with salt water.

Pieter de la Court[42] explains that Amsterdam's history really began with the tidal wave which broke through the protective strip of dunes near Texel creating the Zuyder Zee in 1282; after this, it was possible 'for large ships to cross the Tey' and the sailors of the Baltic made Amsterdam, hitherto merely a village, a rendezvous for trade. Despite this assistance from the elements, access to the town remained difficult and dangerous, or at the very least a complex business. Ships sailing to Amsterdam had to wait at Texel or Vlie, at the mouth of the Zuyder Zee, where sandbanks were a constant menace; ships leaving the city had to wait in the same ports for a favourable wind. All shipping thus had to stop both on the way in and on the way out, something the authorities controlled very closely. In 1670, great scandal, entertaining in retrospect, was caused by a French frigate, a royal warship moreover, which casually sailed from Texel to Amsterdam without permission.[43] To make things even more difficult, large merchant ships were unable to cross the shallows north of Amsterdam because of the barely submerged Pompius sandbank, until a plan was devised in 1688:[44] two tugs, known as 'camels', approached the big vessel from port and starboard respectively and passed chains across under its hull, by which means it was lifted over the obstacle and brought into harbour.

Obstacles or no obstacles, Amsterdam harbour was always full to bursting. 'I have never seen anything which surprised me so much', writes a traveller in 1738. 'It is impossible for one who has not seen it to imagine the superb effect of two thousand Vessels enclosed in the same Harbour.'[45] A French guide, published in 1701, quotes a figure of eight thousand, 'whose masts and rigging form as it were a forest so dense that it seems the sun could hardly penetrate it'.[46] 2000 or 8000 – the figure does not really matter. What is undeniable is the variety of flags one could observe at leisure from the Damplatz. This boat, 'which looks brand new', the same guide explains, 'is German, flying quarters of or and gules. That one ... is from Brandenburg, it flies argent with a sable spread eagle'; there is one from Stralsund, with a golden sun. And there are ships from Lübeck, Venice, England, Scotland, Tuscany, Ragusa (argent with a shield and a strip inscribed *Libertas*). There is even a 'Savoyard' vessel, if that is possible. Further off are large

Amsterdam: the Haringpakkerstoren Tower, by A. Storck Nieuwershuis, B. de Gensvan Collection. (Photo Giraudon.)

ships, specializing in whale-fishing. There is no need to tell the reader 'what the white flags are, since you are French'.[47] If the same reader had sat down to read the *Amsterdam Gazette*,[48] he would have found the names and itineraries of hundreds of ships sailing into the harbour. On 8 February 1669, there arrived at Texel from Bordeaux the *Stork,* the *Flax-Cart,* the *Rising Sun,* the *Fox of Bilbao* and the *Double Cutter of Nantes*; on the 12th, the *Fig Tree of Terceira*, the *Striped Whale* also from Bordeaux; a little later the *Haywain* from Bilbao, the *Greyhound* from Calais, the *Spotted Lamb* returning from Galicia; in June the *Flowerpot* 'coming from Muscovy [probably Archangel] where she spent the winter; in February it was learnt that the *Butterpot* had reached Alicante'. This maritime traffic made Amsterdam 'the warehouse of the World, the Seat of Opulence, the rendezvous of riches and the darling of the gods'.[49]

But none of this could have happened without the contribution made by the other Dutch provinces and towns. They were the *sine qua non* of Amsterdam's greatness. According to Jan de Vries, the heart of what I have called the world-economy centred on Amsterdam was not merely Holland, as is usually assumed, but the whole Dutch seaboard open to maritime trade, Zeeland and Friesland, Groningen and part of Utrecht. Only Gelderland, the Generality Lands and Overijssel were cut off from this bustling centre, as being poor, archaic and still 'medieval' regions.

Cooperation between this 'core' region and Amsterdam itself meant a division of labour: industry prospered in Leyden, Haarlem and Delft; shipbuilding in Brill and Rotterdam; Dordrecht made a living from the heavy flow of traffic along the Rhine; Enkhuisen and Rotterdam controlled the fisheries of the North Sea; Rotterdam again, the most important city after Amsterdam, handled the lion's share of trade with France and England; the Hague, the political capital, was something like Washington in the United States, both now and in the past. So it was no accident that the Dutch East India Company was divided into its various 'chambers'; if alongside the Bank of Amsterdam, created in 1609, similar though less active banks were established in Middelburg (1616), Delft (1621) and Rotterdam (1635). Pierre Baudet has a point when he adapts the famous slogan about General Motors and says that 'what was good for Amsterdam was good for the United Provinces', but Amsterdam had to reckon with a strong supporting cast, to put with the jealousy and hostility of the other towns; she had no choice but to make the best of things.

A variegated population

The cities were great consumers of labour. The urban complex of the United Provinces could not have prospered without population expansion: one million inhabitants in 1500, two million in 1650 (a million of whom were resident in the towns). This progress was not accounted for by natural increase alone. The expansion of the Dutch economy called for, indeed demanded, foreign workers: it was in part their achievement. Not that Holland turned out to be the Promised Land for everybody. Dutch prosperity had as its by-product the existence of a huge proletariat, crowded into slums and reduced to inferior food. Fishing for 'lean' herring in the month of November 'was prohibited in Holland by public notice, [but] it was tolerated because it helped to feed the poor'.[50] The situation was masked, as in Genoa, by charitable activity which tempered potential class struggles. As a recent exhibition in the City Hall in Amsterdam nevertheless demonstrated, there were many pathetic scenes of poverty in seventeenth-century Holland, where the rich were richer than anywhere else, and the poor as numerous and perhaps even worse-off, if only because of the chronically high cost of living.

Not all the immigrants came to Holland simply to seek a doubtful fortune. Many of them were fleeing from the wars and religious persecution which were the scourge of the sixteenth and seventeenth centuries. After signing the peace treaty with Spain in 1609, the United Provinces were on the point of splitting up and demolishing what passed there for a state, on account of the violence of their religious quarrels (Remonstrants versus Contra-Remonstrants) and political conflicts (the regents of the towns versus the Stadtholder Maurice of Nassau). But this wave of violence, marked by the victory of Reformed orthodoxy at the synod of Dordrecht in 1619 and of the stadtholdership after the execution of the *Landsadvokaat* (Grand Pensionary of Holland) Johan Van Oldenbarnevelt, did not last; nor could it in a country where there were many Catholics, where Lutherans were to be found in the eastern regions and where dissident Protestants were still active. In the end, toleration prevailed and was strengthened along with the individual liberty encouraged by the fragmentation of political authority. 'The ministers of the Church could have only a very limited success in turning the Republic into a Protestant state somewhat on the Genevan model.'[51]

Toleration meant accepting people as they were, since whether workers, merchants or fugitives, they all contributed to the wealth of the Republic. It is in any case hard to imagine the 'centre' of a world-economy as anything but tolerant; it was compelled to be tolerant, obliged to take all the men it needed, from wherever they came. The United Provinces unquestionably offered a place of asylum, a life-raft; hence 'the great press of people whom war has driven here … like fish off the coast of Norway when they sense the approach of a whale'.[52] Freedom of conscience was inevitable and became the rule. 'In this Commonwealth', wrote Sir William Temple in 1672, 'no Man [has] any reason to complain of oppression in Conscience.'[53] Or as a Dutch writer put it later, in 1705, 'All the peoples of the world can serve God here according to their hearts and following the movement of their conscience and although the dominant religion is the Reformed Church, everyone is free to live in the faith he confesses and there are as many as 25 Roman Catholic churches where one may go to worship as publicly as in Rome itself'.[54] Historical demographers are particularly aware of the diversity of creeds in Holland, since they may be faced (in Rotterdam for example[55]) with as many as ten different kinds of parish register (Dutch Reformed, Scottish Reformed, Walloon Reformed; Presbyterian, Episcopalian, Lutheran, Remonstrant, Mennonite, Catholic and Jewish). The Catholics incidentally were usually represented by the lower classes, especially in the Generality Lands.

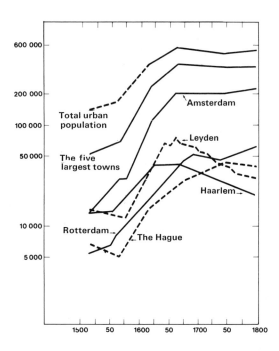

600 000

200 000

Total urban
population

100 000

The five
largest towns

50 000

Amsterdam

Leyden

Haarlem

10 000

Rotterdam

The Hague

5 000

1500   50   1600   50   1700   50   1800

20   THE URBAN POPULATION
INCREASE
This increase, affecting Amsterdam
most of all, was crucial to the rise
of the United Provinces.
(From Jan de Vries, *The Dutch
Rural Economy, op. cit.*, p. 89.)

Immigrants were generally content with the most menial trades, but as a Dutchman said in 1662, 'a man who is willing to work in Holland cannot die of hunger ... and even those who drag rubbish out of the canals with hooks and nets on the end of poles can earn a half-crown a day *if they are prepared to work hard*'[56] (my italics). The danger of fairly high wages of course was that once a poor man had earned enough to live on, he might offer himself the luxury of working only now and then. But such poor men were badly needed as rubbish-collectors, labourers, porters, dockers, boatman, haymakers in Friesland, or peat-diggers, who had to make haste to extract the turfs before the floods and ice of winter. The latter tasks were generally allotted to German immigrants, poor wretches who seem to have become more numerous after 1650 and who were known generically as the *Hollandgänger*, those who go to Holland, usually to work on the earthworks of the polders. Nearby Germany was a pool of cheap labour providing the United Provinces with men for the army, the navy, overseas service and work in the fields (the *Hannekemaaier*) or the towns to which so many *poepen* and *moffen* flocked.[57]

Pride of place among immigrant workers must go to the skilled craftsmen who were numerous in the textile centres of Leyden (serges, camlets, broadcloth), Haarlem (silk and linen-bleaching), Amsterdam where most types of industry were gradually becoming established:[58] wool, silk, cloth of gold and silver, ribbons, gilded leather, morocco, kid, sugar-refining and various chemical industries; and Saardam 'the village of carpenters' near the metropolis which had 'the biggest shipyard in the world'. For all these activities, foreign labour was vital. Workers from Ypres and Hondschoote were responsible for the textile boom in Haarlem. And in the late seventeenth century, the industry of the entire United Provinces was given a considerable boost by the massive invasion of French Huguenots after the Revocation of the Edict of Nantes (1685).

Among the stream of refugees – French Protestants, Antwerpers, Jews from Spain and Portugal – were many merchants, often in possession of substantial capital. The Sephardic Jews[59] in particular contributed to Holland's fortune. Werner Sombart[60] claims that they brought with them to Amsterdam capitalism, no less, which is going rather too far. But they certainly gave the city valuable aid, in the sphere of currency exchange for instance and even more in stock exchange transactions. In these domains they were masters, indeed pioneers. They were also good advisers, and were instrumental in setting up commercial links between Holland and the New World and the Mediterranean.[61] A seventeenth-century English pamphleteer even suspected that the merchants of Amsterdam had lured them to the city out of commercial interest, 'the Jews and other foreigners having opened their own world-wide commerce to them'.[62] It would perhaps be nearer the truth to say that the Jews, being experienced businessmen, naturally gravitated towards prosperous economies. Their arrival in a country generally meant that business was good there or improving. If they withdrew, it did not always mean that business was bad, but it was probably not so good. Did the Jews begin to leave Amsterdam in about 1653?[63] Thirty years later, at any rate, they followed William of Orange to England. Does this mean that, appearances to the contrary, Amsterdam was actually less prosperous then than during the first decades of the century?

The Jews were in any case not the only people who 'made' Amsterdam what it was. Every trading city in Europe sent a contingent to the town which would soon be, if it was not already, the commercial centre of the world. Pride of place undoubtedly went to the merchants of Antwerp. When in August 1585, the city of Antwerp fell to Alexander Farnese after a memorable siege, its citizens obtained generous conditions, notably that merchants were permitted either to stay or to leave the city, taking their property with them.[64] So those who chose exile in Holland did not arrive there empty-handed: they brought capital, competence and commercial contacts and this was unquestionably one of the reasons for Amsterdam's rapid takeoff. Jacques de la Faille, an Antwerp merchant who had settled in the new capital of the North, was not exaggerating when he wrote on 23 April 1594: 'Here is Antwerp itself changed into Amsterdam'.[65] No less than one-third of the city's population was of foreign birth or extraction in about 1650. Fifty per cent of the first deposits in the Bank of Amsterdam, created in 1609, came from the southern Netherlands.

As a result, Amsterdam grew fast – from 50,000 inhabitants in 1600 to 200,000 in 1700 – and quickly became a melting-pot of nations, transforming into 'Dutchmen' the throng of Flemings, Walloons, Germans, Portuguese, Jews

Amsterdam, the fishmarket, the City Hall and the public weighing scales. Engraving by Wright and Schutz, 1797. (Atlas van Stolk.)

and French Huguenots, making a country-wide Dutch 'nation' in effect. Craftsmen, merchants, novice mariners and labourers transformed this narrow strip of land into another country. But it was the rise of Holland in the first place which had created the original demand and provided the conditions for success.

Fisheries from the first

The United Provinces were 'the Egypt of Europe', the creation of the Rhine and Meuse: this was how Diderot[66] described the mixture of land and water that made up the United Provinces. But the country was above all the creation of the sea. The Dutch people 'are so given to seafaring that one might think water rather than land their element'.[67] They had served their apprenticeship on the often troubled waters of the North Sea, in fishing, coasting, long-haul navigation and naval warfare. According to an Englishman in 1624, the North Sea was 'the

Academy of the mariners and pilots of the Dutch rebels'.[68] So Sir William Temple was right when he said: 'As the Dutch Commonwealth was born out of the Sea, so out of the same Element, it drew its first Strength and consideration'.[69]

The fishermen of Holland and Zeeland had sailed the North Sea and neighbouring waters since time out of mind. Fishing was the national industry – or rather at least four different 'industries'. The first, inshore or on inland waterways, secured a varied supply of 'most delicate fish';[70] this was known as 'the ordinary' but in terms of money it was worth as much as half the 'great fishery', the herring industry,[71] alongside which the other two categories – catching cod off the shores of Iceland or on the Dogger Bank,[72] and whaling (oddly enough known as 'the little fishery') were quite modest enterprises.

In about 1595,[73] the Dutch had discovered Spitzbergen and learned from Basque fishermen how to harpoon whales.[74] In January 1614, the monopoly of this fishing was granted to a Northern Company, 'from the coasts of Nova Zemblaya to the Davis Straits, including Spitzbergen, Bear Island and other places'.[75] The company was wound up in 1645,[76] but Amsterdam jealously controlled and pocketed the profits[77] from the wholesale massacre of whales in the great North, which brought her tons of oil (for the manufacture of soap, to light the lamps of the poor and for the treatment of cloth) and hundredweights of whalebone. In 1697,[78] a good year, 'a hundred and twenty-eight vessels left the ports of Holland to go "fishing" for whales, seven were lost in the ice, and 121 returned to port having captured 1255 whales which yielded 41,344 barrels of blubber. Each barrel was normally sold at 30 florins, which makes a total of 1,240,320 florins. Every whale normally yielded two thousand pounds weight of whalebone, reckoned at 50 florins a quintal, which worked out at 1,255,000 florins from 1255 whales; these two sums together came to 2,495,320 florins'.[79] This record suggests that a whaler brought home an average haul of ten whales, although in July 1698, a single ship returning to Texel had slaughtered 21.[80]

These riches were however as nothing compared to the herring fisheries off the Dogger Bank, near the English coast, during the two seasons (from St John's Day to the feast of St James and from the Exaltation of the Holy Cross to St Catherine's Day).[81] For the first half of the seventeenth century, the figures are staggering: 1500 fishing boats – large vessels with space enough on board for preparing, salting and packing the fish, which was then fetched in small boats from the fishing-grounds themselves and taken back to Holland or Zeeland (or even to England where 'Dutch' herring was sold more cheaply than that caught by English boats).[82] On these 1500 *buyssen* sailed 12,000 fishermen and something like 300,000 tons of fish. Sold all over Europe, salt and smoked herring were 'the Dutch Gold Mine'.[83] Dutch trade would be halved, Pieter de la Court reckoned, 'if the trade in fish and allied merchandise were to be subtracted from it'.[84] As Sir George Downing remarked on 8 July 1661[85] without satisfaction, 'The herring trade is the cause of the salt trade, and the herring and salt trade are the causes of this country [Holland] having, in a manner, wholly engrossed the trade of the Baltic sea, for that they have the bulky goods to load their ships with' – and the Baltic trade was after all the true source of Dutch wealth.

Can it be though, that the importance of fishing to the Dutch economy has been exaggerated? After Cromwell's Navigation Act and the first Anglo-Dutch war, (1652–4) the miraculous Dutch fisheries did lose more than two-thirds of their value,[86] but contrary to Pieter de la Court's forecast, the Dutch economy did not collapse. As for the decline of the fisheries, this is explained by the falling-off of profits as a result of rising prices and wages. Only the victuallers still derived a good living from it. But capital outlay was soon to become too onerous. Competition from foreign fishermen – French, Norwegian and Danish – did the rest. And since the same factors were at work elsewhere as well, English herring fishing never really prospered, despite being given much encouragement – here too, high costs were the explanation.[87]

The Dutch fleet

The real instrument of Dutch greatness was a fleet the equivalent of all the other European fleets put together.[88] A French estimate dated May 1669,[89] which leaves aside the very numerous '*heus* and little galliots with only one mast which cannot make long-haul voyages', arrives 'by means of calculations which I find satisfactory', writes Pomponne, at the figure of six thousand for the whole of the United Provinces. At 100 tons and eight crewmen per ship, this amounts to at least 600,000 tons and perhaps 48,000 sailors, fantastic figures for the time and probably not much of an overestimate.

Quantity went hand in hand with quality. By 1570, the Dutch boatyards had come up with a sensational merchant vessel, the *vlieboot* or *fluyt*, variously known as the 'flute' or 'flyboat', a sturdy, round-sided ship of great capacity but which could be handled by a small crew – twenty per cent smaller than on other ships of equal tonnage. This was a considerable advantage when one bears in mind that on a long voyage, labour costs (wages and food) had always been the greatest single item of expense. In this respect, Dutch thrift was much in evidence: rations on board were frugal,[90] consisting of 'Fish and Corn'; even the captains 'had to be content ... with a piece of cheese or a slice of salt beef two or three years old';[91] no wine; small beer and perhaps if the sea was rough a miserly ration of spirits. 'Of all the nations', concluded a Frenchman, 'the Dutch are the most thrifty and sober, indulging in the least luxury or idle expense.'[92]

A long French report, dated 1696, details, not without a hint of envy, all the advantages the Dutch fleet had over its rivals:

> The Dutch rarely use any ship for trade but *flutes* which are escorted in wartime by armed frigates. These *flutes* are big vessels with large holds able to contain much merchandise; they are poor sailing-ships, to tell the truth, but although of clumsy and heavy build, they stand up better to the sea and need fewer crewmen than other vessels. The French are obliged to put four or five

men aboard vessels of 20 to 30 tons in order to sail them, the Dutch put two or three at most; on a vessel of 150 to 200 tons, the French put ten or twelve men, the Dutch but seven or eight. The French put 18, 20 or 25 men on a vessel of 250, 300 or 400 tons, the Dutch only 12, 16 or at the very most 18. The French seamen earns 12, 16, 18 or 20 *livres* a month, the Dutch sailor is content with 10 or 12 *livres* and the officers are paid in proportion. French sailors have to be fed bread, wine, biscuit made of pure wheatmeal and it must be white, fresh and salt meat, cod, herring, eggs, butter, peas, beans and when they eat fish it has to be well-seasoned, and even then they will only accept it on meatless days. The Dutch are satisfied with beer, bread and rye-biscuit, often very black though with an excellent taste, cheese, eggs, butter, a little salt meat, peas, gruel, and they eat a great deal of dried fish without seasoning, every day without distinction, which costs far less than meat. The French having a hotter and more active temperament, eat four meals a day, the Dutch having a cooler temperament eat two or three at most. The French build their ships of oak timbers, with iron bolts, which costs a great deal; most of the Dutch ships, especially those which sail no further afield than France, are merely made of pine, with wooden pegs and although they are twice as big, they cost half as much to build as ours. They also have cheaper rigging, they are nearer than we are to the North, from which they can obtain iron, anchors, and hemp for cables and ropes which they manufacture themselves, as they do their sail-cloth.[93]

This was another respect in which Dutch shipping excelled: the unbeatable costs of their naval shipyards, 'the secret they have' as a French correspondent puts it, 'of building [ships] more cheaply than anyone else'.[94] No doubt this was because they were able to obtain timber for the ships, tar, pitch, rigging and all the other precious naval stores straight from the Baltic – even masts were transported on special ships.[95] But it was also because they used the most modern technology: mechanical saws, hoists for masts, the manufacture of interchangeable spare parts – and they had expert craftsmen and overseers. Consequently the famous yards at Saardam near Amsterdam could undertake, 'provided they were given two months' notice, to turn out a warship ready for rigging every week for the rest of the year'.[96] Add to this the fact that in Holland, whatever the branch of activity, credit was abundant, easy to come by and cheap. It is not surprising then that from very early on, Dutch ships were being exported abroad, notably to Venice, Spain and even Malta[97] where the Knights used them for privateering in the waters of the Levant.

Amsterdam also became the major European market for second-hand ships. If your ship was wrecked on the Dutch coast, you could within a matter of days buy a new one and transfer yourself and your crew to it without losing any time; Dutch brokers would even get hold of some freight for you. If on the other hand you had come overland to buy a ship, it was best to bring your own sailors. For the only problem about transport in Holland was the shortage of labour.

But the men did not have to be experienced mariners. It was sufficient for the responsible jobs on board ship to be in good hands. For the rest, any raw recruit

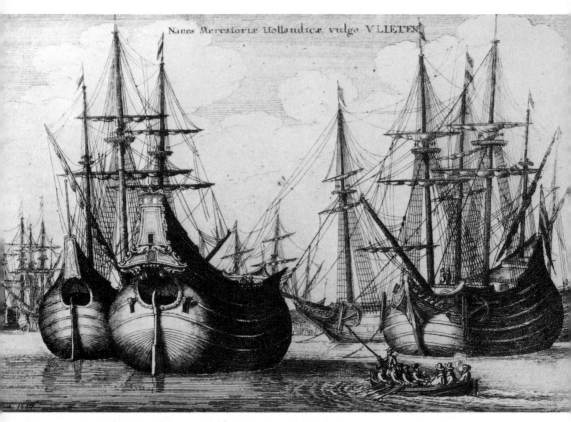

Dutch flyboats. Engraving by W. Hollar, 1647. (Atlas van Stolk.)

would do – if he could be found. Domestic recruiting – which was actively pursued in the inland villages – was not enough, any more than it had been in Venice or would be in England. So foreign seamen volunteered or were pressed into service. *Hollandgänger* who had come to work with pick, shovel or scythe, might find themselves on board ship. In 1667, there were 3000 Scottish and English sailors serving on the ships of the United Provinces[98] and according to some French correspondence, Colbert's shipbuilding programme *may* have enticed back to France 30,000 seamen, mostly from Dutch ships.[99]

These figures cannot be vouched for, but it is clear that Holland could only fulfil her role as freighter of the high seas if she could obtain the necessary extra labour from among the wretched of Europe. The wretched of Europe were only too eager to oblige. In 1688, when William of Orange was preparing to sail for England to expel James II, crews for his navy, which sailed out under the nose of Louis XIV's fleet, were not hard to find: it was enough simply to increase the enlisting bonus.[100] It was not the laziness[101] of the rest of Europe so much as its poverty which enabled the Dutch to 'set up' their Republic. Even in the eighteenth century, the shortage of native sailors, so acute in Britain, was still making itself felt in Holland. When, during the reign of Catherine II, some Russian ships put in to Amsterdam, several of their sailors jumped ship; the Dutch recruiting officers clapped hands on them and before they knew where they were, the poor wretches found themselves in the West Indies or the Far East, piteously begging to be allowed to go home.[102]

Can the United Provinces be called a 'state'?

The government in the Hague had the reputation of being weak and inconsistent. This might suggest the conclusion that an ineffective political apparatus favours the success of capitalism – indeed that it is a necessary condition. Without going as far as this, most historians would willingly endorse P. W. Klein's opinion[103] that one can hardly talk of 'anything resembling a state' in the United Provinces. Pierre Jeannin confines himself[104] to the remark that Dutch prosperity owed virtually nothing to a 'state with little capacity for intervention'. Contemporaries thought much the same. According to Sousa Coutinho, the Portuguese envoy who was negotiating in the Hague in the spring of 1647 and trying to corrupt anyone he could, the government 'being one of so many different heads and judgments, its representatives can rarely all agree on what would be best for them'.[105] Turgot writes in about 1753-4 of 'Holland, Genoa and Venice, where the state is powerless and poor, although individuals are wealthy'.[106] As an estimate of Venice, this may be true (perhaps) of the eighteenth century, though clearly not of the powerful city of the fifteenth century; how true is it of Holland?

The answer depends on what one means by the words 'government' and 'state'. If, as is only too often the case, the state and its social bases are not examined as a whole, there is a risk of jumping to false conclusions. It is true that the institutions of the United Provinces inclined towards the archaic. Their roots lay in an ancient heritage. It is true that the seven provinces considered themselves sovereign, and that they were moreover divided into tiny urban republics. It is also true that none of the central institutions – the Council of State or *Raad van Staat* (which was 'properly speaking the superintendent[107] of all the Republic's affairs',[108] a sort of executive or more accurately a Ministry of Finance) and the States-General which also sat in the Hague and was a permanent delegation of ambassadors from the provinces – had in theory any real power at all. Every important decision had to be referred to the provincial States and approved by them unanimously. Since the interests of the provinces diverged considerably – in particular those of the coastal from those of the inland provinces – this system was a perpetual source of conflict. As Sir William Temple remarked in 1672, a better name would have been the Disunited Provinces.[109]

Such clashes and internal conflicts were translated, at government level, into an endless struggle between the province of Holland, which used its financial power to impose its leadership, and the princes of the House of Orange, who 'governed', as Stadtholders, five provinces out of the seven, who presided over the Council of State and commanded the armed forces on land and sea, with the title and functions of Admiral and Captain General of the Republic. The province of Holland, represented by its Grand Pensionary, the secretary of the Council of State, always upheld the sovereignty and freedom of the provinces, for if the central authority was weak, Holland would be better placed to impose her will, thanks to her overwhelming economic superiority, and to the simple fact that she furnished more than half the total revenue of the state.[110] The Stadtholders for their part obstinately sought to establish personal power similar to that of a monarch, thus reinforcing the central authority in order to curb the predominance of Holland; to do so they drew on the jealousy the other provinces and cities felt towards Holland and Amsterdam, having been only too often in their shadow.

The resulting tensions and crises meant that the two rivals alternated at the head of the state. In 1618, during the intense religious crisis in which Arminians opposed Gomarists, Prince Maurice of Nassau ordered the arrest of Johan van Oldenbarnevelt, the Grand Pensionary of Holland, who was condemned to death and executed the following year. On 1 July 1650, the Stadtholder William II launched an attempted coup d'état, which succeeded in the Hague but failed miserably in Amsterdam. At this point, the premature death of the prince left the way clear for the 'republicans' who abolished the stadtholdership and ruled for almost a quarter-century until 1672. On the French invasion, William III restored the stadtholdership which assumed the mantle of national saviour. The Grand Pensionary Johan de Witt and his brother were massacred in the Hague. Similarly, at the much later date of 1747, the disturbing successes of the French in the Spanish Netherlands enabled William IV to restore his authority.[111] Finally in 1788, the revolution of the Dutch 'patriots', teleguided as much from outside as from inside the country, brought about by reaction the triumph of William V and unleashed the 'Orangist' persecutions.

Foreign policy had a great deal to do with these swings of power. Was the real question, as early as 1618, not so much religious passion as the dilemma of whether or not to resume the war against Spain? The victory of the Stadtholder over Holland – which as usual favoured peace – would lead two years later to the breaking of the Twelve Years' Truce.

Thus, depending on the fortunes of the wars afflicting Europe, the centre of political power in the Netherlands oscillated between the Stadtholders on one hand and Holland and the enormous power of Amsterdam on the other. For the regents of the provinces and towns, these alterations meant being subjected by turns to 'purges' or 'spoils systems', to use rather strong and anachronistic terms; as some families fell from power, certain sections of the social elite gained, others lost heavily. The exceptions were the 'weathercocks'[112] or the prudent, who lay low and emerged unscathed when everything was over; or in some cases the very patient, who were prepared to bide their time: a family might be cast out of power by one of these crises and restored by the next, twenty years later.

But whoever was in power, the United Provinces were careful to maintain their prestige and power. Johan Van Oldenbarnevelt or Johan de Witt were just as firm rulers as Maurice of Nassau or William III. What distinguished these adversaries however was ends and means. Holland was prepared to subordinate everything to commercial interests, hoping to preserve peace and to direct the Republic's military policy towards the building up of a powerful fleet as a guarantee of security (in 1645, this fleet intervened in the Baltic to put an end to the war between Sweden and Denmark which was damaging Dutch interests). The provinces loyal to the Stadtholders, on the other hand, were more concerned with the army which protected them against threats from their ever-dangerous neighbours and which offered a career to their gentlemen; they willingly succumbed to the temptation of joining in the long-running struggles of the European mainland. But whether fleet or army, war or peace, Stadtholder or Grand Pensionary had the upper hand, the United Provinces were determined to impose respect. Could a country at the heart of a world-economy have done otherwise?

Internal structures: little change

At home, changes in the colour of the government did have some importance. Burgomasters and aldermen were ousted from office and replaced; thus creating a degree of mobility *within* the privileged class, a sort of musical chairs among those eligible to exercise political power. The ruling class as a whole remained in position, however, whether Holland or the princes of Orange had the upper hand. As E. H. Kossman[113] notes, 'the princes of Orange were rarely willing and never able to supersede the Holland plutocracy'. No doubt this was because, as another historian puts it, 'in the last resort, they were themselves aristocrats and upholders of the existing social order'.[114] Perhaps it was also because they could only oppose Holland up to a point and because their interventionist foreign policy itself warned them not to disturb the internal order and the social foundations of the country.

> When the Prince of Orange, having been crowned King of England, came back for the first time to the Hague, the States-General asked him whether he wished to be received into their Assembly as the King of England, or as Admiral and Captain General of the Union. He replied that having retained with much pleasure the offices which he and his predecessors had had under the Republic, it was in the position which they conferred upon him that he desired to be received, and indeed he continued to take his usual place in the assembly of the States-General, with the difference only that instead of a chair like that of the President which he had formerly used, he was given a higher one, embroidered with the arms of the Kingdom of Great Britain.[115]

A mere matter of protocol perhaps, but was not respect for institutions a major safeguard of the Dutch oligarchy? Indeed in the eighteenth century, the latter would more than once see a guarantee of social order in the presence and actions of the Stadtholder.

In short, this privileged class was located at the centre of the entire political system. But analysing it is no straightforward matter. Like the institutions which supported it and which it operated, it went a long way back, to the 'burgher class' which had controlled the aldermen's office in the days of Burgundian and Spanish rule. The long War of Independence (1572–1609) had brought this burgher class to power; in most of the provinces, the war had ruined the aristocracy, and in spite of the religious crisis of the years 1618–19, the Reformed Church remained subordinate to the provincial and urban authorities. In the end, the 'Revolution' consecrated the power of the regent class, that is the political elite which held all the important posts in every town and province and which had virtually unlimited power over taxation, justice and the local economy.

These regents formed a group apart, above the bourgeoisie of trade which did not find it easy to penetrate their ranks. But their offices barely supported their incumbents: their salaries were derisory, a factor which kept those without fortunes away. In one way or another, the regents were bound to share in the growing wealth of the United Provinces. They had contacts with the business world; some of them even came directly from this milieu, since families which had acquired wealth might one day find their way into an apparently closed political oligarchy, either through marriage or during a political crisis. This power elite nevertheless formed a very special group, a kind of patriciate. There were perhaps 2000 regents, who called on one another's services, who came from the same background (money and power), who controlled not only the towns and provinces, but the States-General, the Council of State and the Dutch East India Company, who had connections with the merchant class and often continued to participate in commercial and industrial enterprises. B. M. Vlekke has referred to an 'oligarchy' of about 10,000,[116] but this seems rather a high figure unless it is read as including all the members of every family.

During the Golden Age of the seventeenth century however, the regents did not indulge in patrician hauteur or ostentation. For a long time, they cultivated a sober and discreet image in their dealings with a population of which contemporaries tell us that it was habitually insolent and violently attached to its liberty. 'It is by no means new', writes the author of *Délices de la Hollande* (1662),[117] 'to hear a *gallefretier*[118] in some small dispute with an honest Burgher, uttering injurious words such as, "I am as good a man as you, even if you are richer …", and other similar things which are hard to stomach. But wise men are sensible enough to avoid such encounters, and the rich retreat as much as they can from communication with common people, that they may be the more respected by them'.[119]

This text would be more helpful to us if it shed some light on the motives of such 'small disputes'. It is however clear that in the supposedly peaceful seven-teenth century, social tensions were already present. Money was the means by which anyone could be brought to order, but a means which it was prudent to conceal. Was it out of good taste or instinctive shrewdness that the rich men of Amsterdam over a long period refrained from flaunting their wealth and opulence, quite naturally and good-humouredly? 'However absolute the Magistrate', remarks a guidebook of 1701, 'there is no pomp displayed, and one may see these illustrious burgomasters walking about the town with no train of attendants, being in every way indistinguishable from the Burghers who are subordinate to them.'[120] Sir William Temple was himself astonished in 1672 that men as eminent as Johan de Witt, the Grand Pensionary of Holland, or Michael de Ruyter, the greatest mariner of his day, were not distinguished respectively from 'the commonest burgher of the town', or 'the commonest sea-captain'.[121] The houses on the Herengracht, Amsterdam's Quality Street, did not have magnificent facades. And inside them one would not, during the Golden Age, have found the luxury of rich furniture.

But this discretion, tolerance and lack of distinctions began to change with the coming to power in 1650 of the 'republicans'. From now on, the oligarchy would have to take on many new tasks and would lend itself to progressive bureaucratization, very largely withdrawing from business. And the temptation was great for Dutch high society, now prodigiously wealthy, to yield to luxury. 'Seventy years ago', notes Isaac de Pinto in 1771, 'the wealthiest businessmen [in Amsterdam] did not have gardens or country houses comparable to those their brokers own today. The worst thing is not so much the building and immense expense of maintaining these fairy-tale palaces, or rather bottomless pits, it is that the distraction and negligence occasioned by this luxury often causes great prejudice to business and trade.'[122] Indeed, by the eighteenth century, trade was progressively becoming a secondary activity for the moneyed class. Surplus capital forsook trade and turned to government stocks, finance and credit operations. And this society of rentiers with too much money gradually closed its ranks, becoming more and more cut off from the rest of society.

The gulf was deeply felt in the cultural sphere. The elite of the time abandoned its national tradition and welcomed with open arms the French influence which was to carry all before it. The Dutch school of painting barely survived the death of Rembrandt (1669). 'While the French invasion of 1672 failed militarily and politically, it succeeded almost completely on the cultural plane.'[123] The very language of the French gained ascendancy here as elsewhere in Europe, and this was one more way of standing aloof from the mass of people. In 1673, Pieter de Groot was already writing to Abraham de Wiquefort of 'French which is for intelligent people' and 'Flemish which is only for the ignorant'.[124]

Overleaf: The Damplatz in Amsterdam in 1659, by Jacob van der Ulft, Musée Condé, Chantilly. (Photo Giraudon.)

Taxing the poor

Dutch society being what it was, it is no surprise to find that the fiscal system spared capital. Foremost among personal taxes was the *Heere Geld*, a tax on domestic servants: 5 florins 16 sous for one servant; 10 florins 6 sous for two; but only 11 florins 12 sous for three, 12 florins 18 sous for 4, 14 florins 14 sous for 5 – a curiously *regressive* tax. There was a form of income tax, undemanding by present standards: 1%, or 15 florins on an income of 1500 florins, 12 florins on one of 1200. Under 300 florins, no tax was paid. Finally, 'those who have no fixed income and who only live by commerce or by the profession they exercise, are taxed according to the estimated product of their commerce or profession'.[125] It was always possible to find ways of defending oneself against an *estimate* of taxable income. Lastly, a privilege which was as valuable here as it was in France, no death duties were payable on a direct inheritance.[126]

The main fiscal burden fell on indirect taxes, a weapon used by the States-General as well as by the provincial or urban authorities. The consumer came under a continuous fiscal barrage. Observers all agree that no other state, in the seventeenth or eighteenth century, laboured under such a weight of taxation. In the eighteenth century, there were purchase taxes, known as excise duties, on 'wines and strong spirits, vinegar, beer, grain of every kind, flour, fruit, potatoes,[127] butter, timber and firewood, peat, coal, salt, soap, fish, tobacco, pipes, lead, tiles, bricks, stone of all kinds, marble'.[128] There was some talk in 1748[129] of scrapping the whole complicated edifice. But the plan had to be abandoned, for no general tax was capable of absorbing so many particular taxes which had gradually been established and to which the consumer had more or less grown accustomed. No doubt a large number of small taxes were easier to manœuvre than one big one. At all events, the large number of minor taxes was the major feature of the fiscal system. One observer found it amusing: 'A cow that is sold for sixty francs will already have paid 70 *livres*. A plate of meat cannot come to table without first paying excise about twenty times over'.[130] In fact [says a memorandum of 1689]:

> there is no kind of foodstuff which does not pay the excise or consumption tax; that which is levied on milled grain and beer is so heavy that it is always equal to the value of the goods at normal prices; they have even found a way of making beer dear, using their usual skill, for in order to prevent a given product being sold in their country, when their commitments do not allow them openly to prevent it crossing the border, they tax consumption of the product in their country so heavily that no private individual wants to bring in any for his own consumption, nor any merchant for sale, for fear of finding no custom.[131]

Indirect taxes, an essential element in a high cost of living, hit the poor hardest. The rich evaded them or could stand the burden better. Merchants for instance had the right, at customs posts or tolls, of declaring in person the value of the taxable goods. They could say whatever they pleased,[132] and once past the barrier there was no further check. Can a more systematically unjust society or state possibly be imagined? Under the stadtholdership of William IV, it took a riot, which he had to some extent provoked, to put an end to the system of tax-farming.[133] But the establishment of a state customs service (50,000 employees in the province of Holland alone)[134] did nothing to alter the fundamental unfairness of the system.

This was logical enough: the rich taxpayer, who could find ways of resisting a remarkably tough fiscal system, was a regular subscriber to loans launched by the States-General, the provinces or the towns. In about 1764, the United Provinces, with an assured income of some 120 million florins, had a debt of 400 million at very low interest – evidence surely that here was a strong state never short of money whether for public works, mercenary armies, or fitting a fleet? It was also a state which managed its national debt skilfully. 'Since it never fails to pay the interest', Isaac de Pinto explains, 'nobody ever dreams of withdrawing his capital; moreover, whenever they want money, *they can negotiate government stocks advantageously.'*[135] The last words are in my italics: they explain this item from the *Journal du commerce* in January 1759: 'Public stocks in Holland ... yield only 2½ per cent interest, but they can make four or five per cent on the market',[136] that is they could be sold at 104 or 105 having been issued at 100. If the state needed a loan, subscribers came running. 'A proof of the wealth of private individuals in Holland and the great abundance of money in the country', writes a correspondent from the Hague in August 1744, 'is that three million annuities at six per cent and repayable bonds at 2½ per cent were accounted for in ten hours, and if the stock had been 15 million it would have been spoken for similarly; but the state coffers are not like private purses – the latter are full but the treasury is almost empty; however in cases of need, it is possible to raise ample resources by some manoeuvring of the finances, in particular by a tax on each family.'[137]

'Cases of need' occurred regularly: wars were bottomless pits; what was more, this 'artificial' country had to be rebuilt physically every year. In fact 'maintenance of the dykes and the highways costs the state more than [tax on] land brings in'.[138] 'However the product of commerce and consumption is immense, in spite of the miserliness of the artisans who outbid French sobriety without reaping the same benefits, since labour is much dearer here than in France.'[139] This brings us back to the high cost of living – normal at the core of a world-economy: the privileged country may even find it to its advantage. But like all advantages, this might be overturned one day. Did its beneficial effects only develop when it was underpinned by thriving production? In the eighteenth century, it so happened that production fell, while wages, to use Jan de Vries's expression, remained 'petrified', 'fossilized'[140] at high levels. Taxation was certainly to blame. But if the needs of the state were met at the expense of the community, is that really the sign of a 'weak state'?

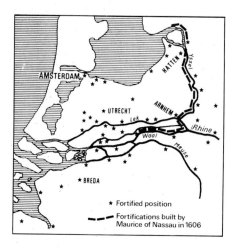

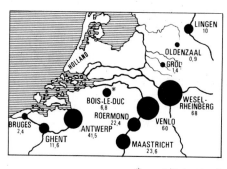

* now 's Hertogenbosch

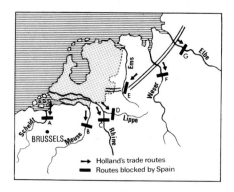

→ Holland's trade routes
▬ Routes blocked by Spain

21 THE UNITED PROVINCES AND SPAIN

I *The United Provinces turned into a fortified island*

During the last decades of the sixteenth century, all the towns in the Netherlands, like those of the rest of Europe, built fortifications 'in the Italian style', with bastions. From now on, cannon would not be able to breach the walls as they had those of medieval towns. Long and costly sieges were now the only way of capturing towns. In 1605–6, Maurice of Nassau completed these 'modernized' defences by building a continuous line of small forts and earthworks along the major rivers, turning the United Provinces into a fortress. (From Geoffrey Parker, *The Army of Flanders and the Spanish Road, 1567–1659*, 1971, pp. 14–15 and 7.)

II *The importance of inland trade to the United Provinces*

The real danger as far as the United Provinces were concerned was being cut off from the waterways linking their commerce with Germany and the Spanish Netherlands. The importance of these links is shown by the receipts of customs posts under Spanish control: 300,000 crowns a year in 1623 (the renewed outbreak of war in 1621 when the Twelve Years' Truce was broken did not immediately interrupt trade with the United Provinces). Alongside the name of each town is the contribution it paid in thousands of crowns. (From José Alcala-Zamora y Queipo de Llano, *España, Flandes y el mar del Norte, 1618–1639*, 1975, p. 184.)

III *An attempted blockade in 1624–7*

In 1624, the Spanish set up a blockade of waterways and of the route travelled by cattle on the hoof from Denmark (marked with a double line). But they were unable to continue this expensive policy after 1627. Was the reason the economic crisis and the bankruptcy of the Spanish state in that year? (*Ibid.*, p. 185.)

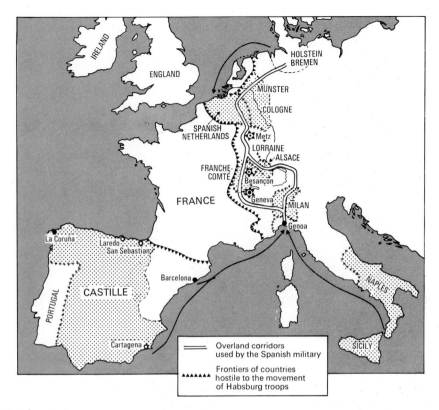

IV *Land against sea*

Since communication by sea was difficult the Spanish war effort depended on a logistic system (based on Sicily, Naples, the Milanese, Franche-Comté, and the Spanish Netherlands and dependent on the friendship or neutrality of many German states) which consisted of a series of permanent corridors carrying traffic over the Alps and up to the North Sea. The Spanish route is shown on the map as extending to Holstein, which was an area of recruitment of soldiers for the Flanders army. (From Geoffrey Parker, *op. cit.*, p. 51.)

The United Provinces and the outside world

That the United Provinces had, on the contrary, a strong state is demonstrated by their foreign policy during the Golden Age of the Republic, until the 1680s or so, when their decline as an important power in Europe began to be visible.

Between 1618 and 1648, during the Thirty Years' War, when we historians tend to have eyes only for the Habsburgs or the Bourbons, Richelieu, Mazarin or the count duke Olivares, was the leading role not very often played by Holland? The threads of diplomacy were woven and unwoven at the Hague. It was here that the successive interventions of Denmark (1626), Sweden (1629) and even France (1635) were organized. Nevertheless like any self-respecting economic centre, the United Provinces kept war at arm's length: a string of forts

The capture, by the Dutch West Indies Company, of Spanish ships carying silver, off Havana, 8 September 1628. Engraving by Visscher. (Atlas van Stolk.)

along the frontiers reinforced the obstacles created by the many waterways. Mercenary troops, few in number but 'hand-picked, very well paid and well-fed',[141] trained in the most advanced kind of warfare, had the task of seeing that the Provinces remained an island sheltered from conflict.

Note also how the Dutch fleet in 1645 intervened in the Baltic to put an end to the war between Denmark and Sweden which was damaging Dutch interests. If the United Provinces held back, despite the efforts of the princes of Orange, from any policy of conquest in the Spanish Netherlands, it was not out of weakness. Was it in the interests of the merchants of Amsterdam to go and liberate Antwerp, when the mouth and the blockade of the Scheldt were in their hands? Note how in Münster, the delegates from the Dutch states made repeated demands on the French, then played them false. 'It is pitiful to see how these deputies treat us', wrote Servien.[142] Or to take another landmark, note how the United Provinces succeeded in concluding a Triple Alliance with England and Sweden and bringing a halt to the worrying incursions of Louis XIV into the Spanish Netherlands. In the years 1669 and 1670, which were crucial to the entire history of Europe, Johan de Witt, the Grand Pensionary in whose firm hands the Dutch forces were concentrated, and Louis XIV's ambassador, the admirable Pomponne, held courteous talks, on an equal footing. I do not have the impression, from a careful study of their relations, that the Dutchman felt the slightest inferiority complex in dealing with the representative of the

Sun King. He explained very calmly (and to my mind lucidly) to the incredulous ambassador, exactly why France was hardly in a position to impose her will on Holland.

No, it certainly cannot be said that the Dutch government was non-existent, though it was not so much a matter of government as of sheer economic weight. During the negotiations for the Peaces of Nijmwegen (1678), Ryswick (1697) and Utrecht (1713), the United Provinces continued to carry weight. The rise of England and France was taking place slowly but surely at Holland's expense, increasingly revealing its inadequacy and fragility but this was a development whose fruits would take time to show.

When business was king

The interests which Dutch policy and life were unceasingly defending and safeguarding, throughout all these favourable and hostile circumstances, were those of commerce as a whole. Such interests dictated and outweighed all else, something which neither religious passion (after 1672 for instance) nor national sentiment (after 1780) were ever able to do. Foreign observers often claimed to be scandalized at the spectacle, and whether their remarks are sincere, or objective, or neither, they do help us to see it a little more clearly.

How indeed could one fail to be astonished that Dutch merchants, annoyed by the V.O.C.[143] and jealous of its privileges, should have launched, or supported with their own capital, rival Indies companies – in England, Denmark, Sweden, France and even Ostend? That they should have invested money in French privateering out of Dunkirk, which was occasionally directed against ships belonging to their compatriots?[144] That Dutch merchants should be in league with the Barbary corsairs operating in the North Sea (though it is true that many of these so-called 'Barbary' pirates were in fact renegade Dutchmen)? That in 1629, after the capture of a number of Spanish galleons off Havana, the shareholders of the Dutch West Indies Company should have insisted on the immediate division of the spoils – a request which being granted, opened the first chink in the Company's armour?[145] Similarly it was with arms bought from the Dutch that the Portuguese expelled the latter from Recife in 1654 and that Louis XIV attacked the Republic in 1672. During the War of the Spanish Succession, payments to the French troops fighting in Italy were made through Amsterdam, to the infuriation of the English who were allied to the Dutch against France. In short, for the Dutch, commerce was king, and in Holland commercial interests effectively replaced *raison d'état*: 'Commerce desires to be free', wrote Pieter de la Court in 1662.[146] 'Gain is the sole and unique compass by which these people are guided', exclaims La Thuillerie,[147] the French ambassador, in a letter to Mazarin on 31 March 1648. At about the same period, in 1644, the directors of the Dutch East India Company were energetically arguing that 'the places and strongholds which [the *Heeren XVII*][148] captured in the East Indies should not be regarded as national conquests but as the property of private merchants, who were entitled to sell those places to whomsoever they wished, even if it was to the King of Spain or to some other enemy of the United Provinces'.[149] Holland's enemies – of whom there was no shortage – had no difficulty in drawing up long lists of such charges, in all good conscience, as if the faults of others were somehow a proof of one's own merit. A Frenchman wrote for instance:

> In Holland, the interest of the State in matters of commerce serves that of the private individual, they go hand in hand [in other words, the state and commercial society were one and the same thing.] Commerce is absolutely free, absolutely nothing is forbidden the merchants, they have no rule to follow but that of their own interests: this is an established maxim which the State regards as a thing essential to itself. So when an individual seems to do, in his own commercial interests, something contrary to the State, the State turns a blind eye and pretends not to notice, as is easy to judge by what occurred in 1693 and 1694. France was short of grain, famine was widespread in the provinces. The war had reached a critical point, this appeared to be the fatal moment for France and one favourable to the allies united against her. Could there have been any greater *raison d'état* than for the said Dutchmen and their allies to have contributed to France's defeat and to have obliged her at the very least to agree to peace on terms which they would dictate? Far from providing her with grain, should they not have sought every means within their power to deprive her of it completely? They were not ignorant of this political circumstance, for they published stern prohibitions forbidding all merchants and masters of vessels under their rule to go to France on any pretext; but did that prevent Dutch merchants communicating with the said French merchants in order to send grain to France, using Swedish and Danish vessels, or their own vessels flying the assumed flag of neutral nations, or what was even worse, their own ships flying the Dutch flag?[150]

In Amsterdam, however, no one voiced any criticism of such attitudes, nor of the speculation and series of embezzlements typified by Isaac Le Maire's criminal activities at the end of the seventeenth century.[151] Business was business. According to the self-appointed moralists from abroad, anything could happen in this country 'which is not like any other'. During the second Anglo-Dutch war (1665–7) the French ambassador, the count d'Estrades, even imagined that there was 'a risk of this country submitting to the English. There is a great cabal within the state with this aim'.[152]

Traders to Europe, traders to the world

The first condition for Dutch greatness was Europe. The second was the world – could it not be said indeed that the one followed from the other? Once Holland had conquered the trade of Europe, the rest of the world was a logical bonus, thrown in as it were. But in both cases, Holland used very similar methods to impose her commercial supremacy or rather monopoly, whether close to home or far away.

The seeds of success had all been sown by 1585

During the Middle Ages, the Baltic was a sort of America on Europe's doorstep. By the fifteenth century, Dutch ships carrying fish and salt were competing there with Hanseatic shipping. At Speyer in 1544[153] Charles V obtained from the king of Denmark free passage for Flemish vessels through the Sound. Ten years later, following a serious shortage in their homelands, the Genoese and Portuguese merchants of Antwerp were addressing their requests for grain to Amsterdam, which had become in the intervening years and to Antwerp's detriment, the major redistribution port for grain,[154] 'the Cornbin of Europe' as it was soon to be known. Success came on a grand scale: by 1560, the Dutch had succeeded in attracting 70% of the heavy Baltic trade.[155] From now on the takeover was secure. Grain and naval stores – planks, beams, masts, tar, pitch – flowed into Amsterdam and what the Dutch called the 'mother commerce'[156] was still, in Holland's Golden Age, absorbing up to 60% of the circulating capital of the United Provinces, and up to 800 ships a year. According to Astrid Friis, the flow of raw materials from the Baltic was the motive force behind the economic and political changes of the seventeenth century.[157]

Important though it might be, Baltic trade was only one piece in the Dutch jigsaw. Trade from these countries could not fully prosper without the exploitation of the far-off Iberian peninsula, the source of the metal currencies which were increasingly becoming the key to trade in the Baltic. A way had to be forced into the trade of countries bordering the latter sea, and the gap between sales and purchases there made good with specie.

But it was precisely the redistribution of Baltic grain which led to the successful penetration of the south by Dutch shipping. Having triumphed in the Baltic, it was soon to triumph in Laredo, Santander, Bilbao, Lisbon and later Seville. By 1530, or at latest 1550,[158] Flemish hookers were handling most of the maritime trade between the North and the Portuguese and Spanish ports. They would soon be carrying five-sixths of the goods exchanged between the Iberian peninsula and the north Atlantic: wheat, rye, naval stores and the industrial products of northern Europe (which Seville re-exported to the New World) in exchange for salt, oil, wool, wine and above all silver.

The capture of this shipping route coincided moreover with the opening of the Amsterdam Bourse (Stock Exchange); and a further coincidence was the rebuilding of the Bourse (1592) immediately after the large-scale shipping of grain to Mediterranean countries began (1590-1);[159] not long afterwards, a Chamber of Insurance was founded (1598).[160]

The north-south link was and remained vital for both parties, so much so that the revolt of the Netherlands (1572-1609) did not sever it. The relationship betwen the rebel provinces and the Spain-Portugal bloc was, to repeat the term Germaine Tillion used in 1962 to describe France and Algeria during the Algerian war, that of 'complementary enemies'.[161] They were neither willing nor able to break off relations. In Spain there were irritation, anger and even repressive measures loudly proclaimed. In 1595, Philip II had 400 Dutch ships seized in peninsular ports (in those days trading with the enemy was not subject to an embargo as would be the case today); they were said to represent two-fifths of the Dutch fleet, reckoned at one thousand vessels at this period.[162] But the confiscated ships, although at first commandeered for service, were eventually released, or released themselves. In 1596 and again in 1598, Spanish ports were once more closed to them, but the measures were impossible to enforce. Similarly, various grand designs, entertained briefly, of bringing the rebels to their knees by refusing them the salt of Setubal and Cadiz, remained at the planning stage.[163] In any case, the salt-marshes of the French Atlantic seaboard, at Brouage and Bourgneuf, were always accessible – and indeed produced salt superior, for northern preserving purposes, to that of the Iberian peninsula. Last and most important of all, Spain, once self-sufficient in grain, had since 1560 been the victim of a crisis which had thrown her agriculture into upheaval.[164] She was at the mercy of foreign grain, hardly any of which, by the end of the sixteenth century, came from the Mediterranean. When Portugal was conquered in 1580, the occupied country was literally at starvation point; appeals had to be sent to the north and the payments, which had to be made in gold, threw into confusion the normal specie transfers of the Spanish system, even in the Mediterranean.[165] Some weight was also attached to the arguments of Philip II's advisers, to wit that to ban trade with the rebels would mean depriving the Spanish exchequer of a million ducats in customs revenue a year.[166] In fact Spain had no choice but to accept this distasteful but necessary exchange; and the United Provinces were in the same situation.

Investigations held in Seville in 1595[167] revealed the presence in the city of individuals in scarcely-concealed communication with merchants in the north; their correspondence was seized and certain Spanish persons in high places – so high in fact that the investigator dared not name names – were compromised. By this date, the silent takeover of Seville by the Dutch had already been accomplished.[168] Until 1568, the Genoese bankers had been financing Seville's trade with the Americas, offering credit to local merchants, and thus enabling them to overcome the long delays occasioned by the interminable Atlantic crossings.

After 1568, the Genoese had withdrawn this source of credit, preferring to invest their money in loans to the king of Spain, and leaving a gap which the merchants of the north hastened to fill. They advanced not money – this was still beyond their means – but merchandise, payment for which they would recover when the fleet returned. Thus a further section of the web was spun: the northerners had now gained a permanent footing in Spanish trade with the West Indies. Spanish merchants in Seville, from now on increasingly tools in other people's hands, became factors or front men for northern merchants, since in theory trading with the *Carrera de Indias* was exclusively reserved for Spanish nationals. This helps to explain the curious incident which occurred in 1596. Sixty ships carrying merchandise bound for the Indies were captured in the bay of Cadiz when the English sacked the port. The victors made a proposal: they would not burn the ships – worth altogether more than 11 million ducats – on condition an indemnity of two million ducats was paid over immediately. But on this occasion, it was not the Spanish who were threatened with losses: all the merchandise belonged to Dutch merchants. Was this why the duke of Medina Sidonia – while remaining the friend, not to say the accomplice of the Dutch – refused the tempting offer? The ships, at any rate, went up in flames.[169]

To sum up then, the first major boost for Dutch fortunes resulted from the liaison established by Dutch ships and merchants between a northern pole consisting of the Baltic trade and the industry of Flanders, France and Germany, and a southern pole, that of Seville, the gateway to America. Spain received raw materials and manufactured articles; the Dutch received, officially or otherwise, the equivalent in cash. And this money, the key to their trade in the Baltic, where they had a deficit, was the means of putting pressure on these markets and eliminating competition. One can only shake one's head at the effort made by the earl of Leicester when he was sent by Elizabeth I, in 1585-7, to the Netherlands, at a time when they were nominally under the protection of the queen of England: he seriously proposed to the Dutch that they sever their trading links with Spain![170]

Holland's fortune was evidently built on *both* Spain and the Baltic. To neglect either of these would be to fail to understand a process in which wheat on one hand and American bullion on the other played indissociable roles. If a greater share of the precious metals arriving in Seville (and after 1650 in Cadiz) was being diverted into fraudulent channels, this was because the flow of bullion had *not* declined catastrophically, as we now know from Michel Morineau's work.[171] And if Spain, undoubtedly in difficulties at this time, decided or was compelled to issue so many bad copper currencies after 1605,[172] it was because as bad money drove out good, this was the price she had to pay for pursuing her political designs in Europe. In 1627 moreover, Olivares, having got rid of the Genoese moneylenders (or having been forsaken by them), was beginning to turn to Portuguese *marranos* for assistance with the finances of Castile. And these new financial backers were in close contact with northern merchants and

Dutch installations for processing whale oil, on Jan Mayen Island, east of Greenland. Painting by C. de Man, seventeenth century. (Rijksmuseum, Amsterdam.)

capital:[173] a strange and ambiguous situation of which mention has already been made.

Finally, was not the finishing touch to Amsterdam's emergence as a world centre contributed once more by Spain? The Spanish had devastated the southern Netherlands, where the war dragged on for years; they had recaptured Antwerp in August 1585, thereby destroying, albeit unintentionally, the life force of Amsterdam's chief rival; and they had made the young Republic the unchallenged rallying-point of Protestant Europe, while still allowing it considerable access to American silver.

The rest of Europe and the Mediterranean

If one were to draw a series of maps showing Holland's trade expansion, one would see her empire gradually reaching all the major axes of European trade, travelling up the Rhine, as far as the Alpine passes, reaching the important fairs of Frankfurt and Leipzig, Poland, the Scandinavian countries and Russia. In the 1590s, when there were cereal shortages in the Mediterranean, Dutch ships passed through the Straits of Gibraltar and, like the English who had preceded them here by a good twenty years, were soon sailing the major routes of the sea, while also participating, to the discomfiture of the Italian cities, in the profitable coasting trade. It has been claimed that Jewish merchants[174] helped the Dutch to penetrate the Mediterranean, but the circumstances of the time also drew them south. Before long, they had been welcomed into all the Mediterranean ports, but were particularly to be found on the Barbary coast, in Livorno, that strange city rebuilt by the Medicis, and also in the Levant ports and Istanbul where the door was opened for them by the capitulation signed in 1612. In any general evaluation of the rise of Holland, the essential part played by Europe and the eminent part played by the Mediterranean should not be underestimated. The success of their expeditions in the Indian Ocean did not divert the Dutch, as might have been expected, from the traditional circuits of the Mediterranean. R.T. Rapp has even proved in a recent article that the Dutch, quite as much as the English, found in the rich inland sea a goldmine, which they thoroughly exploited and which, even more than their activities in the Atlantic, helped their early fortunes.

In any case, how could the Dutch, once Holland had become the centre of a world-economy, afford to neglect any of its peripheries, or to allow any other rival economic empire to be built up outside their own?

The Dutch versus the Portuguese, or the art of the takeover bid

If Europe accepted the early stages of Dutch supremacy without taking much notice, it may have been because the process was at first discreet and seemed to pose little threat; and also because the centre of European gravity had shifted northwards almost imperceptibly, as the reversal of the secular trend between 1600 and 1650 divided the continent in two: one half, the south, was becoming poorer, while the other, the north, maintained above average living standards.

Long-term control of the European world-economy evidently called for the capture of its long-distance trade, and therefore of American and Asian products. America was tackled belatedly and unsuccessfully by its diminutive challenger, but the Dutch waged a brilliant campaign in the Far East, the realm of pepper, spices, drugs, pearls and silk, forcing their way in and winning the lion's share of trade; it was here that their economic leadership of the world was finally consolidated.

The way had been paved for their venture by voyages of reconnaissance, J.H. Van Linschoten's in 1582;[175] and Cornelis Houtman's in 1592[176] – the latter in conditions worthy of a spy thriller. Houtman disguised himself and took passage aboard a Portuguese ship to the Indies; on arrival, he was unmasked and thrown into jail. The reader may be glad to learn that the merchants of Rotterdam paid for his ransom, got him out of prison and as soon as he returned, equipped him with four ships which sailed from Rotterdam on 2 April 1595. Houtman reached Bantam in the East Indies and was back in Amsterdam on 14 August 1597.[177] His return journey was modest: less than a hundred men and a few goods in three vessels, bringing derisory profits. Economically, the voyage had not been worthwhile. But it brought certain promise of future profits, so was regarded as a major pioneering event (and is celebrated by a rather bad painting in the Amsterdam City Museum).

There was to be nothing sensational however about an expansion which happened slowly but steadily and was, in the early stages at any rate, deliberately discreet, preferring peaceful methods to compulsion.[178] The almost-centenarian Portuguese empire was in no fit state to bar the way to the newcomers. As for the merchants of the United Provinces, they were prepared to communicate with the enemy himself if it would assure their ships a safe passage, witness one Noel Caron, an agent in England for the *Estados rebeldes*, who privately fitted a ship for the East Indies, putting all his wealth, his *caudal*, into the venture, and in order to do so carried on a correspondence with a Spanish agent of his acquaintance in Calais.[179]

Was it the desire to avoid trouble that led Dutch captains to sail directly to the East Indies? From the Cape of Good Hope, there was a choice of routes: one could take the 'inner' route, along the coast of Mozambique, which caught the northern monsoon and went by India; or the 'outer' or rather high seas route, which went by the east coast of Madagascar, the Mascarene islands, then took the channel through the hundred or so Maldive islands before making straight for Sumatra and the Sunda Strait in order to reach Bantam, the chief port of Java. This route used not the monsoons but the trade winds; it was the itinerary chosen by Cornelis Houtman who arrived in Bantam on 22 June 1596, after a long crossing on the open sea. Was the choice of this route dictated by the desire to avoid India, where the Portuguese presence was more firmly established than elsewhere? Or, as is perfectly possible, did it correspond to a deliberate decision from the start in favour of the East Indies and fine spices? It was the route taken, incidentally, by Arab navigators making for Sumatra and also anxious to avoid the Portuguese.

It is at any rate quite clear that Dutch merchants at first nursed the hope that their expeditions might be regarded as purely commercial operations. In June 1595, Cornelis Houtman had reached the equator in the Atlantic Ocean when he met two enormous Portuguese carracks on their way to Goa: the meeting was a peaceful one, during which 'Portuguese conserves' were exchanged for 'cheese and hams', and the ships parted company only after 'saluting one another civilly with a cannon-shot apiece'.[180] Jacob Cornelis Van Neck[181] protested loudly (though how sincerely we do not know) when he returned to Holland in April 1599, at the rumours spread about Amsterdam by Jews of Portuguese origin, according to which his rich and profitable cargo (400% profits) had been extorted by force and fraud. There was not a shred of truth in this, he declared, for he had followed the instructions of his directors and taken care not to 'rob anyone of [his] property, but to trade uprightly with all foreign nations'. Nevertheless on the voyage of Etienne Van der Hagen, 1599–1601, the Portuguese fort of Amboyna was subjected to a regular attack, although to no purpose.[182]

The creation on 20 March 1602,[183] on the initiative of the States-General, the Grand Pensionary Barneveldt and Maurice of Nassau, of a chartered East India Company, the *Vereenigde Oost-Indische Compagnie* (V.O.C.) which brought together under a single body the previous companies (*voorkompagnien*) and which was to conduct itself like an independent power, a state within a state (*staat-builen-de-staat*), would change everything. It meant the end of undisciplined voyages: between 1598 and 1602, 65 ships had been sent in 14 fleets.[184] From now on there would be a single policy, a single direction and a single control of Asian affairs: that of the Company, an empire in itself, and one given to continuous expansion.

However, the power of good conscience was such that, even in 1608, merchants who had participated in voyages to the East Indies from the start, were still objecting to any violence, protesting that their ships had only been equipped to handle honest trade, not to build forts or to capture Portuguese carracks. They still shared the illusion at this time – and *a fortiori* after the signing in Antwerp on 9 April 1609 of the Twelve Years' Truce[185] which suspended hostilities between the United Provinces and the Catholic king – that they could calmly collect their share in the Asian bonanza, particularly since the peace treaty said nothing about areas south of the equator. The south Atlantic and the Indian Ocean were virtually free zones. In February 1610, a Dutch vessel bound for the East Indies put in to Lisbon, and asked the viceroy for the Catholic king's consent that the truce be announced and applied in the Far East, an indication incidentally that fighting was still going on there. The viceroy sent to Madrid for instructions, which took so long to come that the Dutch vessel, having orders to wait only twenty days, left Lisbon without the desired response.[186] This is only a single incident. Does it prove that the Dutch wanted peace, or merely that they were prudent?

Their eastward expansion meantime was proceeding with brio. In 1600 a Dutch ship reached Kyushu, the southernmost island of the Japanese archipelago;[187] in 1601, 1604 and 1607, the Dutch attempted to trade directly with Canton, by-passing the Portuguese station at Macao;[188] by 1603 they were landing in Ceylon;[189] in 1604, they launched an unsuccessful attack on Malacca;[190] in 1605, they captured the Portuguese fortress at Amboyna in the Moluccas which thus became the first solid base of the Indies Company;[191] in 1610, they were harassing Spanish ships in the Malacca straits, and captured Ternate.[192]

From now on, in spite of the truce, conquest was pursued, not without difficulty. The Company had indeed to face not only the Portuguese and the Spanish (the latter, based in Manila and active in the Moluccas, hung on to Tidore until 1663)[193] but also the English, who without having any precise plan of action, tended to appear here and there; and last but not least, the active

An attack made on 8 June 1660 against the town of Macassar in the Celebes by Dutch warships. The fortifications and Portuguese vessels were destroyed and burned. The Dutch did not however gain control of the island until 1667-9.
Drawing by Fred Woldemar, B.N., Paris, Maps dept., Y832. (Photo B.N.)

throngs of Asian merchants: Turks, Armenians, Javanese, Chinese, Bengalis, Arabs, Persians, Muslims from Gujerat. Since the East Indies were the major trade crossroads between India on one hand and China and Japan on the other, domination and control of this centre was the extremely difficult task the Dutch set themselves. One of the first governors of the Company in the Indies, Jan Pieterszoon Coen[194] (1617-23, 1627-9) viewed the situation with astonishing clairvoyance: he called for effective and permanent occupation; urged that the enemy should be relentlessly attacked; that fortresses be built; and that the islands be peopled, or as we would say, colonized. The Company finally shrank from the cost of this ambitious programme and the debate ended with a defeat for the imaginative governor. This was an early version of the eternal conflict between colonizer and merchant, which the merchant invariably won.

But the logic of events would one day bring about the inevitable. The foundation of Batavia in 1619 had concentrated on one privileged spot most of Dutch power and trade in the East Indies. And it was from this stable point and from the 'spice islands', that the Dutch wove the immense web of traffic and exchange which would eventually make up their empire, a fragile and flexible one built, like the Portuguese empire, 'on the Phoenician model'. By about 1616, constructive contacts had already been made with Japan; in 1624, Formosa had been reached; it is true that an attack on Macao had failed two years earlier in 1622. And it was only in 1638 that Japan expelled the Portuguese, consenting to receive only Dutch vessels, apart from Chinese junks, after this date. Finally, in 1641, the Dutch took Malacca whose swift decline they engineered to their own advantage; in 1667, the kingdom of Achem in the island of Sumatra surrendered;[195] in 1669 it was the turn of Macassar;[196] and in 1682 that of Bantam, an ancient and prosperous port, the rival of Batavia.[197]

But it was impossible to maintain any presence in the East Indies without some contact with India, which dominated the whole Asiatic world-economy, from the Cape of Good Hope to Malacca and the Moluccas. Whether they wanted to or not, the Dutch were forced to approach Indian ports. They could not resign themselves in Sumatra, or anywhere else where pepper was exchanged for Indian cottons, to settling their accounts in cash or buying cottons from Coromandel or Gujerat 'at second hand'. So they had found their way to Mazulipatam by 1605, and to Surat by 1606,[198] although they were not entirely at home in the latter port, the biggest in all India, until 1621.[199] They founded factories between 1616 and 1619, in Broach, Cambay, Ahmedabad, Agra, and Burhanpur.[200] Their penetration of primitive and fertile Bengal was slow (and not really achieved until 1650 or so). In 1638, they secured a footing in Ceylon, the 'cinnamon isle'. 'The shores of the island are full of it', reported one of their captains at the beginning of the century, 'and it is the best in all the Orient: when one is down wind of the island, one can still smell cinnamon eight leagues out to sea.'[201] But they did not become the masters of the coveted island until 1658–61. Next they were able to force their way into the hitherto reticent markets of the Malabar coast. In 1665, they captured Cochin.[202]

It was in about the 1650s or 1660s that the Dutch empire reached its true dimensions. So the ousting of the Portuguese had not been achieved overnight. Their empire had been a fragile one, true, but it was protected by its very size: scattered over an area from Mozambique to Macao and Japan, it was no tightly-knit structure, to be pushed over by the first determined thrust. And as is revealed by the papers of Ferdinand Cron, the representative of the Fuggers and Welsers at Goa,[203] news travelling overland always reached the Indian Ocean more quickly than the Dutch or English ships sailing towards it. The Portuguese authorities were always forewarned via Venice and the Levant, of the Dutch expeditions on their way to attack them. Lastly, the assailants did not always have the means, or the men, to occupy all the positions captured from their predecessors. Their very success meant that their resources had to be more thinly spread. In short, although the Dutch attack had begun before the end of the sixteenth century, pepper and spices were still being shipped directly to Lisbon in 1632.[204] Only the fall of Malacca in 1641 really dealt a mortal blow to the Portuguese empire in Asia.

The Dutch were by and large stepping into other men's shoes. In 1699, Bonrepaus, Louis XIV's ambassador, accused them of having built their fortune 'as far as possible on the ruins of the Europeans who had preceded them, taking advantage of the trouble others had taken to civilize the Indians, to domesticate them and give them the taste for commerce'.[205] But if Holland had not first pushed aside and then destroyed the Portuguese maritime empire, the English, who were familiar with the Indian Ocean and the East Indies, might very well have done so instead. After all, Drake in 1578 and Lancaster in 1592 had circumnavigated the globe.[206] And the English had created their own East India Company in 1600, two years earlier than the V.O.C. Had they not also on many occasions captured richly-laden Portuguese carracks?[207] These huge vessels, the largest ships in the world at the time, were incapable of moving quickly or using their firepower effectively; and they suffered terribly from the long return journeys: hunger, sickness and scurvy all took their toll.

So if the Dutch had not overthrown the Portuguese Empire, the English would cheerfully have done it for them. Indeed no sooner had the Dutch captured it than they were having to defend it against these persistent enemies. It proved difficult to keep them out of Japan and the East Indies, impossible to ban them from India or push them into the western Indian Ocean, towards Arabia and Persia. It took force in 1623 to drive them out of Amboyna.[208] And the English long remained a presence in the East Indies, buying pepper and spices, persistently selling Indian cottons in the open market at Bantam.

The coherence of trade within the Dutch empire

The greatest source of wealth in the East was trade between regions of Asia that were economically different from one another and very far apart: what the French called *le commerce d'Inde en Inde*, the English 'the country trade', and the Dutch *inlandse handel*. In this long-distance coasting trade, one commodity was the key to buying another, which could be exchanged for a third and so on. This takes us *inside* the Asian world-economies which were a thriving world of their own. The Europeans had found their way into this world to a greater extent than is usually recognized, first the Portuguese, then the Dutch. But the latter, possibly because of their experience in Europe, had a better grasp of the way trade was articulated between the different markets of the Far East. 'They contrived [therefore]', writes the Abbé Raynal,[209] 'to take over the coasting trade of Asia, just as they had that of Europe'; for the good reason that they considered this 'coasting trade' to be a coherent system, in which it was important to seize the key products and the key markets. The Portuguese, although not ignorant of this, had never brought the system to such a peak of perfection.

Like exchange elsewhere, trade in the Far East was based on goods, precious metals and credit instruments. Precious metals were used when goods could not be bartered in sufficient quantities. Credit was called upon when money in turn was unsuitable, either because there was not enough of it, or because it did not circulate quickly enough to settle trade balances immediately. In the Far East however, European merchants could not draw on the ready reserves of credit they were used to at home. It had to be a palliative or a last resort here rather than a dynamic force. They could apply to the moneylenders in Japan[210] or in India (in Surat)[211] but these 'bankers' offered their services primarily to local intermediaries rather than to western agents or merchants. In the end, the Europeans had to have recourse to precious metals, particularly American silver, which was the 'open sesame' of these trades.

But such imports from the West were never sufficient. So the Dutch applied to every local source of precious metals afforded them by Far East trade. Thus they used Chinese gold (in particular for buying goods on the Coromandel coast) as long as they had their base on Formosa (which was attacked in 1622 and recaptured by the corsair Coxinga in 1661); silver from the Japanese mines was an important makeweight from 1638 until its export was banned in 1668; after this, Dutch traders had to buy *koubangs*, Japanese gold coins. When in the 1670s, these were devalued, while retaining their former value for internal Japanese transactions, the Company reduced its gold purchases and went over to buying Japanese copper exports on a massive scale.[212] It did not of course overlook the gold produced in Sumatra and Malacca, nor indeed the gold and silver coins which the Levant trade continued to pour into Arabia (especially Mocha),[213] Persia and north-west India. It even made use of the silver which the Acapulco galleon regularly brought to Manila.[214]

In this context, the long crisis during which the Dutch were absent from the Persian silk market, beginning in mid-century, may not be quite what it seems at first sight. In October 1647, a correspondent of the Chancellor Séguier reported that the Dutch no longer found it convenient 'to go and buy silk in the East', since they had 'given orders to their correspondents in Marseille to buy some for them, and to send them as much as they could'.[215] And indeed the Dutch ships which sailed from the Indies in 1648 did not carry a single bale of Persian silk.[216] Since the Persian market was controlled at source by Armenian merchants, I thought for a while that the crisis could be attributed to these astonishing merchants who were themselves transporting bales of silk to Marseille. But this explanation is probably insufficient. The Dutch, who had been negotiating with the Shah of Iran since 1643 (and reached an agreement with him only in

1653) were not in fact at all anxious to carry off large quantities of Persian silk (the price of which was in any case rising), because they were determined to maintain a favourable trade balance with Persia at all costs, one which meant receiving gold and silver coins in payment for their goods.[217] In any case, they had access to Chinese silk, and more particularly to silk from Bengal,[218] which was by mid-century gradually accounting for a larger place in the goods shipped by the Company to Europe. So the V.O.C. was not the victim of the Persian silk crisis, rather it had provoked it, in order to safeguard one of its sources of specie. In short, the Dutch were constantly obliged to adapt their monetary policy to counter the hazards of an ever-changing situation, which was not improved by the daily fluctuation of exchange rates between the innumerable Asian currencies.

On the other hand, the system of compensatory trading established by the Company operated almost without a hitch until the 1690s – when the lean years began. But until then, the circuits and networks of Dutch trade in Asia, as described in a long and detailed report by Daniel Braams[219] (ironically written in 1687, just as the clockwork machinery was for the first time starting to go wrong), were linked together in a coherent system, based as was the Dutch network in Europe, on a combination of efficient shipping links, credit, and advance payments from home, together with systematic prospecting for potential monopolies.

Apart from the privilege of access to Japan, the only effective and permanent monopoly in Dutch hands was that of fine spices: mace, nutmeg, cloves and cinnamon. The process was identical in each case: production was confined to a small island territory, closely controlled and exclusively marketed, while cultivation of the product elsewhere was prevented. Thus Amboyna became the clove island, the Bandas the mace and nutmeg islands and Ceylon the cinnamon island. Such monoculture rendered these islands almost entirely dependent on regular imports of food and textiles. Meanwhile clove trees growing in the other Molucca islands were systematically uprooted, if necessary against payment of a pension to the local ruler; Macassar in the Celebes was taken by force in 1669, because if the island had been left to itself, it would have been a base for free trade in spices; Cochin in India was similarly occupied, 'although its possession costs the Company more than it brings in',[220] because this was a way of preventing competition from the production of inferior, but cheaper cinnamon. Even in Ceylon, an island really too big to patrol, and held only by expensive garrisons, cinnamon plantations were confined to restricted plots in order to limit supply. It was therefore by means of force and strict supervision that the Company maintained its monopolies – effectively it must be said, since throughout its existence, profits on fine spices remained high.[221] 'No lover is as jealous of his mistress', wrote a Frenchman in 1697,[222] 'as the Dutch are of their trade in spices.'

For the rest, Dutch superiority is explained by the discipline, for many years legendary, of their agents, and by the pursuit of long-term aims. The historian,

The V.O.C.'s factory in Bengal, painting, 1665. (Rijksmuseum, Amsterdam.)

while horrified by such a record of brutality, cannot but be entertained by the calculated, extraordinary and sometimes grotesque web of interlocking purchases, cargoes, sales and exchanges. Fine spices did not find a ready market only in Holland: India consumed twice as much as Europe,[223] and in the Far East they were a sought-after exchange currency, the key that opened many markets, just as the grain and ships' masts of the Baltic were in Europe. There were plenty of other exchange currencies too, if one was prepared to take the trouble to search out the right goods and the right places. The Dutch bought enormous quantities of Indian textiles of every quality for instance, in Surat, on the Coromandel coast, and in Bengal. They exchanged them in Sumatra for pepper (which provided an opportunity, with the help of politics, to draw up a privileged contract), gold and camphor. In Siam, they sold the cottons of Coromandel, though at no great profit (there were too many competitors here) but also spices, pepper and coral; on the return journey, they carried pewter, production of which had been granted to them as an exclusive privilege and which they sold as far afield as Europe, plus an impressive quantity of deer pelts, which were greatly prized in Japan, elephants (which were in demand in Bengal) and a great deal of gold.[224] The factory at Timor operated at a loss, but the sandalwood it produced sold extremely well in China and Bengal.[225] As for Bengal, where the Dutch arrived later but which they vigorously exploited, it provided silk, rice and quantities of saltpetre which was perfect ballast for the return trip to Europe, as was Japanese copper or sugar from various sources.[226] The kingdom of Pegu had attractions too: lacquer, gold and silver, precious stones, and a market for imported spices, pepper, sandalwood and cottons from Golconda and Bengal.

This list could be extended indefinitely: everything was grist to the Dutch mill. Who could fail to be surprised that wheat grown at the Cape, in South Africa, was shipped to Amsterdam? Or that Amsterdam became a market for cowrie shells brought back from Ceylon and Bengal, which found enthusiastic customers, including the English, who used them for trade with black Africa or for the purchase of slaves destined for America? Or that sugar from China, Bengal, sometimes Siam and, after 1637, Java, was alternately in demand or out of it in Amsterdam, depending on whether the price could compete in Europe with that of sugar from Brazil or the West Indies? When the market in the mother country was closed, sugar from the warehouses in Batavia was offered for sale in Persia, Surat or Japan.[227] Nothing better demonstrates how Holland in the Golden Age was already living on a world scale, engaged in a process of constant partition and exploitation of the globe.

Success in Asia, lack of success in America

The perennial problem for the V.O.C. was to select from its operations in Asia the quota of goods needed by Europe, or to put it more accurately the quota Europe could be persuaded to consume. It was a perennial problem because the V.O.C. had to operate a double timetable, Batavia–Amsterdam, Amsterdam–Batavia and so on. The transition from one world-economy (Asia) to another (Europe) was fraught with difficulties in itself, as both theory and experience taught; what was more, the two zones were constantly acting on one another, like the two unequally laden trays on a scale: it only took an extra weight on one side to throw the whole construction out of balance. As the European invasion of Asia developed, for instance, it sent up the purchasing price of pepper and spices, which had long been the standard prices for establishing terms of trade between the two continents. Pyrard de Laval noted in 1610 that 'what formerly cost the Portuguese only one sou now costs [the Dutch] four or five'.[228] (By contrast, selling prices tended to fall of their own accord in Europe, since larger shipments of these exotic products were arriving there). Gone were the days in that far-off year of 1599 when a 'bar' of cloves (525 Dutch pounds) cost 45 pieces of eight in Banda, and a bar of nutmeg six reals – those prices had disappeared for ever.[229]

Struggle and success

In Asia, the spice monopoly, authoritarian price control, and supervision of the quantities marketed (with excess goods being destroyed if necessary)[230] had for many years given the Dutch the advantage over their European rivals. But competition in Europe was increasing with the creation of rival Indies companies (all or almost all financed by Dutch capital reacting against the V.O.C.'s monopoly) and with the appearance on the market of products similar to those of the Far East but from different sources: copper, indigo, cotton and silk. So the Dutch success was by no means a foregone conclusion. As a Dutch traveller[231] explained in 1632:

> We should be under no illusion; when we have managed to drive out the Portuguese [who still controlled Goa, Malacca and Macao, all key positions] it will be impossible for the [Dutch] Company's funds to meet even the sixth part of this trade. Moreover, if it were possible to find sufficient funds to undertake it, we should find ourselves in the awkward position of being unable to consume all the merchandise derived from it, or to get rid of them.

In addition, a monopolist policy of coercion and supervision cost money. In Ceylon, where the task was particularly arduous, since the hilly island interior was governed by the king of Kandy 'who has never been tamed either by the Portuguese or the Dutch', the maintenance of a garrison and upkeep of the forts consumed almost 'all the gains made by the sale of cinnamon' harvested in the island.[232] What was more, the peasants one day rebelled against the Company because of the wretched wages they were paid. In the Banda islands, where the Dutch monopoly had been achieved by force, war, and the deportation of the natives as slaves to Java, the V.O.C. at first made substantial losses.[233] Production had fallen dramatically and had to be reorganized on a new basis: in 1636, the native population consisted of no more than 560 persons, as against 539 Dutch and 834 free foreigners. About two thousand slaves had to be 'imported' from Bengal and the kingdom of Arakan.[234]

In order to establish, consolidate and maintain its monopolies, the V.O.C. found itself drawn into long-term commitments which would reach some kind of resolution only with the conquest of Macassar in 1669 and the bringing to heel and eventually to the ground, of the great port of Bantam (1682). The company was engaged in a perpetual battle with native shipping and trade, forever punishing, deporting, becoming embroiled in police operations and colonial wars. In Java, the struggle against the local states, Mataran and Bantam, was a running tragedy. The countryside around Batavia, even the town's suburbs, were by no means safe.[235] This did not prevent successes, but it made them more costly. In Java, the plantations of sugar cane (from the early part of the seventeenth century) and of coffee-bushes (after 1706-11) were indeed successful.[236] But these had to be turned into controlled production, and the savagely-repressed uprising of the Chinese in 1740 led to an irreversible crisis in sugar production: the island took ten years to recover and did not do so completely even then.[237]

The history of the Company can logically be read as the sum of advantages and disadvantages. On the whole, during the seventeenth century the record was a positive one. And it was during the three or four decades straddling the year 1696 – the watershed which emerges from calculations based on the far from clear accounts of the V.O.C. – that the situation began to deteriorate steadily. Kristof Glamann[238] sees this period as marked by a veritable revolution which threw the established order into total confusion, both on the Asian front and in European markets.

In Europe, the crucial factor was the patent decline after 1670 of pepper as a prime market commodity. As if to compensate, fine spices maintained their position, or even progressed comparatively, while Indian textiles, silks and cottons, printed or unbleached, were taking a larger share of the market and new commodities were gaining ground: tea, coffee, lacquer and Chinese porcelains.

If these had been the only changes, we might be sure that the V.O.C., which followed the trend like the other Indies companies, would have been able to adapt without too much trouble. But they were accompanied by upheaval in the old routes and markets, as breaches were opened in the well-worn circuits of the Company. As often happens in such cases, the survival of an ancient system sometimes hindered the necessary capacity to adapt. The major innovation of this time was undoubtedly the expansion of the tea trade and the opening up of China to all foreign merchants. The English East India Company had rapidly engaged, in 1698, in direct purchases (that is for cash payments)[239] whereas the V.O.C., whose standard practice had been to receive Chinese goods via the junks which came to Batavia chiefly to buy pepper, but also cinnamon, sandalwood and coral, maintained these indirect arrangements which avoided the use of cash. Finally, the Bengal–China trade link – whereby tea was exchanged for cotton, silver or eventually opium – operated to the benefit of the English. This was all the harsher a blow for the V.O.C. since internal warfare in India had meanwhile devastated the Coromandel coast, the scene of one of its greatest successes.

Faced with such competition, was the V.O.C. not equipped to defend itself? The statistical records show that throughout the eighteenth century, and almost up to the last day of its existence in 1798[240] the company was capable of dispatching ever-greater quantities of silver to Asia. And silver, even in the transformed and almost unrecognizable world of Far East trade, was still the key to every problem. Yet for some reason difficult to identify, the V.O.C. continued to decline throughout the eighteenth century.

A Dutch merchant pointing out to his wife the ships belonging to the V.O.C. in Batavia bay. Detail from a painting by A. Cuyp (1620–91). (Rijksmuseum, Amsterdam.)

The rise and fall of the V.O.C.

When did the rot set in? A study of the Company's accounts appears to bring out the importance of the year 1696. But is it appropriate to pinpoint a precise year? Kristof Glamann[241] suggests focusing on the forty years or so surrounding the turn of the century, which seems more sensible.

Contemporaries certainly did not notice serious signs of decline until quite late in the day. In 1712 for instance, in the French seaport of Dunkirk (which Louis XIV was about to cede, for the sake of peace, to an England still insecure though on the threshold of greatness), a conversation took place between two men, one an unimportant informant of the French controller-general Desmaretz, the other an English 'milord' St John. 'When I replied to him', writes the Frenchman, 'that the restoration of their Indies trade [i.e. that of the English] through the decline of the Dutch would be a sovereign remedy to appease the British nation and bring it round to anything, he told me point blank that the English would sell their shirts to achieve this.'[242] So they did not think it was yet the case! Twelve years later, Ustariz, whose judgment is usually good, did not hesitate to write: 'Their Indies company [i.e. that of the Dutch] is so powerful that the trade of the other Indies companies is of small account compared to theirs'.[243]

Such figures as are known do not really resolve the problem. At least they can tell us something of the scale of the enterprise. On its creation in 1602, the Company had a capital of 6.5 million florins,[244] divided into shares of 3000 florins – ten times as much as the English company created two years earlier, which was to suffer considerably from the original lack of funds.[245] An estimate of 1669 tell us that this initial capital, which was subsequently neither repaid nor increased, corresponded to 64 tons of gold.[246] So when we talk about the V.O.C., we are talking from the start about very large sums of money.

It is not remarkable then that in the record years 1657 and 1658, the Company sent to the Far East two million florins in gold, silver and ingots.[247] Nor is one surprised to learn that in 1691, it had about 100 ships on the books,[248] or even, according to a serious French document of 1697, over 160 vessels with 30 to 60 cannon apiece.[249] If so, and if the average crew is taken to be 50 men,[250] the Company was employing some 8000 sailors. To these must be added the soldiers of the garrisons, which also included 'many people from the locality bearing arms and whom they [their Dutch masters] make march in front when there is fighting'. In time of war, the Company could add a further 40 large ships to its number. 'There is more than one crowned head in Europe who would find it hard to do as much.'[251] J. P. Ricard was very impressed in 1722 when he saw with his own eyes that the 'Chamber of Amsterdam' alone employed over 1200 persons in its warehouses and yards, 'whether building ships or doing everything necessary to fit them'. He was struck by one detail in particular: 'There are 50 men who do nothing year in year out, but sort and trim spices'.[252] It would be more helpful of course if we had some overall figures. Jean-François Melon, sometime secretary to John Law,[253] remarked in 1735: 'All these great establishments do not occupy 80,000 men' – as if that were not a prodigious figure for the time! And it was no doubt an underestimate: in about 1788, the Company was literally dying from over-staffing and Oldecop,[254] the Russian consul in Amsterdam, suggests that it had a payroll of 150,000 persons. One result has at any rate emerged from a study now well under way:[255] that a total of a million people sailed on the ships of the V.O.C. during the seventeenth and eighteenth centuries, that is 5000 a year. It is difficult to imagine on the basis of these figures what the Dutch population in Asia would have been, but it was probably much greater than the Portuguese population out there, estimated in the sixteenth century as 10,000 persons,[256] to whom must be added, as in the Dutch case, the mass of native servants and auxiliaries.

There was also talk of massive dividends – 20 or 22%, Savary calculates, between 1620 and 1720.[257] But on close inspection this is less clear. In 1670, there were very substantial returns, and in the euphoria following the victory over the king of Macassar, the Company proceeded to 'pay out' at 40%. Shares immediately shot up on the Stock Exchange 'to 510%', 100 being par when the Company was set up in 1602. This was a big leap, 'for since I have been here,' says Pomponne, 'they have not gone above 460'. But, he goes on, 'this big dividend and these new advantages will not have an effect, for if one takes an average of all the different prices the shares have been sold at, and the dividends which have been paid out over thirty years, those who own them will not have received more than 3 or 4 per cent interest on their money'.[258] To make sense of this sentence, one has to bear in mind that the dividend was not reckoned on the share price quoted on the Bourse but at par, i.e. the 3000 florins of the original share. If I had owned a share worth 15,300 florins in 1670, I would have received a dividend coupon worth 40% of the 'old capital', in other words 1200 florins, representing an exceptional interest payment of 7.84%. In 1720, the dividend payable on a share quoted at 36,000, which was again 40%, in fact represented interest of 3.33%.[259]

This means:

1) that the Company deprived itself of the advantages which would have resulted from increasing its capital. Why? We are offered no answer. Perhaps it was to avoid increasing the power of the shareholders, who were as a rule kept at arm's length? This is one possibility.

2) that in about 1670, according to the prices quoted on the Bourse, the total share capital was of the order of 33 million florins. Was it because this mass offered too little scope for the speculation mania of the Dutch that there was so much investment and speculation in English stocks and shares in Amsterdam?

3) finally that if the original 6.5 million florins brought in on average 20% a year, the shareholders received more than a million florins a year. But historians and observers all agree that the distribution of dividends (sometimes paid in spices or public bonds) was not an important factor in the difficulties experienced by the V.O.C. Now the payment of a million florins would hardly have been a negligible item if the Company's profits were as modest as some people would have us believe.

This takes us to the heart of the problem. What were the Company's profits? It seems to be impossible to find the answer, not only because too little research has yet been done, and because the documents have sometimes disappeared; not only because the accounts that have survived do not correspond to present-day

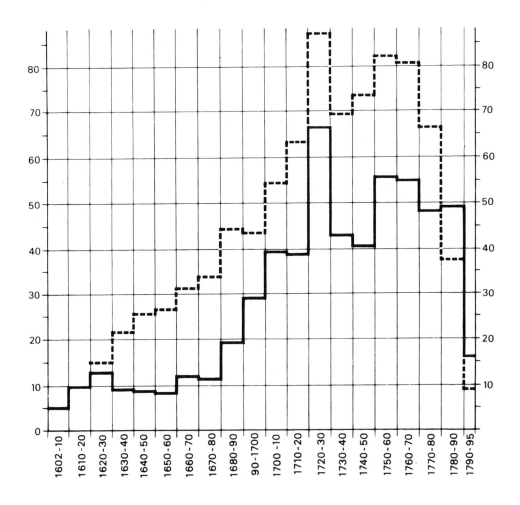

22   CALCULATING THE ACCOUNTS OF THE V.O.C.

Dutch ships engaged on the 'country trade' in the Far East (after F. S. Gaastra)
A team of Dutch historians (Bruyn, Schöffer and Gaastra) has begun to quantify the activity of the
V.O.C. in the seventeenth and eighteenth centuries. According to the table shown here, in about
1680-90, the number of ships the V.O.C. was using in the Far East begins to fall, a sign of trade
recession in the region. On the graph, the continuous line shows shipments of precious metals
from Holland to Asia; the broken line, commodities shipped back, valued in the price at the
point of origin, in millions of guilders. Trade appears to have expanded regularly. But the
relationship between these two sets of data is still difficult to estimate since no account is taken
of goods sent out from Holland, nor of metal money received from the 'country trade' in the Far
East.

practice and leave out important items, both on the credit and debit side (such as fixed capital, buildings and ships, goods and cash sent by sea, share capital etc.[260]), but above all because the system of accounting used makes it impossible to arrive at any overall balance sheet and consequently to calculate with any precision what real profits were. For practical reasons (above all distance, the difficulty of converting currency, etc.) the accounts are imprisoned within the structural bipolarity of the enterprise: there are the accounts of the 'factory Nederland' as Glamann calls it, which drew up an annual balance sheet of the accounts of the six chambers; and there are the accounts of the government in Batavia which received the ledgers of all the *factorijen* of the Far East and then worked out the annual balance for all overseas activity. The only link between these two sets of accounts was that the debts of the one were eventually paid by the other, but each was ignorant of the internal workings of its opposite number, and of the realities behind the surpluses or deficits.

Johannes Hudde,[261] the president of the *Heeren XVII* at the end of the seventeenth century, was so conscious of this that he planned a complete overhaul of the system; but it came to nothing, for various reasons and in the face of real difficulties. But perhaps too, it was because the directors of the Company were not particularly anxious to present the public with a clear set of books. From the start there had been friction between the *Heeren XVII* and the shareholders, who were calling for a statement of accounts and thought their dividends inadequate. And unlike the English company, which was placed in difficulties from the start by demands of this kind (and by the repayments forced out of it by shareholders who had no wish to finance military operations in Asia), the Dutch company always had the last word: its shareholders could only recover their funds by selling their shares on the stock market. In short, the accounts produced by the Company's management may have been presented in such a way as to conceal many aspects of the enterprise.

From the balances that have been studied, what emerges, somewhat to one's surprise, is the modesty of the profits made during the century when business ran smoothly – the seventeenth. The present writer has always maintained that *long-distance* trade was a kind of super-trade in the history of merchant enterprise. Can I have been wrong? I have argued that it offered an opportunity for a few privileged merchants to accumulate considerable capital for themselves. But where profits are small or non-existent, how can there be individual enrichment? Let us return to this double question in a moment.

Why the collapse in the eighteenth century?

The most complete set of accounts relating to the problem is provided by the calculations made in 1771 by B. Van der Oudermeulen[262] (based, for certain years, on documents which have since been lost). Between 1612 and 1654, total profits for the 22 years are reckoned to have been 9,700,000 florins, that is a modest average annual profit, of under 441,000 florins. If this is so, the Company was making only a third as much as its own shareholders – is that conceivable? Between 1654 and 1674, total profits were 11,300,000, the annual average 538,000. Between 1674 and 1696, total profits were 19,000,000, the annual average 826,000. After 1696, the decline sets in; in about 1724 the figure reaches zero. After that, the Company went hopelessly into debt. It was even borrowing money to pay its shareholders' dividends – the last resort of a bankrupt. During the summer of 1788, the situation was simply catastrophic. 'The company of the East Indies is said to be drawing 15 millions in bills of exchange on the state, payable in four or five years. This is what allows it to survive. But in fact, its debt which is already 90 million [florins] is thus increased to 105.'[263] How did the V.O.C. come to be in this financially disastrous position?

The only plausible explanation – but will any single explanation do? – is that suggested by Kristof Glamann:[264] the 'country trade' must have shrunk, or at least the profits of this vital enterprise must have done so. It is certainly true that the Batavia end was always going into debt, and that the *Heeren XVII* made good its deficits for a while with the still-thriving profits of the 'factory Nederland' (helped to some extent by price rises) and thereafter by allowing its own debts to pile up. But how is one to explain the decline of the *inlandse handel*? Since in general economies were prospering during the latter half of the eighteenth century, it cannot have been because of any widespread recession. K. Glamann believes that the reason was essentially competition from other companies,[265] in particular from the English, combined with a revolution in trade and markets which the Dutch agents in Batavia only imperfectly understood. The *Heeren XVII* tried in vain to persuade them of the advantages of direct trading with China, without going through the East Indies. Their English competitors were undoubtedly the gainers here.[266]

But the decline of Dutch fortunes was also accounted for by the notorious amount of fraud committed by the V.O.C.'s agents. Unlike its English counterpart, the Dutch company did not allow them to engage in *inlandse handel* on their own account. And corruption which was never absent from the Dutch East Indies, thrived. Are we to believe that in the beginning, the Company was served by exceptional men? The Abbé Raynal, in his famous work *Histoire philosophique et politique des établissements et du commerce des Européens dans les deux Indes* (1770),[267] suggests that no illicit and fraudulent fortunes were made by its agents before 1650, that the Dutch expatriates of the early years were of unparalleled frugality and integrity. Is this possible? As early as 1640, J.-B. Tavernier permitted himself some doubts, and there is at any rate one case, that of Pieter Nuyts the governor of Fort Zeelandia on Formosa in 1624, who was as stupid as he was venal, declaring quite openly that 'he had not come to Asia to eat hay'.[268] In the second half of the century at all events, luxury and corruption were quite unbridled, as even the official documents report (1653, 1664).[269] Daniel Braams, in his report of 1687, refers to it only in veiled terms. He does

The Dutch as seen by the Chinese: porcelain belonging to the Indies Company, Khang-Hi period, former Espiritu Santo Collection, Lisbon. (Photo, Connaissance des Arts.)

however speak of 'employees of the Company lacking in honesty' or more discreetly of competition from 'other businessmen' and the impossibility of 'preventing private citizens damaging the interests of the Company', on account of the large number of convenient harbours on the coasts of the East Indies and 'the large profits ... [which] make them more eager to engage in as much fraud as they can'.[270]

There was economic change then, though its origins are obscure, but changes had also been taking place in colonial society, thousands of miles away from Holland; it is more than probable that there was a clash of interests between this society and the Amsterdam oligarchy. On one hand were the imperturbable burghers at home, full of their own importance and respectability, on the other the colonial milieus of lower social status, the agents who had so to speak risen from the ranks to form a heterogenous and *cosmopolitan* society. Amsterdam and Batavia were not only opposite poles economically, but also the twin social poles of the imperial architecture of the United Provinces. Between them there was a great gulf fixed, as Giuseppe Papagno rightly points out in his brilliant sketch.[271] Disobedience, contraband, semi-independence and disorder became the rule in the East Indies, where the Dutch 'colonies' undoubtedly liked to live in style. The conspicuous luxury of the rich quarters of Batavia, which was already a commonplace in the seventeenth century, had continuously grown and become more extravagant over the years. Money, alcohol, women, armies of slaves and servants: Batavia was reproducing the strange, heady and morbid atmosphere of Goa.[272] There can be little doubt that in Batavia, part of the Company's deficit was quietly transforming itself into private fortunes.

But was the same thing not equally true back home in the strictly-run and still austere society of Holland in the Golden Age? Here the crucial question is to discover who bought the shipments from the Far East and on what terms. The Company sold its wares either by contract, or at auction in the warehouses, always in very large lots and generally to a syndicate of the top merchants.[273] The *Heeren XVII* were not supposed to figure among the purchasers, but the latter belonged to the same social circles and sometimes the same families as themselves. And in spite of the protests from shareholders, the ban did not apply to the administrators of the various chambers, the *bewindhebbers*, who were closely connected to the patriciates of the interested cities. It is not surprising in these circumstances to find that contracts were often accompanied by promises to block sales of a commodity by the Company, for periods of up to one or two years (which meant that the purchasing group was secure in its domination of the market) or by promises to place orders in the Indies for certain quantities of a given product. If the Company offered for sale a commodity of which a large Amsterdam wholesaler possessed substantial stocks, lo and behold, no buyer came forward and in the end the said wholesaler would buy it, on his own terms. Significantly it is the same names that crop up again and again among partners interested in the Company's transactions. The *Heeren XVII* who managed to

Dutch traders amusing themselves as best they can during their sequestration in the island of Deshima: geisha girls and bottles are much in evidence. The decor is Japanese, the floor is covered with rush mats, but the tables and chairs are western. Tokyo, Gijutsu Daigaku. (Photo T. Chino, Tokyo.)

fob off the shareholders so easily, were in the pockets of the great capitalist merchants, from the very start of profitable trading. Violet Barbour and Kristof Glamann have identified many examples. The fact that such merchants – like the very rich wholesaler and *bewindhebber* Cornelis Bicker[274] – in the seventeenth century made indiscriminate purchases of pepper, spices, cottons, silks and moreover traded in Russia, Spain, Sweden and the Levant (thus proving that they did not specialize); then in the eighteenth *did* specialize (proving that commercial life was being modernized) – does not alter the terms of the problem: the V.O.C. was a machine which stopped where the profits of trade monopolies began.

This takeover mechanism at the top was in fact clearly perceived by contemporaries. In 1629, protesting against the contracts which had just been signed and against the presence of *bewindhebbers* in the syndicates of buyers, the Chamber of Zeeland refused to hand over the goods just sold which happened to be stocked in Middelburg, and the Zeeland delegates did not hesitate to say in

front of the States-General (not that it did them any good) that such a policy
took neither the interests of the shareholders nor those of the Company into
consideration.[275]

Such evidence does not in the end contradict, but rather confirms my original
claims for the 'capitalist' virtues of long-distance trade. If one were to record
systematically the names of these large-scale buyers, one would be composing
the list of the men who really controlled the Dutch economy, those who survived
and kept afloat. But were these not also the men who really controlled the state
of the United Provinces,[276] the architects of all its decisions and its successes?
This would make an admirable subject for research although the result can be
predicted in advance.

Failure in the New World: the limits of Dutch success

The failures of the Dutch in the New World provide a kind of explanation. At
one time, I did wonder whether since America had to be built up from scratch
before it could be exploited, it lent itself to colonization by the large states, rich
in population, food supplies and different products: Spain, France and England.
Holland, being a parasite plant, might have found it hard to reproduce itself in
the New World. However, the stream of men sent out from the United Provinces
to the Far East, or the success of the Portuguese in Brazil contradict what might
seem a natural assumption. Holland *could* have built up an empire in America
if she had really wanted to, and if she had restricted the flow of migrants to the
East – an impossible condition perhaps, as no doubt the Dutch concluded after
their unsuccessful experience in Brazil.

This experience was a belated one. The Dutch, like the English in Elizabethan
times, preferred to live off plunder than to assume the burdens attendant upon
any stable settlement in empty or hostile lands. By 1604, they had acquired a
terrible reputation in Brazil, after sacking the port of Bahia in that year.[277] Ten
years earlier, in 1595, they had been active privateers off the coast of Black
Africa[278] which had economic links with the American plantations. Such expeditions, the ones that have left no traces as well as the ones we know about,
served as an initial contact, a whetting of the appetite.

In 1621, the situation changed. The Twelve Years' Truce, signed with Spain
in 1609, had not been renewed. War broke out once more and on 9 June of the
same year 1621, the new West India Company received its charter.[279] The task
facing the new company was to break into the great block of Latin America,
composed since 1580 of both the Spanish and Portuguese possessions in the New
World. The weak link in 1621 was Portuguese America, and it was here that,
logically enough, the Dutch attack was concentrated. In 1624, they captured San
Salvador, Brazil's capital city, built on the miniature sea of All Saints' Bay,
behind which lay the rolling plain of Reconcavo with its *enghenos*. In the course
of looting the town, the victors filled barrels with gold and silver coins. But a

Spanish fleet seventy strong surprised them on 28 March 1625 and a month later it recaptured the town.[280]

Trouble started once more five years later, in the sugar-growing *Nordeste*, where the Dutch occupied the two neighbouring towns, hostile but indispensable to each other, of Recife, the merchant city down at sea level, and Olinda, up on the cliffs, the town of the lords of the *enghenos*, the plantation-owners. The news travelled world-wide. In Genoa, it was said that the victors had carried off booty worth 'a million in gold'[281] without striking a blow, but this is probably untrue, since the Portuguese had burnt 'all the sugar and dye-wood in the warehouses'.[282] In 1635, the Dutch occupied Parahyba in the north and thus gained possession of '60 leagues of the Brazilian coastline, the best and the nearest to Europe',[283] but even so the territory they occupied was not great. Inland, the victors had left intact Portuguese Brazil which still had freedom of manœuvre, with its plantation owners, its sugar mills and its black slaves, and which was able to draw support from Bahia and its hinterland after its liberation in 1625. The worst of it was that the Dutch still could not get their hands on Brazilian sugar, since the large merchantmen from Holland could not moor in the shallow inlets on the coast where the smaller Portuguese vessels came and went as they pleased, although of course they might be captured on the high seas, or off the coast of Europe. The odd paradox of the Dutch occupation of the sugar-producing *Nordeste* was that it interrupted the flow of Brazilian sugar to Amsterdam, where it had previously been plentiful; and the price went up as well.[284]

In fact, this war, of which mention has already been made,[285] meant that Dutch-occupied Brazil was in a permanent state of siege. In July or September 1633, two Capuchin friars travelling home to England were waiting for a passage in Lisbon; they happened to meet a Scottish trooper who had just returned from service with the Dutch in Brazil. 'For months on end', he told them, 'he had seen nothing resembling meat, and by the end there was no fresh water, except what was shipped from Holland'.[286] He was probably exaggerating, but the Dutch were in real difficulties. Their mistake had been to try to erect a commercial superstructure without gaining control of production, without colonizing the territory in the modern sense of the word.

On 23 January 1637, there was a dramatic development: Maurice of Nassau[287] arrived in Recife, having been appointed governor-general of Dutch Brazil, where he was to spend seven years. He was undoubtedly a great man, who developed a passion for the country and its flora and fauna, and made clear-sighted attempts to create a viable colony. It was no accident that 1637, the first year of his governorship, was marked by the conquest, previously attempted several times without success, of the fortress of São Jorge da Mina, which the Portuguese had built on the coast of Guinea in 1482. The following year, it was the turn of the Portuguese island of São Paulo de Loanda, off the coast of Angola, then the sugar island of São Tomé in the Gulf of Guinea which was a transit station for the American slave trade. This was logical enough: maintaining Dutch-occupied Brazil would have been impossible without black slaves; from now on, they began to arrive. But at this juncture, Portugal revolted against Spanish dominion and regained her independence (1 December 1640). The danger of peace loomed, and a ten-year truce was even signed in 1641 between Portugal and the United Provinces.[288]

The truce was not respected in the Far East. In America, on the contrary, hostilities came to an end, the West India Company being only too glad to see the conclusion of a costly war. Maurice of Nassau, who saw things rather differently, used the newly-released forces against Spain, sending five ships off to the Pacific, where they caused inestimable havoc on the coasts of Chile and Peru, but for want of reinforcements were obliged to return to Brazil; they arrived there just as Maurice of Nassau was preparing to leave, having been recalled – probably at the request of the merchants.

The Dutch thought that from now on they were free to exploit Brazil to their hearts' content. The successors of the prince of Nassau, 'admirable men for commerce but very poor politicians', thought only of making money, of encouraging trade; they even sold arms and powder to the Portuguese, 'on account of the excessive price [the latter] paid for it'. In these circumstances, the war continued under cover, a war of attrition based on the interior, the *sertão*,[289] which was in the end to prove too much for Dutch Brazil in 1654. Since everything stood or fell together, the Portuguese soon recovered most of the positions they had lost on the African coast, including São Tomé and São Paulo de Loanda. The official declaration of war against Portugal in 1657 allowed the Dutch West India Company to attack the enemy openly, to seize its ships. But the war did not pay for itself. Two Dutchmen in Paris in December 1657 summed up the situation clearly, having received recent news from Holland: 'The booty taken from Portugal', they said, 'is only a million and a half [*livres*], insufficient to pay for our armaments, which are costing us close on 3,500,000 *livres*'.[290] The war was a stalemate, so peace gradually broke out of its own accord. It was signed on 16 August 1661, through the mediation of Charles II, the new king of England, who had just married the Infanta of Portugal. Brazil remained in the hands of Portugal, which had however to pay a price for this solution: opening the doors of her American colonies to Dutch shipping; lowering the price of salt in Setubal;[291] and recognizing the conquests made in the Far East at her expense. She would eventually have to pay off the war debt by shipments of salt spread over several years.[292]

In Holland, responsibility for this failure was laid at the door of the West India Company management. There were two Indies Companies, one good, one bad. 'God grant', writes Pieter de la Court in 1662, 'that the East India Company [the good one] learns a lesson from all this before it is too late.'[293] The unfortunate West India Company was refloated by the state in 1667 but never recovered from the disaster. It had to be content from now on with trading between the coast of Guinea and the Dutch possessions of Surinam and Curacao – Curaçao had been occupied in 1634, and Surinam had been handed over by the English at the Peace of Breda[294] in 1667, as meagre compensation for the Dutch cession of New Amsterdam which was to become New York. Curaçao was to remain an active centre for the resale of slaves and profitable smuggling with Spanish America, while Surinam with its sugar plantations would bring Holland a handsome income, but also considerable trouble. It was with these two outposts that the West India Company now continued its mediocre existence. This enterprise which had dreamed of seizing the Azores[295] and had once controlled a substantial part of Brazil, was now reduced to allowing private transporters to operate within its territory on payment of indemnities.

Where is the blame to be laid in the last analysis – on the Company management alone? On the province of Zeeland which provided its financial backing, as Holland did that of the V.O.C.? Or on excessive ambition expressed too late in the day? Was not the real mistake perhaps to think that the New World could be taken over like the islands of the Far East – Amboyna, Banda or Java – whose native populations could be ill-treated with impunity? Whereas in America Holland was up against European opposition: England which encouraged Portuguese resistance, and Spanish America which was more solid than appearances suggested. In 1699, a Frenchman maliciously claimed that the leaders of the United Provinces had 'noticed the extraordinary labours and the considerable expense which the Spanish had been obliged to devote to the establishment of their commerce and government in Countries hitherto unknown; they therefore determined to have as little as possible to do with such undertakings'[296] – in other words, to seek out countries which could be exploited rather than settled and developed. But perhaps the answer is rather (to take us back to our original starting-point) that little Holland was simply not big enough to swallow the Indian Ocean, the Brazilian forests and a sizeable chunk of Africa?

World-domination and capitalism

The Amsterdam experience undoubtedly has much to tell us, in a rather repetitive mode, it is true, about the forms of domination exercised by an urban centre with an imperial vocation. We need dwell no longer on this subject. What is interesting on the other hand is the opportunity to observe in a precise case, and in the context of world-domination on this scale, the nature of the capitalism at work there. I prefer to look at concrete examples than to attempt definitions in the abstract – particularly since the kind of capitalism observable in Amsterdam tells us something both about the experiences which preceded it and about those which would follow. At least two contexts must be explored here:
1. What was happening in Amsterdam itself? What were the trading methods and practices in force there?

2. How was this world centre related to the different zones of the world-economy which it controlled from near or afar?

The first question is a simple one: Amsterdam will hold few surprises for us. The second poses more of a problem, in that its aim is to reconstruct the architecture of the overall area dominated – *from a very great height* – by Amsterdam. This architecture is by no means evident: it is camouflaged by a multitude of particular cases.

What was good for the entrepôt trade was good for Amsterdam

In Amsterdam, everything was crammed together, concentrated: the ships in the harbour, wedged as tight as herrings in a case, the lighters plying up and down the canals, the merchants who thronged to the Bourse, and the goods which piled up in warehouses only to pour out of them. No sooner had a fleet arrived, relates a seventeenth-century eye-witness, 'than through the good offices of the brokers, the entire quantity of merchandise is bought at the first meeting of merchants at the Bourse, the ships are unloaded within four or five days and ready to set sail on a new voyage'.[297] It would certainly take a little longer to find buyers. But the warehouses of Amsterdam could absorb and then disgorge any amount of goods. There was an extraordinary volume of property, materials, goods and services on the market, all available at a moment's notice. At a given command, the entire machine went into action. This was the means whereby Amsterdam maintained her superiority – an abundance of ever-ready goods and a great mass of money in constant circulation. When they belonged to a certain class, the merchants and political leaders of Holland could hardly fail to be aware, through their day-to-day practice, of the immense power they wielded. Their trump cards allowed them to have a hand in any game, licit or illicit.

'Since I have become particularly acquainted with Amsterdam', writes a contemporary in 1699, 'I compare it to a fair where merchants from many parts bring their merchandise which is sure to find a customer; as in ordinary fairs the merchants one meets there do not use the things they sell, so the Dutch, who collect goods from every corner of Europe, keep for their own use only what is strictly necessary for life and sell to other nations the products they consider superfluous and which are always more expensive.'[298]

The comparison with a fair is banal, but it identifies the crucial elements in Amsterdam's role; collecting, storing, selling and re-selling the goods of the universe. It was a policy which had already been practised by Venice; and Antwerp, according to Lodovico Guicciardini, was a 'permanent fair'.[299] This storage capacity undoubtedly seemed by the standards of the time excessive and indeed pernicious, since the force of attraction could lead to quite ridiculous itineraries for the merchandise. In 1721,[300] Charles King, in *The British Merchant*[301] expresses surprise that English goods bound for France should be embarked on Dutch vessels, unloaded at Amsterdam, and from there conveyed

Rotterdam, the bank and an unloading derrick, about 1700. Engraving by P. Schenk. (Atlas van Stolk.)

by the Meuse or the Rhine! They would have to pay duty on the way in and out of Holland, then the tolls on the Rhine or Meuse, and finally customs duties at the French frontier. 'Why should we imagine then', he asks 'that our goods had not come cheaper to Champaign, Metz and other French countries near the Meuse and Rhine, if we had first landed them at Rouen and paid the single duty of that City?' King, being an Englishman, was of course misinformed if he thought that one would pay a single duty once and for all on entering France.[302] But it was clear that the diversion via Amsterdam lengthened and complicated the circuit. When, in the eighteenth century, Amsterdam's power to attract and divert goods towards herself had waned, the direct dispatch of merchandise would eventually prevail.

But this was not yet the rule in 1669, when we can follow the exchange of views between Pomponne, Johan de Witt and Van Beuningen,[303] who expressed himself more bluntly than de Witt. It is impossible, Van Beuningen told Pomponne, for us to go on buying French goods, if our manufactured products are refused entry to France. To make the Dutch consumer forget his taste for French wine – which had largely supplanted beer as a drink – would be quite easy: it would simply take an increase in purchase tax (a drastic means of rationing). But, added Van Beuningen, while the Dutch might decide among themselves to 'establish sobriety among their people and the curtailment of luxury', by forbidding the use of costly French silks, they would continue to carry to other countries 'the same things they would wish to ban from their own'. In other words, French wines, spirits and luxury fabrics would be admitted to the Dutch market, on condition they were exported: the domestic sales outlet would be blocked, but the entrepôt and transit trade would be allowed full freedom.

Storage and warehousing lay at the heart of Dutch commercial strategy. In 1665, there was serious talk in Amsterdam of a project that had frequently cropped up in the past, of seeking a northern passage to the Indies. The East India Company tried to block the proposal. Why? It was, one of the interested parties explained, because if the venture were successful, the trip would be reduced by six months and the Company would not have time, before the expedition returned, to dispose of the ten million florins' worth of goods which piled up every year in its warehouses.[304] If new goods flooded the market, they would bring down the price of existing stocks. In the end, the project collapsed of itself, but these fears shed light on a certain mentality and even more on the degree of maturity of the economy.

For the stockpiling of goods practised at the time was occasioned by the slowness and irregularity of circulation. It was the solution to trading problems which all, or almost all, derived from the intermittent nature of arrivals and

1786: THE DUTCH WERE STILL SHIPPERS FOR THE REST OF EUROPE

Statistics compiled by the French consul in Amsterdam in 1786, of the 1504 ships arriving in the harbour. In spite of the late date, almost all the ships were Dutch.

Coming from	Number of ships	Dutch-registered
Prussia	591	581
Russia	203	203
Sweden	55	35
Denmark	23	15
Northern Germany	17	13
Norway	80	80
Italy	23	23
Portugal	30	30
Spain	74	72
Levant	14	14
Barbary Coast	12	12
France	273	273
American colonies (not the United States)	109	109

From Brugmans, *Geschiednis von Amsterdam*, IV, pp. 260–1.

departures, from the delays and uncertainty of orders and information. If a merchant was in a position to store stocks of a commodity, he was able to react quickly to any opening on the market as soon as it appeared. And if Amsterdam called the tune for European prices, as all the documents tell us, it was because of the abundance of reserve stocks which the city's warehouses could at any moment release or hold back.

Commodities and credit

The Amsterdam entrepôt trade verged on a monopoly. And if the Dutch really were 'the Carryers of the World, the middle Persons in Trade, the Factors and Brokers of Europe', as Defoe wrote in 1728,[305] this was not, as Le Pottier de la Hestroy[306] thought because 'all the other nations were willing to suffer it to be so', but because they were unable to prevent it. The Dutch system was built on a network of commercial relations of interdependence which combined to produce a series of virtually obligatory channels for the circulation and redistribution of goods. It was a system that could only be maintained by constant vigilance, by a policy designed to thwart all competition, and by subordinating the whole of the Dutch economy to this essential objective. The Dutchmen who discussed with Pomponne in 1669–70 the 'application making itself known among other nations that they should not be dependent on them alone [i.e. the Dutch] for all the trade in Europe',[307] were not mistaken when they claimed that 'those who would relieve them [of this trade, which was known as *Entrecours*] and have it no longer pass through their hands', might well make them 'lose . . . the great advantage which they derived from the trade and transport of merchandise which they alone carried to all corners of the world', but would not be able to replace them in this role, nor acquire the benefits of it.[308]

This over-developed function of warehousing and redistribution was only possible because it shaped, oriented and even deformed the other trading functions, as Jean-François Melon points out in his *Essai politique*, apropos banking – not with the greatest of clarity it is true, but his comment has a fairly broad application. 'The good Bank', he says, 'is that which doth not pay', in other words one that does not issue bank notes.[309] The Bank of Amsterdam and its model the Bank of Venice[310] both corresponded to this ideal: everything was 'in Transfers'. The depositor settled his account by a payment, using fictional money, known as bank money, which was reckoned at an agio of 5% in Amsterdam (and 20% in Venice) compared with ordinary money (*courantgeld*). Melon compares Amsterdam and London as follows: 'The Bank of Amsterdam has been obliged to deal in Transfers', he explains, 'because Amsterdam receiveth abundance of Commodities and consumeth little. This City receiveth Commodities by the Sea in large Parcels, to send them away in the same manner [the definition of the entrepôt trade]. London abounds in native Commodities, and its Bank ought to deal in Notes payable on Demand'.[311] The quotation is not of the

An exchange dealer's office. Dutch engraving, 1708. (Atlas van Stolk.)

clearest, I admit, but it is contrasting a country dealing above all in entrepôt and transit trade with one where the range of commodities in circulation, largely integrated into domestic networks of consumption and production, required a constant supply of specie.[312]

If Amsterdam had no bank of issue, preoccupied by the daily payment of coin, it was because such a bank was scarcely necessary in the city. The entrepôt trade required above all easy arrangements for quick settlement, enabling a very large number of transactions to balance each other, without recourse to the hazards of cash; through clearing operations, such transactions could very largely cancel each other out. In this respect, the banking system in Amsterdam was fulfilling the same function as the old-fashioned fairs, including the ultra-modern Genoese fairs, but in a far more flexible and rapid manner because it operated continuously. According to a report by the 'book-keepers of the bank', a firm such as Hope and Co. would, in normal circumstances, before the 1772 crisis, be responsible every day for '60 or 80 entries on the bank register', either credit or debit.[313] According to a reliable witness in 1766, transfers within the Bank of Amsterdam 'amounted to ten or twelve million florins a day'.[314]

On the other hand, the Bank of Amsterdam was not a source of credit, since depositors were forbidden to overdraw on pain of fines.[315] And credit, indispensable in any trade centre, was a vital necessity in Amsterdam, not only because of the abnormal volume of goods which were bought and stored only to be exported a few months later, but also because the secret weapon of the Dutch merchant against foreign competitors was money, the many advance payments made in order to secure better terms for buying and selling. The Dutch were in fact credit suppliers for the whole of Europe – and this was the real secret of their prosperity. This cheap credit, widely available from the firms and leading merchants of Amsterdam, flowed through such a variety of channels, from the most respectable trade to the wildest speculative ventures, that it is hard to follow all its twists and turns. But it clearly played a role in what were known at the time as the commission trade and the acceptance trade, which in Amsterdam took on particular and multifarious forms.

The commission trade

The commission trade was the opposite of trading in person, also known as 'proprietorial trade'. It meant handling goods on behalf of someone else.

A *commission* was properly 'the order which one Businessman gives to another for trading purposes. The person giving the order is the *Commettant*, the person to whom it is given the *Commissionnaire*. We may distinguish between a commission to purchase; a commission to sell; a banking commission which consists of withdrawing, accepting, paying and having money accepted or received on behalf of another; and a warehousing commission which consists of receiving consignments of goods in order to dispatch them to their destination'. Consequently, 'one can buy, sell, have ships built, fitted and refitted, insure or have insured, on commission'.[316] Every aspect of trade could be included in the system, where a great variety of situations could be found. There were even cases where the giver and the receiver of a commission acted side by side: when a merchant came for instance to buy goods 'out of the first hand' in a manufacturing town (let us say to choose silks in Lyon or Tours) he would replenish his stocks accompanied by a commission agent (*commissionnaire*) who acted as his guide and discussed prices with him.

If Holland did not invent the commission trade, which was a very ancient practice, she certainly made it from the first, and for a long while, her chief trading activity.[317] Consequently every variation possible under the terms of the arrangement could be found there: equal and unequal terms, dependence and reciprocal autonomy. One merchant might act as the commission agent for another merchant who did the same for him.

But in Amsterdam, unequal terms tended to become the rule. Either the Dutch merchant had official commission agents abroad, in which case they were factors or indeed touts working in his service (this might be the case in Livorno,

Seville, Nantes, Bordeaux, etc.); or the Amsterdam merchant acted as commission agent for someone else, in which case, by using the weapon of credit, he could have the upper hand over the merchant calling on his services either for sale or for purchase. Dutch merchants, Accarias de Sérionne tells us, every day grant 'credit to foreign Businessmen who commission them to buy [commodities or stocks quoted on the Bourse] on the understanding of repayment which only happens two or three months after the dispatch of the goods, so the purchasers have been given four months' credit'.[318] The commanding position was even more patent in the case of sales: when a merchant sent a consignment of goods to a leading commission agent in Holland, with instructions to sell at such and such a price, the commission agent advanced him perhaps a quarter, half or three-quarters of the agreed price[319] (an arrangement very similar of course to the ancient practice of advance payment on wheat in the ear, or wool before the shearing). The advance would be made at a rate of interest payable by the vendor.

Thus the commission agent in Amsterdam was financing his correspondent's trade, as a document dating from 1783[320] demonstrates quite well apropos of linens from Silesia known as *platilles* (originally made in Cholet and Beauvais before being imitated in Silesia where, since they were produced more cheaply and from high quality Polish flax, they soon had no rivals). *Platilles* were exported to Spain, Portugal and America, the chief distribution points being Hamburg and Altona.

> A large quantity of these linens also come to Amsterdam. The manufacturers themselves send them there when they have not been able to sell them in nearby regions or centres, because they can easily find [in Amsterdam] people who will advance them three-quarters of the value of the goods at a modest rate of interest, while waiting for a favourable opportunity to sell. Such opportunities are frequent, because the Dutch colonies, particularly Curaçao, buy them.

In this case, as in so many others, commission *along with credit*, brought into Amsterdam a considerable volume of goods which obediently followed, as they had to, the ebb and flow of credit. When in the second half of the eighteenth century, the entrepôt trade of Amsterdam deteriorated, the commission trade also suffered so that, to take a fictional example, goods bought in Bordeaux could travel to St Petersburg without stopping in Amsterdam, although the Dutch city was still providing the financial backing without which no transaction would have been easy or even possible. This decline brought new prominence to another 'branch' of Dutch commercial activity, the so-called acceptance trade, which operated exclusively under the heading of finance, or as Accarias de Sérionne would have said, of 'banking' in the general sense of credit.[321] Thus Amsterdam remained the 'cash box'[322] and the Dutch 'the bankers of Europe'.[323]

There was perhaps nothing very abnormal about this development. Charles P. Kindleberger[324] explains it very well:

The monopoly of a port or transit station is difficult to maintain. As well as on risk and capital, such a monopoly is based on good information about available goods and the places where they are in demand. But such information is rapidly communicated, and the trade of the central market replaced by direct traffic between producer and consumer. So Devonshire serges and common cloth from Leeds no longer needed to transit through Amsterdam in order to reach Portugal, Spain or Germany; they were dispatched directly. [In Holland] capital remained abundant, but trade was declining, with a tendency to transform the financial side of commodity exchange into a foreign banking and investment service,

since the advantages of a major finance market to lenders and borrowers were longer-lived than those of a central market to buyers and sellers of commodities. Was this switch from commodities to banking not precisely what had happened in fifteenth-century Genoa? And would it not be repeated in nineteenth- and twentieth-century London? Was supremacy based on banking the most durable kind? This is certainly what the fortunes of the acceptance trade in Amsterdam suggest.

The acceptance trade

'To agree to accept a bill of exchange', Savary explains, 'is to underwrite it, to sign it, and make oneself the principal debtor of the sum mentioned on it, to accept the obligation in one's own name of paying it on the agreed date'.[325] If the due date had been fixed by the drawer, the acceptor (or *acceptator*) merely signed it; if the date was not specified, the latter signed and dated it – the date written down would be the future deadline.

Again, there was nothing very new about this: the acceptance trade related to the countless bills of exchange which had long been the vehicle of credit throughout Europe, and which would from now on be gathering like an enormous cloud over Holland – not by accident, needless to say. The bill of exchange remained 'the first ... among all papers of commerce and the most important', alongside which bearer bills, commodity bills, etc. played only a modest and local role. Throughout all the trade centres of Europe, 'bills of exchange circulated in trade in lieu of cash and always with this advantage over money that they bore interest, through the discounting between one transfer[326] or endorsement and another.'[327] Transfers, endorsements, discounting, drafts and deposits[328] made the bill of exchange an indefatigable traveller from one centre to another, one merchant to another, from a commissioning merchant to a commission agent, from a businessman to his correspondent or to a discounter (as he was known in Holland) or *escompteur* (as he was known in France), or even from a businessman to a 'cashier', i.e. his own cashier. To grasp the problem, it is essential therefore to view it as a whole, through the astonished and admiring eyes of contemporaries trying to understand the Dutch system.

Given the slow rate of consumption – which took time – the slow pace of production, the slow speeds at which goods and even orders and bills of exchange travelled, and the time it took the mass of consumers and customers to produce from their assets the cash required for purchases, a wholesaler had to be able to buy and sell on credit, by issuing a bill which could circulate until he was in a position to repay his creditor in goods, or cash or in some other form of paper. This was the solution already devised by the Italian merchants of the fifteenth century, with endorsement and re-exchange, further expanded in the seventeenth century within the framework of the *ricorsa* pact[329] so discussed by theologians. But there is no comparison between these early expansions of credit and the deluge of paper that occurred in the eighteenth century: 4, 5, 10 or 15 times the specie in circulation. It was a deluge which might represent either the solid fortunes and routine practices of respectable merchants, or chains of unsecured bills, known as *cavalerie* in France and *wisselruiterij* in Holland.[330]

Whether licit or illicit, this mass of paper logically converged on Amsterdam, leaving it only to return, depending on the pulses of the arterial system of European commerce. A merchant who launched himself into these currents usually found them to offer invaluable advantages. In 1766, merchants who were buying wholesale silk in Italy and Piedmont in order to sell it to manufacturers in England and France, would have found it hard to do without Dutch credit. The silk they bought 'out of the first hand' in Italy, had to be paid for in cash, and they were 'obliged by general usage' to deliver it to the manufacturers with about two years' credit, that is the interval required before the raw material could be transformed into a manufactured product and put on sale.[331] This long and irregular delay explains the part played by frequently-renewed bills of exchange. These wholesalers can therefore be numbered among the many European merchants 'who circulate', that is who 'draw bills on [their] correspondents [Dutch of course] in order to take out, with the help of their acceptance, funds in the centre [where they were doing business] and who once the first bills have fallen due, draw new ones or have someone else draw them'.[332] It was a rather expensive form of credit in the long run, since the debt increased from bill to bill, but it was borne without difficulty by a particularly profitable 'branch of commerce'.

Dutch trade and credit machinery functioned therefore by multiple criss-cross movements of bills of exchange, but it could not run on paper alone. It required funds in cash from time to time, in order to supply the Baltic and Far East trades, and also in order to fill the coffers of the merchants and discounters in Holland whose occupation it was to change paper into metal currency and vice versa. Specie was plentiful in Holland which almost always had a positive balance of payments. In 1723, England is reported as having dispatched to Holland gold and silver worth £5,666,000.[333] Sometimes the day to day arrivals were viewed as events of note. 'It is extraordinary', wrote the Neapolitan consul in the Hague on 9 March 1781, '[to see] the quantity of payments made in this country [Holland] both from Germany and France. Over a million gold sovereigns have been sent from Germany[334] and these will be melted down to make Dutch ducats; a hundred thousand gold louis have been sent from France to trading houses in Amsterdam.'[335] And he adds, as if wanting to provide a good retrospective example of the gold point standard[336] for the economic textbooks: 'The reason for this dispatch is that the exchange rate is very advantageous in this country [Holland] at present'. As a rule, to the eyes of an everyday observer, the mass of cash in Amsterdam was hidden behind the mass of paper. But if some accident disturbed the smooth running of business, its presence was quickly revealed. At the end of December 1774 for instance,[337] when the recent crisis of 1773 was still making its effects felt, and when news was beginning to arrive of trouble in England's American colonies, business was so sluggish that 'money has never been as abundant as it is today ... bills of exchange are being discounted at two per cent and even one and a half, when these bills are accepted by certain houses, which is evidence of the inactivity of trade'.

Only through such an accumulation of capital were the risky operations of *wisselruiterij* possible, that is the easy and automatic recourse, for any promising business deal, to paper secured by nothing except the prosperity and superiority of the Dutch economy. I would readily apply to this eighteenth-century situation what Wassily Leontieff has recently written of the mass of dollars and Eurodollars created by the United States: 'The fact is that in the capitalist world, states and even sometimes adventurous bankers and entrepreneurs have used and abused the privilege of minting money, in particular, the United States, which has so long been flooding other countries with non-convertible dollars. The secret is to have enough credit – that is power – to be able to indulge in this process'.[338] Is this not, *mutatis mutandis*, saying exactly the same as Accarias de Sérionne:

> If ten or twelve Businessmen of Amsterdam of the first rank meet for a banking [i.e. a credit] operation, they can in a moment send circulating throughout Europe over two hundred million florins in paper money, which is preferred to cash. There is no Sovereign who could do as much ... This credit is a power which the ten or twelve businessmen will be able to exert over all the states in Europe, in complete independence of any authority.[339]

There were precedents, it seems, for the multinational firms of today.

The loans mania or the perversion of capital

Holland's prosperity led to surpluses which were, paradoxically, an embarrassment, surpluses so great that the credit she supplied to the traders of Europe was not enough to absorb them; the Dutch therefore offered loans to modern states who were particularly adept at consuming capital, if not at repaying it on the promised date. In the eighteenth century, when money was lying idle all over Europe, and finding uses only with difficulty and on poor terms, princes had only to snap their fingers and the rich Genoese, Genevans or Amsterdammers came running to offer their money. In the spring of 1774, just after a severe depression, the coffers of Amsterdam were open to all callers: 'The facility with which the Dutch are giving their money to foreigners today has persuaded several German princes to take advantage of this willingness. The prince of Mecklenburg-Strelitz has just sent an agent here to negotiate a loan of 500 thousand florins at 5 per cent'.[340] At the same time, the court of Denmark was successfully negotiating a loan of 2 million florins, which brought its debt with Dutch moneylenders to 12 million.

Was this burst of financial activity an aberration as some historians, taking a moral tone, have suggested? Was it not rather a normal development? Already in the latter part of the sixteenth century, another period when capital was superabundant, the Genoese had followed the same itinerary, as the *nobili vecchi*, the official lenders to the king of Spain gradually withdrew from commercial activity.[341] It looks very much as if Amsterdam, repeating this process, dropped the bird in hand to go chasing shadows, abandoning the money-spinning entrepôt trade for a life of speculation and rentierdom, and leaving all the best cards to London – even financing her rival's rise. But then, did Amsterdam really have any choice? Indeed had the rich Italians of the sixteenth century had any choice? Was there even the remotest chance of stopping the rise of the North? At all events, every capitalist development of this order seems, by reaching the stage of financial expansion, to have in some sense announced its maturity: it was a sign of autumn.

In Genoa as in Amsterdam, the extremely low interest rates show that capital was no longer finding employment at home through the usual channels. The over-plentiful supply of money in Amsterdam was being loaned at 3 or even 2 per cent, just as in Genoa in 1600.[342] England, after the cotton boom of the early nineteenth century, found herself in precisely the same position: there was too much money about, and it was not bringing in enough, even in the cotton industry. It was at this point that English capitalists agreed to invest massively in the metal industries and the railways.[343] Dutch capital had no such opportunity. Consequently interest rates only a little higher than local ones inevitably lured it away from home, sometimes very far indeed. Again, the position was not quite the same as that of London in the early twentieth century when, after the fantastic venture of the industrial revolution, English capital was once more in over-plentiful supply and without useful domestic employment. London did, like Amsterdam, export capital, but the loans were often made to finance foreign sales of British industrial products and were thus another way of re-stimulating national growth and production. There was nothing of the kind in Amsterdam, since the commercial capitalism of the Dutch city was accompanied by no major industrial development.

Nevertheless these foreign loans were quite worthwhile investments. Holland had been granting them since the seventeenth century.[344] In the eighteenth century, when the English loan market opened in Amsterdam, from 1710 or so onwards, the 'lending branch' was considerably expanded. By the 1760s, all the states of Europe were queuing up in the offices of Dutch moneylenders: the emperor, the elector of Saxony, the elector of Bavaria, the insistent king of Denmark, the king of Sweden, Catherine II of Russia, the king of France and even the city of Hamburg (although it was Amsterdam's successful rival) and lastly, the American rebels.

The procedure for foreign loans, invariably the same, will be familiar to the reader: the firm which had agreed to put the loan on the market, in the form of stocks[345] which would afterwards be quoted on the Bourse, would open a subscription list, in theory to the public. (In practice, if the loan had good guarantees, the subscriptions would have almost all been taken up before the public announcement.) Interest rates were low, barely one or two points higher than the current rate: 5% was considered a high rate of interest. But in most cases, collaterals were obligatory: land, revenue, jewels, pearls, precious stones. In 1764,[346] the elector of Saxony deposited '9 million [fl.] worth of precious stones' in the Bank of Amsterdam; in 1769, Catherine II sent her crown jewels.[347] Sometimes huge quantities of commodities were pledged – mercury, copper, etc. For the firm managing the operation, there were also 'bonuses' (or perhaps 'under the counter payments' would be more accurate). In May 1784, the newly independent States of America negotiated a loan of 2 million florins which was subscribed without difficulty. 'It remains to be seen', said an informant who had 'first-hand' knowledge, 'if Congress will approve the bonuses which have been offered without its knowledge.'[348]

As a rule, the private firm which had issued the loan would itself deliver the capital to the borrower and undertake to distribute the interest it received – all in return for a commission. The firm would then sub-contract with the professional brokers who would, each in his different circle, place a number of bonds. Thus savings were mobilized. Finally, the bonds would be introduced on the Bourse and the manoeuvres we have already seen at work in England would begin here too.[349] It was child's play apparently to send the price of such stocks above par, over 100. It merely required a well orchestrated campaign, perhaps simply a false report that the loan had closed. Naturally those who indulged in such practices whether in a small or a big way, took advantage of the rise to sell any bonds they had bought or had been left with. Similarly in cases of war or political crisis, which might bring prices down, they were the first to sell.

These operations were so commonplace that a special vocabulary developed: the lenders were known as negotiating bankers, merchant bankers, fund brokers; the stock jobbers and canvassers were 'entrepreneurs': they had to distribute and 'market' the *obligations* to private investors. They were also known as traffickers in funds. To leave them out of the process would be to court disaster since they could ruin any operation. This information comes from the correspondence of J.H.F. Oldecop, Catherine II's consul in Amsterdam: year after year, he reports how hard-up princes and their agents are going, with more or less success, through the same motions: 'There is at present', he writes in April 1770, 'some negotiation afoot with Messrs. Horneca, Hoguer and Co. [the firm which specialized in French and pro-French affairs] on behalf of Sweden, which is said to be for five million, and which began with one million. The first million was taken up, about half of it being placed in Brabant, it is even said against money from the Jesuits.'[350] But everyone thinks that the sum remaining to be negotiated will 'be difficult to get together'. Oldecop then found himself, on orders from the Russian government, engaged upon negotiating a loan from Hope and Co., André Fels and Son, and Clifford and Son, where he had 'contacts', and who were among 'the principal businessmen of this city'.[351] The problem was that St Petersburg was 'not a money market where one can send money or withdraw it by every mail'. The best solution would be to make the payments in Amsterdam itself, and for repayment and interest to arrange for shipments of copper to Holland. In March 1763,[352] it was the turn of the elector of Saxony to ask for a loan of 1,600,000 florins, to be paid, at the request of the merchants of Leipzig 'in Dutch ducats which are at present fetching very high prices'.

The French government was one of the last to apply to Amsterdam, and then it was for a series of loans which proved catastrophic for itself as well as for the subscribers, who were thunderstruck when on 26 August 1788, the French government suspended payments. 'This bolt from the blue ... which is threatening to crush so many families', writes Oldecop, 'has given a violent and terrible shock to all foreign dealers'. Loan bonds fell from 60 to 20%.[353] The big firm of Hope, deeply committed to English stocks, had been very well-advised to steer clear of French loans. Was it by luck or good management? The Hopes certainly had no cause to regret their decision. In 1789, the head of the firm exercised 'such sway' over the Amsterdam Bourse 'that it is unthinkable that the exchange rates should be fixed before he arrives'.[354] He also acted as intermediary, on the occasion of the 'Batavian revolution', for English subsidies to Holland.[355] In 1789, he was even able to thwart the French government's attempts to buy grain in the Baltic.[356]

A change of perspective: away from Amsterdam

Let us now leave the heart of this great network and move away from Amsterdam, the central control tower. Our next problem is to see how this entire network, which I see as a superstructure, connected at lower levels with lesser economies. It is with these connections, meeting-points and multiple links that we shall be particularly concerned, since they reveal the way in which a dominant economy can exploit subordinate economies, while not soiling its own hands with the less profitable activities or types of production, or even, most of the time, directly supervising the lesser links in the chain of trade.

The solution varied from region to region, depending on the nature and the effectiveness of the domination exerted by the central economy. Four examples will suffice, I think, to indicate such differences: the Baltic countries, France, England and the East Indies.

The armaments industry was developed in Sweden with the help of the Dutch and became one of the most important in Europe. This is the foundry at Julitabroek. (Rijksmuseum, Amsterdam.)

The Baltic countries

The lands bordering the Baltic are too diverse for the sample we shall consider to be thought representative of the whole. And a number of inland regions – mountainous, forested or marshy, scattered with lakes and peat-bogs – in any case remained outside normal communications.

The severe depopulation of these zones turned them into semi-deserts. The Swedish Norrland for instance, running north from the Dalälven valley, was an immense stretch of forest, between the bare mountains of Norway to the west and the narrow cultivated strip along the Baltic coast to the east. The swift rushing rivers crossing it from west to east still carry down impressive masses of tree-trunks when the ice melts, even today. Norrland alone is bigger than the rest of Sweden put together,[357] but at the end of the Middle Ages, it contained barely 60,000 or 70,000 inhabitants. It was a primitive region, essentially exploited, to the limited extent that it was exploitable at all, by the merchant guild of Stockholm: in other words a truly peripheral zone. And the Dalälven valley has always been recognized as a crucial dividing line. According to an old Swedish saying, 'oaks, crayfish and noblemen [and, one might add, wheat] are not found north of the river'.[358]

The Norrland was far from an isolated example: one has only to think of the many parts of Finland empty of all but woods and lakes, or of the many desolate inland regions of Poland and Lithuania. But everywhere above this elementary level, economies could be found: inland economies in which agriculture and its surpluses represented the sum of economic activity; lively coastal economies, sometimes animated by extraordinary villages of sea-faring traders; urban economies, developing and imposing their presence more often by force than by persuasion; and increasingly, territorial economies, gradually taking shape and moving into action: Denmark, Sweden, Muscovy, Poland, the Prussian state of Brandenburg, which was in the throes of a deep and irresistible transformation since the coming to power of the Great Elector, in 1640. It was these potential giants, the national economies, which were gradually to gain political leadership and fight for domination of the Baltic region.

This region therefore offers to our observation the whole range of economies existent in the seventeenth and eighteenth centuries, from the *Hauswirtschaft* to the *Stadtwirtschaft* and the *Territorialwirtschaft*.[359] And the web of complicities covering the Baltic brought into being a world-economy which capped the whole. As if superimposed on the lower-level economies, it surrounded them, constrained and disciplined them, but also carried them along, for the basic inequality between dominant and dominated was not without its compensations in the form of mutual services: I may exploit you, but from time to time I may do you a favour.

In short, let us say, in order to have a fixed perspective, that neither the voyages of the Norsemen, nor the Hansa, neither Holland nor England, while they successively built up this series of dominant economies in the Baltic, had created the economic foundations without which exploitation from above would have had nothing to connect with. I have already shown how Venice,[360] in a former age, had similarly taken hold of, but not created, the economy of the Adriatic.

Sweden, which will be our chief example, was a territorial economy in the making, at once precocious and retarded. It was precocious in the sense that a Swedish political unit had very early taken shape, centred on Uppsala and the shores of Lake Mälar in the eleventh century, later developing southwards into east and west Gottland. But it was economically backward in the sense that by the beginning of the thirteenth century, the merchants of Lübeck were already settled in Stockholm which commanded the narrow passage between the Baltic and Lake Mälar (twice the surface area of Lake Geneva) and they remained active there until the end of the fifteenth century.[361] The city did not aspire to its own fully-fledged career free from rivals until the advent of the Vasa dynasty in 1523.

In the Swedish case then, *as for so many other national economies*, an economic area slowly took shape around a political area which had already been defined. But there were also fairly obvious special reasons in Sweden why this development was so slow.

In the first place, communications were difficult or non-existent (Sweden's good road system dates from the eighteenth century)[362] in this immense area of more than 400,000 km² which long wars had expanded to the dimensions of an empire (embracing Finland, Livonia, Pomerania, Mecklenburg and the bishoprics of Bremen and Verden). In 1660 or so, this empire still measured 900,000 km² (including Sweden itself). Part of it would be lost in 1720 (by the Peace of Stockholm signed with Denmark) and 1721 (by the Peace of Nystadt with Russia), but Finland, a huge colonial dominion,[363] would remain in Swedish possession until its annexation by Russia under Alexander I in 1809. If one adds to these regions the surface area of the Baltic which Sweden tried to surround with her possessions (about 400,000 km²) the total amounts to over a million square kilometres.

Another of Sweden's weaknesses was her low population: there were 1,200,000 Swedes, 500,000 Finns and a million other nationals[364] scattered along the shores of the Baltic and North Sea. Claude Nordmann[365] was right to point out the contrast between the 20 million subjects of Louis XIV's France and the barely three million inhabitants of the Swedish empire. Its 'greatness'[366] was only possible by dint of superhuman effort. A centralized bureaucracy going back a long way and itself expensive had established a degree of fiscal exploitation going well beyond what was reasonable, and which alone made possible the imperialist policies of Gustavus Adolphus and his successors.

The last and perhaps the cruellest of Sweden's inadequacies was that the waters of the Baltic, the essential area for transport, were not under Swedish control. Until the war of the Augsburg League (1689-97) her merchant navy was mediocre: she had plenty of ships, true, but they were of very small tonnage, mere open boats from villages engaged in coastal trade. Her war fleet, first built in the seventeenth century, was not, even after the foundation in 1679 of the naval base at Karls Krona,[367] the equal of either the Danish or later the Russian navy. In fact shipping in the Baltic had been monopolized in turn by the Hanseatic ships, then after the sixteenth century by Holland. In 1597, almost 2000 Dutch vessels entered the Baltic,[368] which was by now entirely caught in the close-knit web of Holland's trade network. Sweden, despite all the benefits derived from conquest, or from the customs income which she appropriated by controlling the waterways and trade of northern Germany, was in turn caught in the toils of the capitalists of Amsterdam. In the fifteenth century, Stockholm, as the turntable of foreign trade, had passed everything on to the Hansa, and in particular to Lübeck;[369] but from now on, it would all be travelling to Amsterdam. The yoke was solidly in position: even the Swedes were well aware that getting rid of the Dutch, should favourable circumstances present themselves, would effectively mean suspending the vital commodity trade of the Baltic and striking their own country to the heart. So although they were hostile to their demanding masters, they were not anxious to place themselves in the hands of either the French or the English in order to liberate themselves. Indeed in 1659, the English were warned by Swedish officials[370] not to drive the Dutch out of the Baltic, unless they were prepared to take their place.

Until about the 1670s when the English penetration of the Baltic became more marked, the Dutch kept all competitors at bay. Their merchants were not content merely to manage Swedish affairs from Amsterdam. Many Dutch families, and not the least among them – the de Geers, the Trips, the Cronströms, the Blommaerts, the Cabiljaus, the Wewesters, the Usselincks and the Spierincks[371] – settled in Sweden, sometimes took out Swedish nationality, obtained letters of nobility and thereby acquired total freedom of manoeuvre.

Dutch enterprise penetrated deep into the Swedish economy, even in the sector of production, and in the employment of cheap peasant labour, Amsterdam controlled not only the products of the northern Swedish forests (timber, beams, planks, masts, tar, pitch, resin) but also all the activity of the mining districts of Bergslag, a little way from the capital and the shores of Lake Mälar. Imagine a circle of 15,000 km² surface area, within which gold, silver, lead, zinc, copper and iron were mined – the last two being crucial to Swedish production, copper until 1670 when the Falun mines were exhausted, and iron thereafter it was increasingly being exported to England in the form of iron castings and plates). Outside Bergslag stood the blast furnaces and foundries, the cannon and shot factories.[372] This impressive metal industry helped Sweden to achieve political power, but not economic independence, since the mining sector was dependent on Amsterdam in the seventeenth century, as it had been on Lübeck in earlier centuries. The model industries built up by the de Geers and the Trips were not in fact as new as is sometimes thought. It was the Walloon workers of the Liège district (the birthplace of Louis de Geer, the 'iron king') who introduced the great brick blast furnaces to Bergslag, but long before this German workers had built very large furnaces there from timber and earth.[373]

When in 1720-21, Sweden was reduced to the Sweden-Finland bloc, she looked westward for compensation for her losses in the Baltic. This was when Göteborg, founded on the Kattegat in 1618 as Sweden's window on the West, began its rise to fame. The Swedish merchant navy was expanded, increasing both the number and the tonnage of its ships (228 in 1723; 480, three years later in 1726) and it was beginning to venture outside the Baltic: in 1732, the first Finnish ship reached Spain from Abo.[374] In the previous year, on 14 June 1731,[375] the Swedish Indies Company received its charter from the king. This company, with headquarters in Göteborg, was to have quite a long and prosperous career (the dividends reaching 40 and even 100%). For Sweden had been able to take advantage of her neutrality and of naval conflicts in the West to exploit her opportunities. Sweden frequently offered ships flying her flag of convenience to other powers if they asked for them, a profitable service.[376]

This expansion of the Swedish merchant fleet was the sign of a comparative liberation: it meant direct access to the salt, wine and textiles of the West, as well as to colonial products; and by the same token it eliminated the middlemen. Being compelled to compensate for her trade imbalance by exports and services, Sweden needed the cash surplus that would enable her to maintain a monetary circulation saturated with notes from the *Riksbank* (founded in 1657 and re-founded in 1668).[377] A careful mercantilist policy strove to set up industries, with varying degrees of success: shipbuilding was very successful, high quality silk and wool less so. In the end, Sweden continued to depend on the trade circuits of Amsterdam; and her prosperous Indies Company allowed large-scale foreign participation, notably by the English, both in investment and in the provision of crews and cargo-masters.[378] The moral of the story is that it is hard to shake off the heavy hand of an international economy which is never short of resources or subterfuges.

Through the recent work of Sven Erik Astrom,[379] we can next pay a brief visit to Finland, which has the advantage of taking us to the lowest stratum of exchange, to the markets of Lappstrand and Viborg, a little fortified town in the south, on the edge of the Gulf of Finland. Here we find a form of peasant trading described by G. Mickwitz, V. Niitemaa and A. Soom as *söbberei* (from the word *sober* = friend, in Estonia and Livonia) and by Finnish historians as *majmiseri* (from the Finnish word *majanies* = guest). The use of such terms warns us that this was a form of exchange outside the usual norms, and confronts us once more with the still not entirely resolved problems of the theories of Karl Polanyi and his disciples.[380]

Less accessible to the West than Norway and Sweden, since it was farther away, Finland tended to offer for foreign export processed forest products, foremost among which was tar. At Viborg, tar was incorporated into a three-sided arrangement, consisting of the peasant producer; the state which hoped that the peasant as a taxpayer would be able to pay his dues in money; and the merchant, who was the only source able to provide the peasant with money, though only to take it back again via an essential piece of barter, in which salt was exchanged for tar. This was a three-handed operation between merchant, peasant and state, with the bailiff, a sort of administrator, acting as both commission agent and arbiter.

The merchants or 'burghers' of the little town of Viborg were German. By custom, when the peasant, their supplier and client, came to town, the merchant would put him up, and see to his board, lodging and bills. Predictably the peasant ran into debt, which debt is duly recorded in the account books of the German merchants of Viborg.[381] But these merchants were themselves simply agents, since orders for the goods and advance payment was sent to them from Stockholm – and the Swedish capital was in turn only passing on orders and credit from Amsterdam. Since tar was very big business (between a million and a

million and a half trees were cut down every year)[382] and since the peasant who
treated the wood was a peasant capable of visiting the market or finding out
from the little fishing-ports of the neighbourhood the price of salt (a crucial
element in this case), and since he was moreover a free peasant, he gradually
managed to extricate himself from the bonds of the *majmiseri*. But he could not
escape from the higher links in the chain, notably the Royal Tar Company set up
in Stockholm in 1648, which supervised and in fact fixed the price both of salt
and of tar. Lastly, he was as subject as anyone else to the general economic
situation. Thus, since the price of rye went up faster than that of tar towards the
end of the eighteenth century, there was extensive deforestation and development
of cereal-growing. So the Finnish peasant was not his own master, although he
did have a degree of freedom of movement at his own level.

Why did he have this comparative freedom? Sven Erik Astrom, who knows
this question better than I do, says that it was guaranteed by the peasants'
participation in the diets of the grand-duchy which, like the *Riksdag* in Stockholm, included a Fourth Estate, that of the peasants. Politics and the law thus
safeguarded the liberty of this peasant of the remote regions, as they did that of
the Swedish peasant who had also never been a serf. In part, this was because the
monarchical state, an enemy of the nobility, intervened on the peasants' side. In
short, masters of their own property, their *hemman*,[383] the Swedish peasants
were privileged compared to the growing mass of farm workers and the throng
of vagabonds and paupers, the *torpare*.[384] It is true that both Sweden and Finland
had large pioneer zones, and pioneer zones have a reputation for creating and
preserving peasant liberty.

But this is not our main concern. The interesting thing about the Finnish case
is that it enables us to see a little more closely into the 'market' situation of the
peasant, and in particular to note the point at which the large wholesale firm
took over from the merchant who collected the goods at the point of production
– to see how far down the scale the wholesaler intervened himself. The variable
height or connection where the upper chain joins the lower chain is an indication,
almost a gauge. As a rule, there were no Dutchmen in Viborg – they were all in
Stockholm.

My last example is that of Gdansk (Danzig), a strange town in many ways,
rich, populous, admirably situated, and having contrived better than any of the
other Hanseatic towns to keep the precious rights of its staple. Its small patriciate
was extremely rich.[385] 'Its burghers have the exclusive privilege of buying grain
and other goods which come from Poland ... to their town, and foreigners are
not permitted to trade with Poland, nor to send their goods through the town to
Poland; they are obliged to do their trade with the burghers, whether buying or
selling goods.' Savary des Bruslons[386] puts it with his customary clarity and
conciseness. In a few words, the Gdansk monopoly is defined: between the wide
world and the vast expanse of Poland, this city was if not the only[387] certainly by
far the most important point of entry and exit. This privilege was however linked

A Swedish foundry in 1781 (painting by Pehr Hilleström, National Museum of Stockholm). Labour is plentiful, technology is comparatively primitive (hammering by hand). And yet at this period, Swedish iron, imported in large quantities by England, was the best in the West for both quantity and quality.

to strict external control exerted by Amsterdam: there is a fairly close correlation between prices in Gdansk and those in Amsterdam[388] which dictated them, and if the latter city was so anxious to preserve the liberty of the port on the Vistula, it was because in so doing it was preserving its own interests. Moreover Gdansk had given way on the most important point: between the sixteenth and the seventeenth century, Dutch competition had put an end to Gdansk's shipping activities in the West and had stimulated, as if by way of compensation, a brief burst of industrial activity[389]

The respective positions of Gdansk and Amsterdam were therefore essentially no different from those of Stockholm and Amsterdam. What was different was the situation of Poland, the hinterland of the port which exploited it, a situation similar to that existing, for the same reasons, behind Riga,[390] another dominant port with a stranglehold over a hinterland of peasants reduced once more to serfdom; whereas in Finland, where western exploitation had reached the end of the line, and in Sweden, the peasantry remained free. It is true both that Sweden had not experienced a feudal regime in the Middle Ages, and that grain, wherever it was the object of a large-scale export trade, was an instrument of 'feudalization' or 'refeudalization', while it seems probable that mining or forest activities might predispose to a degree of liberty.

The Polish peasantry was at any rate caught in the toils of serfdom. But it is odd that Gdansk preferred to recruit for its trade the free peasants nearest the city or the minor gentry – rather than the magnates who were no doubt more difficult to deal with but whom the Danziger merchants eventually managed to manipulate too, by advancing to them, as to everyone else, down payments on the wheat or rye before it was delivered, and providing in exchange for grain the luxury goods of the West. In his dealings with the nobles, the merchant was able to dictate the terms of trade.[391]

It would be interesting to know more about these internal exchanges: to find out whether potential vendors were approached on the spot or whether they went in person to Gdansk; to discover the exact role of the intermediaries used by the city to make contact with the suppliers; to know who controlled or at any rate managed the boats that plied on the Vistula; who controlled the warehouses of Thorun where the grain was dried and stored from one year to the next as it was in the many-storeyed silos of Gdansk; or who was in charge at Gdansk of the *bordings*, the lighters which unloaded the ships and which could, because of their shallow draught, sail up and down the canal linking the town to the Vistula. In 1572, 1288 small boats and fishing smacks (Polish and Prussian) entered the lower Vistula, whereas over 1000 sea-going vessels arrived in the port, providing quite enough cargo to occupy full-time the 200 burgher wholesalers who met every day in the Junckerhoff, the active Stock Exchange of Gdansk.[392]

It is only too clear how Gdansk, cocooned in her egotism and comfort, exploited and betrayed the great Polish hinterland, moulding it to her own ends.

France versus Holland: an unequal struggle

In the seventeenth century, France was literally subjugated by the tiny Dutch Republic. The entire length of the coastline between Flanders and Bayonne, there was not a single port which did not see increasing numbers of Dutch vessels, usually manned by very few hands (perhaps seven or eight men) tirelessly loading wine, spirits, salt, fruit and other perishable goods,[393] or even linens and grain. In all these ports, but particularly in Bordeaux and Nantes, Dutch merchants and commission agents had come to settle. In appearance, and often in reality, these were modest individuals, towards whom the local population (though perhaps not the local traders) do not seem to have been unduly hostile. But they were making fortunes, amassing substantial capital and one fine day they would return home. For years they would have been integrated into local economic life, frequenting the market-place, the port and the neighbouring markets. I have already described how in the Nantes region they bought up in advance the local

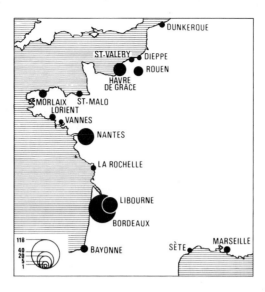

23 SHIPS FROM FRENCH PORTS ARRIVING AT TEXEL,
THE GATEWAY TO THE PORT OF AMSTERDAM
Almost all of these were Dutch ships, which were active along the entire French coast of the
North Sea, the Channel and the Atlantic. There was little contact, by contrast, with the French
Mediterranean ports. (From documents in the Archives Nationales, Paris, A.E., B1-165, f° 2,
12 January 1775.)

wines of the Loire valley.[394] Local merchants might fret and fume, but they could
never get the better of these competitors nor eliminate them: the goods exported
from the French Channel ports or those on the Atlantic were too often perishable,
so the steady stream of ships they provided was a trump card in Dutch hands,
not to mention others they held. And if a French boat attempted to carry wine or
local foodstuffs directly to Amsterdam, it came up against systematic opposition.[395]

Faced with French retaliatory measures of which there was no shortage, the
Dutch had the means of striking back. In the first place, they could do without
French imports. They could simply turn to other suppliers – hence the success of
Portuguese and Spanish wines, of those from the Azores and Madeira, and of
Catalan spirits. Rhine wines, which were scarce and costly in Amsterdam in
1669, were plentiful by the eighteenth century. Salt from Bourgneuf and Brouage
had long been preferred by the Dutch fish-salters to that of Setubal and Cadiz,
which was too caustic, but the Dutch learned to make Iberian salt milder, by
mixing it with sea-water from their own coast.[396] French luxury goods were
greatly in demand abroad, but they were not irreplaceable. It was always possible
to imitate them, to make goods in Holland of almost the same quality. Pomponne, Louis XIV's ambassador at the Hague, was most annoyed, when he met
Johan de Witt in 1669, to see that the Grand Pensionary's beaver hat had been

made in Holland, whereas a few years earlier, all such hats had been imported from France.[397]

What even the most intelligent Frenchmen did not always understand was that this was a dialogue on unequal terms. Compared to France, Holland with her trade networks and credit machinery could change policy at will. This was why France was no more successful than Sweden, despite her superior resources, despite all her efforts and displays of bad temper, at getting rid of the Dutch middlemen. Neither Louis XIV, nor Colbert, nor the latter's successors, were able to break out of the straitjacket. By the treaties of Nijmwegen (1678) and Ryswick (1697), the Dutch had systematically removed the obstacles previously placed in the way of their traders. 'Our plenipotentiaries in Risvic [Ryswick]', says the comte de Beauregard (15 February 1711), 'forgetting the importance of the maxims of M. Colbert, thought that it was a matter of indifference to agree to suppress the tax of fifty sols per barrel.'[398] What a mistake! And the mistake was repeated at Utrecht in 1713. Even before this, throughout the long war of the Spanish Succession, thanks to the passports issued generously by the French government, thanks to the 'disguised' ships of neutral countries, thanks to the accommodating attitudes of the French, and the overland trade which, with the help of smugglers, thrived along the French borders, Holland never went short of French products.

A long French report, written just after the Peace of Ryswick, gives yet another catalogue of the devices resorted to by the Dutch, their flagrant subterfuges, and the innumerable attempts to retaliate by the French who wanted both to respect and to get round the clauses in the treaties signed by Louis XIV's government, but who failed to catch their elusive enemy, 'the Dutch, whose genius, which has a certain subtlety in its very grossness, is disturbed only by reasons to do with their own interest'.[399] But 'their own interest' consisted of flooding France with goods either produced in Holland or re-exported from Holland. Only force could have made them loosen their grip, but force was not used. All the plans dreamed up by the French – closing all the kingdom's ports and frontiers, disturbing the Dutch fisheries, interrupting 'the private trading' of the merchants of Amsterdam (as distinct from the public trading of the Dutch companies in America, Africa and the Indies) – were easier said than done. For the French had no great merchants, 'those whom we regard as such being for the most part factors or foreign commission agents',[400] in other words front men for the Dutch firms. French gold and silver all seemed to end up in Holland.[401] And lastly, the French did not have enough ships. The prizes captured by French privateers 'during the last war, brought us a fairly good number fit for [long-distance] trade, but for want of merchants to fit them and navigators to sail them, we got rid of them to the English and the Dutch, who came to buy them back after the peace'.[402]

The same incapacity to resist is found if one goes back to Colbert's day. When the French *Compagnie du Nord* was founded in 1669, 'in spite of the

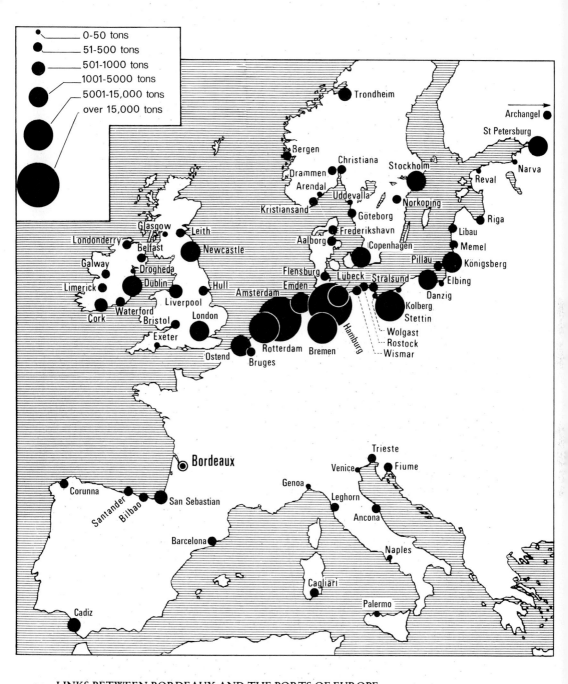

Legend

- 0–50 tons
- 51–500 tons
- 501–1000 tons
- 1001–5000 tons
- 5001–15,000 tons
- over 15,000 tons

Place names (north to south):

Archangel, St Petersburg, Narva, Trondheim, Reval, Riga, Libau, Memel, Königsberg, Elbing, Danzig, Pillau, Stettin, Kolberg, Wolgast, Rostock, Wismar, Stralsund, Lübeck, Stockholm, Norkoping, Göteborg, Frederikshavn, Aalborg, Copenhagen, Flensburg, Bergen, Drammen, Christiana, Arendal, Uddevalla, Kristiansand, Emden, Hamburg, Bremen, Amsterdam, Rotterdam, Bruges, Ostend, Glasgow, Leith, Londonderry, Belfast, Newcastle, Galway, Drogheda, Dublin, Hull, Limerick, Liverpool, Waterford, Cork, Bristol, London, Exeter

Bordeaux

Corunna, Santander, Bilbao, San Sebastian, Barcelona, Cadiz

Genoa, Leghorn, Ancona, Naples, Venice, Trieste, Fiume, Cagliari, Palermo

24 LINKS BETWEEN BORDEAUX AND THE PORTS OF EUROPE

Annual average tonnage sailing from Bordeaux between 1780 and 1791. The diagram clearly shows the predominance of the North in this shipping which sailed for the most part under the Dutch flag (all 273 boats arriving in Amsterdam from France in 1786 were Dutch according to the record kept by the French consul, De Lironcourt). The cargoes consisted chiefly of wines, sugar, coffee, indigo; and on the return journey of timber and grain. (From Paul Butal, 'Les aires commerciales européennes et coloniales de Bordeaux'.)

efforts of the Controller General and of the brothers Pierre and Nicolas Fromont, the merchants of Rouen refused to participate in the Company ... Those of Bordeaux for their part only entered it under constraint and compulsion'. Was it because 'they did not feel themselves to be rich enough either in ships or capital compared with the Dutch'?[403] Or was it because they were already operating as transmission belts in the Dutch network? If we are to believe Pottier de la Hestroy,[404] who wrote his long reports in about 1700, by this date French merchants were certainly acting as middlemen for Dutch firms. This was at least progress compared to the situation described by Father Mathias de Saint Jean in 1646,[405] when the Dutch were themselves acting as intermediaries in French trade centres; they seem to have given these positions up, in part at least, to local merchants afterwards. But it was not until the 1720s, as we have already seen,[406] that commercial capitalism in France began to shake off foreign control, with the emergence of a category of French merchants of international standing. And even then, we should not jump too hastily to conclusions: in Bordeaux, a city whose commercial rise had been spectacular, a witness reports at the end of the eighteenth century that it was 'of public notoriety that more than a third of trade was under Dutch control'.

England and Holland

English reaction to Holland's encroachments on trade began very early. Cromwell's Navigation Act dates from 1651, and Charles II confirmed it in 1660. Four times, England engaged in fierce wars with the Dutch (1652-4; 1665-7; 1672-4; 1782-3). Every time, Holland registered the blow. At the same time, increasingly prosperous production was being developed in England, sheltered by vigilant protectionism – proof no doubt that the English economy was better balanced than the French, less vulnerable to external forces, and that its products were more necessary to the Dutch, who had in any case always sought to placate the English, since the Channel ports were the safest refuge for their ships in bad weather.

But we should not imagine that England entirely eluded the clutches of the Dutch. Charles Wilson[407] has pointed out that any quick-witted Dutchman could find ways round the Navigation Acts. The Treaty of Breda had indeed granted some concessions in 1667. Whereas the Act forbade any foreign vessels to bring to England goods that were not manufactured in the shippers' own country, it was agreed in 1667 that certain goods from the Dutch hinterland should be 'regarded as Dutch' – that is goods brought down the Rhine or bought in Leipzig or Frankfurt and warehoused in Amsterdam, including German linens – provided they were bleached at Haarlem. Moreover the big Dutch trading firms had branches in London: the Van Necks, the Van Nottes, the de Neufvilles, the Cliffords, the Barings, the Hopes and the van Lenneps.[408] So there were plenty of friendly and accommodating relationships, necessitating voyages from one side of the Channel to the other, with mutual gifts of tulip and hyacinth bulbs, barrels of Rhine wine, hams and Dutch gin. Some English firms even conducted their correspondence in Dutch.

By such channels, openings and connections, the Dutch carrying trade handled goods both entering and leaving the British Isles, until at least 1700, and perhaps 1730. In the way of imports, they brought furs, hides, tar, timber, amber from Russia and the Baltic, and fine linens (from Germany though bleached in Holland) 'which the young men who were at this time growing more nice', wanted for their shirts in the eighteenth century, whereas the old ones 'were satisfied with necks and sleeves of the fine, which were put on loose above the country cloth'.[409] In the way of exports, a large proportion of colonial produce was bought by the Dutch at the auctions held by the East India Company; they also bought a great deal of tobacco, sugar, sometimes grain, pewter, and an 'incredible' quantity of woollen cloths – to the tune of over two million pounds sterling a year, Defoe said in 1728[410] – which were stored in warehouses in Rotterdam and Amsterdam before being re-exported, chiefly to Germany.[411] Thus England long remained a link in the Dutch entrepôt trade. An English pamphlet of 1689 even said 'All our merchants must turn Dutch factors'.[412]

A detailed study would certainly bring to light many effective links – in particular those created by credit and forward purchasing – which enabled the Dutch system to prosper in England, and indeed for a long time to do exceedingly well, so that the English (like the French) often had occasion to discover to their stupefaction that their own goods were being sold more cheaply in Amsterdam than in their country of origin.

It was only after 1730 that the Dutch commercial system began to break down in Europe, after fifty years of renewed activity from 1680 to 1730.[413] And it was only in the second half of the century that Dutch merchants began to complain that they were being 'reduced to mere shipping agents or expediteurs who no longer intruded into the actual exchange transactions of goods'.[414] There could be no better sign that the tide had turned. From now on, England was free from foreign interference and ready to take over the sceptre of world trade.

She was even better placed to do so in that the Dutch withdrawal had helped her to obtain what she had so sorely lacked in the seventeenth century: the possibility of large-scale borrowing by the state. The Dutch had always refused hitherto to place their capital at the disposal of the English state, since the guarantees offered had appeared unacceptable to them. But during the last decade of the century, the Westminster Parliament had accepted the principle of a fund secured on earmarked taxes, to guarantee both loans floated by the state and interest payments. From now on, the Dutch opened their purse-strings increasingly wider as time went by. English 'funds' afforded them not only a convenient investment, but higher interest rates than their money could earn in Holland and a choice focus for speculation on the Amsterdam Bourse – none of which, significantly, was available in France.

It was to England then that the surplus capital of Dutch businessmen now began to flow. Throughout the eighteenth century, they were major subscribers to English state loans, and also speculated in other English investments – shares in the East India Company, the South Sea Company or the Bank of England. The Dutch colony in London was richer and more numerous than ever. Its members came together at the Dutch church at Austin Friars, rather as the Genoese met at the church of San Giorgio in Palermo. If one counts alongside the Christian merchants (many of whom were Huguenot emigrés who had taken refuge in Amsterdam), the Jewish merchants who made up another powerful colony, though a smaller one, the picture is one of a veritable Dutch invasion.[415]

This was certainly the impression formed by the English, and Charles Wilson[416] regards this as an explanation of their 'phobia' about loans and the national debt, which they saw as dominated by foreigners. In fact, this influx of Dutch money gave English credit a boost. Less rich than France, but having more 'brilliant' credit as Pinto called it, England was always able to obtain the money she needed in sufficient quantities and at the right time – a great advantage.

The great shock for Holland was the violence with which England turned against her in 1782-3 and cast her to the ground. But had the end of the story not been foreseeable for some time? In the seventeenth century, Holland had in fact allowed herself to be seduced by the English national market, by the social milieu of London where her businessmen found themselves more at ease, made more money, and even found distractions not available in strait-laced Amsterdam. In the complicated game played by the Dutch, the English card was a joker – a winning card which suddenly lost the game.

Outside Europe: the East Indies

Is it possible to see in the first Dutch voyages to the Indies something quite different – the creation *ex nihilo* of a process of subordination which rapidly became a weighty structure?

Three stages can be distinguished in the early Dutch penetration of Asia (as no doubt in all European penetration there). W.H. Moreland listed them long ago in 1923:[417] first there was the 'Voyage' – the trading vessel, like a travelling bazaar, peddling its wares on a grand scale; then came the 'Factory', a concession operated within a country, or in a trade centre; and the last stage was territorial occupation. Macao was not much more than a factory, but with Batavia the colonization of Java began. As for the travelling bazaar, in the early years of the seventeenth century, there are plenty to choose from.

Take for example Paul Van Caerden's four ships – sent to the East Indies between 1599 and 1601[418] by a *voorkompanie*[419] (the New Brabant Company) – of which only two returned. The first leg of their voyage took them to Bantam on 6 August 1600. Because there were too many Dutch ships in the port, and therefore too many buyers, two of the boats were re-routed to the little port of

Passamans, where there was rumoured to be a glut of pepper. But the vendors were rogues, and the sea conditions dangerous. So it was decided, not without hesitation, to sail on to Atjeh (Achem) at the western tip of Sumatra. The two ships arrived there on 21 November 1600. They had already lost a lot of time: seven months and 15 days from Texel to Bantam, plus three months and 15 days to reach what they hoped was the ideal port. In fact the travellers had walked into the lion's den. The crafty and quick-witted king of Atjeh kept them hanging about, after extorting 1000 pieces of eight from them. In order to regain the advantage, the Dutch took refuge on their ships and seized nine merchant vessels which happened to be in port, three of them opportunely laden with pepper which their prudent captors 'placed under strong guard'. And negotiations began again until, having burned two of their prizes to set an example, the Dutch had to resign themselves to leaving this inhospitable port during the night of 21 to 22 January 1601. They had lost another two months in these dangerous tropical waters where the worms gnawed through the timbers of the ships. They had no choice now but to return to Bantam, where they arrived on 15 March after a further seven weeks at sea. Here by contrast there was no problem: Bantam was the Venice of the East. Some other Dutch ships had arrived at the same time and sent prices up, but the goods were taken on board and the two ships finally set sail for Europe on 22 April.[420]

What emerges from this experience is the difficulty, in this still unfamiliar world of the East, so complicated and so different from Europe, of making one's way into a trade circuit, let alone dominating it. In a metropolis of trade like Bantam, middlemen were available, and would present themselves immediately but they had the advantage of the newcomers. The situation could only start to move the other way when the Dutch had gained control of the Moluccan spice trade. This monopoly was the *sine qua non* for entry to all the currents of trade, one by one, first as a privileged partner and eventually as an indispensable presence. But perhaps the major fault committed by the Dutch was their insistence on controlling *everything* in the East – restricting production, ruining native trade, impoverishing and decimating the population – in fact killing the goose that laid the golden eggs.

Is is possible to generalize?

Our four case studies can be regarded as a series of samples. They are intended simply to indicate an overall situation, to show how a world-economy functioned by making use both of the high voltage at the centre and of the weaknesses and compliance of others. Success was only possible if the inferior and subject economies were accessible, in various ways but on a regular basis, to the dominant economy.

The connection with the ring of second-rank powers, that is Europe, operated smoothly with no need for undue pressure: the attraction and mechanisms of

Batavia, the sea-front, 1764

exchange, the interplay of capital and credit sufficed to keep it in working order. And Europe represented four-fifths of the whole of Dutch trade; the overseas trade was an extra, though an important one. It was the presence of these neighbouring countries – developed, competitive, although in an inferior position – which nourished the energy and effectiveness of the centre, as we have already seen. If China was not a magnetic world-economy, was this simply because of her insufficiently central position? Or, and this is perhaps another way of saying the same thing, was it because China lacked a semi-periphery sufficiently strong to provide energy for the core?

It is clear at any rate that the 'true' periphery, on the outer margins of a world-economy could only be controlled by force, violence, and subjugation – why not indeed say colonialism, classifying this incidentally as an ancient, indeed very ancient experience. Holland practised colonialism in Ceylon as she did in Java; Spain invented it in Latin America; England made use of it in India. But even in the thirteenth century, Venice and Genoa were acting as colonial powers, on the outer margins of the areas they exploited: the Genoese in Caffa and Chios; the Venetians in Cyprus, Candia and Corfu. Were these not forms of domination as absolute as anything achievable at the time?

On the decline of Amsterdam

We have explored the file on Dutch supremacy. Its brilliant history loses its lustre at the end of the eighteenth century. This dimming of the radiance should be described as withdrawal or decline rather than decadence in the full sense of the word as used and abused by historians. Amsterdam undoubtedly gave way to London, as Venice did to Antwerp and as London would one day to New York. The Dutch city nevertheless continued to lead a profitable existence – and it is still today one of the high altars of world capitalism.

In the eighteenth century, Amsterdam abandoned some of her commercial advantages to Hamburg and London or even Paris, but gained new ones, maintained certain trades, and her Stock Exchange activity continued to be very vigorous. Through the increase of the 'acceptance' trade, she expanded her banking sector to meet the enormous burst of growth in Europe, which she financed in a thousand ways, particularly in time of war (long-term commercial credit, marine insurance and re-insurance, etc.). As we have seen it was of 'public notoriety' that a third of the trade of Bordeaux depended on Dutch money.[421] What Richard T. Rapp has told us about Venice, during her so-called decline in the seventeenth century – how she contrived through adaptation, reconversion or new ventures, to maintain a G.N.P. as high as in the preceding century – counsels one to be careful in charting the losses of a declining city.[422] Yes, it is true that the expansion of banking represented a process of change and deterioration of capital in Amsterdam; yes, the city's social oligarchy became inward-looking, withdrawing as in Venice and Genoa, from active trade, and tending to turn into a society of rentier investors on the look-out for anything that would guarantee a quiet and privileged life, including the protection of the Stadtholders. But if this handful of privileged persons may be reproached for choosing this role (though it was not always one they had chosen freely) they cannot be faulted for their calculations: they survived unscathed the troubles of the revolution and the empire and, according to some Dutch authors, were still there in 1848.[423] Yes, there was certainly a move from the elementary and as it were healthy tasks of economic life to the more sophisticated games of the money market. But Amsterdam was the prisoner of a destiny leading beyond her own responsibilities: it was the fate of every dominant capitalism to be caught up in an evolution already visible centuries earlier, in the Champagne fairs, and fated by its very success to come up against the threshold of financial activities or rather acrobatics, where the rest of the economy found it difficult to follow – or refused to do so. If one seeks the causes or the motives for Amsterdam's decline, in the last analysis one is likely to fall back on those general truths which hold for Genoa at the beginning of the seventeenth century as much as for Amsterdam in the eighteenth, and perhaps for the United States today, which is also handling paper money and credit to a dangerous degree. This at any rate is what is suggested by a study of the series of crises which hit Amsterdam in the latter part of the eighteenth century.

DUTCH CAPITAL IN 1782

According to an estimate by the Grand Pensionary Van der Spieghel, this amounted to a thousand million florins, invested as follows:

Loans to foreign states	335 million (of which 280 to England, 25 to France, 30 to other powers)
Colonial loans	140
Domestic loans (to provinces, companies, admiralties)	425
Silver, gold, jewels	50

(From Jan de Vries, *Rijkdom der Nederlanden*, 1927.)

The crises of 1763, 1772–3, 1780–3

Beginning in the 1760s, the mighty Dutch system experienced several serious and incapacitating crises: crises which all resemble each other and appear to be connected with credit. The mass of commercial paper, the total sum of 'artificial money', seems to have enjoyed a degree of autonomy vis-à-vis the economy in general, but there were limits which could not be overstepped. At the height of one crisis (18 January 1773) Maillet du Clairon, the watchful French consul in

Amsterdam, sensed these limits when he explained that the London market was as 'close-pressed' as that of Amsterdam, which was 'proof that there is in all things a point after which one has necessarily to fall back'.[424]

Were all these accidents caused by the same simple, indeed too simple process? Was a certain volume of paper money simply too much for the European economy, which periodically let the burden fall? The collapse even seemed to happen with regularity every ten years: 1763, 1772–3, 1780–3. In the first and third of these crises, war undoubtedly played some part: war is naturally inflationary, it holds up production, and the day it ends, the cost has to be counted and the resulting imbalance rectified. But there was no war to explain the 1772–3 crisis. Was this what is known as an *ancien régime* crisis, sparked off by a failure in agricultural production whose consequences spread to all other economic activities? An ordinary crisis in other words? There were certainly catastrophic harvests throughout Europe in 1771–2. A report from the Hague (24 April 1772) says that in Norway there is famine so intense 'that they are grinding up the bark of trees instead of rye flour' and the same extremity is reported from some parts of Germany.[425] Was this the reason for the violent crisis, aggravated possibly by the consequences of the disastrous famine which also hit India in the same years 1771–2, throwing into confusion the workings of the English East India Company? No doubt these were all factors, but is the real cause not once more the periodic return of a credit crisis? At all events, in every case, at the centre of each of these crises, whether as consequence or cause, there was a shortage of currency and the bank rate suddenly shot up to intolerable levels of 10 or 15%.

Contemporary observers always connected such crises to some major bankruptcy – such as the Neufvilles' in August 1763,[426] the Cliffords' in December 1772,[427], the Van Faerelinks' in October 1780.[428] While understandable, this interpretation is not very convincing. The five million florins of the Clifford bankruptcy, or the six million florins of the Neufvilles' were certainly not negligible; they played the role of detonator on the Amsterdam Bourse, placing a bomb under business confidence. But are we to believe that if the Neufvilles had not engaged in some disastrous deals in Germany, if the Cliffords had not entered into hare-brained speculation in East India Company shares on the London Stock Exchange, or if the burgomaster Van Faerelink had not suffered very bad losses in the Baltic, the crisis mechanism would not have rolled into motion and become general? On each occasion the shock created by a major bankruptcy touched off the collapse of a system already under severe strain. It is therefore worth enlarging our field of vision, both in time and space, and above all comparing the crises in question – because they happened one after another, because they punctuated the evident decline of Holland and finally because they are both similar and dissimilar and the explanation would benefit from making the comparison.

In what ways were they similar? They were all modern credit crises, which entirely sets them apart from so-called *ancien régime* crises[429] rooted in the rhythms and processes of the agricultural and industrial economy. Yet how different they are! Charles Wilson[430] considers that the 1772-3 crisis was more serious and far-reaching than that of 1763 – and he is right – but was the 1780-3 crisis not even more far-reaching? Between 1763 and 1783, I would suggest that the degree of disturbance to Dutch affairs had become greater and more marked, and that while these ten-year crescendos had been taking place, the underlying economic context had been profoundly transformed.

The first crisis, in 1763, followed on the heels of the Seven Years' War (1756-63) which had been for Holland – a neutral throughout – a period of unparalleled commercial prosperity. During the hostilities,

> Holland effected almost single-handed ... all the trade of France, especially that carried on with America and Africa which is in itself a great affair, and has done this with an increase in profits of a hundred and often over two hundred per cent ... Some Dutch merchants have grown rich on this, despite the loss of a great number of their ships, captured by the English and estimated at over a hundred million [florins].[431]

But this revival of trade, this return to the good old days, meant that Holland had to engage in huge credit operations, and there was an undisciplined free-for-all of acceptances, extensions of bills of exchange through new bills on other firms, plus a series of *wisselruiterij* operations.[432] 'Only the imprudent took on large commitments', one good judge tells us.[433] But was this true? How could even the wise resist being caught up in the machinery of 'circulation'? Natural credit, forced credit and 'make-believe' credit piled up to produce a paper mountain, 'of such size that according to exact calculations, it is fifteen times greater than the cash or real money in Holland'.[434] We may not be as sure of the accuracy of this figure as our informant, a Dutchman from Leyden, but it is clear that the Dutch firms were faced with a dramatic situation when suddenly the discounters refused to discount paper – or rather could no longer do so. With the currency shortage, the crisis spread, leaving a trail of bankruptcies: it reached not only Amsterdam but Berlin, Hamburg, Altona, Bremen, Leipzig,[435] Stockholm,[436] and hit hard in London which was appealed to by the Dutch money market. A Venetian writing from London on 13 September 1763,[437] reported that the previous week, according to rumours in the City, a 'remarkable' sum of £500,000 had been sent to Holland, to the aid of the beleaguered trading community of Amsterdam.

But can one really speak of 'aid' when all the Dutch were doing was recalling the capital they had invested in English stocks?[438] Since the crisis had begun on 2 August, with the bankruptcy of Arendt Joseph (with debts totalling 1,200,000 florins) and the Neufville brothers (6 million) the arrival of the money from England had taken a whole month of lamentation, despair and frantic appeals. There had been spectacular developments: bankruptcies in Hamburg for instance – many among Jewish merchants[439] – four in Copenhagen, six in Altona,[440] 35 in Amsterdam[441] and 'something which has never happened before, is that at the beginning of this week, bank money dropped to one and a half per cent below cash'.[442] On 19 August, the bankruptcies totalled 42,[443] and 'we already know some of the next victims'. Oldecop, the Russian consul, viewing the catastrophe, did not hesitate to blame 'the great avidity for gains which some merchants wished to make on shares during the war'.[444] 'Pride comes before a fall' he wrote on 2 August – what had been predicted and feared for so long had just come to pass.

The Amsterdam Stock Exchange was immediately paralysed: 'The Bourse is at a standstill ... there is no discounting[445] or exchange; there are no prices quoted; everyone distrusts everyone else'.[446] The only solution would be to play for time,[447] or for 'extensions' to use the language of the fair. One would-be author of a rescue plan[448] talks in his paper of a *surchéance*, a moratorium, in other words a breathing-space granted by the state, so that the usual channels of circulation could be set moving again. His mistake was to suppose that a decision by the United Provinces alone would be sufficient, whereas the situation required the agreement of all the crowned heads and states of Europe.

But was not the best remedy the arrival, in Amsterdam, of coin or ingots? The Neufvilles (and they were not the only ones) had installed in their country residence near Haarlem a factory for 'purging and refining the bad money from Prussia, of which several million [fl.] had been sent them from Germany by the barrel'. This bad money, issued by Frederick II during the Seven Years' War, was collected by local Jewish merchants in touch with Jewish merchants in Amsterdam.[449] The latter, who were almost all engaged in currency exchange and who had been hit very hard by the crisis, drew bills of exchange on this providential metal travelling towards them. 'The Jewish merchants Ephraim and Jizig', wrote the Neapolitan consul in the Hague, 'who are entrepreneurs of the currency of the king [of Prussia], the day before yesterday (16 August 1763) sent three million crowns to Hamburg by post-chaise under escort, and I have learned that other bankers are also sending considerable sums to Holland to maintain their credit.'[450]

The cash injection was the right answer. Indeed the Bank of Amsterdam had, from 4 August, contrary to its usual rules, consented to accept 'gold and silver ingots as deposits',[451] which was one way of drawing bullion straight into circulation.

We need follow no further this liquidity crisis, violent, drastic, hurting only the weaker firms and emptying the market of its shady speculators – a healthy and useful crisis on the whole from a certain point of view, at least if one was in the epicentre of this financial earthquake: not so if one was in Hamburg, where since the beginning of August and before the bolt from the blue of the Neufville bankruptcy, the port had been crammed with boats vainly waiting to load goods and thinking of going east towards other ports;[452] or in Rotterdam, where already in April[453] there had been an uprising by the 'common people' and where 'the burghers had had to take up arms and disperse the mutineers'. But reactions were different in Amsterdam, which apparently escaped such distress and disturbances and which regained her balance without too much difficulty when the storm had passed over: 'The city's merchant bankers were to rise again like the phoenix, or rather to emerge from their own ashes and identify themselves in the end as the creditors of the ruined stock markets'.[454]

In 1773, triggered off by the Clifford bankruptcy of 28 December 1772, the crisis began again and followed the same course: the same sequence of events, the same inevitable progression. Oldecop could have copied out the letters he had sent ten years earlier. The Bourse ground to a halt. 'Several houses', wrote the Russian consul, 'have followed the failure of Clifford and Son. Messrs Horneca, Hogger and Co., who do everything for France and Sweden, have been ... two or three times on the point of insolvency. On the first occasion, 300,000 florins were collected for them in one night – and they had to pay them out the next day'; on the second occasion 'a coachload of gold coin' arrived most opportunely from Paris. 'Messrs Rijé, Rich and Wilkieson, who are the correspondents of Messrs Frédéric in St Petersburg, have had silver dispatched from England.' (The French gold was worth a million florins, the English silver two million.) 'Messrs Grill, who do much trade with Sweden', have had to suspend payments because they could not 'discount their bills of exchange on other people'. Messrs César Sardi and Co., an ancient firm which had handled various negotiations for the court of Vienna, 'has been obliged to follow the torrent'.[455] It is true that these Italians who preferred entertainment to hard work had already seen their credit sink.[456] The most recent catastrophe was the last straw as far as they were concerned. But other firms, which also found themselves insolvent had in fact been quite solid, having simply been taken by surprise by the general collapse, and other bankruptcies would have followed unless immediate action had been taken.[457] Once more, the city decided, with the aid of the bank, to advance two million florins in cash, guaranteed by the leading businessmen in town, in order to assist those who needed money and could offer sureties, either in the form of goods or valuables. 'They are not prepared however to accept endorsed bills of exchange, even if these are on the foremost houses, or in that case, two million' would be of no use at all.[458] Clearly the spectacular – and definitive – bankruptcy of Clifford's, a firm which had existed for a hundred and fifty years, had brought about a general collapse of business confidence, and demands for repayment far exceeded the amount of liquid cash available.

Was this a carbon copy of the 1763 crisis? Contemporaries certainly thought so. It was a similar short-lived crisis, of which the most dramatic moments were over quite soon, by the end of January. But the fact that it was more serious than the previous one raises a problem which Charles Wilson has in the main solved.[459] The decisive difference was that this time the initial incident occurred in London, not in Amsterdam. The disaster which engulfed the Cliffords and their associates was the collapse in the shares of the East India Company, as it sought to cope with a difficult situation in India, particularly in Bengal. And the share prices fell too late for the English speculators who had been waiting for a fall, and too early for the Dutch who were banking on a rise. Both were badly hit, particularly since speculative purchases were usually made by paying only 20% of the share price in question, and the rest on credit. So losses were enormous.

The crisis originating in London led to intervention by the Bank of England which quickly brought about the suspension of discounting of any doubtful bills and eventually of all paper. It would be fruitless to speculate whether the Bank of England was tactically mistaken in thus hitting Amsterdam, centre of the money and credit market. What can be said is that if there was a phoenix in this case which came through the fire unscathed, it was London, which once the scare was over continued to attract investment, from the revived 'surpluses' of Amsterdam.

In Amsterdam, things were not so good: even in April 1773, three months after the end of the alert, trading was uneasy: 'for two weeks past, one hears of nothing but thefts committed nightly. In consequence, the ordinary night watch has been doubled, and citizens' patrols have been sent to the various districts, but of what avail is this vigilance if the cause of the evil is not destroyed and if the government has no means of remedying it?'[460] In March 1774, more than a year after the crisis, an air of discouragement still pervaded the merchant class:

> What will be the last straw for credit in this market [writes the consul Maillet du Clairon] is that five or six of the richest firms have recently quitted trade; among them is the house of André Pels and Son, which is even better-known in foreign centres than in Amsterdam, of which it has often been the mainstay. If rich Houses are forsaking the Stock Exchange, big business will soon disappear from it as well. Since it will no longer be able to sustain large losses, it will not dare to try to make large profits. It is true however that there is still more money in Holland than in any other country, relatively speaking[461]

But what was really at stake, in the eyes of historians that is, was leadership within the European world-economy.

Even in February 1773, our consul, on learning that there had been an enormous bankruptcy (1,500,000 piastres) in Genoa, put this incident (and all the others occurring in the money markets of Europe) down to Amsterdam, this city 'being the centre from which they almost all derive their movement'.[462] I believe that, on the contrary, Amsterdam was no longer the centre or epicentre of Europe. This had already shifted to London. Can one suggest that a highly-convenient rule might operate in this context, to wit, that any city which is becoming or has become the centre of a world-economy, is the first place in which the seismic movements of the system show themselves, and subsequently the first to be truly cured of them? If so, it would shed a new light on Black Thursday in Wall Street in 1929, which I am inclined to see as marking the *beginning* of New York's leadership of the world.[463]

From the historian's point of view then, Amsterdam had already ceased to be a world leader by the time of the third crisis, in the 1780s. This was in any case a crisis differing from the preceding ones not only in length (it lasted from 1780 until at least 1783), in the particularly devastating character it assumed in Holland, and in its association with the fourth Anglo-Dutch war, but also because it fits into a much broader economic crisis of altogether another type: the *intercycle*[464] which Ernest Labrousse identified as having affected France between 1778 and 1791.[465] It is within this phase, lasting over a decade, that we should place the episode of the Anglo-Dutch war of 1781–4, which ended with the occupation of Ceylon by the English, who also gained access to the Moluccas. Holland was by then like the rest of Europe, grappling with a long-term crisis affecting the whole of the economy and not merely the credit system, a crisis similar to that suffered by France under Louis XVI as she emerged financially ruined, if politically triumphant, from the War of American Independence.[466] 'By succeeding in rendering America free, France has so exhausted herself that in her triumph, having sought to humiliate English pride, she has ruined herself and now sees her finances exhausted, her credit diminished, the Ministry divided and the whole Kingdom in factions' – such was Oldecop's verdict on France on 23 June 1788.[467] But neither the weakness of Holland nor that of France are entirely to be explained by war, which is too often evoked as an explanation.

The outcome of a long and widespread crisis is often that the map of the world is simplified, brutally cutting powers down to size, strengthening the strong and further weakening the weak. Defeated politically, according to the wording of the treaty of Versailles (3 September 1783), England emerged the economic victor, since from now on the centre of the world was in her capital, with the consequences and imbalances which that entailed.

At this moment of truth, Holland's weaknesses, some of which were already several decades old, stood suddenly revealed. Her government, whose former efficiency we have described, had become inactive and divided against itself; the urgent armaments programme had remained a dead letter; her arsenals were incapable of modernizing;[468] the country seemed to be falling into irremediably hostile sections; new taxes introduced to try to restore the situation were causing general discontent; and the Stock Exchange itself had become 'gloomy'.[469]

The 'Batavian' revolution[470]

To crown everything, Holland suddenly found herself faced with a domestic political and social revolution – launched by the 'patriots' who were partisans of France and of 'freedom'.

In seeking to explain this revolution, one might regard it as beginning in 1780, which saw the start of the fourth Anglo-Dutch war; or in 1781, with the appeal to the Dutch people (*Aan het Volk von Nederlande*) by Van der Capellen, the founder of the 'Patriot Party'; or on 20 May 1784, with the peace treaty signed in Paris between England and the United Provinces, which sounded the knell of Dutch greatness[471].

An English satirical engraving: the pro-French 'patriots' are practising marksmanship against a drawing of a Prussian hussar. (Armand Colin Photo Library.)

Seen as a whole, this revolution is a string of violent and confused events, accidents, speeches, rumours, bitter enmities and armed confrontations. Oldecop's temperament naturally inclined him to disapprove of the revolutionaries, whom he misunderstood but instinctively condemned. From the start, he fulminated against their claims and not least against their use of the word freedom – *vrijheid* – as if Holland were not already free! 'The most amusing thing of all', he writes, 'is the affected expression of these tailors, shoemakers, cobblers, bakers, cabaret-keepers, etc.... transformed into soldiers.'[472] A handful of real soldiers would soon bring this rabble to its senses, he thought. These improvised soldiers had come together to form insurrectionary popular militias, 'armed corps' to defend democratic municipalities in certain towns, though not all. For the 'patriotic' terror was soon countered by the 'Orangist' violence of the partisans of the Stadtholder. Rumour, riot and repression followed on one another's heels and the disorder spread. Utrecht rose up, there was pillage and looting:[473] a ship bound for the Indies was completely sacked and even the silver coin for paying the ship's crew was taken.[474] The people threatened the aristocrats, whom Oldecop from time to time calls 'the moneybags' (*les richards*). But this was a class struggle as much as a 'bourgeois revolution'.[475] The patriots were predominantly petit-bourgeois: French dispatches call them simply 'the bourgeoisie' or 'the republicans' or 'the republican system'. Their ranks were swelled by certain 'regents' who were enemies of the Stadtholder and who hoped to use the patriotic movement to rid themselves of the insignificant William V. But this limited republican movement could in no circumstances count upon the ordinary people, who were fervently imbued with the Orangist myth and always ready to mobilize, strike, loot and burn.

This revolution, which I would in no sense under-estimate (it is proof *a contrario* of Dutch success) has been insufficiently recognized for what it was, the first revolution on the European mainland, the forerunner of the French Revolution, and unquestionably a serious conflict, which 'divided even bourgeois families, father against son, husband against wife ... with unbelievable ferocity'.[476] And it had its own militant vocabulary, revolutionary and counter-revolutionary, an extremely forceful and surprisingly precocious one. As early as November 1786, a member of the government, irritated by all the debates, tried to define liberty:

> The wise man and the impartial judge, [he explained in the course of a long speech] do not understand the meaning of this word which is so exaggerated at the present time; they see on the contrary that this cry ['Long live Freedom!'] is the signal for general revolt and imminent anarchy ... What does freedom mean? ... It means peacefully enjoying the gifts of nature, being protected by the laws of the land, cultivating land and the sciences, trade, the arts and professions in security ... meanwhile nothing is so hostile to these precious benefits as the conduct of the so-called patriots.[477]

And yet the revolutionary agitation, energetic as it was, only contrived to divide the country into two opposing factions. As Henry Hope wrote[478]: 'It can only end in some absolute tyranny, whether by the Prince[479] or by the people' (his identification of the people with the patriots is odd, to say the least); and it would have taken very little on one side or the other to push the country into the arms of either one. But in its present state of weakness, the country was not to be the sole arbiter of its fate. The United Provinces were caught between England and France, as the prize of a trial of strength between the two great powers. At first, France seemed to have gained the upper hand, and signed a treaty of alliance with the United Provinces at Fontainebleau on 10 November 1785.[480] But this was as much an illusion for the patriots as for the Versailles government. English policy, based on the Stadtholder and his supporters, was helped by having an exceptional man on the spot, James Harris, the ambassador. Subsidies were skilfully distributed in the province of Friesland for instance, through the good offices of Hope and Co. Finally, the Prussians intervened and France, which had advanced a few troops into the Givet region,[481] did not respond. A Prussian detachment arrived, almost without firing a shot, at Amsterdam and at the gates of Leyden which was occupied. The city could have defended itself, but capitulated on 10 October 1787.[482]

Once the power of the Stadtholders was restored, a violent and systematic reaction set in, one that we would today describe as having fascist overtones. Everyone was supposed to wear the Orange colours in the street. Thousands of patriots fled abroad; some of the exiles, the *matadors* caused some stir, but from a great distance. In the country itself, the opposition put up a measure of resistance: some people wore very tiny orange cockades, others arranged them in the form of a V (for *vrijheid*); others did not wear them at all.[483] On 12 October, the associates of Hope and Co. presented themselves at the Stock Exchange wearing the colours, but were driven out and had to return home under the protection of the civil guards.[484] On another occasion, a fight broke out at the Exchange – a Christian merchant had turned up without his cockade[485] and had been challenged by some Jewish merchants who were all supporters of the Stadtholder.[486] But these were trifles compared to the violence and executions by the Orangist mob. In the 'regencies', burgomasters and aldermen were replaced, and a spoils system became established, with the members of old and illustrious families being ousted by newcomers, the nobodies of yesterday. Many burghers and patriots fled to Brabant or France – perhaps 40,000 in all.[487] To crown it all, the small Prussian army was billeted on the conquered land.

> From the moment the troops of the king of Prussia entered the territory of this Province [Holland] their pay was suspended and ... they have no other wages but looting, which is said to be the Prussian practice in wartime; what is certain is that the soldiers act according to this rule, and the flatlands are completely devastated; they do not exactly loot in the towns, at least not here [in Rotterdam] but they come into the shops and take goods without paying ... It is also the Prussian soldiers who demand and keep for themselves the dues paid on entering the town.[488]

The Prussians left in May 1788; but the pro-Orange reaction was by then well-established and took its full course.

The revolution continued to smoulder however in next-door Brabant. Brabant meant Brussels, which had become, like Amsterdam, an active money market, open to the needs and the boundless appetites of the Austrian government. Oldecop who had gradually reassured himself, nevertheless wrote prophetically on 26 February 1787: 'When Europe has amused herself long enough with the follies in Holland, there is every sign that people will start looking at France'.[489]

4

National Markets

NOTHING SEEMS so self-evident (to the historian at least, for the expression is not to be found in today's economic reference books)[1] as the classical notion of the *national market*. This is the term used to denote the economic coherence achieved within a given political unit – a unit that is of a certain size, essentially corresponding to what I have called 'the territorial state' or, as it might also be called, 'the nation-state'. Since within such units political maturity preceded economic maturity, our problem is to discover when, how, and for what reasons these states achieved in *economic* terms a degree of internal coherence and the faculty of acting as a unit vis-à-vis the rest of the world. We shall try, in other words, to locate an occurrence which changed the course of European history and relegated to the second rank those economic complexes which had centred on a single city.

The emergence of the national market inevitably corresponded to the faster pace of circulation and to an increase in both agricultural and non-agricultural production, as well as to the expansion of overall demand – all conditions which one might in the abstract suppose to have been achieved without the intervention of capitalism, as a natural consequence of regular overspill from the market economy. In practice however the latter often tended to remain regional, continuing to operate within the limits suggested by the exchange of diversified and complementary products. So the move from the regional to the national market, welding together a number of short-range, quasi-autonomous and often highly individualized economies, had nothing spontaneous about it. The national market was a form of coherence imposed both by political ambitions – not always realized in the event – and by the capitalist tensions created by trade – in particular by foreign and long-distance trade. As a rule, a measure of expansion in foreign trade *preceded* the laborious unification of the national market.

This is what inclines me to think that national markets are more likely to have developed in or near the centre of a world-economy, within the very interstices of capitalism, and that there was some correlation between their development and the differential geography implied by the progressive international division of labour. Contrariwise, the *weight* carried by the national

Frontispiece, by W. Hollar, to John Ogilby's book *Britannia* (1675), depicting a road leading out of London. This image corresponds by and large to the idea an Englishman of the late seventeenth century would have had of his native land's wealth: there is already a balance between foreign, seaborne trade (the ships in the background, the globe in the foreground), ordinary overland traffic (the coach coming down the road on the right, the riders on horseback, the pedlar on foot), animal husbandry (sheep, cattle, horses) and agriculture. Only industry is missing. (British Museum.)

market played its part in the endless struggle between the different aspirants to world domination – which in the eighteenth century meant the duel between Amsterdam (a city) and England (a 'territorial state'). The national market was one of the contexts within which there occurred, under the impact of both internal and external factors, the transformation essential to the take off of the industrial revolution – namely the growth of a diversified domestic demand, capable of stimulating production in a number of sectors and of opening pathways to progress.

The interest of studying national markets is not in dispute. The trouble is that it calls for the appropriate methods and instruments. Economists have, it is true, over the last thirty or forty years devised methods and instruments for the purposes of 'national accounting' – but they did not of course have the particular problems of the historian in mind. Is the historian entitled to appropriate these macro-economic services for his own use? Clearly the impressive masses of data one sees being processed today in order to produce national economic statistics, are out of all proportion to the scanty material available for past centuries. And as a rule the problems increase the further back one moves from the directly observable past. To make matters worse, there has as yet been no attempt to adapt the theoretical perspectives of the present to a study of the past.[2] And the few economists who have ventured on to the territory of the historian (in most enterprising ways, it must be said), such as Jean Marczewski or Robert William Fogel,[3] have not undertaken research in periods earlier than the eighteenth and nineteenth century respectively. Their work relates to periods for which comparatively plentiful statistics exist, but beyond these half-lit zones they can offer us nothing, not even their blessing. Only Simon Kuznets, whose work I have already quoted,[4] has offered us any assistance here.

And yet this really is the heart of the problem. We need what Pierre Chaunu has called a *pesée globale*[5] – a considered weighing-up of the national economy, following the spirit rather than the letter of the work of Kuznets and W. Leontieff, just as the early twentieth-century historians transposed the pioneering thought of Lescure, Aftalion, Wagemann and above all François Simiand, in order to write the history of wage and price fluctuations. That historical enterprise was a remarkably successful one. But this time the venture is more risky. And since national product does not really fit the patterns of traditional economic cycles,[6] not only can we not call on the latter to help us, but we can also never take one step forward without destroying what we know, or think we know. The only advantage of this approach – and it is not negligible – is that by venturing to use unfamiliar methods and concepts, we are forced to look at things in a new light.

Elements and compounds

Since it covers a large area, the national market naturally falls into several divisions: it is the sum of smaller areas, similar yet separate, which it embraces and forces into certain relationships. *A priori*, it is impossible to say which of these areas, living at different rhythms yet constantly interacting, have been the most important, which have determined the shape of the whole. In the slow and complex process of coordinating markets, it was frequently possible for a country's *international* markets to prosper, along with its lively local markets, while the intermediate level – the national or regional market – on the contrary lagged behind.[7] But this rule was sometimes reversed, especially in areas with a long history, where the international market was often merely a late addition to a long-established and diversified provincial economy.[8]

The formation of any national market has therefore to be studied in the diversity of its elements: each new combination is likely to be a special case. Here as in every other area, it will be difficult to generalize.

A hierarchy of units

The most elementary unit, the most deeply rooted, is what demographers call the *isolate* – the minimum unit of rural settlement. No human group can live and above all survive *to reproduce itself*, unless it contains at least four or five hundred individuals.[9] In *ancien régime* Europe, that would mean a village, or several neighbouring villages in touch with each other, forming both a social community and an area distinguished by cultivation, land-clearance, roads, paths and dwellings. Pierre de Saint-Jacob[10] describes this as a 'cultural clearing' – a term which takes on its full force when (as so often in, say, rural Burgundy) the reference is to an open space literally hacked out of the forest; in such cases, the unit can be understood and read like a book.

Within the charmed circle of these thousands of small units[11] where history passed in slow motion, lives repeated themselves from one generation to the next; the landscape obstinately remained the same or very nearly so – in one region a patchwork of ploughed fields, meadows, gardens, orchards and hemp-plots; elsewhere woodlands alternating with clearings for grazing herds; and everywhere the same implements: pick, shovel, plough, mill, blacksmith's forge and wheelwright's shop.

At the level above these little communities,[12] linking them together (whenever, that is, they were less than completely self-sufficient) came the smallest possible *economic* unit: a complex consisting of a small market town, perhaps the site of a fair, with a cluster of dependent villages around it. Each village had to be close enough to the town for it to be possible to go to market and back in

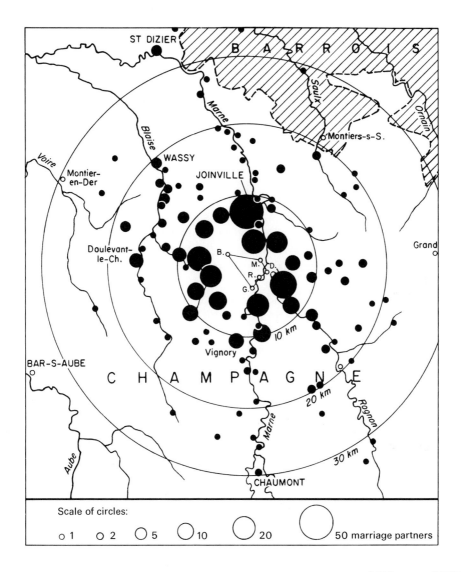

Scale of circles:

○ 1   ○ 2   ○ 5   ◯ 10   ◯ 20   ◯ 50 marriage partners

25   MARRIAGES IN FIVE VILLAGES IN CHAMPAGNE BETWEEN 1681 AND 1790
In this rich wine-producing countryside, the five villages of Blécourt, Donjeux, Gudmont, Mussey
and Rouvroy (designated by their initials on the map) accounted for a combined area of about
1500 hectares, rather more than a typical isolate of the *ancien régime*. Nevertheless, of the 1505
marriages recorded over the hundred years, 56.3% were contracted between spouses living in the
same parish, and 12.4% between spouses from within the five parishes. In the remaining 31.3%,
one of the partners was an 'outsider' (471 in all) and these are the only ones shown on the map.
The great majority of 'outsiders' in fact came from within a radius of only ten kilometres.
(From G. Arbelot, *Cinq Paroisses du Vallage (XVIIe–XVIIIe siècles). Étude de démographie
historique,* 1973.)

a day. But the actual dimensions of the unit would equally depend on the available means of transport, the density of settlement and the fertility of the area in question. The more scattered the population and the more barren the soil, the greater the distances travelled: in the eighteenth century, the mountain dwellers of the remote little Alpine valley of the Vallorcine, north of Chamonix, had to come on foot down the long and difficult route leading to the market town of Martigny in the Valais, 'to buy rice, sugar, perhaps a little pepper and also butcher's meat, there being in this place [the Vallorcine valley] no butcher's shop' – even in 1743.[13] At the opposite end of the spectrum were the many prosperous villages attached to large cities, like the *pueblos de los montes*[14] around Toledo, which were even before the sixteenth century bringing produce (wool, fabrics, leather) to sell at the market in the Zocodover square. These villages had been as it were weaned away from farm labour by their proximity to the city, and were now ensnared in a semi-suburban status. We should visualize most short-range village contacts as coming somewhere between these two extremes.

But how can we form some idea of the weight, area and volume of these little worlds and their elementary economies? Wilhelm Abel[15] calculated that a small town of 3000 inhabitants would require 85 square kilometres of 'village territory' to be able to live off its immediate neighbourhood. But in the pre-industrial world, 3000 would be an above-average population for a small town; and as for the 85 square kilometres, the figure seems very inadequate to me, unless that is 'territory' refers only to arable land, in which case the figure should be doubled to include woodland, pasture and clearings, as well as the land under crops,[16] giving a total area of some 170 km². In 1969, there were, according to the *Dictionnaire des communes*, 3321 *cantons* in France. If the canton (an ancient land division sometimes based on boundaries going even further back) is accepted as a *very rough* equivalent of the elementary economic unit, and since the total area of France is 550,000 km², the 'average canton' would measure between 160 and 170 km², and would today be inhabited by fifteen or sixteen thousand people.

Were the cantons in turn embraced by a superior and therefore larger regional unit? French geographers have long maintained that this is the case[17] using the concept of the *pays* (a term without a precise English equivalent, meaning a local region with a recognizable identity) – which they see as fundamental. The 400 or 500 *pays* in France have certainly varied in size over the centuries and their frontiers have been far from fixed, bearing a more or less close relation to determining features such as landscape, climate and political and economic links. On average, these areas with their strong local colouring might be anything from 1000 km²[18] to 1500 or 1700 km²: so they are quite sizeable units. To give some idea of what I mean, this is about the area covered by the Beauvaisis, the Bray, the pays d'Auge, the Woevre in Lorraine, the Othe, the Valois,[19] the Toulois (1505 km²),[20] the Tarentaise[21] which is close on 1700 km², or the Faucigny

(1661 km²).[22] The Val d'Aosta on the other hand, with its vast Alpine zones, for which a good historical guide now exists,[23] is far larger than this (3298 km²), while the Lodévois, although an original *pays* if ever there was one, confined to the catchment basin of the Lergue, measures only 798 km²; but this is one of the smallest dioceses in Languedoc: those of Béziers (1673 km²), Montpellier (1484 km²) and Alès (1791 km²) are nearer the norm.[24]

Our quest for dimensions, norms and distinctive regions could be pursued throughout France and outside France, across Europe. But would this solve all our problems? It would certainly be an important step forward to find out which of these *pays*, from Poland to Spain and from Italy to England, were attached to a town or city which extended patronage over them. This was the case – to take examples where precise information is available – in the Toulois, of which Toul was the dominating centre;[25] or in the region round Mantua (between 2000 and 2400 km²) which was bound hand and foot to Mantua and its grandees, the Gonzaga family.[26] Any *pays* with such a centre would surely qualify as an economic unit. But the *pays* was also – perhaps above all – a cultural entity: one of the coloured stones providing at once diversity and harmony within the mosaic making up the western world – especially in France, 'which spells diversity'.[27] Perhaps then we should turn to folklore, to costume and dialect, to

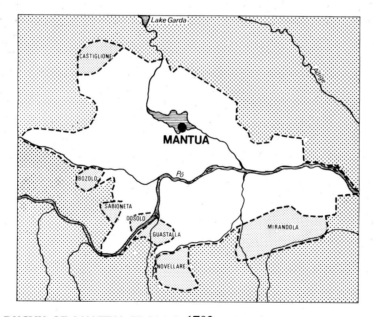

26 THE DUCHY OF MANTUA FROM A 1702 MAP
On the outer edge of the duchy (which measured *in toto* some 2000 or 2500 km²) lay smaller states: the duchy of Mirandola, the principality of Castiglione, Bozolo, Sabioneta, Dosolo, Guastalla, the county of Novellare. Further away lay Venice, Lombardy, Parma and Modena. The city of Mantua itself was surrounded by the lakes formed by the Mincio. Was the duchy of Mantua, with its long past, the equivalent of what would in France be known as a *pays*?

local proverbs and customs (those found only within a certain radius), to the architecture and building materials of houses, to roofs, domestic interiors, furniture, cooking habits – to all the things within a locality that go to make up a way of life, the various arts of living, of adapting, of balancing needs and resources, of enjoyment, which may not be the same as those in the next *pays*? It might also be possible to distinguish certain administrative functions at *pays* level – though there is almost certainly only a rough correspondence between the arbitrary frontiers of the 400 *baillages* and *sénéchaussées* in France and the geographical reality of the 400 or 500 *pays*.[28]

Moving up another level, we come to the *province*,[29] a much larger entity, with varying dimensions of course, since the history which fashioned the provinces did not make them identical. Vidal de la Blache, in a book which is unfortunately no more than an essay, *États et nations d'Europe* (1889), refers to what he calls 'regions', in fact corresponding to the provinces into which the western world is divided. But in the same writer's admirable *Tableau géographique de la France* (1911), which opens Lavisse's famous history of France, he accords more importance to the *pays* than to the 'natural region' or province. And in the end it is once more in Michelet's *Tableau* that one will find the liveliest representation of that diversity of the provinces which was for him 'the revelation of France':[30] a diversity which did not disappear when the provinces were amalgamated – often against their will – to form the early administrative framework within which modern France would gradually take shape. Machiavelli[31] admired and envied what he regarded as the masterpiece of the French monarchy, a political unit constructed, it is true, over several centuries, by the patient conquest of territories which had once been as independent as Tuscany, Sicily or the Milanese, and some of which were even larger: in France a *pays* is about ten times the size of a canton, and a province about ten times the size of a *pays* – 15,000 or 25,000 km^2 – an enormous area by the standards of the past. Measured by the speed of transport of the time, Burgundy alone, in the age of Louis XI, would have been hundreds of times greater than the whole of France today.

This being so, was the province not its inhabitants' true 'fatherland'? As J. Dhont has written apropos of Flanders, 'the living context of medieval [and post-medieval] society lay here; neither in the kingdom, nor in the *seigneurie* – the former being too vast and rather unreal, the latter too small – but in the regional principality, whether organized or not'.[32] In other words, the province long continued to be the 'political unit of optimum size' and nothing, even in the Europe of today, has really broken these ancient bonds. Italy and Germany indeed long remained assemblies of provinces or of 'states', until their unification in the late nineteenth century. Even France, although a 'nation' from an early stage, could on occasions be quite easily dismembered into autonomous provincial worlds, during the long and serious crisis of the Wars of Religion (1562–98) for instance, which was particularly revealing in this respect.

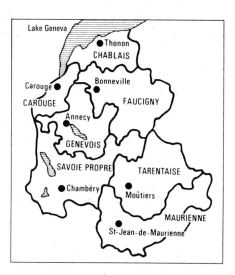

**27 A PROVINCE AND ITS SEVERAL 'PAYS':
SAVOY IN THE EIGHTEENTH CENTURY**
Every province was divided into fairly
coherent units most of which have survived
to the present day. (Paul Guichonnet,
Histoire de la Savoie, 1973, p. 313.)

Provincial units and markets

These provincial units, of differing sizes and degrees of homogeneity, were in fact ancient nations on a small scale, which built or sought to build their own national markets – or as we shall call them for the sake of clarity *regional markets.*

It even seems possible, *mutatis mutandis,* to see in the fortunes of the provincial units, a parallel or a foreshadowing of national and even international fortunes. The same patterns, the same processes repeat themselves. Like the world-economy, the national market was both superstructure and envelope. And so in its own way was the provincial market. In other words, the province was once a national economy, indeed a world-economy, in miniature; despite the difference in scale, all the theoretical analysis of the opening chapter of this book (relating to the world-economy) could be applied word for word to the province: it too was made up of dominant regions and cities, and peripheral *pays* or districts; of more or less developed zones and of others almost self-sufficient. And it is indeed from such *complementary* diversities and their range of possibilities that these rather large zones derive their cohesion.

At the centre of a province then, one or more cities are always to be found dominating the whole. Burgundy had Dijon; Dauphiné had Grenoble; Aquitaine had Bordeaux; Portugal had Lisbon; Venetia had Venice; Tuscany had Florence; Piedmont had Turin. But Normandy had two centres, Rouen and Caen; Champagne had both Reims and Troyes; Bavaria had both Ratisbon (Regensburg), the free city dominating the Danube from its vital bridge, and Munich, the capital created by the Wittelsbachs in the thirteenth century; Languedoc had both Toulouse and Montpellier; Provence had both Marseille and Aix; the area now covered by Lorraine had Nancy and Metz; Savoy had first Chambéry, then

F. Hackert: View of the port and the bay of Messina. Naples, San Martino Museum.
(Photo Scala.)

Annecy and most of all Geneva; Castile had the trinity of Valladolid, Toledo
and Madrid; and to end with a significant example, Sicily had both Palermo, the
grain capital, and Messina, the silk capital: during the long years of Spanish rule,
the authorities took good care not to choose between them, preferring to divide
and rule.

When primacy was shared of course, conflict soon followed: one or other
city would, or should, emerge triumphant. A protracted and unresolved rivalry
could only be the sign of poor regional development: a fir tree with a divided
trunk is unlikely to thrive. Such a duel might indicate that a provincial unit was
torn in two directions or composed of two conflicting fabrics: there was not one
Languedoc but two; not one Normandy but at least two. In such cases, the
provincial market was insufficiently unified, unable to weld together areas either
tending towards self-sufficiency or looking outwards to external trade circuits –
for every regional market was of course concerned both in the international and
the national market. Splits, divisions and inequalities could result, as one sub-
region pulled one way and another in the opposite direction. And there were
plenty of other impediments to the unity of the provincial market – interventionist policies by states and princes in the mercantilist era, or powerful or scheming
neighbours. At the time of the Peace of Ryswick, Lorraine was flooded with

French currency – a form of domination which the new duke was powerless to oppose.[33] In 1768, even the United Provinces regarded themselves as injured by the tariff war waged against them by the Austrian Netherlands. 'The count of Cobenzel[34] is doing everything in his power', the Hague complained, 'to attract trade to the southern Netherlands, where they are building causeways and dikes everywhere to aid the transport of foodstuffs and merchandise.'[35]

But would not an *autonomous* provincial market have been the sign of a stagnant economy? One way or another, the province had to be opened up to external markets, national or international. So the influx of foreign currency was after all beneficial to eighteenth-century Lorraine, which no longer minted its own coin, and where smuggling was a prosperous industry. Even the poorest provinces, with almost nothing to buy or sell abroad could, like Savoy, Auvergne or the Limousin, export their labour force. In the eighteenth century, this openness to the outside world, these pendulum movements became increasingly important: they can be regarded as reliable indicators. By this period, in any case, with the rise of the nation-state and the expansion of the economy and of foreign trade, the days of provincial glory were surely over. The *long-term* destiny of the provinces was to merge into a national unit, whatever the resistance they offered or the repugnance they felt. In 1768, Corsica became French in circumstances too well-known to repeat; but it was quite clear that the island could not aspire to independence. Not that provincial particularism by any means died out – it is still alive today, in Corsica and elsewhere, where latter-day developments and revivals can be seen.

The nation-state, yes – but the national market?

At the top of the hierarchy, the national market was a network of irregular weave, often constructed against all the odds: against the over-powerful cities with their own policies, against the provinces which resisted centralization, against foreign intervention which breached frontiers, not to mention the divergent interests of production and exchange (one thinks of the conflicts in France between the Atlantic ports and those of the Mediterranean, and between inland and coastal regions); and finally against all the enclaves of self-sufficiency beyond anyone's control.

Not surprisingly then, there was inevitably behind the national market a centralizing political will – fiscal, administrative, military or mercantilist. Lionel Rothkrug[36] has defined mercantilism as the transfer of control of economic activity from the local community to the state. Perhaps one should say from the cities and provinces to the state. All over Europe, privileged zones established themselves at an early stage as commanding centres, from which the long task of political construction and the beginnings of the territorial state were launched. In France, the vital region was the Ile-de-France, the fabulous realm of the Capets, where 'yet again everything happened between the Somme and the

Loire'.[37] In England it was the Thames valley; in Scotland, the Lowlands; in Spain, the windswept plateaux of Castile; in Russia, the vast clearing on the Moskva river. Later, similar roles would be played by Piedmont in Italy, Brandenburg or rather the Prussian state between the Rhine and Koenigsberg; and Lake Mälar in Sweden.

All or almost all development took place in relation to strategic communications. I appreciated in its time (1943) Erwin Redslob's book *Des Reiches Strasse*, which underlined the importance in the old days of the road from Frankfurt-am-Main to Berlin as an instrument or indeed detonator of German unity. Geographical determinism is not everything in the creation of territorial states, but it does play a part.

The economy had one to play as well. It took the economic revival of the mid-fifteenth century before the early modern states could *reassert* themselves, whether in the west under Henry VII in England, Louis XI in France, Ferdinand and Isabella in Spain, or in the east with the triumphs of Hungary, Poland and the Scandinavian countries. The correlation is obvious. And yet at this time, England, France, Spain and East Europe were by no means the most advanced zones of the continent. They were after all marginal to the dominant economy which cut a swathe through the middle of Europe, from northern Italy through the Germany of Danube and Rhine to the crossroads of trade in the Netherlands. And this economically dominant zone was based on the nationalism of the old *city-states*: there was no place in it for the revolutionary political formation of the territorial state. The Italian cities rejected the political unification of the peninsula dreamed of by Machiavelli, and which the Sforzas might perhaps have been able to achieve.[38] Venice does not even seem to have contemplated it; and the states of the Holy Roman Empire were no more enthusiastic about the projects of the impecunious Maximilian of Austria.[39] The Netherlands had no intention of being integrated into Philip II's Spanish Empire, and their resistance took the form of a religious revolt, religion being in the sixteenth century an ambiguous language, more than once the translation of political nationalism, newly-created or re-affirmed. So a gulf developed between nation-states on the one hand, the locus of *power*, and urban centres on the other, the locus of *wealth*. Would the threads of gold be strong enough to ensnare the political giants? The wars of the sixteenth century gave an unclear answer to this question. In the seventeenth century, it is patently obvious that Amsterdam, in a sense the last of the cities, was holding back the rise of England and France. It took the economic miracle of the eighteenth century to remove the last obstacle, leaving the economy from now on under the aegis of the states and their national markets, the heavyweights to whom the future belonged. It is not so surprising then that the territorial states, though having tasted political success early on, should have come late to the economic success represented by the national market, the promise of their material triumphs.

What we do not know is how this transition, though prepared in advance, was effected, or when and why. The problem is the lack of landmarks, and more particularly of criteria by which progress can be measured. *A priori*, it might be expected that a political area would become economically coherent when it was thoroughly penetrated with intense market activity which would eventually channel and invigorate if not all, then the greater part of the total volume of exchange. One might also expect to find a certain relationship between the volume of output appropriated by the market and the volume consumed on the spot. One might also think in terms of a certain level of overall wealth, of particular thresholds to be crossed. But what were these thresholds? And above all, which were the crucial turning points?

Internal customs barriers

Traditional explanations have set too much store by authoritarian measures, taken within a political unit, to remove the internal customs barriers and tolls which divided it up or at any rate hindered the circulation of goods. Once these obstacles had been lifted, the argument goes, the national market became effective for the first time. But is this explanation not a little too simple?

The example most often quoted is England, where most internal barriers were indeed removed at an early date.[40] The precociously established central power of the English Crown was, by 1290, ordering toll-owners to maintain the roads they controlled, and reducing their privileges to a few years only. Consequently the obstacles to the free flow of goods, while they did not entirely disappear, certainly dwindled; in the end they were hardly perceptible. Thorold Rogers's massive history of prices in England records only a few isolated and insignificant figures relating to the cost of tolls for the last centuries of the Middle Ages.[41] Eli Heckscher[42] explains this process not only by the early concentration of power in the Crown, but also by England's comparatively small surface area and in particular by the 'overwhelming importance of sea transport', which rivalled the roads and reduced their importance. Certainly foreign visitors were regularly surprised by what they found: a Frenchman, the Abbé Coyer, wrote in 1749 to one of his friends:

> I forgot to tell you, in my description of the roads, that one sees no Offices or Clerks. When you enter this island, you will be very carefully inspected at Dover, after which you may travel the length of Great Britain without meeting the least enquiry. If Foreigners receive such treatment, so much the more do Citizens. The Customs posts are set round the circumference of the Kingdom; one is inspected there once and for all.[43]

This information is confirmed by a French report of 1775: 'On arriving in England, [one's luggage] is carefully inspected piece by piece, and this first inspection is the only one in the kingdom'.[44] A Spaniard[45] in 1783 recognized that it was a great blessing for the traveller, not to be subjected to customs inspection in any part of the kingdom, having once undergone it upon landing. For my part, I did not experience the rigour I had been led to expect in the operation, either at my entry to Dover, or on my departure from Harwich. It is true that the customs officers have a flair for detecting those who intend to take money out of the country by fraud and those who are likely to spend it here, having been drawn here by curiosity.

But not all travellers were so lucky or showed such equanimity. Pétion, the future revolutionary mayor of Paris, on going through customs at Dover on 28 October 1791, found the inspection 'disagreeable and fatiguing: almost every object paid duty: books, especially if they were bound, objects made of gold or silver, leather, powder, musical instruments and engravings. It is true that after this first search you do not have to suffer any others within the Kingdom'.[46]

When he wrote, it was almost a year since the French Constituent Assembly had abolished all internal customs barriers, following the general trend among continental countries to roll back to the political frontier all customs posts which would from now on be patrolled by armed guard and form long protective cordons.[47] But the measures came rather late in the day (1775 in Austria, 1790 in France, 1794 in Venice)[48] and were not always immediately enforced. In Spain, the decision had been taken as early as 1717, but the government had subsequently had to back-pedal, notably with regard to the Basque provinces.[49] In France, over 4000 tolls had been abolished between 1726 and the Revolution – but with only limited success, to go by the interminable list of internal duties abolished by the Constituent Assembly from 1 December 1790 on.[50]

If the birth of the national market had been dependent upon this tidying-up operation, there would have been no national markets on the European mainland until the late eighteenth or early nineteenth century. This is obviously not the case. Did the abolition of tolls even do anything to stimulate trade? When in 1664, Colbert set up the customs union of the *Cinq Grosses Fermes* (tax farms) covering an area the equivalent of the whole of England (see Figure 28), there was no immediate upsurge of economic activity. Perhaps the prevailing economic circumstances were simply not propitious, since in favourable circumstances the economy seems on the contrary to have been capable of overcoming any obstacles, of adapting to any situation. Charles Carrière in his book on the trade of Marseille, calculated that the tolls along the Rhône, including the customs posts at Lyon and Valence which we historians (relying on the complaints of contemporaries) have tended to regard as serious obstacles, were only confiscating some 350,000 *livres* in the eighteenth century, out of traffic worth 100 million *livres* – that is to say 0.35 per cent.[51] And the same could be said of the Loire. I do not dispute that the tolls – 80 of which survived into the nineteenth century – were an obstacle, that they forced the boatmen to pull in out of the current and call at the checkpoint, that they gave rise to extortionate practices, abuses and illicit payments and that they brought further delays to the already slow and difficult

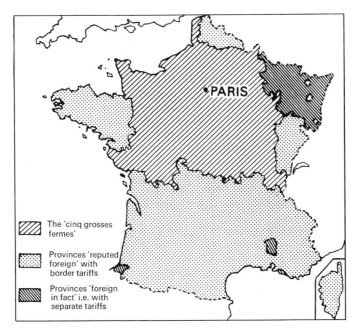

28 THE AREA COVERED BY THE CINQ GROSSES FERMES
From W. R. Shepherd, Historical Atlas, in J. M. Richardson, *A Short History of France*, 1974, p. 64.

river transport. But if we assume the volume of traffic down the Loire to have been the equivalent of that of the Rhône (it is generally supposed to have been superior) – namely 100 million *livres*, and if the total dues paid were 187,150 *livres*, this works out at a percentage, if my information is correct, of 0.187%.[52]

What was more, *acquits-à-caution* (bond notes) allowed the free passage through France of goods in transit, and there are plenty of examples of this from the early days.[53] In December 1673, some English merchants complained that having travelled across France from Marseille to Calais, they were required in the latter port to pay one *sou* in the *livre* on their goods.[54] What they wanted was of course total exemption. In 1719, 1000 camlets from Marseille were dispatched to Saint-Malo on behalf of MM. Bosc and Eon, the packages to be sealed at Marseille on departure and 'on arriving at Saint-Malo, they will be placed in the *entrepôt* warehouse to be sent abroad without paying any further dues'.[55] And these operations were as nothing compared to the free passage granted to grain, flour and vegetables, which were 'exempted from all dues, even those of tolls' by the royal proclamation of 25 May 1763[56] – which was, it is true, revoked on 23 December 1770. See also the decision of the *Conseil d'Etat* (28 October 1785)[57] which made it an offence 'to charge any tolls throughout the kingdom on coal, except if specifically displayed on tariff or placards'. There are thus many examples of unrestricted circulation in a country reputed to be bristling with barriers, where important men like Vauban (1710) had long dreamed of 'relegating [customs posts] to the frontiers and reducing them greatly'.[58] Colbert worked on the problem, and if the target was not achieved in 1664, it was because the *intendants* resisted it in the fear, not entirely unjustified, that the free circulation of grain in this vast kingdom might precipitate famine.[59] Turgot's experiment in 1776 led to near-disaster with the Flour War. Ten years later, in 1786, if the government, despite its intentions, failed to abolish all tolls, it was, so people said, because the operation, 'being calculated', would have meant compensating the toll-proprietors to the tune of eight or ten million *livres*, which 'the present state of [the nation's] finances could hardly bear'.[60] In fact this figure seems a very modest one in the French fiscal context of the time, and if it is accurate, it confirms yet again how insignificant the tolls were.

Such details suggest that the patchwork of customs barriers was not an outstanding problem in itself but a difficulty related to other problems of the time. We could seek confirmation *a contrario* from the English turnpikes – which levied tolls in the same way that French (but not British) motorways do today, and which were authorized in England after 1663 as an encouragement to road building. According to an article in the *Gazette de France* on 24 December 1762, 'the tolls [derived from the turnpikes] are sufficient to produce a sum of three million pounds sterling a year'[61] – a sum much higher than that raised by the Rhine or Loire tolls.

In the end, one cannot avoid the impression that economic growth alone was the truly decisive factor in the expansion and consolidation of national markets. Otto Hinze makes the implicit assumption that everything proceeded from political origins, from the Acts of Union with Scotland in 1707 and Ireland in 1801, which created the market of the British Isles and strengthened the economic weight of the whole. But surely things were not as simple as this. Political factors certainly counted but Isaac de Pinto wondered in 1771 if Scotland had really brought much wealth to England: would France be any better off, he asked, if she annexed Savoy?[62] The argument is not convincing, in that Scotland cannot really be compared to Savoy. But as we shall see in this chapter, it was surely above all the rising tide of the eighteenth century which floated the entire British economy and made union with Scotland so profitable to both sides. If the same cannot be said of Ireland, it was because the latter found herself in the position of a colony, rather than an equal partner in the Union.

Against a priori *definitions*

Let us therefore beware of peremptory *a priori* definitions, such as the assumption that near-perfect coherence (as indicated for instance by simultaneous price variations over a given area) is an indispensable condition for the existence of a national market. If such a criterion were to be applied, there would have been no such thing as a national market in France. The French grain market – as

Toll on an English road. The toll-keeper is asking for payment before he will allow the coach through. Engraving by Eugène Lami (1829). (Photo B.N., Paris.)

fundamental here as everywhere else in Europe – was divided into at least three zones: a north-east zone with low prices and zigzag variations; a Mediterranean region with high prices and less extreme variations; and a zone, more or less bordering the Atlantic, of intermediate character.[63] This certainly would not fit the picture. We might conclude with Traian Stoianovich that 'the only regions of Europe in which the "nation" coincided with the national market were England and possibly the United Provinces'. But the size of the latter made them at best a provincial market. And even the British Isles may not have had a uniform pattern for grain prices, since shortages and famines did occur, sometimes in England, sometimes in Scotland or Ireland.

Michel Morineau is in his own way even more restrictive:

Unless a nation is protected from the outside world and internally unified as a market, how can it be the primary unit appropriate for calculations [i.e. for national accounting purposes]? Regional disparities, to which the present situation in Europe has once more alerted us, already existed in the sixteenth, seventeenth and eighteenth centuries. One hesitates to talk of an 'Italian' or 'German' G.N.P. in these far-off days; both because these countries were politically divided and because it would be economically meaningless: Saxony was a very different place from the bishoprics on the Rhine; and the kingdom of Naples, the Papal States, Tuscany and the Venetian republic [all lived] by their own rules.[64]

Without taking up this argument point by point (could it not be said that there were regional differences between England proper, Cornwall, Wales, Scotland and Ireland, or simply between highland and lowland economies throughout the British Isles? Are there not still pronounced regional disparities everywhere in the world today?), let us note that Wilhelm Abel[65] was nevertheless tempted to calculate the German G.N.P. of the sixteenth century; that according to Otto Stolz,[66] the specialist on customs history, by the end of the eighteenth century the major traffic routes across the Reich had 'created a measure of unity'; that Iorjo Tadic[67] has persistently argued that there *was* a national market in the Turkish Balkans from the sixteenth century, engendering lively and much-frequented fairs such as that of Doljani near Strumitsa, on the Danube; that it is Pierre Vilar's[68] opinion that 'in the latter part of the eighteenth century a truly national Spanish market was being created, to the benefit of the Catalan economy'. So why should it be absurd to attempt to calculate the G.N.P. of Spain under Charles IV? As for the concept of a nation 'protected from the outside world', it is very hard to imagine this in an age when contraband was a widespread and prosperous activity. Even eighteenth-century England had difficulty patrolling her apparently unbreachable frontiers – since tea was being blithely smuggled across them until 1785; and a hundred years earlier in 1698, England was described as 'being open on all sides; smuggling is all the easier in that once the goods are inside the country they are safe'.[69] Thus silks, velvets and spirits – goods coming mostly from France – after landing at some lonely spot on the coast, could make their way calmly towards markets and retailers without fear of further checks.

In any case, we are not looking for a 'perfect' national market – none such exists even in our own day. What we are looking for is a system of internal mechanisms and connections with the outside world – what Karl Bücher[70] called a *Territorialwirtschaft* as opposed to a *Stadtwirtschaft*, the city-based economy we have considered at length in earlier chapters: in other words a large-scale economy, covering a wide area, 'territorialized' so to speak, and sufficiently coherent for governments to be able to shape and manoeuvre it to some extent. Mercantilism represents precisely the dawning of awareness of this possibility of manoeuvring the entire economy of a country – in fact it could be described as the first attempt to create the national market.

The territorial economy and the city-centred economy

Only by relating them to the problems posed by the national market can one understand the underlying differences between *Territorialwirtschaft* and *Stadtwirtschaft*.

I say 'underlying' because the immediately visible differences – those of size and area – are less important than they appear. One can of course say with very little exaggeration that a territory is an area, a city merely a point. But around either a dominant territory or a dominant city, there is an outer zone of influence, an extra area which in the case of Amsterdam, Venice or Great Britain, was nothing less than a world-economy. In both types of successful economy then, mere surface area is so effectively transcended that its literal dimensions, as perceived on first sight, lose importance as a distinguishing feature. Indeed in this respect the two systems resemble each other. Venice was just as much a colonial power in the Levant as Holland was in the East Indies, or England in India. *Cities* and *territories* both attached themselves in identical fashion to an international economy which ferried them along and which they in turn helped to strengthen. In both cases the means of domination and everyday surveillance, if that is the right word, were the same: the fleet, the army, violence and if necessary cunning or even treachery – think of the Venetian Council of Ten, or much later, the British Intelligence Service. 'Central' banks[71] appeared in Venice (1585), Amsterdam (1609) and finally England (1694) – the central banks which Charles P. Kindleberger[72] has called 'the lenders of last resort', and which seem to me to have been above all instruments of power and international domination: I may bail you out but you will be my prisoner ever after. Imperialism and colonialism are as old as the world, and any reinforced form of domination secretes capitalism, as I have often repeated to convince the reader and to convince myself.

So if the world-economy is our starting point, moving from Venice to Amsterdam or from Amsterdam to England means remaining within the same trajectory, the same overall reality. What distinguishes, and indeed contrasts the nation-system and the city-system is their structural organization. The city-state avoids carrying the heavy burden of the so-called primary sector: Venice, Genoa and Amsterdam consumed grain, oil, salt, meat, etc., acquired through foreign trading: they received from the outside world the wood, raw materials and even a number of the manufactured products they used. It was of little concern to them by whom, or by what methods, archaic or modern, these goods were produced: they were content simply to accept them at the end of the trade circuit, wherever agents or local merchants had stocked them on their behalf. Most if not all of the primary sector on which such cities' subsistence and even their luxuries depended lay well outside their walls, and laboured on their behalf without their needing to be concerned in the economic and social problems of production. In all likelihood, the cities were but dimly aware of the advantages this brought and rather more conscious of the drawbacks: obsessed with their dependence on foreign countries (although in reality such was the power of money that this was reduced almost to nothing), all leading cities desperately tried to expand their territory and to develop their agriculture and industry. What kind of agriculture and industry though? The richest and most profitable of course. Since Florence had to import food anyway, why not import Sicilian grain, and grow vines and olives on the hills of Tuscany? So the city states from the start were noted for 1) a very 'modern' relationship between their rural and urban population; 2) an agricultural sector, where it existed, which tended to go in for cash crops and was a natural focus for capitalist investment; it was neither by accident, nor on account of any special quality of the soil that Holland so quickly developed such an 'advanced' agricultural sector; 3) a number of luxury industries, so often the most profitable.

The *Stadtwirtschaft* thus automatically avoided the 'agricultural economy' defined by Daniel Thorner as the stage to be gone through before any effective development can take place. The territorial states by contrast, as they grappled with their slow political and economic construction, long remained embedded in that agricultural economy which was so resistant to progress, as can be seen in so many Third World countries of today. The political creation of a large state, particularly if achieved through war as was generally the case, called for a large budget, and thus for increasing recourse to taxation, which in turn required a bureaucracy, itself creating a need for more money and more taxes. But if more than 90% of the population lived in rural areas, taxation to be successful required both that the state should effectively communicate with the peasantry, and that the peasantry should have moved beyond self-sufficiency to produce surpluses to be sold on the market, in order to feed the towns. And that was only the first step. For the peasant had also – though much later – to become sufficiently well-off to create an increased demand for manufactured goods, thus in turn providing a living for the artisan. The territorial state as it gradually took shape had far too much to do at home to commit itself to the immediate conquest of the major markets of the world. In order to survive and balance its budget, it had to promote the marketing of agricultural and artisan production and to set in motion its mighty administrative machine. All its energies went into this task. I should have liked to consider in this light the history of France under Charles VII and Louis XI – but it is such a familiar story that its cutting edge has been blunted for today's readers. So we should think rather of the state of Muscovy or even – an extraordinary example to which we shall be returning – the sultanate of Delhi, which preceded the Mogul Empire: in the first half of the fourteenth century, the sultan introduced to the huge area which he controlled a monetary economy, complete with markets through which the village economy was both exploited and stimulated to greater efforts. State revenues depended so closely on the success of agriculture that the sultan Muhammad Tughlak (1325–51) had wells dug, offered the peasants money and seed-corn, and induced them, through the good offices of his administrators, to go in for more productive crops such as sugar cane.[73]

It is hardly surprising that in such conditions, the first dazzling successes in creating world-economies should have been achieved by the big cities, or on the other hand that London, the capital of a nation-state, took so long to catch up with Amsterdam, a more alert centre with greater freedom of movement. Nor however is it at all surprising that once the difficult balance of agriculture, trade, transport, industry, supply and demand – called for by the establishment of any national market – *had* been achieved, England turned out in the end to be an infinitely superior rival to little Holland, now inexorably eliminated from all pretentions to world supremacy: once it had been constituted, the national market brought a renewed surge of power. Charles Kindleberger[74] wonders why the commercial revolution which led to the rise of Holland did not also bring about an industrial revolution there. Among other reasons it was no doubt because Holland did not have at her command a truly national market. The same answer might perhaps be given to the question raised by Antonio Garcia-Baquero Gonzàlez[75] about eighteenth-century Spain, where despite the increased volume of colonial trade, signs of an industrial revolution were slow to emerge (except in Catalonia). Was not the answer once again that the national market in Spain was still imperfect, inadequately integrated, and punctuated with areas of patent inertia?

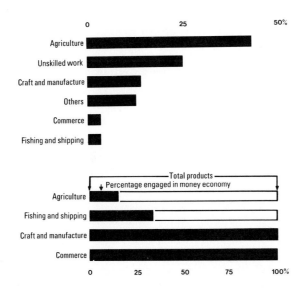

29 HOW INDUSTRY AND TRADE ENCOURAGED THE GROWTH OF THE MONETARY ECONOMY
Since they predominated to an overwhelming extent in the economic activity of the cities, trade and industry explain the long-lasting superiority of the city-centred economy over the territorial economy. From data provided by K. Glamann.

Weights and measures

What we really need is an overall estimate of the national economies already formed or taking shape, a record of their size at certain moments (were they growing or shrinking?) and a comparison of their respective levels at a given time. This means going over ground covered by a respectable number of pioneers in the past, well before Lavoisier's classic calculations of 1791. William Petty[76] (1623-87) long ago tried to compare the United Provinces and France, concluding that the ratio for population was 1 to 13; for cultivated land, 1 to 81; and for wealth, 1 to 3. Gregory King[77] (1648-1712) similarly tried to compare the leading trinity of nations in his own time – Holland, England and France. But a good dozen or so other 'calculators' deserve a mention, from Vauban to Isaac de Pinto and Turgot himself. Some words written by Boisguilbert (1648-1714) – in pessimistic vein, true, but then France in 1699 did not exactly present an encouraging or reassuring spectacle – can even strike us by their modern ring:

> ... Not to speak of what might be, but only of what has been, it is maintained that the [French national] product is today five or six million [*livres*] less in income per annum whether in funds or industry than it was forty years ago. And the evil is increasing every day, that is to say the decrease; since the same causes persist and are even growing, without our being able to render the King's revenues responsible, for these have never increased so little as after 1660, since which date they have grown by only a third, whereas over the previous two hundred years they had always doubled every thirty years.[78]

A remarkable text, as is the listing under eleven headings (from land to mining) into which Isaac de Pinto[79] divided the national product of England – a division not too far removed from the headings used by national accounting even today.

Is it possible, by consulting these ancient enquiries into national 'wealth' and the scattered statistics which one can assemble, to look at the past 'through the lens of global quantities'[80] to which we have become accustomed by national economic accounting as practised since 1924?[81] Such calculations have their shortcomings, needless to say, but for the time being, as Paul Bairoch[82] rightly says, they provide the only way to approach the vital question of *growth*, through the study of present-day – and, I would add, past economies.

I even agree with Jean Marczewski[83] that national accounting is not merely a technique but a science in its own right, and that by its alliance with political economy, it has turned the latter into an experimental science.

But I would not wish the reader to misinterpret my intentions: I shall not be blazing a trail towards some revolutionary new form of economic history. I would merely like, after defining a few of the concepts of national accounting useful to the historian, to return to some elementary calculations – the only kind possible given the documentation available to us and within the scope of this book. My aim is merely to propose certain orders of magnitude, to try to bring to light certain relations, coefficients and multiplicators that seem plausible (but which cannot claim to be accurate); to take the first few steps towards the enormous body of research which has not yet been undertaken – and which may not be for some time. These putative orders of magnitude will at least enable us to guess at the potential of retrospective accounting.

Three variables, three sets of dimensions

The first of these is the national *patrimony*, a store of wealth which changes only slowly; the second is *national income*, or the flow of wealth; and the third is *per capita income*, an estimated relationship.

Patrimony means total wealth, the sum of the accumulated reserves of a given national economy, the mass of capital which is or could be involved in the production process. This concept, which used to fascinate the 'arithmeticians',[84] is the one least in use today, which is a pity. No such thing yet exists as 'an audit of national wealth'. 'This means', as an economist wrote to me in reply to a question, 'that this type of measurement is unreliable and that our accounting methods are imperfect'.[85] Such a gap is certainly to be regretted by the historian seeking to evaluate the role of accumulated capital in growth; he finds that sometimes it was clearly effective; at other times it was unable to move the economy forward unaided, as it sought unsuccessfully for suitable investments; and that at other times again, it was slow to move at the right time to support forward-looking initiatives, being the prisoner apparently of inertia and routine. The industrial revolution in England, for instance, was very largely financed by sources on the margins of mainstream capital and indeed outside London.

I have already referred to the importance of the relationship between national income and national capital stocks.[86] Simon Kuznets[87] thinks that this relation can be established at between 7 and 3 to 1; that is to say, an economy of the past would have had to immobilize the equivalent of up to seven normal years of labour in order to guarantee the process of production; but that this figure falls the nearer we come to the present day. Capital was therefore becoming more efficient – that is in terms of economic efficiency of course – which seems quite plausible.

National income is at first sight a simple concept: does not national accounting consist of 'assimilating the economy of a nation to that of a great business firm'?[88] But this apparent simplicity has in the past been the occasion for many 'scholastic' debates and 'verbal duels'[89] between experts. Time has blunted their edge, and the definitions current today (while certainly much clearer in appearance than in reality) resemble each other very closely, whether we take Simon Kuznets's simple formula (1941) 'the net value of all the economic goods produced by a "nation" in a year',[90] or the more complicated definition given by Y. Bernard and J. C. Colli: 'the representative aggregate of the flow of national resources, goods or services created over a given period'.[91] The main thing is to realize that national income can be considered, as Claude Vimont puts it,[92] from three perspectives: that of *production*, that of the *incomes* received by private individuals and the state; and that of *expenditure*. We shall not have one sum to do but at least three, and the more one thinks about it, the more the number of aggregates to be distinguished increases, depending on whether or not one sets aside the mass of taxes, or the regular wear and tear on fixed capital used in the production process, or whether one's calculations are based on production (with factor costs) or on market prices (which include taxation). I would therefore recommend any historian entering this labyrinth to consult Paul Bairoch's explanatory article[93] which tells one how to relate one aggregate to another, by adding or subtracting as it might be 2, 4 or 10 per cent.

There are three basic equations to bear in mind: (1) Gross National Product (G.N.P.) = Net National Product (N.N.P.) plus taxation, plus replacement of worn-out capital. (2) N.N.P. = Net National Income (N.I.); (3) N.I. = consumption plus savings.

For the historian embarking on research of this kind, there are at least three possible approaches: he can start with consumption, with income, or with production. But let us be realistic: the aggregates we bandy about so casually today are subject to a margin of error of between 10 and 20 per cent, and when it comes to economies of the past, that figure is nearer 30 per cent. Accuracy is out of the question. We have to work with very rough and ready figures and calculations. What is more, historians have fallen into the habit, rightly or wrongly, of talking about G.N.P. without distinguishing it from *net* product. The distinction after all is not very relevant: national income or national product (whether gross or net) come to much the same thing from the historian's perspective. We can only seek, and are only likely to find, for a given economy in a given period, a single measure of its wealth, an approximate figure which is only interesting when compared to the levels of other economies.

Per capita national income is a relationship: G.N.P. divided by population. If production increases faster than the size of the population, per capita income goes up; in the opposite case it goes down; and the third possibility is stagnation, if the relationship remains unchanged. For anyone seeking to measure growth, this is the key statistic, the one that determines average living standards in a given nation, and the variations in those standards. Historians have for some time been seeking to measure living standards using data from price series or real wages, or by means of the statistic known as the 'housewife's shopping basket'. The results of such attempts are summarized in the diagrams produced by J. Fourastié, R. Grandamy and Wilhelm Abel (see Volume I, p. 133) and by E. H. Phelps Brown and Sheila Hopkins (see below, Figure 58). They shed light if not on the exact level of per capita income, at least on its variations over time. It has long been thought that the lowest wage (earned by that unparalleled witness for historical research, the builder's mate, on whose pay a good deal of

The 'means of subsistence' or the G.N.P. of the United Provinces in 17 pictures. Engraving by W. Kok, 1794. (Atlas van Stolk.)

1. Weaving.
2. Butter and cheese production.
3. Herring fishing.
4. Whaling.
5. Peat-cutting.
6. Shipbuilding.
7. The city hall and public weighing station in Amsterdam.
8. The timber industry, sawmills and paper-mills.
9. Texel.
10. Mining.
11. The wine trade.
12. Agriculture and the grain trade.
13. Tobacco, sugar and coffee trades.
14. Tea, spice and linen trades.
15. The Rotterdam Bourse.
16. A trading house.
17. The Amsterdam Bourse.

data happens to exist) on the whole followed the fluctuations of the average standard of living. Conclusive evidence for this is provided in a recent article by Paul Bairoch[94] which I can only describe as revolutionary. If we have some fragmentary knowledge of the wage of a manual labourer (in other words a rock-bottom or minimum wage) that is if we know how much he was paid for one day's work or for several, we have only, says Paul Bairoch, to multiply this daily wage by 196 to obtain per capita national income; if, that is, the field of reference is nineteenth-century Europe, which Bairoch has studied *statistically*. In a structuralist perspective, this is the discovery of a powerful explanatory correlation. This unexpected statistic, which provokes incredulity at first sight, has been calculated *pragmatically* – not theoretically – that is by working on the abundant statistical material of the nineteenth century.

Having fairly well established this equation for nineteenth-century Europe, Paul Bairoch looked at England in 1688 and in 1770-8[95] and deduced, perhaps a little hastily on this occasion, that the multiplier for 1688 – in Gregory King's day – should be about 160, and for 1770-8 in the region of 260. Whereupon, even more hastily, he concluded that 'the body of data thus calculated allows one to postulate that the adoption of an average coefficient of the order of 200 could be regarded as a valid approach in the context of European societies of the sixteenth, seventeenth and eighteenth centuries'. I am not as entirely convinced of this as he is; the element of his findings that most interests me is his claim that the coefficient has had a constant tendency to rise, which, other things being equal, must mean that per capita income was tending, comparatively, to move upwards.

In Venice, where a workman in the Arsenal in 1534 earned 22 *soldi* a day (24 in summer, 20 in winter)[96] the proposed coefficient of 200 would give a per capita income of 4400 *soldi*, or 35 ducats – which is only a *quarter* of the annual wage of a journeyman in the *Arte della Lana* (148 ducats). No doubt a craftsman in the woollen industry was in a privileged category, but the figure of 35 ducats does seem rather low to me. If it is accepted, it corresponds to a G.N.P. for Venice of 7 million ducats (for a population of 200,000).[97] My own calculations, which specialists on Venice have also regarded as rather too low, produced an estimated G.N.P. of approximately 7,400,000 ducats.[98] All the same, these conclusions are not too far apart.

To take another example, in about 1525, the daily wage of a labourer in Orleans was 2 *sols*, 9 *deniers*.[99] If one were to apply the multiplier of 200 (in a country with a population of 15 million) one would end up with a national income very much higher than the maximum allowed by Frank Spooner's calculations. So the correlation of 200, which is probably rather low for Venice, is certainly much too high for Orleans in the same period.

One last example: in 1707, Vauban in his *Dixme Royale*, took as the average 'workman's wage' that of a weaver who worked an average 180 days in the year for about 12 *sols* a day, thus earning 108 *livres* in a year.[100] With this wage as a basis, per capita income (200 × 12 *sols*) would work out at 2400 *sols* or 120 *livres*.

And in this case, the weaver's standard of living would, as one might expect, be slightly lower than average (108 to 120). France's G.N.P., with a population of 19 million, would be about 2280 million *livres*. And it so happens that this is exactly the figure calculated by Charles Dutot in the eighteenth century, using Vauban's sectorial estimates.[101] So in this case, in 1707, Bairoch's coefficient of 200 seems valid.

It would of course require hundreds of similar calculations in order to confirm whether there is indeed a hard and fast rule or anything like it. Such research could quite easily be undertaken: there is no shortage of data. Charles Dutot[102] whom I have just mentioned, set out to discover whether the *real* budget of the French monarchy had increased or not over time. In other words, he was trying, as we would say today, to calculate these budgets *in current prices* – at the time in *livres*. So he had to compare prices from different periods. His choice of prices is amusing (whether they were the really significant ones is another question): a kid, a hen, a gosling, a calf, a pig, a coney or rabbit; and alongside these prices which he certainly regarded as characteristic, he set the daily wage of 'a labourer with his hands': in 1508 in Auvergne this was 6 *deniers*; in Champagne at the same date, one *sol*. Then he tried to relate these prices to those of the year 1735 in the reign of Louis XV: by then the labourer's daily wage had risen to 12 *sols* in summer and 6 in winter. In this context, where would the coefficient of 200 get us? It certainly does not seem to apply to the sixteenth century, except in the most advanced areas.

All in all though, Paul Bairoch's hypothesis gives new significance to the many isolated wage-figures we have and which have hitherto been neglected. It makes comparisons possible. And it also brings new light to bear, if I am not mistaken, on the never satisfactorily resolved question of the number of working days and holidays in the *ancien régime*, obliging us to try once more to push our way into the unrewarding thickets of wage history. What did a wage really mean in the eighteenth century? And should it not in the first place be related not to the life history of an individual but to the family budget? A whole research programme is waiting to be undertaken.

Three ambiguous concepts

Having defined our working tools, our means of investigation, it remains to define our concepts. Three words, at least, govern this debate: *growth*, *development* and *progress*. The first two are often used interchangeably in both English and French (*croissance* and *développement*), and also in German (*Wachstum* and *Entwicklung*; indeed the latter term, which was used by Schumpeter[103] is tending to die out). Italian for practical purposes has only the one term, *sviluppo*; and the two Spanish words *crecimiento* and *desarollo* are rarely distinguished except in the parlance of Latin American economists who, according to J. D. Gould, make a distinction between structural development (*desarollo*) and growth (*crecimiento*) which relates primarily to a rise in per capita income.[104] And indeed for those seeking to plan without too many risks for rapid economic modernization, it is essential to distinguish between two methods of observation which are not always identical, one concerning G.N.P., the other per capita income. Generally speaking, if I concentrate on the G.N.P. aggregate, I am thinking in terms of 'development'; if I turn my attention to per capita income, I am more concerned with 'growth'.

In the present-day world, there are indeed economies where the two coincide, as in western Europe, where the tendency is consequently to use only one word; there are other countries, by contrast, where the two concepts are distinct and even contradictory. As for the historian, he may find himself faced with even more complicated situations: he finds periods of *growth* – but also periods of *reverse growth*; *development* (in the thirteenth, sixteenth and eighteenth centuries) but also *stagnation* and *recession* (in the fourteenth and seventeenth centuries). In fourteenth-century Europe, there was a move back towards ancient urban and social structures, a temporary halt in the development of pre-capitalist structures, while at the same time there was a disconcerting growth of per capita income: never before had the western population eaten so much bread and meat as in the fifteenth century.[105]

And even these distinctions do not account for all eventualities. In terms of European rivalry for instance, eighteenth-century Portugal – where there was no structural innovation, but which was benefiting from the increased exploitation of Brazil – enjoyed a per capita income probably superior to that of France. The Portuguese king was probably the richest ruler in Europe. It is not possible to talk of Portugal in this period in terms either of development or of regression, any more than it is of Kuwait today, although it has the highest per capita income in the world.

The almost complete elimination from our vocabulary of the word *progress* is to be regretted in this context. It had almost the same meaning as development, and a convenient distinction could be made (convenient that is to historians) between *neutral* progress (that is without alteration to existing structures) and *non-neutral* progress – which broke down the framework within which it had developed.[106] Rather than quibble over vocabulary, may I suggest that development is the same thing as *non-neutral* progress, and that we should classify as *neutral* progress the influx of wealth which oil brought to Kuwait, or Brazilian gold to Pombal's Portugal?

Orders of magnitude and correlations

As the 1976 Prato conference showed,[107] many historians are sceptical if not hostile towards the idea of retrospective national accounting. The only figures available are fragmentary and irregularly concentrated. A statistician of today would disregard them because he has better ones to work with. Unfortunately we cannot do likewise. All the same, it is surely permissible, if the figures for the past do not come in complete series, to look for possible correlations between them, to relate one estimate to another, to build up aggregates and to use our results to calculate others – in other words to proceed as Ernest Wageman recommends in his curious – and little-read – book, *Das Ziffer als Detective.*[108]

In short, since orders of magnitude are all we have, our aim must be to relate them to each other, so that they may to some extent substantiate and confirm each other. And there are, surely, some ratios about which there is no dispute. The population figures before the nineteenth century, for instance, are such that an approximate ratio of urban to rural population can be worked out: in this respect, eighteenth-century Holland held the record, with 50% living in the towns and 50% in the country.[109] In England at the same period, the urban population was probably about 30% of the whole,[110] while in France it was

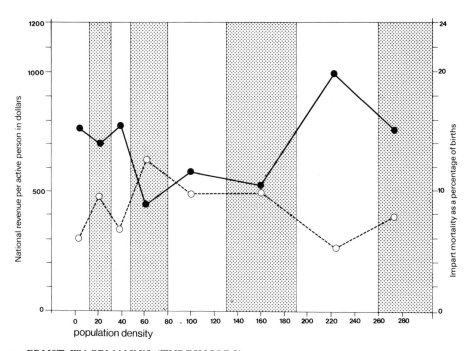

30   ERNST WAGEMANN'S 'THRESHOLDS'
This graph (by F. Braudel in *Annales* E.S.C., 1960, p. 50, from data given by E. Wagemann in *Economia mundial*, 1952, I, pp. 59 and 62) distinguishes rates of population density which are either consistently beneficial (white columns) or consistently detrimental (shaded columns), whatever the country under consideration. The data comes from statistics for about thirty countries in the year 1939. Three figures have been used: population density; per capita income of active population (black circles) and infantile mortality (white circles). Jumping from space to time, Wagemann rather hastily concluded from these figures that as a population increases it moves alternately into a beneficial or a detrimental situation every time it crosses one of the thresholds marked here.

between 15 and 17%.[111] These percentages are in themselves indicative of a wider reality.

It would be interesting for example to speculate about the role of population density, a little-studied theme. The grid worked out by Ernst Wagemann[112] for the year 1939 is not, *pace* its inventor, automatically valid for all periods. If I have nevertheless reproduced it here, it is because it contains an element of truth, namely that there may well be *density thresholds* which herald good or bad times. Favourable or unfavourable demographic densities weighed heavily on pre-industrial economies and societies, as they still do on some Third World countries today. The maturity – or the breakdown – of a national market might be partly explained by these factors. A rising population does not always have the positive and progressive effects often attributed to it – or rather it may have such effects for a while only, and the process may go into reverse once a certain threshold is crossed. The trouble is that the threshold changes, in my view, depending on techniques of marketing and production, and depending on the nature and the volume of trade.

It would also be useful to see how the active population was distributed throughout the various branches of the economy.[113] We have some idea of this distribution in the United Provinces in 1662;[114] in England in the period around 1688;[115] in France in about 1758;[116] and in Denmark in 1783.[117] Of the £43 million at which Gregory King estimated the national product of England in 1688, agriculture represented over £20 million, industry a little less than £10 million, and commerce just over £5 million. The proportions are not the same as those in Quesnay's model[118] (agriculture represented 5000 million *livres tournois* and industry and commerce together 2000 million): Louis XV's France was still up to its knees in agricultural activity compared to England. In an essay of approximate calculation using Quesnay's model, Wilhelm Abel[119] estimated that sixteenth-century Germany, before the ravages of the Thirty Years' War, was much more deeply embedded in agriculture even than eighteenth-century France.

Everywhere in Europe, the ratio agricultural product : industrial product (A:I) was shifting towards industry, but only slowly. In England, industry did not overtake agriculture until 1811–1821.[120] In France this only happened in 1885; in Germany and America it occurred slightly earlier, in 1865[121] and 1869[122] respectively. From my own *very approximate* calculations for the whole of the Mediterranean in the sixteenth century,[123] I have suggested a possible equation of A = 5 times I, a ratio which *might* be valid for the whole of Europe in that century. If so, it is evident that Europe has come a long way.

Another correlation is that between patrimony and the national product. Keynes was in the habit of regarding capital stocks in his own day as three or four times national income. And ratios of 3 or 4 to 1 have also been established by Gallman, Howle and Goldsmith[124] for the United States in the nineteenth century; in a number of today's Third World countries, the ratio varies from 5 : 1 to 3 : 1. According to Simon Kuznets,[125] in the economies of the past, the ratio might have been anywhere between 3:1 and 7:1. It is difficult to know what to do with Gregory King's estimates in this context. In his view the national wealth of England in 1688 was the equivalent of £650 million, of which land accounted for £234 million, labour £330, while the rest consisted of livestock (£25 million), bullion (£28 million) and 'various' items of wealth (£33 million). If one subtracts labour from the total, one has a figure of £320 million for a national product of £43.4 million – or a ratio of 7 to 1.

Alice Hanson Jones[126] used these suggested coefficients to estimate per capita income in several of the American 'colonies' in 1774, after preliminary research had enabled her to calculate their patrimony. She obtained a per capita figure of between $200 (i.e. a ratio of 1:5) and $335 (1:3) and concluded that the United States on the eve of Independence enjoyed living standards superior to those of Europe. If these conclusions are correct, they are not without significance.

National debt and G.N.P.

In the sphere of public finance, where statistics are plentiful, some correlations are detectable: they provide the initial framework for any further reconstruction of national accounting.

There was for instance a relationship between the national debt (the role of which in eighteenth-century England is well-known) and G.N.P.[127] The debt could reach twice G.N.P. without risk. This being so, the healthy state of English finances is proven, since even at the most critical junctures, in 1783 or 1801 for example, the national debt never reached double the G.N.P. There was never any danger of going through the ceiling.

If we suppose for a moment that this ratio was the golden rule, France was not after all in desperate straits when, on 13 January 1561, amid general alarm, the chancellor Michel de l'Hôpital admitted that the state was in deficit to the tune of 43 million *livres*,[128] that is four times the sum of the state budget, whereas G.N.P. at the same time was probably at least 200 million *livres*. Nor was Maria Theresa's Austria at risk: the state's revenues after the War of the Austrian Succession (1748) amounted to 40 million florins; its debts were considerable (280 million) but G.N.P. must have been of the order of 500 or 600 million florins. Even if G.N.P. had been no more than 200 million, the burden of debt would, in theory at least, have been tolerable. It is true that the Seven Years' War before long led to such a drain on funds that Maria Theresa decided to abandon a belligerent policy, and indeed improved her financial position by reducing the rate of interest on the debt to 4 per cent.[129]

In fact the problems associated with the national debt also depended very largely on the efficiency of financial management and the degree of confidence shown by the public. In France in 1789, state borrowing was not beyond the nation's means (3000 million *livres* compared to a G.N.P. of about 2000 million *livres*): the situation was or should have been manageable, but at the time France had a finance policy which was neither coherent nor effective (she was far from showing the skill of the English in this respect). And she found herself faced with a financial crisis combined with a political crisis; it was not simply a question of state insolvency.

Some other equations

The other equations which will concern us are those connecting the mass of money in circulation, national wealth, national income and state budgets.

Gregory King[130] reckoned that the amount of bullion in circulation in his country was £28 million, compared to a patrimony of £320 million – that is 8.75 per cent. Let us accept an *approximate* ratio of 1 to 10; France in the time of Louis XVI had monetary stocks estimated at 1000 million or 1200 million *livres tournois* (a rather low estimate in my view); so her national wealth should have been at least 10,000 or 12,000 million. One might also compare the money supply of England in 1688 with her G.N.P. (and not simply with her patrimony) but these comparisons with money in circulation will not get us very far. The latter figure was only estimated or measured by contemporaries at long intervals: sometimes we have only a single figure for a whole century and not always that.

Budgets by contrast, are usually recorded year by year; they bring us back to the reassuring world of *serial* documents – hence the theme of the 1976 Prato conference: *Public finance and Gross National Product*. While the conference did not reach a conclusion it did at least clear the ground. G.N.P. divided by budget would – *in pre-industrial economies* – work out at somewhere between 10 and 20: 20 being the lower coefficient, representing only 5% of national product (a light burden for the taxpayers) and 10 the higher (10%) – provoking more than the usual volume of complaints. Vauban who had modern notions about taxation (his *Project de Dixme Royale* proposed the abolition of all existing taxes, direct and indirect, as well as of provincial customs duties, and their replacement by a tax 'on anything that brings in income [from which] nothing will escape', since every man would pay 'in relation to his income')[131] was of the opinion that the 10% threshold should never be reached. And he proved it by estimating French national income, sector by sector, and calculating what would be brought in by his tax, which he proposed to adjust according to the means of the social categories concerned. He concluded that 10% of total income would far exceed the largest *war* budget France had yet experienced – 160 million *livres*.

But in the eighteenth century, things changed. The incidence of taxation calculated for both France and England after 1715 is set out in a most stimulating article by P. Mathias and P. O'Brien.[132] Unfortunately their figures are not really comparable with Vauban's, since they relate only to physical output (agricultural and 'industrial') whereas Vauban's also covered rent from urban property, revenue from mills, and all private and public services (servants, the royal

Taxpayers, by Bruegel the Younger (1564–1636). Ghent, Musée des Beaux Arts. (Photo Giraudon.)

administration, the professions, transport and commerce). It is nevertheless interesting to compare the tax burden with physical output in England and France. In France between 1715 and 1800, the percentage was almost always over 10% (11% in 1715, 17% in 1735, but 9 and 10% in 1770 and 1775, 10% in 1803). In England, the tax burden was exceptionally high: 17% in 1715, 18% in 1750, 24% in 1800 during the Napoleonic Wars. It had fallen back to 10% by 1850.

The degree of fiscal pressure is clearly always a significant indicator, since it varies according to country and period, if only because of wars. One method suggests itself for approaching the question and as an initial hypothesis: to see where we get by applying the 'normal margin' of taxation – between 10% and 5%. For instance, if in 1588, the state income of the Signoria of Venice was 1,131,542 ducats[133] then Venetian G.N.P. would have been somewhere between 11 million ducats and 22 million ducats. If in 1779, the revenues of the Tsar (the Russian economy being still archaic at this time) reached between 25 and 30 million roubles,[134] Russian G.N.P. would have been somewhere between 125 and 300 million.

The range of possibility thus established is of course very wide. But once it has been established, cross-references will enable us to appreciate whether fiscal pressure was greater or lesser. In the case of Venice at the end of the sixteenth century, as in other urban economies, fiscal pressure certainly exceeded the usual rate in territorial states – these as a rule kept closer to the lower figure of 5%, whereas Venice seems to have exceeded even the 10% threshold. Indeed the calculations of Venetian G.N.P. which I have attempted using different methods, and based on the wages of the journeymen in the *Arte della Lana* and the labourers in the Arsenal,[135] yield a figure for G.N.P. far below even 11 million ducats, between 7 and 7.7 million, which suggests fiscal pressure quite extraordinary for the time, between 14 and 16%.

It would be worthwhile trying to establish – by going beyond the Venetian example – whether city-based economies in general exerted the highest levels of fiscal pressure (as Lucien Febvre suspected, without finding explicit evidence for his view, in the case of Metz in the year of its reintegration with France, 1552).[136] Were the city-states of the sixteenth century reaching that dangerous fiscal threshold beyond which an *ancien régime* economy was in danger of destroying itself? Is this a further factor to explain the deterioration of the city-centred economies, including eighteenth-century Amsterdam?

Present-day economies seem to be capable of tolerating a quite remarkable increase in state levies. In 1974, revenue from taxes represented 38% of G.N.P. in France and Germany, 36% in Great Britain, 33% in the United States (in 1975), 32% in Italy and 22% in Japan.[137] This rise in fiscal levies is comparatively recent but it is growing more quickly every year both because of the welfare state and because of recourse to taxation as a counter-inflationary measure likely to cut consumption. Since inflation has nevertheless continued unabated, some dissident economists[138] have concluded that excessive taxation is largely responsible for the present crisis and inflation. The idea has been formulated that a tax threshold has been exceeded, thus endangering the economies of the developed nations. Although the present limit is at a very different level, is the problem so very different from the one we can glimpse in the most advanced economies of the West several centuries ago?

To accept that there is a correlation between budget and G.N.P. means accepting that the budget may have an indicative value, and realizing that it is not enough to say, as most contemporaries did and as indeed so many historians still do, that if the all-powerful state, so-called, was short of funds it had only to give another turn to the fiscal screw or juggle with indirect taxes – that perennial resort of all régimes, especially authoritarian ones. It is generally held that Richelieu was driven by the necessities of 'open' war, which broke out in 1635, to increase taxation out of all proportion: did French taxes not double or triple between 1635 and 1642? In fact taxation cannot really be increased enough to bring lasting higher revenues to the state unless the national product is expanding simultaneously. Perhaps this was indeed the case in the early seventeenth century; if so, we should have to follow René Baehrel and revise our usual verdicts on the economic climate in the age of Richelieu.

From consumption to G.N.P.

To estimate G.N.P., one can legitimately start either from production or from consumption. Joan Robinson has defined national income as the 'sum of the expenditures made in a year by all the families composing the nation (plus expenditure on investment for new capital goods and the balance, positive or negative, of exports over imports)'.[139] This being the case, if I know the average consumption of the 'agents' of a given economy, I can work out its total consumption, and by adding to the result whatever has been economized from production – broadly speaking savings – and the positive or negative trade balance, I shall obtain an approximate figure for G.N.P.

Eli Heckscher[140] was one of the early pioneers of this method in his economic history of Sweden (1954), and it was on similar principles that Frank Spooner worked out the graph showing French G.N.P., reproduced here in Figure 31, and that Andrezcj Wyczanski studied Poland's national income in the sixteenth century.[141] 'Even when they are inaccurate', writes the latter, 'these figures [retrospective national accounting] are always more concrete and closer to historical reality than [the] vague verbal descriptions' with which historians had hitherto been content. 'My hypothesis', he goes on, 'is very simple: the entire population of a country has to eat, so the cost of food represents the greater part of national income; or more precisely, it represents agricultural production plus the costs of processing, transport, etc. The rest of national income is made up of the value of the labour of that part of the population which does not produce what it consumes.' So there are three essential elements: C^1, food consumption by the agricultural population; C^2, consumption by the non-agricultural population; and L, the labour of the non-agricultural population. Leaving aside the trade balance, $G.N.P. = C^1 + C^2 + L$, with this advantage for simplicity of calculation that L is very roughly equivalent to C^2: after all, the wage-earning population – who mostly lived in towns – earned hardly more than the minimum to survive and reproduce.

Andrézcj Wyczanski concludes by distinguishing two national incomes, one in the towns and one in the countryside. (Let us not raise too many questions at this stage about the distinction between urban and rural zones, but assume this problem to be resolved.) Of these two incomes, that of the towns is the more likely to expand, and if it expands, the rest of the economy will follow. Hence the simple observation that the demographic evolution of cities can shed light on the progression of G.N.P. itself. If for instance, drawing on Georges Dupeux's work,[142] I have a more or less complete series of figures for the growth of the urban population of France between 1811 and 1911 – growth which occurred at an average rate of 1.2% a year – this graph should indicate that French G.N.P. must have risen at a similar rate.

There is nothing very surprising about this: towns, as all historians agree, have been the essential instruments of accumulation, the motors of economic growth, the forces responsible for all progressive division of labour. Superstructures of the European bloc as a whole, and perhaps, like all structures, semi-parasitical systems,[143] they were nevertheless indispensable to the general process of growth. It was the towns which, from the fifteenth century on, were responsible for the massive movement of *proto-industry*, that transfer (or return) of urban trades to the countryside, in other words the use, or indeed requisitioning of under-employed rural labour in certain regions. Merchant capitalism, by circumventing the restrictive practices of the urban guilds, thus created a new industrial arena – in the countryside but controlled from the towns. For everything came from the towns, everything started there. The English industrial revolution was created in the pioneer towns of Sheffield, Leeds, Manchester and Liverpool.

Frank Spooner's calculations

In the edition in English of his classic study (originally published in French), *The International Economy and Monetary Movements in France, 1493–1725*, Frank C. Spooner[144] included a previously unpublished graph of exceptional interest for French history, since it translates into graphic terms national income, the royal budget and the amount of money in circulation. Only the budget, for which official statistical data is abundant, is represented by a solid line. National income and money stocks are each represented by two curves, an upper and a lower estimate, thus visibly expressing our uncertainties in this field.

G.N.P. (i.e. national income) has been calculated from average consumption expressed in terms of bread prices (on the arbitrary assumption that the number of calories consumed were provided by bread alone). Bread prices and population size varied, yet the G.N.P. constantly goes up – and this is the essential characteristic of the graph.

If, as I believe, this graph is substantially valid, there is a ratio of roughly 1:20 between budget and G.N.P. – proof that taxation was not excessive and that there was no unbearable fiscal tension. As for the stock of money (cumulative coinage), it went up at the same pace as the budget until 1600; then it stagnated and even fell between 1600 and 1640, while the budget continued to rise. But after 1640, the coinage curve radically parts company from the other two, and shoots up vertically – as if France, in the heartland of Europe, was suddenly being flooded with specie and bullion. Was this because of the revival of the American mines after 1680? (But the increase in French money stocks had begun in 1640.) Or was it a result of the revival in French maritime ventures? The expeditions of the sailors of Saint-Malo along the Pacific coast (though at a much later date) probably played a part – they were said to have brought home more than 100 million *livres* of silver. For whatever reason, France seems to have become for a long time a collector of precious metals – without this apparently affecting either budget or G.N.P. An odd situation, especially since if France was

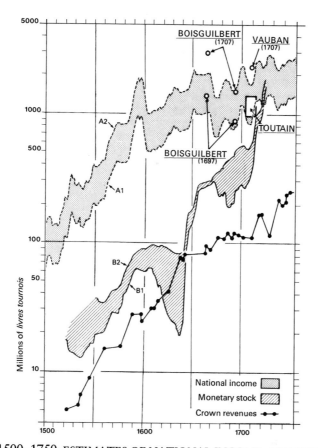

31 FRANCE 1500–1750: ESTIMATES OF NATIONAL INCOME, MONEY STOCKS AND ROYAL REVENUES
Graph from Frank Spooner, *The International Economy and Monetary Movements in France, 1493–1725*, 1972, p. 306. For commentary on this graph see the text.

constantly supplied with specie by her positive trade balance with Spain, she had to make up for a number of outgoings in other directions, notably the Levant trade, and was also exporting money across Europe (through the good offices of Samuel Bernard, Antoine Crozat and the merchants of Geneva among others) to pay for Louis XIV's wars and the upkeep of many troops outside France. And yet France was hoarding money (witness the suggestive remark passed casually by Boisguilbert in 1697 '... although France is more full of money than she has ever been').[145] Or the complaint of the merchants at the end of Louis XIV's reign about the comparative insignificance of 800 million bank notes (which had quickly depreciated) by comparison with the mass of silver which was circulating – or being prudently concealed – throughout the kingdom. The rise in the money supply is certainly not explained by Law's System – indeed I would argue that on the contrary it was the other way about. Only the money supply made the system possible and the process continued into the eighteenth century, becoming a curious feature of the French economy. The problem remains finally without a satisfactory answer.

Visible continuities

Visualizing overall quantities throws into relief clear continuities in European history.

The first of these is the regular rise of G.N.P. come hell or high water: look for example at English G.N.P. during the eighteenth and nineteenth centuries. And if Frank Spooner is correct, France's G.N.P. had been rising since the reign of Louis XII and probably even longer: it was increasing visibly until 1750 and it has continued its ascent beyond the reign of Louis XV and right up to the present day. Such fluctuations as there were were short-lived, the barely-perceptible waves on the surface of a long rolling tide. This picture, in short, has nothing in common with the medium-term movements to which we are used, the *conjoncture* or indeed the secular trend. Even the violent interruptions caused by two world wars were in the end only, after all, interruptions, dramatic though they seemed at the time. Wars were even more easily compensated for in the past. And after disasters – often self-inflicted – societies seem to have been admirably adept at picking themselves up again: France throughout her long history has often had to recover her balance and she is certainly no exception.

A second continuity is the rise of the state, measured by the growing proportion of national income which it has appropriated. It is a fact that budgets are always growing and states becoming larger, devouring everything. It is important to state this in the light of our national accounting, even if it means coming back to traditional wisdom, or to the declarations of principle so often expressed by German-speaking historians. As Werner Näf unhesitatingly put it, *Vom Staat soll an erster Stelle die Rede sein*: 'We must speak in the first place of the state'.[146] The state is 'a gigantic enterprise', wrote Werner Sombart, 'whose leaders have as their chief aim the acquisition ... of as much gold and silver as possible'.[147] We must give the state its due then: the overall economy obliges us to restore it to its very considerable place. 'The state', as Jean Bouvier says 'is never to be taken lightly.'[148]

It certainly could not be so regarded after the 1450s and the return of a more favourable economic climate. Is not the rise of the state, considered over the long term, to some extent the same as the history of Europe as a whole? Having vanished with the collapse of Rome in the fifth century, the state was reconstituted with the 'industrial revolution' of the eleventh to thirteenth centuries, then fell apart once more after the disasters of the Black Death and the awe-inspiring recession of the mid-fourteenth century. I admit to being both fascinated and horrified by the spectacle of this disintegration, this headlong tumble into darkness – the greatest drama ever registered in European history. More catastrophic tragedies have indeed occurred in the course of the world's long existences – the Mongol invasions of Asia, the wiping out of the greater part of the Amerindian population after the arrival of the white man. But nowhere else did a disaster of such magnitude engender such recovery: that uninterrupted movement which began in the mid-fifteenth century and led eventually to the industrial revolution and the economy of the modern state.

France: a victim of her size

France was without question the first modern nation, in political terms, to emerge in Europe, receiving her final shape from the cosmic midwifery of the 1789 revolution.[149] At the level of economic infrastructure however, France was far from being a perfect national market even at this late date. It has been claimed that Louis XI was a pioneer of mercantilism, a 'Colbertian' before Colbert,[150] a prince who cared about the economy of his kingdom as a whole. But what could one man's political will achieve confronted with the diversity and archaism of the French economy in his day – archaism which would long persist?

Piecemeal, regionalized, the French economy was the sum of separate units all tending towards self-sufficiency. The larger trade currents flowing through the country (one is tempted to say flying through her air-space) benefited only those particular cities or regions which served as distribution centres, points of arrival or departure. Like other 'nations' in Europe, the France of Louis XIV and Louis XV was essentially agricultural: industry, commerce and finance were hardly likely to transform it overnight. Progress was patchy and barely visible before the wave of growth in the later eighteenth century. 'The France of the minority', writes Ernest Labrousse, 'with its wide horizons [i.e. looking to the outside world] contrasts with the inward-looking France of the vast majority, encompassing all the rural areas, most of the smaller towns and some of the larger ones.'[151]

The emergence of a national market was a battle against this omnipresent inertia, a battle which would eventually generate exchange and communications. But was the major source of inertia in the French case perhaps the very size of the country? The United Provinces and England – the former a small and the latter only a medium-sized country – had more compact nervous systems and were more easily unified. Distance was not such an obstacle for them.

Diversity and unity

France was a mosaic of small *pays* with their local colourings, each living primarily on its own resources in a confined space. Little affected by the outside

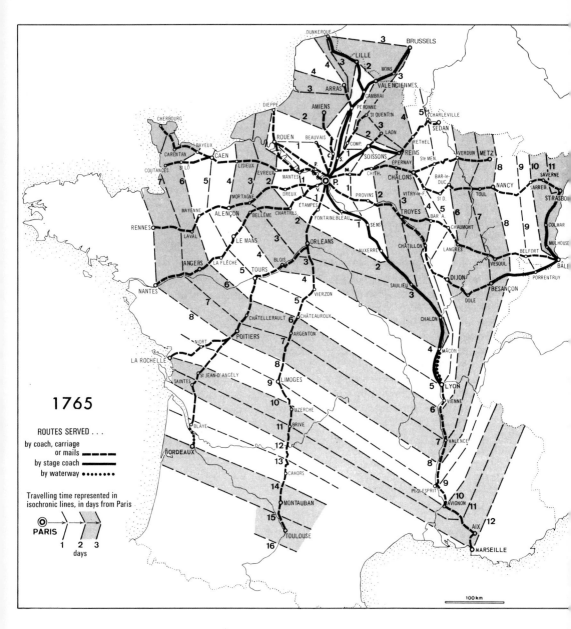

1765

ROUTES SERVED . . .

by coach, carriage
or mails ■ ■ ■ ■ ■

by stage coach ▬▬▬▬

by waterway ●●●●●●●

Travelling time represented in
isochronic lines, in days from Paris

PARIS

1   2   3
days

**32   OVERCOMING THE TYRANNY OF DISTANCE: THE PROBLEMS OF
THE FRENCH NATIONAL MARKET**

These two maps by G. Arbellot (*Annales E.S.C.*, 1973, p. 790) show the 'great road revolution'
which thanks to the new roads capable of taking 'carriages at full gallop', and to the use of the
turgotines – fast stage-coaches – and the larger number of staging posts, had cut sometimes by
half the time taken to travel across France between 1765 and 1780. In 1765, it took at least three
weeks to go from Lille to the Pyrenees, or from Strasbourg to Brittany. Even in 1780, France still
seemed like a solid landmass to be crossed slowly. But progress in road-building was by now

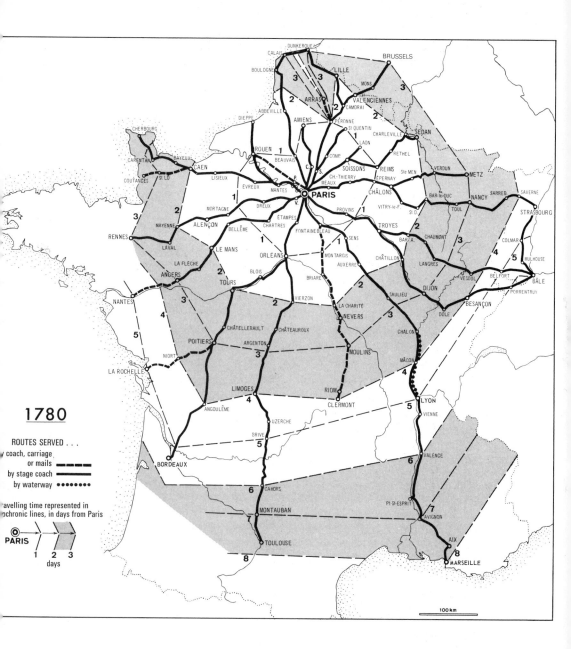

1780

ROUTES SERVED . . .
by coach, carriage
or mails ------
by stage coach ———
by waterway •••••••

travelling time represented in
isochronic lines, in days from Paris

PARIS ◎ → → →
1   2   3
days

tending to reach all parts of the kingdom. On the first map, we can already see several privileged
routes: Paris–Rouen, for instance, or Paris–Péronne (1 day, the same as Paris–Melun); Paris–Lyon
(5 days, the same as it took to travel to Charleville, or Caen or Vitry-le-François despite the
greater distance). On the second map there is a much clearer correlation between distance and
time of journey (hence the near-concentric circles round Paris). The time of travel remained the
same on the former privileged routes such as to Lyon or Rouen. The decisive factor was the
creation by Turgot in 1775 of the *Régie des diligences et messageries*, the state mailcoach service.

world, they spoke a single economic language: what can be said of one can be applied to another, whether nearby or distant. Knowing one, we can imagine the rest.

Some idea of this enclosed world can be glimpsed in the accounts book kept by the prudent and thrifty little monastery of Lazarist fathers[152] in Bonneville, 'capital' of the Faucigny, in Savoy before its annexation to France. In the eighteenth century, the inhabitants of this remote monastery depended on their own resources, buying a few items at the local market, but mainly living off the grain and wine contributed by their tenant-farmers. Grain was delivered to the baker as advance payment for the fathers' daily bread. Meat on the other hand had to be bought for cash from the butcher. Village craftsmen and labourers, paid by the day, were on hand to transport planks, firewood or a load of dung; a peasant woman came in to kill the pig which the fathers had been fattening; the shoemaker delivered shoes to them and to their only manservant; the monastery's horse was shod at Cluses by a blacksmith of their acquaintance; the mason, carpenter and joiner were prepared to come and work on the spot, by the day. Everything happened within a small radius: the horizon was bounded by Tanninges, Sallanches, La Roche-sur-Foron. But since there is no such thing as perfect autarky, the circumference of the little circle round the Bonneville monastery was breached at one or two points. From time to time a special messenger (unless the ducal mails would oblige) was dispatched to Annecy or more often Geneva, to buy out-of-the-way goods: medicine, spice or sugar. But by the end of the century – a little revolution this – sugar was available in the grocer's shop at Bonneville.

The language of exchange here is a simple one, and can be heard in other confined regions if one listens carefully. The Auxois for example, rich in farm-land and grazing, lived on its own resources, particularly since its chief town, Semur, 'has no great highway in it' and is 'far from the navigable waterways'.[153] It did nonetheless have some communication with neighbouring regions of Auxerre and Avallon.[154] Some parts of the Breton interior and the Massif Central were almost self-sufficient, as was the Barrois, although it had contacts with Champagne and Lorraine, and even exported its wine down the Meuse to the Netherlands.

If on the other hand, we turn to a region or town situated on the major axes of communication, the picture changes, with traffic bustling in all directions. This was the case in Verdun-sur-le-Doubs, a little town in Burgundy on the banks of the Doubs and very near the Saône, two waterways which joined up to the south. 'Trade is very busy here', says a report in 1698,

> because of its favourable site ... There is much dealing in grain, wine and hay. Every year on 28 October, there is a free fair, beginning eight days before the Feast of Saint Simon and Saint Jude and continuing for eight days afterwards; in the old days, a very large number of horses were sold here.[155]

Moret-sur-Loing in 1610

The distribution zone around Verdun included Alsace, the Franche-Comté, the Lyonnais and 'the districts lower down'. Lying at the crossroads of several different trade currents, this little town was bound to be outward-looking and open to change. People were tempted to set up businesses here and several possibilities were open to them.

There was plenty of traffic too in the Mâconnais, whose inhabitants however lacked any spirit of initiative. But their wines practically exported themselves in all directions. Other activities were on a small scale, it is true – cereal-growing, calf-rearing, linen-weaving and tannery. But the wine trade was sufficient in itself, not to mention the manufacture of casks accompanying it. 'Although the cask-wood is almost all taken out of Burgundy by the river Saône, there are many coopers busy all year round on this very necessary work, since in the Mâconnais, where wine is sold by the cask, many of them are needed every year.' And the price had even gone up, since the people of Provence had 'ordered ... a great quantity of them, which they have been using in order to save their big barrels which are heavier and made of thicker wood, and to make the carriage of their wines to Paris easier and less costly'.[156]

France was thus criss-crossed with short- medium- and long-range trade routes. Towns like Dijon and Rennes were in the seventeenth century, as Henri Sée suggested,[157] 'almost exclusively local markets' – the word 'almost' tells us that long-distance trade also reached such towns, however discreet its role might seem; and this trade was destined to grow.

Long-distance trade, which is more visible to the historian than the many local exchanges, mostly concerned those indispensable goods which in a way determined their own journeys: salt, for instance, or grain, especially the latter with its necessary and sometimes dramatic transfers from one province to another. In both value and tonnage, grain was 'the most important traffic in the Kingdom'. In mid-sixteenth century, the supply of grain to the city of Lyon alone was equivalent to one and a half times the value of all the Genoese velvets sold on the French market – and these were by far 'the most widespread of the silkstuffs'.[158] To say nothing of wine, which seemed to be drawn as if by a magnet towards the countries of the north. Or the streams of textiles of every kind and origin which flowed through France virtually all year round, seemingly impervious to seasonal rhythms. Then there were exotic goods like spices, pepper and before long coffee, sugar and tobacco, the craze for which filled the coffers both of the French state and the Indies Company. Apart from the river boats and the ever-present waggoners, the flow of traffic was also quickened by the regular mails, created by the monarchy for the fast dispatch of its agents and orders. People could move about even more easily than merchandise: the rich and mighty took the mail coach, the poor went on foot on fantastic journeys through France.

The patchwork of French regions, though 'bristling with exceptions, privileges and constraints',[159] was thus being stitched together. In the eighteenth century, as trade expanded, the barriers between provinces were vigorously pushed down.[160] Boisguilbert's France of separate provinces was fading away, and since almost every region was affected by the increased volume of exchange, each began to specialize in particular activities found to be profitable, evidence that the national market was beginning to play its role in encouraging the division of labour.

Natural and artificial links

It could perhaps be argued that this increased circulation, with its long-term unifying tendencies, was achieved with the help of France's geography. Apart from the awesome bulk of the Massif Central, France had obvious natural advantages for the transport of goods by road or water. Short-haul shipping operated up and down her long coastlines: it may have been inadequate, but at least it existed and while it was largely composed of foreign – notably Dutch – vessels[161] for many years, it nevertheless filled a gap. In terms of waterways, rivers and canals, France, while not as well-endowed as England or the United Provinces, had considerable facilities. The Rhône and the Saône ran along the very axis of the 'French isthmus', in a straight line from north to south. The merit of the Rhône, explained a traveller in 1681, is that it offers 'great convenience to those who wish to go to Italy by way of Marseille. This was the route I took. I went aboard at Lyon and arrived on the third day at Avignon. The next day I went on to Arles'.[162] This could hardly be bettered.

All the French rivers performed their tasks admirably. Wherever a waterway permitted, local craft were adapted to its features; at the very least it could be used for floating down logs, either singly or in trains. There were of course, all over France as elsewhere, mills with their mill-races, but these could be opened if necessary and the boats propelled downstream by the force of the unpent water, as regularly happened on the shallow-running Meuse: between Saint-Mihiel and Verdun, three mills allowed boats to pass in return for a modest fee[163]

- a little detail which tells us that the upper reaches of the Meuse were being used for shipping in the seventeenth century, as well as the waters lower down towards the Netherlands. It was indeed thanks to this means of transport that Charleville and Mézières so long remained distribution points for coal, copper, alum and iron from the north.[164]

But this was nothing compared to the intense flow of traffic along the major waterways: the Rhône, Saône, Garonne and Dordogne, the Seine and its tributaries, and the Loire, queen of French rivers despite frequent flooding, many sandbanks and the tolls which punctuated its course. The Loire played a vital role, thanks to the ingenuity of its boatmen and the convoys of vessels which hoisted their large square sails to travel back upstream; if there was no wind, they had to be hauled. The Loire was the means of joining north to south, east to west: the portage at Roanne linked it to the Rhône, while the Orleans and Briare canals linked it to the Seine and Paris. To contemporary observers, the traffic both up and downstream was enormous.[165] And yet Orleans, which should have been the hub of French trade, remained a second-rank town in spite of its distributive role and its industries – no doubt because of competition from nearby Paris, served as it was by the Seine and its tributaries (the Yonne, the Marne and the Oise) which formed an outstanding system of waterways immensely convenient for supply.

France also had the advantage of an extensive road network, which the monarchy developed in spectacular fashion in the eighteenth century, often changing the very foundations of economic life in the regions it cut through, since the new road did not always follow the same route as the old. Not all these roads were thronged with traffic, it is true. Arthur Young described the magnificent highway between Paris and Orleans as 'a desert compared with those around London. In ten miles, we met not one stage or diligence; only two *messageries* and very few chaises; not a tenth of what would have been met had we been leaving London at the same hour'.[166] It is true that London fulfilled all the functions of Paris, as well as those of a redistribution centre for the whole kingdom, and of a major seaport. And the Thames valley, being smaller than the Paris basin, was more densely populated – as Baron Dupin later repeatedly observed in his classic works on England. Other observers were in any case less dismissive than the learned Arthur Young. The Spanish traveller, Antonio Ponz, had been most impressed four years earlier, in 1783, by the traffic on the road between Paris, Orleans and Bordeaux: 'The vehicles which carry goods are terrible engines: very long, proportionately broad, and above all solid, made at fabulous cost and drawn by six, eight, ten or more horses, depending on their weight. If the roads were not what they are, I do not know what would become of this traffic, whatever the industry and activity of the men of this country'. It is true that unlike Young, Ponz could only compare France with Spain rather than with England, and this enabled him to appreciate the progress that had been made in road-building rather better than the Englishman.[167] 'France', he said, 'needed more roads than other countries, [because of] all her waters and marshy zones'; he might also have referred to her mountains and above all her very large surface area.

It is undoubtedly the case that France's great expanse was gradually being penetrated by a network of roads: by the end of the *ancien régime* there were 40,000 km of roads, 8000 km of navigable rivers and 1000 km of canals.[168] The expanding network captured one area after another, creating a hierarchy of regions and a tendency to diversify means of transport. Thus while the Seine remained Paris's chief supply route, foodstuffs could also arrive in the capital from Brittany up the Loire, or from Marseille by way of the Rhône, Roanne, the Loire and the Briare canal.[169] In December 1709, following appeals from dealers and suppliers, grain was transported from Orleans to the Dauphiné.[170] Even the circulation of specie, which had always been given priority treatment, was made easier by the reorganization of transport routes, as a report by the *Conseil d'Etat* notes in September 1783: several bankers and businessmen from Paris and the principal towns in the kingdom,

> taking advantage of the great facility which commerce now enjoys thanks to the roads driven throughout France, and the establishment of the *messageries* (royal mails), the stage-coaches and the haulage trade ... have made the transport of gold and silver coin the chief object of speculation, sending the rate of exchange up or down as they please and creating abundance or scarcity in the capital and the provinces.[171]

Given the huge dimensions of France, it is clear that progress in transport was crucial to the unification of the country, though it was by no means adequate at this stage, as has been pointed out with reference to periods closer to our own time by the historian Jean Bouvier (who maintains that the national market did not exist in France before the completion of the railway network) and the economist Pierre Uri (who goes even further, claiming categorically that present-day France will only be a true economic unit when her telephone system has reached 'American-style perfection'). They are no doubt right. But the admirable engineers of the *Ponts et Chaussées* who built the eighteenth-century roads were certainly responsible for progress towards a French national market.

The primacy of politics

But the national market was not an exclusively economic reality, especially in the initial stages. It emerged from a a pre-existing political unit. And the correspondence between the nation's *political* structures and its *economic* structures was only gradually established in the seventeenth and eighteenth centuries.[172]

This was perfectly logical. As I have already said several times, an economic area always extends far beyond the borders of political areas. 'Nations' or national markets were consequently built up *inside* an economic system greater than themselves, or more precisely they were formed *in opposition* to that system. A long-range international economy had long existed and the national market was carved out within this wider unit by more or less far-sighted and certainly resolute policies. Well before the age of mercantilism, princes were already intervening in the economy, seeking to constrain, encourage, forbid, or facilitate movement, filling a gap here or opening an outlet there. They sought to establish regular systems which would assist their own survival and political ambitions, but they were only successful in this endeavour in the end if it coincided with the general tendencies of the economy. Was this what happened in the case of 'Enterprise France Ltd'?

The French state, or at any rate a version of it, undeniably made an early appearance. If not the very first of all the territorial states, it had certainly soon outstripped the others. This growth should be seen as the constructive reaction of a central zone to the periphery, at whose expense it was seeking to expand. (In the early stages of her existence, France had to face outwards in many directions simultaneously – north, south, east and even west.) By the thirteenth century, France was already the major political unit of the continent: 'almost a state', as Pierre Chaunu has rightly said,[173] having all the requisite ancient and modern characteristics of a state: the charismatic aura, the judicial, administrative and above all financial institutions without which the political unit would have been completely inert. But if in the time of Philip Augustus and Louis XI, political success turned into economic success, it was because the benefits of the progress of the most advanced sector of Europe spilled over into the French economy. As I have already indicated, historians have still not sufficiently acknowledged the importance of the Champagne and Brie fairs. Imagine for a moment that in about 1270, during the heyday of the fairs, when St Louis lay dying before Tunis, the economic pattern of Europe had been frozen in the form then existing: one consequence would have been a predominant French economic unit, perfectly capable of creating its own coherence and expanding at the expense of others.

This was not of course how things worked out. The great recession which struck in the early fourteenth century brought about a series of collapses, and the economic balance of Europe had to find other foundations. By the time France – the battlefield of the Hundred Years' War – recovered her political and indeed economic coherence in the reigns of Charles VI (1422–61) and Louis XI (1461–83), the outside world had profoundly altered.

And yet by the beginning of the sixteenth century[174] France had once more become 'the first by far of all the states' of Europe – 300,000 km² in area, between 80 and 100 tons of gold in fiscal revenues, a G.N.P. possibly the equivalent of 1600 tons of gold. In Italy, where everything was rated on a scale – power as well as wealth – when a document simply refers to 'il Re', it means the Most Christian King of France – *the* king par excellence. This super-power status alarmed France's neighbours and rivals, all those whom the new economic upsurge in Europe had helped to rise in the world and filled with a mixture of ambition and fear. This was why the Spanish rulers, Ferdinand and Isabella, encircled France, now seen as a threat, with a pre-emptive series of princely marriages; and this was also why François I's victory at Marignan (1515) turned the European balance of power against him – the balance having already been a recognizable mechanism since the thirteenth century. When in 1521, war broke out between Valois and Habsburgs, the mechanism worked against the king of France and favoured Charles V – at the risk, as soon became evident, of engineering the supremacy of Spain, which would in any case have been brought about sooner or later by the flood of American silver.

But was not the real reason for France's political setback simply that she was no longer and could not hope to be the centre of the European world-economy? The headquarters of European wealth now moved in turn to Venice, Antwerp, Genoa and Amsterdam – all of them outside France's frontiers. There was one brief moment when France seemed once more to be moving to the top of the table, during the War of the Spanish Succession, when Spanish America was being plundered by the ships of Saint-Malo. But the opportunity was no sooner glimpsed than it vanished again. All in all, history was not over-favourable to the formation of a French national market. The division of the globe was carried out without her participation, and even at her expense.

Was France vaguely aware of this? She tried – unsuccessfully – to gain a foothold in Italy in 1494; but in any case, between 1494 and 1559, the magic circle of Italy forfeited its leadership of the European world-economy. The attempt was repeated, again without success, a century later in the Netherlands. But it is more than likely that even if the Dutch Wars had ended in 1672 with a French victory – which was certainly a possibility – the centre of the European world-economy would have been transferred straight from Amsterdam to London – not to Paris. It was firmly established in London when the French armies eventually occupied the United Provinces in 1795.

Was France simply too big?

Was one reason for these failures simply that France extended over too great an area? To William Petty's observant gaze in the late seventeenth century, France was a country thirteen times the size of Holland and three or four times the size of England; she had four or five times the English population and perhaps ten times the Dutch. William Petty even claims that France had eighty times more arable land than Holland, whereas her 'wealth' was only three times that of the United Provinces.[175] If one were to take present-day France as a unit of measurement (550,000 km²) and look for a state thirteen times as big (7,150,000 km²) the answer would be something like the United States. It was all very well for Arthur Young to sniff at the low volume of traffic on the road between Paris and Orleans, but if by some sleight of hand we were to transpose the communications network centred on the Ile de France and Paris to London and the Thames valley, most of the routes would be somewhere out in the sea. In a larger space, traffic of equivalent volume is diluted.

Abbé Galiani noted in 1770 that 'France is no longer [the country] of Colbert and Sully'.[176] France had, he thought, reached the limits of territorial expansion. With a population of 20 million, she could not increase her volume of manufactured goods without exceeding the limits imposed by the worldwide economy. Similarly if France had had a navy proportionately the equivalent of the Dutch fleet, such a navy, multiplied by 3, 10 or 13, would have been out of all proportion to what was acceptable by the international economy.[177] Galiani, the most clear-sighted man of his century, had put his finger on the problem. France was the victim of her own dimensions. Size did have some advantages of course: if France regularly resisted foreign invasion, it was because distance could protect: it was impossible to travel across the country to strike at its heart. By the same token, France's own communications, government orders, all the movements of the internal economy, and technical progress found it hard to overcome the tyranny of distance. Even the Wars of Religion, which spread with revolutionary contagiousness, did not sweep the country in a single movement. Alphonse Aulard, the historian of the French Revolution, argued that even the Convention had the greatest of difficulties 'in making its will known throughout France'.[178]

Moreover, certain French statesmen, and not the least among them, sensed that the expansion of the kingdom would not necessarily lead to an expansion of its power. This is at any rate how I would interpret the rather obscure phrase that occurs in a letter from the duke of Chevreuse to Fénelon: 'France, which should above all remain within *sufficient limits*'.[179] Turgot, in the eighteenth century was writing in general terms, not about France in particular, but can one possibly imagine an Englishman or a Dutchman writing: 'The maxim that says one should lop off provinces from states, like branches from a tree, in order to strengthen them, is likely to remain in books for a long time before it is listened to in the councils of princes'?[180] We may wonder what would have happened if France had not grown so quickly. For her territorial expansion, beneficial though it was in several ways to the monarchical state and probably to French culture and the long-term future of the country as well, seriously hampered her economic development. If communication between the provinces was difficult, it was because they formed part of a country where distance was a perennial problem. Even for grain, the country-wide market did not function at all well. France was a huge grain-producer, but most of her own produce was consumed on the spot. Shortages and even famines were paradoxically quite possible, even in the eighteenth century.

This would continue to be the case until the railways reached remote country districts. Even in 1843, the economist Adolphe Blanqui could write that the little communes of the district of Castellane in the Basses-Alpes 'were more cut off from French influence than the Marquesas islands ... Communications here are neither major nor minor: they simply do not exist'.[181]

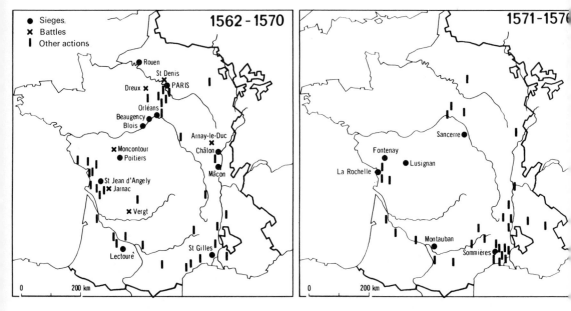

**33 THE WARS OF RELIGION FAILED TO SPREAD TO THE WHOLE OF FRANCE
EVEN AFTER THE COMING TO POWER OF HENRI IV**
These maps show only the more important encounters (from the volume by Henri Mariéjol in
Lavisse's *Histoire de France*) which simplifies the picture of course. Even so, it is clear that there
was nothing simultaneous about the spread of hostilities, that distance was an obstacle to
contagion. Even the final phase of the wars, in the time of Henri IV, was concentrated for the
most part in northern France.

Paris plus Lyon, Lyon plus Paris

It is hardly surprising that an area so immense and so resistant to integration
should have failed to produce a single natural centre. Two cities – Paris and
Lyon (Lyons) – vied for first place in the French economy. And this is surely one
of the less well-known sources of the weakness in the French system.

General histories of Paris often disappoint by failing to set the story of the
capital in the context of French history as a whole, or by paying insufficient
attention to the city's economic activity and authority. In this respect, histories
of Lyon are equally disappointing: they all too regularly explain Lyon in terms
of Lyon. They do, it is true, clearly indicate the link between Lyon's rise to fame
and the fairs which made it in the late fifteenth century the economic pinnacle of
the kingdom. But in the first place, too much credit for the fairs is given to Louis
XI; secondly, it cannot be too often repeated that as Richard Gascon has shown,
the Lyon fairs were the invention of Italian merchants who located them within
easy reach just inside the French border, and that they were actually a sign of
French subordination within the international economy. With only a little ex-

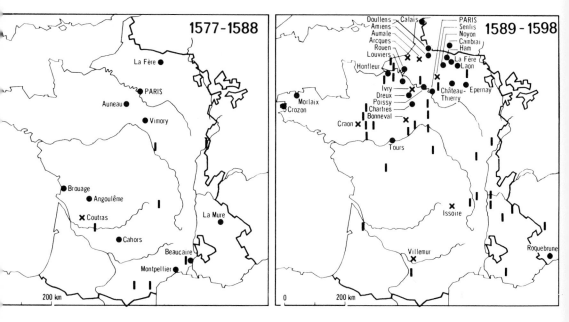

aggeration, it could be said that sixteenth-century Lyon was to the Italians what eighteenth-century Canton was to the Europeans who exploited China. Thirdly, historians of Lyon are not sufficiently alert to the bi-polarity between Paris and Lyon, which is a constant structure in French development.

Since Lyon had been the creation of Italian merchants, things went well while the Italians ruled the European economy, but after 1557, the situation deteriorated. The 1575 crisis and the 'crashes' of the years 1585-95,[182] followed by years of dear money and depression (1597-8)[183] hastened the decline. The major functions of Lyon were transferred to Genoa – that is to a city outside the French sphere, within the embrace of the Spanish Empire, a city deriving strength from the strength and effectiveness of that empire, or rather from the far-off mines of the New World; and while that strength and effectiveness lasted, as a source of mutual support, until about the 1620s, Genoa virtually dominated European finance and banking.

So Lyon found herself back in the second division. There was no shortage of money there – indeed the reverse at times – but it could no longer find the same advantageous employment. J. Gentil da Silva[184] is right: Lyon remained open for trade with the rest of Europe, but was increasingly becoming an exclusively French money-market, attracting native French capital in search of the gilt-edged investments to be found in the fairs, or the regular interest payable on the *dépôts* (deferred payments from one fair to another). The days were past when Lyon could be said to 'lay down the law in all the centres of Europe', or when its trading and financial activity animated 'a sort of polygon from London to Nuremberg, Messina and Palermo, from Algiers to Lisbon, from Lisbon to

Nantes or Rouen', not to mention the vital trade crossroads at Medina del Campo.[185] By 1715, the Lyonnais were content to boast rather modestly: 'Our market usually dictates terms to *all the provinces*'.[186]

Did Lyon's decline further the primacy of Paris? Having been ousted by the Lucchese in the last years of the sixteenth century, the Florentines of Lyon had turned increasingly to 'public finance, becoming firmly established in Paris, in the profitable shadow of political power'.[187] From observation of this move by Italian firms, especially the Capponi, Frank Spooner diagnosed a shift towards the French capital which he regarded as comparable to the all-important takeover by Amsterdam from Antwerp.[188] There certainly was some transfer, but Denis Richet, who has re-examined the evidence, rightly argues that the opportunity presented to Paris – if such there was – was never seriously followed up. 'The climate which brought about the decline of Lyon', he writes, 'ripened the seeds for Paris's growth, but did not lead to a reversal of functions. Even in 1598, Paris still had neither the necessary infrastructure for large-scale international trade, nor fairs comparable to those of Lyon or Piacenza, neither a well-organized currency market, nor a solid body of tried techniques.'[189] That is not to say that Paris as political capital, collecting-point of royal taxes and massive reservoir of wealth, the consumer market which squandered a substantial share of the 'nation's' income, carried no weight in the kingdom's economy or in the redistribution of capital. Parisian capital was present in Marseille by 1563 for instance.[190] And the Parisian mercers of the *Six Corps* were at a very early date engaging in profitable long-distance trade. But on the whole, the wealth bottled up in Paris was only imperfectly channelled into production or indeed into commodity trading.

Was this a missed opportunity for Paris – and through Paris for France – to 'modernize'? It is possible: and if so, the blame can fairly be laid at the door of the wealth-owning classes of Paris who were too strongly attracted to office and land, investments which were 'socially enriching, individually lucrative and economically parasitical'.[191] Even in the eighteenth century, Turgot,[192] taking up a point made by Vauban, accused Paris of being 'an abyss swallowing up all the riches of the state, to which trifles and manufactured articles draw money from all over France, in a traffic as ruinous to our provinces as it is to foreigners. The product of taxation is largely dissipated here'. The trade balance between Paris and the provinces is indeed an outstanding example of unequal exchange. 'It is certain', wrote Cantillon, 'that the provinces always owe large sums of money to the capital.'[193] This being so, Paris continued to grow more handsome and more populous, and to dazzle visitors, at the expense of the rest of the country.

The power and prestige of Paris were also of course those of the command-centre of French policy. Whoever controlled Paris controlled France, even then. From the start of the Wars of Religion, the Protestants had had their eye on Paris, but it escaped them. In 1568, Orleans, the gateway to the capital, was recaptured from them to Catholic rejoicing: 'We have taken Orleans from them', said the Catholics, 'because we did not wish them to come courting so near our good city of Paris.'[194] Paris was later captured by the Leaguers, then by Henri IV, and subsequently by the Frondeurs who could not think what to do with the city apart from disrupting it – to the great indignation of a businessman living in Reims, that is in the shadow of the capital: if the everyday life of Paris were disturbed, he wrote, 'business [would come to a halt] in other cities, whether in France or in foreign kingdoms, as far away as Constantinople'.[195] To this provincial bourgeois, Paris was the centre of the world.

Lyon could not claim such prestige, nor compare itself to the unique reputation of the French capital. But if not a 'monster', Lyon was still, by the standards of the time, a very big city, covering an area so great, as a traveller from Strasbourg explains, 'that there are contained within the city boundaries shooting-ranges, cemeteries, vineyards, fields, meadows and other sites'. 'It is said', the same writer adds, 'that Lyon does more business in a day than Paris in a week, because the merchants here are mostly wholesalers. But Paris has the greater retail trade.'[196] And a level-headed Englishman agreed: Paris was certainly not the greatest trading city in the kingdom. 'Anyone who thinks so is

The new Bourse at Lyon, built in 1749. (Photo B.N.)

confusing tradesmen with shopkeepers. Lyon derives its superiority from its wholesale merchants, its fairs, its *Place au Change* and its many industries.'[197]

A report written by the *intendant*'s administration in 1698 gives Lyon a fairly reassuring bill of health.[198] It lists at length the natural advantages conferred upon the city by the waterways linking it to neighbouring provinces and to other countries. Its two-hundred-year-old fairs continued to prosper: as in the past, they were held four times a year according to the same rules: accounts were always settled one morning between ten o'clock and midday, in the loggia of the *Place au Change*, and 'such large payments are made that two million [*livres*] worth of business is transacted, yet no more than 100,000 *écus* in coin changes hands'.[199] *Le dépôt*, the credit mechanism whereby payment was deferred from one fair to another, worked smoothly since it was supplied by 'the purses of the bourgeois who come to invest money in the market'.[200] The machinery continued to operate, although many of the Italians, in particular the Florentines, the original 'inventors of this market', had moved on. Their places had been taken by merchants from Genoa, Piedmont or the Swiss cantons. In addition, a thriving type of industry (perhaps a form of compensation for the falling-off in trade and finance) was developing in the city and its outlying areas. Silk was its mainstay, including black taffetas of high quality and the famous cloth of gold and silver which supplied a substantial wholesale trade. Even in the sixteenth century, Lyon had been the centre of an industrial zone covering Saint-Etienne, Saint-Chamond, Virieu and Neufville.

The 1698 balance sheet shows Lyon exporting about twenty million *livres* worth of goods and importing twelve million, that is with a surplus of eight million *livres*. But if we accept, for want of better figures, Vauban's estimate for the whole of France – a 40 million surplus – then Lyon's contribution represents only one-fifth of it; this certainly cannot compare with the position of London in the context of English trade.

Lyon's most important trading partner was Italy (10 million *livres* exports, 6 or 7 million imports). Is this evidence that some parts of Italy were more active than is usually allowed? Genoa certainly acted as intermediary between Lyon and Spain where the Genoese had retained an amazing network of sales and purchases. On the other hand, Lyon had few links with Holland, and hardly more with England, continuing rather to concentrate on the Mediterranean region, remaining faithful to her past and her heritage.

Paris takes the crown

While Lyon remained a vigorous centre, it had little contact then with the most advanced sectors of Europe and the up and coming international economy. In its rivalry with the capital, only an injection of energy from outside could have enabled Lyon to assert itself as the heart of French economic activity. In this tale of two cities, obscure and hard to follow as it is, Paris eventually emerged the winner.

But the superiority of the capital, which took time to become evident, would be achieved only in a very particular way. Paris did not get the better of Lyon commercially. Even in Necker's day (about 1781) Lyon was still far ahead in trade: exports, 142.8 million *livres*; imports, 68.9 million; total transactions, 211.7 million; gross balance, 73.9. And if one ignores variations in the value of the *livres tournois*, these figures are nine times those of the 1698 report. Paris at the same date had a total (exports plus imports) of 24.9 million *livres* - hardly more than one-tenth of the Lyon figure.[201]

Paris's superiority was in fact the result - earlier than is generally allowed - of the emergence there of 'financial capitalism'. This outcome could only have been achieved by Lyon's relinquishing part, if not most of her former activity in this sphere.

Viewed in this perspective, might it be argued that the machinery of the Lyon fairs received its first serious upset during the 1709 crisis - itself a crisis in the finances of the French state which had been since 1701 engaged in the War of the Spanish Succession? Samuel Bernard, the accredited moneylender to Louis XIV, virtually went bankrupt on the government's behalf over the payments due in April 1709. There is no lack of documents and testimony concerning this controversial affair.[202] But much remains to be discovered about the true story behind a set of complicated manoeuvres leading from Lyon to the bankers of Geneva, of whom Samuel Bernard had been for years the correspondent, accomplice and, at times, the determined adversary. In order to obtain funds payable outside France - in Germany, Italy and also Spain, where Louis XIV's troops were fighting - Samuel Bernard had offered to the Genevans, as pledges against repayment, bank notes issued by the French government since 1701; the actual repayment would be made later at the Lyon fairs, on settlement days, thanks to bills of exchange which Samuel Bernard drew on Bertrand Castan, his correspondent in Lyon. In order to supply the latter, 'he sent him drafts for the payments, *after* the fairs'. The whole operation was a chain of confidence, in which nobody lost money as long as everything went smoothly, the moneylenders of Geneva and elsewhere being paid either in cash or in depreciated banknotes (the 'loss' being taken into account) while the bulk of the repayment undertaken by Samuel Bernard himself was deferred until a year later. The trick of the trade was to play for time, and then for more time, until Bernard was finally repaid by the king himself - never the easiest part of the enterprise.

Since the controller-general had quickly exhausted all the easy and safe ways of raising money, others had to be dreamed up. Thus in 1709, there was persistent talk of setting up a bank - managed either privately or by the state. Its function would be to lend money to the king, who would immediately pass it on to the businessmen. The bank would issue interest-bearing bills which could be exchanged for royal bank notes - thus revaluing the said bank notes. The news was greeted with pleasure in Lyon.

It is clear that if the operation had succeeded, all the money-handlers would have been brought under the supervision of Samuel Bernard; the 'concentration' would have favoured him and he would have managed the bank, underwritten its notes and handled transfers. The controller Desmaretz did not view this prospect entirely with pleasure. And there was also opposition from business-men in the large seaports and trading towns – 'nationalist' opposition it might be called. 'It is said', reports an obscure witness, probably someone's straw man, 'that Messrs Bernard, Nicolas and other Jews have offered to take charge of the establishment of this bank. ... It would be fairer if this bank were managed by French subjects, Roman Catholics who ... could assure His Majesty of their loyalty.'[203] In fact, the whole bank project was a gamble similar to the moves which led in 1694 to the creation of the Bank of England. In France, the manoeuvre failed and the situation rapidly deteriorated. Individuals took fright and the system began to collapse like a house of cards, especially when, during the first week of April 1709, Bertrand Castan, feeling some doubt, not without reason, about Samuel Bernard's soundness, refused, on being called as usual to the *Loge des Changes*, to honour the drafts in his name, declaring that he could not 'settle his account'. 'Indescribable panic' followed. Samuel Bernard, himself in a difficult situation, as we must recognize, his services to the king having drawn him into untold complexities, finally, on 22 September obtained from the controller Desmaretz,[204] after difficult and prolonged negotiations, 'a decree allowing him three years' grace' to settle his own debts. His bankruptcy was therefore averted. The king's credit had in any case been restored on 27 March 1709 by the arrival of '7,451,178 *livres tournois*' of bullion 'in reals, bars and plate', which were landed at Port-Louis by vessels registered in Saint-Malo and Nantes returning from the South Seas.[205]

Our chief concern at present however is not this complex and tangled financial drama, but the Lyon money market. How sound was it in 1709, when faced with the suspensions of payments? It is difficult to be sure, because of the Lyonnais themselves, who were quick to complain and to paint an unduly black picture of their situation. Still the market had been in serious difficulties for some fifteen years. 'In 1695, the Germans and Swiss deserted its fairs.'[206] A memoran-dum of 1697 even refers to a rather curious practice (also found as it happens in the active though traditionalist Bolzano fairs): the deferred payments from one fair to another were effected by 'notes recorded on one's own balance sheet'.[207] This was a question of juggling with figures in the most literal sense, since debts and credit *did not circulate* in the form of bearer bills or bills to order. In other words, this was not Antwerp. A small group of 'capitalists' had cornered the profits on the 'active debts' of the deferred fair payments; it was a closed shop. If these 'notes' had circulated with a series of endorsements, we are airily told, 'small traders and shopkeepers' would have been 'able to do more business', to join in a traffic from which the 'rich businessmen and accredited practitioners on the contrary seek to exclude them'. Such practices contravened what had become the rule 'in all the financial centres of Europe', but were carried on at the Lyon fairs to the very end.[208] It could be argued that this did not help to make Lyon a more active money market, or to defend it against foreign competition.

The latter certainly existed: Lyon which received Spanish piastres via Bayonne, sent silver and gold coins out to normal destinations like Marseille, the Levant and the Strasbourg mint, but allowed even more to escape to swell the clandestine flow of specie to Geneva. In exchange for cash sent to Geneva, certain Lyon merchants could obtain Amsterdam bills of exchange on Paris, at a substantial profit. Was this early evidence of Lyon's inferiority? The letters sent to the controller-general of state finance by Trudaine the *intendant* of Lyon, repeat the complaints – exaggerated or not – of the local merchants.[209] According to them, Lyon was threatened with losing its fairs and credit operations to Genevan competitors. On 15 November 1707, a letter from Trudaine to Desmaretz was already saying: 'It is to be feared that all the trade of the Lyon market will shortly be transferred to Geneva. For some time now, the Genevans have wanted to set up a money market where fairs and payments can be settled, as in Lyon, Novi and Leipzig'.[210] Was this really so? Or was it a threat invented to influence government thinking? Two years later, at any rate, in 1709, the situation was indeed serious. 'This Bernard business', Trudaine writes, 'has upset the Lyon market beyond repair; things are getting worse every day.'[211] Technically speaking, the merchants were in fact preventing the money market from operating. As a rule, the payments made in Lyon 'are almost all effected in paper money or by transferring sums from one account to another, so that very often for a payment of 30 million *livres*, less than 500,000 [*livres*] in specie changes hands. This facility of transfer being removed, payments have become impossible, even if there were a hundred times more specie about than usual'. This credit strike by financiers even slowed down production in the Lyon manufacturing industry which operated entirely on credit. As a result, 'the manufactories have partly closed down and have reduced to alms-begging more than ten or twelve thousand workers, who have nothing to live on while there is no work. Their numbers are growing every day, and it is to be feared that there will be no manufacturing or commerce left unless help comes promptly'.[212] The alarm may have been excessive but it was not unwarranted. The crisis in Lyon certainly had repercussions in all the French fairs and finance centres. A letter of 2 August 1709 reports that the Beaucaire fair was 'deserted'; 'everything [has] dried up'.[213] Our conclusion must be that the deep-seated crisis which came to a head in Lyon in 1709, while it cannot be fully elucidated or exactly measured, was certainly very severe.

It is quite clear however that once Lyon's eminence had been challenged, it could not stand up to the sudden violent onslaught launched by Law's System. Was it a mistake to refuse to have the Royal Bank located in Lyon? It would undoubtedly have competed with, harmed or even eliminated the traditional fairs,[214] but it might also have held back the rise of Paris. For now all of France, gripped with speculation fever, was rushing to the capital, crowding into the rue

Quincampoix – a Stock Exchange in all but name, as noisy as 'Change Alley in London, if not more so'. The failure of the system eventually deprived both Paris and Lyon of the Royal Bank created by Law in 1716, but it was not long before the government presented Paris with a new Bourse (1724) worthy of the financial role the city would from now on play.

After this, Paris's career could only go from strength to strength. In this steady climb, the unquestionable and decisive turning-point was not reached until quite late in the day however, in about 1760, between the reversal of alliances and the end of the Seven Years' War:

> Paris, which was now placed in a privileged situation, at the very heart of a sort of continental bloc covering Western Europe, was the point of convergence of an economic network whose expansion was no longer thwarted, as in the past, by hostile political frontiers. The ring of Habsburg possessions which had encircled France for two hundred years had been breached ... From the establishment of Bourbon dynasties in Spain and Italy to the reversal of alliances, it is possible to trace the development of an area surrounding France and open to her influence: Spain, Italy, southern and western Germany, the Netherlands; from now on, the roads from Paris to Cadiz, from Paris to Genoa (and on to Naples), from Paris to Ostend and Brussels (a stage on the road to Vienna) or from Paris to Amsterdam, were all open to traffic, and war did not interrupt them for thirty years (1763-92); Paris therefore became the political and financial crossroads of continental Western Europe: hence the growth of business and the increased influx of capital.[215]

The superior force of attraction of Paris made itself felt both inside and outside France. But could a landlocked capital, with its distractions and big-city spectacles really be a major economic metropolis, the perfect centre for a national market engaged in cut-throat international competition? No, said Des Cazeaux du Hallays, the Nantes representative to the *Conseil du Commerce*, in a long memorandum penned at the very beginning of the century.[216] Deploring the lack of regard in which French society held businessmen, he attributed it in part to the fact that:

> foreigners [he was evidently thinking of the Dutch and the British] have a much more active and present image and conception than we do of the importance and nobility of trade, because the Courts of these states are all located in sea-ports so they have occasion to see with their own eyes, as they watch the ships that sail in every direction laden with the wealth of the world, how greatly commerce is to be recommended. If commerce had the same good fortune in France, no further attractions would be required to make all of France go into trade.

But Paris was not on the Channel. In 1715, John Law, at the outset of his venture, clearly saw 'the limits of the ambitions one might entertain for Paris as an economic metropolis, this city being far from the sea, and the river not being navigable [by sea-going vessels, he meant presumably] one cannot make it a capital of foreign trade, but it could be the leading foreign exchange market in

The Hôtel de Soissons in 1720: it was here that Law established his 'trade in paper' before transferring it to the rue Quincampoix.

the world'.[217] Even in the age of Louis XVI, Paris would never in fact be the leading financial centre in the world, but it was undoubtedly the most important in France. However, as Law implicitly foretold, the supremacy of Paris would never be complete: France would continue to have more than one economic pole.

A plea for a differential history

The Paris-Lyon rivalry is far from the only example of tension and opposition within the political unit of France. But did these differences and tensions add up to something of general significance? Certain historians have suggested that they do.

Frank C. Spooner[218] regards sixteenth-century France as being divided, very roughly, along the meridian running north-south through Paris: to the east lay most of the continental regions – Picardy, Champagne, Lorraine (not yet a French possession), Burgundy, the Franche-Comté (still Spanish), Savoy (under the rule of Turin but occupied by the French between 1536 and 1559), Dauphiné,

Provence, the Rhône valley, part of the Massif Central, and at least part of Languedoc: west of the line were the provinces bordering the Atlantic or the English Channel. These two zones were distinguished, Frank Spooner argues, by the volume of specie in circulation – a valid criterion in some respects but one which could be criticized, for instance, because both Marseille and Lyon lie inside the 'less-favoured zone'. There is nevertheless a clear contrast between Burgundy, the land of copper money,[219] and Brittany or Poitou with their Spanish pieces of eight. The active centres of western France penetrated by the wealth of the Atlantic were Dieppe, Rouen, Le Havre, Honfleur, Saint-Malo, Nantes, Rennes, La Rochelle, Bordeaux and Bayonne – with the exception of Rennes, a roll-call of seaports.

What we do not know is when and why this advance of the West slowed down and finally disappeared, in spite of the growing numbers of French mariners and privateers. It is a question which has been tackled by A.L. Rowse[220] and other historians without any very clear answer having emerged. To suggest the date of 1557, the year of a violent financial crisis, probably aggravated by the intercyclical recession of 1540–70, would mean laying the blame on a breakdown in merchant capitalism.[221] We can be reasonably sure that there was such a breakdown but not that there was immediate decline in the Atlantic provinces of France. Pierre Léon[222] has argued that Western France was 'wide open to the influences of the ocean and was still (even in the seventeenth century) that rich France ... of woollens and linens, from Flanders to Brittany and Maine, far superior to inland France with its mines and metallurgy'. So the east-west dichotomy *may* have lasted until the beginning of the personal reign of Louis XIV – the chronological break is not a clear one.

Sooner or later however, a new dividing line was to emerge, running from Nantes to Lyon,[223] this time resembling a parallel more than a meridian. To the north lay a hyperactive and industrious France, with open fields and horse-drawn ploughs; to the south, a France which with a few outstanding exceptions was falling further and further behind. Pierre Goubert [224] has even suggested that there were two economic climates: in the north, the barometer was set fair, in comparative terms, while the south was suffering the onset of an early and severe depression. Jean Delumeau has gone further: 'Seventeenth-century France should be removed, at least in part, from the southern economic constellation, and indeed we should stop systematically considering the French kingdom as an undivided whole'.[225] Once again, if this is correct, France must have adapted to the external conditions of the world economy which were shifting the balance in Europe towards the northern countries and thus pulling France – still a fragile and malleable unit – towards the Channel, the Netherlands and the North Sea.

The line dividing north from south hardly budged after this until the beginning of the nineteenth century. D'Angeville in 1819 made it run from Rouen to Evreux and then to Geneva. South of the line, 'rural life resists urbanization', 'uncivilized France begins with its scatter' of peasant dwellings. This is putting it rather strongly perhaps, but the contrast was clear enough.[226]

Eventually, in our own time, the line has once again gradually moved and the Paris meridian seems once more to be relevant. But now the zones it separates have changed: the west is now the under-developed 'French desert', the east the scene of progress, communicating with the dominant and all-invading German economy.

So the game of spotting 'the two Frances' changes over the years. There is no single and indelible dividing line running through the country, rather a series of successive lines, at least three, probably more. Or perhaps a more accurate description would be a single line swivelling like the needle on a dial. This suggests:—

1 that within a given area, the division between progress and backwardness is constantly shifting, that development and under-development are not fixed geographically once and for all; that advance may turn into decline, and that overall contrasts may be super-imposed on underlying local divergencies which nevertheless still show through;

2 that France as an economic unit can only be explained if it is replaced in the European context, and that the obvious progress of the regions north of the Nantes–Lyon line between the seventeenth and the nineteenth century cannot be interpreted simply by endogenous considerations (the superiority of triennial rotation, the increase in the numbers of horses for ploughing, the vigorous pattern of demographic growth) but must take account of exogenous factors as well: France was altered by contact with the prevailing supremacy of the north, just as she had been attracted in the fifteenth century by the brilliant exploits of Italy, and in the sixteenth by the lure of the Atlantic.

For and against the Rouen–Geneva line

The foregoing description of the different ways of dividing France into two zones between the fifteenth and eighteenth century, may suggest guidelines for but cannot resolve the unending debate concerning the historical diversity of the territory. French territory as a whole does not divide up neatly into identifiable zones to be labelled once and for all: the subdivisions are continuously adapting, regrouping, changing shape and voltage.

Take for instance the map (Figure 34, I) drawn by André Rémond for the remarkable *Atlas of eighteenth-century France* which he may have completed but has never, alas, published: this suggests not a bi-partite but a tri-partite division, based on the different rates of biological growth of the population in Necker's day. The major feature of this map is the great bite into central France, from Brittany to the Jura, representing a zone of depopulation, stagnation, or at best very slow population growth. This wasteland separates two more thriving areas: to the north the *généralités* of Caen, Alençon, Paris, Rouen, Châlons-sur-Marne, Soissons, Amiens, Lille, with record growth in Valenciennes, the Three

Bishoprics, Lorraine and Alsace; to the south, a flourishing area from Aquitaine to the Alps. It was here, in a band including the Massif Central, the Alps and the Jura that the population accumulated, in towns which were absorbers of popu-lation and rich lowlands which could not do without the temporary influx of seasonal migrants.

So the line from Rouen (or Saint-Malo, or Nantes) to Geneva is not an all-purpose division, indicating all the possible contrasts in France. André Rémond's map does not of course show national wealth, or economic progress or decline; it only shows demographic progress and decline. Wherever population figures are high, emigration and industrial activity are the rule – either separately or in combination.

Michel Morineau is always reluctant to accept over-simple explanations. So the idea of a diameter dividing France, running through the Paris region, is unlikely to satisfy him. He is sceptical for instance about the 'Saint-Malo-Geneva line', roughly that accepted by d'Angeville and re-examined by Emmanuel Le Roy Ladurie.[227] His grounds for attack are the trade figures for each of the two zones: while they do not eliminate the line, they reverse its significance: the south was in surplus, the north in deficit. In 1750, no doubt is possible:

> the southern zone by far outstrips the northern. Two-thirds or more of France's exports come from this side of the line. This superiority is accounted for partly by the wine trade, partly by the distribution of colonial goods from the ports of Bordeaux, Nantes, La Rochelle, Bayonne, Lorient and Marseille. But it is also accounted for by a thriving industry capable in Brittany of selling linens to the value of 12.5 million *livres tournois*, in Lyon of selling silks and ribbons worth 17 million and in Languedoc cloth and draperies worth 18 million.[228]

It is my turn to be sceptical now. I confess that I am not convinced by the conclusions of this comparison of the trade balances of the 'two Frances'. It is clear that the volume of industrial goods for export is not the sole determinant here: industry was often, in yesterday's world, a way of trying to make up for the poverty and harsh existence of certain regions. The 12 million *livres*' worth of Breton linens do not make Brittany a vanguard province of the French economy. The proper classification must concern G.N.P. And this is more or less what J.C. Toutain tried to establish in his paper at the 1978 Edinburgh conference, ranking the French regions of 1785 by *physical output* per inhabitant (related to national average).[229] Top of the list was Paris with 280%; the Centre, Loire and Rhône were close to the national average of 100; below came Burgundy, Languedoc, Provence, Aquitaine, the Pyrenees, Poitou, Auvergne, Lorraine, Alsace, Limousin, Franche-Comté; and bottom of all was Brittany. The map in Figure 34, IV, which plots this ranking order, does not clearly vindicate the Rouen-Geneva line, but it certainly identifies the south as an area of poverty.

Border zones, coastal and continental

In fact, in these problems of differential geography as in any other, perspectives may differ depending on the time-scale adopted. Underneath the changes produced by slow-moving economic circumstances, are there not perhaps even longer-term contrasts? Is France (or indeed any other 'nation') any more than the sum of accumulated and different realities, the deepest-seated of which (or at least those I take to be so) being by definition, and indeed observably, the slowest to disappear and the most persistent? Geography, an indispensable lantern in this respect, shows up any number of these structural, *permanent* differences: mountains and plains, north and south, the continental east and the sea-mists of the west. Such contrasts weigh on human existence as much as, or more than the economic changes that pass over our heads, sometimes improving, sometimes discriminating against the zones where we live.

But when all is said and done, the most striking structural contrast, for our purposes at least, is that between the narrow *outer margins*, and the *central blocs*. The 'margins' or border zones follow the lines bounding France and dividing it from what is not France. I shall not use the term *periphery* to refer to them, although it might seem a natural one to choose, because it has been given a particular sense in my terminology and has come to mean for many writers, including myself, those backward regions removed from the privileged centres of a world-economy. The margins then, follow either the natural coastline or what is usually the artificial line of an inland frontier. And the rule here, curiously enough, is that the French margins, with very few exceptions, have always been comparatively rich, while the interior of the country has been comparatively poor. The distinction comes quite naturally to D'Argenson:

> Concerning trade and the interior of the kingdom [he notes in his *Journal* in 1747] we are much worse off than in 1709 [which had itself been a very bad year]. Then, thanks to the naval policies of M. de Pontchartrain, we were harassing our enemies with our privateers,[230] we enjoyed the trade of the South Sea. Saint-Malo was bringing a hundred million [*livres*] into the kingdom. And the interior of the country was twice as well off in 1709 as it is today.[231]

A year later, on 19 August 1748, he once more refers to the 'inland provinces of the kingdom south of the Loire, [which] are plunged into the deepest poverty. The harvest has been only half as much as last year, which was itself a bad one. The price of grain has risen and we are besieged by beggars on all sides'.[232] Abbé Galiani is infinitely clearer and more categorical in his *Dialogue sur les blés* (Dialogue on the grain trade): 'Take note that France at present being a trading, seafaring and industrious kingdom, all her wealth is concentrated on her frontiers: all her large and wealthy cities are on her borders; the interior is terribly poor'.[233] The growing prosperity of the eighteenth century does not seem to have attenuated the contrast, rather the reverse. An official report dated 5 September 1788 declares that 'the resources of the sea ports have been infinitely multiplied, while the trade of the inland towns is confined to their own consumption and

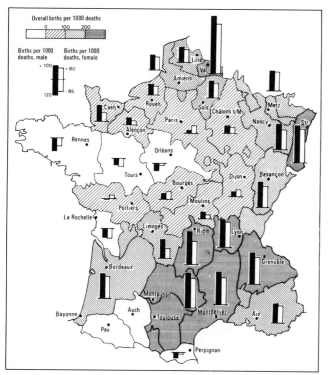

I. BIRTHS AND DEATHS C. 1787
This map, one of the very few which were published, would have been part of André Rémond's eighteenth-century atlas. It draws a curious distinction between regions in demographic decline (the *généralités* of Rennes, Tours, Orleans, La Rochelle, Perpignan) and those which rise above the modest average to score substantial surpluses (Valenciennes, Grenoble, Lyon, Montpellier, Riom, Montauban, Toulouse, Bordeaux). This 'biological' superiority may possibly be related to the spread, in precisely these regions, of the new crops, maize and potatoes.

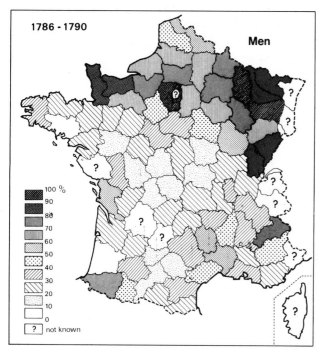

II. LITERACY ON THE EVE OF THE FRENCH REVOLUTION
In this map, based on the number of bridegrooms able to sign their names on the marriage register, the superiority of the north is obvious. (From F. Furet and J. Ozouf, *Lire et écrire*, 1978.)

III. TAXATION AS MEASUREMENT

In 1704, the French government decided to tax the merchant companies in the towns of the kingdom. Tax revenue from Lyon and Rouen was 150,000 *livres*; for Bordeaux, Toulouse and Montpellier the figure was about 40,000; Marseille 20,000. This is the scale used here. Paris is not included in the list. It would be difficult to divide the kingdom up according to these tax levels. The only striking observation to be made is perhaps that north of the latitude of La Rochelle (6000 *livres*) there is a large number of medium-sized towns, while in the south there are a few large merchant cities. (From data in A.N., G⁷ 1688.)

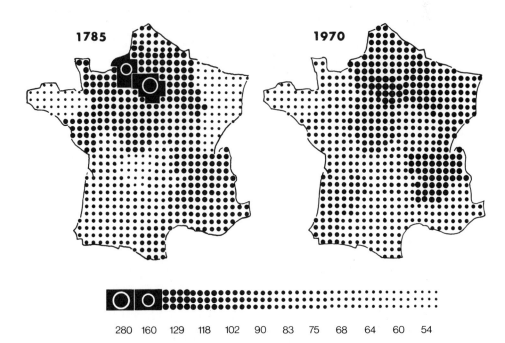

280 160 129 118 102 90 83 75 68 64 60 54

IV. THE GEOGRAPHY OF REGIONAL PER CAPITA INCOME

Per capita income (in *physical product*) of the regions as a percentage of the national average (= 100). In 1785, the figure for Paris was 280 per cent, Haute-Normandie 160, Loire-Rhône 100 etc. Does this mean, as the map suggests, that the north was clearly ahead? Yes, though it might be necessary to check the complicated calculations in question. The situation in 1970 is shown for the sake of comparison. The regional distribution of per capita income has clearly changed. From J.C. Toutain, 'La croissance inégale des revenus régionales en France de 1840 à 1970', *Seventh International Conference of Economic History*, Edinburgh, 1978, p.368.

that of their neighbours; they have no means for the people to live except by manufacturing'.[234] Was industrialization not as a rule the economic revenge of the inland areas?

Certain historians are conscious of this persistent opposition between inner and outer provinces. Michel Morineau has written that in the latter years of Louis XIV's reign, all the wealth and activity of France moved out to the seaboard.[235] Perhaps so – but was this a recent movement or had it not rather begun much earlier? Above all, was it not destined to last?

The merit of Edward C. Fox's book with its provocative sub-title 'The Other France', is that it plumps unequivocally for this *structural* contrast. There have always, he argues, been two Frances, one turning its face to the sea, dreaming of free trade and distant adventures, and the other, the France of the land, stuck-in-the-mud and embedded in inflexible constraints. French history has been a dialogue of the deaf between the two, neither changing place nor direction, each one obstinately drawing on its own resources and understanding nothing about the other.

In the eighteenth century, the more modern France, 'the other France', was represented by the major sea ports, where wealth and an early version of capitalism had taken up residence – an England in miniature, dreaming of a bloodless revolution along the lines of the Glorious Revolution of 1688. But could it achieve anything on its own? No, as was proved, to take a well-known example, by the Girondin episode of 1792–3. As under the *ancien régime*, it was the France of the landlocked interior which triumphed during the revolution and empire and even later. On one side was trade, which would have done better if it had been given more freedom; on the other, an agriculture doomed perpetually to suffer from the subdivision of peasant holdings, and an industry doomed to stagnate for lack of means and initiative: these are Edward Fox's two Frances.[236]

But despite the author's talent, the whole of French history cannot be compressed into this prolonged and repetitive dialogue – if only because there was more than one border-zone. France looked both westwards, to the sea (this is really Fox's 'other France') and eastwards towards continental Europe, Northern Italy beyond the Alps, the Swiss Cantons, Germany, the Spanish Netherlands (which became Austrian in 1714) and the United Provinces. I am not trying to prove that the eastern margin of France was as important or as fascinating as the western seaboard, but it existed, and if its 'marginality' has any meaning at all, it must give it some original features. To sum up, along the western seaboard, France had a string of 'terminals', ports like Dunkirk, Rouen, Le Havre, Caen, Nantes, La Rochelle, Bordeaux, Bayonne, Narbonne, Sète (built by Colbert), Marseille and the series of Provençal ports – making up what we might call France I. France II was the huge and varied interior of which more later. France III consisted of a long string of towns – Grenoble, Lyon, Dijon, Langres, Châlons-sur-Marne, Strasbourg, Nancy, Metz, Sedan, Mézières, Charleville, Saint-Quentin, Lille, Amiens – over a dozen cities with secondary towns in between, forming an uninterrupted chain from the Mediterranean and the Alps to the North Sea. The problem is that this urban border zone to which Lyon holds the key, is not as easy to understand as the string of ports; it lacks the homogeneity and clear outline of France I.

The logical extension eastwards of France as an economic unit (may I say with the benefit of hindsight, and in no spirit of retrospective imperialism, if the reader will believe me) would have been into an area bounded by Genoa, Milan, Augsburg, Nuremberg and Cologne and as far as Antwerp and Amsterdam, in such a way as to include the turntable of trade in the Lombardy plain, to benefit from an extra Alpine pass, with the St Gothard, and to control the 'Rhine corridor' – that essential axis and string of towns. For the same reasons which prevented her controlling Italy and the Netherlands, France failed, except in Alsace, to take her frontier up to the Rhine, that is to a communications route as important or very nearly as important as the maritime routes. The Italy-Rhine-Netherlands axis was for a long time a privileged belt, the 'backbone' of European capitalism. And it did not admit all comers.

It is also true that the kingdom expanded eastwards only slowly and with difficulty, negotiating with the provinces it succeeded in annexing over the maintenance of at least some of their liberties and privileges. Thus Artois, Flanders, the Lyonnais, Dauphiné and Provence remained outside the net of the *Cinq Grosses Fermes*, the tax farms, in 1664. More significantly, provinces known as 'effectively foreign' were completely outside the French customs system: Alsace, Lorraine, the Franche-Comté. Mark these provinces on a map and you will be looking at France III. In Lorraine, the Franche-Comté and Alsace, there was complete freedom of foreign trade: goods could come in from abroad and with the aid of smugglers, make their way profitably into the kingdom.

If I am not much mistaken, a degree of freedom of action seems to be the characteristic of these border zones. It would be useful to know more about the activity of these frontier provinces between the French kingdom and its neighbours. Did they incline one way or the other? What part for instance was played by merchants from the Swiss Cantons in the Franche-Comté, Alsace and Lorraine, which were almost home ground to them in the eighteenth century? Were the same (not always favourable) attitudes towards foreigners to be found from Flanders to the Dauphiné, during the revolutionary crisis of 1793 and 1794 for example? And what role was played, in these provinces where freedom was greater than in inland France, by the towns – Nancy, Strasbourg, Metz and more particularly Lille, which is an excellent test case since its location, very near the Netherlands and not far from England, might have put it in touch through its neighbours with the rest of the world?

Lille raises all the problems of France III. By all the standards of the time, Lille was a considerable place. After the end of the Dutch occupation (1713) both the city and the surrounding countryside quickly recovered. According to the reports of the inspection by the tax-farmers in 1727-8, Lille's 'strength is so great that she gives sustenance to over a hundred thousand people in the town and in the provinces of Flanders and Hainault, by her manufacturing and trade'.[237] Inside and around the town, a whole range of textile industries, furnaces, forges and foundries were at work. Lille produced luxury fabrics as well as cast-iron firebacks, cooking pots, gold and silver braid and ironmongery; from the neighbouring districts and provinces, food came in plenty: butter, meat on the hoof, grain. Lille took maximum advantage of the roads, rivers and canals, adapting without too much difficulty to the government-inspired diversion of traffic towards the west and north, to Dunkirk and Calais instead of to Ypres, Tournai and Mons.

Above all, Lille was a turntable of trade, receiving goods from Holland, Italy, Spain, France, England, the Spanish Netherlands, and the Baltic countries; taking from one to sell to another, redistributing French wines and spirits to the north, for instance. But her trade with Spain and America was undoubtedly the most significant. Four or five million *livres*' worth of Lille products (mostly linen and cloth) were exported every year, either at the vendors' risk or using commission agents. Returns came in the form of cash rather than commodities, to the tune of three or four million *livres* a year according to an estimate for 1698.[238] But this money did not travel directly to the 'province' of Lille: it went to Holland or England where it could be negotiated more easily and cheaply than in France, if only because of different procedures for assaying metals. In short, Lille while as deeply engaged as any other town in the French economy, at the same time stood head and shoulders above it.

This explanation may perhaps make it easier to understand certain alignments of the towns lying inland, some way from the frontier, such as Troyes, Dijon, Langres, Châlons-sur-Marne, or Reims: these had themselves been border posts once, but were now inland towns where deep-rooted memories still survived; it is as if France III, that France which looked east and north, had been formed in successive deposits, like the cortex of a tree-trunk.

The towns of 'the other France'

In the case of the seaboard towns of 'the other France', the picture, as I have already said, is clearer. Here too, success was related to freedom of action and initiative. The trade of these active ports certainly plunged its roots deep into the French interior and drew nourishment from it, but their interests were consistently in the outside world. What was Nantes's greatest desire in 1680?[239] That entry to France should be forbidden to the English, who were racing everyone else back from Newfoundland in their small and speedy ships and landing the first (very profitable) catches of cod: could they not at least be discouraged by high customs tariffs? By the same token, why not give priority to tobacco from Saint-Domingue over English tobacco, which was flooding the French market? Or what about trying to get back the whaling profits which the Dutch and

Hamburg whalers had snatched from the French? And so on – a whole series of preoccupations outside French frontiers.

Thinking along similar lines, Edward Fox wonders whether Bordeaux was Atlantic or French?[240] Paul Butel unhesitatingly calls it 'an Atlantic metropolis'.[241] Certainly, according to a report of 1698, 'the other provinces of the kingdom, except perhaps part of Brittany, do not consume any of the produce of Guyenne'.[242] Were the wines of Bordeaux and its region only satisfying the thirst – and the good taste – of northern buyers? Bayonne, likewise, was preoccupied with the routes, ports and silver coin of nearby Spain. The Jewish merchants in the Saint-Esprit suburb were no exception, and in 1708 they were accused, probably not without foundation, of smuggling into Spain 'the worst cloth they could find in Languedoc and elsewhere'.[243] Or to take the two extremities of the long French coastline, Dunkirk set about beating English prohibitions and dabbled in every activity, from cod-fishing to the slave trade,[244] while Marseille was the most extraordinary and exotic of these seaboard towns, a 'port more Barbaresque and Levantine than typically French', as André Rémond mischievously put it.[245]

In order to take a closer look, let us concentrate on one port, perhaps one of the most significant, Saint-Malo. Yet it was a tiny little town – 'about the size of the Tuileries gardens'.[246] And even at the peak of its career, between 1688 and 1715, its inhabitants deliberately belittled it: our town, they said in 1701, 'is but a barren rock, without any other local property than the industry [of the inhabitants] which makes them so to speak the carriers of France' – but carriers whose 150 ships sailed the Seven Seas.[247] If we are to believe them – and their boasts are almost credible – they were 'the first to discover cod-fishing and to know about Brazil and Newfoundland before "Amaric Vespuce" and "Capral" (*sic*)'. They pointed out that they had been granted privileges by the dukes of Brittany (in 1230, 1384, 1433, 1473) and by the kings of France (in 1587, 1594, 1610, and 1644) – privileges which ought to set them apart from the other Breton ports, but which the *fermiers-généraux* had whittled away with their judgments and harassment after 1688. Saint-Malo therefore applied – unsuccessfully – to be declared a 'free port', like Marseille, Bayonne, Dunkirk – and 'only recently, Sedan'.

The merchants of Saint-Malo were clearly not in any sense outside Brittany (they exported its linens); nor outside France, since they sent on the regular voyages by their frigates to Cadiz the most precious and sought-after of French merchandise: satins from Lyon and Tours, cloth of gold and silver, beaver pelts. And they naturally distributed in France goods from abroad, whether shipped in their own vessels or not. But the pivot of Saint-Malo's trade in general was England: so many trips were made there to fetch goods that the balance had to be paid in bills of exchange on London. Next in order came Holland, which brought to Saint-Malo pine planks, masts, rigging, hemp and tar, in Dutch ships. Off Newfoundland, the men of Saint-Malo fished for cod, which they sent to

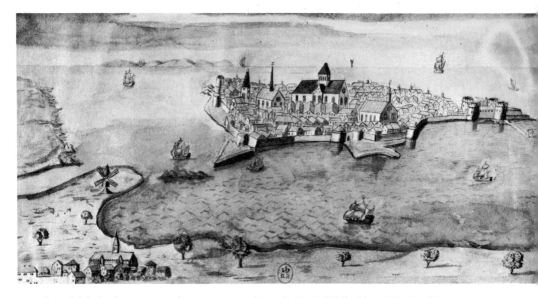

Saint-Malo in the seventeenth century (wood panel). Paris, Bibliothèque Nationale. (Photo Giraudon.)

Spain and the Mediterranean; they sailed to the West Indies, where for a while Saint-Domingue was 'their' colony. They made fortunes in Cadiz which had in practice been Spain's port for America since 1650; they were present and active there before 1672,[248] trafficking in silver; later they settled there, establishing powerful and thriving business-houses. So in 1698 and even later, the chief preoccupation of the Saint-Malo merchants was to make sure of catching the galleons which left Cadiz for Cartagena in the Indies and which had no fixed timetable; and it was even more important not to miss the '*flota*' which reached New Spain 'necessarily on the 10th or 15th July'. The 'American' returns to Saint-Malo did not usually reach the town 'until 18 months or two years after the ships' departure'. On average, the returns represented seven million *livres* in cash, but there were some outstanding years when the figure was 11 million, and Saint-Malo ships returning from the Mediterranean would put into Cadiz and bring home 'some 100,000, others 200,000 piastres'. Even before the War of the Spanish Succession, 'the South or Pacific Sea Company was established by letters patent in the month of September 1698'.[249] Consequently there was an unprecedented boom in contraband and direct shipments of American silver. Lasting from 1701 to the 1720s, this was the most remarkable, one might almost say the most sensational exploit by the sailors of Saint-Malo, or indeed by any French sailors on the stage of world history.

Such wealth placed the little coastal oasis of Saint-Malo firmly on the outskirts of the French kingdom. The abundance of specie in the town even released it from the need for a foreign exchange market linked with other centres,[250] and it had poor road communications even with Brittany, let alone with Normandy and Paris: in 1714, there was no 'regular post [from Saint-Malo] to Pontorson, 9 leagues away'.[251] Pontorson was on the Couesnon, the little coastal river east of Saint-Malo which marked the boundary between Brittany and Normandy. So the mail was slow to arrive: 'The post only comes by the Caen road on Tuesdays and Saturdays and by Rennes on Thursdays; so if one fails to catch the post, there are delays'.[252] The people of Saint-Malo complained, no doubt, but did not hasten to do anything about it. There was perhaps no great urgency.

The French interior

On one hand then were the border zones of the circumference; on the other, the huge expanse of the interior – the first a slim ribbon of precocious development, *comparatively* wealthy, with some grand towns (Bordeaux in Tourny's time was a combination of Versailles and Antwerp);[253] the second a landmass marked by frequent poverty and, with the monstrous exception of Paris, a country of sleepy towns spinning out a grey existence, their beauty, however impressive, usually a relic of their past, their glories those of tradition.

But before going any further, mention must be made of the problem facing the historian approaching this huge field of observation. There is an overwhelming amount of evidence, and literally thousands of monographs have been written, but the great majority of these are case-studies of particular provinces. What mattered to the national market were of course the relations between the different provinces. It is true that in 1664 the practice began of 'general surveys' carried out simultaneously in all the *generalités*[254] of the kingdom. These provide us with a series of synchronic 'sections'. The best-known of these are first the series usually described as 'the *intendants'* surveys for the Duke of Burgundy', begun in 1697 and completed, with difficulty, in 1703; and secondly the survey for the controller-general Orry, carried out with great flourish, finished in 1745 just as its patron fell into disgrace, and subsequently shelved – so effectively that it was almost by accident that in 1952, F. de Dainville came across a summary of the exercise written by an anonymous member of the French Academy.[255]

But the defects of these synchronic surveys are obvious: they are primarily descriptive, where we should prefer to have figures enabling us to construct tables or at least maps to render the descriptions intelligible – which they are not always at first sight. I did make an attempt to construct a map from the *intendants'* survey: to mark the trade links of the various *généralités*, I used a red pencil for foreign trade, blue for exchange between one *généralité* and another, and black for short-distance trade links within a *généralité*. The results convinced me that by the end of the seventeenth century France was indeed on the way to having a closely-knit network, which could properly be called a national market. But the map remains at a very preliminary stage of refinement. To be worthwhile,

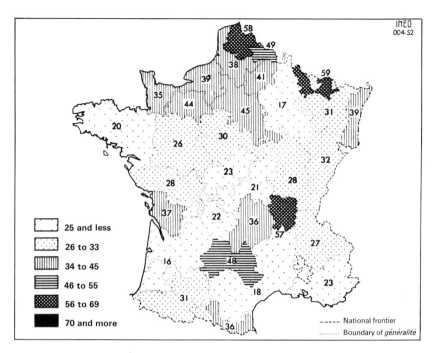

35 POPULATION DENSITY IN 1745
Map drawn by François de Dainville (cf. note 255).

it would require a team of researchers, since the arrows ought to be distinguished according to the products exchanged; and other documents should be consulted in order to weigh the findings, which would mean comparing the volume of internal and external trade – a crucial problem regarding which we only have *a priori* statements, to the effect that internal trade was greatly superior to external trade, by about three or four times.

A further disadvantage of these 'synchronic' views is that they resemble and repeat themselves too much, since they are all contained within a comparatively short time-span of under a hundred years, between 1697 and 1745 or 1780, making it impossible to distinguish lasting structural reality from circumstantial change. It would have been nice to find out whether a pattern of underlying regularities could be derived from a study of the provinces: the system, if it exists, is certainly not easy to uncover.

The survey undertaken for the controller-general Orry does however offer some clues. This one distinguishes between provinces according to what were described as the 'faculties [i.e. the living standards] of the people' living there. Five categories were used: *they are well off; they manage; some manage, others are poor; they are poor; they are indigent.* Making the dividing line run between category 3 (some manage, others are poor) and the bottom categories 4 and 5 (poverty and indigence) enables us to distinguish the poor regions from the

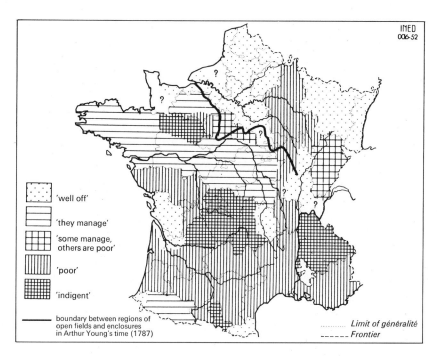

36 'FACULTIES' (LIVING STANDARDS) OF PROVINCIAL POPULATIONS IN
THE EIGHTEENTH CENTURY
From the same source. For details, see the text. (*Population*, 1952, no. 1, pp. 58–9.)

comparatively rich. The resulting map does indeed show that on the whole the
north was privileged and the south underprivileged, but some qualification is
needed. In the first place, there are exceptions to the rule both in the north and
the south: to the north, depopulated Champagne (17 inhabitants to the km²) was
poor, and the *généralité* of Alençon is classed as a zone of unequivocal indigence; in
the south the *généralité* of La Rochelle was 'well off', as were the Bordeaux region
and Roussillon. Secondly, the geographical frontier between north and south
does not correspond, as one might have expected, to the intermediate regions in
category 3, halfway between affluence and poverty. The frontier seems to run,
from west to east, first through a group of 'poor' regions west of Poitou, then
through a band of 'indigent' regions, in the *généralités* of Limoges and Riom
(although Basse-Auvergne is a pocket of affluence here), then again through poor
or indigent regions in Lyonnais, Dauphiné and Savoy (which was not yet a French
possession). These regions in the very heartland of France are the classic under-
developed provinces, often regions of high emigration like the Limousin, the
Auvergne, Dauphiné and Savoy. It must be remembered that emigration, which
usually meant that money was sent home, may have improved the quality of life
locally (Haute-Auvergne, although 'indigent' was perhaps no worse off than
Limagne which was described officially as 'well-off').

One can also see the outline of another axis of inland poverty, running north and south, from poor Languedoc to equally poor Champagne. Was this perhaps (as I am inclined to think) a survival of the north-south axis marking the frontier in the sixteenth century between continental and Atlantic France? At all events, Orry's survey shows that the differential geography of France is more complex than one might have thought in advance.

This conclusion also emerges from the maps devised by André Rémond[256] which give us three series of indicators for the 1780s: cereal yields, grain prices and fiscal pressure. And we are free to add to these some generally accepted demographic findings. These maps, the fruit of prodigious labour, are unfortunately difficult to interpret as soon as one tries to correlate the different indicators. Thus Brittany seems to maintain its very modest balance, because it was not subject to excessive taxation (this was one of the privileges of a *pays d'Etat*) and above all because the export of grain explains its high cereal prices (a potential source of profit when circumstances were favourable as in 1709).[257] Burgundy, where grain yields were high, had the advantages of an only moderate tax burden, and frequent export of grain along the Saône and the Rhône. Here again, high grain prices might be a beneficial element. In Poitou, the Limousin or Dauphiné on the other hand, poverty straightforwardly coincides with low yields and high prices.

Comparing this data with population and density figures does not take us very far. We would first have to accept on trust Ernst Wagemann's hypothesis that rates of density are an indication of general levels of economic activity. Just for interest, we could then test the value of a threshold, say 30 inhabitants per km²: areas below this would be classed as unfavourable, areas with higher density favourable. In southern France on the whole, this criterion works – but in 1745, the *généralité* of Montauban, with a density of 48, contradicts it.

Might this be tackled another way? Yes, but it would be a complicated business. André Rémond's economic maps make it possible to work out average annual grain production and the price of this production per *généralité*; using the *vingtiéme*[258] which is an index of income from land, the latter could be calculated or at any rate (since the theoretical ratio of 1 to 20 was rarely reached) an approximate ranking order could be obtained. One would then have to total this income from *land* and compare it to France's G.N.P. This would give us a coefficient which, if applied to the income from land of a *généralité* would yield both gross production and per capita income – the most significant for our purposes. We would then have a series of provincial per capita incomes enabling us to estimate with at least a measure of accuracy the differential wealth of France. André Rémond is the only person who could carry out an enterprise of this kind with the right combination of prudence and boldness. Unfortunately, he has not done so, or at any rate has not published his results.

So it is no exaggeration to say that the internal realities and relationships of France during the *ancien régime* have yet to be discovered. Jean-Claude Perrot's recent book, *L'Age d'or de la statistique régionale française*, gives for the period between Year IV and Year XII (1796-1805) – which was indeed a golden age of regional statistics – an impressive catalogue of the available printed sources, this time not by *généralité* but by *département*.[259] There is a whole body of research which could now be carried out on a new basis, and the enterprise would certainly be worth the trouble. But we also need research that is prepared to move back beyond the charmed circle of the eighteenth century and its plentiful statistics to explore as far as possible into the past. It is surely essential to look forward into the nineteenth century as well, to see whether, as it developed, the system of interlocking relationships in France allowed the same structural imbalances to persist.

The interior colonized by the periphery

That the French interior – with a few exceptions to prove the rule – took second place in the nation's economic life, is unequivocally shown by the inroads made into this 'neutral', that is to say unresisting central space, by the towns on the periphery: they organized forays inland and controlled communications, dominating and undermining the only too malleable landward regions. Bordeaux for instance annexed the Périgord.[260] But there are some even better examples.

Georges Frêche's recent book[261] sets the problem out well. The Midi-Pyrenees region, centred in the eighteenth century on Toulouse, consisted of a large slice of continental France 'imprisoned in its lands', in spite of the river Garonne, the valuable Canal du Midi and many usable roads. Being landlocked was only part of the problem: there was also the triple attraction of Lyon, Bordeaux and Marseille: the Toulouse area and Toulouse itself became 'satellized'. In this context, the routes taken by the grain trade require no comment. And if one adds the attraction of Lyon for silk, the triangle in which Toulouse's destiny was imprisoned is firmly outlined. So neither grain nor silk – and in the sixteenth century not even woad – offered a way out for Toulouse, a town historically predestined for the second rank in which it was now firmly embedded. Georges Frêche refers characteristically to its 'dependent trade' and 'subordinate merchant network'. Even the grain trade was out of the hands of local merchants, and in those of commission agents working for wholesalers in Bordeaux or Marseille.[262]

France was thus carved up, by these key towns on her coastal or continental margins, into dependent zones, corridors or sectors, which communicated through urban mediators with the all-controlling European economy. And it is in this perspective that the dialogue between 'trading France' and 'territorial France' can best be grasped. If the trading community despite all these advantages, did not succeed in taking over territorial France it was because the latter was an awesomely dense mass, which did not lend itself easily to mobilization; but it was also because France did not occupy in the international order a position comparable to that of Amsterdam or London, and thus lacked the

The Tower and the mills of the Bazacle in Toulouse (seventeenth-century engraving). (Photo C.A.P. Roger-Viollet.)

vigour characteristic of a front-rank economy that would have been required to stimulate and develop regional economies which did not always spontaneously thirst after expansion.

England's trading supremacy

To ask the question how England became a coherent *national market* is important because it immediately leads to a second: how did the English national market succeed, through a combination of its own weight and the circumstances of the time, in imposing its supremacy within the enlarged European economy?

This gradually developing supremacy could already be glimpsed by 1713 and the Treaty of Utrecht; it was clearly visible by the end of the Seven Years' War in 1763, and had been achieved beyond a shadow of doubt by the time of the Treaty of Versailles (1783) – when England appeared (quite misleadingly) to be the defeated power, and when she was unquestionably, with Holland out of the way, the beating heart of the world economy.

This, the first of England's victories, determined the second – the coming industrial revolution – but its roots lie deep in the English past, so it seemed logical to separate England's trade supremacy from her later industrial supremacy, which will be considered in another chapter.

How England became an island

Between 1453 and 1558, between the end of the Hundred Years' War and the recapture of Calais by François de Guise, England, without realizing it at the time, became (if I may be forgiven the expression) an island, in other words, an autonomous unit, distinct from continental Europe. Until this turning-point, despite the Channel, the North Sea and the Straits of Dover, England had been bodily linked with France, the Netherlands and the rest of Europe. Her long conflict with France during the Hundred Years' War (which was in fact the second Hundred Years' War, the first having been between Plantagenets and Capets) had, as Philippe de Vries rightly says 'taken place at a more or less provincial level'.[263] In other words, England acted as a province (or a group of provinces) within the Anglo-French unit which was in its entirety, or virtual entirety, both battlefield and prize in the interminable struggle. For many years, over a century, England was enmeshed in and absorbed into the huge field of operations in France, before the two sides gradually disentangled themselves.

Thus England was late in developing her own identity: she engaged in the temptation, or rather dangers of gigantism – until having been driven out of France, she found herself back home. Henry VIII's failure to reinsert her into Europe once more was probably another piece of good fortune. His minister Thomas Cromwell had warned the king of the huge expense of a foreign war, and the speech he is said to have made in the House of Commons in 1523[264] is significant in more ways than one: war, he argued, 'would cost just as much as the whole of the circulating money in the country'. This in his opinion would force England to adopt a leather currency. He personally had nothing against this, but it would become awkward if, say, the king were taken prisoner and ransom had to be paid. 'The French ... would probably refuse to return the English king on payment of leather, as they refused even to sell their wine except on payment of silver'. Henry VIII nevertheless embarked upon the venture, which eventually failed. But later on, Elizabeth expended little more than strong words towards regaining Calais, which had been lost by Mary Tudor and which the French had promised (insincerely) to return by the Treaty of Cateau-Cambrésis, (1559). For a moment, but for a moment only, she gained possession of Le Havre, but it was recaptured in 1562.

From now on, the die was cast. The Channel, the Straits of Dover and the North Sea had become a barrier, 'a floating bulwark' protecting the island. A learned Frenchman could say of England in 1740: 'An island appears ready made for commerce, and its inhabitants ought to think rather of defending it than of extending their conquests on to the Continent. They would have too much difficulty in maintaining them, because of the distance and the hazards of the sea'.[265] But the same was of course true of the continental Europeans vis-à-vis the island. When in May 1787, Arthur Young crossed the Straits of Dover on his way to France, he expressed pleasure that the Channel 'so conveniently separates England from the rest of the world'.[266] It was indeed an advantage, although for a long time it had not been perceived as such.

At the beginning of the modern period, the fact that they had (to put it brutally) been sent packing, made the English set more store by domestic tasks: the improvement of land, the reclamation of forest, marsh and heath. They began to pay more attention to the dangerous Scottish border, to the threatening presence of Ireland, and to the anxieties occasioned by Wales, which having temporarily regained its independence in the early fifteenth century with Glendower's rebellion, had been restored to order but remained 'unabsorbed'.[267] In short, what England had derived from her apparent defeat was a reduction of her territory to modest proportions, which would later prove much more amenable to the rapid formation of a national market.

At the same time, the break with the continent was paralleled in 1529-33 by a break with Rome, which set an even greater distance between England and the rest of the world. The Reformation, as Namier rightly said, spoke the language of nationalism. England had adopted it abruptly and then plunged or was plunged into an adventure heavy with consequences: the king became the head of the Anglican Church; in his own country he was Pope; and the confiscation and sale of Church lands gave a boost to the English economy. It received an even greater boost when after the Great Discoveries, the British Isles, for so long an excrescence at the far end of the European continent, became the point of departure for the new worlds. England had certainly not deliberately cut herself off from the European mainland with the express intention of turning to the outside world, but this was effectively what happened. And a relic of the past which gave an extra impetus to separation and autonomy was the deep hostility to nearby Europe which still haunted the minds of the English. 'It is certain', noted Sully[268] when he came to London as ambassador-extraordinary of Henri IV in 1603, 'that the English hate us, and with a hatred so strong and so widespread that one is tempted to number it among the natural dispositions of this people.'

But feelings do not arise without cause, and the wrongs, if they can be so described, were always on both sides. England had not yet retreated into 'splendid' isolation; she felt if not besieged, which is too strong a word, at any rate threatened by an unfriendly Europe, by a politically dangerous France, before long by a newly-rich Spain, by Antwerp and her all-powerful merchants and later by Amsterdam – envied and detested for her success. Am I hinting that England suffered from an inferiority complex? It would have been understandable, particularly since her textile 'industrialization' of the late fifteenth and early

The Royal Exchange in London in 1644. Engraving by W. Hollar. (B.N. Cabinet des Estampes.)

sixteenth century, the transition from raw wool to cloth production, had placed her more firmly than ever inside the trade circuits of Europe; the commercial radius of England had expanded; her ships were exploring the outside world and repercussions from the world – a world in which England saw dangers, threats, even 'plots' – came back to England. Gresham's contemporaries were convinced that the merchants of Italy and Antwerp were conspiring to bring down the exchange rate of sterling in order to obtain the craftsmanship of English weavers at cheaper prices. In the face of such threats – not wholly imaginary, though often exaggerated – England's reaction was vigorous. The Italian merchant bankers were driven out in the sixteenth century; the Hanseatic merchants were stripped of their privileges in 1556 and deprived of the *Stahlhof* in 1595; it was against Antwerp that Gresham founded in 1566-8 what would later become the Royal Exchange; it was against Spain and Portugal that the Stock Companies were in fact launched; against Holland that the Navigation Act of 1651 was directed; and against France that the aggressive colonial policy of the eighteenth century was aimed. England as a country was tense, watchful and aggressive, determined to lay down the law and to enforce it both at home and even abroad, as her position grew stronger. As a mischievous Frenchman ironically observed in 1749, 'the English consider their own Pretentions as Rights, and the Rights of their Neighbours as Usurpations'.[269]

The pound sterling

If one wished to prove that 'they order these things differently in England', the remarkable history of the pound sterling would serve the purpose well. This was a money of account, like countless others. But while every other money of account fluctuated, either being manipulated by the state or upset by economic conditions, the pound sterling, having been stabilized in 1560-1 by Elizabeth I, never thereafter varied, maintaining its intrinsic value until 1920 or indeed 1931.[270] This is little short of a miracle, and almost inexplicable at first sight. The equivalent of four ounces of sterling silver,[271] the pound alone among European currencies ploughs its straight furrow through an astonishing three hundred years. Does this mean that like contented peoples it has 'no history'? Certainly not, since the story begins in the reign of Elizabeth in difficult and troubled circumstances and takes its course through a series of crises which could very well have changed it, in 1621, 1695, 1774, and 1797. These well-known events have been studied in detail and intelligently analysed. But the real problem, and an impossible one to solve, is to make sense of the story as a whole, as the sum of these incidents and successes, a story pursuing its imperturbable course: we understand the milestones it reaches but not the pathway that links them. It is as irritating as a mystery novel that withholds its secret, chapter after chapter: and yet there must be a secret, an explanation.

I need not emphasize how important a problem this is: the fixed value of the pound was a crucial element in England's fortunes. Without a fixed currency, there would have been no easy credit, no security for those lending money to the sovereign, no confidence in any contract. And without credit there would have been no rise to greatness, no financial superiority. We might note in this context that the great fairs of Lyon and Besançon had created respectively, in order to safeguard their transactions, the fictional and stable moneys of account, the *écu au soleil* and the *écu de marc*. Likewise, the Banco di Rialto, created in 1585, and the Bank of Amsterdam, set up in 1694, both obliged customers to use bank money, quoted at a rate higher than ordinary currencies which were so variable: the agio on bank money as compared to ordinary money was a guarantee of security. The Bank of England, created in 1694, needed no such guarantee: its usual money of account, the pound, brought it the security of fixed value. This is all beyond dispute but it is important to draw the consequences. Jean-Gabriel Thomas, a banker turned historian, has in a recent study (1977)[272] referred to the wisdom of the English, and argued that the failure of Law's System had one important cause not usually mentioned, namely the untimely devaluations of the *livre tournois* as a money of account: these upset the normal operation of credit, ruined confidence, and killed the goose that laid the golden eggs.

To return to the pound sterling, the answer seems to be that there is not one single explanation but a series of explanations; not that the English were privy to some general theory which guided a far-sighted policy, but that they devised a series of pragmatic expedients to solve short-term problems – which regularly turned out in the long run to form the wisest course of action.

In 1560-1, Elizabeth I and her advisers, foremost among them the great Thomas Gresham, sat down to remedy the unspeakable chaos resulting from the Great Debasement,[273] the phenomenal inflation of the years 1543-51. During these difficult years, the silver content of the denominations in circulation (the shilling and the penny) had been excessively reduced. From 11 ounces 2 penny-weight[274] of silver in every 12 ounces of alloy (that is 37/40 of pure silver) the measure had fallen to 10 ounces in 1543 and in the course of further debasements to only 3 ounces in 1551 – that is only 1 part fine metal to 3 parts base metal. The Elizabethan reform consisted of a return to the old standard, 'the ancient right standard' of 11 ounces two pennyweight in every 12 ounces. It was a measure urgently required: the situation was one of extreme disorder, with the coins in circulation all of different weight and silver content, many of them clipped, yet with the same face value; they were mere fiduciary currencies, what the French might have described as metal *assignats*. Prices had doubled or tripled in a few years and the English exchange rate in Antwerp had deteriorated – two calamities which reinforced each other, for England as a big cloth exporter was like a trading vessel moored to Europe; her entire economic life depended on the mooring-rope, the rate of exchange on the Antwerp market. The rate of the pound was the motor or 'governor' of English foreign economic relations. Even as lucid an observer as Thomas Gresham was convinced that the Italian exchange dealers in London and Antwerp were manipulating exchange rates to suit them-selves and by so doing obtaining English workmanship at advantageous prices. This view, which fails to see the connection between exchange rates and trade balance, contains some truth but also an element of illusion: the illusion consisted of seeing exchange rates as a dialogue between two markets (London and Antwerp in this case) whereas it was actually a chorus in which every financial centre in Europe had a say – a sort of round, as Italian practice had long recognized. Under these conditions, the exchange dealer had no control over exchange rates, but he was in a position to benefit from their fluctuations and to speculate in them, if that is he had sufficient means and expertise. The Italians did indeed meet these two conditions and on this point Gresham was not mistaken to be wary of them.

At any rate, by fixing the intrinsic value of the pound at a visibly high level, and by recalling all the specie in circulation for re-coining, the government in London hoped for two results: (1) that the exchange rate in Antwerp would improve; and (2) that prices at home would fall. Only the first of these hopes was fulfilled.[275] The English people who had borne the cost of the operation (since the government had bought up coin in circulation at only a fraction of its face value) received no compensation in the shape of lower prices.[276]

So the Elizabethan reform was not immediately beneficial: indeed it imposed a straitjacket on the currency, since the volume of good money minted out of the bad was not even sufficient to maintain normal circulation. It is true that the situation was rescued shortly afterwards by the influx of silver from America, which flowed into every country in Europe after the 1560s.[277] These shipments from the New World also explain the successful stabilization in 1577 of the *livre tournois*, the French money of account, which was on the gold standard: the gold *écu* was declared to be equal to three *livres*, and from now on all trading books were to be kept in *écus*. In fact this reform had been forced upon Henri III by the merchants in Lyon, both foreigners and nationals, because it suited them; credit should not be too hastily given to Henri III himself. In the French case, as in the English, the system was preserved thanks above all to the mines in New Spain and Peru. But what changed circumstances could give they could also take away: in 1601 the French stabilization collapsed, and the *livre tournois* had to leave the gold standard. In England on the contrary, the Elizabethan system remained intact. Can this be attributed to the island's trade expansion, to economic circumstances favouring northern Europe? This would clearly be going too far. But it is certainly true that England was both a participant in the world economy on her own terms, while at the same time remaining retrenched in her island fastness behind her watchful defences. France, on the contrary, was open and vulnerable to the rest of Europe: she was the sounding board on which all her neighbours' actions echoed, the meeting point of every kind of currency; she was at the mercy of fluctuations in the price of precious metals on the 'market place' and these fluctuations could upset the prices quoted at the very doors of the Mints.

In 1621,[278] the stability of the pound was once more threatened, but the incident passed without trouble. The English clothiers, suffering from surplus production, wanted a devaluation of the pound which would reduce their production costs while improving their competitiveness abroad. Was Thomas Mun the man responsible for saving the stability of the pound, which had become a fetish in public opinion probably because of the memory of the Great Debasement? I would certainly not question the intelligence of Mun, who was the first person in England to grasp the connection between exchange rates and trade balance and who had acquired considerable commercial experience at the head of the young East India Company. But can one man, however brilliant and far-sighted, have been responsible for a monetary process affecting the entire English economy and even developments in Europe? Mun's arguments might not have prevailed had it not been for the agreement reached in 1630 between England and Spain (which had once more gone to war with the United Provinces in 1621) by which English ships were granted the monopoly of transporting the silver which financed the Spanish Netherlands. It was indeed a strange alliance and one which historians have (with one exception) ignored.[279] The silver landed in England was minted in the Tower of London and then re-exported (but not *in toto*) to the Netherlands. This was manna from heaven. But the beneficial flow dried up in about 1642 or 1648, at least in this form. And yet for reasons which this time remain a mystery, despite the violent disorders of the Civil War, the pound sterling held its value – in circumstances which seem frankly extraordinary.

For throughout the difficult latter half of the seventeenth century, the money in circulation in England consisted of very old silver coins, worn down, clipped and lightweight, since they had lost up to 50 per cent of their volume. Despite the intermittent sallies of pamphleteers, no one was seriously concerned. Indeed good money benefited only from a very small agio over the rest: the golden guinea was worth only 22 shillings as against its face value of 20. So things cannot have been too bad! In fact, with the growing spread of goldsmiths' notes (which were already a form, albeit a private one, of paper money) and above all with the fixed rate of the money of account setting all minds at rest, these lightweight silver coins were becoming a fiduciary currency, just as copper denominations were elsewhere in Europe; and people simply accepted the situation.

Until, that is, the sudden and violent crisis of confidence, in 1694, which interrupted this astonishing tranquillity and tolerance.[280] England had just experienced a series of bad harvests: a typical *ancien régime* crisis was getting under way, with repercussions in the 'industrial' sector. What was more the war waged against France since 1689 had forced the government to make large foreign payments and therefore to export specie. The best gold and silver coins were leaving the country. The atmosphere of crisis and the scarcity of coin led (in London more than in the provinces) to a systematic flight from bad money and a powerful impulse to hoard. The golden guinea[281] broke all past records, soaring from 22 shillings to 30 shillings in June 1695 (that is 50 per cent above the official value of 20 shillings). Both gold and silver prices soared, and the collapse of the pound on the Amsterdam market is sufficient indication of the gravity of the situation which was greeted by a hail of pamphlets and sowed panic in public opinion. Currency and notes (those of the goldsmiths and those of the Bank of England which had been created in 1694) lost much of their value, and to obtain cash one had to pay 12, 19 or even 40% over the odds. Loans, when they could be obtained, were at usurious rates; bills of exchange circulated with difficulty if at all. The crisis reached every corner of life: 'There are in one single street of London called Long Lane, twenty-six houses to let', writes an eyewitness. '... And even in the district of Cheapside there are at present some thirteen shops and houses closed and to let, an extraordinary thing, because not a quarter of this number of houses has ever been empty before ... in living memory'.[282] In 1696, 'the disorder is so great, for want of coin, that many gentlemen of quality have left London, being unable to live there, although having incomes of six or seven thousand pounds sterling, because no money can be extracted from the provinces'.[283]

Pamphleteers naturally discoursed to their hearts' delight, endlessly discussing the true causes of the crisis and the remedies to be applied. Everyone was agreed on one point: the coin in circulation had to be improved, the silver had to be re-coined. But was the new money to be issued on the same basis as during the Elizabethan reform? Or would a devaluation be announced? Another worrying question was who would bear the expenses of the operation – likely to be very heavy if the first course was followed, though lighter of course if the pound was to be devalued. The secretary to the Treasury, William Lowndes,[284] was in favour of a devaluation of 20 per cent, among other reasons because he was seeking to protect the government's finances. The best-known of his opponents, John Locke, the philosopher and economist, fought tooth and nail for the immutability of sterling, which he said should remain 'an invariable fundamental unit'.[285] Perhaps he had in mind not only the defence of a sound policy but also the rights of property-owners, the validity of contracts, the inviolability of funds lent to the state – in short the property of the minority ruling class. But why should the views of John Locke have prevailed over those of the secretary to the Treasury?

One reason no doubt was that the government of the former prince of Orange, now on the throne of England, when faced with serious financial problems, had committed itself to a policy of loans and long-term debt, an unaccustomed policy in England and one that inspired distrust and criticism on the part of many Englishmen, particularly since the new king was Dutch – and among the state's creditors were to be found moneylenders from Amsterdam who were beginning to invest in public stocks and shares in England. An absolutely unassailable credit standing was necessary if the state was to pursue the still unpopular policy of appealing for large loans, and if the newly-created bank was not to be placed in difficulties, its funds having been scarcely assembled before they had been lent to the state. This is probably the most satisfactory explanation of the government's decision not to devalue, and to adopt, for all its difficulties, the costly solution called for by Locke and speedily approved by both the Commons and the Lords in January 1696. The expenses of the huge re-coining operation (£7 million) were entirely borne by the state which was already burdened by the war. But the object was attained: as a sign of the recovery of credit, the pound went up in Amsterdam, prices in England began to return to reasonable levels, and English stocks were soon to be found in greater quantities on the London and Amsterdam markets.

This problem had scarcely been resolved before a new tension declared itself, pointing towards the future adoption of the gold standard – which took so long to become an official reality, imposed as it was by force of circumstance, not by conscious reflection.[286] Silver indeed fought a long rearguard action, with defenders such as Locke, who saw the silver standard as unquestionably the more convenient and the better adapted to trade. 'Let Gold, as other commodities, find its own Rate', he wrote.[287] This is not exactly what happened though, since the guinea (whose rate could be fixed simply by the king's decision) was pinned by an authoritarian decree to the rate of 22 silver shillings – which had indeed been its price on the 'free' market – but before the crisis. Now this meant 22 shillings in good money so that the gold/silver ratio was established at 1:15.9 and gold was thus over-valued: in Holland the ratio was only 1:15. So gold came streaming in to England, where it fetched higher prices, and brand new silver coins went the other way, out of the country. On a renewed plea from John Locke, the guinea was brought down to 21s 6d in 1698, but this was still not enough to prevent the two-way flow from continuing. Even after a further reduction, to 21 shillings in 1717, this time following intervention by Sir Isaac Newton, the Master of the Mint, the ratio of 1:15.21 still over-valued gold, and England went on exporting silver while attracting gold currencies.

The situation persisted throughout the eighteenth century, leading to a *de facto* gold standard – not officially recognized until the proclamation of the gold standard in 1816, when the pound sterling became the equivalent of the sovereign (a real gold coin weighing 7.988 grammes, and 11/12 fine metal). But already in 1774, gold had clearly overtaken silver as a monetary regulator. Worn gold coins were being withdrawn from circulation to be reminted at their proper weight, while it was decided to discontinue the expensive process of melting down silver coins for re-minting; they were consequently no longer allowed in full discharge payment for sums over £25. In practice, if not in law, the pound sterling was attaching itself to gold and thereby taking out a new lease of stability.

All these facts are well-known: but what are the reasons behind them? The constant over-valuation of gold, the real key to the phenomenon, was the direct result of decisions taken by the government alone. To what policy or economic necessity did such over-valuation correspond? Over-pricing gold effectively meant unleashing a reverse movement of silver. It has always been my personal opinion that in the monetary system of the past, an over-priced currency became a sort of 'bad' money, capable of driving out the good. This extension of Gresham's so-called law may simplify our explanation. When England attracted gold, by the same token she exported silver, whether to the Netherlands, Russia, the Mediterranean, the Indian Ocean and China, where silver was essential for trade. Venice had done precisely the same thing, in order to make it easier to transfer to the Levant the silver which was indispensable for her purchases there. What was more, England had been further propelled in this direction since her trade victory over Portugal, sealed by Lord Methuen's treaty (1703) whereby she gained access to the gold of Brazil. So could it be said that the English chose gold rather than silver, without consciously realizing it – and by so doing became a world power?

A flock of sheep and cattle in Soho in the late eighteenth century. (Photo Snark International.)

The Thames embankment, late eighteenth century. (Viollet collection.)

A fashionable district of London, Grosvenor Square in about 1790. (Photo Snark International.)

It is probably no accident that precisely when her trade balance with Portugal went into deficit, thus interrupting or slowing down the flow of Brazilian gold, England should have proceeded towards the next logical stage: that of paper money. It was indeed the case that as she gradually moved to the centre of the world, England, like Holland in her palmy days, had less need for precious metals: easy, not to say automatic credit took care of her payments. Thus in 1774, on the eve of the War of American Independence, England did not interfere as gold and silver coins left the country. She was unperturbed by this apparently abnormal development: high-level circulation of money was now in the form of notes issued by the Bank of England or by the private banks; it would hardly be an exaggeration to say that gold and silver had become lesser currencies. And if 'paper' (that convenient shorthand which the French had long been using and which so irritated Isaac de Pinto)[288] had attained such a significant place, it was because England, by dethroning Amsterdam, had become the point of convergence of all the world's trade – and all the world so to speak settled its accounts in London. In the old days, the fairs had offered similar concentrations, with credit taking precedence over cash. England was merely giving new dimensions to old solutions and found herself flooded with more paper than the Besançon fairs and with just as much as Amsterdam.

Further steps in this direction would inevitably be taken. In 1797, England's monetary problems were still growing: the war required the export of huge quantities of specie to the continent, whose hostility to France had to be bought. With the deepest apprehension of the consequences of his action, Pitt[289] normally so sure of himself, persuaded Parliament to accept the short-term non-convertibility of Bank of England notes. And it was then that a final miracle took place: the Bank Restriction Act which laid down the compulsory exchange rate for notes, was supposed to last for a mere six weeks. Yet it remained in force for twenty-four years without a single serious breach. The bank notes, which had no guarantee whatever behind them, continued to circulate without losing any value in relation to metal until at least 1809-10. For a quarter of a century, until 1821, England was living ahead of her times under the monetary regime we have today. A Frenchman who spent the Napoleonic Wars living in England reported that he had never seen a golden guinea the whole time he was there.[290] Thus a crisis of exceptional gravity in itself was survived without any great damage.

Success of this nature depended on the attitude of the British public, on its civic spirit and the confidence it had long shown in a monetary system which had always opted for stability. But confidence of this order was equally based on the assurance and certainty provided by wealth. Paper money's real guarantee was undoubtedly neither gold nor silver but the huge output of the British Isles. It was with the goods created by British industry and the profits from British trade and redistribution that Britain paid out to her European allies the fabulous subsidies which enabled her to defeat France, to maintain a fleet of fantastic proportions for the time, and the armies which fought in Spain and Portugal to turn the tables on Napoleon. At that period, no other country would have been able to do as much. A lucid observer remarked in 1811 that there was not room in the world for two experiences of this kind;[291] and he may well have been right.

But it has to be admitted in the end that although every episode in the history of sterling is clear and explicable, the steady and unwavering course it followed is amazing: it is as if the English – usually so renowned for their pragmatism – had had a revelation in 1560 of the correct direction to take. And of course that is ridiculous. Perhaps then we should see sterling's history as the repeated result of the aggressive tension characteristic of a country fiercely conditioned by its insularity (as an island to be defended), by its efforts to break through to world status and by its clear identification of the enemy: today Antwerp, tomorrow Amsterdam, the next day Paris. The stability of the pound was a weapon in this battle.

London creates the national market and is created by it

How can one begin to describe the role played by London in making Britain great? The capital city created and directed England from start to finish. London's outsize dimensions meant that other cities hardly began to exist as regional capitals: all of them, except possibly Bristol, were at her service. In no other western country, as Arnold Toynbee remarked, did one city so completely eclipse the rest. In the late seventeenth century, when the population of England as a whole was insignificant by comparison with that of France or Germany, and below that of Italy or Spain, London was already probably the largest city in Europe.[292] In 1700, Londoners numbered 555,000 – a tenth of the English population. In spite of repeated outbreaks of plague and epidemics, the city's population rose steadily and spectacularly. By contrast with France – a vast expanse divided and uncertain whether to obey Paris or Lyon – England had only one capital, and that an enormous one.

To speak of London is to speak of three or four cities at a time: the City was the economic capital; the king, Parliament and high society were all in Westminster; downstream was the Port of London and the poorer districts; and on the south bank was the suburb of Southwark, with its narrow streets and its theatres: the Swan, the Rose, the Globe, the Hope, the Red Bull (a total of 17 in 1629, whereas Paris had only one theatre at the same period).[293]

The entire economy of England was ruled from London. Political centralization, the power of the English Crown, the highly concentrated nature of trade, all combined to make the capital great. But this greatness itself imposed an order on the area it dominated and throughout which it set up a wealth of administrative and trading connections. N.S.B. Gras considered that London was a good hundred years ahead of Paris in the organization of her supplies.[294] Moreover London was also a very active port (handling at least four-fifths of England's foreign trade) as well as being Paris's equal as a parasitical capital, the centre of luxury and extravagance and – since these went hand in hand – of culture and creativity. Last but not least, the virtual monopoly London held of imports and exports enabled the capital from very early on to control all the production and redistribution in the island: it was a central sorting station for the other regions of England. Whether bound inland or abroad, everything had to pass through London.

For a true picture of the establishment and creation of a national market by London, one cannot do better than read – or better still re-read *The Complete English Tradesman* by Daniel Defoe. He is such a precise observer in every detail that although the words 'national market' nowhere appear, the reality of this market, its unity and the interlocking nature of exchange, with the advanced division of labour operating over wide areas, leap from the page to provide a thoroughly instructive sight.

Apart from the extremely busy coastal shipping – carrying heavy goods such as coals from Newcastle – most transport before the days of canals travelled on the roads, since only short stretches of the rivers were navigable: goods went by cart, by packhorse, and even on the backs of a multitude of pedlars.[295] All this traffic converged on London, only to be redispatched to the provinces. Perhaps it was the case that 'the Manchester men [were] saving their wealth, a kind of pedlars, who carry their goods themselves [i.e. without using a middleman] to the county shopkeepers everywhere, as do now the Yorkshire and Coventry manufacturers also'.[296] But at the time Defoe was writing (1720) such direct contact between producer and local retailer was a new phenomenon, interfering with and complicating the usual circuits. *Generally*, says Defoe, once a manufactured product has been finished in some county outside London, it is sent to London to a factor or warehouse-keeper who sells it either to a London shopkeeper who will retail it, or to an export merchant, or perhaps to a wholesaler who will distribute it for retailing in the various regions of England. Thus,

> the sheepmaster who shears and sells the fleece, and the shopkeeper who sells the cloth or clothes ready made, by retale, [sic] are the first and last tradesmen concerned in the whole trade; and the more hands this manufacture ... passes through either in the workmanship, or carriage, or sale of the goods ... so much the greater benefit is that manufacture to the publick stock of the nation, because the employment of the people is the great and main benefit of the Kingdom.[297]

And as if his reader had not yet entirely understood the advantages of a market economy which distributed work and therefore employment, Defoe retraces his steps to describe an example, that of a piece of broadcloth manufactured in Warminster in Wiltshire: the clothier sends it by carrier to London to Mr A, factor at Blackwell Hall, who is to sell it. He sells it to Mr B, a woollen draper, that is a wholesaler who will resell it, sending it by road to Mr C, a Northampton shopkeeper. He will cut it into lengths and retail it to country squires. It was in the end these moves into and out of London which provided the vital constituent framework of the national market.

All goods, including imports, thus travelled along the roads of England – the busiest in Europe as Defoe called them. Everywhere, in the smallest towns or even villages, nobody was content with local manufacture: 'they ... want goods from almost every other part':[298] English cloth from other counties or from India· tea; sugar. There can be no doubt that by the beginning of the eighteenth century, that is very early indeed, the English market had begun to look like a living organism. It was moreover in this first quarter of the century that huge investments (in comparative terms) were made, bringing the network of navigable rivers to 1160 miles and so improving communications that few people now lived more than 15 miles from a waterway.[299] It is not surprising that roads likewise improved. Defoe in 1720 speaks in the past tense of roads that were impassable in winter[300] – impassable by wheeled traffic that is, since pack animals travelled in all weathers in the seventeenth century. Nor is one in the least surprised to learn that markets which stocked, sold and re-sold goods were quickly organized in defiance of all official regulations, and that the middlemen very often never so much as saw the goods in which they were dealing – a sign of near-perfect organization. The London grain market was controlled in mid-century by about fifteen factors who did not hesitate if necessary to store their grain in Amsterdam where warehousing (which varied with interest rates) was cheaper than in England. A further advantage was that grain leaving the country benefited from the export subsidy granted by the English government, and if shortages occurred in England the same grain could come back in without paying any duty.[301] These are all signs of the growing sophistication of the domestic market in the course of the eighteenth century.

In 1815, a former prisoner-of-war who had spent many years in England made an instructive observation: 'If all the interests of England are concentrated in the city of London, which is today the meeting-place of all business, one can also say that London is also present in the rest of England'[302] – that is that goods on sale in London, from all the corners of England or indeed the world, were also to be found in provincial market places and in all the county towns. Uniformity of costume, and particularly the spread of women's fashions are clear signs that the English economy was being reduced to a single unit. There are other criteria too, the spread of banks for example. The first Land Banks appeared in 1695,[303] in a modest way at first since the entire sum of their banknotes that year was £55,000. But it was a significant beginning since credit does not usually make an appearance until last of all, when previous economic development has made it both possible and necessary. Above all, the Land Banks were to multiply in number, in connection with the London banks and the Bank of England created in 1694. Unification was thus going on in the credit sphere – with the provincial economies becoming satellites of the capital.

It can however be argued that while London engineered the original establishment of a coherent national market, the latter subsequently developed and grew in strength by itself. In the eighteenth century, unlike the seventeenth,

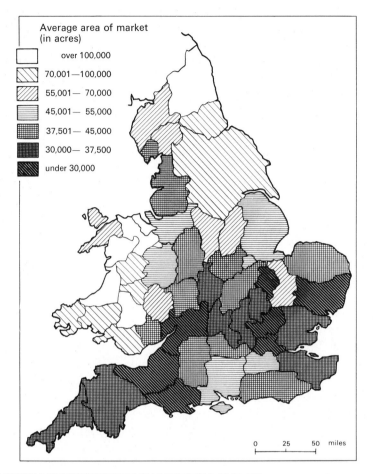

Average area of market (in acres)

☐	over 100,000
◩	70,001 — 100,000
◪	55,001 — 70,000
▤	45,001 — 55,000
▦	37,501 — 45,000
■	30,000 — 37,500
◆	under 30,000

0   25   50   miles

37   THE BRISK MARKETS WERE NEAREST TO LONDON
This map (from *The Agrarian History of England* ... IV, ed. J. Thirsk, (1967), p. 496, shows how London had created an area where trade was brisk and turnover fast. The modernization of the national market began in southern England.

provincial manufacturing centres and ports, particularly those concerned with colonial produce and the slave trade – such as Liverpool, Bristol or Glasgow – underwent rapid development.[304] General prosperity was strengthened all the more thereby. Within the British Isles as a whole, England was by now a national market, compact and densely-woven. There was nothing comparable anywhere else in Europe. Inevitably, sooner or later this exceptional density would begin to weigh heavy within the British Isles transforming the economies of the other three countries in relation to that of England.

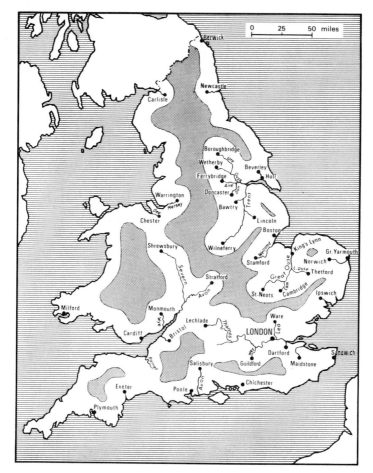

38 THE NATIONAL MARKET AND NAVIGABLE WATERWAYS (1600–1700)
T.S. Willan's map, from *River Navigation in England 1600–1750*, (1964) shows what it was like
before 'canal fever' and the building of the great waterways. It shows the navigable stretches
only of the rivers; the shaded areas are those more than 15 miles from a waterway. When one
compares this map with the previous one, it almost looks like its photographic negative. It was
the existence of waterways as much as the attraction of the capital or the network of coastal
shipping, which helped to set up a national market. By the end of the eighteenth century, the
shaded zones would almost have disappeared with the progress of transport.

How England became Great Britain

To the north and west, England was bounded by remote and mostly pastoral
highland countries, which long remained very poor. Their scattered population
was made up of Celts, usually hostile to English culture. The conquest of these
peoples was the crucial process in the internal history of the British Isles: it was
an enterprise which could only end in the worst solutions, those of force. Politics

as one might expect preceded economics here and the latter had long to be content with minor or isolated successes. Cornwall's tin was appropriated in very early times by London merchants.[305] In Wales, reconquered in 1536, the export of cattle on the hoof to London did not become a major item until after 1750,[306] and the country was only really changed by the heavy industry introduced by the English in the nineteenth century. But the two major offensives were, predictably, launched against Scotland – where events in the end took an unexpected course – and Ireland, which became a colony to be exploited on England's doorstep.

Scotland might in theory have been thought a country designed to retain its autonomy and to escape even the slightest 'marginalization': a large country, half as big as England, mountainous and poor, separated from her southern neighbour by forbidding border country. A long history of bloody battles predisposed her to resist the English. And even after 1603, when James VI of Scotland inherited Elizabeth's throne to become James I of England, uniting the two crowns, Scotland retained a government and an assembly, comparatively weak it is true, but still in existence.[307] Likewise, the frontier between the two countries was maintained, with its customs barriers. But while it enabled Scotland to protect herself against untimely imports, it also enabled England to forbid Scottish livestock and linen products to cross the border, as well as to deny access to English colonies to ships from Edinburgh, Glasgow or Dundee.

Seventeenth-century Scotland was a poor country which it would be ridiculous to compare for a moment with England. Scotland's economy was archaic, her agriculture traditional, and death-dealing famine only too often followed bad harvests, for example in 1695, 1696, 1698 and 1699. 'We shall never know how many people died [in those years]: contemporaries spoke of a fifth, or a quarter, or a third or even more of the inhabitants having died or fled in some areas.'[308]

However foreign trade brought animation to Scottish ports, particularly Leith (the port of Edinburgh), Aberdeen, Dundee, Glasgow and a number of harbours sheltering boats of low tonnage which sailed in all directions: to Norway, Sweden, Danzig, Rotterdam, Verre, Rouen, La Rochelle, Bordeaux, sometimes even to Spain and Portugal: they were intrepid boats, often the last to cross the Sound westwards before it froze in winter. Scottish sailors and traders often broke their journeys and settled abroad, whether as poor *skottars* who took up peddling, or as prosperous merchants who made their fortunes in Stockholm, Warsaw, or Ratisbon.[309] The Lowland seaports handled a thriving trade and the modest volume of shipping continued to grow. The merchants of Glasgow and Edinburgh (who were all local men, a sign of the healthy condition of trade) were enterprising, despite being short of capital. This explains both the creation in 1694, but also the eventual failure of the 'Scottish Africa Company' which sought capital in vain in London, Hamburg and Amsterdam.[310] Attempts to settle a Scottish colony on the banks of the Darien Isthmus in 1699 were equally unsuccessful. England, far from encouraging such ventures watched their

Eighteenth-century Edinburgh: the Grassmarket, looking up at the castle. The vehicle on the left is coming from the West Port of the city. Edinburgh Public Library. (Photo A.G. Ingram Ltd.)

collapse with relief.[311] But in Scotland the Darien tragedy was regarded as a national disaster.

It was probably in the hope of seeing English and American markets open to Scotland that political union with England was voted by a single-figure majority in the Edinburgh Parliament in 1707. The calculation, if that is what it was, was not a bad one, since as Smout has shown, Scotland's increased political dependence was not translated into economic enslavement or 'marginalization': partly because by becoming a 'province' of England so to speak, Scotland was now able to benefit from all the commercial advantages enjoyed by Britons abroad, and her merchants were equal to the occasion; partly because nothing that Scotland possessed was of such economic interest to the English as to lead to any form of imperial colonization. But the hoped-for revival and prosperity did not happen all at once. It took time to take full advantage of the chance to trade throughout the empire – in North America, the West Indies and even India, where so many Scots sought their fortune to the irritation of the English. It was only with the economic growth, in the last fifty years of the eighteenth century in particular, that export and industry really developed. But when success came, it was clear to see. First came the development of a large-scale trade in livestock on the hoof: production prices increased by 300 per cent between 1740 and 1790, because of contracts to supply the English fleet. Wool exports also increased, likewise encouraged by higher prices. This in turn led to a number of logical, but sometimes painful transformations, as land became more profitable than labour, and sheep-grazing was extended at the expense of crofting and farming communities. Lastly, after 1760, Scotland joined vigorously and in an original manner in the industrial transformation of the island. The expansion first of linen then of cotton manufacture, based on a banking system which the English often regarded as superior to their own, eventually created sufficient demand for agricultural produce to bring about a belated but effective change in farming. 'Progress', the favourite word of the age of enlightenment, was the watchword in Scotland. And 'practically all classes in Scottish society were conscious of a momentum which was carrying them towards a richer society'.[312]

There undoubtedly was a Scottish takeoff: 'If Scotland were not prospering', wrote an observer in 1800, 'Glasgow would not be growing as fast as it is, the size of Edinburgh would not have doubled in thirty years, and they would not now be building a New Town whose construction is employing close on ten thousand immigrant workers'.[313] Was this development – so different from the Irish case to which we will turn next – the result of a mere combination of circumstances? Or of the initiative and experience of Scottish merchants? Or of the fact, underlined by Smout, that Scotland's population growth, at least in the Lowlands, was moderate and did not, as it has in so many Third World countries of today, wipe out the benefits of economic growth? No doubt all these had something to do with it. But perhaps too Scotland did not, as Ireland did, encounter the visceral hostility of the English. Scotland was not for instance wholly Gaelic-speaking: in the rich Lowlands, between Glasgow and Edinburgh, the people had for various reasons long spoken English or Scots. An Englishman would not feel he was in entirely a foreign country. The Highlands on the contrary spoke Gaelic (and in the far north, a form of Norwegian dialect had even survived). It certainly is the case that Scottish growth widened the gulf between Highlands and Lowlands. It could almost be argued that the frontier which in the seventeenth century divided an increasingly rich England from an increasingly poor Scotland had moved from the Anglo-Scottish border to the Highland line.

In Ireland, the situation was very different: it was in the twelfth century that the English invaded and settled within the Pale,[314] as they were later to do in their American colonies. The Irish were the enemy, savages simultaneously despised and feared. The consequence was mutual incomprehension, high-handedness by the invaders, and horrors whose sinister catalogue needs no elaboration: the story has been told with lucidity and honesty by English historians themselves.[315]

There can be no doubt, as one of them has put it, that 'the Irish, together with the blacks who were sold as slaves were the victims of the system which brought Great Britain world hegemony'.[316]

But our concern here is neither the colonization of Ulster, nor the 'farce' of the so-called Irish government set up in Dublin (a fiction which was of course destroyed by the Act of Union of 1801); it is the subjection of Ireland to the English market, that total subjection which meant that 'throughout the eighteenth century, trade to Ireland was the most important branch of English overseas trade.'[317] This exploitation originated in the estates of the Protestant Anglo-Irish, who had appropriated for their own advantage three-quarters of the land in Ireland. Out of an annual income of £4 million, rural Ireland paid these absentee landlords annual dues of the order of £800,000; by the end of the eighteenth century, the sum had reached £1 million. In these conditions, the Irish peasant was reduced to severe poverty, aggravated by a rising population.

Thus Ireland sank into the position of a 'peripheral' country, subject to 'cycles' in the sense of the word used by Lucio de Azevedo[318] of the Brazilian economy. In about 1600, since Ireland was covered with forests, she became a supplier of timber to England and developed, again for her masters, an iron industry which collapsed of itself when the island had been completely deforested after a hundred years. Next, to meet the rising demand of the English cities, Ireland specialized in livestock farming and the export of salt beef and pork, and kegs of butter – for the English market was plentifully supplied with meat on the hoof from Scotland and Wales and closed her doors to live animal exports from Ireland. The key port for these huge meat exports was Cork in the south: which supplied not only England but the English fleet, the sugar islands of the West Indies and the fleets of other western nations, notably France. In 1783, during the season 'which lasts through October, November and December', almost 50,000 head of cattle were slaughtered in Cork; plus 'pigs which were killed in the spring' to the same value, not to mention the product of other slaughter-houses.[319] European merchants had their eyes glued to the prices fixed at the end of the season on kegs of salt beef or pork, and bacon, lard, butter and cheese by the quintal. The bishop of Cloyne, reckoning the prodigious quantity of cattle, pigs, butter and cheese exported every year from Ireland was curious enough to wonder 'how a foreigner could possibly conceive that half the inhabitants are dying of hunger in a country so abundant in foodstuffs'?[320] But these foodstuffs did not of course contribute in any way to domestic consumption, any more than the Polish peasant consumed his own grain.

Towards the end of the century, Irish salt meat encountered competition from Russian exports via Archangel and even more from shipments out of the English colonies in America. It was then that the 'grain cycle' began. A French consul wrote from Dublin on 24 November 1789:

> The most enlightened people whom I have been able to consult ... regard the salt meat trade in Ireland as doomed, but far from being distressed at this they

are pleased to see that the big landowners are forced in their own interest to change the system of exploitation which has prevailed hitherto, and no longer to give over to grazing vast and fertile estates which if cultivated would provide employment and subsistence for a much greater number of inhabitants. This revolution has already taken place *and is proceeding with inconceivable rapidity.* Ireland, which was formerly dependent upon England for the grain consumed in the capital [Dublin] *which was the only part of Ireland in which this foodstuff was at all known,* has been in a position for several years now to export considerable quantities of it.[321]

As the reader will know, England, once a grain exporter, had become with the beginnings of industrialization and a rising population, a cereal importer. The grain cycle continued in Ireland until the repeal of the Corn Laws in 1846. But in its early stages, this cereal export was a manoeuvre reminiscent of the situation in seventeenth-century Poland. The Irish, our informant explains,

are only able to export [cereals in 1789] because the great majority of them do not consume it; it is not the surplus that leaves the country, it is what anywhere else would be the vital necessity. The people in three-quarters of this island are content to eat potatoes, and in the north, groats from which they make oatcakes and porridge. Thus a people which is poor, but used to privation, is feeding a nation [England] which has far more natural wealth than itself.[322]

If one looked simply at the statistics for foreign trade – which also included salmon fisheries, profitable whaling expeditions, large-scale exports of linen whose manufacture had begun in mid-eighteenth century – Ireland should have had in 1787 a trade surplus of £1 million: this was precisely what she paid every year to her English landlords.

But for Ireland as for Scotland, a new opportunity arose with the American War. Westminster was prodigal with promises, and in December 1779 and February 1780 suppressed a certain number of restrictions and bans which had previously limited Irish trade; granted permission for direct contacts with North America, the West Indies and Africa; and allowed His Majesty's Irish subjects to enter the Levant Company.[323] When this news reached Paris, it was greeted as 'a revolution' in Ireland: 'the king of England is going to become infinitely more powerful than he has ever been ... and France ... will certainly be the loser unless she promptly opposes this prodigious increase in power. There is one way to do it: and that is to make a new king of Ireland'.[324]

Ireland took advantage of the concessions. The linen industry which occupied perhaps a quarter of the population, expanded further. On 26 November 1783, the *Gazette de France* announced that Belfast had exported to America and the Indies 11,649 pieces of linen, that is 310,672 yards and (certainly with some exaggeration) that 'before long the towns of Cork and Waterford in Ireland will be doing more trade than Liverpool and Bristol'. In 1785,[325] the Younger Pitt even had the perspicacity to propose the total economic liberation of Ireland, but the House of Commons was hostile to the idea, and as usual on such occasions, the Prime Minister did not insist.

A major opportunity was no doubt lost on this occasion, for soon afterwards with the French Revolution and its raids on Ireland, political drama once again overtook the island. The whole story began again. As Vidal de la Blanche rightly remarked,[326] Ireland, too close to England to escape her, and too large to be assimilated, was constantly the victim of her geographical location. In 1824, the first steamship line was created between Dublin and Liverpool and soon 42 ferries were operating. 'In the old days', wrote a contemporary in 1834, 'it took a week on average to cross from Liverpool to Dublin; now it is a matter of a few hours.'[327] Ireland was now closer than ever to England and at her mercy.

To return now to our original question, it will be readily agreed, I think, that the British market developing out of the long-established English market, emerges with a strong and clear identity from the time of the American War of Independence. This war undoubtedly marked a change of pace and a turning point. This confirms our earlier conclusion that England became unchallenged mistress of the European world-economy in about 1780-5. The English market could perhaps now be said to have successfully achieved three things: control of itself, control of the British market and control of the world market.

England's greatness and the national debt

The European economy developed exuberantly after 1750 and England was no exception. There were many signs of visible growth – but which are the most crucial or important? The increasing hierarchy within commercial life? The exceptionally high prices which had disadvantages but also the advantage not only of attracting to England 'the production of foreign countries' but of swelling home demand? The standard of living and per capita income of her inhabitants, inferior only to small and very rich Holland? The volume of trade? All these things counted, but England's greatness – shortly to bring about an industrial revolution which nobody could at the time have predicted – was not the result simply of the rise and organization of the expanding British market, nor entirely of the unrestrained growth common to all developed countries of Europe in the eighteenth century. It was also the result of a series of happy chances which placed England, without her always fully realizing it, on the road towards modern solutions. The pound sterling was a modern currency; the banking system was one which shaped and adapted itself in a modern direction; and the national debt was rooted in the security of long-term or perpetual debt – an empirical solution which would turn out to be a technically effective masterpiece. It is true that this is also in retrospect the clearest indication of the health of the British economy, for however ingenious the system that emerged from what has been called the English financial revolution, it required the prompt and regular discharge of the interest continuously payable on the national debt. The fact there was never any defaulting on the interest payments is an achievement as remarkable as the uninterrupted stability of sterling.

The feat is all the more remarkable in that English public opinion was overwhelmingly hostile to the national debt. England had of course borrowed money before 1688, but always on a short-term basis with high interest paid at irregular intervals – and with repayment at even more irregular ones, sometimes only thanks to a new loan. In short, the state's creditworthiness was not of the soundest, especially since 1672 and the moratoria on the debts of Charles II, who not only failed to repay in time the money lent him by the bankers but also suspended interest payments (and the affair ended up in the courts). After the Glorious Revolution and the accession of William of Orange, the government, finding itself obliged to borrow large sums and to reassure the moneylenders, hit upon the policy of long-term loans (the word 'perpetual' was even mentioned) with interest guaranteed by an earmarked tax. This decision which with hindsight we can see as the beginning of an ingenious financial policy, of amazing rectitude, was in fact improvised in confusion, amid much discussion and disturbance, and under heavy pressure from events. Every solution was tried in turn: tontine, life annuities, lotteries and even in 1694 the creation of the Bank of England which, as we have seen, promptly lent all its capital to the state.

But to the English public, all these innovations smacked of 'jobbing', of speculation in shares and, no less, of foreign practices brought into the country by William of Orange. People distrusted 'these New Notions in Government', wrote Jonathan Swift in 1713, 'to which the King, who had imbibed his Politics in his own Country, was thought to give too much way'. The Dutch idea that 'it was in the public's interest to be in debt', might be true of Holland, but not of England where politics and society were after all very different.[328] Some critics went even further: was not the government seeking, by means of these loans, to buy the support of the subscribers and even more that of the firms who ensured the success of such operations? Moreover, did not the possibility of this easy investment, at interest rates higher than the legal norm, create a powerful competitor for the natural credit which was the lifeblood of the English economy, and in particular its steadily expanding trade? Defoe himself, in 1720, looked back nostalgically on the days when 'there were no bubbles, no stock-jobbing ... no lotteries, no funds, no annuities, no buying of navy-bills and public securities, no circulating exchequer bills', when all the money in the kingdom flowed like a mighty commercial river with nothing to divert it from its ordinary course.[329] As for the claim that the state was borrowing money out of concern not to tax its subjects too heavily, that was absolute nonsense! Every new loan made it necessary to create a new tax, a fresh source of income, so that the interest could be paid.

In addition, many English people were alarmed at the large total of the sums borrowed. In 1748, just after the peace of Aix-la-Chapelle, which he thought disappointing and mortifying, a disputatious Englishman[330] lamented that the debt had reached about £80 million. This level, he explained, seems to be our '*nec plus ultra* and if we were to take one step more, we should be in danger of

A London coffee house in about 1700. From *The Life and Work of the People of England* (British Museum).

general bankruptcy'. This would take us 'to the edge of the precipice and ruin'. 'One does not have to be a wizard', remarked David Hume in about 1750, 'to guess what will happen next. It can only be one of these two catastrophes: either the nation will destroy public credit, or public credit will destroy the nation.'[331] Shortly after the Seven Years' War, Lord Northumberland confided to the duke of Cumberland his anxiety on seeing the government 'live from day to day, whereas France is restoring her finances, paying her debts and setting her fleet to rights'. Anything might happen, 'if France took a fancy to attack us'.[332]

Foreign observers too were amazed at what seemed to them the incredible size of the English national debt. They echoed British criticisms, poked fun at processes they did not understand or, more often, saw this as a signal weakness, an unthinking and facile policy which would take the country to disaster. The chevalier Dubouchet, a Frenchman who had lived many years in Seville, explained in a long report to cardinal Fleury that England was crushed by her debt of £60 million: 'we know her resources, we know her debts, she is in no position to pay them'.[333] Under these conditions, the war which was still being contemplated, would be fatal to her. This illusion is found in the writings of all the political experts. It explains for instance the pessimism of a book published in

Vienna in 1771 by the Dutchman Accarias de Sérionne, entitled *La Richesse de l'Angleterre* (*England's Wealth*) – wealth the author regarded as threatened by the high cost of living, the rising taxes, the extravagant level of the national debt and even by the reputed drop in population. And what about the following confident sally in the *Journal de Genève* of 30 June 1778: 'It has been calculated that in order to pay off the English national debt at a guinea a minute, it would take 272 years, nine months, a week and a day and 15 minutes – which means the debt must stand at 141, 405, 855 guineas'. And yet war swelled the debt to even greater – indeed enormous – proportions, as if to mock the incompetence of the specialists and experts. In 1824, Dufresne de Saint Léon calculated that 'the capital of all the public debts in Europe ... comes to 38 to 40 thousand million francs, three-quarters of which is accounted for by England alone'.[334] At about the same time (1829), Jean-Baptiste Say, who was also severe on English public borrowing, already considered France's debt 'too considerable', 'although it comes to barely 4 thousand million'.[335] Was victory even more expensive than defeat?

And yet all these rational observers were wrong. The national debt was the major reason for the British victory. It had placed huge sums of money at England's disposal at the very moment when she required them. Isaac de Pinto was clear-sighted when he wrote in 1771: 'The scrupulous and inviolable exactness with which this interest [that on the national debt] has been paid, the idea of parliamentary guarantees, have established England's credit to the point where she has received loans that have surprised and astonished the rest of Europe'.[336] He regarded the English victory in the Seven Years' War (1756–1763) as the natural consequence. France's weakness, he claimed, lay in her poor credit arrangements. Thomas Mortimer was also right when in 1769 he admired in English public credit 'the permanent miracle of her policy, which has inspired both astonishment and fear in the states of Europe'.[337] Thirty years earlier, George Berkeley had celebrated it as 'the chief advantage which England has over France'.[338] So a small minority of contemporary writers could see what was at stake and recognized that this apparently dangerous game represented an effective mobilization of England's full resources and a redoubtable weapon.

It was only in the final decades of the eighteenth century that the truth of the matter was generally recognized and that Pitt the Younger could declare to the Commons that on the national debt depended 'the vigour and even the independence of this nation'.[339] As a note written in 1774 put it, 'never could the English nation, which is so weak in itself, have imposed its law on almost the whole of Europe had it not been for its trade, its industry and its credit which only exists on paper'.[340] This was the triumph of 'artificial wealth', claimed some people. But was not artificial wealth a masterpiece of human achievement? In April 1782, during a serious crisis with practically no way out – or so thought France, her allies and many other Europeans – the English government, which had appealed for a loan of £3 million, received offers of £5 million. All it had taken was a word with the four or five biggest firms in London.[341] Lucid as usual, Andrea

Dolfin the Venetian ambassador in Paris, had written the previous year to his friend Andrea Tron, apropos the war launched against England:

> What is beginning is a new siege of Troy, and it will probably finish like that of Gibraltar. We have to admire however the constancy of England which is resisting so many enemies in so many places. It is time to recognize that any plan of bringing her down must be despaired of, and therefore that prudence commands some compromise and sacrifice for the cause of peace.[342]

One could hardly ask for better homage to the power and, no less, to the tenacity of England.

From the Treaty of Versailles (1783) to the Eden Treaty (1786)

Nothing better reveals the might of Britain than the events of the year 1783. Despite the humiliation of the Treaty of Versailles (3 September 1783), despite the self-satisfaction and sabre-rattling of France, England proved on this occasion her strength no less than her political sagacity and economic superiority. As Michel Besnier puts it, she lost the war but immediately afterwards won the peace. She could in fact hardly fail to win, since she held all the trump cards.

Why? Because the true duel for world domination was not really between England and France, but between England and Holland; and Holland had been literally stripped of her substance by the fourth Anglo-Dutch war. In addition, France had clearly failed in her bid for world hegemony by 1783, as would be proved three years later by the signature of the Eden Treaty.

Unfortunately there is some obscurity about this treaty, a commercial agreement signed between France and England on 26 September 1786, bearing the name of the English negotiator, Sir William Eden (later Lord Auckland). The French government seems to have been more anxious than the English cabinet to conclude it. Article 18 of the Treaty of Versailles had specified the immediate appointment of commissioners to draw up a commercial agreement. But the English government would willingly have allowed article 18 to remain a dead letter.[343] The initiative came from the French side, out of a desire to consolidate the peace no doubt; perhaps too to put an end to the vast contraband trade between the two countries which was enriching the smugglers without even reducing prices. The customs authorities of both countries were being cheated of substantial revenues which would have been most welcome, in view of the financial distress occasioned both in England and in France by the expensive American War. In short, France took the first steps. 'No', wrote Simolin, Catherine II's ambassador to London in January 1785, 'England is not reduced to accepting the terms which the French would like to force on her'; and those who thought so 'before seeing things with their own eyes', such as Rayneval the French negotiator in London, 'were misled like him'. Once the agreement was signed, Pitt, in a display of rather unnecessary crowing, 'said before Parliament that the commercial treaty of 1786 was the true revenge for the peace treaty of

Versailles'.[344] Unfortunately the historian has no means of deciding without hesitation whether this was true. The 1786 agreement is not a good test of comparison between the English and French economies – especially since it was not due to come into force until summer 1787;[345] and whereas it was supposed to last twelve years, it was renounced by the Convention in 1793. The experiment did not last long enough to be conclusive.

If we are to believe the French witnesses, who were both judge and plaintiff in the case, the English were up to all sorts of tricks. They understated the value of the goods they brought into French ports and took advantage of the confusion, inexperience and venality of the French customs officers. They so contrived it that English coal never arrived in France in French ships;[346] and they also charged heavy export duties on English goods carried in French ships; so much so that 'two or three little French brigs lying in the river here [in London] can hardly acquire enough goods for the return trip in six weeks to avoid being obliged to return on Ballast'.[347] But was this not an old trick of the English? In 1765, Savary's *Dictionnaire* had already described as characteristic 'of the genius of the English Nation' the fact that they never allowed 'anyone to come and arrange reciprocal trading with them. It must therefore be confessed', he goes on, 'that the manner in which foreign merchants are received in England, the extraordinary and excessive import and export duties they are obliged to pay, and the treatment they often suffer, hardly induce [the latter] . . . to set up correspondents here'.[348] The French should not therefore have been surprised when after the Eden Treaty, 'Mr Pitt, thinking he was carrying out a political action because it was immoral, reduced the import tax on Portuguese wines to the same extent that he had reduced those on ours – completely against the spirit of the treaty'. 'We would have done better to drink our own wine', remarked a Frenchman, with hindsight.[349] On the other side, it has to be said that too many mediocre wines[350] were being imported to England by French speculators who were too ready to believe that English customers would not notice the difference.

It is at any rate clear that the decree bringing the treaty into force on 31 May 1787, which opened French ports to English shipping, opened the floodgates to large numbers of ships and an avalanche of British goods: cloth, cottons, ironmongery and even quantities of china – causing an outcry in France, especially from the textile regions in Normandy and Picardy, where the *cahiers de doléance*, the grievance registers of 1789, called for 'the reform of the trade treaty'. The strongest protest was voiced in the famous *Observations de la Chambre de Commerce de Normandie sur le traité entre la France et l'Angleterre* (Rouen 1788). In fact, the coming into force of the treaty coincided with a crisis in French industry which while it was being modernized in certain regions, Rouen for example, was on the whole still suffering from antiquated structures. Some people in France entertained the hope that English competition would hasten the necessary transformations and further the movement which had already transplanted to France some of the improvements introduced to English industry (cotton-spinning at Darnetal or Arpajon for instance). 'I see with pleasure', wrote M. d'Aragon from London on 26 June 1787, 'that a throng of English workers of all kinds are seeking to set themselves up in France. If they are encouraged, I do not doubt that they will attract their friends to come too. There are among them several of merit and talent.'[351]

But with the beginnings of the French Revolution, fresh difficulties arose; the exchange rate in London was subject to 'convulsive movements': it fell by 8 per cent as early as May 1789, because of the flight of French capital; by December it had fallen by 13 per cent,[352] and worse was to come. Even if this collapse of the currency meant that French exports to England temporarily rose, it undoubtedly disturbed trade circuits. To estimate how much, we need some statistics; all we have are memoranda and polemics. Such for instance is the memorandum *Sur le traité de commerce avec l'Angleterre en 1786*,[353] written in 1798, some time after the treaty was signed. The author was probably Dupont de Nemours. He tries to show that the treaty could have been a success (implicitly admitting that it had not been). By imposing duties of 10 to 12 per cent on goods entering the country, 'our manufactures' had been adequately protected, all the more so since in order to introduce their goods, 'the English had artificial expenses which could not have been less than 6 per cent, so there was a difference of 18 per cent in our favour'. This 18 per cent barrier was protection enough for French industry against English imports. And for 'fine cloth', there had not been 'the slightest protest on the part of the manufactures of Sedan, Abbeville or Elbeuf; it is even evident that they have prospered'. Nor were there complaints from 'the ordinary woollen [producers], namely those of Berry and Carcassonne'. In short, the woollen sector had faced this competition without any great problem. Cotton was another story. But all that was needed was to mechanize spinning. This was the opinion of 'Holker the elder', an Englishman by birth who had become an inspector of the French manufactories. 'Let us, like [the English] set up spinning machines', he says, 'and we shall be able to manufacture as well as they do.'[354] In short, English competition could have given the necessary fillip to the French modernization which was already under way – but as I have already said, it would have required persistence and the argument leaves out England's chief and ultimate trump card: the monopoly of an unlimited market, a worldwide one during the Revolutionary and Napoleonic Wars.

From this point of view, the arguments of those who have blamed the French Revolution and the Napoleonic Wars for France's economic backwardness in the early nineteenth century, have some truth in them. But there is plenty of other evidence besides the obscure Eden Treaty to suggest that the game had already been lost and won before 1786, that England had already gained control of the worldwide economy. It is enough to have seen how London was able to impose terms of trade on Russia, Spain, Portugal and the United States; or the way in which England, pushing aside her European rivals, effortlessly recon-quered the markets of her former colonies in the New World, to the great surprise and discomfiture of America's allies; the manner in which England sailed through the stormy waters of the post-1783 recession; the order and good sense which Pitt restored to finance;[355] the defeat of the tea smugglers in 1785; or the passing of the East India Bill the year before[356] which marked the start of a more honest administration of British India. Not to mention the first settlement of a British colony in Australia, when towards the end of 1789 a flotilla under Commander Phillips 'transported to Botany Bay the first malefactors whom the government had sent there'.[357] Robert Besnier's argument is probably correct: England 'having been defeated in America, abandoned the idea of a military victory by attrition, in order to preserve and extend her markets'. She sacrificed all thirst for revenge to the safeguarding 'of her economic growth and superiority'.[358]

As for France, she fell between Scylla and Charybdis. In the days of Colbert and Louis XIV, she had been unable to escape from the Dutch net; now she was caught in England's toils. France could only breathe the air of the outside world through London, as in the past she had through Amsterdam. There were of course advantages and conveniences in this situation. French trade with India was never so prosperous, in all likelihood, as when the subcontinent was lost to her for good. But the advantages were always short-lived.

Statistics: a contribution but not a solution

Can any light be shed on the rivalry between France and England, so central to world history in the eighteenth and early nineteenth century, by statistics, or better still by statistical comparisons? Can they indeed solve the problem? The operation had never really been seriously attempted before the Prato conference of 1976 when it was tackled by two British historians, Peter Mathias and Patrick O'Brien.[359] This confronts us with a litmus test at first sight disconcerting, then enlightening, but probably still incomplete. It is disconcerting because throughout their demonstration the superiority of France seems to appear at every turn. As a French historian remarked in the discussion which followed this sensational paper at Prato, if all this was true, France should have been the winner in this rivalry for the world, and the industrial revolution should have taken place in France. And that of course is precisely what did not happen. So the problem of the English triumph is merely presented under a new and insistent form. We certainly do not know the answer yet.

The two graphs offered by Mathias and O'Brien, showing English and French growth rates between 1715 and 1810 – even though confined to overall commodity output – establish that in the eighteenth century the French economy was growing faster than the English, and that in terms of value it was greater too. The problem is turned completely on its head. The volume of French output rises from 100 in 1715 to 210 in 1790-1; to 247 in 1803-4; and to 260 in 1810. English output meanwhile rises from 100 in 1715 to 182 in 1800. The gap is very wide, even if one bears in mind that this method of reckoning doubly under-

For this English caricaturist in 1792, England's superiority is clear: taxes or no taxes, who eats better? (B.N., Paris.)

estimates the English figures: (1) it measures only physical output and therefore leaves out services, a sector in which England was certainly ahead of France; and (2) since France's takeoff was later, she probably made more rapid progress compared to her competitor.

But if we turn to the value of total production, expressed in *livres tournois* or hectolitres of grain, the gap is yet again considerable. In terms of production, France was a giant – a giant which did not win the fight, and this is the problem that has to be explained – but a giant all the same. T. J. Markevitch[360] is not therefore guilty of special pleading when he insists that the French cloth industry was the greatest in the world in the eighteenth century.

For a different comparison, one could look at the national budgets. A brief article in the *Gazette de France* of 7 April 1783, gives the respective totals for the budgets of the European countries, which a 'political calculator' (whose identity we shall probably never know) has converted into pounds sterling for comparative purposes. France heads the list with £16 million, England comes a close second with £15 million. If it could be accepted that there was some kind of correlation (of whatever nature) between budget, that is total tax revenue, and G.N.P., then the G.N.P.s of England and France ought to be roughly equal. But it happens to be the case that fiscal tension in England and France was very different as our British colleagues have made clear: taxation in England amounted to 22 per cent of G.N.P., while in France it was only 10 per cent. So if these calculations are right (and there is some reason to think that they are) taxation in England was double that in France. This runs counter to the usual assertions by historians who are prone to imagine France as crippled by a tax burden levied by an absolute monarch. It also oddly enough confirms a French report dating from 1708 at the height of the War of the Spanish Succession: 'After having seen the extraordinary subsidies which the subjects have to pay in England, it has to be said that one is very lucky to be in France'.[361] A hasty judgment, no doubt, coming from a privileged man. In practice, unlike the English, the French taxpayers were subject to a heavy 'social' levy paid to the nobility and the Church. And it was this social levy which forestalled too great an appetite on the part of the French Exchequer.[362]

We are still left with the fact that France's G.N.P. was more than double that of England (France £160 million, England £68). Approximate though these figures are, the difference is so great that even if one throws in the G.N.P. of Scotland and Ireland, it cannot be made up. In this comparison, France comes off best because of her size and population. England's achievement was that she succeeded in reaching budget parity with larger countries than herself. This was a frog, which unlike the one in the fable, managed to puff itself up to the size of the ox.

The achievement only becomes comprehensible in the light of per capita income on one hand and the tax structure on the other. *Direct taxation*, which made up the greater part of the tax burden in France, was always both politically and administratively unpopular and difficult to increase. In England *indirect taxation* levied on the very many consumer goods (including mass consumption) made up the largest share of the tax burden (70 per cent between 1750 and 1780). And these indirect taxes were less visible, easier to conceal under prices, and the more productive in that the national market was more integrated than in France, so that most consumption passed through the market. Finally, even if one accepts the G.N.P. figures of £160 million and £68 million, since the French population was three times that of England, England was of course ahead on per capita income: France £6, England £7.31 – a substantial difference, though not perhaps as great as the English caricaturists liked to think when they habitually depicted the Englishman as a massive John Bull and the Frenchman as a starveling. Was it because he had grown accustomed to this image, or simply out of nationalist reaction that Louis Simond,[363] a Frenchman turned American, said how struck he was in London in 1810–12 by the short stature of the Englishmen he passed in the street? In Bristol, the recruits seemed very small to him – only their officers found favour in his eyes.

What then should we conclude? Perhaps France's growth in the eighteenth century has been underestimated: she was beginning to make up for lost time, no doubt with all the disadvantages that normally accompany structural change usually produced by accelerated growth. But we might also conclude that France's massive wealth did not help her to overcome the 'artificial' wealth (as Accarias de Sérionne would have called it) of England. Once more, I am inclined to sing the praises of the *artificial*. If I am not mistaken, England lived under a situation of greater strain than France, for years on end. But it was this strain which shaped the genius of Albion. And we should not forget that circumstances too played a part in this long duel. If reactionary and conservative Europe had not served England and laboured on her behalf, the victory over revolutionary and imperial France might have been put back for years. If the Napoleonic Wars had not distracted France from world trade, England would not have found it so easy to impose her rule on the globe.

5

For and Against Europe: the Rest of the World

LET US NOW TURN AWAY from the quarrelling giants of the European world-economy – Britain, France and their allies, accomplices and rivals – and try to look more closely at the rest of the world, which for the purposes of this chapter will mean:
– the Americas – slowly but surely becoming 'Europeanized';
– Black Africa – which has perhaps been too hastily dismissed as 'primitive';
– the great expanse of eastern Europe, the self-contained world-economy represented by Muscovy (or indeed by modern Russia until the reign of Peter the Great);
– Islam, its splendour now in decline;
– and lastly a world in itself, the Far East.[1]

While we might have preferred to see this 'non-Europe'[2] on its own terms, it cannot properly be understood, even before the eighteenth century, except in terms of the mighty shadow cast over it by western Europe. Already all the world's problems were beginning to be seen in a Eurocentric perspective; and from this standpoint, limited and misleading though it might be, it is quite possible to describe *America* as a near-total success for Europe; *Africa* as a more promising success than it first appeared; the parallel cases of *Russia* and the *Ottoman Empire* – contradictory yet analogous – as areas of slowly-maturing success, gradual but inevitable; and the *Far East* – from the shores of the Red Sea, Abyssinia and South Africa to the East Indies, China and Japan – as a questionable success, more apparent than real: Europe's presence might be visible there in a thousand details, but that is only because we are looking for it – from a misleadingly privileged position what is more. (If the little continent of Europe were to be cut loose to float among the seas and land-masses of Asia, it would vanish from sight. In the eighteenth century, Europe had not yet acquired that overwhelming industrial superiority which would, for a while, eliminate the disparity.)

It was from all over the world, at any rate, that Europe was now drawing a substantial part of her strength and substance. And it was this extra share which enabled Europeans to reach superhuman heights in tackling the tasks encountered on the path to progress. Without this constant assistance, would Europe's industrial revolution – the key to her destiny – have been possible by the end of the eighteenth century? Whatever answer historians may propose for this question, it is one that must be asked.

It might also be asked whether Europe was somehow of a different human and *historical* nature from the rest of the world; and thus whether the confrontation which is the subject of this chapter, stressing contrasts and differences, will or will not help us to form a clearer judgment of Europe – that is of Europe's success. The conclusions do not in fact all tend in the same direction. For the rest of the world, as we shall see, very often went through economic experiences resembling those of Europe. Sometimes the time-lag was very slight – but it was nevertheless there, essentially as a result of Europe's coherence and effectiveness, which may after all have merely been a function of its comparatively small area. If France was, by the standards of the time, at a disadvantage compared to England because of covering a larger area, what is one to say about Asia, or Russia, or the infant Americas, or under-populated Africa, compared to the tiny but super-charged space occupied by western Europe? Europe's advantage can also, as we have seen, be explained by the particular social structures there, which encouraged capitalist accumulation on a larger scale and on a more secure footing than elsewhere – more often than not with the state's blessing. But it is also clear that if these forms of superiority, comparatively slight as they were, had not been translated into domination in every sense of the word, the European advance would not have occurred with such brilliance and rapidity, nor above all would it have produced the same consequences.

The Americas: playing for the highest stakes of all

Were the Americas Europe's 'periphery', its 'outer skin'? Both expressions are an indication of the way in which the New World, after 1492, was gradually drawn – body and soul, past, present and future – into the European sphere of action and thought,[3] the way in which it became integrated to Europe and eventually assumed its fantastic new meaning. Is not America – which Immanuel Wallerstein unhesitatingly includes in the sixteenth-century European world-economy – perhaps the true explanation of Europe's greatness? Did Europe not discover or indeed 'invent'[4] America, and has Europe not always celebrated Columbus's voyage as the greatest event in history 'since the creation'?[5]

Friedrich Lütge and Heinrich Bechtel[6] may well be right to minimize the *immediate* effect of the discovery of the New World, particularly from the standpoint of German history. But once America had made its entry to European life, it gradually altered all the deepest features of the Old World, drawing Europe's action in a new direction. Ignace Meyerson[7] following certain other writers, tells us that the individual is what he does, that he defines and reveals himself by his acts, and that 'being and doing' are one and the same: if so, I would say that America was Europe's 'doing', the achievement by which Europe most truly revealed her own nature. But it was an achievement which took so long to accomplish and to complete that its meaning can only be grasped when it is seen whole, in the fullness of its history.

America's wide open spaces: hostile but promising

If the discovery of America brought Europe little return in the short run, this was because the new continent was only partly apprehended and settled by the white man. Europe had patiently to reconstruct America in her own image before it began to correspond to her wishes. Such a labour of reconstruction was not of course accomplished overnight: in the early days, Europe indeed seemed insignificant and impotent faced with the superhuman task ahead and as yet only imperfectly perceived. In fact Europe took centuries to build a world in her own image across the Atlantic, and then only with immense variations and distortions, and after overcoming a long series of obstacles one after another.

In the first place, there were those of the natural world, that 'bites, smothers, silts, poisons and crushes',[8] and those caused by the inhuman expanse of territory stretching into the distance. 'The Spanish', complained a Frenchman in 1717, 'have [in America] kingdoms larger than the whole of Europe.'[9] They did indeed: but the extent of their dominions hindered their conquests. It had taken the conquistadors a mere thirty years to overcome the fragile Amerindian civilizations; but this victory had brought them 3 million km² at most, and even these were but imperfectly controlled. A hundred and fifty years later, in 1680, when Spanish and European expansion was coming to an end, only about half the New World had been settled – some 7 million km² out of 14 or 15 million.[10] Once the great American Indian civilizations had been subdued, the struggle would thereafter be waged against an empty landscape or against peoples still living in the Stone Age, foundations on which no conquest could be reliably based. The famous expeditions of the *Paulistas* across the wastes of South America in the sixteenth century, in search of gold, precious stones and slaves, were voyages neither of conquest nor of colonization: they left no more trace behind them than a ship does in the sea. And when in mid-sixteenth century, the Spanish arrived in southern Chile, they found nothing but a barren waste. 'Towards Atacama, near the deserted coast, you see a land without men, where there is not a bird, not a beast, nor a tree, nor any vegetation.'[11] Thus spoke Ercilla. The 'frontier', the open space to be conquered by human settlement, was forever on the horizon of American history, whether in eastern Peru or southern Chile, whether looking across the Venezuelan *llanos* or the wastes of Canada, in the Far West of the United States, the rolling plains of Argentina in the nineteenth century, or even in the Brazilian interior north-west of São Paulo in the twentieth century.[12] Distance on this scale meant wearisome travelling and exhausting and

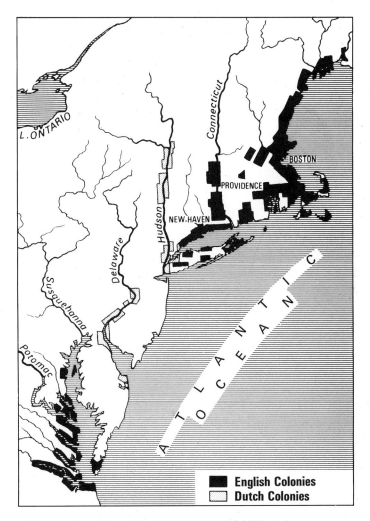

39 THE ENGLISH AND DUTCH IN NORTH AMERICA IN 1660
The small colonial settlements, scattered along the coast, had not yet, by 1660, reached more than a tiny part of the territory to be colonized. The Dutch positions in New Amsterdam and on the Hudson River were handed over to the English at the Treaty of Breda in 1667. (From Rein, *Europäische Ausbreitung*, pl. XVII.)

interminable expeditions on foot. In the interior of New Spain (Mexico), voyagers travelled with a compass or astrolabe at hand, as if on the high seas.[13] Bueno da Silva and his son discovered gold in the far-off Goyaz region of Brazil in 1682; ten years later 'in 1692, the son set off for Goyaz with several companions; they were to take three years to reach the deposits'.[14]

The English colonies, still only sparsely populated, were scattered from Maine to Georgia over 2000 km, 'the same distance as from Paris to Morocco'.

In 1776, 'news of the Declaration of Independence took the same time – 29 days – to travel from Philadelphia to Charleston as it took to reach Paris from Philadelphia'.[15]

Like all natural features, the sheer size of the American continent did, it is true, work in more ways than one: it was both hindrance and opportunity, constraint and freedom. Because land was so plentiful it was cheap, while human labour was scarce. Lacking population, America could only become something if man was shackled to his task: serfdom and slavery, those ancient forms of bondage, appeared once more as if a necessity or a curse imposed by the size of the territory. At the same time, the open country offered a way of escape, a tempting prospect. The Indian who fled from his white masters had unlimited places to hide. Runaway slaves from the workshops, mines or plantations had only to make for the mountains or the impenetrable forests. It is only too easy to imagine the daunting task of the *entradas*, the expeditions sent to pursue them across the dense and trackless Brazilian forests: 'every soldier had to carry on his back weapons, powder and shot, . . . flour, drinking water, meat and fish'.[16] The *quilombo* of Palmares,[17] the republic of runaway slaves which lasted so long, covered a region perhaps the size of Portugal in the hinterland of Bahia.

As for white workers, willing or unwilling immigrants, they were bound by contract to a master who rarely treated them well. But once their term was up, they could go as pioneers to the 'new found lands'. Colonial America offered unlimited paths to 'the ends of the earth', *fines terrae*, awesome in prospect but the equivalent in their way of the 'good earth' which fulfilled the same role in the southern Siberian *taiga*; like the latter, the American frontier was a promised land, since it held out the offer of freedom. This was the major contrast with the Old World in western Europe, already 'full to bursting', where there was no frontier, no virgin lands, where the balance between subsistence and population was restored, if it had to be, only by famine or emigration.[18]

Regional or national markets

Gradually, however, the land was brought under control. Every pioneer settlement, however modest, was another position won; every town that grew was a small but undeniable victory. Every trail blazed (usually thanks to Indian lore and to food provided by the natives) marked progress, the condition of further progress, notably towards improvements in supplying the towns or towards the creation of fairs which sprang up almost everywhere. I refer not only to the internationally recognized fairs at Nombre de Dios, Porto Belo, Panama, Vera Cruz or Jalapa, on the road to Mexico City, but to the local fairs and modest markets which appeared in the middle of nowhere – the fur market at Albany in upstate New York for instance, or the wholesale markets of San Juan de los Lagos and Saltillo, in northern Mexico, which were just beginning to make their fortunes.[19]

The building of Savannah in Georgia. Frontispiece of Benjamin Martyn's book, *Reasons for establishing the colony of Georgia, 1733*. (British Library.)

When towards the end of the seventeenth century, a new breath of life surged through the Americas, the initial structuring of the economic area was almost complete. *Regional* (or even quasi-national) *markets* were taking shape within Spanish America, inside the prematurely-drawn administrative boundaries which at first enclosed half-empty spaces – later to be covered with roads, mule-trains and human settlements: such was the case of the vice-royalty of Peru (whose frontiers were larger than those of present-day Peru); of the *audiencia* of Quito (now Ecuador); or of the *audiencia* of Charcas (now Bolivia). Jean-Pierre Berthe[20] has described how, within the boundaries of the Mexican *audiencia* of New Galicia, drawn up in 1548, a regional market was constituted around the city of Guadalajara and its environs. Marcello Carmagnani's monograph on eighteenth-century Chile[21] is perhaps the best existing study of the formation of a regional or indeed 'national' market, particularly since it is situated within a general theoretical context.

Bringing the land under control was a slow process and at the close of the eighteenth century, there were still – as indeed there are today – unpopulated lands far from any road, territory to spare all over America. This explains why there have always been, and still are, so many wanderers that they have generic names – the *vadios* of Brazil, the *rotos* (ragged ones) of Chile, the *vagos* of Mexico. Mankind has never taken root in any real sense in the expanses of America. In the mid-nineteenth century, the *garimpeiros*, gold- and diamond-hunters wandering in the Brazilian *sertão*, returned to the Atlantic district of the

Ilheos south of Bahia and planted acres of cocoa bushes which can still be seen today.[22] But even farming was not enough to keep people in one spot: they would often move off, masters, men and beasts together, as if the New World had difficulty in creating and maintaining peasant communities attached to the soil like those in Europe. The typical peasant of the Brazilian interior, in the past and even today, the *caboclo*, is almost as mobile as the modern factory worker. The Argentinian *peón*, though not as mobile as the *gaucho* of the past, is still ready to travel.

So man was only partly in control over the country: wild life was still running riot in the eighteenth century – especially in the wide open spaces of North America, the land of the deer and the buffalo, of bison, bears, and animals prized for their fur, as well as of the grey squirrels now familiar in Europe – which migrated *en masse* in extraordinary journeys across rivers and lakes.[23] Cattle and horses from Europe reverted to the wild, where they bred in fantastic numbers, threatening the crops – perhaps the most picturesque form of colonization in the history of early European settlement in the New World. In large areas of New Spain, where the native population had drastically diminished, herds of livestock roamed where once humans had lived.[24]

Patterns of slavery

The everlasting problem in this boundless landscape was consequently a shortage of manpower. For emergent America required a supply of labour that was plentiful, easily controlled, cheap – ideally costing nothing at all – in order to develop the new economy. Eric Williams's pioneering study, *Capitalism and Slavery*,[25] points repeatedly to the causal links between the slavery, near-slavery, serfdom, quasi-serfdom, wage-earning and quasi-wage-earning in the New World, and the rise of capitalism in old Europe. The essence of mercantilism, he concludes, was slavery.[26] Marx had expressed the same thing in another way 'in an inspired sentence of perhaps unrivalled historical density': 'The veiled slavery of the wage-workers in Europe needed, for its pedestal, slavery pure and simple in the New World'.[27]

We are now familiar with the hardships of these American labourers, whatever the colour of their skin: such hardships are not to be laid at the door simply of the planters, the mine-owners, the moneylending merchants of the *Consulado* in Mexico City or elsewhere, the harsh officials of the Spanish Crown, the sugar- and tobacco-dealers, the slave-traders, or the grasping captains of trading vessels. All of these must carry some blame, but they were essentially middlemen, agents for other people. Las Casas accused them of being wholly responsible for the 'infernal servitude' of the Indians and wanted to refuse them the sacraments and expel them from the Church; but not once did he contest the rule of Spain – on the contrary. The king of Castile, *Apostol Mayor*, being responsible for all missionary activity, had the right to be *Imperador sobre muchos reyes*, ruler over all native sovereigns.[28] In reality the root of the evil lay back across the Atlantic, in Madrid, Seville, Cadiz, Lisbon, Bordeaux, Nantes, or Genoa, without question in Bristol, and in later years in Liverpool, London and Amsterdam. It was inherent in the reduction of a whole continent to the status of *periphery*, a result brought about by a distant force, indifferent to human sacrifice, operating by the almost mechanical logic of a world-economy. The word genocide is not too strong to describe what happened to the American Indians or the black people of Africa, but it is worth noting that white men did not survive entirely unscathed and were sometimes lucky to escape at all.

In fact one kind of servitude followed on the heels of another in the New World: the enslavement of the local Indian population led to its collapse; the servitude of white men (French *engagés* and English indentured servants) filled the gap for a while, especially in the West Indies and the English mainland colonies; and black slavery eventually created a community with the strength to put down roots and multiply, against all the odds. Lastly, mention should be made of the waves of immigration from all over Europe in the nineteenth and twentieth centuries, which swelled, as if by coincidence, just as the supply of slaves from Africa was slowing down or about to stop. The commander of a French ship once confided to me in 1935 that there was no more convenient cargo than the emigrants travelling steerage: 'they see themselves on and off the ship'.

Indian servitude could only survive where the population density and co-herence of the pre-existing society were sufficient to create obedience and docility and to guarantee steady supplies of labour. In other words, it was confined to the areas of the former Aztec and Inca Empires. Elsewhere, the indigenous population collapsed on the first impact of the white conquests, whether in Brazil, where the natives fled from the coasts to the interior, or in the United States (the thirteen original colonies): 'In 1790, there were only 300 Indians left in Pennsylvania; 1500 in New York State; 1500 in Massachusetts; 10,000 in the Carolinas'.[29] In the Caribbean, invaded by the Spanish, the Dutch, the French and the English, the original inhabitants were wiped out, either by epidemics brought from Europe or for want of being found employment by the newcomers.[30]

By contrast, in the populated zones which were from the start the target of the Spanish conquest, the Indian population proved easy to regiment. Miracu-lously it survived the hardships of conquest and colonization: the mass murders and pitiless wars, the severing of social ties, the appropriation by force of its 'labour power', the high mortality of the portages and mines, and lastly the epidemics brought from Europe and Africa by both white and black men. Central Mexico, which had once had some 25 million inhabitants, was reduced, it is estimated, to a residual population of one million. The same 'abysmal' demo-graphic collapse occurred in the island of Hispaniola (Haiti), in the Yucatan, in Central America, and later in Colombia.[31] A graphic illustration comes from

This scene probably depicts the mobilization of Indian labourers in front of the *senzalas* (the shanties in which the slaves lived). It is a marginal illustration on the map of the three naval battles in which the Dutch and Spanish united to fight the Portuguese on 13, 14 and 17 January 1640. Map of the Praefectura of Paraiba and Rio Grande, engraved in 1647. B.N., Paris, Map Room, Ge CC 1339, map 133. (Photo B.N.)

Mexico, where in the early days of the conquest the Franciscans were celebrating mass on the steps of the churches, so great was the throng of the faithful; by the end of the sixteenth century, mass was being said inside the same churches, or even in mere chapels.[32] This demographic collapse was quite unprecedented, out of all proportion even to the horrors of the Black Death in fourteenth-century Europe. And yet the native population did not entirely disappear, but began to build up again from mid-seventeenth century, for the greater benefit of its Spanish masters, needless to say. The exploitation of the Indians continued with the semi-serfdom of the *encomiendas*, domestic service in the towns, and compulsory labour in the mines – referred to under the general heading of *repartimiento*, and known in Mexico as *cuatequitl* and in Ecuador, Peru, Bolivia and Colombia as *mita*, forced labour.[33]

In New Spain however, 'free' labour, that is in return for wages, was beginning to appear by the sixteenth century, the result of a crisis of some complexity. In the first place, the sharp decline of the Indian population led to large zones becoming waste lands, as deserted as parts of Europe in the fourteenth and fifteenth centuries after the Black Death. The land farmed by Indian villages shrank to a series of islands and it was in the empty space thus spontaneously vacated or wrongfully confiscated that the large estates, the *haciendas*, were established. The Indian who desired to escape from the collective duties imposed upon him by village society or from the state in its hunt for manpower, could flee to the *haciendas*, where a *de facto* serfdom came into being, and into which later wage-labourers would have to be recruited; or he could flee to the towns, where domestic service or the craft workshops would welcome him; or to the mines, not those nearest Mexico City which still used forced labour, but those further north, in the towns that sprang up in the desert from Guanajuato to San Luis de Potosi. Over 3000 mines, some of them tiny, were scattered over this area, employing a total of ten or eleven thousand workers in the sixteenth century and perhaps 70,000 in the eighteenth; the workers came from all directions, Indians, half-breeds and whites, all mingling together. The introduction in about 1554–6 of the mercury amalgam process[34] made it possible to treat inferior ores, to reduce overheads, and to increase productivity and production.

As in Europe, the mining community was a world apart; masters and men were heavy spenders, poor savers and fond of gambling. The workers received a sort of bonus – the *partido* – according to the quantity of ore they mined. Their wages were very high, by the standards of the time, but the work was terrible (dynamite was not in use before the eighteenth century) and it made for a restless, violent and sometimes cruel community, much given to drinking and feasting. Not only were there 'artificial paradises' on which one historian has wryly commented[35] but a craving for festivity and above all a persistent love of display. In the eighteenth century, such tendencies were aggravated as if prosperity had proved a poor counsellor. If a worker found himself with 300 pesos at the end of the week,[36] they were quickly spent. One man might buy himself fine clothes, cambric shirts. Another might invite 2000 guests to banquet at his expense, and squander the 40,000 pesos he had made by discovering a small mine. So this restless world wagged, in its own peculiar way.

Less dramatic and less lively indeed was the scene in the Peruvian mines, the largest in sixteenth-century America. The amalgam process reached Peru late, in 1572, but did not bring freedom. The forced labour (*mita*) continued and Potosi was still the miner's purgatory. Was the system kept going by its own success? Possibly: not until the end of the century did Potosi lose the lead it never afterwards recovered, despite a spurt of renewed activity in the eighteenth century.

In the end then, the Indian population bore the brunt of the first large-scale development of the New World by Spain: Indians worked in the mines, in agriculture – in particular growing maize, the key to survival in the Americas; they manned the mule- and llama-trains without which neither silver nor anything else could have been carried, officially from Potosi to Arica, or clandestinely from the High Andes, by Cordoba, to the Rio de la Plata (the River Plate).[37]

On the other hand, where there were only scattered tribes of Indians, European colonists had to build with their own hands: in Brazil, before the sugar plantations; in the French or English mainland colonies, or in the West Indies. Until about the 1670s, the French and the English both called very largely on the service of *engagés* (the French term) or indentured servants (the English term). Both *engagés* and servants were virtually slaves.[38] Their lot barely differed from that of the black Africans who were now beginning to arrive; like them, they had been transported across the ocean crammed into the holds of narrow ships and fed on uneatable food. Moreover when they had been brought to America at a company's expense, the company had the right to recoup its losses: the *engagés* were sold, in exactly the same way as slaves, having to suffer being inspected and looked over like cattle by their purchasers.[39] The *engagés* and indentured servants were not of course slaves for life, nor would their descendants be slaves. But this in itself hardly incited their master to treat them well, since he knew he would lose them when their contract was up (36 months in the French West Indies, four to seven years in the English colonies).

In England, as in France, every device was tried to recruit the necessary numbers of emigrants. More than 6000 contracts to serve as *engagés* have been found in the archives at La Rochelle for the period 1635–1715. Half of the recruits came from Saintonge, Poitou and Aunis, provinces whose 'wealth' was illusory. To swell the numbers of emigrants, misleading advertisements were sometimes supplemented by violence. Press gangs would swoop on certain districts of Paris.[40] Men, women and children were kidnapped into emigration in Bristol; or heavy criminal sentences were passed to increase the number of 'volunteers' for the New World who could thus save themselves from the gallows or from the galleys. Large numbers of Scottish and Irish prisoners were transported under Cromwell. Between 1717 and 1779, England dispatched 50,000 deportees[41] to the colonies; the humanitarian evangelist, John Oglethorpe, in 1732 founded the new colony of Georgia to receive the large numbers of transported debtors.[42]

White 'servitude' went on over a long period and on a large scale, as Eric Williams has pointed out, arguing that the different forms of slavery in the Americas followed on each other's heels and in a sense governed each other: as soon as one form ended, another took its place. The sequence was not absolutely automatic, but the general rule is clear enough. White slavery was called upon only when there were not enough Indians; and black slavery, the massive importation of black Africans into the New World, did not develop until the supply of both Indian labour and the white manpower imported from Europe dried up. In areas where black slaves were not employed – in the grain belt north of New York for instance – white indentured servants were still to be found until the eighteenth century. The demands of colonialism thus governed a series of changes, for economic rather than racial reasons: they had nothing 'to do with the colour of the labourer'.[43] White 'slaves' gradually disappeared because they had the drawback of being on fixed contracts – and they may have cost more to keep too, in terms of diet.

Once the *engagés* and indentured servants were released from their contracts, they might clear and farm small-holdings devoted to tobacco, indigo, coffee or cotton. But subsequently, they often lost out to the big plantations developed for the all-conquering sugar industry, a costly and therefore capitalist enterprise which required a large labour force and expensive plant, in other words fixed capital. And under the heading of fixed capital came black slaves. The big sugar plantations drove out the small-holdings which, ironically, had helped them to start up: on land which had been cleared and cultivated by the small farmer, it was easier to establish plantations. Exactly the same process could be seen at work in the 1930s in the pioneer districts of São Paulo state in Brazil, where temporary small farms were preparing the way for the huge coffee-growing *fazendas* which would eventually take over.

During the sixteenth and seventeenth centuries, as larger farms (proportionally) appeared, the numbers of black slaves essential to such enterprises increased. After the dramatic drop in the Indian population, the economic process which drew African populations to America began to operate of its own accord: 'money, not passions, passions of wickedness and goodness, spun the plot'.[44] Stronger than the Indian (it was said that one black slave could do the work of four Indians), more docile and dependent since he was cut off from his community of origin, the black slave was bought and sold as merchandise, or even ordered in advance. The slave-trade made it possible to set up sugar plantations gigantic for the time – going to the very limits of distance in view of the problem of carting the cane, which had to be taken to the mill for processing as soon as it was cut, or it would rot.[45] On these huge plantations, the work was essentially regular, repetitive and unskilled, with only a handful of jobs for technicians or skilled workers.

The docility, permanence and physical strength of the black work-force made it the cheapest, most efficient and before long the most sought-after labour. If in Virginia and Maryland tobacco-growing, originally practised by white smallholders, expanded rapidly between 1663 and 1699[46] – when exports increased sixfold – it was because black labour was replacing white. At the same time, and it comes as no surprise, a semi-feudal aristocracy was becoming established – cultured, sophisticated but also oppressive. Once tobacco was grown on a large scale for export, like wheat in Sicily or Poland, or sugar in the Brazilian Nordeste and the West Indies, it created a similar social order as the same causes produced similar results.

But black slaves were used for many other tasks. Gold extraction in Brazil, which began in the last years of the seventeenth century, was the result of the massive incorporation into the *Minas Geraes*, the Goyaz and the *sertão* of Bahia, of thousands of black slaves. And if black slaves were not on the whole sent to

An engraving illustrating J.-B. Debret's *Voyage pittoresque et historique au Bresil* (1834). The author provides a commentary on pp. 78–9: this slave dealer's shop in Val Longo street in Rio de Janeiro was a 'veritable warehouse' where black slaves arriving from the African coast were brought by their owners. The dealer, sitting in the armchair, is discussing the purchase of a child with a *Mineiro* (owner of the Geraes Mines). The attic behind bars at the back of the room served as a dormitory for the slaves who climbed a ladder to reach it. There were no windows apart from a few loopholes. 'This', writes Debret 'is the Bazaar in which men are bought and sold.' (Photo B.N., Paris.)

the silver mines of the Andes or northern New Spain, it was for the good reason that after the long journey to the interior they cost more than on the Atlantic coast – and not only, as is sometimes claimed, because the cold in the mountains (real enough) made it impossible for them to perform the hard labour required in the mines.

The different kinds of slave-labour in America were in fact more interchangeable than has been thought. Indians could be used as gold-panners, as happened near Quito. And we can dismiss as nonsense the idea that white men could not live as manual labourers in the tropics (as Adam Smith among many others believed).[47] The *engagés* and servants certainly worked with their hands in the seventeenth century. German settlers established themselves a hundred years ago in Seafort, Jamaica and are living and working there still. The Panama canal was dug by Italian navvies. And cane-cutting in the tropical part of northern Australia is done entirely by white labourers. Similarly in the southern United States, white manual labour has taken over to a large extent as black people have moved north to the cold climate of the big cities, Chicago, Detroit or New York, without any particular detriment to their health. So if climate (although it certainly should not be ignored) is not the only explanation of the distribution and settlement of populations in the New World, then clearly we must turn for further enlightenment to history: not only to the complex history of European exploitation, but also to the powerful past of the pre-Columbian civilizations, the Aztecs and the Incas, which left on American soil indelible traces of Indian culture. In the end, history allowed an Indian America, an African America and a white America to survive to the present day: they may have intermingled but not to any great extent, since they can still be unmistakably distinguished from one another.

When the colonies worked for Europe

How many times has it been said that America had to recreate Europe across the sea? This is true only in part, but sufficiently so for one not to take literally Alberto Flores Galindo's view[48] that no European interpretation of any American phenomenon can be entertained. By and large, America was obliged to travel, as best she could and on her own account, through the long stages of Europe's history – without necessarily respecting either the same order or the original models, it is true. The experiences of Europe – Antiquity, the Middle Ages, the Renaissance, the Reformation[49] – can be detected in America, although not clearly distinguished. I still have a very strong visual recollection of the pioneer zones of twentieth-century America, which provide a clearer picture than any learned disquisition could give of what it must have been like when the forests were cleared in thirteenth-century Europe. Similarly, certain features of the earliest European towns in the New World, with their patriarchal dynasties, conjure up for the historian a vision of classical antiquity – part true, part false perhaps, but unforgettable. And I admit to being fascinated by the history of these American towns which sprang up even *before* the countryside was settled, or at much the same time. They make it possible to imagine in a new light that crucial burst of urban growth in eleventh- and twelfth-century Europe – which most medievalists have persisted (rather oddly to my mind) in regarding as the slowly-maturing fruit of agricultural (rather than commercial or urban) advance.

How sensible is it to see such things as mere echoes, when in fact Europe was firmly controlling overseas development and making all the rules? Since every colonial power was determined to hold on to its own share of America without yielding an inch (forcing upon it the 'colonial pact' or the *exclusif*) transatlantic societies would have found it very difficult to detach themselves from the remote control and ever-present model of Europe – a mother which kept her offspring firmly attached to her apron strings and had moments of distraction only in the early days, during the dark hours of the first modest settlements. England and Spain allowed their original American colonies to develop more or less under their own steam. Then when their progeny had grown and prospered, they were taken in hand and brought under metropolitan control: the institutions of the mother country were both the instruments and beneficiaries of 'centralizing' policies.

Such centralization was both natural and the more willingly accepted since it was indispensable if the infant colonies were to be defended against attack from other European colonial powers. For rivalry remained keen among those who had shared out the New World and endless conflicts were waged along the landward frontiers as well as along the interminable American coastline.

A further reason for the ready acceptance of centralization was that it maintained the rule of the white minority within the colony, a minority still attached to the beliefs, thought, language and way of life of what was already regarded as the 'Old World' back in Europe. Although small in numbers, the landed aristocracy which settled the central valley of Chile in the eighteenth century was effective, active and dominant – 'the 200 or so families'[50] of the country. The plutocracy of Potosi in 1692 consisted of a mere handful of persons 'dressed in cloth of gold and silver, for no other costume would be good enough for them'.[51] Their households were unbelievably luxurious. How many wealthy merchants were there in Boston on the eve of the American Revolution, in 1774? What enabled such tiny communities to survive was probably the passivity of the workers in the first place, but they also depended on the complicity of an all-embracing social order which it was in Europe's interests to maintain at all costs.

It is true that these societies might vary in their degree of docility or of dependence on the mother country. But disobedience – when it occurred – did nothing to alter their way of life or the internal ordering and functioning of the colony, itself inseparable from the order and functioning which have formed the backbone of all European societies, past and present. The least subservient and the least easy to control of these societies were those outside the major intercontinental trade routes, those whose 'mediocre economy … was not governed by one dominant product',[52] by some monoculture controlled from the other side of the Atlantic.[53] These neglected societies and economies, receiving little investment and few orders, remaining poor and comparatively undisturbed, were pushed towards self-sufficiency. Such for example were the pastoral regions of Peru on the slopes of the Andes, above the Amazon rain-forests; the Venezuelan *llanos*, where the *encomenderos* did not allow themselves to be dictated to by the authoritarian government in Caracas; or the valley of the São Francisco, the 'sheep-river' in the Brazilian interior, home of half-wild flocks, where the feudal landowner Garcia de Rezende was said to possess an area as big as France under

Louis XIV (but virtually uninhabited). The same would have been true of any remote town so isolated in the great open spaces of America that it was virtually obliged – even if it had no urge for independence – to govern itself. In the late seventeenth century and even in the eighteenth, São Paulo, the old capital of the first *bandeirantes*,[54] was still an example of such involuntary independence. 'The Portuguese', wrote Accarias de Sérionne in 1766, 'have few settlements in the Brazilian interior; the city of São Paulo is the one they regard as the most important ... This city is more than a twelve-hour journey inland.'[55] 'It is a sort of Republic', wrote Coreal, 'originally composed of all kinds of godless and lawless men.'[56] The *Paulistas* considered themselves to be a free race: an apter description of the town would have been a hornet's nest: its inhabitants scoured the roads of the interior and if they took supplies to the mining camps, they also raided the Indian villages of the Jesuit foundations along the Paraña, even venturing into Peru and Amazonia (1659).[57]

Nevertheless, there were docile and obedient economies in plenty. How could tobacco-growing Virginia or sugar-growing Jamaica have rebelled, when they depended on sales to the English market and on credit from London banks? Before the American colonies could gain their independence, a number of conditions not easily united had to be fulfilled. What was more, the right moment had to be chosen, as would be demonstrated by the first great anti-European revolution, that of England's American colonies in 1774.

Rebel colonies also needed sufficient strength of their own to enable the colonial order to be maintained and developed without the assistance of the mother-country. And this order was under constant threat. The planters of Jamaica lived in terror of a slave uprising; the Brazilian interior had its 'republics' of runaway slaves; Indian 'bravos'[58] threatened the vital communications of the isthmus of Panama; in southern Chile, the Araucanians were a threat until far into the nineteenth century; in Louisiana, an Indian rising in 1709 required the dispatch of a small French expeditionary force.[59]

When the colonies worked against Europe

But could the 'colonial pact' be maintained in circumstances of the most glaring inequality? The colonies only existed to serve the wealth, prestige and strength of their mother-countries. Their trade and indeed their entire life was under constant surveillance. Thomas Jefferson, the future President of the United States, baldly described the plantations of Virginia as 'a species of property annexed to certain mercantile houses in London'.[60] Another grievance was the near-critical shortage of currency: England was constantly besieged with complaints on this score from her American colonies. No steps were taken to remedy the situation: the mother-country intended to maintain a positive trade balance with the colonies and therefore to extract currency from them, not to dispatch it to them.[61] So however boundless the patience of these subordinate countries, such a regime might not have lasted long if all the rules and regulations had been scrupulously observed; if distance – to mention only the long sea voyage across the Atlantic – had not created a measure of freedom; and if smuggling – ubiquitous and unstoppable – had not appeared to oil the wheels of commerce.

The result was a certain *laissez-aller*, a relaxation of discipline, so that certain habits and expedients crept in, at first unobtrusively, which it was afterwards difficult to forbid. Thus there were no effective customs posts; and the colonial administration saw itself as being there not to carry out to the letter instructions from home, but to accommodate local and private interests. Moreover, the expansion of trade helped the American economies to acquire their own sources of currency, to see to it that some of the bullion from the American mines, whether by fraud or simply by market forces, remained behind instead of sailing to Europe. 'Before 1785, it was normal to find the Church in Mexico contracting with the peasants to receive tithes in silver'[62] – a significant detail. And credit, a sign of advanced development, had a role to play even in the distant Brazilian interior. It is true that there the presence of gold made all the difference: the *Conselho* of Vila Rica wrote to the king on 7 May 1751 that many miners 'clearly still owe the money for the slaves they own, so that the man who looks rich from outside is really poor, while many who live poorly are actually rich'.[63] The owner of a gold-panning concession would be operating thanks to advance payments made to him by merchants, funds which he would have used in particular to buy slaves. The same development appeared in the silver-mining countries. From D.A. Brading's fascinating book on eighteenth-century New Spain, seen largely from the vantage-point of Guanajuato, the biggest mining town of the time in America or indeed the world, one has the impression that credit could take any of a multitude of forms, combining or mingling them, destroying one combination and inventing another, *ad infinitum*.

The clear lesson of all this is that a by no means negligible accumulation of capital on the part of local merchants was taking place. In Spanish America, there were even such rich Creole merchants that it was said at the end of the eighteenth century that Spain was 'the colony of its colonies'. Was this merely a figure of speech or does it betray Spanish resentment against people who did not know their place? At any rate, during every independence crisis, one finds plenty of evidence of bitter conflicts and animosity between the merchants settled in the New World and the capitalists back home. Such was the case in Boston, in Buenos Aires where local merchants wanted to break off dealings with the wholesalers in Cadiz, and in the Brazilian towns where hostility to Portuguese merchants turned to hatred. In Rio de Janeiro, where murder and theft were commonplace, the Portuguese merchant with rings on his fingers, ostentatiously dining off silver plate, was a hated figure: any stick was good enough to beat him with – failing all else savage ridicule, depicting him as a clumsy and odious figure of fun, perhaps a cuckolded husband. A fascinating study in social psychology could be made of those who were known throughout Spanish America as the *chapetones* or *gachupines* – the recent arrivals from Spain, inexperienced, presumptuous and very often with a fortune secured in advance. They arrived to reinforce the small groups already on the spot who had succeeded in capturing the key places in commerce. The whole of Mexico for instance was under the thumb of merchants originally from the Basque provinces or from the mountains behind Santander. These merchant dynasties brought out from Spain nephews, cousins or neighbours from their home villages, and recruited assistants, successors and sons-in-law. The newcomers romped home in the 'marriage stakes'. In 1810, Father Miguel Hidalgo y Costilla, the Mexican revolutionary priest who, like many other people, would have liked to put an end to this *gachupina* immigration, accused them of being 'unnatural men ... The force behind all their toil is sordid avarice ... They are Catholics through policy, their true God is money', *Su Dios es el dinero*.[64]

The conflict over industry

In industry as in commerce, the conflict between colonies and mother country had roots reaching far back. As early as the end of the sixteenth century, a long crisis hit Latin America and probably the whole of the continent.[65] European capitalism was going through a difficult patch to say the least; so during the seventeenth century, the 'American end' had to find its own salvation. The emergent regional markets extended their trade links: the Brazilians moved steadily out towards the Andes; Chile supplied grain to Peru; ships from Boston brought flour, timber and Newfoundland cod to the Caribbean, and so on. Local industries sprang up. In Quito in 1692, there were 'manufactories of serge and canvas ... coarse fabrics ... which serve to clothe the people. These are sold in Peru and Chile, and even in the Tierra Firme and Panama, by way of Guayaquil which is Quito's port [on the Pacific]. And they are also transported overland to Popayan'.[66] Similar expansion in textile production occurred in New Granada at Socorro,[67] in the Peruvian province of Cuzco, in the Indian provinces of southern Mexico at La Puebla;[68] and in the interior of what would later be Argentina, notably in Mendoza where, reports Bishop Lizarraga, 'the Indians who have been brought up among us make a thread as fine as the finest Biscay thread'.[69] Many other transformation industries of agricultural or animal products developed: soap and tallow candles were manufactured everywhere, and everywhere too leather was processed.[70]

Having been established it seems during the difficult years of the seventeenth century, at a time when much of America was being 'feudalized' as the great *haciendas* appeared, would this elementary industry lead to greater things when the economic climate improved? For this to occur, Europe would have had to surrender its monopoly on manufacture – and this was very far from what Europe had in mind. Lord Chatham is supposed to have said: 'If America so much as considers making a stocking or a horseshoe nail, she shall feel the full

An embroidery workshop in Peru. The workers are women of mixed race. Madrid, Palacio Real, Libro Trujillo del Peru. (Photo Mas.)

weight of British might'.[71] Such a remark, if it really was made, reveals something of Britain's intentions, but also of her ignorance of realities across the Atlantic: the New World was quite prepared to manufacture the things it needed.

In short, the whole of America, as it matured, developed its own reciprocal arrangements and devised its own expedients. Spanish America in particular found in the smuggling networks a measure of freedom and a source of profit. The Manila galleon, as everyone knew, was a means of snatching American silver out of the clutches of Spain or indeed Europe, for the benefit of far-off China and the capitalists of the *Consulado* in Mexico City. What was more, up to the end of the eighteenth century, by far the lion's share of the silver coins and ingots was going not to the king of Spain (now no more than a poor relation) but to private merchants – including the merchants of the New World.

The English colonies choose liberty

The general unrest in the New World first surfaced in the English colonies in America. 'Insurrection' is perhaps too strong a word for the Boston Tea Party when, on 16 December 1774, a number of rebels disguised as Indians boarded three ships owned by the India Company standing at anchor in Boston harbour, and threw their cargo of tea into the sea. But this minor incident marked the beginning of the break between the colonies – the future United States – and England.

The conflict undoubtedly had its origins in the economic progress of the eighteenth century which brought increased prosperity to the English colonies along with the rest of America – possibly more so since they were in the thick of internal and external trade.

The earliest sign of such prosperity was the constant stream of immigrants – English workmen, Irish peasants, Scots – many of the latter in fact from Ulster and having taken ship in Belfast. In the five years preceding 1774, 152 ships left Irish ports carrying '44,000 passengers'.[72] And there was a wave of German colonists too: between 1720 and 1730, they virtually 'Germanized ... Pennsylvania'[73] where the Quakers were soon in a minority compared to Germans and Irish Catholics. German immigration increased even more after independence, since many German mercenaries in the British Army decided to settle in America.

This immigration amounted to 'a trade in human beings'.[74] In 1781, 'one major dealer boasted of having himself, before the war, imported 40,000 Europeans: "Palatines", Swabians, some Alsatians. They emigrated through Holland'.[75] But it was above all the Irish who were the object of a traffic akin in all but name to the slave trade, and which did not cease with independence, indeed the contrary.

> The import trade [sic] from Ireland [explains a report in 1783], which was suspended during the war, has been resumed with large profits for those engaged in it. [One boat has landed] 350 men, women and children, no sooner arrived than immediately hired. [The procedure is a simple one]: a [ship's] captain puts his conditions to the emigrants in Dublin or some other Irish port. Those who can pay for their passage – usually about 100 or 80 [*livres tournois*] – arrive in America free to take any engagement that suits them. Those who cannot pay are carried at the expense of the shipowner, who in order to recoup his money, advertises on arrival that he has imported artisans, labourers and domestic servants and that he has agreed with them on his own[76] account to hire their services for a period normally of 3, 4 or 5 years for men and women and 6 or 7 years for children. The most recently imported have been hired for the sum of 150 or 300,[77] delivered over to the captain, depending on sex, age

and strength. Their masters have only to feed, clothe and lodge them. When their service is up, they are given a suit of clothes, and a shovel and they are absolutely free. Fifteen or sixteen thousand are expected for the next winter, mostly Irish. The Dublin magistrates have great difficulty preventing emigration. And the entrepreneurs are beginning to look to Germany.[78]

As a result, there became established a form of migration 'running from the [Atlantic] coasts to the mountains and even further westwards ... A single dwelling serves for all until one has been built for each [family]'. The newcomers, as soon as they had made some money, 'come to Philadelphia to pay the price of the land' assigned them, which was usually offered for sale by the government of the colony (later the state government). The colonists 'very often ... resell these plots and go elsewhere in search of uncultivated land which they again sell once they have worked it. Many labourers have thus cleared up to six different sites'.[79] This document from the end of the eighteenth century provides a good picture of what had already become the well-established phenomenon of the 'frontier', attracting immigrants eager to make their fortunes once they had served out their contracts. The Scots in particular ventured into the great forests and lived in the Indian style, moving all the time from one clearing to another. Behind them, less adventurous immigrants, often Germans, stayed to farm the reclaimed land.[80]

This human tide, flowing towards the lands and forests of the West, both accompanied and stimulated a general economic advance. Observers felt they were watching a biological explosion: the Americans, they said 'have as many children as they can. Widows with a large family are sure to remarry'.[81] The high birth rate swelled the population figures as a whole. At this rate, even the regions north of Philadelphia gradually ceased to be inhabited by settlers of exclusively English stock. And since the Scots, Irish, Germans or Dutch felt only indifference or hostility to England, this ethnic mixture, beginning early and increasing quickly, no doubt hastened the break with the mother country. In October 1810, the newly-arrived French consul in New York tried, as he had been instructed by Paris,[82] to define 'the present state of mind of the inhabitants of the State and their real feelings towards France'. His reply is interesting:

It is not by the populous city where I live [New York at the time had 80,000 inhabitants] that one should judge: its inhabitants, who are for the most part foreigners and made up of every nation except Americans so to speak, have in general no mind for anything but business. New York might be described as a permanent fair in which two-thirds of the population is always being replaced; where huge business deals are being made, almost always with fictitious capital, and where luxury has reached alarming heights. So trade rarely has a sound foundation: the frequent bankruptcies – often of men of great fortune – cause little stir; what is more, a bankrupt rarely meets anything but the greatest indulgence from his creditors, as if each man hoped to acquire a right to reciprocal tolerance. It is in the countryside and in the inland towns that one must look for the American population of New York State.

As for the human transformations brought about by the 'melting-pot', were these not felt by the entire 'American' population (still quite small at this time – 3 million in about 1774) to be foreign intrusions, as massive in comparative terms as those of the late nineteenth century?

All the same, this phenomenon was more marked in the northern colonies (New England, Massachusetts, Connecticut, Rhode Island, New Hampshire, New York, New Jersey, Delaware and Pennsylvania) than in the southern colonies (Virginia, Maryland, North and South Carolina and Georgia) which were the scene of a completely different society of plantation owners and black slaves. Even today, if one visits Jefferson's magnificent mansion at Monticello, deep in Virginia, one can see parallels between this and the *Casas Grandes* of Brazil or the Great Houses of Jamaica, with the difference that most of the slaves' quarters are here in the basement of the huge building which seems to press down on them with all its weight. Much of what Gilberto Freyre has written about the plantations and the towns of the Brazilian Nordeste could be applied to the American Deep South. But despite their similarities of situation, these two experiences remain distinct in human terms. They are separated by everything that divides Portugal from England – differences of culture, mentality, religion, sexual habits. The amours between the lords of the *engenhos* and their slaves were conducted openly, as Gilberto Freyre reports, whereas Jefferson's long-standing passion for one of his young slave-girls was a closely-guarded secret.[83]

This distinction between North and South was a strongly marked structural feature which would influence the history of the future United States from the start. In 1781, an observer wrote of New Hampshire: 'One does not see here as one does in the southern states, the owner of 1000 slaves and eight or ten thousand acres lording it over his more modest neighbour'.[84] A year later, another writer wrote in the same vein: 'In the South, there is greater wealth of a smaller number; in the North there is more public prosperity and individual happiness, a happy mediocrity, a larger population'.[85] This is perhaps simplifying the picture unduly, and Franklin Jameson has introduced some nuances to it.[86] Even in New England, although they were extremely rare since the aristocracy was mainly city-dwelling, some large estates did exist. In New York State, 'manors' covered a total of 2½ million acres and the Van Rensselaer manor for instance, about a hundred miles from the Hudson River, measured 24 miles by 28, that is two-thirds the size of the entire colony of Rhode Island (which was admittedly very small). The big estates were even bigger in the southern colonies, even in Pennsylvania and more so in Maryland and Virginia, where the Fairfaxes owned a property of 6 million acres. In North Carolina, Lord Granville's estate alone was the equivalent of one-third the area of the colony. It is clear that the southern states, but also some of the northern ones lent themselves to an aristocratic regime, sometimes concealed, sometimes undisguised, amounting to a 'transplant' of the social system from the old country, of which primogeniture

Boston in 1801. View of State Street and Old State House: brick-built houses, carriages in the street, European fashions. Painting by James B. Marston, Massachusetts Historical Society, Boston. (Photo I.P.S.)

was the corner-stone. At the same time, since small properties found corners for themselves in between the big estates, either in the North where the relief made the land unsuitable for large-scale agriculture, or in the West where virgin forest had to be cleared to make way for the plough, the unequal division of the land, in an economy overwhelmingly dominated by agriculture, did not prevent the establishment of a fairly stable social balance, from which the privileged benefited most – that is until the revolution, which destroyed many landed families who took England's side, and which was followed by a wave of expropriations, sales and developments, conducted 'in a quiet, sober Anglo-Saxon way'.[87]

So the agrarian regime was more complicated than a simple North–South contrast might suggest. Of the 500,000 black slaves in the thirteen colonies, 200,000 were in Virginia, 100,000 in South Carolina, 70 or 80 thousand in Maryland, about the same in North Carolina, perhaps 25,000 in New York State, 10,000 in New Jersey, 6000 in Connecticut, 6000 in Pennsylvania, 4000 in Rhode Island, 5000 in Massachusetts.[88] In Boston in 1770, there were 'over 500 carriages and it was a sign of magnificence to have a Negro coachman'.[89] Curiously, it was in the state with most slaves – Virginia – that the aristocracy was most favourable to the Whigs, that is to the revolution, whose success it probably ensured.

It seems that the contradiction between demanding freedom for white settlers from English rule and continuing to acquiesce in black slavery did not yet unduly trouble anyone. In 1763, an English parson preaching to a congregation in Virginia assured his listeners that he did them 'no more than justice in bearing witness, that in no part of the world were slaves ever better treated than, in general, they are in the colonies'.[90] One need not regard this as gospel truth. In any case, the real situation of the slaves, even in the southern plantations, could vary greatly from one place to another and it may well be that, being better integrated into the Spanish or Portuguese American settlements, black slaves were actually happier there, or less unhappy, at any rate in some regions.[91]

Competition and rivalry in trade

The thirteen colonies taken together formed an essentially agricultural unit: in 1789, 'the number of workers employed in agriculture is at least nine out of ten in the United States as a whole and the value of the capital invested in agriculture several times as great as that in all the other branches of industry put together'.[92] But despite the prime importance of land, of pioneering and of crop cultivation, the colonies were in fact driven to rebellion primarily by the growing maritime and mercantile activity of the northern regions, especially New England. While commerce was not the dominant economic activity, it was nonetheless the determining one. Adam Smith (who understood the American colonies he had never seen in his life better than the industrial revolution taking place under his nose at home) perhaps came nearest to the essential causes of the American rebellion, the events and repercussions of which he followed closely: *The Wealth of Nations* was published in 1776, two years after the Boston Tea Party. Adam Smith's interpretation is contained in one little sentence. Duly praising the British government as being so much more generous towards its colonies than other European powers, he points out that 'the liberty of the English colonists to manage their own affairs their own way is complete' – but he is obliged to add a qualification: 'in everything except their foreign trade'.[93] Quite an exception – and one which caused both direct and indirect damage to the whole economy of the colonies, forcing them to go through London for everything, to depend on London credit and above all to stay inside the trading straitjacket of the British 'Empire'. But New England, with its key ports, Plymouth and Boston, which had quickly sensed the possibilities offered by trade, could only consent to such restriction grudgingly, or by cheating and evading the controls. 'American' trade was far too lively and too spontaneous not to seize the freedom it was not granted; but such expedients could never be more than half-satisfactory.

New England had been rebuilt[94] between 1620 and 1640 by Puritans expelled from Stuart England whose ambition was to found a closed society, free from the sins, injustices and inequalities of this world. But the land was poor and the sea offered its services: a small trading community became established there almost from the start – perhaps because the northern English colonies were closest to and most conveniently situated for trade with the old country? Or perhaps because the coast of Acadia, the mouth of the St Lawrence and the banks of Newfoundland were a nearby source of providential food from the sea? The New England settlers 'made most money' from fishing: 'Without delving into the entrails of the earth which they leave to the Spanish and Portuguese, they get [this money] from the fish which they carry to the latter'.[95] Further assets were the sailors who became expert in this hardy enterprise, and the ships which had to be built to carry it out. In New England in 1782, the fishing industry accounted for 600 vessels and 5000 men.

But the New Englanders were not satisfied with this activity on their doorstep. 'They were known [and this in itself is revealing] as the Dutchmen of America. . . . It was said that American ships operated even more economically than those of the Dutch. This quality and the low prices of their goods made them unbeatable freighters.' They had indeed organized to their own advantage coastal shipping between the central and southern colonies and distributed over a wide radius their products: grain, tobacco, rice and indigo. They took it upon themselves to supply the English, French, Dutch and Danish West Indies: they shipped out fish, salt mackerel, cod, whale oil, horses, salt beef, and also timber, barrel-staves, planks, even what we should call pre-fabricated houses, 'readymade, and a carpenter travelled with the load to supervise the construction'.[96] The ships returned carrying sugar, molasses and rum – but also silver coins since they could make contact in the West Indian ports or those of the mainland with the circulation of Spanish American silver. It was no doubt the success of this trade expansion in the south which increased the trading strength of the northern colonies and stimulated the development of their industry: shipbuilding, coarse woollen and cotton textiles, ironmongery, rum distilleries, iron bars, cast iron, pig-iron.

What was more, the merchants and dealers of the northern ports – including New York and Philadelphia – had extended their voyages to the entire North Atlantic, to islands like Madeira, to the African coast, the Barbary Coast, Portugal, Spain, France and of course England. They were even shipping dried fish, grain and flour to the Mediterranean. It is true that this extension of trade on a world scale, creating triangular patterns of traffic, by no means by-passed England. Although American ships were sailing directly to Amsterdam, London was almost always the apex of one of these triangles; it was to London that American trade brought its payments from the various centres in Europe; and from London that it obtained its credit. A considerable share of American profits thus remained there, for the balance between England and her colonies favoured the former. 'By means of purchases and commission', remarked an observer in 1770, before the colonial rebellion, 'all the money of these establishments [the

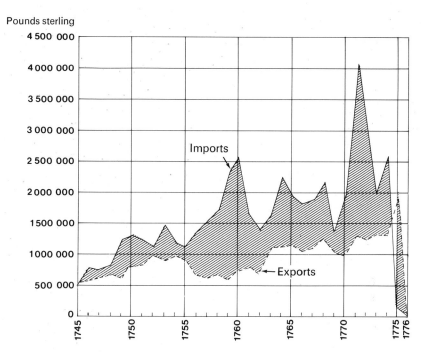

Pounds sterling

40 BRITAIN'S POSITIVE TRADE BALANCE WITH HER AMERICAN COLONIES
Their trade deficit forced the colonies, in order to restore their foreign balance, to engage in
'triangular' trade, with centres in Africa (the slave trade), the West Indies and Europe, including
the Mediterranean. (From H.U. Faulkner, *American Economic History*, 1943, p. 123.)

colonies] goes to England, and all the wealth they have left is in paper [money].'[97]
All the same, America undoubtedly appeared as a rival from the start and her
growing prosperity dented Britain's own prosperity and worried the great merchant houses of London – hence a number of irritating but ineffective measures
of retaliation. As a shrewd witness noted in 1766:

> England now passes pointless laws to hinder and confine the industry of her
> colonists: she palliates the evil but does not remedy it . . . [she] is losing to this
> trade, that of economy and re-export, customs duties, warehousing charges
> and commission and a share of labour in her ports. And in the case of direct
> returns to the colonies, which is today the general habit, is the result not that
> the shippers, especially those of Boston and Philadelphia whose shipping
> numbers over 1500 vessels, are supplying not only their own colonies, but also
> the other English colonies with European merchandise loaded in foreign ports?
> And this cannot be done without causing great prejudice both to England's
> commerce and to her finances.[98]

There were of course other quarrels between the colonies and the Old
Country; and the occupation by the British of French Canada in 1762, sanctioned
the following year by the Treaty of Paris, may have precipitated events by
providing the English colonies with security on their northern frontier. They no

longer required protection. In 1763, both victorious England and defeated France reacted in what (to our eyes at least) is an unexpected fashion. Rather than Canada (which they had captured from the French) or Florida (which Spain ceded to them) the English would have preferred possession of the sugar island of Saint-Domingue (Santo Domingo). But the Jamaican planters disagreed, refusing to share with anyone else the English sugar market, which they had always monopolized. Their protests, combined with France's desire to hang on to Saint-Domingue, queen of the sugar islands, meant that the 'few acres of snow' as Voltaire called Canada, fell to England. But irrefutable evidence survives of England's coveting Saint-Domingue. When war broke out again with France in 1793, the English wasted six years launching costly and profitless expeditions to take the island: 'The secret of England's impotence for the first six years of the war [1793-9] may be said to lie in these two fatal words: St Domingo'.[99]

The ink was no sooner dry on the Treaty of Paris of 1763 at any rate, before tension began to mount between the colonies and England. The Old Country wanted to bring the colonies to heel, to make them bear part of the huge expense of the late war. The colonies went so far in 1765 as to boycott English goods, which was nothing less than *lèse-majesté*.[100] This was sufficiently evident for the Dutch bankers in October 1768 to fear 'that if there is trouble between England and her colonies, the result may be bankruptcies of which this country [Holland] might well suffer the effects'.[101] Accarias de Sérionne was already envisaging the rise of an 'American' Empire in 1766: 'New England is more to be feared than Old England' he wrote, 'as regards the loss of the Spanish Colonies'. And this would be an empire 'independent of Europe',[102] an empire, as he wrote a few years later, in 1771, which 'would in the very near future be threatening the prosperity above all of England, Spain, France, Portugal and Holland'.[103] In other words, the first signs were beginning to appear of the United States' subsequent domination of the European world-economy. And this, surprisingly enough, is what the French plenipotentiary in Georgetown explicitly states, thirty years later it is true, in a letter of 27 Brumaire, Year X (18 October 1801):

> I think that England now finds herself in relation to the United States in a position altogether similar to the situation which brought the great power [i.e. England] face to face with Holland at the end of the seventeenth century, when the latter, worn out with expenses and debts, saw her commercial influence pass into the hands of a rival which was taking its first steps so to speak in commerce.[104]

The exploitation of America by Spain and Portugal

In the other America, Latin America, we shall find quite different realities and a very different history. Not that there are no similarities at all, but what happened in the North was certainly not repeated mirror-fashion in the South. Northern and southern Europe reproduced their own contrasts and differences across the Atlantic. There were also considerable time-lags: the English colonies became independent in 1783, the Latin American colonies not earlier than 1822 and 1824 – and even then the liberation of Latin America was no more than a fiction since colonial rule was replaced by English domination lasting more or less until 1940; after which the United States moved in. In short the North was characterized by strength, activity, independence and individual initiative; the South by inertia, servitude, the heavy hand of the colonial powers, and all the constraints inherent to the condition of any 'periphery'.

Such divergence was obviously the result of different structures, of different experiences and inheritances. The situation is clear enough, but it cannot be adequately expressed in terms of the convenient distinction textbooks used to make between 'settler colonies' and 'exploited colonies'. How could there be settler colonies where there was not also exploitation, or 'exploited' colonies where there were not also settlers? More appropriate perhaps than exploitation would be the term *marginalization*: the condition, within a world-economy, of being condemned to serve others, of being told what to do by the all-commanding international division of labour. For this was indeed the allotted role of Latin America (unlike North America) – both before and after the gaining of political independence.

Spanish America reconsidered

Spanish America gained its independence belatedly and very slowly. The process of liberation began in Buenos Aires in 1810, and since dependence on Spain would only be replaced by a new dependence, on English capital, the end of Spain's rule only became visible in 1824–5,[105] the years which mark the beginning of massive investment in South America by the City of London. (Brazil attained independence without too much upheaval: on 7 September 1822, Pedro I proclaimed the country's independence from Portugal, at Ypiranga near São Paulo, and in December of the same year he took the title of emperor of Brazil. The separation – John VI, the new emperor's father was still ruling in Lisbon – was an extremely complex process in detail, connected with spheres of influence in both European and American politics.[106] But we shall do no more here than record its peaceful outcome.)

In Spanish America on the other hand, independence was a long-drawn-out drama. We shall be less concerned with this for the moment though, than with the history leading up to a break which had international repercussions more

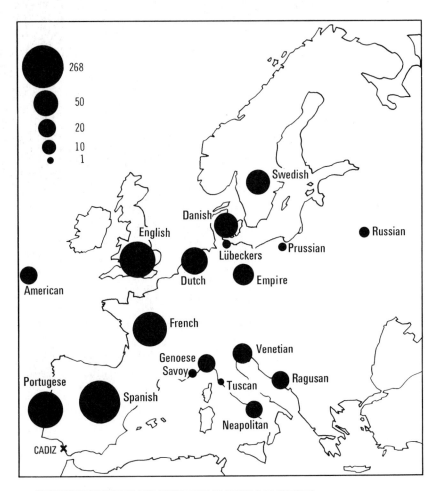

268

50

20

10

1

Swedish

Danish

English

Russian

Lübeckers

Prussian

American

Dutch

Empire

French

Venetian

Genoese

Savoy

Ragusan

Portugese

Tuscan

Spanish

Neapolitan

CADIZ **✗**

41 EUROPE HASTENS TO EXPLOIT SPANISH AMERICA
The number and origin of the ships entering the bay of Cadiz in 1784. (Data from
Archives Nationales, Paris, A.E., BIII, 349.)

important than those of Brazil's separation from Portugal. From the start,
Spanish America had inevitably been a decisive element in world history, whereas
Brazil, once it had ceased to be a major gold producer in the nineteenth century,
mattered much less to Europe.

Even in the early days, Spain had been incapable of exploiting unaided the
'colossal'[107] market of the New World. Even when marshalling all her strength
and all her men, all the oil and wine of Andalusia and the cloth from her
industrial towns, Spain, a still-archaic power, had proved unequal to the task. In
any case in the expansionist eighteenth century, no European 'nation' alone
would have been able to meet the demand. As Le Pottier de la Hestroy explained

in 1700, 'consumption in the West Indies of the goods which they must necessarily fetch from Europe, being very considerable, [is far beyond] our powers [i.e. those of France] however many manufactories we set up at home'.[108] As a result, Spain had to appeal to the rest of Europe, particularly since her own industry had begun to decline by the end of the sixteenth century; and Europe hastened to seize the opportunity. Indeed the Spanish colonies were exploited by other European countries more than by Spain, of which Ernst Ludwig Carl said in 1725 that she was 'hardly more than an entrepôt for Foreigners'[109] – perhaps a go-between would be more accurate. The Spanish laws against the 'transportation' of silver, the principal resource of America, were certainly strict and yet 'this coing [i.e. Spanish coin] is to be seen throughout Europe', as Charles II of England remarked in November 1676.[110]

Twenty years earlier, Father Antonio Vieira, a Portuguese Jesuit, had exclaimed in a sermon delivered at Belem in Brazil: 'The Spanish extract the silver from the mines, and transport it, and it is the foreigners who have all the benefit'. Of what use was all this precious metal, he asked; it was never used to relieve the poor, 'only to help swell and inflate even more the men who order these peoples about'.[111]

If the strict Spanish laws were to no avail, it was of course because of smuggling: fraud, corruption, cheating and jiggery-pokery were by no means confined to the trade and economy of America but they were magnified in this huge arena: they had the entire Atlantic Ocean and the southern seas as their sphere of action. Philip II himself refers to some apparently innocent ships which sailed in 1583, 'claiming to carry wines to the Canary Islands, [but which] in reality made for the Indies, very profitably according to report'.[112] An entire ship could be laden in Seville with goods for the West Indies 'without the officers even being aware of it!'[113] And before long the Dutch, French, English and Italians of all origins, especially the Genoese, were illegally loading cargoes aboard the official fleets for the Indies, without difficulty. In 1704, 'the Consulate [of Seville] admitted that Spanish interests accounted for only a sixth of the cargoes of the fleets and galleons',[114] whereas in theory only Spanish nationals were permitted to engage in this trade.[115]

On the other side of the ocean, in the 'Indies of Castile', smuggling was equally indefatigable. In 1692, a Spanish traveller reported that 'the King's Treasure which leaves Lima is worth at least 24 million pieces of eight [a year],[116] but before it can get from Lima to Panama, Porto Belo or Havana ... the Corregidors, the Excisemen, the Customs officers and so on, all possessed of healthy appetites, have each taken a share'.[117] The galleons themselves, which combined the role of warship and merchantman, provided the opportunity for regular fraud by insiders. And smuggling by outsiders increased in the seventeenth and eighteenth centuries. Alongside the existing colonial systems, flexible and effective counter-systems grew up. Such for instance were the voyages of the Saint-Malo sailors along the coasts of the south Atlantic: they had probably already begun before the War of the Spanish Succession, and they continued after it ended in 1713. A Spanish fleet is supposed to have driven them out in 1718,[118] but they were back in 1720,[119] and again in 1722.[120] Another example is the shipping out of the non-Spanish ports in America, along the interminable and poorly-patrolled coastline of the continent. The Dutch practised this trade (known as trading 'at pikestaff's length') out of St Eustace and Curaçao (which had belonged to them since 1632); the English did it from Jamaica; the French from Saint-Domingue and their other possessions in the West Indies. And the daring group of Scots who landed by force and not without trouble on the isthmus of Darien in 1699, were hoping to do the same thing, with the intention, by settling 'on the coast of the mainland itself', to undercut the English and Dutch whose bases were further away.[121] The mariners of North America were equally ready to take part: in the 1780s, their whalers, on the pretext of standing off the coast of Peru, were in fact shamelessly importing contraband goods which local merchants naturally welcomed with open arms, since they could buy them cheap and sell them at the 'official' price which had not dropped.[122]

But for smuggling on the grand scale, there was nothing to beat the contra-band traffic which diverted silver from the Spanish mines of Potosi to the Portuguese colony of Brazil. The favoured route was down the Rio de la Plata after 1580.[123] After the separation of the two Crowns in 1640, the Portuguese persevered in this trade and for a long time held an ideal base in the little enclave of Colonia do Sacramento, in what is now Uruguay (occupied in 1680). The Spanish had to lay siege to it and eventually captured it in 1762.[124]

Needless to say, smuggling could never have prospered without the compl-icity of local merchants and corruption among the customs officials. If it de-veloped on a massive scale, it was, as Accarias de Sérionne said, because 'the immense profit of this commerce enabled it to bear at once the great risks and the costs of corruption'.[125] In the same vein, speaking of the governorships in America which were up for sale in 1685, an anonymous writer declared roundly that 'these are always tacit licences to allow the importing of foreign goods'[126] – a suggestion confirmed by the case, back in 1629-30 in Lima, of the honourable *Oidor de la Audiencia*, appointed as judge for smuggling offences, who was hoarding forbidden goods in his own house and although caught red-handed, nevertheless continued his career as a respectable *oidor*.[127]

Of course, to listen to the apologists of smuggling, it was entirely in the public interest. 'The Spaniards in America', explains a Frenchman in 1699, 'to whom their own galleons bring less than half the goods they require, were pleased that foreigners [in this case usually French] brought the goods instead.'[128] The former used 'every expedient' to further this illicit commerce, with the result that 'over 200 [vessels] are carrying on in the sight of all Europe and of the Spanish themselves a commerce which is forbidden on pain of the strictest penalties'. A French report of 1707 even reveals that 'the cargoes of the [French] ships the *Triomphant*, the *Gaspard* and the *Duc de la Force*, ... had been sold before they set sail, to merchants in Vera Cruz'.[129] It is true that there was at the time some collaboration between Louis XIV's France and a Spain uncertain of her future under Philip V.

Smuggling was ever-present; but the scale varied according to the period. On the basis of some plausible calculations, one has the *impression* at least that it was exceeding in volume the normal (official) trade of Spanish America by 1619, if not earlier – a state of affairs which lasted until the 1760s or so, that is over a hundred years.[130] But this is only a hypothesis, as yet untested. The answer probably lies in the archives of other European countries as well as in the Spanish documents, if someone is prepared to tackle this research.

The Spanish Empire taken in hand again

In the end, the Spanish government did react to these irregularities. Slowly and with difficulty, matters were taken in hand, but towards the last years of the eighteenth century, the restoration of order was pursued energetically and in 'revolutionary fashion'. Let me point out straight away that due attention has not always been paid to the administrative measures taken on this score by the Spanish authorities – the *intendants* were not simply the establishment in America of a French institution, a sort of cultural transfer: they also corresponded to the deliberate intention of the government in Madrid to break the power of the Creole aristocracies who traditionally held the commanding positions in America. Similarly, the suppression of the Society of Jesus in 1767 proved to be the beginning of a 'military' regime, one of force and authority to replace what had been a kind of moral order. For their greater misfortune, those states which later gained their independence inherited this military regime. Here too, a transformation, almost a revolution was taking place. Should credit for this be given to the Bourbon dynasty, which had brought to Spain from France the principles of a centralized monarchy and an arsenal of merchantilist measures? Or was it rather that Spain was already moved by a strong desire for change, a desire which was shortly to sweep through the whole of Europe during the Age of Enlightenment? Claudio Sanchez Albornoz[131] even goes so far as to say that the Bourbon monarchy was not responsible for Spain's transformation – rather the Spanish desire for change opened the door of the kingdom to a French dynasty.

By 1713, the attention of the reformers was naturally turning to the area where Spain had most at stake, her last chance – the New World. Could Spain hold on to what she had created on the other side of the Atlantic? France, whose ships had prowled with ease along the American coasts, had not given up her ambitions either on the borders of the south Atlantic or in the territories of New Spain. In Law's time, after all, the French government had considered using Louisiana as a base from which to venture into nearby Spanish territory. A Spanish writer gloomily prophesied in November 1720: 'We shall have the misfortune of seeing the kingdom of New Spain divided and falling into the hands of the French, if God does not send some remedy'.[132] The threat from England, though less visible, was even more serious, if only because of the double concession made at the Treaty of Utrecht in 1713, of the *asiento* and the licensed voyage: this gave the English South Sea Company the means of combining the advantages of both licit and illicit smuggling.[133]

But all was not yet lost. The government set to work and in 1714 set up on the French model a ministry of the Navy and the Indies; in the same year a Honduras Company was also created; in 1728 a Caracas Company, destined to thrive; in 1740 a Havana Company;[134] in 1717-18, the *Casa de la contratación*, the mechanism for the Seville monopoly, was transferred to Cadiz, along with the *Consejo de Indias*: in other words Cadiz, for so long Seville's rival, at last became the single port for the Indies traffic. It is true that these chartered companies were not a success; in 1756, their monopolies had to be rescinded.[135] Even so, this failure probably did help free trade to develop outside the 'cumbersome system of fleets',[136] which proved unequal to the task of *regularly* servicing the economies of the New World. The 1735 reform which established the voyages of registered shipping[137] was not immediately effective, since the *registros* found it hard to rid themselves of the habit of sailing in convoy. But 'in about 1764 ... communications between Spain and the New World began to operate on a regular footing'.[138] Monthly packets sailed between Cadiz, Havana and Puerto Rico, and at two-monthly intervals to the Rio de la Plata. Finally the decree of 12 October 1778 declared trade free between America and 13 (later 14) Spanish ports.[139] Trade between Spain and the New World took a substantial upturn and inevitably Spain's hold over her possessions abroad increased.

Another important measure was the creation in 1776 of the viceroyalty in Buenos Aires: this reduced smuggling along the Rio de la Plata. Over the whole of Spanish America, while smuggling no doubt increased in absolute terms, it went into *relative* decline with the general upswing in trade (by the 1790s, contraband was accounting for no more than a third of the value of official trade). Active patrols were introduced, which led to some picturesque or indeed comical incidents. In 1777, it was suddenly discovered that the island of Orna off the coast of Maracaibo had been secretly occupied by the Dutch, and that the governor they had put in had become the regular protector of 'all the malefactors, criminals and smugglers from Spain and other nations who take refuge in this spot'.[140]

But smuggling at the expense of a healthy economy was not as serious a threat as it had been in the previous century to the solidity of the Spanish Empire. The renovated system was even able to withstand two severe trials: the Tupac Amaru rising in Peru in 1780[141] and that of the *Comunidades* in Venezuela in 1781, both massive rebellions provoked in part by the 'Bourbon modernization'. The Tupac Amaru rising, which caused such upheaval in Peruvian society, concerned all the complex currents stirring among the Indians, the half-breeds and the Creoles. But this widespread movement, an extraordinary indicator of

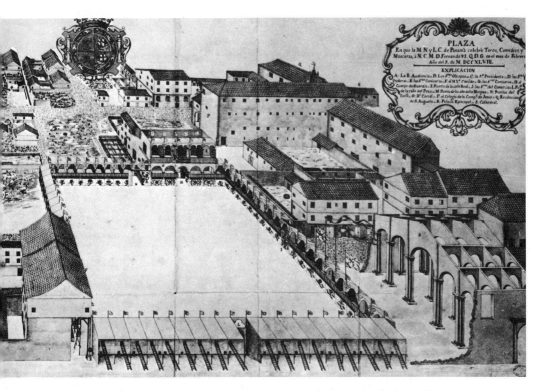

The *Plaza Mayor* in Panama in 1748. Around this square, which is typical of Spanish American towns, with its *Audiencia*, cathedral and *Cabildo*, stands have been prepared for some public holiday with bullfights, plays and masquerades. Watercolour, Archivo General de Indias, Seville. (Photo Mas.)

what was stirring in the depths of that society, was over in barely five months: the destruction of churches, workshops and *haciendas* did not last and the insurrection was finally crushed by Indian auxiliaries armed and trained by the Spanish.

Like all progress everywhere, progress in America brought the destruction of old orders. The Bourbons deliberately chose not to observe long-standing privileges. Alongside the old *consulados*[142] of Mexico City and Lima, other *consulados* were created as rivals of their predecessors and neighbours: the *consulado* of Vera Cruz was thus established as a counterbalance to the ancient powers of the *consulado* of Mexico City. The simultaneous arrival of manufactured goods from Europe (chiefly from England and Spain) swamped local markets, and their high quality and low price brought about the progressive destruction of local industries. Trade circuits were also changing, sometimes favouring local trade, sometimes discriminating against it. Peru for instance[143] on being deprived of the mining areas of the High Andes (which were in 1776 attached to the viceroyalty of Buenos Aires) lost a valuable annex which by its demand for foodstuffs and textiles had helped to balance the Peruvian economy. New Spain is another example: great upheaval was caused there by the terrible famines of 1785 and 1786[144] and order (or at least a semblance of order) could only be restored if the ruling classes (Creoles and *gachupinas*) would consent to sink their passionate and complex differences.

The treasure of treasures

The destiny of Spanish and Portuguese America as a whole (later to be known collectively as Latin America) clearly depended on the fortunes of an even greater area, that is the total European world-economy of which South America was no more than a peripheral and closely controlled zone. Would it ever be able to break out of its bonds? Yes and no – on the whole, no. There are many reasons, the most important being that neither Brazil nor Spanish America, while they did have some ships and even some sailors, were naval powers. (This was not the case in the United States, whose sailors were really the 'founding fathers' of the new country.) Another reason is that Spanish America, even before the eighteenth century but especially during that crucial period, was in double thrall – to the Iberian powers, Portugal and Spain, but also to the rest of Europe (and most of all to England). The English colonies had had to break only one chain, that binding them to England, to achieve their freedom. South America, on the contrary, having freed itself of the shackles binding it to the colonial powers, was still not independent of Europe. It had rid itself of only one of the two masters who had for so long watched over and exploited it. Could Europe be expected to give up the gold and silver of America? Even before the revolutions that led to independence, the European powers were poised for action: each was on the alert for the succession which could confidently be expected. The English occupied Buenos Aires in 1807, but could not hold on to it; the French invaded Portugal in 1807 and Spain in 1808; thus precipitating the emancipation of the Spanish colonies – but without gaining anything from it for themselves.

Was such haste or greed justified? Was the prize real or a mirage? Was America still at the beginning of the nineteenth century the 'treasure of treasures', as Nicole Bousquet has described it? To answer such a question, one needs some figures: the estimated G.N.P. of Spanish America and Brazil, and the surplus available to send to Europe, since this surplus was the treasure in question.

The only credible figures (and they concern only New Spain) are those provided in 1810 by the secretary to the *consulado* of Vera Cruz, Jośe Maria Quiros.[145] And even these give only the *physical output* of New Spain (in millions of pesos and round figures): agriculture: 138.8; manufacturing: 61; minerals: 28; total: 227.8 (so mining output, surprisingly, represents only 12.29 per cent of the whole). But how can we estimate G.N.P. from physical output? In the first place, we should add the vast amount accounted for by contraband; then there is the considerable item of services: since Mexico had few navigable rivers, the chief form of transport was the mule-train – inconvenient and terribly expensive. All the same, G.N.P. can hardly have been more than 400 million pesos. And since it is usually accepted that the mineral output of New Spain was the equivalent of that of the rest of Spanish America put together, are we justified in suggesting that the G.N.P. of the whole (16 million inhabitants) would have been double that of Mexico, that is 800 million pesos at most? Next, Brazilian G.N.P., if J.A. Coatsworth's figures for Brazil in 1800[146] can be accepted, was a little under half that of Mexico, or about 180 million pesos. So 'Latin' America as a whole might have had a total G.N.P. of getting on for 1000 million pesos.

Uncertain though these figures may be, they do at least allow us to draw one conclusion: that per capita income was low: 66.6 pesos for the 6 million Mexicans, 50 pesos for the 16 million inhabitants of the whole of Spanish America; less than 60 in Brazil which had a population of slightly over 3 million. And in 1800, according to the figures accepted by Coatsworth,[147] per capita income in Mexico was only 44% of that in the United States, which must therefore have been (according to my own calculations, since Coatsworth gives them in 1950 dollars) 151 pesos or dollars of the time (the two currencies were equivalent). This is not a totally absurd figure, even compared to Alice Hanson Jones's results in a study of the three most advanced of the North American colonies: somewhere between 200 and 336 dollars.[148] The per capita income of the *most privileged* colony of the South, Mexico, was only 33% or so of that of the privileged northern colonies. With the passage of time, the gap grew even wider: by 1860 this figure had dropped to 4%.

But our problem here is not only to work out the living standards of the population of Latin America, but to calculate the amount by which exports from America to Europe exceeded imports from Europe. The *official* figures for the year 1785[149] record exports to Spain of 43.88 million pesos in bullion, plus 19.41 million in goods, a total of 63.3 million (of which gold and silver accounted for 69.33% and goods, though rising sharply, only 27.6%). Exports in the other direction, from Spain to America were worth 38.3 million pesos, so the difference was 25 million. Let us for the moment simply take this figure on trust, though some doubt surrounds it. If we add to this the corresponding figure for Brazil (25% of the total, or 6.25 million) we reach a further total of 30 or 31 million pesos, or 3% of the G.N.P. of the whole of Spanish America but this figure (since it is based on the official records) must be regarded as a *lower limit*, since it leaves out contraband which we know was considerable. If we convert these 30 million pesos into pounds sterling (5 pesos = £1) the 'treasure' Europe was taking out of America was of the order of at least £6 million. This was of course an enormous sum; by way of comparison, in about 1785, the whole of Europe, including England, was obtaining £1,300,000 from India.[150]

So Latin America (about 19 million inhabitants) was sending back to Europe every year four or five times as much as India (about 100 million inhabitants).

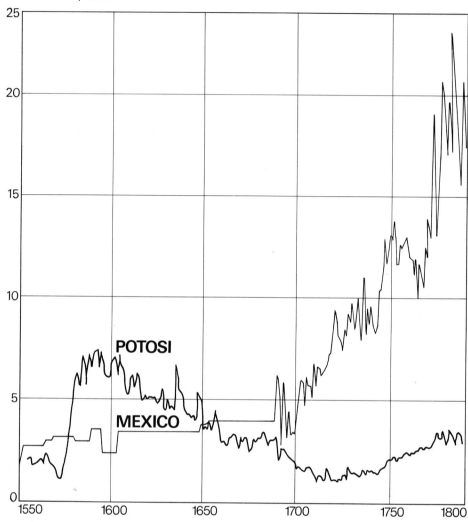

millions of pesos

POTOSI

MEXICO

42 TWO AMERICAN SILVER CYCLES
The curve for Potosi is from M. Moreyra Paz-Soldan's article in *Historia*, IX, 1945; the curve for the Mexican mint comes from W. Howe, *The Mining Guild of New Spain, 1770–1821*, 1949, pp. 453 ff. The first American silver boom occurred in Potosi. But the Mexican mining boom at the end of the eighteenth century reached previously unparalleled heights.

This would certainly make it the greatest treasure-store in the world – and in the popular imagination American treasure swelled to truly fabulous proportions. A French agent wrote in 1806, at a time when the revolutionary and Napoleonic Wars had led to the stockpiling of mined metals on the spot, for fear of sending them by sea:

> If what I have heard is correct, there are over a hundred million piastres in gold and silver ingots lying in the vaults of the mints of the Three Viceroyalties

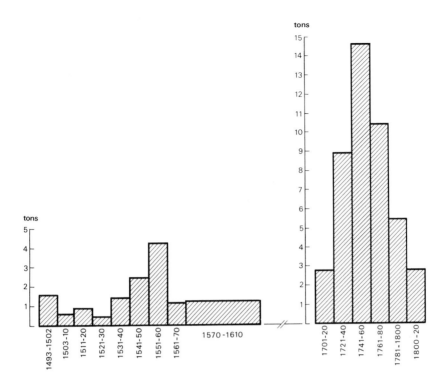

43 TWO AMERICAN GOLD CYCLES
A 'Spanish' cycle (gold from the West Indies, New Spain, New Granada and Peru) gave way to a 'Portuguese' cycle (gold from Brazil). The first brought about 170 tons of gold to Europe over a period of 120 years; the second 442 tons, that is three times as much over a similar period. These figures, calculated in annual averages and in tons are not a hundred per cent reliable. One thing only is certain: the overwhelming superiority of the Brazilian cycle. (Spanish figures from Pierre Chaunu, *Conquête et exploitation des Nouveaux Mondes*, 1969, pp. 301 ff.; Portuguese figures from F. Mauro, *Études économiques sur l'expansion portugaise*, 1970, p. 177.)

of Peru, Santa Fe [Bogota] and Mexico, not forgetting the enormous amount of capital shared out among the owners of the mines ... The capitalist merchants have been obliged by the war to keep back their shipments. [Smuggling] has been able to handle [only] a certain proportion of the circulation of this silver.[151]

England was tempted by such booty, but hesitated for fear of upsetting matters in Brazil, where the king of Portugal had taken refuge in 1808, and Spain which an English army under Wellington was slowly and with difficulty liberating. As a result, the break-up of the Spanish Empire took place in slow motion. But the outcome was inevitable: from the day that Spain, as she industrialized, began to take her colonies in hand again and to become more than a mere intermediary between America and Europe, 'the fall of the empire was at hand, for it was in the interests of no other nation that it should remain Spanish'. In particular of course, it was not in the interests of the nation now towering above the others, the nation which had long temporized, but with France beaten and the American revolutions out of the way, no longer had any cause for prudence. 1825 saw a rush by English capitalists to invest in the markets and mining enterprises in the new (ex-Spanish and ex-Portuguese) states of America.

There was logic behind this: the other countries of Europe had been industrializing in Britain's wake and, like Britain, had sheltered behind protective tariff barriers. European trade was thus stifling for lack of air.[152] Hence the need to look to overseas markets. It was a competition in which Britain was well placed, particularly since she had used the most reliable and the most direct method, that of financial contacts. From now on, bound hand and foot to the City of London, Latin America would remain on the periphery of the European world-economy: even the United States, after their constitution in 1787, despite all their initial advantages, had had great difficulty extricating themselves from a similar position. The ups and downs of American fortunes were now registered by the prices quoted for their loans on the London Stock Exchange (and to a lesser extent on the Paris Bourse).[153]

The 'treasure of treasures' though, to return to this question, while still apparently surviving into the nineteenth century, seems to have diminished considerably. One sign of this is that all 'South American loans' were quoted below par. And the fact that the slump in the European economy (1817–51) began very early in South America (in 1810), that this peripheral crisis brought immense upheaval, and that Mexican G.N.P. declined from 1810 until the 1860s, gives further indication of the depressing history of Spanish America during the first half of the nineteenth century. The 'treasures' of America were being eaten up or squandered, for the wars of independence were ruinous. To give but one example, the mining population of Mexico was torn apart, providing the revolution with its agents, torturers and victims. Abandoned mines were flooded when the pumping stopped, in particular the largest mines, famous only shortly before for their high yields. When extraction did not come to a complete standstill, there was a bottleneck at the crushing stage; more particularly the mercury essential for the amalgam process was obtainable only at excessive prices if at all. The Spanish regime had always maintained a supply of comparatively cheap mercury, since it was brought in by the public authorities. In the early days of independence, the only mines still working were usually small enterprises drained by sloping tunnels instead of pumps.

Finally South America was the scene of the first mistakes made by 'developed' countries about the technology suitable for transfer to 'under-developed' countries. We have for example a report written on 20 June 1826 by the French consul in Mexico City concerning an English venture:

> Dazzled by the prodigies they have acomplished at home by means of the steam engine, they believed it could render similar services here. The steam engines were therefore brought from England, together with wagons for trans-

porting them, nothing was forgotten: except roads for the wagons to travel along. The principal highway in Mexico, the best and most frequented, is the one leading from Vera Cruz to the capital. Your Excellency will be able to judge the state of this road when I say that ten mules have to be harnessed to a carriage holding four persons if they intend to travel ten or twelve leagues a day. It was along this road that the English wagons had to cross the Cordillera: so each of the wagons required no less than twenty mules. Each mule travelled six leagues a day and cost ten francs. Bad this road might be, but it was at least a road; they had to leave it to approach the mines, there were nothing but tracks to follow. Some entrepreneurs, discouraged by the obstacles, have left their machines temporarily in store in Santa Fe, Encerro, Xalappa or Peroti; others, more intrepid, have at great expense built paths which have carried their machines to the mines; but once they arrived, there was no coal to start them up; where there was wood, this was used; but it is scarce on the plateau of Mexico, and the richest mines, those of Guanajuato for instance, are more than thirty hours away from a forest. The English miners were quite amazed to encounter these obstacles which had been pointed out by M. Von Humboldt twenty years ago.[154]

Such for many years were the conditions productive of poor business and low quotations on the London Stock Exchange. But since speculation will always find takers, shares in the Mexican mines, on account of their popularity in public opinion, made huge fortunes for some capitalists before they collapsed. The English government also succeeded in selling to the Mexican state the war *matériel* used by Wellington on the field at Waterloo – some small compensation!

Neither feudalism nor capitalism?

In concluding this section, it is difficult to avoid mention of the intense and highly abstract discussions which have taken place about the forms of society and economy found in the American continent, and whether they are reproductions or altered versions of the models found in the Old World. Historians have sought to define them in terms of concepts familiar to Europe and to produce a model which might bring them together in some kind of unity. The attempt is not a very promising one: some people have talked of feudalism, others of capitalism; the would-be wise have opted for a transitional model sufficiently elastic to satisfy everybody, accepting both feudalism and its variants as well as signs heralding the arrival of capitalism; the truly wise, like B. H. Slicher Van Bath,[155] reject both terms and prefer to start from a completely clean sheet.

In any case, how can one seriously propose a single model of society for the whole of America? Any such thing would immediately have to admit a number of exceptions. Not only do social systems differ from country to country, but they may coexist, mingling elements impossible to classify under any of the suggested headings. The American continent was essentially a *peripheral zone* in our terminology, with the single exception (and there was still some doubt even about this one in the late eighteenth century) of the United States, which became a politically-constituted unit in 1787. But it was a periphery made up like a mosaic with a hundred different colours: modern, archaic, primitive, or curious mixtures of all these.

I have made sufficient mention of New England[156] and the other English colonies to say no more than a few words about them here. Were these capitalist societies? That would be going too far. In 1789, they were with some exceptions, still predominantly agricultural economies; and to the south, as one approached Chesapeake Bay, one would have found regular slave-owning societies. It is certainly true that once peace returned in 1783, an unprecedented wave of enterprise swept through the young States: every kind of industry sprang into existence at once: the domestic system, workshops, manufactories, but also cotton factories using new machines from England; banks and numerous trading companies were created. All the same, in practice, although there were banks, the money in circulation consisted less of hard cash than of drastically devalued banknotes issued by the States, or of clipped foreign coins. Moreover, when the war ended, the fleet – the instrument of independence and greatness – had to be rebuilt. In 1774, it had been divided between coastal shipping and long-haul trade: 5200 vessels (250,000 tons) in the first category; 1400 in the second (210,000 tons). The two branches were approximately equivalent: but while coastal shipping had been 'all-American', the long-distance ships had been English, and these had to be replaced – providing plenty of work for the shipyards of Philadelphia. What was more, England had succeeded in regaining her dominant position in American trade by 1783. So the real capitalism was still in London, the centre of the world: the United States had only a second-best version of capitalism, quite a sturdy one admittedly and one which was to develop during England's absorption in the Revolutionary and Napoleonic Wars (1793–1815), but this spectacular growth was not yet enough to take them into the first rank.

Elsewhere in America, the only signs of capitalism I can detect were in isolated spots, confined to individuals or investments more closely integrated into European capitalism than to any local network. This was even true of Brazil, which had moved further in this direction than Spanish America, but which effectively consisted of a few cities: Recife, Bahia and Rio de Janeiro, which had a 'colony' of its own in its vast hinterland. Similarly in the nineteenth century, Buenos Aires, with the vast Argentine pampas stretching away to the Andes behind it, would be a striking example of the all-devouring city, capitalist after a fashion, dominating, organizing and attracting to it the wagon-trains of the interior and ships from all over the world.

Alongside these islands of merchant capitalism, is it too fanciful to identify patches of 'feudalism' here and there? German Arciniegas[157] argues that in the seventeenth century great tracts of the Spanish New World partly abandoned by Europe were subject to 'refeudalization'. I am willing to accept that the Vene-zuelan *llanos* or parts of the Brazilian interior were subject to a seigniorial

An 'industrial village' in New England. (New York State Historical Association, Cooperstown.)

regime, but this can hardly be described as 'feudal' unless one simply means an autarkic or near-autarkic system, of the type Gunder Frank refers to: 'a closed system only weakly linked with the world beyond'.[158]

It is no easier to draw clear conclusions from a study of land tenure. In Spanish America, three forms of ownership co-existed: the plantations, the *haciendas* and the *encomiendas*. We have already discussed the plantations:[159] this was capitalism after a fashion, but only in the person of the planter or the merchants who gave him financial backing. The *haciendas* were large estates, chiefly created in the seventeenth century during the 'refeudalization' of the New World – which operated to the advantage of the landowners, the *hacendados* and, no less, that of the Church.[160] These great estates were partly self-supporting, and partly in contact with the market. In some areas, Central America for instance, they remained largely self-sufficient; but the estates belonging to the Jesuits – often enormous in area and better known to us than the rest because of their archives – were divided between a natural subsistence economy and an exchange economy based on money. The fact that the accounts of the *haciendas* were kept in money does not rule out the possibility that the wages they refer to may have been paid only at the end of the year – in which case the peasant would not receive any coin, since payments in kind already received might have cancelled out or even exceeded the sum due to him.[161] Similar situations certainly occurred in Europe.

The *encomiendas* in theory at least take us closer to 'feudalism', although these concessions of Indian villages to Spanish citizens took the form of 'livings' rather than 'fiefs'. In theory these were temporary concessions entitling the *encomendero* to the dues paid by the Indians, but not to the outright ownership of the land or the right to dispose of the labour force. But that is only the position on paper: the *encomenderos* often broke the rules. A report in 1553 for instance[162] criticizes both unscrupulous masters who sell their Indians 'under cover of selling an *estancia* or some livestock', and 'frivolous or prevaricating *oidores*' who shut their eyes to this practice. The proximity of local authorities limited such infringements, but the further one went from the large cities[163] the less possible it became to exert control. The *encomendero* as one element in the colonial command structure, was only theoretically in the service of the Spanish authorities, on the same terms as officers of the Crown. In practice, *encomenderos* were tending to shake off this constraint and a crisis in the *encomienda* system began in 1544 with the revolt of the Pizarro brothers in Peru. It was to continue for long years, for conflict between *encomenderos* and officials of the Crown was inevitable. The officials – the *corregidores* and *oidores* of the *audiencias*, the colonial assemblies modelled on the *audiencias* in Spain – could hardly be other than opposed, most of the time, to landowners who, if left to themselves, would quickly have created or recreated a feudal regime. Much, though not all, of the activity of Spanish America, as George Friederici has suggested[164] rapidly turned it into a classic instance of bureaucracy and officialdom. This is hard to reconcile with the standard image of feudalism, just as the lord of the *engenho* in Bahia and his slaves cannot be easily assimilated to a properly capitalist model.

Should we conclude that neither feudalism nor capitalism had crossed the Atlantic? America as a whole could be seen as a collection, a miscellany of different societies and economies. At the lowest level came the semi-closed economies, however we choose to label them; immediately above these, the partially-open economies, if such there were; and lastly, at the highest levels, came the mines, the plantations, some (not all) of the major grazing concerns, and wholesale trade. Capitalism was at most no more than one of the higher echelons of commercial life: its representatives were the *aviadores* of the mining towns, the privileged merchants of the *consulados*, the merchants of Vera Cruz (constantly at odds with those of Mexico City), the merchants who could indulge themselves behind the facade of the metropolitan-based companies, the merchants of Lima, the merchants of Recife (by contrast with the 'seigniorial' city of Olinda) or those of the lower town of Bahia as opposed to those of the upper town. But with all these men of business, we are really still caught in the mesh of the European world-economy which cast its net over the whole of America; we

The Dutch colony on the Cape of Good Hope. (Drawing, J. Rach, 1762. Atlas van Stolk.)

are not in the presence of national forms of capitalism, but within a system extending across the globe and controlled from its nerve centre in Europe.

In Eric Williams's view[165] Europe's superiority (by which he means her approaching industrial revolution and which I would extend to include British world supremacy and the emergence of an even more powerful form of merchant capitalism) can be directly explained by her exploitation of the New World, in particular by the fresh stimulus imparted to the European economy by the regular profits from the plantations and above all, he says, from the sugar plantations worked by black slaves. The same thesis, simplified further, is advanced by Luigi Borelli,[166] who attributes the modernity of the Atlantic and European economy entirely to sugar and therefore to America, where sugar, capitalism and slavery are all combined. But can it really be argued that America, including the gold and silver mines, was the sole source of European greatness? Surely not, any more than it can be argued that India is the single explanation of European supremacy, although Indian historians can certainly maintain today, with convincing arguments on their side, that the English industrial revolution drew much sustenance from the exploitation of their country.

Black Africa: collaborator as well as victim?

I should like now to concentrate on the heartland of Black Africa, leaving aside the countries of the Maghreb – a 'White Africa' contained within the orbit of Islam; leaving aside too, with less obvious justification perhaps, the eastern part of Africa, from the Red Sea and the coast of Abyssinia to the southern tip of the continent.

This southernmost tip of Africa was, in the eighteenth century, still only semi-inhabited. The Cape Colony, founded in 1657 by the Dutch, although its 15,000 inhabitants made it the largest European colony on the continent, was no more than a stopping-point on the way to the Indies, strictly serving the *Oost Indische Compagnie*,[167] which remained fiercely watchful over this strategic position. As for the long east coast of Africa, looking out on the Indian Ocean, it belonged to the Indian world-economy for which it had been at once an important route and a *peripheral* zone, well before the arrival of the Portuguese in 1498.[168] The long interlude of Portuguese commercial activity did of course bring many changes. It was indeed along this coast that Vasco da Gama sailed, after rounding the Cape, as he headed north towards India, putting in at Mozambique, Mombasa and Malindi; from the latter port the Gujerati pilot, Ibn Majib, guided him without too much difficulty, thanks to the monsoon, straight to Calicut. So the coast of Africa was a valuable route both on the way to and from the Indies: its ports enabled the crews to take on fresh provisions, to repair their ships and sometimes to wait for the right time to put to sea when, late in the season, it was dangerous to sail back round the Cape of Good Hope.

There was for a long time, another attraction on the Contra Costa:[169] the existence of gold-panning deep in the vast state of Monomotapa.[170] The gold was exported through the port of Sofala south of the Zambezi delta. The small conurbation long dominated by the town of Kilwa, to the north, became a centre for Portuguese enterprise. Force was effectively applied in 1505, and the situation was well in hand by 1513. Since the gold could only be brought to the coast in exchange for goods, whether grain from Malindi or more often cotton from India, the Portuguese had to use the fabrics of Gujerat for the purpose, and quickly learnt to do so. But this profitable traffic did not last long: Monomotapa was riven by constant wars; gold became scarce and meantime Portuguese control was slipping. Arab merchants were regaining the upper hand in Zanzibar and Kilwa, where they picked up slaves to be re-sold in Arabia, Persia and India.[171] The Portuguese did manage to hold on to Mozambique where they maintained a sort of presence. Towards the end of the eighteenth century, they were said to be exporting several thousand slaves from here every year, and the French even took part in this trade, between 1787 and 1793, in order to obtain manpower for the Ile de France (Mauritius) and the Ile Bourbon (Réunion).[172]

But we can on the whole accept the pessimistic conclusion reached in a memorandum addressed to the Russian government on 18 October 1774, concerning this long coastline. 'It is a long while since the river of Sofala or any of the adjacent streams rolled any gold down with their waters.' The ports of Malindi and Mombasa north of Mozambique were all but deserted and the few Portuguese families still residing there were 'more barbarians than civilized'; their trade consisted of 'the dispatch to Europe of a few degenerate Negroes, most of whom are good for nothing'.[173] The message thus conveyed to the Russian government, which was looking for international outlets, was that this was not a promising spot. So we shall not lose a great deal by leaving aside the 'Indian' side of southern Africa; its great days were by now over.

The western half of Africa

Things were very different on the Atlantic coastline of Africa, from Morocco to Portuguese Angola. Europeans had, as early as the fifteenth century, prospected these mostly unhealthy shores and made contact with local populations. Was it lack of curiosity which stopped them bothering to explore the interior, as has often been said? They certainly did not find in Black Africa terrain as well prepared[174] as that of the Aztec and Inca Empires in America, where Europeans could appear to the many subjugated peoples in the guise of liberators,[175] and where they could eventually base their rule on well-ordered societies which were comparatively easy to exploit.

In Africa, Portuguese and other European explorers had found near the coast only a scatter of tribes, or weak states on which it was impossible to build. The more solid states, such as the Congo[176] or Monomotapa, lay inland, protected both by the continental landmass and by the coastal belt of societies whose political organization was minimal or feeble. Perhaps too, the tropical diseases so prevalent in coastal areas were another obstacle. But this may not be entirely the case, since the Europeans overcame similar obstacles in the tropical regions of America. A more serious reason may be that the African interior was protected by its comparatively dense settlement and by the resilience of societies which, unlike those of the pre-Columbian Americans, were acquainted with iron metallurgy and often harboured warlike populations.

The Europeans did not in any case have much incentive to venture far from the sea, since within easy reach of the coast were ivory, wax, Senegal gum, malaguetta, gold dust and the highly profitable merchandise of black slaves. And at the beginning at any rate, these goods could be obtained in exchange for mere trifles: glass beads, brightly-coloured fabrics, a little wine, a skin of rum, one of the rifles known as 'trading' guns, and the copper bracelets known as *manillas*, 'a rather strange ornament' which the African 'puts on his leg just above the ankle ... or on the arm just above the elbow'.[177] In 1582, the black people of the Congo were being paid by the Portuguese 'with old iron, nails and so on, which they prize more highly than gold coins'.[178] All in all, these were suppliers and customers whom it was easy to dupe, easy-going, sometimes lazy, 'taking each day as it comes'. But 'as a rule, the crops produced by these people are so meagre that the European captains who go there to buy men are obliged to bring from Europe or America enough provisions to feed the slaves who will be their cargo'.[179] In short, the Europeans were confronted everywhere with still primitive economies. For them André Thevet's terse comment in 1575: money 'is not in use there', said it all.[180]

But what is money after all? The African economies had their own currencies, that is to say 'a means of exchange and a standard of recognized value', whether these were pieces of cloth, blocks of salt, livestock or, in the seventeenth century, imported iron bars.[181] Dismissing such currency as 'primitive' in no way authorizes us to conclude forthwith that African economies were lacking in energy or that they would never be roused to activity before the nineteenth century and the repercussions of the industrial and commercial revolution in Europe. In mid-eighteenth century for instance, these backward regions were after all sending *possibly as many as 50,000* black slaves every year to the trading ports (whereas Spain in the sixteenth century could drum up only about 1000 emigrants a year in Seville,[182] and the immigrants to New England between 1630 and 1640[183] numbered on average about 2000 a year). What was more, the raids which produced this human merchandise did not even interrupt the rhythm of everyday life, since the thousands of slaves, harnessed together by leather collars round their necks, were dispatched to the Atlantic with their numerous slave-drivers during the dry season, when there was no work in agriculture.[184]

The regular consignments of slaves, year in, year out, point inescapably to the existence of a fairly vigorous economy – a conclusion repealed with varying degrees of emphasis by the authors of several recent studies of Africa. The comings and goings of the slave-ships are not therefore sufficient in themselves to explain the slave trade, which must also be analysed in the African context. 'Just as the slave trade was a sub-system of the Atlantic economy', writes Philip Curtin, 'it was also a sub-system of a broader pattern of West African society, attitudes, religion, professional standards, self-identity, and much else.'[185] Africa's share of rights and responsibilities in this matter should be acknowledged.

Black Africa: isolated yet accessible

Black Africa consists of a great triangle between three equally large masses: the Sahara to the north, the Indian Ocean to the east, and the Atlantic to the west. As already indicated, we shall not here consider the east coast. As for the wastes of the Sahara and the shores of the Atlantic, these were endless hostile fronts from which foreigners (whoever they were, whatever the period, whatever the circumstances) could approach the very gates of Black Africa and, with unfailing regularity, find their way in. Was this so surprising, since the black continent was after all inhabited by peasants who had turned their backs both on the sea

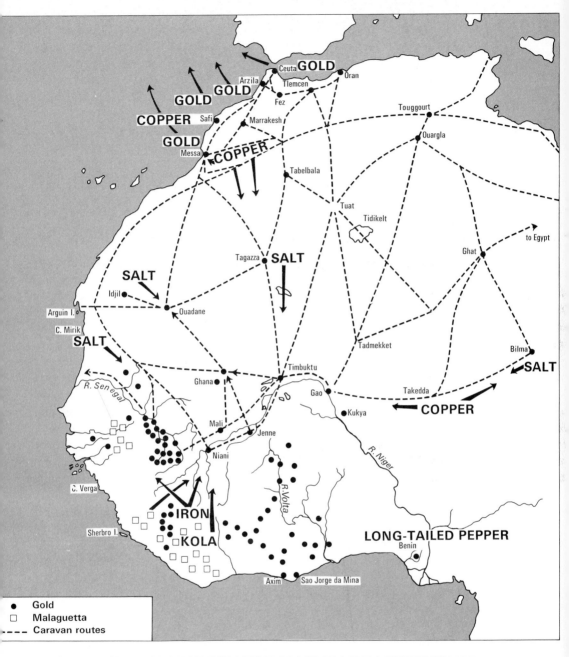

Gold
Malaguetta
Caravan routes

44 THE PORTUGUESE CONQUEST OF THE COAST OF AFRICA (FIFTEENTH AND
SIXTEENTH CENTURIES)
By the sixteenth century, the maritime routes were outpacing the ancient roads across the
Sahara. The gold which used to travel to the Mediterranean was now being diverted towards the
coast. To the various sources of wealth exploited by the Portuguese, we should of course add
that of black slaves. (From V. Magalhaẽs Godinho, *L'Économie de l'Empire portugais aux XVᵉ et
XVIᵉ siècles*, 1969.)

and on the Sahara desert which 'functioned in many respects like the sea'?[186] Curiously, no black explorers ever undertook any of the voyages across either the desert or the ocean which lay on their doorstep. On the Atlantic coast, the only shipping was from one side to the other of the mouth of the Congo river.[187] To the African, the Atlantic was, like the Sahara, an impenetrable obstacle much more than a mere frontier.

To West Africans, the white men were *murdele*, men from the sea.[188] Even today, traditional accounts tell of the black people's surprise at their appearance:

> They saw a great boat appear on the wide sea. This boat had white wings, flashing like knives. White men came out of the water and spoke words no one could understand. Our ancestors were afraid, they said these were *Vumbi*, ghosts of the dead. They drove them back to the sea, with flights of arrows. But the *Vumbi* spat fire with a noise of thunder. . . .[189]

In these first encounters, the blacks did not even imagine that the whites lived or had any existence outside their boats.

On the Atlantic coasts of Africa, the European ship met neither resistance nor surveillance. It had complete freedom of manoeuvre, could travel wherever it wished, trade wherever it pleased, compensating for failure in one place by success in the next a few days later, or simply going from strength to strength. The Europeans even introduced trading 'to Africa from Africa', the equivalent of 'the country trade' in the Far East, though on a much smaller scale. The forts built along the coast made solid operational bases, and the nearby islands could be used as look-out posts: hence the settlements in Madeira, the Canaries and the curious island of São Tomé in the Gulf of Guinea, the island of sugar and slaves which was developed on a prodigious scale in the sixteenth century – no doubt because the west winds and the southern trades met at this point, so that shipping could leave in either direction, westwards to America or eastwards to nearby Africa.

If I am not much mistaken, the same process occurred along the edge of the Sahara. Islam's camel-trains were as free to choose their entry-points as Europe's ships. Ghana, Mali and the Empire of Gao were gateways apparently linked to the commercial exploitation of ivory, gold dust and slaves. And the day this traffic was surprised from the rear by the arrival of the Portuguese in the Gulf of Guinea, the ancient political structures began to crumble. Timbuktu was captured in 1591 in a raid by Moroccan adventurers.[190]

Once more we can observe the profound identity of action between Islam's imperialism and that of the West. Here were two aggressive slave-trading civilizations, to whom Black Africa paid the price for her weakness and lack of vigilance. It is true that the invader appeared at her door carrying unfamiliar offerings guaranteed to fascinate potential customers. Greed played a part in the tragedy: 'thieves and men without conscience come in the night to carry off [the sons of our nobles and vassals]', said the king of the Congo, 'goaded by the desire to possess the goods and merchandise of Portugal, for which they hunger'.[191] 'They will sell each other', wrote Garcia de Resende in 1554, 'and there are many merchants who specialize in this and deceive them and hand them over to the slave-traders.'[192] The Italian Gio Antonio Cavazzi, who lived in Africa from 1654 to 1667, noted that 'for a coral necklace or a little wine, the Congolese would sell their own parents, their own children, or their brothers and sisters, swearing to the purchasers that these were household slaves'.[193] It cannot be denied that greed was a motive, nor that the Europeans deliberately encouraged it. The Portuguese, who liked to use costume as a badge of rank, introduced the same love of *vestir* to the Africans under their influence. Perhaps this was not without ulterior motive, since a Portuguese in Sofala in 1667 even proposed that the ordinary black people who unashamedly went naked, should be *obliged* to wear loin-cloths: then 'all the cloth of India would not be enough to meet the needs of even half the blacks'.[194] Any and every means were indeed used to impose trading, including the practice of paying in advance: in cases of non-repayment, a creditor had the right to seize the goods and finally the person of the defaulter. Straightforward violence was also widely used; whenever it met no resistance, profits broke all records. In 1643, a witness reported that he was 'absolutely certain that this kingdom [Angola, where the hunt for slaves was at its height] has enabled some men to grow even richer than in the East Indies'.[195]

It has to be said that if there was a traffic in human beings in Africa, it was undoubtedly because the Europeans desired and dictated it. But it is also true that Africa had already developed this bad habit long before the Europeans arrived, sending slaves to Islam, the Mediterranean and the Indian Ocean. Slavery was endemic in Africa, part of the structure of everyday life, within a social framework we can only wish we knew better. Even the patience of the historian accustomed to fragmentary documentation, even the bold hypotheses of the comparatist, or the ingenuity of a Marian Malowist[196] are insufficient to recreate this society. Too many questions remain unanswered: what role did the towns play in relation to the clusters of villages? What was the place of craft working and long-distance trade? What was the role of the state? Besides, there cannot have been a single model of society. Slavery came in different guises in different societies: there were court slaves, slaves incorporated into princely armies, domestic and household slaves, slaves working on the land, in industry, as couriers and intermediaries and even as traders. Recruitment was both internal, drawing on the local population (if delinquency in the West led to the galleys, here it led to a death sentence or slavery) and external, following wars or raids against neighbouring peoples, as in the days of ancient Rome. In the long run, these wars and raids became something of an industry. Was there perhaps a risk that the batch of slaves resulting from a war might be too numerous, too difficult to feed and keep, and thus superfluous to needs? By selling them on the foreign market, Africa may have been getting rid of a surplus of hungry mouths.

Slavery in Islam. The slave market in Zabid, in the Yemen, thirteenth century. From an illustration of the Maqamats 635/1237, of al Hariri. B.N., Paris, Ms. ar. 5847. (Photo B.N.)

The slave trade developed out of all recognition in response to demand from America, and had repercussions throughout the black continent. It played a dual role between interior and coast: weakening and sapping the strength of the inland states such as Monomotapa and the Congo; encouraging by contrast a host of little states near the coast, which acted as go-betweens supplying European merchants with slaves and merchandise, just as the successive empires of the Niger had acted as go-betweens for Islam, providing North Africa and the Mediterranean with gold dust and slaves. The same thing had happened in tenth-century Europe, when the zone along the Elbe had been a collecting point for slavs (slaves) to be dispatched to the countries of Islam. And had not the Crimean Tartars in the sixteenth century provided Istanbul with the Russian slaves it requested?[197]

From the coast to the interior

By such processes Black Africa was more thoroughly enslaved than the history books of the past might suggest. Europe sent its roots deep into the heart of the continent, far beyond the coastal bases, the island lookouts, the moored ships rotting away at anchor, the well-known slaving ports or the forts (the first and most famous of which was São Jorge da Mina which the Portuguese built on the coast of Guinea in 1454). These forts, first the Portuguese and later the Dutch, British or French, though so costly to maintain, gave protection against possible attacks either from the blacks or from rival Europeans. For whites engaged in similar trading operations attacked each other on every occasion, seized each other's forts, and waged an active if not very rewarding war of their own on the fringes of major conflicts. They could only unite against a common enemy: for instance the English Royal Africa Company and the French *Compagnie du Sénégal* (later absorbed into the French Indies Company in 1718) could reach a measure of agreement in their hostility to the privateers and 'interlopers', English or not, that is against any merchants trading outside the big companies. The latter, including the Dutch V.O.C, were admittedly in a sorry state, unable to keep up their fortresses and garrisons without grants from the government; in the end they abandoned many of their claims and let things slide.

Trade was taken inland from the coast in light boats which were rowed up the rivers to the upstream ports and to the fairs where European traders met African caravans. The natural intermediaries for this traffic were for many years the mixed-race descendants of the Portuguese, half-black and half-white, who had become 'children of the land' and whose services were much sought after. Later, both the English and the French decided to go upstream themselves and settle in the interior. 'Captain Agis [an Englishman] is not at present in Bintam', noted Father Labat. 'The English employ him to do their trading up-river; he is an enterprising man, and has been seen on the Faleme river, a day's journey from Fort St Stephen of Caynoura.'[198] In the latter part of the eighteenth century, when the English Royal Company gave up most of its activities and Fort St James at the mouth of the Gambia river was abandoned, European trade fell once more into the hands of native middlemen; black oarsmen, who were cheaper than white labour, went upstream with European goods and returned with African commodities, including ebony often destined for a privateer's ship. The blacks had become the subsidiary masters of trade.

This development is curiously reminiscent of the early pattern followed in trade by the Portuguese, who had been the first Europeans to penetrate Africa just as they had the Far East. The earliest *lançados*[199] had been Portuguese; and so were the merchants on the island of São Tome, who were very soon operating an Africa-with-Africa trade from the Gulf of Guinea to Angola, as merchants one day and pirates the next. At the end of the sixteenth century, there were in San Salvador, the capital of the Congo, over a hundred Portuguese merchants and about a thousand adventurers of the same nationality. Then the expansion slowed down, as subordinate roles were handed over to African middlemen and commission agents, notably the Mandingos, who were known by the generic name of *mercadores*; and to subordinate assistants, both black and mixed race, known as *pombeiros*. The latter, whoever the master they worked for, exploited their African brothers even more cruelly than the whites had.[200]

The three-cornered traffic and its terms of trade

Everyone knows where the slave trade led: to the Middle Passage, the terrible Atlantic crossing endured by the slaves crammed into the crowded holds of the trading-ships. But this voyage was only one element in the three-cornered operation in which every ship setting sail from the African coast was engaged, whether under the Portuguese, Dutch, French or English flag. An English ship might for instance land its slaves in Jamaica, return to England carrying sugar, coffee, indigo, and cotton, then set out for Africa again. The pattern was the same, *mutatis mutandis*, for all the ships in the slave trade. At every corner of the triangle a fresh profit was made, and the total return of the voyage was the sum of these profits.

Ships leaving Liverpool or Nantes would be carrying substantially the same cargoes: many textiles of course – including Indian cottons and striped taffetas – copper utensils, pewter plates and pots, iron bars, knives in leather sheaths, hats, glass trinkets, fake crystal, gunpowder, pistols, 'trading guns', and spirits. This is in fact literally the manifest of the cargo a French banker loaded on to his three-hundred tonner, *Le Prince de Conty*, before she sailed from Nantes, France's leading slave-trading port, in April 1704.[201] At this late date, the list would hardly have differed in Liverpool or Amsterdam. The Portuguese always took care not to carry either firearms or spirits to Africa, but their successors no longer displayed such scruples – or such prudence.

As European demand began to rise sharply, the African market had in the end to offer a degree of elasticity to accommodate the increased supply of European goods. This was what happened in Senegambia, a curious region between desert and ocean, on which Philip Curtin has written a remarkable new study[202] laying particular emphasis on the African economy itself, on the volume of trade despite the difficulty of transport, on the high attendance at markets and fairs, on the vigorous growth of the towns which necessarily demanded surpluses, and on the so-called primitive systems of currency which nonetheless proved quite effective.

As time went by, African buyers became more selective about European goods, no longer blindly buying everything. If Senegambia continued to buy iron bars or even iron scrap, it was because unlike other African regions, it had no metal industry; if some other region (or rather sub-region) bought quantities of textiles, it was because local weaving capacity was insufficient, and so on. Finally

– and here comes the surprise – faced with Europe's still-voracious demands, Africa in the end reacted according to the classic rules of economics: by putting up her prices.

I
THE TERMS OF TRADE OF SENEGAMBIA

1680	100	The terms of trade are obtained by relating the indices of exports and imports (to be precise E/I × 100)
1780	475	
1830	1031	

The benefit to African exporters multiplied about 10 times over the period. Even allowing for a large margin of error, the rise is striking.

II
SENEGAMBIA'S EXPORTS

(by commodity, as a percentage of total exports)

	1680	1730	1780	1830
gold	5.0	7.0	0.2	3.0
gum	8.1	9.4	12.0	71.8
hides	8.5	—	—	8.1
ivory	12.4	4.0	0.2	2.8
slaves	55.3	64.3	86.5	1.9
wax	10.8	14.5	1.1	9.9
peanuts	—	—	—	2.6
total	100	100	100	100

Tables from P. D. CURTIN, *Economic Change in Precolonial Africa*, 1975, pp. 336 and 337.

The evidence in support of Philip Curtin's thesis[203] comes from a study of prices and of the terms of trade, which the primitive nature of the 'currency' did not prevent him from conducting effectively. He explains that when the iron bar, the money of account in Senegambia, was quoted by an English merchant at £30, this was not in fact a price, but a *rate of exchange* between the pound sterling (one fictional currency) and the iron bar (another fictional currency). Goods, quoted in bars (and later in pounds), varied in price as can be seen from the tables below; it is therefore possible to calculate plausible totals for Senegambia's exports and imports and thus to work out approximately the terms of trade, 'an indicator enabling one to appreciate the advantage which an economy derives from its foreign trade'.[204] By comparing exports and imports, prices of goods entering and leaving the country, Curtin concludes that Senegambia was deriving increasing benefits from its foreign trade. The fact was that in order to obtain more gold, slaves and ivory, Europe had to increase supply, thus lowering the price of its merchandise in comparative terms. Having been established in Senegambia, this rule could probably be applied to the whole of Black Africa which in response to the demand from the plantations, goldmines and towns of the New World, was sending increasing consignments of slaves off with the slave traders: 900,000 in the sixteenth century, 3,750,000 in the seventeenth, between 7 and 8 million in the eighteenth, and despite the abolition of the slave trade in 1815, 4 million in the nineteenth century.[205] If one remembers the modest means employed and the primitive nature of the transport of the time, the slave trade really broke all the records.

The impact of European demand led to increasing specialization in Senegambia, as first one then another commodity dominated the market: in the early seventeenth century it was hides; then until the nineteenth century, slaves; later, gum; and later again, peanuts. (A comparison could be made with the 'cycles' of colonial Brazil: dyewoods, sugar, gold.)

The end of the slave trade

Such trading strength, once it had been achieved, explains why traffic did not come to an end overnight when the slave trade was officially abolished, on the proposal of the English, at the Congress of Vienna in 1815. According to an English traveller in 1817,[206] Rio de Janeiro, Bahia and above all Cuba became the new centres for a 'traffic in human beings' which continued to thrive. Was Havana the most prosperous of these reception stations? Seven slave ships entered the harbour there at one time – four of them French. But it was the Portuguese and the Spanish who took over the best part of what remained of the trade, taking advantage of the drop in purchases and prices occasioned in Africa by the withdrawal of the English (£2 to £5 per slave, whereas the price was £100 in Havana and twice as much in Florida or New Orleans because of the difficulties of smuggling). The fall was only temporary, but our English traveller was very indignant at such profits being made from a traffic voluntarily renounced by his own country to the greater gain of the Spanish and Portuguese. The latter, he argued, taking advantage of the low price they were paying for slaves, would have 'the means to sell cheaper than we can in foreign markets, not only sugar and coffee but all tropical products'. At the time, many Englishmen would have shared the sentiments of the outraged Portuguese who in 1814 claimed that it was 'both the interest and the duty of the great continental powers formally to refuse their assent to the insidious proposal of England that the Slave Trade be declared contrary to the rights of man'![207]

Did these wholesale transportations in the end disturb the fundamental balance of the black societies of Angola, the Congo and the regions on the Gulf of Guinea? To answer this question one would have to know the size of the population before the arrival of the first Europeans. But it seems to me that in the last analysis such huge totals were only made possible by the extraordinary demographic vitality of the African population. And if as may be the case, the population actually continued to increase in spite of the slave trade, the entire question would have to be looked at afresh.

(I do not mean, by saying this, in any way to diminish the blame or responsibility attaching to Europe, as regards the African population. If such had been my aim, I would have pointed to the gifts which, intentionally or unintentionally, Europe took to Africa: maize, manioc, American beans, sweet potatoes, pineapples, guavas, coconuts, citrus fruits, tobacco, vines; domestic animals – the cat, the Muscovy duck, the turkey, the goose, the pigeon. Not to mention the impact of Christianity which was often welcomed as being a way of acquiring the strength of the white man's God. And one could go even further: whatever the rights and wrongs of the past, black America now exists – is it to be so lightly dismissed?)

The Russian world-economy – a world apart

The world-economy centred on Europe[208] did not extend to the whole of the old continent. Beyond Poland, there was always the remote and marginal world of Muscovy.[209] On this point it is impossible to disagree with Immanuel Wallerstein who unhesitatingly places it outside the western sphere, outside 'European Europe', at least until the beginning of the personal reign of Peter the Great in 1689.[210] The same could be said of the Balkans, where for centuries the Turkish conquest had smothered and subdued a Christian civilization – and of the rest of the Osmanli Empire in Asia and Africa, where huge areas existed in autonomy or near-autonomy.

Vis-à-vis Russia and the Turkish Empire, Europe exerted her monetary superiority, the attractions and temptations of her technology and merchandise, and her strength. But whereas in Muscovy European influence spread almost naturally, as the huge country gradually swung towards the West, the Turkish Empire remained obstinately aloof from Europe's destructive intrusion, or at any rate put up resistance to it. Only force, exhaustion and the passage of time would eventually wear down its visceral hostility to the West.

The return of the Russian economy to quasi-autonomy

Muscovy had never been completely closed to the European world-economy,[211] even before 1555 when the Russians took Narva, the little Estonian port on the Baltic, or before 1553, when English merchants first settled in Archangel. But opening a window on to the Baltic, 'whose waters are worth their weight in gold',[212] allowing the new English Muscovy Company to push open a door in Archangel (even if this door was closed early in the season every year by the winter ice) meant directly accepting European intrusion. At Narva, which had soon been taken over by the Dutch, shipping from all over Europe crowded into the little harbour before scattering again to a variety of European ports.

The so-called Livonian War however ended disastrously for the Russians: they were only too glad to sign an armistice on 5 August 1583 with the Swedes, who had entered Narva.[213] The Russians now lost their only access to the Baltic, keeping only the inconvenient port of Archangel on the White Sea. This blow put an end to any further opening up of Russia to Europe. But the new masters of Narva did not forbid the passage of goods being imported or exported by Russian merchants.[214] So trade with Europe continued, either via Narva, or via Reval and Riga[215] and the trade balance in Russia's favour was made good with gold and silver. The purchasers of Russian grain and hemp, particularly the Dutch, usually brought to settle their account bags of money each containing 400 to 1000 *riksdalers*.[216] 2755 bags arrived in Riga in 1650; 2145 in 1651; 2012 in 1652. In 1683, trade via Riga ended in a Russian trade surplus of 823,928 *riksdalers*.

In these circumstances, if Russia remained somewhat inward-looking, it was for a number of reasons: her unmanageable size, her still sparse population, her limited interest in the West, and the difficult and ever-renewed attempt to establish an internal equilibrium – and not so much because Russia was cut off from Europe or hostile to trade with the rest of Europe. The Russian experience was not unlike that of Japan, but with this major difference that Japan had in 1638 taken the political decision to cut herself off from the world economy, whereas Russia was the victim neither of her own deliberate action, nor of some categorical exclusion on the part of the outside world. It was simply that Russia tended to manage her affairs on the margins of the rest of Europe, as an autonomous world-economy with its own communications network. If M.V. Fechner is correct, the centre of gravity of Russian trade and the Russian economy in the sixteenth century lay closer to the south and east than it did to the north and west, that is to Europe.[217]

At the beginning of the sixteenth century, Russia's principal foreign market was Turkey. Contact was made through the valley of the Don and the Sea of Azov, where goods were transferred exclusively to Ottoman ships: the Black Sea was at the time a jealously guarded Turkish lake. The horseback courier service between the Crimea and Moscow is clear evidence that there was regular and substantial traffic along this route. Towards mid-century, the occupation of the lower reaches of the Volga (by the capture of Kazan in 1552 and of Astrakhan in 1556) opened up further the road to the south, although the Volga flowed through still-unpacified regions, making the land route difficult and the river route dangerous: every time one set foot ashore one was running a risk. But the Russian merchants organized river convoys which were large enough to defend themselves if necessary.

From now on, Kazan and particularly Astrakhan became turntables for

The port of Archangel in the seventeenth century. B.N., Paris, Cabinet des Estampes.
(Photo B.N.)

Russian trade with the steppes of the Lower Volga and, above all, with Central
Asia, China and nearby Iran. Merchants travelled to Kasvin, Shiraz and the
island of Hormuz (which it took three months to reach from Moscow). A
Russian fleet, built at Astrakhan in the latter part of the sixteenth century, was
active on the Caspian Sea. Other trade routes ran to Tashkent, Samarkand and
Bukhara and even as far as Tobol'sk – in those days the gateway to the Siberian
East.

This trade with the South and East, although we have no figures for it, must
have been greater in volume than trade to and from Europe. The Russians
exported untanned skins, furs, ironware, coarse fabrics, wrought iron, arms,
wax, honey and other foodstuffs, besides re-exporting European goods: Flemish
and English cloth, paper, glass and metals. Back in return came spices (especially
pepper) and silks from China and India, all of which passed through Iran; Persian
velvets and brocades; sugar, dried fruits, pearls and gold ornaments from Turkey;
cheap cottons from Central Asia. All this exchange activity was controlled,
protected and sometimes even developed by the state.

To go by the few available figures, which relate to the state monopolies (thus only to a certain proportion of all exchange, and that not necessarily the greatest) trade with the East brought Russia a positive balance and on the whole acted as a stimulus to the economy. Whereas the West took from Russia only raw materials, sending in exchange manufactured articles and currency (which had its importance, it is true), the East bought manufactured goods from Russia and provided in return dyestuffs for Russian industry, some luxury goods admittedly, but also cheap silks and cottons for the popular market.

A strong state

Whether deliberately or not, Muscovy had chosen the East rather than the West. Was this the reason for Russia's economic backwardness? Or did Russia, by postponing contact with European capitalism, avoid the unenviable fate of nearby Poland, whose economic structures were reshaped by European demand, where fortune had singled out Gdansk (the 'eye of Poland') and where the great noblemen and magnates had become all-powerful, while the state's authority diminished and the development of the towns was held back?

In Russia on the contrary, the state was like a great rock in the middle of the sea: omnipotent, strongly-policed, the authority of the Russian state extended everywhere, to the towns (whose air did not 'make a man free'[218] as in the West), to the conservative Orthodox Church, to the peasant masses who belonged to the Tsar before they belonged to their overlord, or even to the boyars themselves, who had been brought to heel, whether they were hereditary nobles or the holders of *pomestye* (the livings granted for services rendered to the sovereign, and which may remind the reader of the *encomiendas* of Spanish America or the Turkish *sipahiniks*). In addition, the state had taken control of essential commodity trades, holding a monopoly in salt, potassium, spirits, beer, hydromel, furs, tobacco and later coffee. The grain market operated well at national level, but the export of grain was subject to permission from the Tsar, who often used it as a form of pressure to further his territorial conquests.[219] It was the Tsar too who arranged for the official caravans which, from 1653 onwards, left at what were supposed to be three-yearly intervals for Peking, carrying precious furs and returning with gold, silk, damask, porcelain and later tea. For the sale of alcohol and beer which were subject to state monopoly, special taverns were opened, 'which are known in the Russian language as *kobaks*, and which are exclusively the property of the Tsar ... except in the part of the Ukraine inhabited by Cossaks'. He derived a large annual income from them, perhaps a million roubles, and 'since the Russian nation is accustomed to strong liquor, and since soldiers and workers receive half their pay in bread or flour and the other half in cash, [they] spend the second half in the taverns so that all the coin circulating in Russia ends up in His Imperial Majesty's coffers'.[220]

Everyone took liberties, admittedly, with state property. Fraud was 'unlimited'; 'boyars and other private individuals contrive to sell clandestinely tobacco from Circassia and the Ukraine where it grows in great quantities'. And what can one say about the black market in vodka which operated at all levels of society? Smuggling on the grandest scale, which the authorities were powerless to prevent, concerned Siberian pelts and furs which were reaching nearby China in such quantities that the official caravans sent to Peking were soon unable to do business. In 1720, 'they cut off the head' of 'Prince Gagarin, former governor of Siberia, for having amassed so much wealth that so far they have only sold [the] furniture and merchandise [he owned in] Siberia and China, and there are still several houses full of unsold goods, not to mention precious stones, gold and silver, said to be worth over 3 million roubles'.[221]

But fraud, smuggling and breaking the law were not peculiar to Russia, and however widespread they may have been, they did not greatly impede the Tsar's arbitrary rule. We are very far removed from the political climate of the West, as can be seen from that peculiarly Russian institution, the *gosti*,[222] great merchants whom long-distance trade here as elsewhere had enriched, but who were firmly attached to the state. There were twenty or thirty of them in the service of the Tsar, endowed both with enormous privileges and enormous responsibilities. The *gosti* were required by turns to levy taxes, to collect customs duties in Astrakhan and Archangel, to sell furs and other goods belonging to the treasury, to handle foreign trade on the state's behalf, in particular the sale of commodities under state monopoly, and to supervise the management of the Mint and of the 'ministerial' department of Siberia. They were answerable for all these duties with their lives and personal property.[223] In return, their individual fortunes were sometimes colossal. In the reign of Boris Godunov (1598-1605) the *annual* wages of a worker have been estimated at 5 roubles. The Strogonov family – the richest of all the Russian merchants it is true, having made their fortune from usury, the salt trade, mining, industry, the conquest of Siberia, the fur trade and the acquisition of large colonial estates in the Perm region east of the Volga in the sixteenth century – advanced to the Tsar during the two Polish wars of 1632-4 and 1654-6[224] the sum of 412,056 roubles. And they had already, in the early days of Michael Romanov's reign, provided him with massive quantities of grain, salt, precious stones and money in the form of loans or extraordinary taxes.[225] As the owners of land, serfs, paid workers and household slaves, the *gosti* thus formed the very pinnacle of society, making up a very particular 'guild'.[226] There were two other guilds consisting of merchants of the second and third category, who also enjoyed certain privileges. The functions of the *gosti* declined however with the reign of Peter the Great.

It is clear then, that by contrast with what happened in Poland, the jealous and sharp-eyed authority of the Tsar in the end succeeded in preserving an autonomous trading system covering the whole of Russia and contributing to the country's economic development. And just as in the West, the great wholesale merchants did not specialize. One of the richest *gosti*, Gregor Nikitnikov, handled not only sales of salt, fish, cloth and silk, but also had businesses in Moscow, a share in the trade down the Volga, owned boats at Nizhniy-Novgorod (now Gorkiy) and had dealings in exports via Archangel; at one time he was negotiating with Ivan Strogonov for the purchase of a hereditary estate, a *votchyna*, for the fabulous price of 90,000 roubles. A certain Voronin owned more than 30 shops in the *radjs*[227] of Moscow; the merchant Shorin transported goods from Archangel to Moscow, from Moscow to Nizhniy-Novgorod and the Lower Volga; together with a partner, he bought up 100,000 poods of salt in a single purchase.[228] And these great wholesalers also went into the retail trade in Moscow to which they systematically transferred the surpluses and wealth of the provinces.[229]

The yoke of serfdom in Russia: an ever-increasing burden

In Russia as elsewhere, state and society went hand in hand. A strong state corresponded to a tightly controlled society, condemned to produce the surpluses from which the state and the upper class lived – for without the latter the Tsar would have been unable to control unaided the great mass of peasants who represented the essential source of royal income.

Every Russian folk tale has four or five main characters – the Peasant, the Landlord, the Prince, the Artisan and the Merchant (the two last-named usually being, in Russia, peasants who had gone up in the world but who remained socially and in the eyes of the law peasants still, subject to the constraints of the seigniorial society). And this was a regime becoming more and more oppressive: from the fourteenth century the lot of the peasants grew steadily worse from the Elbe to the Volga.

But Russia did not follow the usual pattern. In Poland, Hungary and Bohemia, the 'second serfdom' was established to the advantage of the nobles and magnates who stood between the peasants and the market and who controlled supplies to the towns, that is when the latter were not purely and simply their personal property. In Russia, the leading role was taken by the state: everything was governed by the state's needs and undertakings and by the heavy weight of the past: three centuries of fighting against the Tartars of the Golden Horde was even more effective than the Hundred Years' War which had given rise to the authoritarian monarchy of a Charles VII or a Louis XI. The solution adopted by Ivan the Terrible (1544–84) who founded and shaped modern Muscovy, was the displacement and if necessary suppression of the old aristocracy and, in order to have an army and an administration obedient to his desires, the creation of a new service nobility, the *pomechtchiki* to whom were granted for life the lands confiscated from or abandoned by the old nobility, or the virgin lands in the southern steppes which the new 'nobleman' would have to bring under cultivation with the aid of a few peasants or slaves. For slavery persisted among the Russian peasants longer than is sometimes thought. As in early colonial America, the problem was the supply of labour, which was scarce, rather than land, which was plentiful.

And this was what in the end led to serfdom and extended it. The Tsar had brought his nobility to heel – but the nobility had to live. If its peasants deserted it to colonize the newly-conquered lands, how was it to survive?

Seigniorial property,[230] previously based on a regime of free tenants, was transformed in the fifteenth century with the appearance of the *domain*, an estate which the landlord farmed himself, as in the West, and which was established at the expense of peasant holdings. The movement began among the lay nobility and spread to monastery-owned estates and those of the state. The domain sometimes employed slave-labour, more often that of indebted peasants who voluntarily enslaved themselves to pay off their debts. The system tended increasingly to demand payment of dues in the form of labour from the free tenant, and compulsory labour increased in the sixteenth century. But the peasants always had the possibility of flight – to Siberia after the late sixteenth century or better still to the black earth lands of the south. Their constant movements had become an endemic problem, as they persisted in changing masters or making for the virgin lands of the 'frontier' or perhaps trying their luck at craftworking, peddling or small shopkeeping.

This was all perfectly legal: according to the code of 1497, during the week of the feast of St George (25 November) when the year's heavy labour was over, every peasant was entitled to leave his master, provided he paid whatever he owed him. Other feast-days were also the signal to move on: Lent, Shrove Tuesday, Easter, Christmas, the feast of St Peter. Landlords used every means at their disposal to halt such flights, including corporal punishment or increasing the indemnities payable. But once a peasant had taken to the road, how could he be brought back to the fold?

Such peasant mobility threatened the foundations of seigniorial society, whereas it was the policy of the state to shore up this society, turning it into an instrument adapted to serve the crown: every subject had his place in an order which laid down the duty of one and all to the prince. The latter had therefore to call a halt to the escapades of the peasants. For a start, the feast of St George was declared the only legal day for departures. Then in 1580, an edict by Ivan IV suspended all freedom of movement 'temporarily' until further notice. The temporary ban was to last – especially since peasant flight continued despite further ukases (24 November 1597 and 28 November 1601), culminating in the code of 1649 which, in theory at any rate, marked the point of no return. This ukase declared illegal, once and for all, any movement by the peasant without the consent of his landlord, and abolished the old rules which granted runaway peasants the right not to be brought back to their masters, once a certain interval had elapsed (originally five years, later fifteen). This time no interval was specified: however long he had been away, a fugitive could be forced to return to his former landlord, along with his wife, children and worldly goods.

Such a development was only possible to the extent that the Tsar whole-heartedly took the side of the nobility. Peter the Great's ambitions – to develop a fleet, an army and an administration – required the reduction of the whole of Russian society, noble and peasant alike, to obedience. The priority accorded to the needs of the state explains why, unlike his Polish opposite number, the Russian peasant although in theory reduced to total serfdom in 1649, was in fact subject to *obrok* (dues payable in money or in kind, and to the state as much as to the landlord) rather more than to *barchina*[231] or forced labour. Where this did exist, even in the worst periods of serfdom, in the eighteenth century, it never exceeded three days a week. The payment of dues in cash clearly implies the existence of a market to which the peasant always had access. Indeed it is the market which explains the development of direct farming by the landlord of his domain (he wanted to sell its product) and no less the development of the Russian state, which depended on income from taxation. Depending which way one looks at it, one could equally well say either that the early appearance of a market economy in Russia was consequent upon the opening up of the peasant economy, or that it was the condition of such opening. In the process, Russia's foreign trade with Europe (which some people would no doubt dismiss as comparatively insignificant compared to the huge domestic market) had a part to play since it was Russia's positive balance with the West which injected into the Russian economy the minimal monetary circulation – silver from Europe or China – without which market activity would scarcely have been conceivable, certainly not at the level reached in practice.

The market and rural society

This basic freedom – access to the market – explains many contradictions. On one hand, the status of the peasant clearly deteriorated: in the age of Peter the Great and Catherine II, the serf had become a slave, 'a thing' (in the words of the Tsar Alexander I), a chattel which his master could sell when he pleased; the peasant was powerless in the face of seigniorial justice which might sentence him to deportation or imprisonment; moreover, he was liable for military service, could be enlisted as a sailor in the navy or merchant fleet, or drafted to work in the manufactories. This was indeed why so many peasant revolts erupted, to be regularly suppressed in bloodshed and torture. The Pugachev rebellion (1774–5) was only the most dramatic episode in this stormy history. On the other hand, it is quite possible that, as Le Play later thought,[232] the living standard of Russian peasants was comparable to that of many peasants in the West – in some cases at least, since one might find on the same estate serfs living in near-comfort alongside destitute peasants. And seigniorial justice was not equally harsh every-where.

It is also true that there were loopholes: serfdom allowed odd little pockets of freedom. Russian serfs frequently obtained permission to engage either full-

The Volga between Novgorod and Tver

or part-time in artisan trades, in which event they could sell the product of their work. When the princess Dashkov was in 1796 exiled by Paul I to a village in the northern region of Novgorod province, she asked her son where this village was and to whom it belonged. He made enquiries without success. 'At last by good fortune, a peasant from this village was found in Moscow: he had brought with him [to sell of course] a load of nails of his own making.'[233] Or a peasant could often obtain from his master a passport entitling him to ply some industrial or commercial trade far from the estate; and all without ceasing to be a serf, even after making his fortune, that is without ceasing to pay dues – at a rate proportionate to his wealth.

Some serfs became, with their master's blessing, pedlars, travelling salesmen, shopkeepers in the suburbs or in the town centres, or carriers. Every winter, millions of peasants hauled goods accumulated during the fine season into town on sledges. If by misfortune the snowfall was inadequate, as happened in 1789 and 1790, making it impossible to use sledges, the city markets remained empty and famine followed.[234] In summer, the rivers were thronged with boatmen. And from transporting goods to trading in them was but a short step. When conducting his survey of Russia, the naturalist and anthropologist Pierre Simon

Pallas stopped in 1768 at Vyshniy Volochek near Tver (now Kalinin) 'a large village, almost a small town. It owes its increase in size to the canal joining the Tvertsa to the Msta. This link [between the] Volga and Lake Ladoga is the reason why almost all the peasants of this region have turned to commerce: so that farming has virtually been abandoned'; the village had become a town, 'the local capital of the region of this name'.[235]

Furthermore, the ancient tradition of the rural craftsmen who worked for the market – the *kustari* who had all but abandoned agriculture by the sixteenth century – developed to an extraordinary degree between 1750 and 1850. This huge craft production far outweighed that of domestic outworking by peasants for city manufacturers.[236] The serfs were even able to take part in the rapid and wide expansion of manufactories encouraged by the state during and after the reign of Peter the Great: in 1725 there were 233 manufactories in Russia; by 1796 when Catherine II died, there were 3360, not counting mines and ironworks.[237] These figures admittedly include some very small undertakings besides large-scale enterprises. But they undoubtedly represent a remarkable increase. Most of the non-mining industrial expansion took place around Moscow. North-east of the capital for instance, in the village of Ivanovo (the property of the Sheremetev family), the local peasants who had traditionally been weavers eventually opened no less than 49 manufactories of printed fabrics (first linens, then cotton) in 1803. Their profits were fantastic and Ivanovo became the major Russian textile centre.[238]

No less spectacular were the fortunes made by certain serfs in wholesale trade. This was a profession in which there were comparatively few bourgeois – something peculiar to Russia.[239] As a result, peasants hastened to take it up and prospered – sometimes against the law but also with the protection of their landlords. Speaking in the name of the Russian government in the middle of the eighteenth century, Count Munnich stated that for a century, 'in spite of all the prohibitions, the peasants have constantly been engaging in trade, investing considerable sums of money in it', so that the growth and 'present prosperity' of wholesale trade 'are due to the competence, hard work and investment of these peasants'.[240]

For these *nouveaux riches* who remained serfs in the eyes of the law, the drama, or perhaps one should say the comedy, began when they tried to buy their freedom. Their master was usually reluctant to cooperate, perhaps because it was in his interest to continue to collect substantial rents, perhaps because his vanity was tickled by keeping these millionaires under his command, or because he wanted to raise their emancipation money to preposterous heights. The serf for his part, in an effort to release himself at least cost, took great pains to conceal the size of his fortune and frequently succeeded. In 1795 for instance, Count Sheremetyev demanded as the price for the freedom of Gratchev, the great textile manufacturer of Ivanovo, the exorbitant sum of 135,000 roubles, plus the factory, land and serfs owned by Gratchev – apparently almost the whole of his fortune. In fact, Gratchev had secreted away large amounts of capital under the names of merchants acting for him. Even after buying his liberty at so dear a price, he remained one of the barons of the textile industry.[241]

Such huge fortunes were of course acquired only by a minority. But the presence of innumerable peasants in small- and medium-scale trade was nevertheless a feature of the very special climate of serfdom in Russia. Whether well-to-do or miserable, the serf class was not imprisoned within village self-sufficiency; it remained in contact with the country's economy and found ways of surviving and making a livelihood. Moreover, between 1721 and 1790, the population doubled, a sure sign of vitality. What was more, the number of 'state peasants' gradually increased to the point at which it embraced half the rural population, and these state peasants were comparatively free, often being subject to no more than notional authority.

In the end, Mother Russia was absorbing into her bloodstream not only silver from the West but also a kind of capitalism. The innovations the latter brought with it were not necessarily earnest of progress; but under their weight the old regime began to crumble. Wage-labour made a very early appearance and developed in the towns, in transport, and even in the countryside for urgent seasonal tasks like haymaking and harvest. The workers who hired themselves out were often ruined peasants setting out to seek a living as farmhands or labourers; artisans who had lost all their money and continued to work in the *posad*, the worker's district, but now on the payroll of a more fortunate neighbour; or poor men who were hired as sailors, boatmen, hauliers (there were 400,000 *burlaki* on the Volga alone).[242] Labour markets came into existence, in Nizhniy Novgorod for example – a sign of the future fortune of this remarkable centre. The mines and manufactories needed not only serfs, but also wage-labourers who were given a bonus on being hired – at the risk of seeing the newly-engaged workman slip quietly out of town.

But the picture should be presented neither in too favourable nor in too gloomy a light. We are speaking in all cases of a population accustomed to privation, to surviving in harsh conditions. Perhaps the most telling image is that of the Russian soldier who was, we are told, 'really easy to feed ... He carries a little tin box, and has a small flask of vinegar, a few drops of which he pours into his drinking water; if he comes across a piece of garlic, he eats it with flour mixed with water. He can withstand hunger better than any other man, and when meat is given out to the troops he regards this largesse as a treat'.[243] When the army stores had run out of food, the Tsar had only to declare a day of fasting and crisis was averted.

A small-town society

A national market took shape early in Russia, one broadly based on the produce from noble or ecclesiastical estates and the surpluses of peasant farms. But this profusion of rural productivity was perhaps counterbalanced by the mediocrity of the towns. These were essentially small towns rather than cities, not only in size, but because they had not developed to any great extent the true functions of a city. 'Russia is one big village.'[244]: such was the impression of European travellers, correspondingly surprised by the abundance of the Russian market economy – which was however still at an elementary stage. It had its origins in the villages and included the small towns – which were themselves barely distinguishable from the surrounding countryside. The peasants had invaded the suburbs, taking over the bulk of artisan activity there, and even in the town they had set up an incredible number of small artisan shops. The German traveller J.P. Kilburger remarked in 1674 that 'there are more shops in Moscow than in Amsterdam or in an entire German principality'. But they were all tiny: a dozen of them would easily have fitted into the average Dutch shop. Sometimes two, three or four shopkeepers shared the same premises, so that 'the vendor can scarcely turn round amid his goods'.[245]

These shops, arranged according to their specialities, would run into two rows along a *radj* (literally 'row'). The word *souk* would not be an inappropriate translation since these districts with their close-packed shops were more reminiscent of Muslim towns than of the specialized streets of a western medieval town. In Pskov, 107 icon-makers had their shops in the *ikonnyi ryad*.[246] In Moscow, the site of what is now Red Square was 'covered with shops, as are all the streets around; every trade has its own street and district, so that the silk merchants do not mix with the cloth or canvas merchants, nor the goldsmiths with the saddlers, shoemakers, tailors, furriers and other artisans ... and there is one street where they sell nothing but Images of their Saints'.[247] One step further took the visitor to the larger shops, the *ambari*, which were in fact wholesale stores but also engaged in the retail trade. Moscow also had its markets and even specialized markets – including fleamarkets, where barbers operated in the open air among the old clothes, or meat and fish markets of which a German traveller insisted that 'you can smell them before you see them ... The stink is so strong that foreigners have to hold their noses'.[248] Only the Russians themselves do not seem to notice it, he claimed.

Apart from these small-scale market activities, there was also long-distance trade. This had inevitably developed on a national scale because of the diversity of the Russian regions, some of which were short of grain, others of wood or salt. Certain imported goods, or furs, crossed the country from end to end. Fairs rather than towns were the true generators of this trade, which made the fortunes of the *gosti* and later of other great merchants. There were probably between three and four thousand fairs in the eighteenth century[249] – that is ten or twelve

The *piroshki* seller (*piroshki* were little meat pies very popular in Russia). Engraving by K.A. Zelencov, eighteenth century, from *The Cries of Petersburg*. (Photo Alexandra Skarzynska.)

times the number of towns (in 1720 apparently there were only 273 towns). Some of the fairs, like those of Champagne, had the function of linking regions as distant from each other as Italy from Flanders. Among the major fairs[250] was Archangel in the far north; further south was the very lively fair, 'one of the most considerable in the Empire',[251] of Sol'vychegodsk; there was Irbit, on the road from Tobol'sk to Siberia; Makaryev, the early version of the great fair of Nizhniy Novgorod which really came into its own only in the nineteenth century; Briansk, between Moscow and Kiev; Tikhvin, on the approaches of Lake Ladoga, on the way to the Baltic and Sweden. These are by no means to be dismissed as archaic means of trading, since the age of fairs lasted until the eighteenth century in the West as well. But the problem about Russia is the comparative insignificance of the towns compared to the fairs.

Another sign of the lack of urban maturity was the absence of a modern system of credit; hence the reign of usury in both town and countryside on unimaginably harsh terms: at the slightest default, everything fell forfeit, including human life and liberty. For 'anything could be lent ... money, food, clothing, raw materials, seed-corn'; and anything could be pawned, shop, workshop, booth, wooden cabin, garden, field, plot, even the pipes from a salt pit. Incredible rates of interest were commonplace: when a Russian merchant lent money to a fellow countryman in Stockholm in 1690, the interest was 120 per cent over nine months, or more than 13 per cent per month.[252] In the Levant, where usury was commonly practised between Jewish or Muslim moneylenders and Christian borrowers, interest rates were no more than 5 per cent a month – modest by comparison. In Moscow, usury was the high road to capital accumulation. And the rate of return specified in the agreement mattered less than the acquisition of the goods pledged – property, workshops, hydraulic pumps. This was another reason why the interest rate was so high and the time limits so strict: everything was calculated to make the agreement impossible to keep, so that at the end of the day, the pound of flesh could be seized without hope of remission.

A world-economy – but what kind of world-economy?

Mighty Russia, for all its surviving archaisms, was unquestionably a world-economy in itself. Viewed from its centre, Moscow, it possessed not only vigour but also a certain power of command. The axis running north-south along the Volga was a crucial dividing line, just as the capitalist backbone of fourteenth-century Europe had run from Venice to Bruges. And if we imagine a map of France magnified to the scale of Russia, Archangel would be Dunkirk; St Petersburg, Rouen; Moscow, Paris; Nizhniy Novgorod, Lyon; and Astrakhan, Marseille. Later in 1794, the southern terminus would have moved to Odessa.

An expanding world-economy, pushing its conquests into the almost trackless peripheries, Muscovy was an immense unit, and it is this immensity which places it in the first rank among the economic monsters. Foreign observers were not mistaken when they regularly stressed this fundamental question of dimensions. Russia is so vast, wrote one of them, that at the height of summer 'at one end of the Empire the daylight lasts only 16 hours, while at the other it lasts for 23'.[253] It is so vast, with its reputed 500,000 square leagues, writes another,[254] 'that all the inhabitants [of the world] could easily fit [into it]'.[255] But, he adds, they would probably 'be unable to find enough to live on'.

In such surroundings, journeys became interminable, inhuman undertakings. Distance bedevilled and complicated every aspect of life. Transactions took years to complete. The official caravans leaving Moscow for Peking took three years to make the round trip. In the course of their long journey, they had to cross the Gobi Desert – at least 4000 versts (about 4000 km).[256] One merchant who had done the trip several times, assured two Jesuit fathers inquiring about it in 1692 that it was no worse than crossing Persia or Turkey[257] – as if that was not bad enough! In 1576, an Italian observer remarked of the realm of Shah Abbas,[258] *che si camina quatro mesi continui nel suo stato*, that it took four months to cross it. The journey from Moscow to Peking took even longer: as far as Lake Baikal, sledges were used, after that horses and camel trains; and one had to reckon with the inevitable halts and the harsh necessity of stopovers lasting the entire winter.

The same problems affected the north-south route from the White Sea to the Caspian. It is true that in 1555, a party of English merchants had succeeded in travelling from Archangel to the Iranian border. But the long-nourished plan to capture the Indian Ocean spice trade from the rear by crossing the 'Russian isthmus' north to south, took little account of the real problems of such an endeavour. Yet even in 1703, the news (probably premature) of the recapture of Narva by the Russians,[259] was inspiring much excitement in London: what could be simpler than to use this port as a starting-point for crossing Russia to the Indian Ocean, and thus beating the Dutch to it? But the English failed on several occasions to carry out the venture. In the 1740s, they did succeed in establishing themselves on the shores of the Caspian, but the indispensable permission of the Tsar, which had been granted in 1732, was withdrawn in 1746.[260]

Distance, which was the underlying reality of the Russian world-economy, and indeed gave it its shape, also had the advantage of protecting it against foreign invasion. Distance also encouraged the diversification of production and a more or less hierarchical division of labour between one zone and another. The claims of Russia to be a world-economy are also supported by the existence of its peripheral zones: the south and the Black Sea;[261] or the endless wastes of Siberia stretching eastwards to Asia. The Siberian case is a fascinating one, so let us take it as an example.

The invention of Siberia

If Europe 'invented America', Russia had to 'invent' Siberia. In both cases the 'inventors' were overwhelmed by the scale of the task. Europe in the early sixteenth century was however at the height of her powers, and America was firmly linked to the old continent by prime transport routes across the Atlantic. Sixteenth-century Russia by contrast was still short of resources and of people, and the sea-passage between Siberia and Russia, although at one time exploited by Novgorod, was not a convenient one: this was a sub-polar route leading to the wide estuary of the Ob, blocked by ice every year for months on end. The Tsarist government eventually closed the route entirely for fear that it would make contraband in Siberian furs too easy.[262] So Siberia was linked to the Russian 'hexagon' only by the long overland routes, to which fortunately the Urals did not prove too great an obstacle.

It was only in 1583 that communication by these routes, although initiated long before, became a reality with the expedition led by the Cossack Yermak on behalf of the brothers Strogonov, merchants and manufacturers who had received from Ivan IV large land concessions beyond the Urals, 'with the right to install cannon and arquebuses there'.[263] This was the start of a comparatively rapid conquest (100,000 km² a year).[264] Within a century, in their pursuit of furs, the Russians had moved progressively from the valleys of the Ob, the Yenisey, and the Lena, and had reached the banks of the Amur on the outposts of China (1689). The Kamchatka peninsula was taken between 1695 and 1700; Alaska, across the Bering Strait which was discovered in 1728, saw its first Russian settlements in the 1740s.[265] Towards the end of the eighteenth century, a report mentions the presence of two hundred Cossacks on the American mainland, roaming the country and trying 'to accustom the Americans to pay tribute' – tribute as in Siberia, consisting of sable and fox furs. And, it adds, 'the vexations and cruelties which the Cossacks exercise in the Kamchatka will no doubt soon be introduced to America'.[266]

The Russian advance had on the whole preferred to concentrate on the area stopping short of the Siberian forests, moving into the southern steppes where the frontier became established in about 1730 from the banks of the Irtys, a tributary of the Ob, as far as the Altay range. This was truly a *limes*, a continuous frontier held by the Cossacks, unlike the less systematic occupation of Siberia as a whole with its scatter of wooden fortresses (*ostrugi*). And this key frontier maintained its 1750 shape until the reign of Nicholas I (1825–55).[267]

Siberia then was a vast expanse of the unknown, originally conquered by a few unprompted expeditions and individual ventures, a process carried on independently of official intentions or schemes which would make an appearance only later. There was even a term to denote these early obscure pioneers: the *promyslenniki* – hunters, fishers, graziers, trappers, artisans and peasants, 'axe in hand, bag of seed-corn over shoulder'.[268] Not to mention genuine adventurers, who were feared and made unwelcome: or religious dissidents, merchants of other nationalities and, from the end of the seventeenth century, deported prisoners. The number of immigrants was derisory in relation to the great wastes of Siberia – 2000 a year at most on average; this was barely enough to establish scattered settlements of peasants, who possessed the priceless advantage of being virtually free, along the southern borders of the forests (silver birch forests here, by contrast with the dark conifer forests of the north). On these light soils, the swing-plough with beechwood ploughshare was adequate to cultivate a few fields of rye.[269]

The Russian settlers naturally chose the most fertile regions and the banks of fish-filled rivers, pushing the indigenous population back towards the deserts of the southern steppes or the deep forests of the north: to the south were the Turco-Tartars, from the Kirghizes on the shores of the Caspian to Mongolian peoples such as the amazing and warlike Buriats of Irkutsk province where a fort was built in defence against them in 1662; to the north were the Samoyeds, the Tunguses and the Yakuts.[270] The south was a world of merchant caravans and tent-dwelling nomads who grazed their flocks over immense stretches of the steppes; the north a world of log cabins in forest clearings, where the fur-trappers had to use compasses to find their way.[271] European travellers inclined to amateur ethnography have left many observations about these unfortunate peoples driven back into hostile natural surroundings:

> The Tunguses of the Ona valley [notes Gmelin the elder] almost all speak the Russian language, and wear Russian dress but it is easy to tell them by their height and the patterns they draw on their faces. Their clothing is of the

simplest, they never wash, and when they go into a tavern, they have to bring their own glasses: they would never be given any. Apart from the marks by which they can be distinguished from Russians, it is also very easy to recognize them by their smell.[272]

By the end of the eighteenth century, Siberia probably had a population of a little under 600,000, counting the native peoples who were easily dominated because of their poverty and small numbers, and who might even be incorporated into the small detachments of troops guarding the forts. They were frequently used for heavy labour: hauling barges, transport, mining. And they also provided the outposts with fur, game or goods from the south. The few Mongol or Tartar slaves – who were usually sold on the market in Astrakhan[273] – or those who were sold in the Siberian markets of Tobol'sk or Tomsk, were insignificant in number. There was nothing here comparable to what was happening in the slave-plantations of America or even in some parts of Russia.

Transport was crucial and never an easy matter. The rivers, running from south to north, were ice-bound for months on end, and the thawing of the ice in spring could be terrifying; portages for flat-bottomed boats (*strugi*) made it possible in summer to cross from one valley to another at key watersheds, where towns sometimes grew up, at first on a modest scale, like the towns built by Europeans in the American interior. Despite the intense cold, the winter was comparatively favourable for travelling since sledges could be used. The *Gazette de France* for 4 April 1772 records, passing on a dispatch from St Petersburg, that 'there have arrived by the latest sleds a considerable quantity of gold and silver ingots from the Siberian mines [probably from Nerchinsk] and the Altay mountains'.[274]

Confronted with the slow formation of Siberia, the Russian state had time gradually to take precautions, to instal controls and post detachments of Cossacks and active if prevaricating officials. The assertion of control over Siberia was given concrete expression in 1637 by the creation in Moscow of a Siberian department (*prikaz*) – a sort of ministry for Siberian affairs to handle the 'colony', not so very different in its attributions from the *Consejo de Indias* or the *Casa de la Contratación* in Seville. Its role was at once to organize the administration of Siberia and to collect such merchandise as was the object of state monopoly. This did not mean precious metals, since mining was a later development. The mines of auriferous silver at Nerchinsk were not discovered until 1691: they were first worked by Greek entrepreneurs and did not yield their first silver until 1704 or their first gold until 1752.[275] So for many years deliveries from Siberia consisted simply of fantastic quantities of furs, known as 'soft gold', strictly controlled by the state: trappers, whether indigenous or Russian, and merchants had to pay tribute or taxes in furs, and these were collected and re-sold by the *prikaz*, either in China or in Europe. But not only was the state often obliged to pay its agents in the same currency (keeping only the best pelts for itself), it was also unable to keep an eye on the entire output of the trappers. Siberian furs were being smuggled out of the country and sold in Gdansk or Venice at cheaper prices than in Moscow. And it was even easier of course to smuggle them into China, which was a major purchaser of furs – sea-otter and sable particularly. Between 1689 and 1727, fifty caravans of Russian merchants left for Peking – only a dozen of them on official business.[276]

For the Russian hold over Siberia was far from complete. As late as 1770, according to a contemporary (a Polish exile whose adventures would later take him to Madagascar), 'it is even part of the policy of the Russian government to close its eyes to such infringements [i.e. smuggling]: it would be too dangerous to arouse the Siberians to revolt. The slightest trouble would make the inhabitants rise up in arms, and if things reached this pass, Siberia would be quite lost to Russia'.[277] Benyowski was exaggerating, and in any case Siberia would never be able to escape the Russian grip: it was imprisoned by its primitive level of development, revealed by the low prices in its new towns, the near-autarky of many of its regions and what was in some ways the artificial character of its long-distance trade, which nevertheless locked it into a chain of obligations.

For the fact was that however slow or long-drawn-out, these exchanges formed a system of interdependence. The great Siberian fairs – Tobol'sk, Omsk, Tomsk, Krasnoyarsk, Yeniseysk, Irkutsk, Kyakhta – were all connected. The Russian merchant leaving Moscow for Siberia would stop first at Makaryev and Irbit, then at all the Siberian posts, sometimes making return journeys (between Irkutsk and Kyakhta for instance). The round trip could last four and a half years with some long halts; at Tobol'sk, 'the caravans of the Kalmucks and Burkaskis ... stay all winter'.[278] Into such places would crowd men and draft animals, with sleds to which both dog and reindeer teams were harnessed, unless there was a strong wind, when a sail was hoisted and the animals ran behind the 'ship' as it sailed along under its own power. These staging-post towns with their shops were places of congregation and amusement. The press of stall-keepers was so 'thick on the market-place of Tobol'sk that it was hard to push a way through'.[279] Irkutsk possessed numerous taverns where travellers systematically drank all night long.

The towns and fairs of Siberia were thus hosts to a twofold network of commerce: long-distance trade in which Russian or European goods were exchanged for those of China or even India and Persia; and the sale of local products (above all furs) in exchange for the supplies necessary to all these settlements lost in the wastes of Siberia – meat, fish, flour and the sacrosanct vodka which had rapidly conquered northern Asia (it was the only thing that made exile bearable). The further east and north one went, of course, the wider the range of prices. At Ilimsk, well beyond Irkutsk, capital of the province of the same name, a kind of fur market was held with certain western goods being handed over in exchange. In 1770, a merchant could make a profit of 200 per cent on such goods and double his profit again by selling the furs in China. Out here, a pound of gunshot was worth three roubles, a pound of tobacco, one and

A meeting of Russian and Chinese merchants at the house of the 'burgomaster' (*gorodnitski*) of Kyakhta, the town where the Russo-Chinese fairs were held. After C. de Rechberg, *Peuples de la Russie*, Paris-St Petersburg, 1812, vol. I. (Photo B.N.)

a half; ten pounds of butter cost six roubles, a keg of eau-de-vie of eighteen pints, fifty roubles; forty pounds of flour, five roubles. In return, a sable pelt was worth only one rouble, a black fox fur, three; a bearskin, half a rouble; fifty grey squirrel pelts, one rouble; a hundred white rabbit pelts, one rouble; twenty-four ermine pelts, one rouble – and so on. It is easy to see who got rich at these prices.[280] On the Chinese frontier, a beaver pelt was 'valued at exchange at 80 to 100 roubles'.[281]

On the other hand without the lure of gain, what merchant would ever have ventured out into these infernal regions, where there were no roads, where there was danger from wild beasts and no less from human marauders, where horses dropped dead in harness, where the last frosts were in June and the first began again in August,[282] where wooden sledges easily broke and might be caught and buried in lethal snowstorms? If horses went off what was literally the beaten track, they might plunge into soft snow up to their necks. To make matters worse, after the 1730s North American furs began to compete with the 'soft gold'

A. *Forteresse*
B. *Vatzka*
C. *Eglise Lutherienne*
D. *Cloitre de Poxryff de N.° D.°*
E. *Moulin de Pierre*
F. *Demeures des Tartares*
G. *Montagnes d'ou on tire du Sel*

H. *La Ville Blanche*
J. *Le Dome*
K. *Maison du Gouverneur*
L. *L'Arsenal*
M. *La Chancelerie*
N. *L'Eglise S.° Jean*
O. *L'Eglise de la Resurrection*

P. *Le Magasin des Vivres*
Q. *L'Eglise S.° Nicolas*
R. *Cloitre de Salvateur*
S. *Chantier pour les Vaisseaux*
T. *Magasin pour les Vaisseaux*
V. *Les Ecuries*
X. *Le Cloitre de Dolbinoff*

PLAN DE LA
VILLE D'ASTRACAN
Echelle de Cinq Cent Toises

Plan of the town of Astrakhan in 1754. *Atlas maritime*, III, 1764. B.N., Paris, Ge. F F 4965. (Photo B.N.)

of Siberia, where a cycle was coming to an end, or at any rate deteriorating. It was now that the mining cycle began, as dams, mill-wheels, hammers, forges and furnaces were built. But northern Asia, an imperfect version of America, had no black slaves or Indian peoples to draw on. The only available manpower here was Russian or Siberian, and this was in reality forced rather than voluntary labour. During the first fifty years of the nineteenth century, there was an extraordinary and fantastic gold rush, of which haunting images have survived: the frantic searches for gold up the Siberian rivers; the long marches through the swamps of the *taiga*; the recruitment of workers from among deportees and peasants for the four summer months. The workers were rounded up and supervised and were no sooner freed than they spent all their money on drink; they had no choice, after surviving the winter as best they could, but to answer the recruiters' call again in the spring, to receive the signing-on bonuses and the rations required for the long trek back to the mine.[283]

Inferiorities and weaknesses

Russian expansion was not uniformly steady or unchallenged. It was an extraordinary achievement, but it had its vulnerable points. The weaknesses of the Russian world-economy showed up most clearly in the north and west, by comparison with the western world, as one might expect; but they were also evident in the south, from the Balkans and the Black Sea to the Pacific, as it faced the double presence of Islam and China.

Under the rule of the Manchus, China was turning out to be a politically powerful, aggressive, and victorious state. The Treaty of Nerchinsk (1689) virtually brought to a halt Russian expansion into the Amur valley. After this, Russo-Chinese relations thoroughly deteriorated and in January 1722, the Russian merchants were expelled from Peking. An improvement was brought about by the double treaty of Kyakhta (20 August and 21 October 1727) which established the frontier between Mongolia and Siberia and created a Sino-Russian fair on the frontier itself, south of Irkutsk: from now on, this would handle the bulk of trade between the two countries, although a few official caravans[284] for a while continued to reach Peking. The Chinese derived most benefit from this arrangement, since they had now banished Russian traders far from their capital to the outer edge of Mongolia, and they stepped up their conditions. From now on Chinese gold, in flakes or ingots, could be exchanged only for silver. And in 1775, the Russians in the caravan were arrested and hanged in Peking.[285] The Kyakhta fair still had some good days ahead of it, but Russian penetration into the Chinese sphere had been effectively halted.

The Russian position was rather different as regards Islam, which was weakened by political splits between the Turkish Empire, Persia and the Mogul Empire. There was no continuous political front from the Danube to Turkestan. On the other hand trading networks here were ancient, solidly-established and almost impossible to intercept or dislodge. It is an indication of Russian weakness that the merchants of India, Iran and the Balkans invaded (there is no other word for it) Russian territory: there were Indian merchants in Astrakhan and Moscow, Armenians in Moscow and Archangel. And if the latter in 1710 obtained privileges from the Tsar, or if the Tsar agreed in 1732 to grant English merchants facilities to trade with Persia through Kazan, it was because the Russians had encountered setback after setback on the Caspian.[286] Communications were only effective in this direction if they could count on local communities in the key staging-towns – starting with Astrakhan, which contained a Tartar suburb, an Armenian district, and Indian colony, and a caravanserai for 'foreigners' (which in 1652 for instance, put up two Jesuit fathers who were hoping to travel to China). Similarly, for communications with the Black Sea and the Turkish markets in the Balkans, including Istanbul, it was the Turkish merchants (often of Greek origin) and a handful of Ragusan traders, who carried the most weight.

It was indeed a Ragusan, born in Bosnia, brought up and educated in Venice, Sava Lukitch Vladislavitch Raguzinskii, newly arrived in Russia in 1703, whom Peter the Great employed for negotiations with the Balkans and later appointed to organize Siberian trade.[287] And in Siberia itself, there were Greek fur-buyers and mining entrepreneurs in the Altay region. On 20 January 1734, when the Irbit fair opened and the roads were 'thronged with horses, men and sledges ... I saw there', a traveller reports, 'Greeks, Bukhars and Tartars of all kinds....

The Greeks brought with them chiefly foreign goods purchased at Archangel, such as French wines and spirits'.[288]

Foreign superiority was even clearer to see on the European side, where the beneficiaries were Hanseatic, Swedish, Polish, English and Dutch merchants. In the eighteenth century, the Dutch were gradually being ousted; poorly served by their local correspondents, they were going bankrupt one after another, as the English took over the commanding positions: by the time of the negotiations at the end of the century, the latter were dictating their terms. In competition with foreign merchants, in Moscow and later in St Petersburg, Muscovite merchants rarely proved much of a challenge. It is surely curious that the richest merchant in Siberia in the 1730s – a man who had travelled to Peking as agent for Muscovite caravans and who later became vice-governor of Irkutsk, Lorents Lange – was probably a Dane.[289] Similarly, when after 1784 Russia began direct trading with the Black Sea, once again this was handled by foreign intermediaries – Venetians, Ragusans and Marseillais. That is not to mention the adventurers, tricksters and 'persons of ill repute', who had been active in Russian affairs since before Peter the Great. As late as April 1785, Simon Vorontsov was writing from Pisa to his brother Alexander: 'All the scoundrels in Italy, whenever they are at a loss what to do, publicly declare that they are off to Russia to make their fortunes'.[290]

The conclusion is obvious: on its far-flung frontiers the Russian giant was not firmly established. Russia's foreign trade was always manipulated by hidden hands in Peking, Istanbul, Isfahan, Leipzig, Lwow, Lübeck, Amsterdam or London. It was only within the domestic markets or at the huge fairs scattered over the country that the Russian merchant could take his revenge, by dealing in European goods imported through St Petersburg or Archangel and used as exchange currency all the way to Irkutsk and beyond.

The price of European intrusion

Peter the Great's military victories and his far-reaching reforms are said to have 'brought Russia out of the isolation in which she had hitherto lived',[291] a formula which is neither entirely false nor entirely correct. Was Muscovy not already looking towards Europe before Peter the Great? Above all, while the founding of St Petersburg, around which the Russian economy was reorganized, certainly opened a window or rather a doorway on to the Baltic and Europe, making it easier for Russians to reach the outside world, by the same token Europeans coming the other way found it easier to penetrate the Russian stronghold and by increasing their share of trade to conquer the Russian market, shaped it to suit their own purposes as far as possible.

Once more, all the means Europe ordinarily employed to further her ends were pressed into service – above all flexible credit arrangements (buying stocks in advance) and the European secret weapon, ready money. A consul in France's

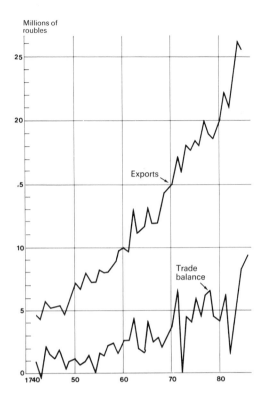

Millions of roubles

Exports

Trade balance

45   THE POSITIVE RUSSIAN TRADE BALANCE (1742–1785)
From a document in the Moscow Central Archives (Vorontsov collection 602-1-59) which gives
the Russian trade balance overland and by sea. There were two short lived drops in the surplus,
in 1772 and 1782, probably as a result of arms purchases.

service at Elsinore on the Sound noted on 9 September 1748: 'Considerable sums
of money in Spanish pieces of eight pass through here on every English vessel
bound for St Petersburg'.[292] This was because the trade balance measured in St
Petersburg, Riga and later at Odessa (1794) always worked out in Russia's
favour – with a few exceptions, at moments when the Russian government was
engaged or about to engage in some large foreign operation. The best way to
promote trade in poorly-developed countries was to import precious metals: the
European merchants allowed the same 'haemorrhage of specie' to Russia as they
did to the Levant ports or the Indies – with the same results: the progressive
takeover of the Russian market, with the real profits being made on the return
journey by the resale or redistribution of merchandise in the West. What was
more, the manoeuvring of foreign exchange on the Amsterdam and later the
London money market,[293] meant that Russia was sometimes fobbed off with
meaningless promises.

   Russia thus became accustomed to receiving the manufactured articles and luxury goods of Europe. Having been a late entrant to international trade, she would subsequently find it hard to disengage from it. Her rulers came to think that the development taking place under their eyes was their own work, and they encouraged and helped it to penetrate their country as a new structural element, seeing it as bringing advantage both to themselves and to a Russia now open to Enlightenment. But was Russia paying too high a price? That is the suggestion in a memorandum, probably from the pen of a Russian doctor, dated 19 December 1765 – an almost revolutionary document, certainly running against the received wisdom of the time. It calls upon Russia more or less to close the door to all foreign penetration. The proper models to follow, suggests the writer, are the policies of India and China (as he imagines them at any rate). 'These nations carry on much trade with the Portuguese, the French and the English, [who] buy from them all their manufactured goods and some raw materials. But neither the Indians nor the Chinese buy the slightest amount of European goods, except for watches, ironware, and a few arms.' So the Europeans are obliged to pay for their purchases with money, 'the method adopted by these nations ever since they have been known to history'.[294] The writer is of the view that Russia ought to return to the simplicity of the time of Peter the Great; since those days, alas, her nobles have become accustomed to luxury which 'has continued to increase for forty years'. The worst temptations are aboard French ships, of which there are not many, but 'the cargo [of one of them] being entirely made up of luxury goods', is generally worth ten or fifteen times that of other nations' ships. If such luxuries were to continue to be imported, they would bring about 'the desolation of agriculture and of the few factories and manufactories of the Empire'.

Is there however not a little irony in the fact that this 'nationalist' memorandum which was communicated to Alexander Voronstov, and therefore brought to the attention of the Russian government, was written in *French*? In itself it illustrates another side of the European intrusion, an acculturation which changed the way of thinking and the way of life not only of the aristocracy, but also of the Russian bourgeoisie and of the entire intelligentsia which was also contributing to build the new Russia. The philosophy of the Enlightment now spreading throughout Europe deeply penetrated Russian intellectual and ruling circles. In Paris, the engaging Princess Dashkov felt the need to exonerate herself from charges of tyranny towards her peasants. She explained in 1780 to Diderot, who had used the word 'slavery', that the greatest threat to the serf lay in the greed of 'governments and their provincial officials'. It was in the interests of the landlord on the contrary that his peasants should be rich, since they 'create his own prosperity and increase his income'.[295] Fifteen years later, she congratulated herself on the results of her management of her estate of Troitskoe near Orel: in 140 years the population had approximately doubled and no woman 'wishes to marry away from my estate'.[296]

But along with ideas, European influence also communicated fashions and undoubtedly contributed to the thorough penetration of Russia by all the luxuries condemned by the good doctor. Rich and leisured Russians became as intoxicated with European ways, with the refinements and pleasures of Paris and London, as westerners had been for centuries with the dazzling civilization of the Italian cities. Simon Vorontsov – who had himself tasted and praised the charms of the English way of life – nevertheless wrote with irritation from London on 8 April 1803: 'I hear that our gentlemen are making extravagant purchases in Paris. That fool Demidov has ordered a porcelain dinner service, every plate of which costs 16 gold louis'.[297]

When all is said and done however, there was no comparison between the Russian situation and the complete dependence of, say, Poland. When the European economy launched its assault on Russia, the latter had already embarked on a course of action which protected her domestic market and the development of her own artisan production, her own manufacturing enterprises created in the seventeenth century,[298] and her own active commerce. And Russia had even adapted very well to the 'industrial pre-revolution', that is to the general upturn in production of the eighteenth century. On state orders and with state assistance, mines, foundries, arsenals, new manufactories of silks and velvets and glassworks sprang up from Moscow to the Urals.[299] And an enormous substratum of domestic and craft industry continued to operate. On the other hand when the real industrial revolution came, in the nineteenth century, Russia was to mark time and fall further and further behind. This was far from the case in the eighteenth century when, according to J. Blum, Russian industrial development was equal and sometimes superior to that of the rest of Europe.[300]

None of this prevented Russia from – more than ever – fulfilling her role as provider of raw materials: hemp, flax, tar, ships' masts; and of foodstuffs: grain and salt fish. Sometimes it was even the case that – as in Poland – exports did not correspond to a genuine surplus. In 1775, for example, 'Russia allowed foreigners to extract her grain, although famine was devastating part of her Empire'.[301] Indeed, the same note dating from 1780 continues, 'the scarcity of specie obliges the farmer to deprive himself of necessities in order to pay taxes' (which were collected in cash). And this scarcity of coin was a burden to landowners who were obliged 'commonly to buy on one year's credit and to sell their foodstuffs for cash six months or a year before the harvest', letting their crops go for 'low prices in order to compensate for the interest on the advance'. Here as in Poland, advance payments for future harvests distorted the terms of trade.

This was the easier in that the landlords, or at any rate the richest of them, were within easy reach of the European merchants. The Russian nobles had been bidden in authoritarian manner to live in St Petersburg 'which they hate', says a report of 1720, 'because staying here ruins them, by keeping them away from their estates and their old way of life which they love above all things in the world, so that if the Tsar does not establish before his death a successor capable of maintaining what he has so auspiciously begun, his people will revert, like a torrent, to their former barbary'.[302] The prophecy was not fulfilled however,

The port of St Petersburg in 1778. Engraving after a drawing by J.B. Le Prince. (Photo Alexandra Skarzynska.)

since although the Tsar died suddenly in 1725, Russia continued to have contacts with Europe, and to sell increasing quantities of raw materials over there. On 28 January 1819, Rostopchin wrote from Paris to his friend Simon Vorontsov in London, 'Russia is an ox which they are eating and turning into stock cubes for other countries' (a metaphor which tells us incidentally that the process for evaporating beef stock to make dried extract had been discovered before Liebig (1803–73) who is usually credited with the invention).[303]

Rostopchin's imagery may be strong but he was not entirely mistaken. It should not be forgotten however that these deliveries of raw materials to Europe provided Russia with a positive trade balance and thus with a constant supply of money. And this in turn was the pre-condition for the introduction of the market into a peasant economy, an essential element in the modernization of Russia and in her powers to resist foreign invasion.

The Turkish Empire

The case of the Turkish Empire is reminiscent of Russia, but with several important differences. An early creation and from the start a vigorous one, by the fifteenth century the Ottoman Empire was an anti-Europe, a counter-Christendom. Fernand Grenard rightly saw the Turkish conquest as something very different from the barbarian invasions of the fifth century: it was 'an Asiatic and anti-European revolution'.[304] And the empire was also unquestionably from the very beginning a world-economy, one which had inherited the ancient ties between Islam and Byzantium and was firmly controlled by effective state authority. 'The *Grand Seigneur* is above the law', said the French ambassador, M. de la Haye, in 1669, 'he may have his subjects put to death without formality and often without any foundation in justice, and may seize their goods and dispose of them as he wishes'.[305] But the counterpart of this despotic power was the long-lasting *pax turcica* – a latter day *pax romana*, the envy of the West. By the same token, the Ottoman rulers were visibly capable of keeping their indispensable western interlocutors firmly in their place. Even Venice was obliged to wheel and deal to get anywhere in Istanbul, penetrating the Turkish economy so far and no further. Only when the authority of the Grand Signor declined would the Ottoman world-economy show signs of disorganization. Even the 'decadence' about which historiography has been so eloquent was 'less rapid and far-reaching than is generally thought'.[306]

The foundations of a world-economy

A fundamental condition of Turkey's autonomy was its physical area: the Ottoman Empire was of planetary dimensions. Who could fail to join the western chorus of amazement and alarm at its fabulous size? Giovanni Botero in 1591 estimated that it had 3000 miles of coastline, and noted that the distance from Tauris to Buda was 3200 miles, that from Derbent to Aden the same, and that the distance from Basra to Tlemcen was just under 4000.[307] The sultan reigned over thirty kingdoms, over the Black Sea and 'the White Sea' (the Aegean), the Red Sea and the Persian Gulf. The Habsburg Empire in its prime was even larger, but that was an empire dispersed worldwide and broken up by great oceans. The Osmanli Empire was in one piece: a jigsaw of interlocking landmasses in which potentially divisive stretches of water were held prisoner.

Lying between the frontiers traced by the long-distance international trade routes, this landmass was a complex of permanent communications and constraints, virtually a fortress and also a source of wealth. It was certainly the overland traffic which turned the Middle East into a crossroads of trade, providing the Turkish Empire with the lifeblood that made it mighty, especially after the conquest of Syria in 1516 and Egypt in 1517 which rounded off its triumphs. It is true that by this time the Middle East could no longer claim to be the centre of the world it had still been in the days of Byzantium and of the first triumphs of Islam. The Europeans had meantime benefited from the discovery of America in 1492 and of the route round the Cape in 1498. And if Europe was too preoccupied in the New World to devote herself whole-heartedly to resisting the Ottoman Empire, this was partly because a number of obstacles had providentially appeared to block Turkey's conquering advance, which failed to go beyond the regency of Algiers to capture Morocco, Gibraltar and the gateway to the Atlantic. Turkey did not achieve overall mastery of the Mediterranean, nor did she ever succeed in conquering Persia, the insurmountable barrier to the east which deprived the Ottomans of the key positions overlooking India and the Indian Ocean. C.R. Boxer suggests that the battle of Lepanto (7 October 1571) which ended Turkish control of the Mediterranean (acquired thirty years earlier by the Turkish victory at La Preveza in 1538) and the more aggressive posture of Persia under Shah Abbas were the basic reasons for the halt of the Turkish advance.[308] I agree; but neither should one underestimate the presence of the Portuguese who were running rings round Islam in the Indian Ocean: for this triumph of European maritime *technology* continued to prevent the Turkish monster from establishing any real presence outside the Persian Gulf and the Red Sea.

So the Middle East as a crossroads of trade had declined in value, but it was far from being reduced to insignificance. The precious Levant trade, so long unparalleled, was not suspended when the Turks occupied Syria in 1516 and Egypt in 1517, nor were the routes through the nearby Mediterranean by any means abandoned. The Red Sea and the Black Sea (the latter as important to Istanbul as the 'Indies' were to Spain) continued to offer their services. After 1630, pepper and spices bound for Europe seem to have been permanently diverted to the Atlantic route but their place was taken by silk, before long by coffee and drugs, and eventually by cotton and cotton textiles, both printed and plain.

Furthermore, the sheer size of the empire ensured that, given the modest level of local consumption, there would be abundant surplus production: animals for butchering, grain, hides, horses – even textiles. The Turkish Empire had also inherited the towns and great conurbations of Islam: it was scattered with merchant cities with their many crafts and trades. Indeed almost every eastern city surprised the western visitor by its noise and bustle: there was Cairo, a great parasitic growth yet at the same time a powerhouse, and a capital in its own way; Aleppo, on its marvellous site surrounded by fertile land, a town about the same size as Padua, *ma senza nessun vacuo e populatissima*, but without any empty spaces, and densely-populated;[309] even Rosetta, 'a very large town, well peopled and pleasantly constructed [with] brick houses standing [twelve feet] above the street';[310] Baghdad and its busy city centre, with 'six or seven streets

... of tradesmen's and craftsmen's shops, streets [which] are closed at nights, some by gates, others with heavy iron chains';[311] Tabriz, on the Persian border, a town 'remarkable for its size, its commerce, its multitude of inhabitants and the abundance of all the necessities of life'.[312] Edward Brown of the Royal Society described Belgrade on his visit there in 1669 as 'a large, strong, populous and great trading city'.[313] The same could be said of almost every Turkish city in Africa, Asia and the Balkans (where they were 'white cities' by contrast with the 'dark' world of the villages).[314]

How then is one to believe that all these cities, ancient and restored, or new and sometimes very close to the western pattern, could possibly have prospered in a Turkey supposedly in decline? Why should something generally considered to be a sign of progress here be thought a sign of deterioration?

An even greater misunderstanding arises from seeking to relate the Turkish Empire's economic history to the chronology of its political history. There is great uncertainty about the latter, to judge by the hesitations of Turkey's historians. One of them has argued [315] that the empire reached its political zenith in 1550, during the last years of Sulaiman the Magnificent (1521-65); another [316] no less convincingly suggests that Turkey's decline set in after 1648 (a whole century later) but this, the year of the Treaty of Westphalia and the assassination of the sultan Ibrahim I, is more of a European than a Turkish landmark. If any date is to be singled out, I should prefer to take 1683, just after the dramatic siege of Vienna (14 July - 12 November 1683), when the Grand Vizier Khan Mustapha, the unfortunate hero of the undertaking, was put to death in Belgrade on the sultan's orders.[317] But no political landmark seems entirely valid to me. Yet again, while politics clearly bears some relation to economics and vice versa, the political 'decline' of the Ottoman Empire, whenever that decline occurred, did not immediately bring about that of the economy. After all, between the sixteenth and the seventeenth century, the population of the empire grew spectacularly, almost doubling in size. In the Balkans, according to Iorjo Tadic,[318] the *pax turcica* and the demand of Istanbul created a genuine *national market*, or at the very least stimulated trade. And in the eighteenth century, there are clear signs of revival.

It was certainly at some cost to themselves that the Ottomans controlled 'not only all the Islamic Mediterranean ports (except those of Morocco) but also the ports providing outlets on the Red Sea and Persian Gulf',[319] plus the towns on the Black Sea which connected with Russian trade routes. The major axes of trade running through the empire themselves gave it a certain coherence. These axes might shift, but they remained in existence. In the fifteenth century, the major crossroads of trade was probably not so much Istanbul, the top-heavy capital which needed rebuilding, as Bursa, city of many trades, and a centre for transit and commerce. The Turkish advance into Syria and Egypt then moved the centre of the Ottoman economy towards Aleppo and Alexandria, thus setting up throughout the sixteenth century a sort of trade diversion operating against

The city and the bazaar of Ankara in the eighteenth century. Detail of painting by J.B. Van Mour, a French artist living in Istanbul between 1699 and 1737. (Rijksmuseum, Amsterdam.)

Istanbul, so that the internal balance of the empire shifted southwards. It is known that the centre moved yet again in the seventeenth century, this time to Smyrna, though this has never been satisfactorily explained. And in the eighteenth century, it seems to me, the economy was re-centred on Istanbul. Could it be that in the course of these little-known episodes, the world-economy corresponding to the Ottoman Empire had a series of different centres of gravity, depending on the period and the economic climate?

In or around 1750 at any rate, Istanbul recaptured its dominant position in the economy. The customs tariffs of the city, a list of which was passed on in 1747 to Moscow, do not in themselves prove anything about the volume of trade. But they do have the particular feature of distinguishing between merchandise 'quoted at the old tariff' and goods added in 1738 or later. The list of imported goods is interminable: numerous textiles, mirrors, panes of glass, paper, pewter, sugar, brazil-wood and campeachy wood, English ales, mercury, every kind of drug and spice, Indian indigo, coffee, etc. Among the *new* products, various other kinds of textiles are listed: cloth, silks, cottons from France, England and Holland; steel, lead, furs, calicoes, indigo from St Domingue, 'coffee from Christendom'; all in a wide range of qualities. The catalogue of outgoing products is shorter, listing the classic exports of Constantinople: buffalo hides, 'black ox' hides, morocco, shagreen, goat's hair and camel hair, wax; only a few articles were added later: fine camlets, silk and goat's hair processed for wigs'. In other words, the list of imports grew ever longer and more varied from distant countries, especially Europe which sent to Constantinople luxury articles and even products from the New World. But there were few additions to the list of exports.[320] A long French report on the Levant trade confirms this impression:

> [French] ships carry more goods to Constantinople than to all the other ports in the Levant. Their cargoes consist of cloth, spices, sweetmeats, dyestuffs and various other goods. Merchandise to the same value cannot be bought in Constantinople, because the only goods the French merchants take on there are hybrid hides, serges and plush, sheep- and goat-skins, printed cottons, a little wax, timber and shagreen. The surplus funds are transferred to other ports by means of bills of exchange which the French merchants of Smyrna, Aleppo and [Port] Said provide for the Pashas who have to make returns to the treasury of the *Grand Seigneur*.[321]

So Constantinople as well as being a major consumption centre was also a currency exchange market, on which large profits could be made; the export trade on the other hand, was as a rule livelier in the other ports of the Levant.

The scale of European penetration of the Turkish Empire

But the key question concerns the place European trade occupied within the overall volume of Turkish trade. In many cases European trade scarcely scratched the surface of the Turkish economy, or merely passed quickly through.

A halt at a caravanserai (manuscript in the Museo Correr, Cicogna collection, Venice). The Italian legend reads as follows: 'Here is an open caravanserai, with the doorway guarded by chains, with hearths and fires for the convenience of travellers. Their arms are hung up on the wall, and their horses stand below the platform inside the building. Turks of all conditions stop here, as [we would] in the taverns of Christendom'. (Photo by the museum.)

It was at grassroots level that the real economy of the Turkish Empire, an elementary but vigorous one, was to be found. Traian Stoyanovich has invented a picturesque name for it, 'the bazaar economy', that is a market economy articulated around the cities and regional fairs where exchange continued to obey traditional rules and was still, he argues, characterized by transparency and good faith. Even in the eighteenth century, credit was poorly developed, apart from usury which was ever-present even in the countryside. True, it was no longer the case that as Pierre Belon had noted in 1550, 'Everything in Turkey is exchanged for cash. So there are not so many papers, record-sheets of loans[322] or ledgers, and between neighbour and neighbour for any retail merchandise, there is no more credit accorded than if they were foreigners from Germany'.[323] But the old ways still survived to some extent, even if western merchants did make advance payments for goods to their suppliers and even if as we have seen the positive balance of their sales in Constantinople enabled them to sell in Smyrna or Aleppo bills of exchange on Constantinople. Overall, commercial life in Turkey still had some archaic features, one of which was the disconcertingly low price of everything compared with western Europe. In Tabriz in 1648, 'one could buy for a sou enough bread to feed a man for a week'.[324] According to the *Gazette of Amsterdam* of 13 December 1672, in Kaminiec which had been captured by the Turks, 'one could buy a horse for 4 rixdales and an ox for 2'.[325] Near Tocat in Asia Minor, Gardane in 1807 met 'inhabitants dressed like ancient patriarchs and equally hospitable. They hasten to offer you lodgings and food, and are most astonished if one offers them money'.[326]

The reason was that money, the sinews of western trade, usually made only fleeting appearances in the Turkish Empire. Part of it found its way to the ever-open jaws of the sultan's treasury, some was used to oil the wheels of top-level trade, and the rest drained away in massive quantities to the Indian Ocean. The West was correspondingly free to use its monetary superiority on the Levant market and even, when circumstances permitted, to deal in money itself, trading on the variable silver-gold ratio and on the preference accorded to certain coins – Spanish silver reals for instance, or the Venetian gold sequin which was always overvalued in the Levant. In 1671, the director of the Venetian *Zecca*[327] pointed out that if one bought a gold sequin in Venice for 17 Venetian lire, or an *ongharo*[328] for 16 lire, it was possible to make a profit of 17.5 per cent on the first and 12 per cent on the second by selling them in Constantinople. A few years later, the rate of profit on a sequin had risen to 20 per cent.[329] By the end of the sixteenth century, it had become a profitable business to send gold by clandestine means from Turkey to Persia.[330] And when Venice witnessed a decline in her eastern trade in the seventeenth and eighteenth centuries, she continued to mint sequins to send to the Levant as a means of ensuring the extremely profitable returns she required.

Similarly, by the end of the eighteenth century, Marseille was exporting hardly any goods to the Middle East, but instead was sending silver coins, mostly Maria-Theresa thalers minted in Milan.[331] It was the easiest way for the French port to keep its position in the Levant markets.

Did the survival of such archaic elements in the Turkish economy bring about its decline? Not as long as the domestic market remained lively and while the arms industry and shipbuilding survived alongside thriving craft production and considerable textile industries (in Chios and Bursa for instance) as well as the multitude of local weaving enterprises so small that they are lost to historical record. Charles Sonnini's astonishing voyage on the Black Sea in the late eighteenth century[332] reveals what is by any standards an extraordinary catalogue of local textiles. Moreover, if we are to believe a letter from Charles de Vergennes, the French ambassador in Constantinople (8 May 1759)[333] all the fabric im-

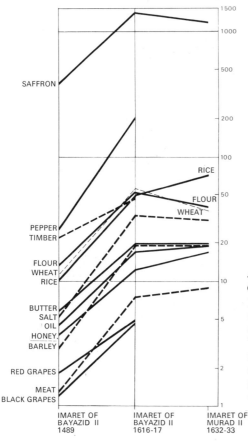

Y-axis values (top to bottom): 1500, 1000, 500, 200, 100, 50, 20, 10, 5, 2, 1

Left labels (top to bottom): SAFFRON, PEPPER, TIMBER, FLOUR, WHEAT, RICE, BUTTER, SALT, OIL, HONEY, BARLEY, RED GRAPES, MEAT, BLACK GRAPES

Line labels: RICE, FLOUR, WHEAT

X-axis:
IMARET OF
BAYAZID II
1489

IMARET OF
BAYAZID II
1616-17

IMARET OF
MURAD II
1632-33

**46 TURKISH PRICES AND SIXTEENTH-
CENTURY INFLATION**
I am indebted to Omer Lütfi Barkan for these
examples of prices which show that the price
rise of the sixteenth century extended to
Turkey. The *imarets* were religious
foundations which provided board for
students and the needy. These are nominal
prices expressed in aspers and do not take
account of devaluations of the asper.

ported from the West would clothe no more than 800,000 people; and the empire
had a population of 20 to 25 million. So there was bound to be a market for the
output of the empire's textile trades – indeed they would not be seriously
disrupted until the increase in imports from Austria and Germany at the end of
the eighteenth century. And as Omer Lütfi Barkan has explained,[334] it was really
only the flood of English textiles after the industrial revolution, in the nineteenth
century, which eventually brought about their almost total collapse.

So while the gates of the Turkish economy had long since been stormed, that
economy had still not been entirely conquered or totally marginalized, even in
the eighteenth century. The products consumed in Turkish cities mostly came
from domestic producers. Grain exporters were, as in Russia, subject to political
control. There was certainly widespread grain smuggling from the islands in the
Aegean, in which Greek sailors were profitably engaged. And a few of the
principal owners of *çiftliks* also indulged in it, but these *çiftliks*, of comparatively
recent creation, had been developed above all to supply Istanbul, not necessarily
for export; this was the case for example of the rice-producing *çiftliks* in

Pack-horses and a camel caravan on the road out of Ankara. Detail of the picture on p. 470.

Rumelia.[335] All in all, Turkish markets functioned reasonably well, relying on a long-established and still efficient transport system.

A land of caravans

The Ottoman possessions were indeed remarkable for the presence everywhere of camel caravans. Even in the Balkans, where trains of pack-horses were still used, it seems that camels had by the end of the sixteenth century invaded all the routes of the peninsula. So the 'Levant ports' seemed now to extend as far as Spalato (Split) in Dalmatia; and the Venetian *galere da mercato* instead of sailing to Syria, had only to cross the Adriatic.[336] Before the war, in 1937, there was still in Dubrovnik a vague folk-memory of these caravans as a romantic feature of the past.

A map of the caravan routes would show them running from Gibraltar to India and northern China, from Arabia and Asia Minor to Astrakhan and Kazan. Both camels and dromedaries were used. Contained within this world of caravans, indeed central to it, was the whole movement-in-space which made up the Ottoman economy.

Western travellers have often described this means of transport, the crowds of travellers herded together, the long journeys during which 'one does not find towns or inns to lodge in every night, as in England', the nights spent in the open, under 'tents when the weather permits', or in the khans and caravanserais, 'built out of charity, for the use … of all passers-by', large and convenient buildings where lodgings were cheap. 'But [visitors] must expect nothing here generally but bare walls: as for other accommodations, of meat, drink, bed, fire, provender, with these it must be everyone's care to furnish himself'.[337] Many of the caravanserais, still standing or in ruins, can be seen in the East even today. Mapping their sites on a map as Albert Gabriel has done, is one way of reconstructing the old road networks.[338]

But although Europeans could use this form of transport for their goods and if necessary their persons, they were not permitted to take any share in its organization. The caravans were a monopoly of Islam. If western merchants went no further than Aleppo, Damascus, Cairo or Smyrna, it was largely because the caravan routes were out of their hands; the Ottoman economy itself took sole charge of this traffic so crucial to its own existence and saw that it was strictly run and supervised, frequent, and above all regular, more regular than transport by sea. The secret of independence in this sector was clearly efficiency. If it was difficult to divert Persian silk from the Mediterranean routes, if the Dutch and English failed to do so whereas the same Dutch merchants had succeeded in cornering pepper and spices, it was because silk travelled from its point of origin by caravan, whereas pepper and spices were 'sea-borne' products from the start, travelling in the holds of ships. The Ottoman economy owed its suppleness and vigour to the tireless convoys which converged from every direction on Istanbul or on Scutari, across the Bosphorus; to the distant routes which wove a network round Isfahan, penetrated Persia, and reached India at Lahore; and to the caravans which set out from Cairo for Abyssinia and returned carrying precious gold dust.

Turkish waters: a well-protected sector

Turkish waters were also quite well protected from outsiders, with most sea-borne transport taking the form of coastal shipping in the seas of the Levant or the Black Sea, a sort of Turkish equivalent of the Asian 'country trade'. It is true that the coasts of the Levant had been threatened in the early days by Christian corsairs from the waters of the west Mediterranean, and the coasting trade had all but been taken over by westerners, in particular by fifty or sixty French ships. But by the end of the eighteenth century, western piracy was less of a threat and the coastal trade had, it seems, been won back from western ships, perhaps because the galleys in the Ottoman fleet had by then long been replaced by sailing vessels, and because the fleet had taken to cruising the Aegean.[339] In December 1787, Captan Pasha sailed into Istanbul with a squadron of battered ships, in poor condition but carrying 25 million piastres taken on board in Egypt.[340] In the past, tribute from Egypt had often been transported overland to Constantinople for security reasons. Was this the beginning of a real change? Between 1784 and 1788, according to French observers, that is several years after the battle of Chesme, the Turkish fleet nevertheless included 25 vessels 'with more than 60 guns', one of which, a huge 74-gunner, had 'just been built by French engineers'.[341] Even though this mighty vessel was manned by a crew of 600, among whom 'there were no more than eight experienced seamen, the rest [being] men who had never seen the sea', the fleet did manage to move about and on the whole to accomplish what was asked of it.

As for the Black Sea, it may not have been fully exploited by ships from Istanbul, but it long remained – and this was what mattered – closed to 'Latin' ships. In 1609, the ban was reiterated after an English expedition got as far as Trebizond. Historians who accuse the Turkish government of negligence and disregard would do well to remember that the Black Sea, so crucial to the supplies of Istanbul and to the building of the Turkish fleet, remained strictly closed to foreign shipping until the end of the eighteenth century. In March 1765, Henry Grenville wrote in a report to the English government:

> The Turks do not share the shipping on the Black Sea with any other nation, and all Foreigners are excluded from it ... The Black Sea is literally the Nursing Mother of Constantinople and provides it with all necessities and foodstuffs such as Grain, Wheat, Barley, Millet, Salt, Cattle, Sheep on the hoof, Lambs, Hens, Eggs, fresh Apples and other Fruits, Butter, another very considerable article, this Butter comes in great buffalo-skin bags, it is rancid, mixed with Mutton fat and very bad, but the Turks ... give it ... preference over the best butter of England and Holland, Tallow, very cheap Candles, Wool, Cow Hides, Ox Hides, Buffalo Hides, both dry and salt, yellow Wax and Honey ... [which the Turks] use as sugar ... much Potash, Grindstones ... Hemp, Iron, Steel, Copper, Timber for building, Firewood, Coals ... Caviar, Fish dried and salted

– plus slaves, mostly provided by the Tartars. In the other direction went goods warehoused in Istanbul: raw cotton, incense, wine, oranges, lemons, dried fruits from the Greek islands, textiles from Turkey or imported from Christendom – all to be ferried to destinations in Russia, Persia, the Caucasus, or the Danube. Coffee and rice however were forbidden to leave 'so that abundance shall reign in Constantinople'.[342]

This huge market used the most rudimentary means of transport: on land goods were carried in wooden wagons 'with no irons' (that is their wheels were not bound with iron, so they were fragile and unable to transport heavy loads) and they were drawn by buffaloes – much stronger than oxen but infuriatingly slow; on sea they travelled in a thousand ships, but these were mostly small boats with the irregular rectangular 'leg o' mutton' sails, or flimsy *caïques* which often went down on this stormy sea with its sudden squalls. Only the ships carrying grain or timber were three-masters with large crews, since the vessels often had to be hauled along and when timber was being loaded, the crew had to land to chopdown trees and make charcoal.[343] It used to be said that if only one in three of these ships returned from the Black Sea trip, the merchant would still make his profit; and that if Constantinople, a city built entirely of wood, were to burn down every year, the Black Sea would provide enough timber to rebuild it every time. 'I need hardly say', writes Grenville, 'that this is an exaggeration'.[344]

In this context, the access gained by the Russians to the Black Sea, the opening of the straits in 1774[345] and especially after 1784,[346] and the arrival of the first Venetian, French and Russian ships, were so many serious blows to the might of the Ottoman Empire and to the equilibrium of the enormous capital. But the new traffic did not become really significant until large-scale exports of Russian grain began in the early decades of the nineteenth century – one of the major events in European history, though rarely recognized as such.[347]

The situation in the Red Sea, a 'second Mediterranean' almost completely encircled by the Turkish Empire, was at once worse and better than in the Black Sea. Turkey had strengthened her hold on it in 1538-46 when she consolidated her position in Aden. Even earlier than this, realizing the commercial, strategic, political and religious importance of the Red Sea, Turkey had captured Mecca and the holy places of Islam. As a sea sacred to Muslims, and forbidden to Christians, the Red Sea would long remain, under Islamic control, the essential route for the ships carrying pepper and spices to Cairo, Alexandria and the Mediterranean. But the Dutch appear to have succeeded in about 1630 in diverting all the eastern pepper and spices bound for Europe to the route round the Cape of Good Hope. So Ottoman prosperity was hit much earlier in the Red Sea, a shipping corridor of international importance, than in the protected waters of the Black Sea.

The diversion of the spice trade did not however mean that the Red Sea was emptied of shipping. The difficult entrance at Bab el-Mandeb was regularly crossed every year by hundreds of ships and long boats (*germes*) carrying southwards rice and beans from Egypt or the European goods stored in the warehouses which the rather insouciant merchants of Cairo owned in Suez. And every year a convoy of seven or eight vessels, including the 'royal' flagship, probably sailing on the sultan's own account, carried the 400,000 piastres and the 50,000 gold sequins which normally travelled to Mocha and Aden, while a caravan from Aleppo to Suez, Mecca and beyond, transported about the same amount overland, though with a greater proportion of gold coins. According to a present-day historian, 'the Red Sea connection remained as a vital channel in the outflow of Spanish-American silver to India and further east', well after the sixteenth century.[348] So it was certainly by using the Mecca caravans that the most could be made of Venetian sequins and Spanish piastres[349] accompanying consignments of European and Mediterranean goods, chiefly cloth and coral. Even in the 1770s, the Red Sea trade, now mostly in Indian hands, was still bringing considerable supplies of gold and silver to Surat. There is no shortage of evidence for this. In 1778-9, an Indian ship brought back from Mocha 300,000 rupees in gold, 400,000 in silver and over 100,000 in pearls; another carried 500,000 in gold and silver. As a historian of the Mediterranean, I was astonished to find that at the end of the eighteenth century the position was still the same as it had been in the sixteenth: gold and silver coins – the most favoured merchandise – were continuing to reach the Indian Ocean by the shortest (and surest?) route.[350]

In the other direction, the major stimulus to trade was increasingly coffee from southern Arabia. Mocha was the centre of the coffee trade and with Jeddah became the leading port on the Red Sea. Ships arrived there carrying merchants and merchandise from all over the Far East. Spices were naturally prominent among their goods. A report of May 1770 does claim that 'drugs and spices' had 'entirely' ceased to travel through the Red Sea 'by the year 1630'.[351] All the same, ten ships a year from the Indian Ocean, from Calicut, Surat or Masulipatam, and the odd Portuguese ship out of Goa, were still arriving in Mocha with cargoes of pepper, cinnamon, nutmeg and cloves. And these spices travelled on with the increasingly large cargoes of coffee heading for Jeddah and Suez.

Should it be assumed that they went no further west? In Cairo, the centre which the French preferred to Alexandria or Rosetta, and where thirty or so French merchants were established, 'the number of merchants from the Indies', one of them reports, 'is beyond reckoning, in coffee, incense, gum, aloes of all sorts, senna and tamarind, saffron-bulbs, myrrh, ostrich plumes, fabrics of all kinds of thread and cotton, stuffs and porcelains'.[352] It is true that this list does not include spices. But with the new 'royal' commodity of coffee, the Red Sea was enjoying a fresh burst of prosperity. By way of Alexandria and Rosetta, coffee could reach Turkish and European customers more quickly than it did in the capacious hulls of the ships belonging to the Indies companies – which did however often go out of their way on the return journey to call at Mocha. As the scene of the revival of the Levant trade, a virtually free port and the queen of the coffee markets, Mocha was visited by many ships from the Indian Ocean. In spite of what today's historians and yesterday's documents say, I find it hard to believe that some pepper and spice was not still finding its way beyond Jeddah into the Mediterranean.

Suez, Egypt and the Red Sea were certainly arousing European appetites once more. In Constantinople and Cairo, there was keen rivalry between the French and the English.[353] In France, and even outside France, schemes to build a Suez canal were legion. One undated project goes into great detail:

> The workmen [who are to dig] the canal should be lodged in sheds barricaded at night for security. And so that these workers may be recognized at all times, it would be wise to clothe them all, men, women and children in uniform: red smocks, white turbans, hair cut short.[354]

The French ambassador, M. de la Haye applied to the sultan for free shipping in the Red Sea, 'and even to create settlements there'.[355] His request was turned down. But the careful and tenacious English East India Company was worried about the possible revival of the ancient Levant route and appointed an agent in Cairo in 1786.[356] In the same year, a French colonel, Edouard Dillon, left on a reconnaissance mission with a view to the possible 'opening of communications with the Greater Indies through the Red Sea and the isthmus of Suez'[357] with the blessing of the 'beys' of Egypt. Simolin, Catherine the Great's ambassador in Paris sent word of it to his monarch. 'From what I know of the emissary', he added, 'he seems a man of limited views and knowledge.' Was it all much ado about nothing? It was at any rate another hundred years before the Suez Canal was finally built (1869) and the revival of the ancient route to the Indies became a reality.

The merchants serving the Ottoman Empire

The economic empire which underpinned the Turkish Empire was defended by a multitude of merchants who thwarted and reduced penetration by westerners. France (that is Marseille) was represented in the Levant by perhaps 40 trading posts, staffed by 150 or 200 persons at most, and the same was true of the other 'nations' in the Levant ports. Everyday transactions were handled by Arab, Armenian, Jewish, Indian or Greek merchants (the latter category including besides authentic Greeks, Macedo-Rumanians, Bulgarians and Serbs) and even by Turks, though on the whole a career in commerce held little attraction for the latter. The Levant swarmed with ambulant salesmen, retailers, shopkeepers in their dark little stores, commission agents from every geographical and ethnic group and of every social status. Tax farmers, wholesalers and real businessmen, capable of lending money to governments, were not far away either. The fairs, gigantic meetings where business worth millions of piastres was transacted, channelled an uninterrupted flow of men, merchandise and beasts of burden.

In this busy domestic market, thronged with people, the western merchant had very little elbow-room. He might have his entrée to certain centres – Modon, Volos, Salonika, Istanbul, Smyrna, Aleppo, Alexandria, Cairo. But according to the ancient pattern of Levantine trade, in none of these places would the merchant from Venice, Holland, France or England come into direct contact with the eventual retailer of his goods. Westerners had to operate through middlemen, usually Jews or Armenians 'who needed an eye keeping on them'.

What was more, eastern merchants did not hand over to the Europeans the monopoly of exports of goods to the West. By the sixteenth century, the easterners had implanted colonies in the Italian Adriatic ports. In 1514, Ancona granted trading privileges to the Greeks of Vallona, the Gulf of Arta and Ianni: its *palatio della farina* became the *Fondaco dei mercanti turchi et altri musulmani*. Jewish merchants arrived at about the same time. By the end of the century, the eastern merchants had invaded Venice, Ferrara, Ancona, even

The square and fountain of Top Hane, Istanbul. (Photo B.N.)

Pesaro,[358] Naples and the fairs of the Mezzogiorno. The strangest of these were
perhaps the Greek merchants and seamen, honest or dishonest, sometimes
frankly pirates, who came from islands with practically no arable land and were
therefore doomed to roam the world. Two centuries later, in October 1787, a
Russian consul in Messina noted that 'sixty or more ... Greek ships bound for
Naples, Livorno, Marseille and other Mediterranean ports' sailed through the
straits every year.[359] When the long crisis of the Revolutionary and Napoleonic
Wars (1793–1815) put an end to the presence of the French traders in the Levant,
their place was taken by Greek merchants and seamen – a success which played
a part in the approaching independence of Greece itself.

Less spectacular, but no less curious was the diaspora in the eighteenth
century of these 'orthodox' merchants throughout the countries acquired by the
Habsburgs under the Peace of Belgrade (1739) which moved the Austro-Hun-
garian border to the Sava and Danube. The Viennese government set out to

colonize the newly conquered territories: the countryside was repopulated, towns sprang up though still on a modest scale, and Greek merchants moved into this virgin territory. They were carried by their own impetus beyond its frontiers and were soon to be found all over Europe, in the Leipzig fairs, using the credit facilities provided by Amsterdam, and even in Russia or indeed Siberia as we have already seen.[360]

Economic decadence, political decadence

The question now arises, were these merchants inside the Turkish Empire foreign bodies? Were they, as I am inclined to think, the artisans of the survival of the Turkish economy – or rats ready to leave the sinking ship? It is a question which brings us back to the irritating problem of the decadence of the Turkish Empire – a problem to which there is unfortunately no solution.

It is my view that one cannot properly speak of the decadence of the Turkish Empire before the first decades of the nineteenth century. If I had to suggest rather more precise dates, I would say that decline set in 1800 in the Balkans, the living heart of the empire and the zone which provided the bulk of its armies and its taxes, but was also the most threatened; in Egypt and the Levant, the downturn perhaps occurred during the first quarter of the nineteenth century; in Anatolia, in the 1830s. Such at any rate are the conclusions of a seductive and controversial article by Henri Islamoglu and Çaglar Keyder.[361] If these dates are correct, the advance into the Ottoman Empire by the European world-economy (an advance both destructive and constructive) moved progressively from the most active part of the empire, the Balkans, to the secondary regions like Egypt and the Levant, and finally to the least developed and thus least susceptible region, Anatolia.

That still does not answer the question whether the first third of the nineteenth century was also the period which hastened the political decline of the Ottoman Empire. That dangerous word *decadence*, which springs easily to the lips of Turkish specialists, contains so many different elements that it begs questions when claiming to answer them. No doubt if concerted action by Austria, Russia, Persia and, briefly, Venice had ever come to anything, Turkey might have been carved up in the same way as Poland. But Turkey was altogether a tougher proposition than the Polish republic; and she was offered a reprieve during the Revolutionary and Napoleonic Wars (although the Egyptian expedition did briefly pose a threat).

Turkey's fatal weakness, we are told, was her inability to adapt to the military technology of Europe. Such a failure only seems apparent with hindsight. Simolin,[362] Catherine the Great's ambassador at Versailles, was protesting in March 1785 against the constant stream of French officers entering Turkey – and being answered by Vergennes that these were 'means far too insignificant' to cause any alarm. A diplomatic answer no doubt, but if the Russian government was anxious, it was because it was not so sure of its superiority over the Turks as historians would have us think. Orlov's fleet did indeed in 5 July 1770 at Chesme, off the island of Chios, destroy all the Turkish frigates, which stood high out of the water and were perfect targets for the cannon balls and blazing brands fired at them.[363] But the Russian fleet was on this occasion commanded by English officers, and it proved incapable thereafter of effecting any serious landing on Turkish soil. The Ottoman artillery certainly left much to be desired, but thinking Russians, such as Simon Voronstov, realized that their own was not much better. The sickness or sicknesses that attacked Turkey came from all quarters at once: the state had lost its authority; its servants were being paid wages at the old rates, while the cost of living had gone up: they 'compensated themselves by embezzlement'; the money supply was probably inadequate – or at any rate the economy was hard to get moving. To introduce reform, while defending itself and at the same time remodelling the army and the navy, would have been a long-term task requiring massive expenditure proportionate to the dimensions of the weighty body of the empire.

The new Grand Vizier saw this very clearly in February 1783. His first decision was:

> to bring back into the bosom of the Empire the domains of the Grand Signor alienated during the last war under the reign of the sultan Mustafa. The government would derive 50 million piastres from this. But these alienated domains are at present in the hands of the greatest and wealthiest personages of the Empire who are employing all their credit to bring down the project, and the sultan lacks all firmness.[364]

This piece of information from Constantinople, passed on by the Neapolitan consul in the Hague, confirms Michel Morineau's recent remarks about the narrow base of Ottoman taxation:

> When bad times came, and the financial demands of the Ottoman Empire increased, greater fiscal pressure was exerted on the population and since the only means the people had of obtaining the piastres needed to pay their taxes was to sell goods abroad, they got rid of their products at rock-bottom prices. This is not so very different from the absurd trade balance quoted for twentieth-century China.[365]

The triumphal entry of industrialized, active and insatiable Europe, blundering as it were into this troubled world, would sound the death-knell of Ottoman greatness. Even so, we should be wary of adopting the conventional chronology and would do well to distrust contemporary declarations, since eighteenth-century Europe was already beginning to take her success rather for granted. In 1731, an author who does not deserve to be famous, wrote: 'All it would require against this Nation [the Ottoman Empire] which observes no Discipline or Order in its combats, is to pitch the right moment to drive it [out of Europe presumably] like a flock of Sheep'.[366] Twenty-five years later, the Chevalier Goudar did not even see the need for the 'right moment': 'We have only to reach agreement about the spoils of the Turk', he writes, 'and the Empire is as good as gone'[367] – an absurd claim. It was the industrial revolution which in the end got the better of an empire whose undoubted vigour was nevertheless insufficient to haul it out of its archaic ways and the legacy of its past.

The Far East – greatest of all the world-economies

The Far East[368] taken as a whole, consisted of three gigantic world-economies: Islam, overlooking the Indian Ocean from the Red Sea and the Persian Gulf, and controlling the endless chain of deserts stretching across Asia from Arabia to China; India, whose influence extended throughout the Indian Ocean, both east and west of Cape Comorin; and China, at once a great territorial power – striking deep into the heart of Asia – and a maritime force, controlling the seas and countries bordering the Pacific. And so it had been for many hundreds of years.

But between the fifteenth and eighteenth centuries, it is perhaps permissible to talk of a *single* world-economy broadly embracing all three. Did the Far East, favoured by the regularity and the usefulness for shipping of the monsoon and the trade winds, actually combine to form a coherent whole, with a series of successive dominant centres, a network of long-distance trading connections and an inter-related series of prices? This combination – gigantic, fragile and inter-mittent – is the true subject of the following pages.

One has to use the word intermittent since the relationship between these huge areas was the result of a series of pendulum movements of greater or lesser strength, either side of the centrally positioned Indian subcontinent. The swing might benefit first the East then the West, redistributing functions, power and political or economic advance. Through all these vicissitudes however, India maintained her central position: her merchants in Gujerat and on the Malabar or Coromandel coasts prevailed for centuries on end against their many com-petitors – the Arab traders of the Red Sea, the Persian merchants of the Gulf, or the Chinese merchants familiar with the Indonesian seas to which their junks were now regular visitors. But sometimes the pendulum malfunctioned or stopped working altogether: at such times the loose garment of Asia was more than usually divided into autonomous fragments.

The crucial feature in this simplified model is precisely this ebb and flow, favouring by turns the West, that is Islam; and the East, that is China. Any advance on the part of these two economies, one each side of India, might have incalculable repercussions, sometimes lasting many centuries. If the West forged ahead, ships from the Red Sea and/or the Persian Gulf would invade the Indian Ocean, crossing it from side to side, and appearing (as they did in the eighth century) off Canton (Han Fu to Arab geographers).[369] If, on the other hand, the usually home-loving Chinese ventured abroad, it meant that seamen from the

Arab-style boat photographed in Bombay harbour: boats like this are still plying between India and the Arabian coast and Red Sea. (Photo F. Quilici.)

south coast of China sailed to the East Indies, which they never lost from sight, and to the other 'Indies' east of Cape Comorin. There was nothing to prevent them from going further still.

In the thousand years or so before the fifteenth century, Far Eastern history is simply a monotonous repetition of the same events; one port would rise to prominence on the shores of the Red Sea, only to be replaced in time by one of its identical neighbours. The same thing happened along the coast of the Persian Gulf or in India, or in the islands and peninsulas of the East Indies; and maritime zones too might dominate by turns. For all the changes, however, history followed essentially the same course.

The beginning of the fifteenth century, the starting-point of this work, was marked by the revival of China under the Ming dynasty which liberated the country from the Mongols in the years after 1368, as well as by an extraordinary wave of maritime expansion, an event which has been much discussed but still remains in many respects a mystery, from its origins to its interruption in about 1435.[370] The foreign expeditions by Chinese junks, which went as far afield as Ceylon, Hormuz and even the Zendj Empire on the African coast,[371] drove back or at any rate disrupted Muslim trading. The voice of the East now spoke louder than the Centre or West. And it was at this time as I shall try to show, that the centre of gravity of this huge super-world-economy became stabilized in the East Indies, with their busy ports of Bantam, Atjeh, Malacca and – much later – Batavia and Manila.

It might seem absurd to attribute such importance to these ports in the East Indies – which were certainly not large in size. But then Troyes, Provins, Bar-sur-Aube and Lagny were also small towns in the days of the Champagne fairs; lying along a strategic communications axis commanding all traffic between Italy and Flanders, they nevertheless became the centre of a very great trading complex. Was this not exactly parallel to the position of the East Indies, a crossroads of trade with its fairs sometimes prolonged for months on end as the merchants waited for the monsoon to change direction so that they could set sail for home? Perhaps these East Indian ports even positively benefited – like the trading towns of medieval Europe – from not being strictly integrated into any very powerful political units. Despite all the kings and 'sultans' who ruled them and maintained order there, these were virtually autonomous towns: wide open to the outside world, they could orient themselves to suit the currents of trade. So whether Cornelius Houtman arrived in Bantam in 1595 by chance or calculation, he had landed unerringly at the complex heart of Far Eastern trade – hitting the jackpot first time so to speak.

All things considered, how wise is it for one historian to try to bring together in a single analysis the scattered fragments of a history still insufficiently explored by research? It is true that we still know very little about this world – though more than we used to. We can for instance challenge the traditional image (briefly revived by J.C. van Leur)[372] of Asiatic traders as high-class pedlars hawking about in their small packs tiny quantities of valuable merchandise – spices, pepper, pearls, perfumes, drugs and diamonds. The reality is rather different. Everywhere, from Egypt to Japan, we shall find genuine capitalists, wholesalers, the rentiers of trade, and their thousands of auxiliaries – the commission agents, brokers, money-changers and bankers. As for the techniques, possibilities or guarantees of exchange, any of these groups of merchants would stand comparison with its western equivalents. Both inside and outside India, Tamil[373], Bengali and Gujerati merchants formed close-knit partnerships with business and contracts passing in turn from one group to another, just as they might in Europe from the Florentines to the Lucchese, the Genoese, the South Germans or the English. There were even, in medieval times, merchant kings in Cairo, Aden and the Persian Gulf ports.[374]

Thus we are gradually becoming more and more clearly aware of 'a network of maritime traffic comparable in volume and variety to that of the Mediterra-

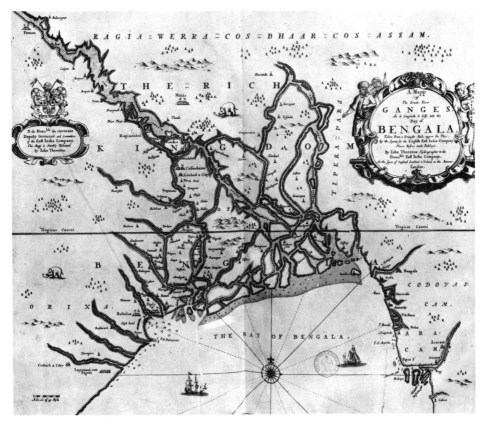

The huge Ganges delta, mapped for the East India Company by John Thornton, early eighteenth century. (Photo B.N., Paris.)

nean or of the northern and Atlantic coasts of Europe'.[375] Everything and anything could be found here: luxury goods alongside commonplace commodities, silk, spices, pepper, gold, silver, precious stones, pearls, opium, coffee, rice, indigo, cotton, saltpetre, teak (for shipbuilding), Persian horses, elephants from Ceylon, iron, steel, copper, pewter, shimmering fabrics for the rich and powerful, coarse cloth for the peasants of the spice islands or the black population of Monomotapa.[376] The 'country trade' had been in existence long before the arrival of the Europeans, since complementary products attracted and balanced each other: in the seas of the Far East they maintained a perpetual flow of trade, like that in the seas of Europe.

The fourth world-economy

Three world-economies in the Far East might already be thought a lot. But the arrival of the Europeans brought into being a fourth – conjured up by the Portuguese, the Dutch, the English, the French and others. When Vasco da Gama sailed into Calicut on 27 May 1498, he pushed open the door. But the Europeans were not yet strong enough to force their way into this unknown world which they had yet to discover (for all the sensational tales brought back by their celebrated predecessors, the first western travellers). Asia was still a *terra incognita*, another planet; even the plants and animals were different here[377] in this whole continent of different peoples, different civilizations, religions, forms of society or types of land tenure.[378] Everything was strange and new: even the rivers were not like European waterways. What was large in the West was multiplied immeasurably here. The towns of the East were vast ant hills teeming with people. How strange the westerners found these civilizations, societies and cities!

And these distant lands could only be reached after months at sea in difficult conditions. The fourth world-economy was liable to find itself out of its depth here. The possession of bases in the Middle East (which Christian forces had tried to capture during the Crusades) gave the states and traders of Islam the means to intervene in strength and as they pleased in the Indian Ocean; whereas the ships from Europe brought only derisory forces with them in their ventures to the societies and territories of Asia. So far from home, even at the time of their most brilliant successes, the Europeans never had superiority of numbers. There were no more than 10,000 Portuguese settlers in all in the sixteenth century, from Hormuz to Macao and Nagasaki.[379] For years the English were equally poorly represented, despite the scale of their early successes. There were a mere 114 English 'civilians' in Madras, in about 1700; 700 or 800 in Bombay; 1200 in Calcutta.[380] In September 1777, Mahé (a very secondary French base it is true) contained no more than 114 Europeans and 216 Sepoys.[381] In 1805, there were only '31,000 English in [the whole of] India', a tiny contingent, but one capable of ruling the entire country.[382] At the end of the eighteenth century, employees of the Dutch V.O.C. both at home and in the Far East numbered 150,000 at most.[383] Even supposing that less than half of these served overseas, the Dutch were still by far the largest group. One might add that the *strictly European* armies, in the time of Clive and Dupleix were very small.

The disproportion between the *apparent* means employed and the results of the European conquest, is striking, 'A chance happening, the merest puff of public opinion', wrote an American of French origin in 1812, 'might ... blow away English rule in India.'[384] Twenty years later, Victor Jacquemont repeated the same sentiments with emphasis: 'In the singular construction of English power in India, everything is artificial, abnormal and exceptional'.[385] The word 'artificial' is not pejorative: artifice was generally a synonym for intelligence and in this context for success. A handful of Europeans managed to impose themselves not only on India but on the whole of the Far East. By all the rules, they should not have succeeded – but they did.

India's self-inflicted conquest

In the first place, the Europeans were never acting in isolation. Thousands of slaves, servants, auxiliaries, associates and collaborators bustled around them – a hundred or a thousand times more numerous than the men who were not yet – but soon would be – the masters. The European ships engaging in the 'country trade' for instance, were manned from the start by mixed crews, largely composed of local seamen. Even those that sailed to the Philippines employed 'a few Spaniards [but] many Malays, Hindus and Filipino half-breeds'.[386] The ship carrying Father de Las Cortes from Manila to Macao in 1625, which went off course and was wrecked on the Cantonese coast, had no fewer than 37 Lascars among the crew.[387] When in July 1690 the French fleet, under Duquesne's nephew, captured the Dutch flyboat the *Montfort of Batavia* off Ceylon, among the captives figured two 'Lascaris or black slaves, who are terrible to behold. These wretches would let themselves die of hunger rather than touch anything a Christian had touched [i.e. cooked]'.[388]

Likewise, the armies which the companies eventually set afoot were composed overwhelmingly of native troops. In Batavia in 1763, for every 1000 to 1200 European soldiers 'of all nationalities', there were nine or ten thousand Malay auxiliaries, plus 2000 Chinese soldiers.[389] Whose fertile mind hit on the brilliant idea (if indeed it was a new discovery) of enlisting sepoys – thus using Indian troops to conquer India? Was it François Martin?[390] Or Dupleix? Or the English – of whom a contemporary (but he was French) wrote: 'they levied [sepoys] in imitation of M. Dupleix'?[391]

Similarly, the crucial centres of commercial enterprise were occupied by local merchants. A western businessman would find himself besieged by thousands of native brokers pressing their services on him: Moors from Egypt, the ubiquitous Armenians, Banyans, Jews from Mocha, Chinese from Canton, Amoy or Bantam, not to mention the Gujerati, the merchants from the Coromandel coast, or the Javanese – lean and hungry auxiliaries who literally encircled the Portuguese when the latter made their first expeditions to the spice islands. It was after all perfectly natural that they should. In Kandahar where his wanderlust had taken Maestre Manrique in 1641, a Hindu merchant, taking the Spanish traveller for a Portuguese, offered his services because as he explained, 'the people of your nation do not speak the language of these countries so you are sure to encounter difficulties unless you find someone to guide you'.[392] Help, collaboration, collusion, coexistence, symbiosis – all these became necessary as time went by and the local merchant, ingenious and unbelievably frugal, capable of surviving long voyages on a small ration of rice, was as indestructible as couch-grass. In Surat, the 'servants' of the English East India Company had in any case been hand in glove with the big-time moneylenders in the town virtually from the start. And how often we find English factories from Madras to Fort William, asking permission from the board of directors in London to borrow money from Indian merchants! In 1720, when the liquidity crisis resulting from the South Sea Bubble was raging in England, the East India Company borrowed the cash it needed in India – a wise move as it turned out since thanks to this decision 'the crisis passed as quickly as it had come'.[393] In 1726, when the French company began to recover, it kept well away from Surat where it owed the Banyans no less than 4 million rupees.[394]

It thus became impossible to shake off these indispensable collaborators already on the spot and busily creating wealth. Pondicherry, says a report of 1733, will never be a prosperous centre 'unless some means is found of attracting there merchants capable of trading on their own account'[395] – merchants of whatever nationality, but above all Indian. Indeed would Bombay ever have been built without the Parsees and Banyans? What would Madras have been without the Armenians? In Bengal, as elsewhere in India, the English made unlimited use of the local merchants and bankers. Only when British rule was firmly established in Bengal were the native capitalists of Calcutta brutally eliminated from the more profitable sectors (banking and foreign trade) and obliged to fall back on land, usury, tax-collecting or even, in about 1793, 'the greater part of the obligations [i.e. bonds] of the British East India Company'.[396] But at the same time in Bombay, where everything still remained to be done, the British took care not to displace the Parsee, Gujerati or Muslim merchants who continued to amass huge fortunes there in foreign trade or as owners of the port's merchant fleet – until the arrival of the steamship in the 1850s.[397] Nor, despite several attempts, did English banking ever entirely manage to eliminate the *hundi*, the bill of exchange used by the Indian *sarrafs*, the symbol of their freedom of manoeuvre and of a solid banking organization of which the British had taken advantage long before they tried to suppress it.

Gold and silver, strength or weakness?

We are often told that Europe, America, Africa and Asia were complementary. It would be equally correct to say that world trade did its best to render them complementary and often succeeded in doing so. The Far East did not on the whole welcome European products with the frenzy and appetite displayed from an early date by the West for pepper, spices or silk. Since trade balances require that one passion be compensated by another, Asia had retaliated from the days of the Roman Empire by consenting to exchange her goods only for precious metals – gold (which was preferred on the Coromandel coast) but above all silver. China and India in particular became, as I have had numerous occasions to point out, bottomless pits for the precious metals in circulation: they were sucked in, never to re-emerge. This curious but constant phenomenon accounted for the flow of bullion from West to East, which some people have seen as a weakness of Europe vis-à-vis Asia, but which I regard, as I have already said, merely as the usual method employed by Europeans, not only in Asia but elsewhere as well, even inside Europe, when they wanted to break into a particularly profitable market. In the sixteenth century, this method was to assume unprecedented proportions thanks to the discovery of America and the output of the mines of the New World.

American silver reached the Far East by three routes: through the Levant and the Persian Gulf, a route which as Indian historians have proved was still the most important as late as the seventeenth and eighteenth centuries; the route round the Cape; and the route taken by the Manila galleon. Leaving aside the very special case of Japan (which possessed its own silver mines whose output occasionally played a part in Japanese foreign trade) almost all the silver in circulation in the Far East was of European – that is American – origin. So the rupees which a European might borrow from an Indian banker or money-changer were in fact, tit for tat, made of silver imported some time previously by European trade.

As we shall see later, this influx of precious metals was vital to the movements of the most active sector of the Indian, and no doubt the Chinese economy. If the Indian boats sailing from Surat to Mocha by some mischance failed to rendez-vous with the Red Sea ships carrying gold and silver, Surat – for so long the dominant centre of Indian trade – would quickly have plunged into crisis. This being so, it is perhaps not an exaggeration to see Europe, committed to Asia only by her passion for luxury goods, as having a stranglehold in the form of silver over the economies of the Far East, and thus being in a position of strength. But whether this superiority was fully and lucidly appreciated is open to question. European merchants seeking to pursue profitable trade in Asia were themselves at the mercy of the arrival in Cadiz of the American silver fleet – always unpredictable and sometimes disappointing. The need to find at all costs the necessary specie for trading in Asia could only have been regarded as a burden. Between 1680 and 1720 in particular[398] silver was comparatively scarce, and its price on the open market exceeded the price offered by the mints. The result was a *de facto* devaluation of the key silver currencies, the pound sterling and the florin, and thus a deterioration of the terms of trade in Asia for both England and Holland.[399] Silver might give the West an advantage, but it also created difficulties and uncertainties for everyday trade.

The European assault force: merchants with a difference

The Europeans had from the start another source of superiority, one of which they were fully aware and without which their efforts would never have got off the ground: this priceless advantage was the western warship, easy to manoeuvre, capable of sailing against the wind, rigged with a range of sails, and armed with

The Dutch assault on and capture of Tidore, one of the Molucca islands held by the Portuguese, in 1606. On the right of the picture, longboats are landing the attacking troops. (Atlas von Stolk.)

cannon which were even more effective once the use of gun-ports became widespread. When, in September 1498, Vasco da Gama's fleet left the approaches to Calicut, it encountered eight large Indian vessels which had sailed to intercept it. They were all rapidly put to flight and one was captured (the other seven ran aground on a sandbank on a beach which the Portuguese vessels could not approach since the waters were too shallow for them).[400] What was more, Indian maritime customs had always been extremely pacific. There is only one known exception to this rule of non-aggression, the Empire of Chola which had in the thirteenth century built an impressive navy on the Coromandel coast, had several times occupied Ceylon, the Maldive and Laccadive islands, and had been able to cut the Indian Ocean in two at will. By the sixteenth century however, all this was in the past, and despite the presence along certain parts of the coast of pirates (who were not particularly hard to avoid) merchantmen never needed to sail in armed convoys.

The task of the Portuguese was thereby made much easier. Unable to occupy the great landmasses of the Far East, they found it a simple matter to control the seas, the medium of transport and communications. This was what mattered after all: 'If you are strong in ships', Francisco de Almeida wrote to the king in Lisbon, 'the commerce of the Indies is yours, and if you are not strong in ships, little will avail you any fortress on land.'[401] In Albuquerque's opinion, 'If once Portugal should suffer a reverse at sea, your Indian possessions have not power to hold out a day longer than the Kings of the land choose to suffer it'.[402] In the following century, the commander of the Dutch base of Hirado in Japan spoke in similar terms in 1623: '[We have] barely sufficient force to set ashore unless under the protection of the ships' cannon'.[403] And a Chinese resident in Macao remarked with regret: 'We shall know how to put [the Portuguese] at death's door as soon as they nourish any disloyal design. [But] if we move them to the open sea, by what means would we punish the evil doers and how could we ... defend ourselves against them?'[404] Thomas Roe, ambassador of the East India Company to the court of the Mogul emperor, thought the same: hence his advice to the English officials: 'Keep to this rule if you look for profit: seek it out on the seas and in peaceful trading; for there is no doubt that it would be an error to maintain garrisons and to fight in India on land'.[405]

These pronouncements, elevated almost to the status of maxims, should not be interpreted as a desire for peace, merely as the clear recognition over a period of many years that any attempt at territorial conquest would be extremely hazardous. European intrusion could nevertheless, when the occasion arose, take aggressive and brutal form. There is no shortage of examples of assault, pillage and warlike designs. In 1586, shortly before the sailing of the Invincible Armada, Francisco Sardo, the Spanish governor of the Philippines, offered his services for the conquest of China with 5000 men: later, Coen's effective approach to the islands of the East Indies, which were easier to control than the mainland, was characterized by force, colonization and strong-arm tactics.[406] And the time of territorial conquests did eventually come – rather late in the day perhaps – in the age of Dupleix, Bussy and Clive.

But before this burst of colonization, Europeans were already making the most of their overwhelming superiority both *on* sea and *from* the seaward side. When local pirates were active, Europeans could handle freight on behalf of non-European merchants fearful for their goods; they could attack or threaten to bombard a recalcitrant port; or force local vessels to pay for safe-conduct passes[407] (the Portuguese, Dutch and English all practised this form of ransom demand); they could even, in cases of conflict with a territorial power, wield the effective weapon of a blockade. During the war against Aurangzeb in 1688, conducted at the instigation of Sir Josiah Child, director of the East India Company, 'The subjects of the Mogul', Child wrote, 'cannot bear a war with the English for twelve months together, without starving and dying by the thousands for want of work to purchase rice; not singly for want of our trade,

Native pirates off the Malabar coast: they are using oars and sails, arquebuses and arrows.
Watercolour by a Portuguese artist long resident in Goa in the sixteenth century.
(Photo F. Quilici.)

but because by our war, we obstruct their trade with all the Eastern nations which is ten times as much as ours and all the European nations put together'.[408]

This text spells out admirably not only how much the English appreciated the massive strength and indeed commercial might of Mogul India, but also their determination to use all the advantages they possessed, to do business 'sword in hand', as one of the Company's servants put it.[409]

Trading posts, factories, supercargoes

The Great Indies companies were the multinationals of their age. They had to grapple not only with their 'colonial' problems but also with the state which had created and continued to support them. They were a state within – or outside – the state. They did battle with their shareholders, creating a form of capitalism at odds with traditional trading practices. They had not only to handle the capital belonging to the shareholders (who clamoured for dividends), the capital of holders of short-term bonds, and the company's circulating capital (that is liquid assets) but also to see to the maintenance of fixed capital – ships, harbours and fortresses. They had to keep an eye from a distance on several foreign markets and relate these to the possibilities and advantages of their own national market, that is to the sales at auction in London, Amsterdam and elsewhere.

Of all these difficulties, distance was the hardest to overcome – indeed the old Levant route was still used to send letters, agents, important instructions, gold and silver. In 1780, with the aid of a favourable monsoon, an Englishman even set up a record speed for the journey London-Marseille-Alexandria-Calcutta: 72 days.[410] The normal route by the Atlantic and the Cape generally took eight months each way, so that a round trip could hardly be completed in less than 18 months – that is assuming all went well and that the traveller was neither obliged to winter in port nor faced with untoward problems when rounding the Cape of Good Hope. It was this slow turn-around time of ships and goods which made it impossible for the directors in London and Amsterdam to keep control in their own hands. They were obliged to delegate powers and share them with local boards of the company, which might have to take urgent decisions on their own authority (as they did in Madras or Surat) as well as to translate the wishes of the company into action on the spot, arranging 'contracts'[411] and orders at appropriate times (six months or a year in advance), anticipating payments and collecting cargoes.

These trading units far from home had various names: trading posts, factories, settlements. The two first terms were interchangeable in everyday language, but by and large they are listed in order of descending importance. Thus the English 'factory' in Surat set up a series of 'settlements' in Goga, Broach, Baroda, Fatehpur Sikri, Lahore, Tatta, Lahribandar, Jasques, Mocha and Isfahan;[412] and the 'establishments' of the French company at Chandernagor were divided into three categories: surrounding the headquarters, Chandernagor, 'the six great trading posts (*comptoirs*) were Balasore, Patna, Cassimbazar, Dacca, Jugdia, and Chittagong; and there were mere settlements at Supur, Kerpoy, Karagola, Monghur and Serampore', the last two being 'branches where an agent without territory resided'.[413]

The 'territory' of a trading post or company headquarters proceeded from a concession by the local authorities, difficult to obtain and never granted without something in return. Taken as a whole, the system was another form of colonization – of a purely commercial nature: the Europeans settled within easy reach of the points of production and the markets, at the intersections of trade routes, using networks in existence before their arrival, thus saving themselves the trouble of creating infrastructures, and leaving to local communities the tasks of transporting the goods to the ports, organizing and financing production and handling elementary exchange.

Clinging like a parasite to a foreign body, European occupation of the East before the British conquest of India (with the exception of the Dutch successes in the special case of Indonesia) was sporadic, confined to a series of positions and strongholds. Macao, on the outskirts of Canton was no bigger than a village. Bombay, on its island, three leagues by two, had hardly space for its harbour, shipyard, barracks and houses and had it not received supplies from the neighbouring island of Salsetta, its richer inhabitants would not have been able to eat meat every day.[414] Deshima, a settlement within the port of Nagasaki, was certainly smaller than the *Ghetto Nuovissimo* in Venice. Many 'factories' were little more than fortified buildings, or glorified warehouses, where the Europeans lived a life more cut off even than that of the most closed castes in India.

There were exceptions of course: Goa on its island, Batavia, Mauritius (Ile de France) and Reunion (Bourbon). European positions in China on the other hand were even more precarious. Merchants from Europe had no permanent status in Canton, and unlimited access to the free market was refused to them (unlike in India). The companies were represented on each of their ships by travelling salesmen, who made up a sort of mobile factory, a travelling community of supercargoes. If the latter quarrelled or refused to obey the chief who had been chosen for them, problems and disappointments were to be expected.[415]

Should one therefore conclude that until the British conquest, European trading activity did no more than skim the surface of Asia; that it was confined to trading posts which made little impression on this gigantic body; that European occupation was superficial, skin-deep and of no consequence, changing neither societies nor civilizations; and that economically it concerned only the export trade, that is only a minor part of production? This is none other than the old argument about the domestic market and foreign trade raising its head again. The European trading posts in Asia were in fact no less effective than those of the Hanseatic League or the Dutch in the Baltic and North Sea, or than the Venetian and Genoese trading posts throughout the Empire of Byzantium, to take only a few examples among many. Europe sent very small groups of settlers out to Asia, where they were in a tiny minority it is true, but it was a minority in direct contact with the most advanced capitalism in the western world. These European minorities, of whom it has been said that they constituted merely 'an inherently brittle superstructure',[416] were in touch not with the masses of Asia but with other commercial minorities who dominated trade and exchange in the Far East. And it was indeed these *local* minority groups who, partly under pressure, partly of their own accord, paved the way for the European intrusion, teaching first the Portuguese, then the Dutch and English (and even the French, Danes and Swedes) the way through the labyrinth of the 'country trade'. The process had thus begun which was by the end of the eighteenth century to deliver more than 85 or 90 per cent of India's foreign trade over to the English monopoly.[417] But it was only because the accessible markets of the Far East formed a series of coherent economies linked together in a fully operational world-economy, that the merchant capitalism of Europe was able to lay siege to them and to use their own vitality to manoeuvre them to its own advantage.

How to get at the real history of the Far East?

The real object of our interest then is the subterranean history of Asia; but let me at once say that this is not easy to discover. In London, Amsterdam and Paris, there are plenty of excellent archives, but we always see the landscape of India or the East Indies filtered through the history of the big companies. There are also, in Europe, and throughout the world, many eminent Orientalists. But a specialist on Islam cannot also be an expert on China, or India, or the East Indies, or Japan. Moreover Orientalists are more likely to be linguists and cultural experts than social or economic historians.

Today this state of affairs is changing. Specialists on China, Japan, India or Islam are showing more interest than in the past in these countries' societies or political and economic structures. There are even some sociologists who think like historians.[418] Best of all, over the last twenty or thirty years, as they have pursued the identity of their countries now liberated from Europe, historians in the Far East, whose numbers are growing, have begun to catalogue the available sources; various studies now bear witness to what Lucien Febvre used to call a sense of 'problem-based history'. These historians are toilers in the vineyard of the new history and its harvest is beginning to appear in their books and in a number of excellent journals. We are on the brink of some far-reaching reappraisals.

To follow in their footsteps and tackle the whole area at once is out of the question. There is so much material (although many questions remain unanswered) that the time is simply not ripe for an overall view. I have nevertheless tried, rashly perhaps, to convey through *one* example, some idea both of the scope and of the novelty of the problems which are now coming to light. The example I have chosen is India. There are now several fundamental studies in English, and the work of an outstanding team of Indian historians is now available, since they too have fortunately published in English. In them we have excellent guides for exploring the splendours and miseries of 'medieval' India – since the convention is already well-established in India of making the Middle Ages run until the installation of the British Raj. This is the only point in their analysis that I find questionable because of the *a priori* classifications it suggests (notably a lag of several centuries behind Europe) and because it introduces to the picture the so-called problems of 'feudalism', which is described both as surviving and as deteriorating between the fifteenth and eighteenth centuries. But such criticisms are merely points of detail.

If my choice fell on India, it was not only for the reasons just mentioned; nor because Indian history is particularly easy to grasp; on the contrary, by the norms of general history, India seems to me to be a subtly deviant case, and a very complex one, politically, socially, culturally and economically. No, the reason is that India was a world-economy occupying a central position, on which everything depended: every kind of development could take root in this tolerant environment with its weaknesses. It was here that the Portuguese, the French and the English first set foot. The Dutch were the only exception: by hitching their wagon to the East Indies they won the race to obtain a monopoly. But in doing so, did they perhaps forfeit the chance of success in India – which later proved to be the foundation of any durable achievement by the other newcomers to the East, first the Muslims and later the westerners?

The villages of India

India is made up of villages – thousands and thousands of them. It is more appropriate to use the plural than the singular[419] which suggests a misleading image of 'the typical' Indian village, enclosed in its little community, surviving as an intangible, unchanging and always self-sufficient unit, throughout the eventful history of India; and which also seems to suggest that by some second miracle, 'the village' was the same throughout the huge sub-continent, despite the clear identities of different provinces (the particular features of the Deccan, for instance, 'the land of the south'). No doubt a self-sufficient village, producing its own food and clothing and entirely self-absorbed, could still be found in remote and backward regions even today. But it would be an exception.

As a rule, the village community was open to the outside world, subject to various authorities and to the markets which watched it closely, emptied of its surpluses and forced upon it the convenience and the dangers of a money economy. This brings us close to the secret of the entire history of India: the vitality drawn up from the base to animate and nourish the great political and social corpus. In a very different context, the pattern is similar to that of the Russian economy at the same period.

Through recent studies, it is now possible to see how the machine functioned, fuelled as it was by harvests, rents and state-imposed taxes. The ubiquitous money economy was an excellent drive-belt, facilitating and increasing the number of transactions, including compulsory exchange. Credit for the creation of these circuits is only partly due to the government of the Mogul emperor. India had in fact been for centuries subject to a money economy, partly through her links with the Mediterranean world, which had since Antiquity been acquainted with money, and indeed after a fashion had invented it and exported it abroad. If we can believe L. C. Jain,[420] India already had bankers six centuries before Christ, a hundred years before the age of Pericles. The money economy had certainly penetrated Indian trade many centuries before the sultanate of Delhi.

The decisive contribution of the latter, in the fourteenth century, was a coercive administrative organization, with a hierarchy reaching down through the provincial and district authorities to the villages, which it kept under firm control. The weighty mechanisms of this state, inherited by the Mogul Empire in 1526, enabled the latter to stimulate and confiscate surplus output in the

The Mogul emperor's court: an Indian lord approaches the sovereign. (Photo B. N.)

countryside. Consequently it encouraged the maintenance and expansion of such surpluses. For the Muslim despotism of the Moguls contained a measure of 'enlightened despotism', a desire not to kill the goose that laid the golden eggs, a desire to encourage peasant 'reproduction', to extend cultivation, to substitute a profitable crop for a less profitable one, to colonize virgin land, and to increase the possibilities of irrigation by wells and reservoirs. The village was also encircled and penetrated by the network of travelling merchants, by the neighbouring market towns, even by the markets held for the barter of foodstuffs within large villages or out in the country between villages, as well as by the hungry markets of near or distant towns, and by the fairs connected with religious festivals.

To what extent then were the villages controlled from outside? This was certainly the aim of the provincial and district authorities, as it was that of the nobles, who had received from the emperor (theoretically the sole owner of the land) a share of the dues from the estates (*jagirs* or life-holdings); it was also the concern of the vigilant tax-collectors, the *zamindars*[421] who had hereditary rights to land; and of the merchants, usurers and money-changers who bought, transported and sold harvests, and who also converted taxes and dues into cash so that their product could circulate more easily. The landlord would actually live at court in Delhi, keeping up his rank, and the *jagir* was granted him for a fairly short term, usually three years. He exploited it by flying visits quite shamelessly, from a distance; like the state, he preferred to receive his dues in cash rather than in kind.[422] The conversion of crops into coin was therefore the cornerstone of the system. Not only were silver and gold both an object of and an encouragement to hoarding, they were also the indispensable mechanisms which made the whole great machine function, from its peasant base to the summit of society and the business world.[423]

The village was, in addition, controlled from within by its own hierarchy and the caste system (embracing artisans and the proletariat of untouchables). It had a vigilant leader, the village headman, and an exclusive 'aristocracy', the *khud-kashta*, a small minority of relatively wealthy or at any rate comfortably-off peasants, owners of the best land, possessors of four or five ploughs, four or five bullock or buffalo teams and in addition enjoying a favourable tax rating. These men effectively represented the famous village 'community' about which so much has been written. In exchange for their privileges and the *individual* ownership of the fields they farmed themselves with family labour, they were *collectively* responsible to the state for the payment of taxes on behalf of the whole village. Indeed they received a share of the money collected. They enjoyed similar favours regarding the colonization of virgin lands and the creation of new villages. But they were closely watched by the authorities who viewed with suspicion the development of anything like tenant-farming or share-cropping which might benefit these village elders, or even of the introduction of wage-labour (which did exist but to a minimal extent) – that is of any form of land-

An Indian bullock caravan carrying grain from 'Balaguate' (Balaghat in the province of Madhya Pradesh) to the Portuguese settlement in Goa (sixteenth century). (Photo F. Quilici.)

tenure outside the norm, the extension of which might, in the hands of fiscally privileged individuals, eventually diminish the volume of taxation.[424] As for the other peasants who did not own their fields, who came from elsewhere and might move on from time to time to another village taking their bullocks and ploughs, they were more heavily taxed than the elders.

The village also had its own artisans: wedded to their trades by the caste system, they received for their labour a share of the communal harvest, plus a plot of land to cultivate (although certain castes earned wages).[425] The reader may think this a complicated system, but what peasant regime under the sun is simple? 'While the peasant was not unfree or a serf, his status was definitely a dependent one.'[426] The share of his income confiscated by the state, by the lord of the *jagir* and other interested parties might be anything from a third to a half, or even more in fertile regions.[427] So how was such a regime possible? How could the peasant economy support it, while at the same time maintaining a degree of expansion, since seventeenth-century India, despite her growing population, continued to produce enough food for her people, increased her industrial crops and even expanded the production of her many orchards to meet a higher demand for fruit and the new fashion among landowners?[428]

Results like this must be put down to the modest living standards of the peasants and the high productivity of their agriculture.

For in 1600, rural India was farming only a portion of the available land: from the available statistics, it seems probable that in the Ganges basin for instance, only half the arable land under cultivation in the same region in 1900 was being farmed at all in the seventeenth century; in central India, the figure is between two-thirds and four-fifths; in southern India one may *conjecture* the figure was higher. So one thing is certain: almost everywhere in India between the fifteenth and the eighteenth century, only the best land was being farmed. And since there was no agricultural revolution here, since basic tools, methods and essential crops did not change until 1900, it can probably be assumed that the per capita output of the Indian peasant was higher in 1700 than 1900,[429] particularly since land as yet uncultivated, on which new villages were built, offered the peasants extra space which could support more grazing and this in turn meant more draft animals, bullocks and buffaloes for ploughing, more dairy products and more ghee (melted butter used in Indian cookery). Irfan Habib[430] has argued that in view of the two annual harvests, cereal yields in India were higher than those in Europe until the nineteenth century. But even with equivalent yields, India would still have had the advantage. In a hot climate, the needs of a labourer are fewer than in the temperate countries of Europe. The modest quantity subtracted from the harvest for the peasant's own subsistence left a larger surplus available for marketing.

A further source of the superiority of Indian agriculture, besides the two harvests a year (of rice, or of grain plus peas or chick peas, or oil-yielding plants), was the place occupied by cash-crops intended for export: indigo and cotton plants, sugar cane, opium poppies, tobacco (introduced to India in the early seventeenth century), the pepper-bush (a climbing plant which produced peppercorns between the third and the ninth years but which, contrary to popular belief, would not grow unless carefully tended).[431] Such plants brought in more than millet, rye, rice or wheat. And in the case of the indigo plant for instance, 'it is the practice among the Indians to cut it three times a year'.[432] Furthermore it required complicated industrial processes; so like sugar cane, and for similar reasons, the growing of indigo which required substantial investment, was a *capitalist* venture very widespread in India, with active cooperation by large tax-farmers, merchants, representatives of the European companies and of the Mogul government which attempted to create a state monopoly by a policy of granting exclusive tenancy agreements. The indigo most favoured by the Europeans was that grown in the Agra region, especially the first crop whose leaves were 'of a deeper purple'. Given the scale of both local and European demand, the price of indigo rose steadily.[433] In 1633, when wars were affecting the areas where it grew in the Deccan, Persian and Indian purchasers turned increasingly to the Agra indigo which consequently broke the previous record price of 50 rupees a *maund*.[434] The English and Dutch companies thereupon decided to suspend purchases. But the peasants of Agra, forewarned presumably by the merchants and 'indigo-farmers' who had the affair in hand, uprooted the plants and switched temporarily to other crops.[435] Was such adaptability a sign of capitalist efficiency, of direct communication between the peasants and the market?

None of this prevented visible poverty among the rural masses: poverty which was predictable given the general conditions of the system. What was more, the Delhi government levied in taxes a proportion of the harvest – in theory once it had been harvested, but in many regions, local administrators for the sake of convenience estimated the average yield of the land in advance and established a *fixed rate* of taxation on this basis, in kind or in cash, depending on the area under cultivation and the nature of the crop (less for barley than wheat, less for wheat than for indigo, less for indigo than for sugar cane or opium poppies).[436] This being the case, if the harvest did not come up to expectations, if there was a drought, if bullocks from the caravans or elephants from Delhi ravaged the cultivated fields, if prices rose or fell inopportunely, the burden was borne by the producer. And the peasant's life was aggravated further by debt.[437] With the complexity of land tenure systems, of ownership and taxation, depending on the province, the generosity of the local prince or on the presence of war or peace, any kind of variation could be expected – usually for the worse. On the whole, however, as long as the Mogul state remained strong, it was able to maintain the minimum level of peasant prosperity essential to its own prosperity. It was only in the eighteenth century that general decline began to affect the state, the obedience and loyalty of its officials and the security of transport.[438] Peasant revolts became endemic.

Artisans and industry

The other sufferers in India were the countless artisans present in all cities, towns and villages – some of which had been transformed into entire villages of artisans. This increase in the working population was inevitable if it is true that the seventeenth century saw a massive increase in the urban population of India, which some historians put at 20 per cent of the total: if they are right, the urban population of India was some 20 million inhabitants – roughly the equivalent of the total population of France in the seventeenth century. Even if this is an overestimate, the artisan population, augmented by an army of unskilled labourers, must still have represented millions of individuals working both for the domestic and the export market.

Rather than with the history of these countless artisans as such, Indian historians seeking to discover the situation of their country on the eve of the British conquest have been most concerned to discover the nature of India's ancestral industry, and in particular whether her industry was or was not comparable to that of Europe at the same time, whether it might have been capable on its own of engendering some kind of industrial revolution.

Industry, or rather proto-industry, encountered many obstacles in India. Some have been perhaps exaggerated and exist only in the minds of historians – in particular the trammels supposedly imposed by the caste system, which affected the whole of society, including of course the artisan population. Weberian analysis sees the caste system as preventing the advance of technology, stifling initiative among artisans and, since it confined a certain group of people to a single activity laid down once and for all, as inhibiting any new specialization or social mobility from generation to generation.

> There are good grounds [writes Irfan Habib] for throwing doubt on this entire theory.... First, the mass of ordinary or unskilled people formed a reserve from which new classes of skilled professions could be created when the need arose. Thus diamond miners in the [Carnatic] must have come from the ranks of the peasantry or agricultural labourers, for when some mines were abandoned, the miners 'went back to their village'.... More important still, over a long period economic compulsions could bring about a radical transformation in the occupational basis of a caste. A well-documented case is that of the caste of tailors in Maharashtra,[439] a section of which took to dyeing, and another to indigo-dyeing early in the eighteenth century.[440]

Some flexibility among the workforce cannot be denied. Indeed the ancient caste system had developed alongside the division of labour, since in Agra in the early seventeenth century more than a hundred different trades are recorded.[441] And the workers could move about, as in Europe, in search of profitable work. The destruction of Ahmedabad stimulated a vigorous burst of growth in the Surat textile industry, in the second quarter of the eighteenth century. And the European Indies companies attracted to the areas round their branches weavers from the various provinces who, unless subject to specific prohibitions (some castes were forbidden to travel by sea for instance) could travel about to meet demand.

Other obstacles were more serious. Europeans were often astonished at the small number and rudimentary nature of the tools used by the Indian craftsmen – 'a deficiency of tools' which, as Sonnerat explained with illustrations, meant that a sawyer took 'three days to make a plank which would take our workmen but an hour'. Who could fail to be surprised that 'the fine muslins we seek so eagerly are made on looms composed of four pieces of wood stuck in the ground'?[442] If the Indian craftsman nevertheless produced masterpieces, this was the result of extraordinary manual dexterity, further refined by extreme specialization: 'A job that one man would do in Holland here passes through four men's hands before it is finished', remarked the Dutchman Pelsaert.[443] Tools were made almost entirely of wood, unlike those of Europe which already contained a large proportion of iron even before the industrial revolution. And archaic methods prevailed: for example, the Indian version of the Persian-designed wheel for irrigation and pumping water used wooden gears, wooden cogwheels, leather bags, earthenware pots and was propelled by animal or

Native blacksmiths in sixteenth-century Goa: note the elementary technology, with hand bellows and the peculiar hammers which look as if they might also be used as axes. (Photo F. Quilici.)

human power until the nineteenth century. This was not so much for technical reasons, Irfan Habib thinks[444] (since wooden mechanisms such as those used for spinning and weaving could often be sophisticated and ingenious) as for reasons of cost: the high price of European metal machinery would not have been compensated for by the savings made on labour – which was both plentiful and cheap. *Mutatis mutandis*, this is very like the problems raised today by certain kinds of advanced technology requiring heavy capital investment but only a small labour force: the adoption of such technology by Third World countries has been both disruptive and disappointing.

Similarly, although the Indians were not well-versed in mining techniques (confining their efforts to the extraction of surface minerals only) they had succeeded, as we saw in Volume I, in producing a crucible-fired steel of exceptional quality, which was exported at high prices to Persia and elsewhere. In this respect they were ahead of European metallurgy. They worked their own metal, producing ships' anchors, fine sidearms, swords and daggers of every design, good hand guns and respectable cannon (not cast but made of welded iron bars hooped together).[445] The cannon in the arsenal of the Mogul emperor at Baterpore (between Surat and Delhi) were however, according to an Englishman who saw them in 1615, made of cast iron, 'of various calibres but generally too short and too slender'.[446] But he may have been viewing them with the eyes of a seaman used to the long-barrelled naval cannon and for all we know these early pieces may have been improved. By 1664 at any rate, Aurangzeb possessed heavy artillery pulled by massive draft teams (and which had to be moved into position well ahead of battle because it was so slow) as well as pieces of very light artillery (two horses to a gun) which regularly followed the emperor in his travels round the country.[447] By this date, European artillerymen had been replaced by Indian gunners: they may have been less skilful than the foreigners, but they had obviously made technical progress.[448] Rifles and cannon were by now in any case to be found all over India. When Tippoo Sahib, the last nawab of Mysore, was abandoned by the French in 1783, he took refuge in the mountains and conveyed his heavy artillery along impossible roads across the Ghats. (Near Mangalore, he had to hitch 40 or 50 oxen to every piece; one of the elephants pushing a gun from behind lost its footing and fell over the precipice, taking nine or ten men with it.)[449] So India was by no means hopelessly backward in technology. The Indian Mints, for example, were every bit as good as the European: 30,000 rupees were being turned out every day at the Surat Mint in 1660 for the English company alone.[450]

Lastly, there was the wonder of wonders, the naval shipyards. According to a French report, the vessels built in Surat in about 1700 were 'very good and extremely serviceable ... and it would be most advantageous [for the French Indies Company] to have some built there', even if the price was the same as in France, since the teak wood from which they were made guaranteed them a lifetime at sea of forty years, 'instead of ten, twelve or fourteen at most'.[451] During the first half of the nineteenth century, the Parsees in Bombay invested considerable sums in shipbuilding, having vessels constructed both on the spot and in other ports, especially Cochin.[452] Bengal, including Calcutta from 1760,[453] also had shipyards: 'The English have since the last war [1778-83] fitted in Bengal alone four or five hundred vessels of all sizes, built in India for them'.[454] Some of these ships could be very big: the *Surat Castle* (1791-2) 1000 tons, 12 cannon and a crew of 150; or the *Lowjee Family*, 800 tons, manned by 125 Lascars; the flagship of this fleet, the *Shampinder* (1802) ran to 1300 tons.[455] And it was indeed in India that the finest Indiamen were built, vessels of enormous size for the time, which did the China run. In eastern waters, until the coming of the steamship in mid-nineteenth century, the English in fact relied exclusively on Indian-built ships. None of them sailed for Europe: indeed English ports were forbidden to them. In 1794, the war with France and the urgent need for transport ships was responsible for the ban being lifted for a few months. But the appearance of Indian ships and sailors caused such hostile reactions in London that English merchants quickly decided not to use their services.[456]

India's remarkable textile production is so well known that I hardly need

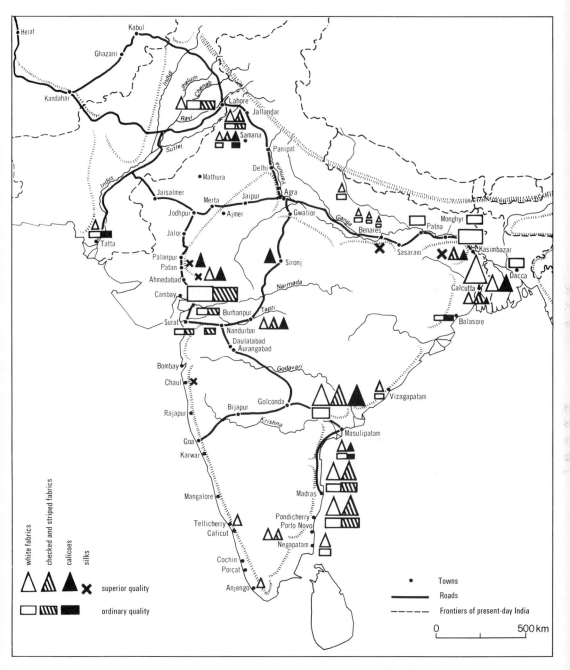

Herat · Kabul
Ghazani ·
Kandahar ·
Lahore
Jallandar
Samana
Panipat
· Mathura
Delhi
Agra
Jaisalmer
Merta · Jaipur
Jodhpur · Ajmer
Gwalior
Jalor
Benares
Monghyr
Patna
Kasimbazar
Sasaram
Dacca
Palanpur
Patan
Sironj
Calcutta
Ahmedabad
Cambay
Narmada
Burhanpur
Tapti
Balasore
Surat
Nandurbar
Daulatabad
Aurangabad
Bombay
Godavari
Chaul
Golconda
Vizagapatam
Bijapur
Rajapur
Krishna
Goa
Masulipatam
Karwar
Madras
Mangalore
Pondicherry
Porto Novo
Tellicherry
Calicut
Negapatam
Cochin
Porcat
Anjengo

white fabrics
checked and striped fabrics
calicoes
silks

superior quality

ordinary quality

· Towns
— Roads
----- Frontiers of present-day India

0   500 km

47 TEXTILE ROUTES AND INDUSTRIES IN INDIA, MID-EIGHTEENTH CENTURY
Except on the Malabar coast which was rich in pepper, textile industry was to be found in every region of India. The different symbols indicate the diversity of output and give some idea of its volume. (Based on K.N. Chaudhuri, *The Trading World of Asia and the English East India Company*, 1978.)

dwell on it. It possessed to the full the capacity so admired in the English cloth trade, to meet any increase in demand. It was to be found in the villages; it kept artisans busy in the towns; from Surat to the Ganges, it nourished a string of craft workshops producing for themselves or for the big export dealers; it was well entrenched in Kashmir; it was poorly represented along the Malabar coast, but had thoroughly colonized the Coromandel coast. European companies tried, in vain, to introduce western working arrangements for the weaving trade, in particular the putting-out system which I have already described at length. The clearest example occurred in Bombay,[457] where thanks to belated immigration by Indian workers from Surat and elsewhere, the attempt could be started from scratch. But the traditional Indian system of advance payments and contracts remained the rule, at least until the conquest of Bengal, when its artisans were brought under direct supervision, in the last decades of the eighteenth century.

The textile industry was hard to take over for this very reason that it was not contained within a single network as in Europe. Different sectors and circuits governed the production and marketing of raw materials; the manufacture of cotton yarn (a long operation especially if the aim was a yarn both fine and strong, to make muslin for instance); weaving; bleaching and preparation of fabrics; and printing. Processes which in Europe were vertically linked (as in thirteenth-century Florence) were here organized in separate compartments. Buyers for the companies would sometimes go to the market where the weavers sold their wares but more often, when a large order was being placed (and orders grew steadily larger)[458] it was better to strike a bargain with Indian merchants who had employees travelling through the production zones and themselves arranging contracts with the artisans. The middleman would undertake to deliver to a company servant on a specified date, at an agreed price, an agreed quantity of specified types of fabric. To the weaver he customarily made an advance payment in money, which was a kind of pledge of future purchase, enabling the worker to buy yarn and to maintain himself while he was working. When the piece of material was finished, the weaver would be paid the market price less the advance. Market prices, which were not fixed at the time of ordering, might vary according to the price of yarn or that of rice.

The merchant was thus shouldering a risk which would of course be reflected in his rate of profit. But the weaver was undoubtedly given a certain amount of leeway: he received his advance in money (not, as in Europe, in materials); and he could always resort directly to the market, something not open to the worker operating in the *Verlagssystem*. What was more, he could always default, change his place of work, even go on strike and give up the loom to return to the land or join the army. This being so, K.N. Chaudhuri finds it very difficult to explain the poverty of weavers, of which there is so much evidence. Could the reason be the antiquity of a social structure which condemned peasants and artisans to minimal remuneration? The huge increase in demand and production in the seventeenth and eighteenth centuries may have widened the range of choices for the artisan, without doing anything to alter the general low level of wages, despite the fact that production operated within a direct money economy.

On the whole this system made manufactories unnecessary, but some did exist, bringing together workers in large workshops – the *karkhanas*, which operated for their owners, the nobles or the emperor himself. The owners were not above letting these luxury goods go for export on occasion. Mandelslo (1638) speaks of a magnificent and very costly fabric of silk and cotton with gold-embroidered flowers, which the workshops had recently begun to manufacture in Ahmedabad when he was passing through, and 'which was confined to [the use of] the Emperor; nevertheless foreigners are permitted to carry it out of the country'.[459]

In fact all India processed silk and cotton, sending an incredible quantity of fabrics, from the most ordinary to the most luxurious, all over the world, since through the Europeans even America received a large share of Indian textiles. The variety of materials can be conjectured from the descriptions left by travellers and the trade lists drawn up by the European companies. Here for example, without comment, is a list taken from a French memorandum on textiles from the different provinces:

> Blue and unbleached cottons from Salem, blue guineas from Madure, bazeens from Gondelur, percales from Arni, table linens from Pondicherry, bettelles, chavonis, tarnatans, organdies, Steinkerques from the coast, cambays, nicannes, bejutapauts, papolis, korotes, brawles, boelans, lemanees, quilts, chittees, caddies, white dullees, handkerchief fabrics from Mazulipatam, sanees, muslins, terrindanis, durries [striped muslins], mulmuls, fine, embroidered in thread of gold or silver, common cottons from Patna [which were exported in such large quantities – up to 100,000 lengths – that they could be obtained 'without a contract'],[460] seersuckers [mixed silk and cotton], baftas, hummums, cossaes, four-thread weaves, common bazeens, gazas, Permacody cottons, Yanaon guineas, conjoos.[461]

And the writer of the memorandum adds that the quality could vary greatly in some types of fabric: in Dacca, which was the market for 'very fine muslins, unique of their kind ..., there are plain muslins from 200 francs for 16 ells, to 2500 francs for 8 ells'.[462] But even this impressive list pales into insignificance beside the 91 varieties of textiles Chaudhuri lists as an appendix to his book.

There can be no doubt that until the English industrial revolution, the Indian cotton industry was the foremost in the world, both in the quality and quantity of its output and the scale of its exports.

A national market

Every kind of commodity went into circulation in India, whether agricultural surpluses, raw materials or manufactured goods for export. The grain collected at village markets was conveyed by chains of local merchants, usurers and

Travelling in India in the sixteenth century: bullock-carts carrying ladies in the kingdom of Cambay; with an armed guard escort. (Photo F. Quilici.)

moneylenders, to small towns (*qasbahs*) then to the big cities through the offices of wholesalers who specialized in the transport of bulky goods – salt and grain in particular.[463] This circulation was by no means perfect: it could be surprised by sudden outbreaks of famine which the great distances between one place and another only too often turned into disaster. But was this not equally true of colonial America or even of the Old World in Europe? And in India the circulation of goods employed every conceivable means, cutting through obstacles, linking distant regions of different cultures and living standards, thus enabling every kind of merchandise to travel, the everyday and the precious (the latter covered by insurance at comparatively low premiums).[464]

On land, transport took the form of large caravans, the *kafilas* of the *banjara* merchants, protected by armed guards. These caravans, depending on the terrain, used bullock-carts, buffaloes, donkeys, dromedaries, horses, mules, goats and if necessary human porters. They suspended services during the rainy season, when their place was taken by waterways – a far less costly and often faster means of transport, but for which insurance premiums were, oddly enough, higher. Caravans were warmly welcomed everywhere; even villages gladly accommodated them.[465]

The term that springs to mind, perhaps an excessive one, is that of a *national market*: the Indian subcontinent, for all its size, had a degree of coherence in which the money economy was an important or rather essential element. This overall coherence created poles of development productive of the asymmetries indispensable to the brisk circulation of goods.

The leading role played by Surat and its region for example must surely be obvious to anyone: this was a place favoured in every sector of material life – trade, industry and exports. The port was the gateway for entry to and departure from India, linked by long-distance trade both to the flow of bullion from the Red Sea and to the distant ports of Europe and the East Indies. Another centre of increasing importance was Bengal, the wonder of India, another but bigger Egypt. A French sea captain who with some difficulty took his 600-ton ship up the Ganges to Chandernagor, rightly said of this river:

> It is the source and centre of trade in the Indies. [Commerce] can be carried on with great ease since one is not subject to the inconvenience found on the coast of Coromandel[466] ... and the country is fertile and extraordinarily populous. Besides the high quality of the merchandise made here, [it] provides grain, rice and generally everything necessary for life. This abundance attracts and always will attract a great number of traders who send vessels to every part of the Indies from the Red Sea to China. Here one can see the assembly of the nations of Europe and Asia, who differ so greatly in their national genius and their customs, reach perfect agreement or perfect disunity, depending on the self-interest which alone is their guide.[467]

More descriptions would be required of course to build up a picture of the trading geography of India in all its richness. One would have to mention in particular the 'industrial bloc' of Gujerat, the most impressive in the Far East; the contributions of Calicut, Ceylon and Madras; and the many merchants, Indian and foreign, who were prepared to embark their money or their merchandise, at considerable risk, in the freighting trade which had all the ships of Europe (except the Dutch) competing for their custom. One would also have to mention the complementary exchanges effected within India (foodstuffs but also textiles and dyes) using the waterways and overland routes, a less spectacular but perhaps even more important form of exchange for India as a whole than the export trade; it was certainly vital to the structures of the Mogul Empire.

The significance of the Mogul Empire

When in 1526, the Mogul Empire replaced the sultanate of Delhi, it took over a well-tried organization; the combination of this inheritance with a rediscovered dynamism proved to be for many years a heavy but effective machine.

Its first achievement (the pioneering work of Akbar, 1556–1605) was to persuade the two religious communities, Hindu and Muslim, to cohabit without too much conflict, although in fact the latter faith, being that of the rulers, received most honour – so much so that Europeans, seeing the countless mosques in northern and central India, long assumed Islam to be the prevalent religion in India, and Hinduism, the religion of the merchants and peasants, a sort of idolatry on the way to extinction, like paganism in Europe before the spread of Christianity. European thought did not really discover Hinduism until the late eighteenth or early nineteenth century.

The second feat of the Moguls was to acclimatize and introduce to almost the whole of India a single civilization, borrowed from neighbouring Persia and ferrying its arts, literature and sensibility. Thus the two cultures present in the country came together and it was eventually the minority culture – that of Islam – which was on the whole absorbed by the Indian masses, though only after it had itself adopted many cultural borrowings.[468] Persian remained the language of the rulers, of the upper, privileged classes: 'I will have someone write to the Rajah in the Persian tongue', a Frenchman in difficulty in Benares informed the governor of Chandernagor on 19 March 1768.[469] The administration used Hindustani, but its organization was also based on an Islamic model.

It is in the first place to the sultanate of Delhi, and then to the Mogul Empire, that responsibility must be attributed for the establishment in the provinces (*sarkars*) and the districts (*parganas*) of an ordered administration to handle the collecting of taxes and dues, but which also had the task of promoting agriculture – that is the basis of the fiscal system – as well as of developing irrigation and encouraging the spread of cash-crops for export.[470] Its activities, backed up from time to time by state subsidies and propaganda missions, were often effective.

Central to the system, housed at the heart of the empire whose existence it guaranteed and from whose resources it lived, was the terrible strength of the army. The nobles around the emperor, the *mansabdars* or *omerahs*, numbering 8000 in 1647, were the commanders of this force. Depending on their rank, they recruited dozens, hundreds or thousands of mercenaries.[471] The total size of the 'standing army' in Delhi was considerable – it would have been unthinkable in Europe: almost 200,000 horsemen, plus over 40,000 matchlockmen or gunners. Both in Delhi and in Agra, the other capital, the departure of the army on campaign left behind a deserted city, inhabited only by the Banyans.[472] If one were to calculate the total numbers dispersed in garrisons all over the empire with reinforcements along the frontiers, the answer would probably be close on a million men.[473] 'There is no little village that has not at least two horsemen and four foot soldiers',[474] detailed to keep order – and also to observe and spy on the population.

The army was itself the government, since the high offices of the regime were chiefly occupied by soldiers. The army was also the leading customer for luxury foreign fabrics, especially woollen cloth from Europe, which was not imported to make clothes in this hot climate but for 'saddlebags[475] and saddles for horses, elephants and camels, which the mighty have embroidered in embossed gold and silver, for palanquins, for gun-cases to protect them from the damp, and for the pomp of their foot soldiers'.[476] Up to 50,000 crowns' worth of cloth was being imported at this time (1724). The horses imported in large numbers from Persia or Arabia (for every cavalryman had several mounts) were themselves a luxury: the exhorbitant prices paid for them averaged four times those paid in England. At court, before the start of grand ceremonies, open 'to great and humble alike', one of the pleasures of the emperor was to have parade 'before his eyes a certain number of the finest horses in his stables', accompanied by 'a few elephants, . . . their bodies well scrubbed and clean . . . painted black with the exception of two broad stripes of red paint', and decorated with embroidered cloths and silver bells.[477]

The state kept by the *omerahs* was almost as grand as that of the emperor himself. Like him they possessed their own craft workshops, the *karkanahs*, manufactories whose refined products were reserved exclusively for their owners.[478] Like him, they had a passion for building. Large suites of servants and slaves accompanied them everywhere and some *omerahs* amassed fabulous hoards of gold plate and jewels.[479] It is not hard to imagine what a burden this aristocracy must have been on the Indian economy, living as it did from grants paid directly out of the imperial treasury, or from the dues paid by peasants on the *jagirs* granted to their masters by the empire, 'to maintain their rank'.

Political and non-political reasons for the fall of the Mogul Empire

The mighty imperial machinery was by the eighteenth century showing signs of wear and fatigue. There is a wide choice of dates for the beginning of what is known as the decline of the Mogul Empire: 1739, the date of the capture and terrifying sack of Delhi by the Persians; 1757, the battle of Plassey, won by the English; 1761, the second battle of Paniput, when Afghans in medieval armour triumphed over the Mahrattas armed with modern weapons, at the very moment when the latter were preparing to reconstitute the Mogul Empire for their own benefit. Historians have generally accepted with little controversy the date of 1707, the year of Aurangzeb's death, as marking the end of the great days of Mogul India. If we accept their account, the empire died from within, rather than being done to death by outsiders, whether Persians, Afghans or English.

It had been a strange empire, founded on the activities of a few thousand feudal nobles, the *omerahs* or *mansabdars*, recruited both inside and outside

India. At the end of the reign of Shah Jahan (1628–58) they were already being drawn from Persia and central Asia – in all from seventeen different sources. They were as foreign to the country they went to govern as the Oxford and Cambridge graduates who governed India in Kipling's day.

Twice a day, the *omerahs* paid their respects to the emperor. Flattery was as essential here as at the court of Versailles. 'The Emperor did not pronounce a word which was not greeted with admiration or which failed to make the principal *omerahs* throw up their hands crying *karamat* that is to say *wonders*.'[480] But what they were doing above all by such visits was reassuring themselves that the emperor was still alive and that thanks to him the empire was still standing. The briefest absence on the emperor's part, the rumour of an illness, or false reports of his death, might immediately unleash the frightening turmoil of a war of succession. Hence the determination of Aurangzeb during the last year of his long life, to make his presence known, even when he was mortally sick, to prove *coram populo* that he still existed and the empire with him. It was precisely the weakness of this authoritarian regime that it had not succeeded in making arrangements once and for all for the imperial succession. It is true that the struggle which almost always took place on such occasions was not necessarily serious. In 1658, Aurangzeb, at the end of the war of succession which marked the bloody opening of his reign, had just defeated his father and his brother Dara Shukoh. But the affliction of the vanquished was not insupportable:

> Almost all the *omerahs* were obliged to come and pay court to Aurangzeb, ... and what is almost unbelievable, not one of them had the heart to make a stir or to attempt the slightest thing on behalf of their King [i.e. the loser] who had made them what they were and who had raised them up out of the dust and perhaps even from slavery, as is quite common in this court, to bring them to richness and greatness.[481]

François Bernier, a French doctor and a contemporary of Colbert, thus reminds us that despite his long stay in Delhi his reactions and habits of mind had not changed. But the high and mighty of Delhi observed a different code of behaviour: they were guided by the precepts of a different world. For what were they but *condottieri*, like the Italians of the fifteenth century, recruiters of soldiers and knights paid for services rendered? They had to levy troops and arm them as best they could (hence the varied armour worn by Mogul troops).[482] As *condottieri*, they were too used to war not to respect its risks; they conducted it dispassionately, thinking only of their own interests. Like the warlords of Machiavelli's time, they might prolong hostilities while avoiding any decisive encounter. A glorious victory could be inconvenient: it might create jealousy towards an over-successful leader; whereas dragging out a campaign, increasing the troops and thus the payments and revenues guaranteed by the emperor, could bring nothing but gain, especially since war was not over-dangerous, largely consisting of taking up positions in front of some fortress which would be reduced to surrender by hunger; the besiegers would pitch a vast military camp the size of a town, with thousands of tents, hundreds of shops and facilities, even a certain degree of luxury. François Bernier has left us a vivid description of the astonishing cities under canvas, which were built and rebuilt along Aurangzeb's route to Kashmir in 1664 and which were inhabited by literally thousands of people. The tents were pitched in a certain order, repeated every time and the *omerahs*, as at court, came to pay their respects to the sovereign. 'Nothing is so magnificent on a dark night in the midst of the countryside as the sight of the long processions of torches threading their way between the tents, escorting all the *omerahs* to the emperor's quarters or bringing them back to their own tents.'[483]

All in all, it was an astonishing machine, rigid yet fragile. To keep it in working order required an energetic and effective ruler, as Aurangzeb perhaps was during the early part of his reign, until say 1680, the year in which he crushed the rebellion led by his own son Akbar.[484] But it also required that the country refrain from disturbing the social, political, economic and religious order which governed it. Yet this contradictory world was always stirring. It was not only the sovereign who changed – growing intolerant, suspicious, indecisive, and more bigoted than ever – but also the whole country and the army itself. Giving itself up to luxury and pleasure-seeking, the army lost its combative qualities; what was more, by over-recruiting it opened its ranks wider. The number of *jagirs* did not however increase at the same pace, and any new ones granted were often in devastated or arid regions. The general strategy of the owners of *jagirs* therefore became to seize any occasion to make a profit. In this climate of disdain for the public good, some members of the Mogul 'life aristocracy' took steps to preserve some of their wealth from the legal provisions stipulating that it revert to the emperor on their death; they even succeeded, as their counterparts were doing in the Turkish Empire at the same time, in transforming life-holdings into hereditary property. A further sign of corruption was that already by the middle of the seventeenth century, princes and princesses of the blood, ladies of the harem and nobles were engaging in trade, either directly or through merchants who lent them their names. Aurangzeb himself possessed a fleet of ships which traded in the Red Sea and the African ports.

Wealth was no longer, in the Mogul Empire, a reward for services rendered to the state. The provincial rulers, the *subahs* and *nawabs*, were showing signs of disobedience. When Aurangzeb attacked and subjugated two Muslim states of the Deccan – the kingdoms of Bijapur (1686) and Golconda (1687) – he found himself, after his victory, confronted with a sudden and widespread crisis of insubordination. Already the Mahrattas, a small tribe of poor mountain-dwellers in the western Ghats, had displayed their keen hostility towards him. The emperor completely failed to stop the raids and pillage by these extraordinary horsemen, their ranks swelled by a throng of adventurers and malcontents. Neither by force, guile nor corruption could he defeat their peasant leader Shivaji, the 'mountain rat'. The emperor's prestige suffered inordinately, parti-

The Great Mogul goes hunting, escorted by a host of nobles and servants most of whom are mounted on horses, elephants or camels, except for the foot soldiers, top right.
(Photo B.N., Paris.)

cularly when in January 1664, the Mahrattas captured and sacked Surat, the wealthiest port in the Mogul Empire, the point of departure for all trade and pilgrim voyages to Mecca, the very symbol of Mogul power and rule.

For all these reasons, N.M. Pearson[485], with some justification, regards the long reign of Aurangzeb as part and parcel of the Mogul decline. He argues that the empire, faced with this domestic war of an unprecedented and persistent kind, proved unfaithful to its vocation and *raison d'être*. This may well be the case; but was this tragic war exclusively brought about, as some historians still maintain,[486] by Aurangzeb's post-1680 policies, inspired both by distrust of his blood-relations and by religious intolerance? Is this not to overestimate the influence of this 'Indian Louis XI'?[487] The Hindu reaction welled up from deep below the surface: we can see surface signs of it in the Mahrattas war, and in the triumphant heresy and determined struggles of the Sikhs,[488] but its origins are still hidden from us. Yet it is here that the explanation is probably to be sought for the deep-seated and inexorable decline of Mogul India and of its attempt to bring together two religions and two civilizations, Islam and Hinduism. Muslim civilization, with its institutions, its characteristic urban achievements and its monuments which were imitated even in the Deccan, apparently offered the spectacle of a rare success. But this success was coming to an end and India was being torn apart. It was indeed this rift which opened the way to the British conquest as Isaac Titsingh, a Dutchman who for many years represented the V.O.C. in Bengal, clearly perceived (25 March 1788): the only obstacle which the English would have found insurmountable would have been an alliance between the Muslims and the Mahrattas: 'their statesmanship is now constantly directed towards the forestalling of such an alliance'.[489]

What is certain is the length of time it took for Mogul India to collapse. The Battle of Plassey (1757) took place fifty years after the death of Aurangzeb (1707). Was this half-century of evident difficulty also a period of economic decline? If so, for whom? For the eighteenth century was of course characterized by the prosperity throughout India of European commerce. But what does this really signify?

It is actually very difficult to estimate the real economic situation of India in the eighteenth century. Some regions undoubtedly went into decline, others kept going, a few made progress. The wars which devastated the country have been compared to the suffering in Germany during the Thirty Years' War (1618–1648).[490] As comparisons go, the French Wars of Religion might provide a useful parallel, since during the struggles which split sixteenth-century France, the economic situation was on the whole quite favourable.[491] Indeed it was the survival of the economy which prolonged and maintained the war, enabling both sides, Protestants and Catholics, to pay the foreign mercenaries they constantly recruited. Were the Indian wars fuelled by a similarly benign economic situation? Perhaps: the Mahrattas were only able to launch their raids with the help of the businessmen allied to their cause, who amassed supplies and arms for them along their chosen routes. War had to pay for war.

The problem in short remains before us: it cannot be resolved without further research into statistics and price series. May I suggest, at the risk of error, that India in the latter half of the eighteenth century seems to me to have been caught up in the new revival of the economy making itself felt from Canton to the Red Sea? The fact that the European companies, the independent merchants or the 'servants' of the companies indulging in 'the country trade' were doing well and increasing the number and size of their ships, might mean either that damage was being done, or that a takeover was occurring; but all the same production in the Far East and notably in India with its central position must have followed the trend. And 'for every piece of cloth made up for shipment to Europe', as Holden Furber writes, 'hundreds of pieces had to be woven for domestic consumption'.[492] Even the African regions bordering the Indian Ocean revived under the impact of Gujerati merchants.[493] Does the pessimism expressed by historians of India about the eighteenth century simply flow from *a priori* assumptions?

At any rate, whether India's doors were opened by economic prosperity or by economic decline, she certainly put up little resistance to foreign conquest – and not only when the conqueror was British: the French, Afghans and Persians were all ready to intervene.

Was this decline confined to the highest political and economic levels, or did it also occur in the teeming life of town and village? At this elementary level, not everything stayed standing, but many structures remained intact. The English certainly did not take over a country without resources. Even after 1783, English, Dutch, Portuguese and French merchants were still doing a lot of business in Surat, although it was by now already in decline.[494] Mahé in 1787[495] was attracting the pepper trade by offering prices higher than those in the English trading-posts. The French 'country trade' handled by French nationals in the trading posts and in particular in Mauritius and Réunion, was still prosperous or at any rate holding its own. And every Frenchman seeking his fortune in the Indies rather late in the day had his own pet projects and anti-British schemes: India was still it seems a desirable prize, worth conquering.

India's decline in the nineteenth century

What is beyond doubt is the general decline of India in the nineteenth century. This was both an absolute and a relative decline, in that India proved unable to keep pace with the European industrial revolution and to imitate her English master. But was the peculiar form of capitalism in India to blame? Or perhaps the economic and social straitjacket of a low wage structure? Does the explanation lie in the difficult political situation, as the wars of the eighteenth century combined with growing intervention by Europeans, in particular by the British? Or in India's technological backwardness? Or was the crucial blow dealt belatedly by the impact, here as in Russia, of the machine revolution in Europe?

Indian capitalism unquestionably had its shortcomings. But it was part of a system which did not after all work so badly, although India was disproportionately large – ten times the size of France, twenty times the size of England. The Indian community, the national market divided against itself by geography, required a certain quantity of precious metals if the community was to live and the market to function. And the economico-socio-political system of India, harsh and even perverse though it might be, forced it to resort as we have seen to the indispensable fluidity and efficacity of the money economy. India had no precious metals of her own but she was importing enough for peasant dues in the central zone to be paid in specie as early as the fourteenth century. This was as advanced as anywhere in the world, including Europe at the time. And since the money economy could only function if it husbanded its reserves, first accumulating them then opening the sluices and creating *artificial* money in advance of harvests or payments, arranging transactions on the market or on credit; and since no economy largely based on money could function without merchants, whole-salers, shipowners, insurers, brokers, middlemen, shopkeepers and pedlars – it is clear that such a business hierarchy did exist and was fulfilling its role in India.

It is in this sense that a certain capitalism was part and parcel of the Mogul Empire. At the crucial bottlenecks, Indian businessmen and bankers controlled key positions for the accumulation and release of capital. If India, like Islam, lacked the continuity provided by the great landed families who in the West accumulated not only wealth but capital in the shape of power and influence, the caste system did on the other hand encourage and stabilize the process of mercantile and banking accumulation which was pursued with determination from generation to generation. Certain families acquired outstanding fortunes, comparable to those of the Fuggers or the Medici in the West. In Surat, there were businessmen who owned entire fleets of ships. We know of literally hundreds of important merchants affiliated to Banyan castes, and an equal number of rich or very rich Muslim merchants. In the eighteenth century, the bankers appeared to have reached the peak of their wealth. Were they (as I am inclined to think, possibly under the influence of European history) carried along by the logical evolution of an economy which was tending, as it reached maturity, to create its own high-level banking functions? Or as T. Raychaudhuri has suggested, were these businessmen driven into finance (tax-collecting, banking and usury) because European competition was tending more and more to squeeze them out of shipping and long-distance trade?[496] Both trends may have combined to make the fortune of the Jagat Sheths who, being honoured with this grand title (literally 'merchants of the world'), in 1715 substituted it for their original family names.

We know a certain amount about this family, originally from the state of Jaipur and belonging to a branch of the Marwari caste. Their fortune became immense after they had settled in Bengal, where we find them collecting taxes for the Great Mogul, lending at interest, making bank loans and running the mint at Murshidabad. One source of their fortune, according to contemporaries, was simply fixing the rate of the rupee in relation to the old coins. As money-changers, they sent huge sums by bill of exchange to the Great Mogul in Delhi. When Murshidabad was taken by a detachment of Mahratta cavalry, they lost 20 million rupees overnight, but business continued as usual. And the Jagat Sheths were by no means unique. We know of many other business families which could stand comparison with them.[497] These Bengali capitalists were to be progressively ruined after the end of the eighteenth century, it is true, but that was because of deliberate action by the British rather than any ineptitude on their own part.[498] On the west coast of India in Bombay, on the other hand, we find that in the first half of the nineteenth century a group of very rich Parsees and Gujeratis, both Muslim and Hindu, prospered in every kind of banking and mercantile activity – shipbuilding, freight, the China trade, even certain industries. One of the richest of these men, the Parsee J. Jeejeebhoy, had 30 million rupees deposited in an English bank in the town.[499] In Bombay, where the collaboration and organization of native business networks was indispensable to the English, Indian capitalism easily proved its capacity to adapt.

Does that mean to say that Indian capitalists always had their own way in India? By no means, for the merchants and bankers had never had the stage to themselves. Above them, before the structures of the British Raj, had been the despotic states of India, and not only that of the Great Mogul: the wealth of the great merchant families singled them out for exactions on behalf of the tyrants. They lived in perpetual fear of torture and dispossession.[500] However brisk the flow of money which was the lifeblood of merchant capitalism and the Indian economy, the world of the Banyans lacked the liberty, security and political tolerance which favoured the rise of capitalism in the West. But to argue on this account as some historians have done, that Indian capitalism was impotent, is taking it rather far. India was not China, where capitalism in itself, that is the accumulation of capital, was *deliberately* thwarted by the state. In India, wealthy merchants might be exposed to extortion, but there were plenty of them, and they survived. The powerful solidarity of the caste embraced and guaranteed the fortunes of the group, ensuring it the collaboration of merchants all the way from the East Indies to Moscow.

I would not therefore accuse capitalism of being responsible for India's backwardness, which is to be explained, as is always the case, by both internal and external reasons.

Among the internal causes, perhaps one should single out low wages. It is a truism to speak of the gap between Indian wages and those in Europe. In 1736, the directors of the East India Company reckoned that the wages of French workmen (and we know that these were far below those of English labour) were six times as high as wages in India.[501] Chaudhuri understandably finds it a little puzzling that highly-skilled workers, who seem to have had some freedom and means of defending themselves within the social context, should have been paid such miserable wages. But could it perhaps be argued that low wages were a structural feature, long embedded in the overall economy of India? Were they not, that is, the *sine qua non* of the flow of precious metals into India, a flow dating back to very ancient times, indeed to the Roman Empire? Is the low-wage economy not a more satisfactory explanation than unbridled thirst for gold on the part of the emperor and the privileged classes, for the cyclonic suction which seems to have drawn precious metals from the West to the East? On reaching India, gold and silver currencies automatically increased in value, compared to

An employee of the East India Company, converted to the pleasures of opium and the *dolce vita*. Indian painting by Dip Chand (late eighteenth century). Victoria and Albert Museum. (Photo by the museum.)

the very low price of human labour, which inevitably meant low prices for food and even, comparatively, for spices. This in turn would explain the powerful rebound – the penetration of western markets by Indian exports, raw materials but above all textiles, cottons and silks: they were more attractive than comparable English, French or Dutch products, not only for their quality and beauty, but because of the price difference, just as the same phenomenon is today flooding world markets with textiles from Hong Kong or Korea.

The labour of a 'foreign proletariat' was the very foundation of Europe's trade with India. Defending the principle of bullion exports in 1684, Thomas Mun had an unanswerable argument: the Indian goods which the East India Company had bought at a cost of £840,000 had been sold in Europe for

£4 million – so that they effectively brought money into England.[502] From mid-seventeenth century on, cotton textiles from India became a leading import commodity and their quantity grew rapidly. In the single year 1785-6, the English company sold in Copenhagen alone 900,000 pieces of Indian cloth.[503] K.N. Chaudhuri is however probably quite right to deduce from such statistics that there could be no incentive for technological innovations which might increase productivity, in a country where the number of artisans ran into millions, and whose output was being fought over by all nations of the world. Business was good, so why change anything? The incentive worked the other way round – providing a stimulus to the threatened industry of Europe. England's first step was to close her own frontiers for the greater part of the eighteenth century to Indian textiles, which she re-exported to Europe and America. Then she tried to capture for herself this profitable market – something that could only be achieved by making drastic reductions in manpower. It is surely no coincidence that the machine revolution began in the cotton industry.

This brings us to the second explanation for India's falling behind: an external not an internal explanation – in a word, Britain. It is not enough simply to say that the British seized India with all her resources. India was for the British an instrument thanks to which they gained access to an even larger area, coming to dominate the Asiatic super-world-economy; and it is within this enlarged framework that one can see how from an early stage India's internal balances and structures were distorted and strained to achieve aims quite foreign to her; how, in the process, India was eventually in the nineteenth century 'deindustrialized', reduced to the role of a major producer of raw materials.

It can at any rate be confidently said that eighteenth-century India was not on the brink of producing some revolutionary form of industrial capitalism. Within her own limitations, India was perfectly at ease, with a natural, strong and successful economy; her agriculture was traditional but productive and high-yielding; her industry was on an ancient pattern, but it was thriving and efficient (until 1810, Indian steel was actually of higher quality than anything produced in England, and inferior only to Swedish steel);[504] the whole country was penetrated by a well-established market economy; there were many efficient trading circuits. Last but not least, India's commercial and industrial strength was based, as one might expect, on a vigorous export trade: she was part of an economic area going well beyond her own shores.

But India did not dominate this area. I have even indicated how passive was India's attitude to this surrounding zone on which the bulk of her trade depended. And it was from outside that the threat came: as she gradually lost control of the 'country trade' routes throughout Asia, India became impoverished and slipped from her throne. The intervention of the Europeans, which had originally given a fillip to Indian exports, in the end operated against her. Ironically India's very strength was used to bring about her own destruction, by forcing open the reluctant gates of China, after 1760, to the greater profit of the English, thanks to cotton and opium. India was to suffer from the repercussions of England's newly-increased strength.

India and China: caught in a super-world-economy

After this long explanatory detour, we are now brought back to the original problem: somehow to account for the Far East as a whole, caught up as it was after 1400 in a super-world-economy – immense, impressive but fragile. This fragility has unquestionably been one of the major elements of universal history. For the Far East, structured enough to be penetrated with relative ease, but not sufficiently structured to defend itself, was asking to be invaded. The intrusion of the Europeans should not therefore be regarded as their responsibility alone; indeed they were only following in the footsteps of other invaders – those of Islam for instance.

The logical confluence of trade, the crossroads lying at the centre of this super-world-economy could hardly be elsewhere than in the East Indies. Geography placed this region on the edge of Asia, halfway between China and Japan on the one hand, and India and the countries of the Indian Ocean on the other. But if geography proposes, history disposes, and in this instance refusal or acceptance could take innumerable forms depending on the actions of the super-powers of the Far East: China and India. At times when both were prosperous, in control of themselves and simultaneously engaged in outside activities, the centre of gravity of the Far East was quite likely to lie, and to remain for a longer or shorter period, somewhere near the Malacca peninsula and the islands of Java and Sumatra. But the sleeping giants were both slow to arouse and invariably slow to act.

Only at the beginning of the Christian era, that is rather late in history, did India really recognize and start to take an interest in the East Indies. Her sailors, merchants and missionaries exploited, educated and evangelized the archipelago, successfully transferring to it her superior political, economic and religious way of life. The islands were thus converted to Hinduism.

The Chinese dragon arrived very much later in the islands, only in about the fifth century. And it failed to impose upon the states and towns by now converted to Hinduism the mark of its own civilization, which could in theory have scored triumphs here as it did in Japan, Korea and Vietnam. The Chinese presence remained confined to the spheres of politics and economics; on several occasions China foisted on to the states of the East Indies protectorates, guardianships and the obligation to send ambassadors as a sign of allegiance; but in essence, and in way of life, these states would long remain true to themselves or to their earliest conquerors. The Indian yoke weighed heavier on them than the Chinese.

Hindu expansion, followed by Chinese expansion, probably corresponded to underlying bursts of economic prosperity which must have inspired and sustained such ventures, but whose chronology, origins and agents are still unknown. Although I can claim no expertise in an area very inaccessible to non-specialists, I imagine that India by expanding eastwards was passing on the impact she had felt from the 'far West', that is the Mediterranean. Is not the connection between Europe and India, an ancient and creative one in every respect, one of the firmest structural features of ancient history? In China's case, the problem is rather different: the East Indies seem to have been for the Chinese the ultimate frontier, rarely if ever crossed. The barrier of the East Indies always proved easier to cross from west to north-east than in the other direction.

Both these expansions, first the Indian then the Chinese, at any rate made the East Indies if not a pole of attraction, then at least a busy crossroads of trade. Various outstanding periods marked the history of this region: the Krivijaya kingdom (seventh to thirteenth centuries) centred on south-east Sumatra and the town of Palembang; then the Mojopahit empire (thirteenth to fifteenth centuries), based this time on the rich rice-growing island of Java. One after the other these political units seized control of the major maritime routes, notably the crucial route through the Malacca straits. These powerful ventures into empire-building both lasted for some time – the first for five or six centuries, the second for three or four, making it possible already to talk in terms of an East Indian economy, if not of a super-world-economy of the Far East.

Probably there was no super-world-economy revolving round the East Indies until the rise of Malacca, from 1403, when the town was founded or 1409 when it began to make an impact, until its capture by Alfonso de Albuquerque on 10 August 1511.[505] It is worth looking a little more closely at this sudden but century-long success.

Malacca's hour of glory

Geography was certainly responsible for a good deal of Malacca's story.[506] The town occupies an advantageous site on the straits which bear its name, lying on the maritime channel connecting the waters of the Indian Ocean to those of the China seas on the edge of the Pacific. The narrow Malay peninsula (which good roads today enable one to cross quickly, even on a bicycle) could only be crossed in the past by beaten tracks at the latitude of the Kra isthmus. But these ran through jungles full of wild animals. Once the peninsula had been circumnavigated successfully the Malacca straits came into their own.[507]

Built on a slight eminence rising above a 'soft' and 'muddy' plain ('one spade thrust finds water')[508] and bisected by a clear running river where boats could come ashore, Malacca was a mooring and shelter rather than a true port: larger junks anchored opposite the town between the two little islands which the Portuguese christened *Ilha de Pedra* and *Ilha da Naos* (the Island of Stones and the Island of Ships), the second being 'no bigger than the square in Amsterdam where the town hall stands'.[509] However as another traveller pointed out, 'one can land at Malacca any time of year, an advantage which the ports of Goa,

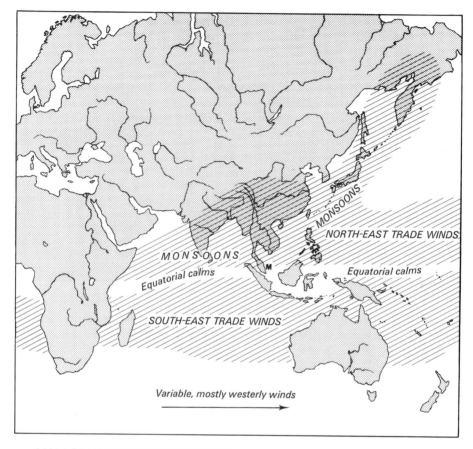

NORTH-EAST TRADE WINDS

MONSOONS

MONSOONS

Equatorial calms

Equatorial calms

SOUTH-EAST TRADE WINDS

Variable, mostly westerly winds

48 MALACCA'S PRIVILEGED POSITION
The band of equatorial calm moves north then south depending on the position of the sun. So Malacca is a connection or corridor between the monsoons and the north-east and south-east trades. (From Vidal de la Blache's *Atlas*, p. 56.)

Cochin or Surat do not offer'.[510] The only obstacles were the tidal currents in the straits: the tide usually 'flowed eastwards and ebbed westward'.[511] As if these advantages were not enough, Malacca stood not only at the meeting place of two oceans but also at the intersection of two zones of atmospheric circulation, the monsoons of the Indian Ocean to the west, and the trade winds to the south and east. Best of all, the narrow band of equatorial calm which moves slowly north or south depending on the position of the sun, stays for quite a long time in the Malacca region (latitude 2°30'N) thus alternately allowing ships free passage towards the trades or the monsoon. 'This is one of the places most favoured by nature', exclaimed Sonnerat, 'it is perpetual springtime here.'[512]

But there were other good sites in the East Indies – the Sunda straits for instance. The earlier fortunes of the Krivijaya and Mojopahit regimes[513] prove that the same control could be exerted from the east coast of Sumatra and from even further east in Java. Indeed in 1522, Magellan's ships, after their leader's death in the Philippines, crossed through the Sunda Islands southwards near Timor on their homeward route, in order to catch the south-east trades. And it was by a similar route that Drake on his voyage round the world in 1580, reached the southern coast of the East Indies.

If Malacca's rise can be explained in terms of geography, history certainly made an important contribution, both at local level and at the more general level of the Asiatic economy. The newly-founded town succeeded for instance in attracting and to some extent controlling the Malay sailors who had always been fishermen, coastal traders and above all pirates. Malacca thus succeeded in ridding the straits of these corsairs, while at the same time acquiring for itself the little sailing ships, crews and even war fleets it needed. As for the large junks indispensable to long-distance trade, these could be found in Java or Pegu. It was here for instance that the sultan of Malacca (who took a great interest in and large share of the town's traffic) bought the ships with which he arranged a voyage to Mecca on his own account.

The town's rapid development soon became a problem in itself. How was it to survive? Perched on a hilly and forested peninsula, rich in tin mines but short of edible crops, Malacca's only source of food was the local catch of fish. It was therefore strictly dependent on Siam and Java, the two nearest rice-growers and exporters. Siam was an aggressive and dangerous state, and Java was still labouring under the ancient but not yet dead imperialism of the Mojopahit Empire. One or other of these states would probably have snapped up this little town that had grown up accidentally, if Malacca had not in 1409 placed itself under Chinese protection, which remained effective until the 1430s: meantime the Mojopahit Empire had collapsed, removing the threat to Malacca's existence.

The town's extraordinary fortune was also the result of a crucial combination of circumstances: the meeting of China and India – China having for thirty years or so encouraged an amazing expansionist venture by her mariners into the Java seas and the Indian Ocean, India having since an earlier date launched an even greater assault. Towards the end of the fourteenth century, under the impulsion of Muslim India and the Delhi sultanate, a wave of Indian traders and transporters, natives of Bengal, Coromandel and Gujerat had reached the East Indies, accompanied by a strong current of religious proselytism. The conversion to Islam which the Arab sailors of the seventh century had not achieved or even attempted, had become a reality centuries later, thanks to trade with India.[514] The coastal towns all went over to Islam one after another. For Malacca, which was converted in 1414, this was a golden opportunity: business and religion went hand in hand. And if the Mojopahit Empire was gradually disintegrating and ceasing to be a threat, it was precisely because the coastal towns had turned to Islam, while the interior of Java and the other islands remained faithful to Hinduism. The spread of the Muslim order only affected about a third or a

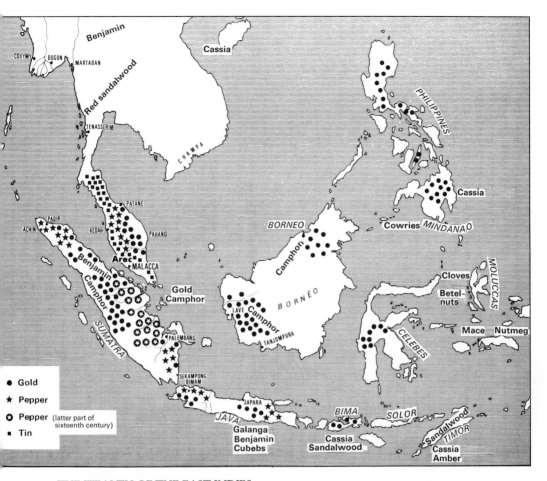

Gold ●
Pepper ★
Pepper (latter part of sixteenth century) ◉
Tin ■

49 THE WEALTH OF THE EAST INDIES
The Portuguese from their base in Malacca rapidly surveyed the riches of the archipelago: above all pepper, fine spices and gold. This first European impact was sufficiently strong to stimulate fresh plantations and new markets, particularly for pepper. The same thing occurred on the Malabar coast in India. (From V. Magalhaẽs Godhino, *op. cit.*)

quarter of the population. Some islands remained untouched by it – such as Bali, which remains today a fantastic museum of the Hindu past. And in the distant Moluccas, the conversion was incomplete: the Portuguese to their astonishment later found nominal Muslims there who were by no means hostile to Christianity.

But the rising fortune of Malacca was a direct consequence of the expansion of Indian trade. There was a good reason for this: the Indian traders had brought to Sumatra and Java an important gift – the pepper-bush. Everywhere, spreading from the points affected by contact with Malacca, a market economy began to replace what had previously been a primitive and largely self-sufficient regime.

> They took little heed of sowing or planting [writes a Portuguese chronicler of the previous history of the inhabitants of the Moluccas] ... they lived as in the first ages of humanity. In the morning they took from the sea or the forest enough to feed themselves for the whole day. Living off plunder, they derived no profit from cloves, and there was no one to buy them from them.[515]

When the Moluccas were integrated into trade networks, plantations were laid out and regular links set up between Malacca and the spice islands. A *keling* merchant (that is a Hindu merchant from the Coromandel coast) Nina Suria Deva, sent eight junks every year to the Moluccas (for cloves) and to the Banda Islands (for nutmeg). These islands, having gone over to a monoculture, depended entirely for their subsistence on the rice brought to them by the junks from Java, which even sailed out as far as the Mariana Islands deep in the Pacific.

So the Islamic invasion had created a new order. 'Sultanates' were set up in Malacca and Tidore, Ternate and later in Macassar. The most curious phenomenon of all was the establishment of a *lingua franca* necessary for doing business, based on Malay, which was commonly spoken in the headquarters of trade, Malacca. Throughout the East Indies with their 'Mediterraneans', remarked a Portuguese chronicler, 'the number of languages is so great that even neighbours do not, so to speak, understand each other. Today they use the Malay tongue, which most people speak, and it is employed throughout the islands, like Latin in Europe'. It is not surprising then that the 450 words of the vocabulary of the inhabitants of the Moluccas brought back to Europe by Magellan's expedition were in fact words of Malay.[516]

The spread of the *lingua franca* was proof of Malacca's expansionist strength. But this was really created by external factors, much as Antwerp's fortune had been in in the sixteenth century. For while the town could offer lodgings, market-places, warehouses and protective institutions, not to mention its very precious code of maritime laws, its trade was kept going by foreign ships, traders and commodities. Among these foreigners, the most numerous group was made up of Muslim traders from Gujerat and Calicut (a million Gujeratis according to Tomé Pires, 'besides four or five thousand ... seamen who came and went'); and another large group consisted of the Hindu merchants of Coromandel, the *kelings*, who had their own district, the *Campon Queling*.[517] The Gujeratis had the advantage of being as solidly established in Sumatra and Java as they were in Malacca, and of being able to control the bulk of re-exports of pepper and spices to the Mediterranean. Cambay (another name for Gujerat) could only survive, it was said, by stretching out one arm to Aden and the other to Malacca.[518] Once more, one becomes aware of India's hidden superiority: she was much more open than China to foreign contacts and had links with the trade networks of Islam as well as with the Middle East – the more so since China after 1430, for reasons which despite the fertile imagination of historians remain obscure, abandoned long-distance expeditions for good. Moreover, China was only moderately interested in spices, of which the Chinese consumed small quantities, except for pepper which they could obtain in Bantam without needing to go through Malacca.

The capture of Malacca by the little fleet commanded by Albuquerque (1400 men, 600 of whom were from the Malabar coast)[519] was inspired by the prosperity and reputation of the town, 'which was then the most famous in the Indies market'.[520] It was a brutal assault: once the bridge over the river had been stormed, the town was sacked for nine days on end. But Malacca's fortunes did not entirely come to an end on that fateful day, 10 August 1500. Albuquerque, who remained in the conquered town until January 1512, quickly re-organized it; he built an imposing fortress, and if he presented himself from Siam to the spice islands as the enemy of Muslims, he also announced that he was a friend of the Gentiles, the pagans and in fact of all merchants. After the occupation, Portuguese policy became more tolerant and conciliatory. Even Philip II as king of Portugal and lord of the Indies after 1580, pursued a watchful religious toleration in the Far East. We must not convert by force, he insisted, *Não e este modo que se deve ter uma conversão*.[521] In Portuguese-occupied Malacca, there was a Chinese bazaar as well as a mosque, though it is true that the Church of St Paul belonging to the Jesuits dominated the fortress, and from its steps one could see the sea. As Luis Filipe F.R. Thomaz has rightly remarked, 'the conquest of Malacca in August 1511 opened to the Portuguese the doors of the Java Seas and the Far East; by capturing Malacca, the victors did not merely acquire a rich town, but also control of a complex of trade routes meeting at Malacca to which the town was the key'.[522] In general, with some exceptions, they held on to these routes. Some of them were even extended when in 1555, in order to counter the mid-century crisis, the Portuguese landed at Macao opposite Canton and even reached Japan. Malacca while in their hands was the centre of communications between the Pacific, India and Europe, as Batavia later would be in the hands of the Dutch.

Before the arrival of the Dutch disturbed their Asian paradise, the Portuguese enjoyed a period of peace and prosperity, bringing profit to the king in Lisbon, to Portugal, to the pepper retailers in Europe, but also to the Portuguese adventurers in the East who often, if not always, had the semi-feudal mentality of the Spanish conquistadors in America. There were a few Turkish attacks, but they were intermittent and accomplished little. On the whole, the Portuguese profited from their quiet life. But 'by dint of travelling through these seas without hindrance, they began to neglect all kinds of precautions for their defence'.[523] So when in 1592, Lancaster's two English ships arrived by the very same route as Vasco da Gama, they had little difficulty in capturing the Portuguese vessels they encountered. And soon everything would begin to change: the Europeans would bring to the Indies their European wars and rivalries, and the reign of Malacca as a Portuguese town would be over. The Dutch took it in 1641 and immediately relegated it to a subordinate role.

The new centres of the Far East

Even before the fall of Malacca, Batavia had become the new centre of the Far Eastern trade, directing and ordering everything. Founded in 1619, it was at the height of its fortunes in 1638, when Japan barred access to the Portuguese while remaining open to ships of the V.O.C. The headquarters of the aristocracy of trade – as well as control of the vital networks of the 'country trade' – thus remained in the East Indies and would continue to do so as long as the Dutch East Indies Company retained its astute, vigilant and authoritarian supremacy, that is for over a century, with some ups and downs. In early 1662 for instance, the Dutch were expelled from Formosa, the island off the Chinese mainland and halfway to Japan where they had been settled since 1634, the date of the building of the fort at Castel Zelandia.[524] The long reign of Batavia, described earlier in this book, thus coincided broadly with the long crisis of the seventeenth century which so severely affected the European world-economy (including the New World) between approximately 1650 and 1750. But it probably did not hit the Far East so hard, since throughout India the seventeenth century was an age of prosperity, of demographic and economic expansion. Perhaps this was one of the reasons why during the European crisis Holland's economy was by far the best protected, as we have already seen, and the one which had the lion's share of what trade there was.

The new town of Batavia was certainly a striking symbol of Dutch supremacy. The two-storey town hall built in 1652 marked the centre of the town, a town criss-crossed with canals and grid-plan streets, surrounded by walls, fortified with twenty-two towers, and punctuated by four gates. Into Batavia flocked all the peoples of Asia, Europe and the Indian Ocean. Outside the walls were the Javan and Amboynan districts and a few country villas; but above all paddy-fields, sugar cane plantations, canals, and on the banks of the re-channelled river flour-mills, paper-mills, saw-mills and powder-mills, as well as sugar-mills, tile- and brickworks. Inside the town, everything was neat, clean and orderly: the market-places, warehouses, stores, butcheries, fishmarket, barracks and the *Spinhuis*, where dishonoured girls were sentenced to spin. I need not reiterate how rich, pleasure-seeking and indolent Dutch colonial society was. This wealth and love of pleasure which we have already seen in Goa, which was already to be seen in Batavia even before De Graaf's arrival in 1668, and which would later appear in identical form in Calcutta, is the unmistakable sign of outstanding success.[525]

But by the beginning of the eighteenth century, the formidable Dutch machine was beginning to break down. This is sometimes attributed to the growing corruption and unreliability of the Company's agents. But the 'servants' of the English East India Company far outdid the Dutch in this respect, yet that did not prevent the English company from moving into first place in about 1760. Was it, as one is tempted to think, because the reversal of the trend in mid-century

Macao in the early seventeenth century by Theodore de Bry. The town had been occupied by the Portuguese since 1557 and was the departure point for merchants trading with China. (Photo, B. N., Paris.)

brought increased activity, a greater volume of trade and encouraged change, upheaval and revolution? Back in Europe, there was a reshuffle of the international cards, resulting in a speedy victory for the English. In Asia, the centre of gravity of the Far East was shifting towards India, but India was only moving into first place under the rule and on behalf of England, by a process admirably described in Holden Furber's book (published as long ago as 1948).[526] The English company ('John Company') ousted its cousin ('Jan Compagnie') the V.O.C., because the latter had lost out in both Bengal and India in the 1770s and had already failed in the middle of the century to seize the first place in Canton, where China was gradually inching open the gates a little wider every day. I do not intend to suggest that John played a shrewder and more intelligent game in Canton than Jan, although this is sometimes maintained, not without some justification. But a French observer who bitterly criticized the French company, argued that in Canton in about 1752, it was the Danish and Swedish companies – the most junior and the least well equipped to succeed – who rose to the occasion best of all.[527] If the English eventually emerged on top, it was because they could combine their own forces with the formidable weight of India. Plassey (1757) did not only mark the political conquest of India, but also that of the trading 'rivieras' running along the coast of the subcontinent and extending on one side to the Red Sea and Persian Gulf and on the other to the East Indies and soon to Canton. It was entirely for the use of the country trade, in particular for the China run, that the Indian shipyards were turning out so many 'Indiamen'. According to Furber,[528] whereas in 1780 the fleet flying the English flag and carrying the country trade totalled 4000 tons, by 1790, it had risen to 25,000! The jump was not quite as big as it looks, since 1780 was a war year, the last-but-one serious confrontation between France and England, and English ships were then prudently sailing under Danish, Portuguese or Swedish flags. When the danger was past they appeared in their true colours again.

At the same time there was a rapid shift of fortunes from Batavia to Calcutta. The sudden rise of the city on the Ganges helps to explain from a distance the somnolence of the V.O.C. Calcutta grew phenomenally, in every direction, and in the greatest disorder. The count of Modave[529] a French traveller and fortune-hunter, arrived there in 1773 just as Warren Hastings' governorship was beginning. He observed both the town's exuberant growth and its lack of order. Calcutta was nothing like Batavia with its trim canals and streets. There was not even a quayside on the Ganges: 'the houses are scattered here and there on the bank, the walls of some of them are washed by the river'. Nor was there a perimeter wall. There were perhaps 500 houses at most, built by the English amid a sea of bamboo huts with thatched roofs. The streets were as muddy as jungle tracks, sometimes broad but closed at either end by barriers made of large beams. There was chaos in every direction. 'It is said to be the effect of the famous British freedom, as if freedom were incompatible with order and symmetry.'[530] Indeed, our Frenchman continues, 'it is not without astonishment mingled with a little anger that a foreigner looks on the city of Calcutta. It would have been so easy to make it one of the fairest cities in the world, simply by taking the trouble to observe a regular plan, that one cannot understand how the English could have neglected the advantages of such a fine site and left everyone complete freedom to build according to the strangest of tastes and the most extravagant dispositions'. It is true that Calcutta which had been a mere settlement in 1689, to which a fortress (Fort William) was added in 1702, was still in 1750 an insignificant town. Prévost does not even mention it. When the count of Modave observed it in 1773, by which time every possible trading population was represented there, the town was growing wildly and in the throes of a building boom. Bricks were being made in the surrounding countryside, wood was being floated down the Ganges or through the sea of Pegu; rents were reaching record levels. Calcutta already had 30,000 or so inhabitants and would have more than doubled by the end of the century. The town was growing without being responsible either for its growth or its fortune. The English behaved there without the least restraint, elbowing aside or bullying anyone who got in their way. Bombay on the other side of India was by contrast a pole of liberty, the compensation or perhaps the revenge of Indian capitalism which would score some extraordinary successes there.

Is any conclusion possible?

Long though this chapter has been, the picture it gives of 'non-Europe' is clearly far from complete.

I could have dwelt at more length on China, and in particular on the centrifugal expansion which affected the province of Fukien, a process which would only be interrupted by the departure of the Dutch from Formosa in 1662, or rather by the conquest of the island in 1683 by the Manchus, but which began again in the eighteenth century with the opening up of Canton to the many-sided trade of Europe.

I could also have devoted space to the special case of Japan which, according to Leonard Bluss's brilliant essay,[531] constructed after 1638 a world-economy for its own use and to fit its own dimensions, consisting of Korea, the Ryukyu islands, Formosa until 1683, and the Chinese junks allowed in on sufferance, together with the privileged 'vassal' trade of the Dutch.

I could have said even more about India, and made room for the analysis recently advanced by J.C. Heesterman[532] who sees as one of the main reasons for the decline of the Mogul Empire the development of urban economies which were by the eighteenth century destroying the unity of the whole.

Lastly I could have included a section on Safavid Persia, on its command economy and its role as indispensable intermediary between India, Central Asia, hostile and hated Turkey, Muscovy and distant Europe.

But even if I had been able to paint the picture in its fullness, at the risk of stretching the chapter to the proportions of a book, would we be any nearer the end of our problems and questions? Certainly not. To reach conclusions about Europe and non-Europe, that is on the world as a whole, we should need some valid measurements and figures. What I have essentially given here is a description, an outline of some of the problems and some hints at possible or perhaps probable explanations. But we have by no means solved the enigma of the relations between Europe and non-Europe. For if it can hardly be questioned that until the nineteenth century the rest of the world outweighed Europe both in population and, while the economic *ancien régime* lasted, in wealth, if it is virtually beyond question that Europe was less rich than the worlds it was exploiting, even after the fall of Napoleon when Britain's hour of glory was dawning – we still do not really know how this position of superiority was established and above all maintained – for the gap grew steadily wider.

The great service Paul Bairoch has once more rendered to historians is precisely to pose this problem in statistical terms. By so doing he does not merely agree with my position but goes well beyond it. But is he right? And am I right?

I shall not go into details and into the validity of the methods my colleague in Geneva has employed. I shall simply assume for the sake of brevity that the procedure he adopted was sufficiently scientifically valid for his results (very approximate ones, as he is the first to admit, and to warn the reader) to be taken into consideration.

The chosen indicator is per capita income, G.N.P. per inhabitant, and so as to give a meaningful picture of the respective positions of the various countries, all the levels have been calculated in dollars at 1960 US prices, so they are all presented in the same units. The results are as follows: England in 1700, between $150 and $190; the English colonies in America, the future United States in 1710, between $250 and $290; France (1781–1790), $170 to $200; India in 1800, $160 to $210 (but in 1900 between $140 and $180). These figures, which reached me as I was correcting the proofs of this book, confirmed my faith in the assertions and hypotheses I had already put forward. Nor was I surprised by the figure for Japan in 1750: $160. Only the high figure for China in 1800: $228 seems rather surprising, although it is true that this high level later declines ($170 in 1950).

But let us concentrate on what interests us most, namely the comparisons, if possible *synchronic*, between the two blocs made up of Europe-plus-the-United States and non-Europe. In 1800, western Europe reaches the figure of $213 (North America $266); not so surprising perhaps, but this figure is hardly any higher than that of the 'Third World' of the time – about $200. And that is a somewhat unexpected figure. In fact the high level reached by China ($228 in 1800, $204 in 1860) raises the average of the less favoured group. Today the figure for western Europe as measured in 1976, is $2325, whereas China – despite recent recovery – is only $369, and the Third World as a whole is at about $355, far behind the developed nations.

What emerges from Paul Bairoch's calculations is that at the time when Europe was scoring dazzling triumphs all over the globe, when her ships commanded by Cook, La Pérouse or Bougainville, were exploring the vastness of the Pacific Ocean, she was (unlike today) far from having reached a level of wealth vastly superior to living standards in the rest of the world. The combined G.N.P. of the developed countries of today (western Europe, the USSR, North America, Japan) was in 1750 only $35,000 million (1960 dollars) – whereas that of the rest of the world was $120,000 million; in 1860, the respective figures were $115,000 million as against $165,000 million; the first group only overtook the second between 1880 and 1900; in 1880 the figures were $176,000 million to $169,000 million; by 1900 they were $290,000 million to $188,000 million. But in 1976, in round figures, they were $3000 million to $1000 million.

This perspective obliges us to take a rather different view of the respective positions of Europe (plus the other privileged countries) and the rest of the world, before 1800 and after the industrial revolution, which now appears to take on tremendous significance. It seems certain that only Europe (perhaps for reasons that have more to do with her social and economic structures than with technological progress) was able to carry out the machine revolution, with England leading the way. But this revolution was not merely an instrument of development in itself. It was a weapon of domination and destruction of foreign competition. By mechanizing, European industry became capable of out-competing the traditional industry of other nations. The gap which then opened up could only grow wider as time went on. The history of the world between about 1400 and 1850–1950 is one of an ancient parity collapsing under the weight of a multisecular distortion, whose beginnings go back to the late fifteenth century. Compared with this predominant trend, everything else is secondary.

6

The Industrial Revolution and Growth

THE INDUSTRIAL REVOLUTION which began or rather became visible in England in the 1750s or 1760s, strikes the observer as an extremely complex process. In the first place it was the culmination of the 'industrialization' which had begun many centuries earlier. And since it is constantly being reproduced, it could be said to be still with us today. Identified in the past as the beginning of a new era, the industrial revolution is likely to influence the future for many years to come. But massive, all-pervasive and innovatory though it may have been, it does not, nor can it, tell the whole story about the modern world.

This is what I shall be doing my best to convey in the following pages, whose purpose is to define this extraordinary phenomenon and, if possible, to place it in its proper context.

Some relevant comparisons

As a first step, some definitions and in particular some preliminary comparisons may be relevant. In the first place, since its original appearance in England the industrial revolution has engendered a series of other revolutions and is evolving before our eyes, still moving on towards new horizons: the revolutions it has spawned can tell us something in retrospect about the English 'takeoff'. On the other hand, we can go back to the days before the English industrial revolution and find many instances of industrialization, something which has always been present in human societies; some of these past experiences were advanced and forward-looking, though in the end none of them came to anything. But the study of failure can sometimes be relevant to the understanding of success.

Revolution: a complicated and ambiguous term

Borrowed from the vocabulary of astronomy,[1] the word *revolution* in the sense of upheaval or overthrow of an existing society, is thought to have appeared in the English language in 1688.[2] It is in this sense, but also in the opposite sense

Honour where honour is due: the industrial revolution began with the coming of steam, the achievement of James Watt (1736-1819). This portrait by James Eckford Lauder, shows him putting the finishing touches to his steam engine in the laboratory. (Snark International.)

meaning *reconstruction*, that one should understand the convenient expression *the industrial revolution* which seems to have been coined not by Engels in 1845[3] but possibly in 1837 by the French economist Adolphe Blanqui[4] (brother of the more famous revolutionary, Auguste)– unless that is it appeared even earlier, in about 1820 in debates between various other French authors.[5] The term certainly does not seem to have been in standard use among historians until after the appearance in print in 1884 of the *Lectures on the Industrial Revolution* which the social reformer Arnold Toynbee gave in Oxford in 1880-1, and which his pupils published after his death.

Historians are often criticized for misusing the word *revolution* which, it is argued, ought to be used in the original sense, to refer only to violent and rapid change. But when one is talking about social phenomena, rapid and slow change are inseparable. For no society exists which is not constantly torn between the forces working to preserve it and the subversive forces – whether perceived as such or not – working to undermine it. Revolutionary explosions are but the sudden and short-lived volcanic eruptions of this latent and long-term conflict. In any attempt to analyse the revolutionary process, the most difficult part is always making the connection between the long and the short-term, recognizing their relationship and the links between them. The industrial revolution in England at the end of the eighteenth century is no exception. It consisted both of a rapid sequence of events and of what was clearly a very long-term process: two different rhythms were beating simultaneously.

Whether we like it or not then, we are faced with a dialectic between the long and the short-term. According to W. W. Rostow[6] for instance, the English economy 'took off' between 1783 and 1802, because a critical investment threshold had been crossed. This explanation has been challenged by Simon Kuznets whose figures tell a different story[7] but it survives in the image of the takeoff, the plane leaving the runway – that is an event precisely located in time. But before there could be any takeoff in the first place, the plane (Britain) had to be built and satisfactory conditions for the flight had to be arranged. In any case, no society is likely to be able – simply because, say, its rate of savings has gone up – to transform at a stroke 'its attitudes, institutions and techniques', as Arthur Lewis claims.[8] There will always have been some earlier experiences, stages of progress and adaptations. Phyllis Deane is right to remind us that all the innovations and even discontinuities of the late eighteenth century were, in the English case, contained within 'a historical continuum', stretching back into the past, covering the present, reaching into the future, a continuum in which breaks and discontinuities lose their identities as unique or decisive events.[9] When David Landes describes the industrial revolution as the formation of a critical mass which eventually produced a revolutionary explosion,[10] the image is an appropriate one, but it must be understood that the mass can only have been formed by the slow accumulation of all manner of necessary elements. Argue as we may, the long-term will always claim its due.

So the industrial revolution was at least twofold. It was a revolution in the ordinary sense of the word, bringing its visible changes in a sequence of short-term events, yet it was at the same time a long-term process, advancing with discreet and silent steps, sometimes barely discernible at all 'and as unlike a revolution as anything that can be imagined', according to Claude Fohlen,[11] who by contrast with Rostow, lays the emphasis on continuity.

It is hardly surprising then that even during the apparently most explosive period (let us say roughly after 1760) this vital phenomenon made very little impression on the most famous observers of the day. Adam Smith, with his example of the little Scottish pin factory, seems in retrospect to have been a rather poor witness to his age – and yet he lived until 1790. Ricardo (1772-1823) who was younger than Smith and thus has even less excuse, hardly gives any place to the machine in his theoretical writings.[12] And Jean-Baptiste Say, after describing the English 'steam chariots' in 1828, makes this short-sighted prophecy: 'Nevertheless ... no machine will ever be able to perform what even the worst horses can – the service of carrying people and goods though the bustle and throng of a great city'.[13] But it is not fair to expect the great men of the age – if Say can be numbered with them – to be skilled at the art of prophecy. And it is only too easy with hindsight to accuse Marx or Weber, or even a later writer like Werner Sombart, of misunderstanding – that is of understanding differently from ourselves – the long process of industrialization. I find T.S. Ashton, usually a fair-minded writer, rather unjust in his hasty condemnation of past historians, based on a remark by Kroebner.[14]

In any case, are the historians of today – so many of whom study the industrial revolution – any more correct in their judgments? Some see the process as beginning before the seventeenth century; some regard the Glorious Revolution of 1688 as a key moment; others again see the radical transformation of England as coinciding with the broad economic revival of the later part of the eighteenth century. They can all make out a convincing case, depending on whether the accent is put on agriculture, demography, foreign trade, industrial techniques, or forms of credit. But should the industrial revolution be seen as a series of sectorial modernizations; as a sequence of stages of development; or as a phenomenon of simultaneous growth on all fronts, taking the word 'growth' in the broadest sense? If by the late eighteenth century, British growth had become irreversible, being by now as Rostow[15] puts it the 'normal condition' of Britain, it was certainly not on account of progress in some particular sector (such as the rate of savings or investment) but on the contrary as the consequence of an overall and indivisible process, the sum of the reciprocal relations of interdependence and liberation that each individual sector as it developed, sooner or later, by accident or design, had helped to create for the greater benefit of the other sectors. Can 'true' growth (or as some people would call it true development – the word does not much matter) be anything but growth which links together, irreversibly, progress on several fronts at once, creating a mutually sustaining whole which is then propelled on to greater things?

Downstream from the industrial revolution: the under-developed countries

The industrial revolution in Britain opened the door to a series of revolutions which are in its direct line of descent: some have succeeded, others have failed. It had itself been preceded by several revolutions of the same order, some of which barely got off the ground, while others were pursued quite seriously – but all of them sooner or later came to nothing. From this historical vantage-point then, one can look in two directions – towards the past or towards the present – and embark on two kinds of historical journey, each offering an approach to the subject which draws on the invaluable insights of comparative history.

If we look down the stream of history to the present, there is no great virtue in studying the example of the industrial revolutions in Europe and the United States, which followed close on the heels of the British model. But the present-day Third World, which is still undergoing industrialization, offers the historian a rare opportunity to observe something in action, something that can be seen, heard and touched. It is certainly no success story. Over the past thirty, forty or fifty years, the Third World as a whole can hardly be said to have made steady progress. Its efforts and expectations have only too often led to bitter disappointment. Can the reasons for the failure, or comparative failure of these experiments help to define *a contrario* the conditions which brought about the exceptional success of the industrial revolution in Britain?

Economists and more particularly historians will of course caution us against the procedure of extrapolating from the present in order to understand the past. They will argue, not without some truth, that 'the mimetic model, which predicated the repetition of the itinerary previously taken by the industrialized countries, has had its day'.[16] The context has completely changed and it would be impossible nowadays for the industrialization of some Third World country to follow the authoritarian state model seen in Japan or the spontaneous growth of George III's England. Agreed; but if 'the crisis in development is also a crisis in development theory' as Ignacy Sachs has said,[17] would not the process of development in itself – including the case of England in the eighteenth century – become more intelligible if we asked ourselves what has gone wrong with the theory, and why the enthusiastic planners of the 1960s so gravely underestimated the difficulties of the undertaking?

The problem, we shall immediately be told, is that a successful industrial revolution calls for a general process of growth, and therefore of overall development, which 'in the last analysis takes the shape of a process of transformation of economic, social, political and cultural institutions'.[18] The entire length and breadth of a society and economy are concerned in this process and must be capable of accompanying, sustaining and actually undergoing change. It only takes one obstacle, what we would today call a bottleneck, at one point in the process, for the whole machine to come to a standstill, for its motion to be halted or even reversed. The leaders of countries today trying to catch up with the advanced nations of the world have learnt this to their cost, and development strategy has now become as prudent as it is complex.

What advice then would a well-informed economist such as Ignacy Sachs give in these circumstances? Essentially that no *a priori* planning model be applied: no single model will do, since every economy presents a particular combination of structures which may appear to resemble each other but do so only approximately. In any given society, the planner would be well advised to take a hypothetical growth rate (say 10%), suppose it to be adopted as a target, and study one by one 'the consequences of the hypothesis'. This would mean checking one after another a number of factors: the amount of investment which would have to come out of national income; the possible types of industry with a view to potential home and foreign markets; the quantity and quality of labour required (skilled or otherwise); market supplies of the foodstuffs required to feed the workforce; the available technology (in particular from the point of view of the capital investment and the size and kind of workforce they would require); the provision of extra imports of raw materials or machine tools; the eventual effect of the new output on the balance of payments and foreign trade. If the growth rate originally posited was deliberately chosen 'at sufficiently high level to show up all the possible bottle-necks that might appear if it really were maintained as a target',[19] the checklist would indicate in which sectors insuperable obstacles might arise. It would then be possible in the second stage, to proceed to scale down, by envisaging 'variants at every level' until a more modest, but theoretically viable target was reached.[20]

The examples described in Sachs's book give a concrete idea of the principal bottle-necks encountered in the Third World today; population growth, when it cancels out the benefits of development; shortages of skilled labour; a propensity to industrialize in luxury and sometimes export sectors, because of low domestic demand for basic industrial products; and perhaps most of all, the 'agricultural barrier', the insufficiency and inelasticity of food supplies provided by an agricultural sector which has remained archaic and largely self-sufficient, and cannot expand to meet the increased consumption automatically engendered by the greater number of wage-earners; an agricultural sector which cannot always even feed its own surplus population and is thus responsible for the exodus to the towns of an unemployed proletariat; one which is lastly unable because of its poverty to swell the demand for basic industrial products. Compared with these major problems, the need for capital, the level of savings, credit arrangements and interest rates seem almost secondary. But it is surely significant that this list enumerates precisely all the obstacles which no longer existed in eighteenth-century (or indeed seventeenth-century) England.

So the prime requirement of growth is intersectorial harmony: one sector should not be allowed to block progress being made in another. This brings us back to what we sensed lying behind the concept of the *national market* – the assumption that the national market is characterized by cohesion, free circulation of goods and a certain level of per capita income. In France, a country notoriously slow to achieve economic takeoff (since the cohesion of the economy was not a reality until the railway network was complete) it might be argued that there was for a long period precisely the same kind of dichotomy which can be observed in Third World countries today: an ultra-modern, rich and advanced sector existing alongside a number of backward areas, the 'lands of darkness' as they were called by an 'entrepreneur' who in 1752 wanted to open up to trade one of these regions and its fantastic forests by rendering navigable the Vere, a small and insignificant tributary of the Aveyron.[21]

But the endogenous conditions for growth are not the only things which shape the national market. Is not the major obstacle facing today's developing nations the international economy in its existing form, and the way in which it divides and distributes tasks – something on which this book has already laid if anything too much emphasis? England successfully carried out her industrial revolution when she was at the centre of the world – when she *was* in fact the centre of the world. Today's Third World countries would like to do the same, but they are firmly on the periphery. Consequently everything conspires against them: the new technology, which they can only use under licence and which does not always correspond to the needs of their own societies; capital which they can borrow only from outside sources; shipping, which is beyond their control; even their own surpluses of raw materials, which sometimes leave them at the mercy of the purchaser. This is why the contemporary world offers such a distressing spectacle; why industrialization persistently makes a progress only in places where it has already made progress, and the gap grows ever wider between the under-developed countries and the others. It may however be the case that we are now witnessing a change in this balance of power. Since 1974, the countries producing oil and other raw materials, and the poor countries whose low wages make it possible for them to produce industrial goods at very low prices, seem to have begun to take revenge upon the highly industrialized nations. Only the history of the next few years will tell. But if the Third World is to make any progress it will somehow or other have to break down the existing international order.

Upstream from the English industrial revolution: revolutions that came to nothing

Today's failures are a salutary warning that every industrial revolution is a combination of elements, a 'family complex', a series of different factors. And it is in relation to this multiplicity of factors that the 'pre-revolutions', the movements which preceded the English revolution, are significant. In their case, there is always something missing, so that they add up to a sort of typology of failure or missed opportunity. Sometimes an invention appears in isolation, brilliant but useless, the sterile fruit of some fertile brain; no more is heard of it. Sometimes there is takeoff of a kind, perhaps as the result of a revolution in energy, or some sudden advance in agricultural or craft technology, a breakthrough in marketing or an increase in the population: there is a burst of progress, the motor seems on the point of starting – and then the whole thing comes to a halt. Is it right to lump together under the same heading this series of abortive revolutions, the reasons for which are never exactly the same? They are at least similar in their rhythm: a burst of progress followed by a collapse. Imperfect repetitions of each other though they may be, they are repetitions all the same and obvious comparisons practically suggest themselves.

My conclusion will surprise no one, certainly not an economist: no industrial revolution, indeed no advance in production or exchange in the broader sense, can be regarded as a strictly economic process. The economy cannot exist in isolation from the other sectors of human life; it depends on them, they depend on it.

Alexandrian Egypt

My first example, an ancient but intriguing one, is Ptolemaic Egypt. Perhaps this looks too like chapter one in a school textbook – but steam[22] had actually made its appearance in Alexandria between 100 and 50 BC, eighteen or nineteen hundred years before Denis Papin or James Watt. Should one dismiss as of no account the invention by the 'engineer' Hero, of the aeolipile, a sort of steam-powered turbine – a mere toy, but one which nevertheless operated a mechanism capable of opening and shutting a heavy temple door some distance away? This discovery followed in the wake of several others – the suction pump, the force pump, some early versions of the thermometer and the theodolite, various engines of war – more theoretical than practical admittedly – which depended on compressed or expelled air, or massive springs. In those distant days, Alexandria was a throbbing powerhouse of invention. Several revolutions had already taken place there during the preceding century or two – cultural, commercial and scientific: this was the age of Euclid, Ptolemy the astronomer and Eratosthenes; Dicaearchus, who seems to have lived in the city early in the third century BC, was the first geographer 'to draw a line of latitude across a map, the line running from the Straits of Gibraltar along the Taurus and the Himalayas to the Pacific Ocean'.[23]

A detailed study of the long Alexandrian episode would of course take us too far, through the extraordinary Hellenistic world resulting from Alexander's conquests, in which territorial states like Egypt and Syria replaced the earlier model, the Greek city-state. It was a transformation which in some ways brings to mind the early development of modern Europe. And it tells us something we shall find frequently repeated: that inventions tend to come in clusters, groups or series, as if they all drew strength from each other, or rather as if certain societies provided simultaneous impetus for them all.

Brilliant though it was, the Alexandrian era eventually came to an end without its inventions giving rise to a revolution in industrial production (despite their being specifically directed towards technical application: Alexandria even had a school of engineering in the third century). No doubt the explanation lies largely in the existence of slavery, which provided the ancient world with the easily-exploited workforce it required. Thus in the East, the horizontal water-wheel remained a rudimentary mechanism adapted only to the heavy tasks of grinding grain, an everyday chore, while steam was used merely to operate ingenious toys, since, as a historian of technology has written, 'no need was felt for a more powerful [source of energy] than those already known'.[24]

Hellenistic society remained indifferent to the inventions of its 'engineers'.

It might also be argued that the Roman conquest, coming as it did shortly after this age of invention, bears some responsibility. The economy and society of the Greeks had been open to the rest of the world for several centuries. Rome by contrast enclosed herself within the Mediterranean world; and by destroying Carthage, and subjugating Greece, Egypt and the East, Rome shut three doors leading to wider horizons. Would the history of the world (as Pascal suspected) have been different if Anthony and Cleopatra had won the battle of Actium in 31 BC? In other words, is an industrial revolution possible only at the heart of an *open* world-economy?

The earliest industrial revolution in Europe: horses and mills, from the eleventh to the thirteenth century

In the first volume of this book, I dwelt at some length on the changes of this period – in the use of horses, the horse-collar (an invention from eastern Europe which increased the animal's traction power); oats (which Edward Fox[25] has argued brought the centre of gravity of Europe back to the great rainswept cereal-growing plains of the north, in the days of Charlemagne and heavy cavalry); and triennial crop rotation, which was quite an agricultural revolution in itself. I also referred to water-mills and windmills, the latter new inventions, the former a revival. I can therefore afford to be brief on this subject, about which information is now increasingly available, especially since many studies of this 'first' industrial revolution have been written, including Jean Gimpel's lively and intelligent book,[26] Guy Bois's vigorous and provocative study[27] and E.M. Carus-Wilson's classic 1941 article[28] which revived[29] and gave wide currency to the term 'the first industrial revolution' to describe the widespread adoption in England of fulling-mills (about 150 between the twelfth and the thirteenth centuries) and sawmills, paper-mills, grinding-mills, etc.

'The mechanising of fulling in the Middle Ages', E.M. Carus-Wilson writes, 'was as decisive an event as the mechanisation of spinning and weaving in the eighteenth century.'[30] The large wooden paddles turned by a water-wheel and introduced to the major industry of the time – woollen cloth – to replace the feet of the fulling-workers, proved to be the instruments of a revolutionary upheaval. Most water courses near the towns, which were generally in the lowlands, did not have the motive force of the upland streams and waterfalls. Fulling-mills therefore tended to be sited in less populated areas, to which they attracted their merchant clientèle. The hitherto jealously guarded craft monopoly of the towns was thus by-passed. The towns inevitably tried to defend themselves by forbidding weavers working within the walls to have their cloth fulled outside. The authorities in Bristol in 1346 forbade 'any man to take outside this city for fulling any kind of the cloth known as raicloth on pain of losing XL d. per cloth'.[31] That did not prevent the 'mill revolution' from taking its course, both in England

This illustration from a French Bible of the thirteenth century depicts the grindstone which Samson was condemned to turn for the Philistines under the lashes of a guard, in the form of what was in the 1230s a modern mill, with a wealth of technical detail. The internal mechanism is meticulously represented, showing the transmission of vertical to horizontal movement. The wheel being turned by the man could equally well be turned by a mill race. This evidence of respect for machinery may be compared to the words of Roger Bacon quoted below. (François Garnier Bible, c. 1220–30, Vienna, B.N., Paris, Codex Vindobonensis 2554.)

and throughout the continent of Europe which certainly did not lag behind on this occasion.

But the point is that this revolution took place alongside a number of other revolutions: a significant agricultural revolution which pitted large numbers of peasants against forest, marsh, seashore and river, and encouraged the adoption of triennial rotation; and a simultaneous urban revolution prompted by demographic expansion – never before had towns sprung up so thickly within such easy reach of one another. A clear distinction of functions, a 'division of labour' between town and countryside, sometimes brutally felt, became the norm. The towns took over industrial activity, became the motors of accumulation and growth, and re-invented money. Trade and traffic increased. With the Champagne fairs, the new economic order of western Europe became first discernible then clearly visible. In the Mediterranean, shipping and overland routes, especially to the east were gradually reconquered by the Italian cities. The whole economic area was undergoing the expansion without which no growth would be possible.

The word *growth*, in the sense of overall development is indeed unhesitatingly used in this context by Frederic C. Lane.[32] In his view, we can undoubtedly talk of a period of 'sustained growth' in the twelfth and thirteenth centuries in, say, Florence or Venice. How could it be otherwise at a time when Italy was the very centre of the world-economy? Wilhelm Abel even maintains that the whole of western Europe was caught up in a wave of general development from the tenth to the fourteenth century, citing as evidence the fact that wages rose faster than cereal prices.

> The thirteenth and early fourteenth centuries [he writes] witnessed the first industrialization of Europe. At this time, the towns with all their commercial and craft activities were undergoing vigorous development, less perhaps because of the technical advances of the age (though these were not negligible) than as a result of the generalization of the division of labour, thanks to which work yields were increased, and it was probably this higher productivity which made it possible not only to resolve the difficult problem of providing a growing population with its essential food supplies, but even to feed it better than ever before. The only analogous occasion was during the 'second industrialization' in the nineteenth century – admittedly on a very different scale.[33]

In other words, the eleventh century saw the beginning of what was effectively a period of 'sustained growth' on the modern pattern, one which would not recur before the English industrial revolution. It is hardly surprising that the 'global development' theory seems the logical explanation. A whole series of inter-related advances were taking place in production and productivity, in agriculture, industry and commerce, as the market expanded. During this first serious awakening of Europe, there was even expansion in the 'tertiary' sector (another sign of development) with a rise in the number of lawyers, notaries, doctors and university professors.[34] We actually have some statistics about the notaries: in Milan in 1288, there were 1500 for a population of about 60,000; in Bologna, 1059 for a population of 50,000; in Verona in 1268 there were 495 for 40,000; in Florence in 1338, there were 500 for a population of 90,000 (but Florence was a special case: business was so well organized there that book-keeping methods often rendered the services of a notary unnecessary). And predictably, with the fourteenth-century recession, the number of notaries declined comparatively; although it climbed again in the eighteenth century it never again reached the heights attained in the thirteenth – no doubt because the abnormal rise in the number of notaries in medieval days was created both by the increase in economic activity and by the need for the services of clerks when the vast majority of people were illiterate.

Europe's great leap forward ended in the monster recession of the fourteenth and fifteenth centuries (roughly from 1350-1450) following the Black Death which may have been as much consequence as cause – the slowing-down of the economy, dating from the cereal crisis and famine of 1315-17,[35] *preceded* the epidemic and may have rendered its sinister work easier. So plague was not the only grim reaper of the prosperity of a previous age: this was already slowing down if not at a standstill by the time the disaster struck.

How then is one to explain Europe's greatest triumph and greatest disaster before the eighteenth century? Most probably by the dimensions of a demon-graphic explosion with which agricultural production found it impossible to keep pace. Falling yields are the mark of any agriculture pushed beyond the bounds of its productive capacity, when it does not possess the methods or techniques which might compensate for the rapid exhaustion of the land. Guy Bois's study, based on the example of eastern Normandy, analyses the social aspects of this phenomenon: the underlying crisis of feudalism which broke up the old partnership between the landlord and the peasant farmer. This destructured society, shorn of its code and vulnerable to disorder and random warfare, was in search both of a new equilibrium and a new code – results not attained until the establishment of the territorial state which would be the salvation of the seigniorial regime.

Other explanations could be suggested – in particular the fragility of the countries most affected by the energy revolution represented by the new mills: northern Europe from the Seine to the Zuyder Zee, from the Low Countries to the Thames valley. New territorial states like France and England, although by now strong political units, were not yet manageable economic units: they were to be seriously affected by the crisis. What was more, in the early years of the century, with the decline of the Champagne fairs, France, having been for a brief moment the centre of European trade now found herself excluded from the circuit of profitable trading links and the first capitalist successes. The cities of the Mediterranean were soon to take over from the new northern states, and this would mark the end, for the time being, of that supreme confidence visible in Roger Bacon's extraordinary glorification of the machine:

Machines may be made by which the largest ships, with only one man steering them, will be moved faster than if they were filled with rowers; wagons may be built which will move with incredible speed and without the aid of beasts; flying machines can be constructed in which man may…beat the air with wings like a bird… Machines will make it possible to go to the bottom of seas and rivers.[36]

The age of Agricola and Leonardo da Vinci: a revolution in embryo

When after this long and painful crisis Europe began to revive again, a wave of renewed trade and vigorous growth ran along the axis linking the Netherlands and Italy, through the middle of Germany. And it was Germany, a secondary zone for trade, which led the way in industrial development: possibly because this was one way of breaking into international exchange, situated as Germany was between the two dominant poles, to the north and south. But it was above all because of the development of mining. The early revival of the German economy in the 1470s, ahead of the rest of Europe, was not the only result. The extraction of metallic ores – gold, silver, copper, tin, cobalt and iron – stimulated a whole series of innovations (the use of lead to separate out silver from copper ore for instance) as well as the creation of machinery, on a gigantic scale for the time, to pump out water from the mines and to bring up the ore. The engravings in Agricola's book provide an impressive picture of the sophisticated technology developed at this time.

It is tempting to see these achievements, which were imitated in England, as the real forerunners of the industrial revolution.[37] The expansion of mining did indeed have repercussions in every sector of the German economy of the time – in fustians, wool, the leather trade, various kinds of metallurgy, tin, wire, paper, the new arms industry and so on. Trade stimulated large-scale credit networks and big international firms like the *Magna Societas* were established.[38] The urban crafts flourished: there were 42 craft guilds in Cologne in 1496; 50 in Lübeck; 28 in Frankfurt-am-Main.[39] Transport was improved and modernized; large firms began to specialize in carrying goods. And Venice, the queen of the Levant trade, established close trading relations with High Germany, since she needed silver. The German cities unquestionably offered for over half a century the spectacle of a rapidly-expanding economy in virtually every sector.

But everything began to slow down or stop in the years around 1535 when, as John Nef's work has shown, silver from America started to compete with the output of the German mines; at about the same time, 1550, Antwerp's commercial supremacy was also being challenged. Was it not a source of inferiority for the German economy to be dependent on external powers, to have been manufactured to meet the needs of the two real centres of the European economy, Venice and Antwerp? The age of the Fuggers, when all is said and done, was the age of Antwerp.

Detail of a miniature dating from the late fifteenth century depicting the silver mine at Kutna Hora, in vertical section as was the custom. The miners are dressed in white; ladders are used for the descent and a winch for hauling to the surface. The part of the miniature not shown here shows a very modern set of equipment (the Germans led the world in mining techniques): winches operated by horse power, drainage and ventilation systems. Vienna, Oesterreiche Nationalbibliothek. (Photo by the library.)

Even more outstanding success was achieved in Italy, at about the time when Francesco Sforza came to power in Milan in 1450. It was outstanding, partly because it had been preceded by a series of exemplary revolutions. The first of these was a demographic revolution which continued until mid-sixteenth century. The second was the appearance in the early fifteenth century of the first territorial states, still small in size, but already modern in structure: it even seemed for a brief moment that Italian unity was in the air. And lastly, an agricultural revolution along capitalist lines was taking place among the canals of the great Lombardy plains. All this in a climate of scientific and technical discovery: this was the age when hundreds of Italians, sharing the enthusiasm of Leonardo da Vinci, were filling their notebooks with designs for extraordinary machines.

Milan now entered upon a singular phase in its history. Having been spared during the terrible crisis of the fourteenth and fifteenth centuries (precisely because of its agricultural productivity, according to Zangheri), the city witnessed a remarkable spurt of manufacturing activity. Woollens, cloth of gold and silver, and armour began to take the place of the fustians which had been Milan's staple industry in the early fourteenth century. The Lombard capital was caught up in a huge wave of commercial activity linking it to the fairs of Geneva and Chalon-sur-Saône, to cities like Dijon and Paris, and to the Netherlands.[40] At about the same time, the Milanese capitalists were completing their takeover of the countryside, with the reorganization of properties into large estates, the development of irrigated meadows and livestock farming, the digging of canals both for irrigation and transport, the introduction of rice as a new crop, and even in many cases the disappearance of fallow land, with continuous rotation of cereals and forage crops. It was in fact in Lombardy that 'high farming' – later to be developed in the Netherlands and transferred with celebrated results to England, first saw the light.[41]

Hence the question put by our informant and guide Renato Zangheri: why did this substantial transformation of both the industry and the countryside of Milan and Lombardy come to nothing? Why did it not lead to an industrial revolution? Neither the infant technology of the time nor the lack of energy supplies seems an adequate explanation. 'The English industrial revolution was not based on any scientific or technical progress not already available in the sixteenth century.'[42] Carlo Poni was astonished to discover the sophistication of the hydraulic machines used in Italy to throw, spin and mill silk, with several mechanical processes and rows of spindles all turned by a single water-wheeel.[43] Lynn White has argued that even before Leonardo da Vinci, Europe had already invented the whole range of mechanical devices which would actually be developed during the next four hundred years, that is until electrical energy, as and when the need was felt for them.[44] As he puts it: 'a new device merely opens a door; it does not compel anyone to enter'.[45] Quite so. But why did the exceptional conditions which were combined in fifteenth-century Milan fail to create any

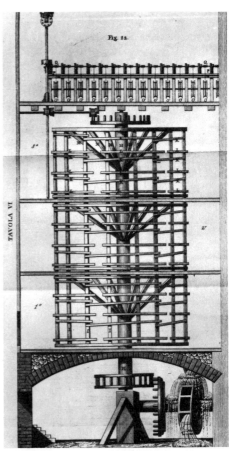

Early machines in Italy: here are two designs for a *filatoio* for producing *organzine* (thrown silk) on the Bolognese model, one dating from 1607 (on the left), the other from 1833. *Organzine* is a double, triple or quadruple thread of thrown silk used as a warp. The first silk-mill to be set up in England in 1716-17, ' a true factory, the first in England', was copied by the English after two years of industrial espionage in Italy. An almost identical model had been working since the early seventeenth century in Bologna, the city of its invention (cf. the work of C. Poni). Totally mechanized – the workers had only to watch it and reconnect the threads that broke – the machine was made up of an internal turning mechanism, the *lanterna* (bottom left) activated by a water-wheel, and surrounded by a fixed frame (top left) holding a very large number of spindles, bobbins and winders. If mechanization had been the only cause of the industrial revolution, Italy would have got there first. On the right is a *filatoio* of 1833. From P. Negri, *Manuale practico per la stima delle case et degli opisizi idrauliti*, Bologna, 1833.

such need or demand? Why did the Milanese revolution crumble instead of thrive?

The available historical data does not really provide enough evidence to answer this question. We are reduced to conjecture. In the first place, Milan did not have access to any large national market. And the profits from land did not outlast the first wave of speculation. The prosperity of the first industrial entrepreneurs, if we are to believe Gino Barbieri[46] and Gemma Miani, was only on a small scale, creating a sort of modest capitalist class. But how strong an argument is that? After all, the first cotton magnates often had very humble beginnings. Was it not rather Milan's misfortune to be so close to Venice, yet so far from sharing Venice's dominant position? And not to be a port, with access to the Mediterranean and the international export trade, free to experiment and take risks? Is the failure of Milan's 'industrial revolution' perhaps proof that an industrial revolution, as a total phenomenon, cannot be built up entirely from within, simply by the harmonious development of the various sectors of the economy; that it must also be based on command of external markets – the *sine qua non* of success? In the fifteenth century, as we have seen, this commanding position was occupied by Venice, and to some extent (for Spanish trade) by Genoa.

John U. Nef and the first British industrial revolution, 1560–1640

The industrial expansion which took place in England between 1540 and 1640 was much more clear-cut and thorough-going than the early experiences either of Italy or Germany. In mid-sixteenth century, the British Isles were still, industrially speaking, far behind Italy, Spain and the Netherlands, Germany and France. A hundred years later, the situation had been miraculously reversed and the speed of the transformation had been so fast that there is no parallel before the equivalent wave of change in the late eighteenth and early nineteenth century, in other words, *the* industrial revolution. By the eve of the Civil War (1642) England had become the leading industrial nation in Europe and was to remain so. It is this 'first industrial revolution' to which John U. Nef drew attention in his article which caused a sensation when it was originally published in 1934 and has lost none of its analytic force today.[47]

But why did this happen in England, when all the major innovations of the period – I am thinking for example of the blast furnaces, the various apparatus used for underground mining: tunnels, ventilation systems, pumps and winding gear – were all borrowings, demonstrated to the English by German miners hired for the purpose? Why England, when it was the craftsmen and workers of more technically advanced countries – Germany, the Netherlands, but also Italy (for glass) and France (wool and silk textiles) – who contributed the necessary techniques and skills for the establishment of a series of industries quite new to Britain – paper-mills, powder-mills, glass, mirrors, cannon-founding, alum and copperas (green vitriol), sugar refining, saltpetre, and so on?

The remarkable thing is that when these industries did arrive, England should have developed them on a scale hitherto unknown: the growing size of firms, the dimensions of the buildings, the rising numbers of workers, soon running into tens or even hundreds, the comparatively high level of investment which was reaching thousands of pounds, whereas the *annual* wage of a worker was only about £5 – all these were completely new and indicate how extraordinary was the expansion of English industry in this period.

On the other hand, the decisive feature of this revolution – a completely home-grown one so to speak – was the increasing dependence on coal, which had become a major element in the English economy. Not as it happened by deliberate choice, but in order to meet a visible deficiency. Wood had become increasingly scarce in England and was costing high prices by mid-sixteenth century; scarcity and expense dictated the move to coal. Similarly, the sluggish flow of most English rivers, which had to be raised by dams and diverted by canals to work overshot wheels, made hydraulic energy much more expensive here than in continental Europe and would eventually provide an incentive to research into the power of steam, or so John Nef suggests.

So England, unlike France or the Netherlands, went in for coal-mining on a grand scale, beginning with the Newcastle coalfields and the many local seams. Mines which had previously been worked open-cast by a part-time rural labour force now began to operate continuously; pits were dug up to 40 or 100 metres deep. From about 35,000 tons in 1560, output had risen to 200,000 tons by the beginning of the seventeenth century.[48] Wagons running on rails carried the coal from the pithead to the docks: specialized ships, in ever-increasing numbers were taking it all over England and even to Europe, by the end of the century. Coal was already being regarded as a form of national wealth:

> England's a perfect world, hath Indies too,
> Correct your maps, Newcastle is Peru

as an English poet put it in 1650.[49] The replacement of charcoal by coal not only made it possible to heat domestic interiors – bringing a sinister pall of smoke to London; it also affected industry which had however to learn to adapt to the new fuel and devise new expedients, in particular to protect the matter being processed from the sulphurous fumes of the burning coals. One way and another, coal was introduced to glassmaking, to breweries, brick-works, alum manufacture, sugar refineries and the industrial evaporation of sea-salt. In every case, this meant a concentration of the workforce and inevitably of capital. Manufacturing industry was born; with it came the great workshops and their alarming din which sometimes proceeded uninterrupted day and night, and their throngs of workers who, in a world used to artisans, were remarkable both for their large numbers and as a rule for their lack of skill. One of the farmers of the 'alum houses' built during the reign of James I on the Yorkshire coast and each employing about sixty workers, explained in 1619 that the manufacture of alum was a 'distracted worke in severall places, and of sundry partes not possible to bee performed by anie one man nor by a fewe. But by a multitude of the baser sort of whom the most part are idle, careless and false in their labour'.[50]

One of the earliest pictures (1750) of an English 'railway': this one was built by Ralph Allen (1694-1764) and operated by gravity, carrying blocks of stone from the hills above Bath down to the wharves on the river Avon which ran through the town. In the background can be seen Prior Park, the luxurious dwelling of Allen himself. Fashionable ladies and gentlemen have come to admire the sight. (Mary Evans Picture Library.)

Technically then, with larger factories and the widespread use of coal, England was certainly innovating in the industrial sector. But what really gave the impetus to industry and probably to innovation as well, was the substantial enlargement of the domestic market, for two complementary reasons. The first was rapid population growth – estimated at 60% in the course of the sixteenth century.[51] At the same time there was a large rise in agricultural incomes, which turned many peasants into consumers of industrial products. To meet demand from the growing population and especially from the visibly-expanding towns, agricultural output was increased in several ways – by the reclamation of land, by enclosures at the expense of commons and grazing, by crop specialization – but without any truly revolutionary measures to increase productivity or the fertility of the soil. These would only begin to appear after 1640 and then only very gradually until 1690.[52] Agricultural output thus began to lag somewhat behind demographic expansion as is proved by an agricultural price rise much greater overall than the industrial price rise.[53] The result was a visible increase in prosperity in the countryside. This was the age of the 'great rebuilding' as rural dwellings were restored, improved and enlarged, as upper storeys replaced attics, windows were glazed, chimneys were built for burning domestic coal. Inventories compiled after death tell us of a new-found affluence reflected in furniture, linen, hangings, pewter vessels. This domestic demand undoubtedly stimulated industry, trade and imports.

Promising though it appeared, this lively burst of industrialization did not carry all before it. Some important sectors continued to lag behind.

In metallurgy for instance, the blast furnace on the modern German model, a heavy user of fuel, by no means ousted all the bloomeries, old-fashioned furnaces some of which were still in operation in 1650 – and in any case even the blast furnaces continued to burn charcoal. Only in 1709 did the first coke-fuelled blast furnace appear – and this remained unique of its kind for another forty years. Several explanations have been suggested for this by T. S. Ashton and others, but Charles Hyde's conclusion in his recent book[54] seems to me to be irrefutable: if coke only replaced charcoal in about 1750, it was simply because until then production costs favoured the latter.[55] What was more, even after the adoption of coke, English metallurgy long remained inferior, both in quality and quantity to that of Russia, Sweden or France.[56] And while light metal industries (cutlery, nail-making, tools, etc.) grew steadily from mid-sixteenth century, they were using imported Swedish steel.

Another backward sector was the cloth industry, now faced with a long crisis in foreign demand which made it necessary to undergo some painful adjustments while output remained virtually stationary from 1560 to the end of the seventeenth century.[57] Still largely a rural cottage industry, cloth production was increasingly brought within the putting-out system. Whereas in the sixteenth century this industry alone had been responsible for 90% of English exports, and the figure was still 75% in 1660, by the end of the century it had fallen to only 50%.[58]

But these problems cannot explain the stagnation that set in in England after the 1640s: while the economy did not decline, neither did it progress. The population had stopped rising, agriculture was producing more and better quality crops; it was investing for the future – but rural incomes had fallen with prices; industry was ticking over but no longer innovating, at least not until 1680 or so.[59] If this standstill had been confined to England, one might perhaps have put it down to the effects of the Civil War which began in 1642 and brought considerable disruption; or one could point to the still inadequate nature of the national market, or England's comparatively poor position in the European world-economy, in which Holland was still the dominant economic power. But England was by no means alone in this experience – one that was undoubtedly shared by all the north European countries which had been progressing alongside her and were now simultaneously retreating. The 'seventeenth-century crisis' might strike at different times, but it left its mark everywhere.

To return to England however, John U. Nef's own diagnosis is that while the industrial advance certainly slowed down there after 1642, it did not collapse; there was no slipping backward either.[60] What may in fact have happened, and we shall return to this point apropos E. L. Jones's analysis, was that the seventeenth-century crisis, like all periods of demographic slowdown, brought some increase in per capita incomes and a transformation of agriculture, which had repercussions on industry too. By taking Nef's arguments further, we might say that the English industrial revolution of the eighteenth century had already begun in the sixteenth and was simply making progress by stages. It is an explanation from which some lessons may be drawn.

But could not the same be said of the whole of Europe, where since at least the eleventh century, a series of linked and in a sense cumulative transformations had been experienced? Every region in turn sooner or later underwent a burst of pre-industrial growth, with the accompanying features one could expect, particularly in agriculture. Industrialization was in a sense endemic throughout the continent. Outstanding and important as Britain's role was in this story, Britain was by no means the sole initiator and inventor of the industrial revolution accomplished on her soil. This explains why that revolution had scarcely appeared, let alone achieved its decisive successes, before it was spreading unopposed to nearby Europe, where it scored a series of comparatively easy triumphs, encountering none of the obstacles which so many under-developed countries have met in the twentieth century.

The industrial revolution in Britain, sector by sector

Britain's success after 1750 is the dazzling burst of light on which all else converges. But we should guard against illusion: this display of fireworks brings us to the heart of our difficulties, as R.M. Hartwell has explained in his challenging book, *The Industrial Revolution and Economic Growth* (1971) – a book which is in fact the sum of all the other books on the topic, a platform from which the writer speaks through the ideas of every other writer, leading us into a huge museum where a series of the most varied and discordant pictures have been placed carefully side by side on the wall. The choice is up to us. Who would not be bewildered by the hundredth debate on this subject?

It is true – and in a way reassuring – that at a conference of specialists on the industrial revolution arranged by the journal *Past and Present* in April 1960[61] agreement turned out to be impossible. And consensus proved equally elusive at the Lyon colloquium of 1970[62] on the same topic, where Pierre Vilar[63] perhaps put his finger on the problem when he confessed frankly that having studied the industrial revolution which transformed Catalonia so rapidly in the eighteenth and nineteenth centuries, he had been unable to come up with any model that entirely satisfied him. The problem was brought no nearer solution when at the same conference the expression *industrial revolution* was replaced by *industrialization*, a more neutral term but in the end equally complex. 'I admit that I am still completely in the dark about what industrialization means', said Jacques Bertin on this occasion. 'Does it mean railways? cotton? coal? metals? gaslighting? white bread?'[64] I would reply that the list is if anything too short: industrialization, like the industrial revolution, means everything – society, economy, political structures, public opinion, and the rest. The most ambitious kind of history cannot embrace it, certainly not in any simple, all-purpose, peremptory definition. In other words, the industrial revolution which was to throw first Britain then the whole world into upheaval, was never at any stage in its career a neatly-definable phenomenon, a combination of given problems occurring in a given area at a given time.

This is why I do not really accept – though I am obliged in turn to adopt it – the approach which tries to explain the industrial revolution sector by sector. Faced with what looks like an inextricable mass of difficulties, historians have indeed proceeded by Cartesian methods, dividing to understand. They have identified a series of headings – agriculture, demography, technology, commerce, transport, etc. – all of which did indeed undergo major change; but the danger of this approach is of making them look like separate stages, affected one after another and thus forming a flight of steps towards growth. This fragmented model comes straight from the most traditional kind of political economy. It is perhaps to be regretted that the advocates of retrospective economics have not designed another model better suited to guide the steps of historical research, that they have not defined another set of indicators, landmarks and quotients which would tell us how the different sectors operated *in relation to each other synchronically*, whether they furthered each other's progress or on the contrary acted as brakes or bottlenecks for rival sectors. If we could take a series of synchronic sections at acceptable chronological intervals, we might conceivably be able to form a more accurate perception of the development of industrial growth. But this requires agreement beforehand between historians on an appropriate research model, which could then be applied to different places and different periods.

Until then we can only continue to use the classifications which have stood the test of time in a number of remarkable studies, too numerous for all of them to be listed. Within the 'industrial revolution' as a whole, they have identified a series of individual revolutions – in agriculture, demography, inland transport, technology, trade and industry. Our first step will be to try to trace these changes from which no sector was actually immune. It may seem a little tedious to follow such a well-worn path of exposition, but there are times when it is necessary.

British agriculture – a crucial factor

Agriculture usually heads the list and rightly so. But of all the problems confronting us, this is by far the most taxing. For we are faced here with a long, seemingly never-ending process, not one revolution but a series of revolutions, changes, developments, breaks and revivals forming a chain down the ages. If we were to trace it from end to end, we could easily go back to the thirteenth century and the first attempts at liming and marling the soil, experiments with different strains of wheat or oats, or the simplest forms of crop rotation. Our task however is neither to find the source nor to plot the course of this river, but to examine how it flows into the sea; we do not want to study all the ramifications of the rural history of Britain, simply to assess its contribution to the great ocean of the industrial revolution. Was agriculture an integral part of this mighty achievement?

To ask this question is to be exposed to a thousand contradictory replies. Some historians would answer yes, some no, and some would hesitate to pronounce either way. M.W. Flinn writes: 'It must remain extremely doubtful whether the agricultural developments themselves would be sufficient to have played more than a modest part in stimulating an industrial revolution'.[65] More generally, H.J. Habbakuk argues that 'This increase in agricultural output is not to be regarded as a pre-condition of growth, if only because it normally accompanied rather than preceded the acceleration of growth';[66] while Paul Bairoch, who is anxious to identify and rank the strategic variables of the English industrial revolution, argues that the takeoff in agriculture was 'the major pump-priming factor', the trigger for everything else.[67] E.L. Jones is even more categorical: from a comparative study of the history of the countries which succeeded in industrializing, he suggests that the primary condition of success was to have 'agricultural output rising faster than the population'.[68] The 'critical period' in Britain, he argues was between 1650 and 1750.

This thesis runs counter to those arguments which essentially define the agricultural revolution in terms of mechanical improvements and therefore regard it as following rather than preceding the cotton revolution or even the railway revolution. It is certainly the case that industrial and mechanized equipment played only a negligible part in agricultural life until the middle of the nineteenth century. The seed-drill described by Jethro Tull in 1733[69] for instance was only sparingly used even in progressive east Norfolk, the home of Townshend and Coke; elsewhere it appeared only in the nineteenth century.[70] The horse-powered threshing machine, invented in Scotland in about 1780, followed after some delay by the steam engine, certainly did not spread very fast. Similarly the triangular or Rotherham plough[71] which made it possible for one man to plough with only two horses (as distinct from the rectangular plough drawn by six or eight oxen with a driver and a ploughman) though patented in 1731, was not used very much before 1870.[72] It has even been calculated that new crops

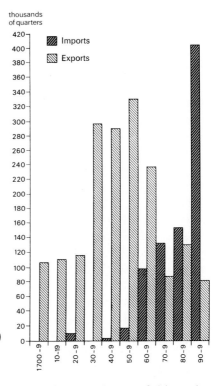

thousands
of quarters

420 —
400 —
380 —
360 —
340 —
320 —
300 —
280 —
260 —
240 —
220 —
200 —
180 —
160 —
140 —
120 —
100 —
80 —
60 —
40 —
20 —
0 —

▨ Imports

▧ Exports

1700 -9 10-19 20-9 30-9 40-9 50-9 60-9 70-9 80-9 90-9

50   BRITISH IMPORTS AND EXPORTS OF
GRAIN AND FLOUR
By and large, England consumed her own grain
until about 1760; between 1730 and 1765 she was
exporting on a considerable scale for the time (2%
of total output in 1750, that is 330,000 quarters out
of a total production of 15 million); imports began
in 1760 and went on rising although output was 19
million quarters in 1800 and 25 by 1820. (From
P. Mathias, *The First Industrial Nation*, 1969, p. 70.)

such as the famous turnip which moved from kitchen garden to field in the
seventeenth century, multiplied at the rate of only about a thousand plants a
year from its point of introduction. And until 1830 the flail, sickle and scythe
remained the basic implements on English farms.[73] So it must be said that the
progress in English agriculture *before the industrial revolution*, of which there is
incontrovertible evidence[74] – came not so much from machines or wonder crops
as from new methods of land use; new timetables for ploughing; new forms of
crop rotation which eliminated fallow and encouraged grazing, a useful source
of fertilizer and therefore a remedy for soil exhaustion; attention to new strains
of crops; selective breeding of sheep and cattle; specialized farming for higher
yields – all with results which varied according to region, to natural conditions
and to the constraints of the market which were never the same in two places.
The resulting system was what would in the nineteenth century be called *high
farming*, 'an extremely difficult art' as a later observer was to write, 'based on
long observation'. It consisted of:

> enclosed fields, divided by frequent ploughing, fertilized with abundant,
> good-quality manure and sowed in turn with plants that either exhaust or
> enrich the soil, without leaving any fallow ... by alternating cereals, plants
> with tap roots which derive their sustenance from a great depth and give
> nothing to the soil, and herbaceous plants with creeping roots which enrich
> the soil and draw sustenance from the surface.[75]

This transformation, which would prove to be a vital one, took place after 1650, at a time when demographic pressure had eased, when the population was increasing only slowly if at all (possibly as a result of conscious efforts to postpone the age of marriage). Whatever the reason, demographic pressure was not as great. Is it not paradoxical therefore that it was precisely at this moment when demand was lower and the price of grain was falling that both output and productivity increased and that innovation spread? This apparent paradox can be quite easily explained however in the light of E.L. Jones's analysis.[76] Demand for cereals remained virtually the same, but with the expansion of the towns and the phenomenal growth of London, demand for meat went up; animal farming became more profitable than arable and therefore tended to take its place. Consequently, farmers went over to forage crops already in existence such as clover, sainfoin, turnips, and to new methods of crop rotation. The key to the paradox is that the massive expansion of livestock, both intended and achieved, had as its side-effect an increase in the quantity of manure, which in turn sent up the yields of cereals like wheat and barley included in the normal rotation. Thus there occurred what Jones calls 'a virtuous circle' (by contrast with a vicious circle) according to which the low price of cereals encouraged farmers to concentrate on livestock, therefore to plant more forage crops; which brought about a rapid rise in the head of livestock especially sheep, and this in turn improved cereal yields. English grain output increased automatically, effortlessly so to speak, to the point of exceeding home demand. Hence the fall in the price of cereals which were increasingly exported until 1760. E.A. Wrigley has calculated that the rise in agricultural *productivity* between 1650 and 1750 was at least 13%.[77]

But high farming had a further consequence. Since forage crops do best on light and sandy soils, these became the most productive land in England. Land previously regarded as poor, fit only for grazing sheep, was put under crops. Heavy clayey soils by contrast, previously regarded as the richest for cereal-growing, and unsuitable for forage crops, were hit by the low prices created by higher yields in rival regions. They went out of cultivation and complaints began to be heard. In the Midlands in the 1680s, a call went up for nothing less than a law to stop the land improvements in the south of England: in Buckinghamshire, the owners of clayey soils in the vale of Aylesbury demanded that clover be a prohibited crop.[78]

Various regions discriminated against by neighbouring success tried livestock instead, especially draft animals or, if they were near London dairy farming. But it was more frequent for agricultural decline to be compensated for by an increase in artisan production. This explains why the years after 1650, when John U. Nef detects a slowing-down in the *large-scale* industry which had developed over the previous century, saw vigorous expansion in *cottage industry*, within the ancient but still effective framework of the putting-out system. In the late seventeenth and early eighteenth centuries, lace-making developed in east

A brickworks in the English countryside. The smoke pouring from chimneys like these was already being accused of polluting the air in the eighteenth century. (Photo Batsford.)

Devon, and to an even greater extent in the counties of Bedford, Buckingham and Northampton; straw-plaiting for hats spread from Hertfordshire to Bedfordshire; nailing was making headway in the countryside round Birmingham; there was paper-making in the Mendips where there were over 200 paper-mills in 1712, many of them in old cornmills; and hosiery in the counties of Leicestershire, Derbyshire and Nottingham.[79]

The 'seventeenth-century crisis' in England thus corresponded to a fairly slow and uneven development of the countryside, which nevertheless favoured the coming industrial revolution on two counts: it encouraged the establishment of a high-yield agriculture which would be capable, by holding grain back from export, of meeting the sudden demographic explosion after the 1750s: and in the poorer regions it was responsible for the rise of cottage industries with a proletariat more or less accustomed to craft working, in short a 'trained and malleable' workforce, ready to meet the demand from large-scale urban industry when this appeared in the late eighteenth century. It was on this reserve labour force that the industrial revolution would draw, rather than on the strictly agricultural workforce which maintained its previous levels, contrary to assumptions made by commentators from Marx to the present day.

If things happened very differently on the European continent, it was probably because the very original development of English agriculture was conceivable only within a context of large land holdings: a large estate for those days was about 200 acres. For such estates to become commonplace, the tenacious seigniorial regime had to be destroyed and adapted, and the archaic relationships between tenant and landlord transformed – something that had long been accomplished in England by the time the industrial revolution occurred. The big landowner[80] had become a *rentier*, who regarded his estate as a sign of social status, but also as a going concern, which it was in his interest to rent out to efficient tenant-farmers (traditionally, the landowner even made good the losses of the tenant in a bad year). A prosperous estate, farmed out at a good rent, moreover guaranteed its owner easy credit, perhaps for investment elsewhere, for landowners were frequently also industrial or mining entrepreneurs. As for the farmer, he was assured of his leasehold by convention, if not by law; he could thus safely invest money in the farm[81] and run it by the rules of the market and capitalist management. The major feature of this new order was the rise of the farmer, a genuine entrepreneur. Farmers are 'truly respectable people', said a French observer. 'Although they put their hands to the plough, in their farm or lodging, they are equal to the bourgeoisie of the towns.'[82] This was in 1819, but even three-quarters of a century earlier in 1745, a visiting Frenchman described the English farmer as a peasant 'who enjoys an abundance of all the commodities of life'; his farmhand 'takes tea before taking up the plough'. He was equally impressed by the 'countryman who wears a frock-coat in winter', with a wife and daughter so elegantly dressed that they might be mistaken for 'shepherdesses in a novel',[83] an impression certainly not contradicted by a nice little engraving of the seventeenth century, claiming to represent a 'paisants woman' riding to market on horseback, with a basket of eggs at her side, but shod and hatted like a woman of property.

The French observer, Maurice Rubichon, struck by the contrast between the rural landscape in England and France, described the British agricultural system at length. The landed gentry – two or three families in each of the 10,000 parishes of England, he estimated[84] – owned roughly a third of the parish's land, divided up into large farms worked by tenant farmers; another third was owned by yeoman, small (or not so small) independent proprietors, while the peasants had little plots and the right to the use of the common land which made up the last third of the cultivated area. Rubichon's estimates are probably very approximate. What does seem certain is that everything combined to increase further the concentration of landed property even before the eighteenth century: the small peasant farmer was more or less condemned either to extend his holding and survive, or to lose it one day and become a wage-labourer. This tendency, combined with the enclosures which eliminated common land and encouraged concentration, meant that large estates, more adaptable and profitable, were gradually extended, benefiting the landed gentry, the rich yeomen and the tenant farmers. This was the direct opposite of what happened in France, where the 'feudal' regime collapsed literally overnight on 4 August 1789, when the capitalist concentration of land was only just beginning; from now on the land was

A paisants Woman riding upon &c:

English peasant woman on her way to market. Illustration from a manuscript of 1623-5. (British Library.)

irremediably divided among many peasant and bourgeois proprietors. Maurice Rubichon, an unconditional admirer of the English rural order, inveighed against the subdivision of France which 'was already carved up into 25 million plots before the Revolution', and now 'the figure is 115 million'.[85] Can this all be laid at the door of the *Code Napoléon*, which provided for equal inheritance? Was England preserved from fragmentation only by the survival of primogeniture among the landed gentry? Or was the establishment of capitalist farming the crucial factor?

Finally in our estimate of the role played by agriculture in the industrial revolution, we should not forget that the English countryside had from a very early date been integrated into the island's national market; as a component part of this network, English farms managed until the early nineteenth century, with a few exceptions, to feed the population of the towns and industrial conurbations; they were the essential component in a domestic market which provided the initial natural clientèle for English industry in its early days. The country's expanding agriculture was the iron industry's leading customer. Farm implements – horse-shoes, plough-shares, scythes, sickles, threshing machines, harrows, rollers – all required considerable quantities of iron; in 1780, this amounted to a demand for about 200 or 300,000 tons a year.[86] These figures cannot be accepted as they stand for the first part of the eighteenth century which is the particular focus of our inquiry, but if during that period iron imports from Sweden and Russia were rising steadily, was this not because the English domestic iron industry had insufficient capacity to meet the increasing demand largely accounted for by agriculture? And does that not suggest that agriculture was on the move before the development of industry?

The demographic revival

During the eighteenth century, the population increased in England as it increased throughout Europe and the entire world: 5,835,000 in 1700; just over 6 million in 1730; 6,665,000 in 1760. Then the movement accelerated: 8,216,000 in 1790; 12 million in 1820; almost 18 million in 1850.[87] Mortality rates fell from 33·7% to 27% in 1800 and 21% for the decade 1811–21, while the birth rate reached the record level of 37% or even higher. The statistics quoted vary somewhat from author to author, but they all tell much the same story.[88]

The massive biological increase meant more intensive cultivation of the countryside, the growth of all the towns, and the record expansion of the industrial conurbations. Historical demographers have identified three reference groups of English counties which in 1701 had comparable population figures.[89] By 1831, all three had expanded in absolute terms, but now the industrial counties represented 45% of the population as compared to a third in 1701; while the agricultural counties now contained only 26% of total population as compared to 33%. Some counties had progressed at a quite spectacular rate: the population of Northumberland and Durham had doubled, while that of Lancashire, Staffordshire and Warwickshire had tripled.[90] No doubt is therefore possible: industrialization unquestionably played a leading role in the rise of the English population. Detailed studies bear out this impression. If we take the single age-group 17 to 30, we find that in industrial Lancashire in 1800, 40% of this age group were married as compared to 19% in the agricultural areas of the county at the same time. So industrial employment also appears to have encouraged early marriage, thus accelerating demographic advance.

A soot-blackened England was coming into being, with its factory towns and workers' terraces. It was certainly no Merrie England. Like many other travellers, Alexis de Tocqueville described it in his travel journal: in July 1835[91] he stayed in Birmingham and went on to Manchester. These were enormous, still unfinished cities, thrown up quickly and badly, without any thought of planning; but they were full of life. The necklace of dense, bustling urban concentrations – Leeds, Sheffield, Birmingham, Manchester, Liverpool – were the heart and soul of the English industrial revolution. If Birmingham was still quite human, Manchester already seemed a vision of hell. Its population had increased tenfold between 1760 and 1830, rising from 17,000 to 180,000 inhabitants.[92] Because of land shortage, the factories perched on its hills had five, six or even twelve storeys. Mansions and workers' two-up-two-downs sprawled all over the town, higgledy-piggledy. There were puddles and mud everywhere: for every paved street, there were ten dirty lanes. Men, women and children herded into squalid housing – up to 15 or 16 people might be crammed into a single basement; the 50,000 Irish immigrants were part of a typically wretched sub-proletariat. The same was true of Liverpool, where Tocqueville observed 'sixty thousand Irish Catholics', adding 'the misery is almost as great as in Manchester, but it is concealed'. So in all these cities spawned by the industrial revolution, even the massive rise in the English-born population was not always enough to provide the necessary mass of workers; immigrants had to come to the rescue from Wales, Scotland and especially Ireland. And since mechanization had multiplied the number of unskilled tasks at all the key points of industrial development, calls were made on the labour of women and children, like immigrants a docile and underpaid workforce.

So the industrial revolution brought together all the manpower it required – whether for manual work or for the 'tertiary sector' where the new age was already creating jobs. All successful industry, as Ernest Labrousse[93] has pointed out, generates its own bureaucracy, and so it was in England. A further indicator of the abundance of the labour supply was the enormous number of domestic servants, probably reflecting a long-standing situation, but one which the industrial revolution did not mitigate, indeed the opposite. At the beginning of the nineteenth century, domestic servants made up over 15% of the population of London.

After 1750 then, England had no labour shortage, indeed she had so many children she hardly knew what to do. Were they a burden or on the contrary a source of energy? Consequence or cause? That these workers were useful, indeed indispensable, is obvious: they provided the necessary human dimension of the industrial revolution. Without these thousands or millions of people, nothing would have been possible. But that is not the point: we need to establish a correlation. The population explosion and the wave of industrialization were two mighty processes taking place side by side. But did one determine the other? Unfortunately both of them are very imperfectly recorded in the available documents. The population history of England has to be reconstituted from incomplete parish records. Any proposition we may make is subject to caution and liable to be overturned by future research when the enormous labour of counting and checking is tackled. Similarly, can we be really sure we know enough to trace an accurate graph of industrialization, broadly identifiable with the output curve? 'It seems reasonable to suppose', Phyllis Deane writes, 'that without the growth of output dating from the 1740s, the associated growth in population would eventually have been checked by a rise in the death rate due to declining standards of living.'[94] 1740 is certainly, on the graph in Figure 51, the

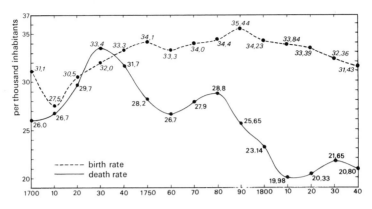

51 BIRTH AND DEATH RATES IN ENGLAND
These two curves are based on estimates we will assume to be valid, though they vary from
author to author. The difference between them shows the rise in the English population after the
1730s. (From G.M. Trevelyan, *English Social History*, 1942, p. 361.)

point at which the birth rate and the mortality rate diverge: from this point on,
births exceeded deaths. If true, this simple observation is proof in itself that the
demographic revolution *followed* the rise of industry and was, in very large
measure, created by it.

Technology: a necessary but probably not sufficient condition

If there is one factor which has lost ground as a key explanation of the industrial
revolution, it is technology. Marx believed it was crucial; recent historiography
has put forward some solid arguments against seeing it as a *primum mobile* or
even a pump-primer, to use Paul Bairoch's expression. And yet inventions often
occur before industrial capacity – but for that very reason they may often occur
in a vacuum. The efficient application of technology lags, by definition, behind
the general movement of the economy; it has to wait to be called on, sometimes
several times, to meet a precise and persistent demand.

In textiles for instance, the two major processes are spinning and weaving. In
the seventeenth century, one weaver required the services of seven or eight
spinners (or rather spinsters, since they were usually women). Logically therefore
it was in spinning, the operation requiring the greatest workforce, that technical
innovation was needed. Nevertheless it was the loom which in 1730 saw the first
labour-saving device, Kay's flying shuttle. This elementary invention – the shuttle
was launched by a spring and manoeuvred by hand – which speeded up the
weaving process, did not come into widespread use until after 1760 – possibly
because it was precisely in the 1760s that three new inventions to speed up
spinning appeared and were very quickly adopted: the spinning jenny in 1765 in
a simple version within the means of cottage industry; Arkwright's water-frame
(1769); and ten years later, Crompton's 'mule', so-called because it combined

the characteristics of the other two machines.[95] From now on, spinning became ten times more productive, and increased quantities of imported raw cotton began arriving from the West Indies, the East Indies and before long the southern colonies in America. All the same the rate of spinning continued to limp along behind the speed of weaving until the 1840s. Even when the steam-engine revolutionized spinning in about 1800, handloom weavers managed to keep pace, the number of weavers increased and their wages rose. The handloom was not in the end displaced until after the Napoleonic Wars and then only slowly, despite the technical improvement introduced by the Roberts power-looms in about 1825. The reason was that until about 1840 it was neither essential nor indeed advantageous (given the sharp drop in weavers' wages resulting from competition from machines and the unemployed) to replace it with the power-loom.[96]

Paul Bairoch is therefore right when he says: 'During the first decades of the industrial revolution, technology was to a much greater extent a factor governed *by* the economy than one governing the economy'. Innovations were quite clearly dependent on the state of the market: they were introduced only when they met persistent demand from consumers. In the case of the English domestic market, average annual consumption of cotton was 1,700,000 pounds in the period 1737–40; 2,100,000 in 1741–9; 2,800,000 pounds in 1751–60; and 3,000,000 pounds in 1761–70. And 'these were small quantities compared to what England was consuming twenty years later': in 1769 (before mechanization) cotton consumption per head was 300 grammes – enough to 'allow the production of one shirt per year per inhabitant'.[97] But this may in fact have been a critical threshold, since in 1804–7, when the same level was reached in France, mechanization of the cotton industry began there too.

If demand stimulated invention however, it was itself dependent on price levels. England really did have from the early eighteenth century, a popular market ready to buy up large amounts of Indian cottons precisely because they were cheap. Defoe, when poking fun at the extravagances of the fashion for printed cottons, points out that chambermaids were wearing these imported fabrics before their mistresses. This domestic market did, it is true, diminish as the craze for printed cottons sent the price up, but the real reason was the authoritarian clamp-down on imports of Indian cottons to England, except for re-export (a step incidentally which indicates how booming the market was). This being so, it may have been not so much pressure of English demand as competitive Indian prices, K.N. Chaudhuri suggests,[98] which stimulated technical inventions. The latter in any case occurred, significantly, in cotton and not in the national industry for which there was the highest demand from consumers, namely wool or even linen. The woollen industry was not mechanized until much later.

The same was true of the English metal industry: the effect of prices on innovation was perhaps as great or even greater than that of demand alone. We have already noted that coke-smelting, a technique invented by Abraham Darby, was practised in his own blast furnaces in Coalbrookdale in Shropshire as early as 1709, but that no other entrepreneur followed his example until the middle of the century. Even in 1775, 45% of the output of pig-iron was being produced by charcoal-fired furnaces.[99] Paul Bairoch attributes the belated success of the process to increasing pressure of demand, which is certainly the case.[100] But Charles Hyde has clearly explained the circumstances surrounding the late introduction of coke-smelting. Why was this method so disdained for the forty years before 1750, by the seventy-odd blast furnaces then operating in England? Why were at least eighteen furnaces built between 1720 and 1750 using the old process?[101] Simply because for one thing these enterprises were very profitable, their high selling prices being protected by heavy duties imposed on imported Swedish steel, by the absence of regional competition on account of prohibitive transport costs, and by a prosperous export trade in finished iron products.[102] Secondly, because production costs were raised clearly by the use of coke (about

The blast furnaces in Coalbrookdale, Shropshire, where Abraham Darby was the first industrialist to use coke as a fuel in England in 1709. Note however on this 1758 engraving, that there are on the banks of the Severn (bottom right) four charcoal-burning ovens. In the foreground, a large metal cylinder produced on the spot is being transported in a horse-drawn wagon. Engraving by Perry and Smith, 1758. (Armand Colin Picture Library.)

£2 per ton) and the cast-iron thus produced, being more difficult to work was not particularly tempting to the steel-masters if its price was no lower than the market price.[103]

Why then did things change after 1750, without any new technical inventions, when in a period of twenty years, twenty-seven coke-fired blast-furnaces were built and twenty-five of the old models were closed down? Why did the steel-masters from now on take far more coke-smelted pig-iron? The answer is that increased demand for ferrous metals sent the price of charcoal sharply up (and this represented about half the cost of producing pig-iron),[104] while after the 1730s, coke-smelting benefited from a drop in coal prices. So that the situation was reversed: in about 1760, the cost price of charcoal-fired smelting was about £2 per ton greater than that of iron produced by the rival method. This being so, one wonders yet again why the old procedure survived so long – still accounting for about half total ouput in 1775. Probably the cause was the phenomenal rise in demand which paradoxically protected the lame duck. Demand was so great that prices remained high, and producers using coke did not bother to drop their prices far enough to eliminate their competitors – until about 1775, after which date the price difference between the different smelting methods increased and charcoal-burning was rapidly abandoned.

So it was not the introduction of steam power or Boulton and Watt's machine which brought about the adoption of coke as fuel for blast-furnaces. The die was already cast: with or without steam, coke would have triumphed in the end.[105] That is not to deny the role played by steam in the coming expansion of British metal-working: on one hand by operating the great power-bellows, it made it possible to increase the size of furnaces considerably; secondly, by freeing the steel industry from the need to be located near running water, it opened up new regions to metal-working, in particular the Black Country and Staffordshire, a region rich in iron ores and coal but short of fast-running rivers.

At about the same time as smelting, iron-refining was also liberated from the constraints and high prices of charcoal. Whereas in 1760, coal was only used in the ironworks in the final stages, for reheating and hammering previously refined iron, the practice of 'potting' introduced coal-firing into the entire refining process in about 1780. National ouput of iron bars went up 70% almost overnight.[106] Here again, Charles Hyde dispels some myths: it was not puddling, perfected after a difficult transitional period between 1784 and 1795, which drove charcoal from the iron-works: charcoal had already been eliminated.[107] Puddling was however, the crucial step in British metallurgy, a revolution both in *quantity* and *quality* which made British iron a world-beater – whereas it had previously been both quantitatively and qualitatively inferior.

Was it perhaps the improved *quality* of metal which was responsible for the fantastic triumph of the machine, not only in the factory but in everyday life too? The various incarnations of the steam-engine, as recorded in histories of technology, make striking reading. The earliest steam-engines used wood, brick,

Iron was beginning to replace wood by the last years of the eighteenth century in England. The bridge over the Wear, at Sunderland, built in 1796. (British Library.)

heavy structures and a few metal tubes; by 1820, they were a network of metal pipes. In the early days, the boiler and the various elements subject to pressure had posed many problems. Newcomen's engine had been built with the aim of remedying the deficiencies in Savery's older model, whose joints tended to explode under the pressure of the steam. But Newcomen's sturdy machine was built with brick supports and hearth, a wooden beam, copper boiler, a tin cylinder and lead piping. Only slowly and with difficulty would these costly materials be replaced with good quality iron. Watt himself was unable to construct an airtight cylinder in the Carron works in Scotland. Eventually it was Wilkinson who solved this problem, thanks to a boring-machine of his own invention.[108]

All such problems seemed to be disappearing by the first decades of the nineteenth century, at the same time as wood was being replaced by metal in mechanical construction and a number of small metal parts of all kinds were being manufactured, making it possible 'to vary the traditional structure of machines'.[109] In 1769, John Smeaton had built the first hydraulic wheel with a cast-iron axle for the Carron ironworks. It was a failure; the porous cast-iron did not stand up to sub-zero temperatures. The wide diameter wheels which had gone into operation on London Bridge the year before, 1768, were still made of wood – but in 1817, they were replaced by iron wheels.[110]

So while it was crucial in the long-term, metallurgy was not in the forefront of development in the eighteenth century. 'The iron industry', writes David Landes, 'has sometimes received more attention than it deserves in histories of the industrial revolution.'[111] This is probably fair comment, if one is a stickler for chronology. But the industrial revolution was a continuous process which had to invent itself as it went along, one that was on tenterhooks, so to speak, for the innovation that was bound to come. The total was always being added to. And it was always the most recent advance which gave meaning to those that had gone before. Coal, coke, cast-iron, iron and steel were all important in their own right. But all of them were as it were validated by steam – and steam itself took time to find its true place with Watt's rotary steam-engine, before the railway age. Emile Levasseur calculated[112] that in the year 1840, when the first phase of the industrial revolution was over, one CV (horse-power provided by steam) was the equivalent of twenty-one men, and that by such reckoning, France had at her disposal a million slaves of a special kind – a total destined to expand at an *exponential* rate: by 1880 this figure would be 98 million, that is two and a half times the real population of France at the time – so what must the figure have been for England?

Why the cotton revolution should not be underestimated

As the curtain-raiser for the English industrial revolution, the cotton boom has long been a favourite subject with historians – but that was in the past and fashions change. Recent research has tended to diminish the role of cotton: it is these days sometimes regarded as rather minor – after all the total volume of cotton production could be measured in millions of pounds, whereas coal was measured in millions of tons. Not until 1800 did the volume of raw cotton processed in England exceed 50 million pounds, that is 23,000 tons, which as E.A. Wrigley has pointed out, is only the equivalent of 'the annual output of 150 miners in a coal mine'.[113] Moreover, since innovations in the cotton industry are part of a long line of changes particular to the older textile industries (wool, cotton, silk and linen) beginning even earlier than the sixteenth century, everything suggests that the cotton industry was an *ancien régime* phenomenon, or, as John Hicks put it, that it was 'the last chapter in the development of the old industry rather than the first in the new, as it is usually described'. Might it not be possible at a pinch to imagine success on a comparable scale in fifteenth-century Florence?[114] It was in rather the same vein that Ernest Labrousse at the Lyon conference of October 1970, described Kay's famous flying shuttle, so much admired in its own day, as 'a child's clockwork toy'.[115] The cotton revolution was accomplished without any major technical innovations. The light weight and comparatively high value of cotton enabled it to use the existing means of transport and the modest power provided by waterwheels in the Pennine valleys and elsewhere. It was only towards the end of the boom that the cotton industry moved over to steam and away from the scarcity and unreliability of the available water-power, but the steam-engine was certainly not invented for this purpose. And last but not least, the textile industry had always called for more labour than capital.[116]

Should we then accept John Hicks's label – an *ancien régime* revolution? There was all the same a crucial difference between the cotton revolution and all previous revolutions: it succeeded. Far from slumping back into stagnation, the cotton boom ushered in a period of long-term growth, which eventually turned into 'continuous growth'. And 'in the first phase of British industrialization, no other industry was of comparable importance'.[117]

The real danger these days is of playing down the cotton revolution. It is true that its antecedents go back a very long way, since cotton was being processed in Europe as early as the twelfth century. But the yarn which could be extracted from the cotton bales imported from the Levant, while fine, was not very strong. So it could not be used alone, but only as the weft to be combined with a linen warp. This hybrid fabric was called fustian (*futaine, Barchent*) – the poor relation of the textile world, coarse in appearance, but rather dear – and what was more, difficult to launder. So when in the seventeenth century traders began importing to Europe not only the raw material but also woven and printed calicoes from India, beautiful all-cotton fabrics, cheap and often patterned in attractive colours which – unlike European dyes – stood up to washing, it was a real breakthrough. Shipped in by the Indies companies, aided and abetted by fashion, these fabrics soon conquered Europe. In order to protect their textile industry (not so much fustian as woollens) England in 1700 and 1720, and France as early as 1686, forbade the sale of Indian cottons on national soil. The cottons however, kept on coming, in theory for re-export, but a roaring contraband trade meant that they found their way everywhere, gladdening the eye and satisfying a long-lasting fashion which laughed at prohibitions, police raids and confiscations.

The cotton revolution, first in England, but very soon all over Europe, began by imitating Indian industry, went on to take revenge by catching up with it, and finally outstripped it. The aim was to produce fabrics of comparable quality at cheaper prices. The only way to do so was to introduce machines – which alone could effectively compete with Indian textile workers. But success did not come immediately. That had to wait for Arkwright's water-frame (1769) and Crompton's mule (1775–8) which made it possible to produce yarn as fine and strong as the Indian product, one that could be used for weaving fabric entirely out of cotton. From now on, the market for Indian cottons would be challenged by the developing English industry – and it was a very large market indeed, covering England and the British Isles, Europe (where various continental cotton industries were however soon putting up their own competition), the coast of Africa, where black slaves were exchanged for lengths of cotton, and the huge market of colonial America, not to mention Turkey and the Levant – or India itself. Cotton was always produced primarily for export: in 1800 it represented a quarter of all British exports; by 1850 this had risen to fifty per cent.[118]

All these foreign markets, conquered one after another, as additional or substitute outlets depending on circumstances, explain the extraordinary rise in output: 40 million yards in 1785; 2025 million yards in 1850.[119] At the same time, the price of the finished product fell, from an index of 550 in 1800 to an index of 100 in 1850, whereas the price of grain and most foodstuffs fell by no more than a third over the same period. Profit margins which were originally fantastic ('not five per cent, or ten per cent, but hundreds ... and thousands per cent', as an English politician later said)[120] were drastically reduced. However, the invasion of world markets was sufficient to make up for the diminishing returns. 'Profits are still sufficient', wrote a contemporary in 1835, 'to allow of a great accumulation of capital in the manufacture.'[121]

If the takeoff did occur after 1787, cotton was certainly responsible. Eric Hobsbawm points out that its rate of expansion closely resembles that of the British economy as a whole. Other industries progressed along with cotton – and were later dragged down with it when it collapsed, something which continued into the twentieth century.[122] The impression the British cotton industry made on contemporaries was one of unprecedented vitality. In about 1820, when machines were on the point of taking over from handloom weavers as well, cotton was already the country's major user of steam-power. In about 1835, it was using at least 30,000 horse-power provided by steam and only 10,000 horse-power of hydraulic energy.[123] To measure the strength of this new intruder, one has only to consider the extraordinary development of Manchester, a thoroughly modern city, with 'its hundreds of factories, five, six or even more storeys high, each topped with an immense chimney-stack and a plume of black smoke',[124] asserting its supremacy over the neighbouring towns including the port of Liverpool, only a short while earlier the great slave-trading port, and now on the way to being the chief entry point for raw cotton, especially from the United States.[125]

The ancient and glorious woollen industry, by comparison, continued for many years to present a rather old-fashioned spectacle. An English manufacturer reminiscing in 1826 about the old days recalled how the appearance of the spinning jenny among artisan families had relegated the antiquated spinning wheels to the attic and converted the whole labour force to cotton in about 1780: the spinning 'of wool had disappeared altogether and that of linen was nearly gone; cotton, cotton, cotton, has become the almost universal material for employment'.[126] The jenny was subsequently adapted for spinning wool, but complete mechanization came twenty years later than in the cotton industry.[127] It was in Leeds (which had now replaced Norwich as the wool capital) that spinning (not of course weaving) began to be mechanized, but the wool was still a rural cottage industry in 1811.

> The [Leeds] cloth market [Louis Simond reports] consists of a large building and a large square market, built round a courtyard, proof against fire, the walls being made of brick, the floors of iron. Two thousand six hundred

Robert Owen's cotton mill at New Lanark, on the Clyde, late eighteenth, early nineteenth century. Industrially, Scotland followed closely in England's footsteps. (Document in possession of T.C. Smout.)

country manufacturers, part-farmers, part-weavers, keep stalls here twice a week, for only an hour at a time. They each have their stall along the walls of a long gallery ... the lengths of cloth are piled up behind them and they hold samples in their hands. The purchasers pass down the double line comparing samples, and since prices are agreed almost unanimously, deals are quickly made. With few words and little wasted time on either side, much business is done.[128]

It is quite clear that we are still in the pre-industrial age. Overall control was in the hands of the purchaser, that is the merchant. So wool did not follow in the steps of cotton's industrial revolution. Similarly, cutlery and ironmongery in Sheffield and Birmingham went on being produced in the many family workshops; and that is not to mention the innumerable old-fashioned trades, some of which were to survive into the twentieth century.[129]

After the cotton revolution which was for a long time the spearhead of the movement, came the iron revolution. But the England of railways and steamships, of heavy equipment which required massive capital investment but yielded relatively low profits, surely owed its existence to the huge amounts of capital which had already accumulated in the country. So even if cotton did not *directly* influence the machine revolution and the coming of the heavy metal industry, profits from cotton certainly paid the first bills. One cycle propelled the other on its way.

Victory in long-distance trade

It is hardly an exaggeration to speak of the English *commercial revolution* in the eighteenth century, of the extraordinary expansion of trade. During this century, industries producing for the home market saw their output rise from an index of 100 to 150; but those producing for export saw theirs rise from 100 to 550. It is clear that foreign trade was far out in front. This 'revolution' has of course itself to be explained, and the explanation will require nothing less than a worldwide survey. As for the links between the commercial and industrial revolutions, these are close and reciprocal: the two revolutions powerfully reinforced one another.

England's fortunes abroad lay in the constitution of a mighty trading empire giving the British economy access to the largest trading area in the world, from the Caribbean to India, China and Africa. If we divide this great empire in two – Europe on one hand and the overseas countries on the other, it may be possible to see more clearly the origins of what is after all an extraordinary career.

In the years either side of 1760 when both British and world trade were steadily expanding, it is interesting to note that England's trade with nearby Europe was declining in relative terms while overseas trade was on the increase. If we divide British trade with Europe into three columns – imports, exports, re-exports – we find that it is only in the last column, re-exports, that the share going to Europe remained a large one, more or less continuously throughout the eighteenth century (1700–1: 85%; 1750–1: 79%; 1772–3: 82%; 1797–8: 88%). This was not true of imports from Europe to Britain whose share fell steadily (65%, 55%, 45% and 43% for the same dates); while British exports to the continent fell even faster (85%, 77%, 49% and 30%).[130]

This double decline is significant: the centre of gravity so to speak of English trade was moving further away from Europe, as British trade increased with the American colonies (soon to be the United States) and with India, especially after Plassey. This bears out a rather shrewd remark by the author of *Richesse de la Hollande* (1778)[131] which may provide us with a clue to the answer. Accarias de Sérionne argues that England, held back by the high domestic prices and labour costs which made her the most expensive country in Europe, could no longer cope with competition from the French and Dutch on the markets closest to home. She was being beaten to it in the Mediterranean, in the Levant, in Italy and in Spain (in Cadiz that is, since England managed to compete quite successfully in Spanish America, operating out of the 'free ports' in Jamaica). Admittedly, in two crucial European markets, England remained ahead: in Portugal, which was one of her most ancient and solid conquests; and in Russia where she acquired indispensable supplies for the navy and for industry (timber, masts, jute, iron, pitch, tar). It is hardly forcing the overall picture however to say that England seemed to be making no further progress in Europe, indeed her trade there was dwindling; but she was triumphing in the rest of the world.

This triumph requires careful analysis. It is easy to see how by and large

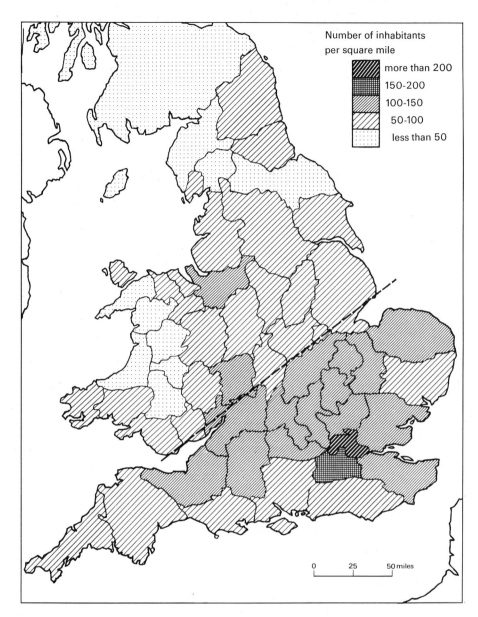

Number of inhabitants
per square mile

more than 200
150-200
100-150
50-100
less than 50

0   25   50 miles

52   THE TWO NATIONS IN 1700
Population and wealth distribution divide the country in two, either side of a line running from
Gloucester on the Severn to Boston on the banks of the Wash. (From H.C. Darby, *op. cit.*,
p. 524.)

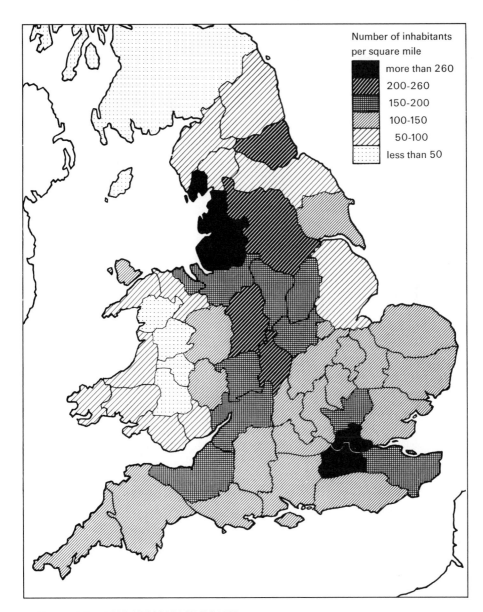

**Number of inhabitants
per square mile**

more than 260
200-260
150-200
100-150
50-100
less than 50

53   THE NEW POPULATION MAP IN 1800
What had previously been the poorest region of England, the north, now experienced a
population explosion, to become modern industrial England. (*Ibid.*, p. 525.)

England pushed her trade to these outer margins. In most cases, success was achieved by force: in India in 1757, in Canada in 1762 or on the coasts of Africa, England shouldered her rivals aside.[132] But it was not always or only a matter of force, since the newly-independent United States continued to increase on a massive scale the volume of goods they bought from the Old Country (though not their exports to it).[133] Similarly after 1793-5, the wars in Europe played into England's hands, obliging her to look to the rest of the world, while France and Holland were now forced out of worldwide trading. 'It is well known', writes a French observer who had lived in England throughout the Revolutionary and Napoleonic Wars, 'that no country in the four quarters of the earth has been able to trade for the last ten years (1804-13) without England's goodwill.'[134]

It is easy to see the advantages England derived from this concentration on the countries of the 'periphery', a reserve to be drawn on by the world-economy she dominated. Her high domestic prices, which were an incentive to modify the means of production (machines were used because labour costs were high) also drove her to seek supplies of raw materials (or even articles suitable for immediate re-sale in Europe) from low-cost countries. But if this was the case, a powerful reason must be the way in which English trade, with the services of the best navy in the world, had triumphed over distance. In no other country in the world, including Holland, was the division of labour so far advanced in the shipping sector as it was in England, whether in shipbuilding, shipfitting, financial backing or maritime insurance. A glance inside the London coffee-houses where the insurers foregathered – the Jerusalem, the Jamaica, Sam's and after 1774 the new Lloyd's coffee house in the Royal Exchange – would tell us more than any long treatise: insurance brokers carried orders from their customers from one insurance firm to another to find takers. Even foreigners knew the best addresses in town.[135] Lloyd's was an unrivalled centre for news and information. Insurers were better informed about a ship's position than her owners: they generally knew very well when they were on to a good thing.

But Britain, protected by her fleet, also knew very well when she was on to a good thing. There is no need here to describe for the hundredth time how during the Revolutionary and Napoleonic Wars, Britain managed to outwit the vigilance and comparative hostility of that part of the European continent which France was trying to blockade against her rival. The British always succeeded in finding a way in – at Tonningen in Denmark (until 1807), at Emden and Heligoland (until 1810); no sooner was one gateway abandoned than another opened.[136] And British trade worldwide continued imperturbably, sometimes benefiting from force of habit. The East India Company confidently carried on shipping Indian cottons home during the Napoleonic Wars: 'Thousands of bales of cotton had been lying idle in the Company's warehouses for ten years, when somebody thought of giving them to the Spanish *guerilleros* to make themselves shirts and trousers'.[137]

The commercial revolution cannot of course in itself explain the industrial revolution.[138] But no historian would deny the effect of commercial expansion on the economy which it certainly helped to reach new heights. Many historians have chosen however to minimize that effect. The problem is fundamentally the same as the bitter dispute between those who attribute capitalist growth exclusively to the virtues of *internal* evolution and those who see it as being created from outside, by the systematic exploitation of the world – a debate which has little purpose since both explanations are perfectly acceptable. Contemporary admirers of Britain were already inclining to the first explanation. Louis Simond wrote in 1812: 'The sources of England's wealth must be sought in her extensive domestic circulation [of goods], in her advanced division of labour and in the superiority of her machines.'[139] 'I suspect that people have exaggerated ... the importance of England's foreign trade'.[140] Another observer even writes: 'The vulgar notion that England owes her wealth to foreign trade is ... as false as it is firmly held, like all vulgar ideas'.[141] And he adds confidently: 'As for foreign trade, it is of no importance to any state, not even England, whatever may be said by those profound political thinkers who dreamed up the Continental system'. The 'system' was the Continental Blockade, an act of folly according to Maurice Rubichon, a Frenchman who hated France under the empire as much as he had hated it under the revolution. Was it not folly to strike at England's trade, folly to blockade the continent, folly to have sent the French fleet and the flower of the French army off to Egypt in 1798, on the inaccessible Indies route – pure folly and a waste of time for, our informant continues, what was England getting out of the Indies? About thirty ships at most, 'and half their cargo consists of the drinking water and provisions required for such a long sea-voyage'.

If such absurd ideas were in circulation at the time, was this not because many people believed, like Cantillon, that there was no such thing as a favourable or unfavourable trade balance: what a country sold could only be the equivalent of what it bought, – what Huskisson the future president of the Board of Trade called 'the Interchange of reciprocal and equivalent benefits'.[142] I need hardly say that England's trading position – with Ireland, India, the United States or anywhere else – was most emphatically *not* one of 'equivalent benefits'.

It is true that while the data available, based on customs records, gives us a fairly good idea of the rising volume of British trade, it does not allow one to calculate the British trade *balance*, as Phyllis Deane[143] has explained in a lengthy analysis impossible to summarize here. Estimates based on these records might incline one to assume only a small positive balance and possibly even a negative one. This brings us back to our previous discussion about the trade balance of Jamaica or the French West Indies. Customs records, besides their intrinsic shortcomings, refer only to goods entering or leaving English ports. They do not register movements of capital, nor the slave trade – that 'triangular' form of commerce which was outside customs control – nor freight handled by the merchant navy, nor the money sent back by planters in Jamaica, or nabobs in India, nor the profits from the country trade in the Far East.

In the port of Bristol: Broad Quay, early eighteenth century. Museum of Bristol City Art Gallery. (Photo by the museum.)

This being so, is it still possible, after recognizing the undeniable volume and extraordinary increase of foreign trade, to minimize its relative importance when total domestic trade is compared to total external trade? David Macpherson in his *Annals of Commerce* (1801)[144] was already estimating the former at two or three times the size of the latter[145] and even in the absence of reliable figures, there can be little doubt that the volume of internal trade was the greater. That by no means solves the problem, as I have already said, and I do not intend to go back over the debate about the relative importance of domestic and foreign trade. But as regards economic growth and the industrial revolution in England, the size of the domestic market by no means eclipses the significance of foreign trade. The mere fact that British industry in the eighteenth century increased its production for export by about 450% (index: 100 in 1700, 544 in 1800) and its production for the home market by only 52% (100 in 1700, 152 in 1800) is sufficiently indicative of the role of foreign markets in British production. After 1800, that role grew steadily greater: between 1800 and 1820, exports of British-made goods increased by 83%.[146] To bring about the industrial revolution, both areas of growth, internal and external, pooled their strength as multipliers. One could not have done it without the other.

Indeed I recognize the force of the argument advanced by the Indian historian Amalendu Guha,[147] who suggests that rather than compare *totals*, we compare *surpluses* – that is the surpluses England derived from India and the surplus savings in England which went into investment. According to various calculations, English investments amounted to about £6 million in 1750 (5% of G.N.P.) and to £19 million in 1820 (7%). Set alongside these figures, are the £2 million regularly derived every year from India between 1750 and 1800 so very insignificant? We do not know in detail how this money, the profits from India (in particular the wealth of the nabobs), was distributed throughout the British economy. But it was certainly neither wasted nor inactive. It went to raise the level of wealth of the island in general; and it was upon such levels of wealth that England's triumphs rested.

The spread of inland transport

However important the multiplier effect of foreign trade, I have already said too much about the national market in this book[148] to run any risk of underestimating its importance. In any case, if one accepts that, broadly speaking, domestic trade amounted to about two or three times foreign trade,[149] and that the latter (after allowing for re-exports) represented on average between 1760 and 1769 about £20 million a year in round figures,[150] then domestic trade must have represented £40 to £60 million; and if profits were 10% of the whole,[151] these must have been of the order of £4 or £6 million a year – an enormous sum. The industrial revolution was directly linked to this active circulation of goods within the economy. But why did it develop so early in England?

We have already seen that this can be explained in part by the revolutionary centralizing role of London, by the growing number of markets and the spread of the money economy which was reaching every part of the island, and by the volume of trade – to be seen in the traditional fatstock fairs, in the long-unrivalled and famous gatherings at Stourbridge fair, in the thriving market-towns which formed a circle round London, in the specialized wholesale markets inside the city itself, and the increased numbers of middlemen, redistributing incomes and profits among a growing mass of economic participants, as Defoe accurately observed. In short, much of the explanation lies in the sophistication and modernization of a network of commercial relations tending increasingly to operate under its own steam. Lastly and perhaps most of all, there was the proliferation of new means of transport, something which preceded the demands of trade, and then helped it to expand.[152]

Here too, we meet a problem already encountered earlier in this book. But it may be worthwhile looking at it afresh with reference to the remarkable circulation of goods in England. The first means of transport by which this was handled was the enormous volume of coastal shipping. The sea from this point of view as from many others, was England's first natural advantage. The coasters or 'colliers' represented three-quarters of the British navy, employing at least 100,000 sailors in 1800.[153] This being so, coasting was the school of seamanship for the crews which England turned to such good use elsewhere. Everything travelled by coaster: grain in bulk, and particularly coals from Newcastle, which sailed from Tyneside to the Thames estuary. Two score or so ports scattered around the English coasts handled this almost continuous stream of traffic, some of them ideally situated and easy of access, others used out of necessity despite their inconvenience. The Channel ports, which offered a handy refuge, were also, Defoe noted, the home or at any rate *a* home of 'smuggling and roguing'.[154]

The second advantage enjoyed by goods circulating in England was the inland network of waterways. The industrial and commercial importance of Norwich, which is a long way from the coast, can very largely be put down to the fact that the town could be directly reached from the sea, 'without lock or stop'.[155] T.S. Willan, with his customary brevity and precision,[156] has demonstrated the revolutionary importance of shipping on the rivers, which could carry sea-going vessels or at any rate their cargoes, far inland, forming as it were an extension of the marine waterway which coastal shipping had woven around the island.

England's navigable rivers, slow-flowing as a rule, were no longer used after about 1600 in the state in which nature had left them. In order to carry coal and other heavy goods in demand in the towns (particularly building materials) they were gradually improved, their navigable stretches extended, some of their meanders by-passed, and locks were built. The lock, T.S. Willan has argued, was an invention worthy to be ranked with the steam-engine.[157] The improvement of rivers was a sort of apprenticeship preparing the way for canals: the earliest canals simply prolonged or connected river routes. But vice versa, some rivers were only made navigable (or virtually 'canalized') when it became clear that they could be used to connect newly-built canals.

So canal fever was not really an attack of fever or folly, simply a speculative endeavour – one which did not pay off in fifty per cent of cases, it is sometimes argued; but one could retort that in the other fifty it did: whenever the route had been judiciously chosen, whenever coal (the crucial commodity) used the new waterway, whenever the necessary credit to launch the scheme had been well-handled by the building corporation or by the individual entrepreneur.

Canal fever began in 1755 with the Sankey canal, built to carry coal from St Helen's to Liverpool,[158] which preceded by a few years the justly celebrated and totally successful Duke of Bridgewater's canal, linking the Worsley coal mines to Manchester.[159] When the Duke of Bridgewater undertook on his own these works 'which required a greater circulation of paper money than is to be found in the feeble establishment pompously known as the Bank of France, he had not of course like the latter seen his paper money discredited; nor was he obliged like the latter to have in his cellars cash to the value of a quarter of his notes in circulation; and this was just as well – for he often did not have so much as a crown to pay the postillion who drove him along the works'.[160]

On this occasion, the entrepreneur played his cards well. He already owned a mine, which made it easier to borrow money: everyone knows that people only lend to the rich. But his plans were well worked out. By delivering the coal from his mines directly to Manchester, he succeeded in selling it for half the old price and was able to make an annual profit of 20% on his outlay and expenditure. Canals were only a folly when built by those without a clear plan in mind, for if the cost of transport by sea is taken as the unit of reference, canal transport cost only three times as much. (Carting was nine times as expensive and pack animals twenty-seven times).

Meanwhile on land, the turnpikes (the first of which was begun in 1654) had made it possible to build up a very respectable network of main roads. Financed, like the canals, by individual entrepreneurs (the state was interested only in strategic roads heading towards Scotland or Ireland) the turnpikes replaced old roads which may not have been as terrible as they are sometimes described, but which were unsuitable for wheeled traffic and often impassable in winter.

But even the new roads with their hard surfaces[161] (produced by simple techniques which had made little advance even on Roman methods) and the craze for canals did not solve all problems, for instance those of transporting coal from the pithead to the dockside. In the last years of the eighteenth century, iron rails made their first appearance – putting the railway before the engine, as Clapham put it.[162] Baron Dupin[163] translated the English 'rail road' as *route-ornière*, misleadingly since *ornière* means a groove and suggests that the rail was hollow in the middle to take the solid wheel of a carriage. But a rail is of course a raised bar and the very earliest rails were in fact made of wood. They carried wagons which also had wooden wheels: these were being used as early as the seventeenth century in the quarries at Bath, in the Cornish tin-mines and for moving coal round Newcastle.[164] On these rails, usually completed by an external sill which prevented the wheel from slipping off, a horse could pull a load three times heavier than on an ordinary road. The really dramatic change was the replacement of the wooden rail by the iron rail in 1767 or so. From 1800 efforts were being made to develop a steam-engine which could pull loads: the first

The Duke of Bridgewater (1736–1803), in front of his canal. Engraving, 1767. (Armand Colin Picture Library.)

locomotive, Stephenson's Rocket, appeared in 1814.

There were already railways (without locomotives) '76 leagues long' around Newcastle in 1816,[165] and they were even longer in the county of Glamorgan in Wales, which includes the ports of Cardiff and Swansea and the mines at Merthyr Tydfil. A Scottish system had also been developed around Glasgow and Edinburgh and it was there that 'the greatest number of schemes of this kind [have been put to] capitalists in recent years'.[166] One of these rail roads went right into the city of Glasgow, observed Baron Dupin who thought that it might be possible to 'lay rails like this down one side of the very sloping streets in the main French towns, in several streets on the Montagne-Sainte-Geneviève in Paris for instance'.[167] In 1833, a book describing 'a voyage from Manchester to Liverpool by railway and steam engine' by M. Cuchetet caused a sensation in France. It gave details of these 'iron roads',[168] of the station in Water Street,[169] of the various engines used, 'among which that of Mr Robert Stephenson, known as

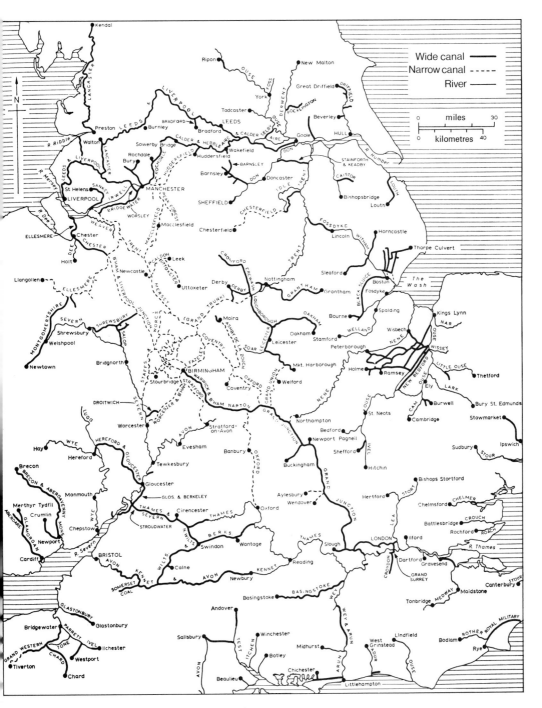

54 PRINCIPAL NAVIGABLE WATERWAYS c. 1830
From H. J. Dyos and D.H. Aldcroft, *op. cit.* T.S. Willan's map, for the period 1660–1700, in
Figure 38.

the "Samson", is the most advanced at present'[170] – engines 'which are no bigger than the average water-barrel carried by a water-carrier'.[171]

From the wooden rail to the steam-train, railways were an important part of the development of the 'carrying trade' in Britain. One does not have to be an expert to be convinced that this increased speed of transport sustained England's growth as a whole. Even in the twentieth century,[172] there is a correlation between growth and ease of transport facilities. The speed of communications also means that instructions and news travel faster and is vital to the business world. Would Thomas Williams have been able to establish and maintain his copper monopoly and all his other business interests, from Cornwall to Shetland in the 1790s, if his business letters from London to Lancashire and Wales had not been able to travel as fast as the modern post?[173]

But when it comes to transport, we must not only think of England's increasingly dense inland network of rivers, canals, roads and railways. Long-distance transport should not be forgotten – these things were all connected. In 1800, a Frenchman observed that when there was a severe shortage of grain at home, 'England shipped in 600,000 quintals of rice from India at 12 francs a quintal in transport costs, whereas it would be impossible to find a carrier in a little town in Brittany who would take a quintal of grain to some other town in Lorraine for less than 40 or 50 francs; yet the distance is no more than 150 leagues'.[174]

> Here in London, we have been able to see over the past twenty years [1797 to 1817 probably] that as soon as England enters into conflict with Italy, and can no longer obtain there as in the past the silk she needs for her factories, the [East India] Company plants mulberry trees in India and annually provides thousands of bales of silk; that as soon as England enters into conflict with Spain, and can no longer obtain there as in the past the indigo she needs for her factories, the Company has this plant too grown in India, and annually provides thousands of chests of indigo; that as soon as England enters into conflict with Russia and can no longer obtain the hemp she needs for her navy, the Company plants it in India to meet the demand; England is threatened with hostilities with America and may be unable to obtain cotton, so the Company provides the amount required by the spinners and weavers; England [is] in conflict with her [own] colonies ... the Company provides the sugar and coffee Europe needs.

These remarks are no doubt open to question. But the interesting thing about them is that they were made by the very same observer who counselled against the 'vulgar notion'[175] that England's wealth was derived from foreign trade and who assured us that she could have been self-sufficient. So she might have been, but it would have been on a very different footing, and would have meant leaving the conquest of the world to some other country.

The West India Dock in London, early nineteenth century. Sugar, rum and coffee being unloaded. (Photo Batsford.)

The mills of history grind exceedingly slow

Everything I have said so far has pointed towards a number of conclusions. In the first place, that in this instance (the industrial revolution) as in every instance that history seeks to study in depth, it is not the short-term, the history of events that matters most. Everything achieved by this revolution took a long time: coke-smelting, the mechanization of weaving, the true agricultural revolution, a steam-engine that worked, railways that ran. The industrial revolution was a long time being born, and before it could develop and begin to move, there had to be a good deal of destruction, adaptation and 'restructuring'. If we are to believe Charles Wilson and Eric Hobsbawm,[176] the industrial revolution was already there in embryo in England by the Restoration (1660), yet nothing emerged very quickly. Throughout the apparently absurdly backward seventeenth century however, the age that seemed to drag its feet, the *ancien régime* was steadily being eroded and overthrown: the traditional structures of agriculture and landed property were being impaired or destroyed; the guilds were losing their grip, even in London after the Great Fire of 1666; the Navigation Act was renewed; and the last constructive measures of a mercantilist policy of protection were being enacted. Everything was really on the move, so that the kingdom, wrote Defoe in 1724, 'changes its face from day to day'; every day something new appeared to engage the attention of travellers.[177] England was ceasing to be an under-developed country in the present-day sense of the word: she was raising her levels of output and her standard of living, perfecting the tools of her economic activity. Above all, she possessed an economy whose different sectors were in harmony, each being far enough developed not to present the risk of creating a dangerous bottleneck at the first serious crisis. England was therefore poised for advance, whatever the direction chosen or the occasion that might arise.

All the same, can we really be satisfied with this image of a smoothly coordinated and evenly developing combination of sectors, capable between them of providing all the interconnected elements of the industrial revolution and meeting demands from other sectors? It conveys a misleading vision of the industrial revolution as a consciously pursued objective, as if Britain's society and economy had conspired to make possible the new Machine Age. At a pinch, this picture of a revolutionary, yet somehow pre-determined experience might be applied to the industrial revolutions being pursued at the present time, with previous models available to act as markers along the road. But this was certainly not how the English revolution developed. It was not moving towards any goal, rather it encountered one, as it was propelled along by that multitude of different currents which not only carried forward the industrial revolution but also spilled over into areas far beyond it.

Beyond the industrial revolution

It is evident from the very vocabulary we use that the industrial revolution, massive phenomenon though it was, was not the only or even the major overall occurrence in a period heavy with developments. *Industrialism*, the adoption by a whole society of an industrial mode of life, is clearly something broader than the 'revolution' itself. And it is even more evident that *industrialization*, the transition from a predominantly agricultural society to one in which manufacture dominates – a far-reaching movement in itself – takes us beyond the radius of the preceding analysis. The industrial revolution proper was an accelerating factor so to speak in this process. As for *modernization*, this is something bigger again than even industrialization: 'Industrial development is not the whole story of the modern economy'.[178] And the ground covered by the term *growth* is even wider – extending to the whole of history.

That said, is it possible to use the data and realities of growth in order to stand back and view the industrial revolution from outside, in the context of a wider movement?

Types of growth

To start us on the way, we may consider the reflection of D.C. North and R.P. Thomas that 'the industrial revolution was not the source of modern growth'.[179] Growth was certainly something separate from the industrial revolution, even if the latter was undoubtedly borne on the back of the former. I would be inclined to agree with John Hicks that 'the industrial revolution of the last two hundred years was perhaps no more than a vast secular boom'.[180] When he refers to a 'boom' does this not simply mean growth – growth which was not confined to the period of the industrial revolution, and which in fact preceded it. The word growth itself, which has only become fashionable recently – since the 1940s[181] – denotes in today's language 'a complex process of *long-term* development'.[182] But do we really have a precise measure of this concept? Economists do not on the whole talk about growth in periods earlier than the nineteenth century. And they are in any case far from agreed in explaining how it works. Some believe that all growth is balanced, others that all growth is unbalanced or uneven. *Balanced growth* (as described by Nurske, Young, Hartwell) affects all sectors at the same time, in a fairly steady forward movement, based on demand, and drawing considerably on the national market which is the principal motive force behind development. The *unbalanced or uneven growth* school (Innis, A.O. Hirshman, Schumpeter, Rostow) views growth as beginning in one privileged sector which transmits the impetus to others. Growth therefore consists of the process of catching up with the leader, and in this perspective it is supply, that is the voluntarist side of economics (as A. Fanfani would say), which comes to prominence; in this kind of development, it is the effect of outside markets rather than the expansion of the domestic market that matters, even if the latter is on the point of becoming a national market.

Having made this distinction, R.M. Hartwell[183] has demonstrated to his own satisfaction that the industrial revolution was the result of balanced growth. His arguments are excellent. But he is thereby extending to the late eighteenth century forms of growth which economists as a rule confine to the nineteenth. He might just as well, without too greatly distorting concrete reality (in so far as it is known) have adapted the second theory – that of unbalanced growth – to the process of the industrial revolution. It is the latter theory which many historians have in fact – not always fully consciously perhaps – preferred in the past; and they might still choose it today on reflection. In the first place, it is a dramatic and *événementiel* explanation, convincing and easy to grasp at first sight. After all there really *was* a cotton boom, and this was unquestionably the first industry to go in for mass production. So could it not be said that cotton started the ball rolling?

But why should the two theories be regarded as mutually exclusive? Why cannot they be valid simultaneously or in succession, in the normal dialectic which contrasts and brings together long-term and short-term movements? Is the distinction between them not more theoretical than practical? There are plenty of examples to show that progress in a single sector can launch a burst of growth, as we have already seen in this chapter, and others could no doubt be cited from the present-day world. But we have also seen that such growth is likely to collapse sooner or later, to run into difficulties, unless it is able to rely on a wider, multi-sectoral response. So rather than discuss the merits of *balanced* and *unbalanced* growth, would it not be better to speak of *continuous* and *discontinuous* growth? This is a very real distinction since it corresponds to that profound, indeed structural break, which took place, in the West at least, in the nineteenth century. Simon Kuznets is quite right, to my mind, to distinguish between 'traditional' growth and 'modern' growth.[184]

Modern growth is that continuous or sustained growth of which François Perroux[185] was able to say long ago that it was independent of rising or falling prices, a remark which surprised, disturbed and even worried historians used to studying 'traditional' centuries very different from the nineteenth. François Perroux and Paul Bairoch, who took up this point, are of course quite right. In the United Kingdom as a whole, total national income and per capita income progressed without faltering through a long period of falling prices (1810–50), a long price rise (1850–80), and another fall (1880–90) – at annual rates of 2.8% and 1.7% for the first period; 2.3% and 1.4% for the second and 1.8 and 1.2% for the third.[186] This was that wonder of wonders, continuous growth. It never came to a total halt, even during times of crisis.

Before this transformation, traditional growth had hiccupped along in a succession of stop-go movements, sometimes even backward jumps, for centuries on end. Several very long phases can be distinguished: 1100–1350; 1350–1450; 1450–1520; 1520–1720; 1720–1817.[187] These phases present contradictory features: population rose during the first, collapsed during the second, climbed again during the third, stagnated during the fourth; and shot up during the last. Every time the population increased, both output and national income grew, as if to prove the truth of the belief that population equals wealth. But on every occasion per capita income declined or even fell sharply, whereas it improved during phases of economic stagnation – as the long-term graph[188] established by E.H. Phelps Brown and Sheila Hopkins has shown. There was thus a clear *divergence* between national income and per capita income: a rise in the national product was always achieved on the backs of those who did the work: this was the law of the *ancien régime*. And I would suggest, contrary to what has been said and repeated elsewhere, that the early phases of the industrial revolution in Britain were sustained by an *ancien régime* pattern of growth. There was no economic miracle, no continuous growth before 1815, or possibly even 1850; some people would argue that it did not occur until after 1870.

How can growth be explained?

Whatever form growth takes, it raises the level of the economy, as the incoming tide floats the boats in a harbour; it engenders an infinite number of inter-related balances and imbalances; it enables slumps to be avoided, it creates employment and conjures up profits. It is the movement that enables the world to regain its secular rhythm after every slowdown or contraction. But this movement which seems to explain everything else is itself difficult to explain. Growth *per se* is a mysterious thing[189] – even for today's economists with their sheafs of statistics. One can only advance hypotheses – without much confidence since as we have seen, at least two possible explanations have been suggested, namely balanced and unbalanced growth: but we are not obliged to choose between them.

In this situation, the distinction made by Simon Kuznets between 'what makes economic growth possible' and 'the way it actually *happens*', could be a crucial one.[190] Is not 'growth potential' precisely that 'balanced' development which is only acquired slowly, through the continuous interaction of the different factors and agents of production, by a transformation of the structural relations between land, labour, capital, the market, the state and social institutions? Growth of this kind is inevitably a matter of *the long-term (la longue durée)*. It enables us to trace back the origins of the industrial revolution to the thirteenth, seventeenth or eighteenth century if we choose to. The 'way growth actually happens' on the other hand cannot but be a question of more immediate circumstances (*la conjoncture*), the product of a comparatively recent time-span, of particular conditions, of technical discoveries, of some national or international opportunity, or even of pure chance. If for instance, India had not been the world's leading producer (both model and competitor) of woven cotton, the industrial revolution would probably have happened just the same in Britain, but would it have started in cotton?

If one accepts this yoking together of the long and the short-term analysis, one can without too much difficulty combine the explanation of the two forms of growth – the one of necessity balanced, the other of necessity unbalanced and advancing by fits and starts, lurching 'from crisis to crisis', replacing one growth industry with another, one market with another, one energy source with another, one means of pressure with another, depending on the circumstances of the moment.

For sustained growth to occur, long-term factors – the forces which accumulate progress over time – must already have produced 'whatever it is that makes economic growth possible', and every time an obstacle is encountered, there must be some new source of dynamism waiting in the wings to take over from the one that is running (or has run) out of steam. Sustained growth is like a relay race with no final whistle. If growth could not be maintained from the thirteenth to the fourteenth century, it was because the mills which had launched it could provide only a limited impetus and there was no other source of energy to take over from them; but a more powerful reason possibly was that the agriculture of the time could not keep pace with population increase and found itself faced with falling yields. Until the industrial revolution, every burst of growth came up against what I called in the first volume of this book, 'the limits of the possible', a ceiling imposed by agricultural output, by the available means of transport, sources of power or market demand. Modern growth begins when that ceiling or limit recedes indefinitely into the distance – which is not to say of course that some kind of ceiling may not be reached in the future.

Growth and the division of labour

Every advance made by growth concerns the *division of labour*. The latter is a derivative phenomenon, trailing along behind growth which drags it in its wake so to speak. But the increasing complexity of the division of labour can eventually be taken as a reliable indicator of the progress made towards growth, or even as a means of measuring it.

Contrary to what Marx believed and wrote in good faith, Adam Smith did not invent the idea of the division of labour. He merely conferred the status of a general theory on an ancient idea already adumbrated by Plato, Aristotle and Xenophon, and mentioned long before his own time by William Petty (1623–87), Ernst Ludwig Carl (1687–1743), Adam Ferguson (1723–1816) and Cesare Beccaria (1735–93). But from the time of Adam Smith, economists regarded the idea as something akin to Newton's law of gravity. Jean-Baptiste Say was one of the first to rebel against the vogue and thereafter the concept of the division of labour rather went out of fashion. Durkheim wrote of it that 'it is merely a derivative phenomenon ... [which] takes place on the surface of social life, and this is particularly true of the economic division of labour, which is but skin deep'.[191] Is this really so? I have often imagined the division of tasks as something like the *intendance* – the supply corps which follows the army and organizes occupied territory. Was the improved organization of exchange – and by the same token the enlargement of its scope – such a small thing? The extension of the services or tertiary sector – a major phenomenon of our own times – forms part of the division of labour and lies at the heart of socio-economic theories of today. The same is true of the destructuring and restructuring of social features which accompany growth, for growth does not merely increase the division of labour, it reshuffles the cards, eliminating old functions and proposing new ones, in a process which reshapes both economy and society. The industrial revolution represented a new and completely disorienting division of labour, preserving and refining the mechanisms at work but bringing disastrous consequences in social and human terms.

The division of labour: the end of the road for the putting-out system

The most frequent form taken by industry in town and country was the putting-out system,[192] a pattern of working which had become general throughout Europe and had enabled mercantile capitalism from a quite early stage to take advantage of the surplus of cheap labour in the countryside. The rural artisan worked at home, helped by his family, while still keeping a field and a few animals. Raw materials – wool, flax, cotton – were provided by the merchant in town who ran the operation, received the finished or semi-finished product and paid the bill. The putting-out system thus combined town and country, craft and farming, industrial and family labour, and at the top, mercantile and industrial capitalism. To the artisan, it meant a life that was balanced if not exactly peaceful; to the entrepreneur, it meant the possibility of keeping fixed capital costs down and more particularly of coping with the only too frequent gaps in demand: when sales fell off, he simply reduced his orders and employed fewer people – perhaps suspending operations entirely. In an economy where it was demand, not supply, which restricted industrial output, out-working provided industry with the necessary elasticity. It could be halted or re-started at a word of command.[193]

Even the manufactories, which were the earliest concentrations of labour, the first attempt at *economies of scale*, often retained this pattern which provided room for manoeuvre: they usually relied on a large number of outworkers. And in any case, manufactories represented only a small fraction of output,[194] until the factory with its machines perfected the all-conquering solution of mass-production; and that took time.

The disruption brought by the new system was indeed slow to emerge. Even in the vanguard industry of cotton, the family workshop survived for a long time, since handloom weaving co-existed with mechanized spinning for a good half-century. As late as 1817, one witness described it as exactly the same as in the old days, 'with the sole exception of the flying shuttle invented and introduced by John Kay in about 1750'.[195] The power-loom, driven by steam, was not operational until the 1820s or so. The long period when rapid spinning in modern factories was out of step with traditional handloom weaving did of course radically upset the former division of labour. Whereas previously the spinning wheels had hardly been able to keep up with the demands of the weaver, the position was reversed as spinning increasingly became mechanized. Handloom weaving was forced to call on more and more workers, who had to work at breakneck speed, but could earn high wages. Rural workers began to abandon their small-holdings and joined the ranks of the full-time weavers which were visibly swollen too by the recruitment of large contingents of women and children. In 1813–14, out of 213,000 handloom weavers, 130,000 – more than half – were under the age of fourteen.

It is of course true that in a society where every man living by the sweat of

While there were from a very early date modern machines in the cotton mills round Edinburgh and Glasgow, the manufacture of woollen cloth in the Highlands of Scotland remained very archaic. Even in 1772, the women in this engraving are fulling the cloth with their feet. On the left, two women appear to be grinding corn at a primitive quern. (National Library of Scotland.)

his brow was always on the borderline between hunger and starvation, it had always been normal for children to work alongside their parents in the fields, in the family workshop or shop. So true indeed that in the early days, new firms and factories hired not individuals but whole families who offered themselves as a team, to mines or cotton mills. In Robert Peel's factory in Bury in 1801-2, out of 136 workers, 95 belonged to 26 families.[196] So the family workshop moved straight into the factory, with all the advantages that this method offered in the way of discipline and efficiency. Small teams (made up of one adult plus one or two children) were not only possible but positively advantageous. Technical progress sooner or later put an end to the practice however. Thus in the textile industry after 1824, the new automatic mule perfected by Richard Roberts required, if it was to work at full stretch,[197] that the man or woman watching the machine had as many as nine young (or very young) assistants, whereas the old mules only required one or two. Thus the family structure was broken up inside the factory, producing a completely different context and atmosphere for child labour.

Shortly before this, another far more disastrous process of disruption had begun with the coming of the power-loom. This time it was the handloom weavers who were doomed to disappear. The power-loom, 'with which a child can produce as much as two or three men',[198] was truly a social catastrophe, on top of so many others. Thousands of weavers were thrown on to the streets. Wages collapsed so drastically that the starvation rates at which labour could be bought kept some wretched handloom weavers in work longer than would rationally have been expected.

At the same time, the new division of labour, as it urbanized working-class society, was tearing apart the world of the poor, as they chased after work which vanished in front of them; it eventually took them to unfamiliar places, far from the countryside they knew and in the end diminished their way of life. Living in towns, deprived of the traditional resources of kitchen garden, cow, and farm-yard fowls, working in great factories under the stern gaze of the overseers, being forced to obey, losing all freedom of movement, accepting fixed working-hours – all these were immediate effects hard to bear. It meant changing a whole way of life and view of the world, to the point of alienation from one's own existence. It meant changing diet – eating poor food and less of it. Neil J. Smelser has given us a sociological and historical account of the life of the uprooted workers in the new all-conquering cotton industry.[199] It was many years before working-class society succeeded in creating protection in the shape of new attitudes and organizations – friendly societies, cooperative banks and so on.[200] Trade unions would only come later. And it is not much use asking the rich what they thought of the new town-dwellers. They saw them as 'mindless, vicious, quarrelsome and rebellious' and to make matters worse, 'as a rule poor'.[201] What the workers themselves thought of factory labour was expressed rather differently – with their feet. In 1838, only 23% of the textile workforce were adult males; the great mass were women and children, who put up less resistance.[202] Never before had social discontent in England been so severe as in the years 1815–45 which saw the rise in turn of Luddite machine-breakers, of political radicals, who would have liked to break down the structures of society, of trade unionism and of Utopian socialism.[203]

The industrialists

The division of labour did not only affect the base but also – perhaps even more quickly – the top levels of industrial firms. Hitherto, in Britain as on the continent, the rule had been the indivisibility of the chief commercial functions – a businessman could be a jack of all trades: merchant, banker, insurer, ship-owner, industrialist. When the English 'country banks' appeared for instance, their proprietors were corn-merchants, brewers, or wholesalers with many in-

A weaving workshop in eighteenth-century England, by Hogarth. In the foreground the owner is looking through the books; behind him, women are working at looms. (Photo British Museum.)

terests, who had been motivated to set up banks by their own needs and those of their neighbours.[204] These men with a finger in every pie were found wherever one turned: they were directors of the East India Company (naturally) or the Bank of England where they influenced decisions and exerted patronage, they had seats in the House of Commons, gradually climbed the ladder of honours, and were soon governing the country which was already subordinate to their interests and passions.

But by the late eighteenth and early nineteenth century, a new type was emerging, the 'industrialist', a man of action who would before long, even before the formation of Peel's second ministry (1841), be making an appearance on the political stage, in the House of Commons itself. In the course of acquiring their independence, these men had broken one by one the ties between pre-industry and mercantile capitalism. With them there appeared a new form of capitalism, one that went from strength to strength, firmly based on industrial production. The new 'entrepreneurs' were above all organizers. 'Relatively few', remarks Peter Mathias, 'were the pioneers of major innovations or inventions in their own right.'[205] The talents they claimed to possess, the tasks they set themselves, were those of being conversant with new techniques, able to handle their foremen and workers and lastly having an expert knowledge of the market so as to be able to direct output themselves, changing course whenever necessary. They tended to do without the merchant as middleman, preferring themselves to supervise the purchase and transport of the raw materials they needed, to see that it was of the correct quality and arrived regularly. Since they were producing for a mass market, they wanted to be able to assess for themselves the state of the market and to adapt production accordingly. The Fieldens, mill-owners in Todmorden, had their own agents in the United States in the early nineteenth century, who bought supplies of cotton for the factory.[206] 'The great London porter brewers bought little malt in the open market at Mark Lane or Bear Quay [but] ... employed factors' in the barley-growing regions of East Anglia – who were kept on a very tight rein if the following letter from a London brewer to his factor is anything to go by: 'I have sent you by coach a sample of the last pale malt you sent in. It is so infamously bad ... that I will not receive another sack of it into my brewhouse. Should I have occasion ever to write such another letter, I shall entirely alter my plan of buying'.[207]

Such behaviour was a sign of the completely new dimensions of industry, including brewing which a Frenchman in 1812 described as 'truly one of the curiosities of the city of London':

> The brewery of Barclay & Co is one of the most impressive. The whole enterprise is powered by a 'fire-pump' of thirty horse-power and although there are employed there nearly 200 men and a large number of horses, they are almost all used for outside tasks. There is nobody to be seen inside this prodigious factory and everything in it operates by a hidden hand. Great rakes move up and down and stir the boilers 12 feet high and 20 feet in diameter, which contain the hops and stand over the fire. Elevators carry 2500 bushels of draff[208] a day to the top of the building from where it is distributed in various pipes to the places where it is to be used; the barrels are transported without being touched; the pumping machine itself which accomplishes all this is so precisely constructed, there is so little friction or shock within it, that without exaggerating, it makes hardly any more sound than a watch ticking, and one can hear a pin drop anywhere in the building. The vats into which the liquid is poured when it has received the final preparations, are of gigantic dimensions: the largest holds 3000 barrels of 36 gallons each, which at 8 barrels to the ton is equal to the cargo of a 375-ton ship; and there are forty or fifty of these containers, the smallest of which holds 800 barrels, that is 100 tons ... The smallest vat, when full of beer is worth £3000 sterling and calculating on this basis the contents of the others, the cellar alone contains a capital of £300,000 sterling. The barrels in which the beer is carried to consumers, themselves cost £80,000 sterling and the

entire establishment probably requires a capital of no less than half a million pounds sterling; the building is fire-proof, the floors being made of metal and the walls of brick; 250,000 barrels of beer a year come out of it, enough to load an entire fleet of 150 ships each carrying 200 tons cargo.[209]

These colossal breweries had moreover organized the distribution of their output, not only in London itself, where they supplied beer directly to half the ale-houses in town, but also in Dublin, where they had agents.[210] This is an important point: industrial enterprise was moving towards total independence. Peter Mathias cites the example of the building entrepreneur Thomas Cubitt, who emerged as a man of fortune in about 1817, having become rich during the Napoleonic Wars. His success owed nothing to technical innovation, and every-thing to new management techniques: he got rid of the sub-contractors who had traditionally handled the building trade; he acquired a permanent workforce and organized his own credit arrangements.[211]

This recently-found independence was the sign of a new age. The division of labour between industry and other kinds of business was nearing completion. Historians tell us that this is the beginning of industrial capitalism, and so it is. But they also tell us that this is when 'true' capitalism begins; I find that a much more questionable proposition. Is there such a thing as 'true' capitalism?

British economy and society by sector

The composition of every society undergoing long-term growth is inevitably affected by the division of labour. This was everywhere at work in England. The division of political power between Parliament and Crown in 1660, at the Restoration, and in particular with the Bill of Rights of 1688, marks the beginning of a division with far-reaching consequences. Another example would be the way a cultural sector (from education to the theatre, newspapers, publishing houses and learned societies) was gradually emerging as an increasingly independent world. The world of commerce was also being split apart, a process I have rather too briefly described. And lastly a modification of the occupational structure was taking place, along the lines of the classic scheme first defined by Fischer in 1930 and by Colin Clark in 1940, namely that the *primary* sector (agriculture) although still dominant, was shrinking as first the *secondary* (industrial) and then the *tertiary* (services) sector expanded. R.M. Hartwell's exceptional contribution to the Lyon Colloquium of 1970[212] provides a good opportunity to consider for a moment a problem which is not often discussed.

It is true that the distinction between the three sectors is far from crystal clear, and there are grounds for uncertainty on the exact borderline between even the first and second sectors (agriculture and industry sometimes overlap); as for the third, which is an amalgam of everything, questions could certainly be asked about its composition or its identification. It is usually taken to include all the 'services' – commerce, transport, banking, administration – but is it right to include domestic servants in this category? Should the hordes of domestic servants (in about 1850, this was the second largest occupational group in England after agriculture, with over a million people)[213] be placed in a sector theoretically marked by superior productivity? This does not seem right. But with this reservation, let us accept the Fischer-Clark proposition that a growing tertiary sector is invariably a sign of a developing society. In the United States today, the services sector accounts for half the population – a record percentage indicating that American society is the most advanced in the world.

R.M. Hartwell argues that historians and economists have seriously overlooked the importance of the tertiary sector in English growth of the eighteenth and nineteenth centuries. The development of a *services revolution* he suggests, could be seen as the counterpart of the agricultural revolution in relation to the industrial revolution.

The place of services in the economy certainly expanded: it cannot be denied that transport developed, that commerce gave rise to many new functions; that the number of shops was always increasing and that they were tending to specialize; that businesses were expanding steadily if not on the whole particularly fast; that they were developing their own bureaucracies; that new categories of occupations were coming into being or taking on new functions: factors, accountants, inspectors, actuaries, commissioners. Banks had very small staffs it is true, but there were large numbers of them. The state, with its thousands of administrative responsibilities was acquiring its own bureaucracy, beginning to swell into an oversize body. There were more top-heavy state bureaucracies on the continent admittedly, but the British state was by no means a slim organization, despite delegating many of its functions. We shall not count the army, the navy or domestic service in the tertiary sector. But we should unquestionably make room in it for the growing numbers of liberal professions – doctors, lawyers, etc. The latter had begun their way up in the days of Gregory King and were being turned out in droves by the Westminster law schools.[214] By the end of the eighteenth century all the professions were expanding steadily and tending to change their structures and traditional forms of organization.

Did the tertiary revolution in eighteenth-century England have any effect on industrial takeoff? It is hard to reply, particularly since as Colin Clark himself explained, division into sectors has always been present in some form, and is still going on as a long-term feature of the economy. There is certainly no evidence that the expansion of the tertiary sector launched growth.[215] But it was unquestionably a sign that growth was taking place.

The division of labour and the geography of Britain

Let us now turn to the devastating effect that the division of labour had on the economic geography of Britain. This was something very different from the elimination of provincial autarkies in France during the economic expansion of the eighteenth century.[216] In England, the process was not one of development so much as upheaval – things were practically turned upside down. The interaction between the different regions of England – projected on to the physical landscape of the island where it has left visible signs – is the most powerful and telling document one could imagine on the growth of the British economy and the industrial revolution it brought with it. It is surprising that this question has not inspired any full-length study, although there is at least one remarkable essay on historical geography[217] and a very rich literature on the history of the regions.[218]

The question has been clearly perceived however, by E.L. Jones in his paper at the 1965 Munich conference,[219] by David Ogg[220] in 1934, by G.M. Trevelyan[221] in 1942: between them they have said the important thing, which is that the economic geography of England had for centuries been articulated either side of a line from Gloucester on the Severn, to Boston, the little town on the Wash which used to export wool to Florence and the Hanseatic ports.[222] Leaving Wales on one side, this line bisected England into two roughly equal parts of contrasting character. South-east England, especially the Thames valley and surrounding areas, had the lowest rainfall in the island, and the most eventful history. Here was to be found 'every type of urban development which had grown up over the centuries: ecclesiastical seats, regional markets, university cities, staging posts, entrepôt towns, [former] manufacturing centres'.[223] All the accumulated advantages of history were combined here – the capital city, a rich commercial life, a countryside domesticated and modernized to meet the needs of the capital; last but not least, between London and Norwich to the north, and between London and Bristol to the west, lay the prime zones of English pre-industry. North-west England by contrast, was an area of high rainfall; on its ancient uplands the main activity was sheep grazing. Compared to the south it was a sort of periphery, a backward area, as indeed the figures indicate: in the seventeenth century, the population ratio between north and south (excluding London) was 1:4; for wealth (calculated from taxes) the figures were 5:14.[224]

This ancient imbalance was completely overturned by the industrial revolution. The previously privileged south saw its traditional industries decline. It did not succeed, for all its capitalist wealth and commercial strength, in attracting and keeping the new industry. It was on the contrary that other England, north of the dividing line, which was 'in the space of a few generations'[225] transformed into a rich and astonishingly modern country.

The road from London to Scotland via Northampton and Manchester today runs through the Pennine coalfield with its series of basins where once men and machines crowded together and where there sprang up almost overnight the most dynamic and the most 'satanic' of industrial conurbations. The evidence is still visible there today: every coal basin had its own speciality, its types of industry, its own history and its own great city – Birmingham, Manchester, Leeds, Sheffield – which grew up simultaneously, shifting the industrial balance of England to the north. Here industrialization and urbanization proceeded at breakneck speed; the various Black Countries of England were machines de-vouring and disorienting the population who flocked to them. Geography is not of course the only explanation for these mighty constructions, but it helps us to see more clearly the harsh determinism exerted by coal, the constraints of communications, the role of manpower resources and, too, the heavy weight of the past. Perhaps the brutal new features of eighteenth- and nineteenth-century England essentially needed some kind of social vacuum as their site.

North-west England was not, it should be said, a desert in the way that journalists describe the west of France for instance as 'the French desert'. But it was undoubtedly in economic terms a *periphery*, like Scotland, compared to the London area. This time however, the periphery, including Scotland, joined up with the core, made up for lost time and reached the same level. In terms of our core-periphery theories, it is an exception of glaring dimensions – as T.C. Smout has pointed out in his work on Scotland.[226] There is no shortage of explanations: the advanced core region (southern England) was within easy access of the periphery (and in any case the term 'periphery', if undoubtedly applicable to Scotland, is perhaps only partly applicable to north-west England). More signi-ficantly, Scotland and the 'other' England caught up with the south by means of very rapid industrialization. And it is well attested that industrialization prospers when it is introduced to low-income areas, where the very poverty of the workforce gives it a competitive advantage – as can be seen today by looking at South Korea, Hong Kong and Singapore, and in the past by comparing northern Europe with Italy.

Finance and capitalism

The history of capital reaches well beyond the first industrial revolution – preceding it, encompassing it and continuing after it. During this period of exceptional economic growth which encouraged progress everywhere, capital, like everything else, was transformed and expanded as industrial capitalism asserted itself, soon becoming all-important. But was this the new form in which capitalism was finally to make its mark as it were in world history, to begin its own 'true' career? Was it only in this form that it reached perfection and became its true self, with modern mass production and the huge weight of fixed capital that this required? Was everything that had come before merely preparing the way, a series of embryonic forms of capitalism, curiosities fit only for the historical museum? This is often the impression more or less directly conveyed by standard historical analysis. While it may not be a totally misleading impres-sion, neither is it entirely correct.

In my view, capitalism is a venture that goes back a very long way: by the time of the industrial revolution it already had a considerable wealth of experi-ence behind it and not only in the commercial sphere. So in England in the early years of the nineteenth century, capital was present in all its classic forms which

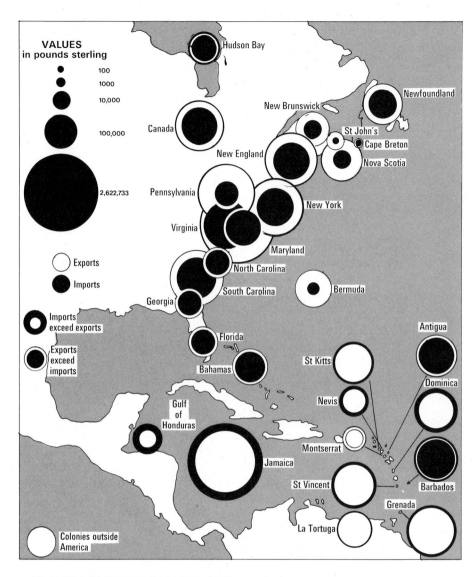

**VALUES
in pounds sterling**

- 100
- 1000
- 10,000
- 100,000
- 2,622,733

○ Exports

● Imports

◉ Imports
exceed exports

◐ Exports
exceed
imports

Hudson Bay

Newfoundland

New Brunswick

St John's

Cape Breton

Nova Scotia

Canada

New England

Pennsylvania

New York

Virginia

Maryland

North Carolina

South Carolina

Bermuda

Georgia

Antigua

Florida

St Kitts

Dominica

Bahamas

Nevis

Gulf
of
Honduras

Montserrat

Jamaica

St Vincent

Barbados

Grenada

La Tortuga

○ Colonies outside
America

55 GREAT BRITAIN'S TRADE WITH WITH THE REST OF THE WORLD IN 1792
From statistics in French archives (A.E. M. et D. Angleterre 10 f° 130). White stands for exports
(E), black for imports (I). The inside of the circle is black or white depending on whether exports
exceeded imports or vice versa. Circles that look empty signify approximate equality between
imports and exports. This was the case in Turkey (I = £290,559; E = £273,715); Italy (£1,009,000
and £936,263); and Ireland (£2,622,733 and £2,370,866). There was an imbalance in Britain's
favour with the United States; Portugal (£977,820 and £754,612); and France after the Eden
treaty (£717,034 and £1,221,666). Some general totals: Europe £11,170,860 and £12,813,435;
America: £5,603,947 and £8,159,502; Asia £2,671,547 and £2,627,887; Africa £82,917 and

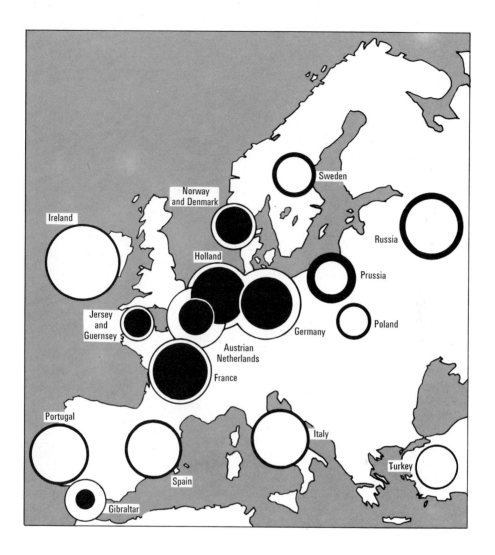

Ireland

Norway
and Denmark

Sweden

Russia

Holland

Prussia

Jersey
and
Guernsey

Germany

Poland

Austrian
Netherlands

France

Portugal

Italy

Turkey

Spain

Gibraltar

£1,367,539. Total imports were £19,529,273 to £24,878,362 exports, that is a positive balance of over £5 million. Exports of 'English-manufactured' goods were worth £18,509,796, re-exports of goods manufactured abroad £6,568,565. British trade was carried by 15,463 ships entering her ports and 15,010 leaving, a total of 30,470 ships, 3620 of which were foreign. The average tonnage of English ships was 122 tons, their average crew 7 men. For Franco-British trade there were 3160 return voyages, 430 by foreign ships. For trade with Asia there were 28 departures and 36 returns, all in English ships, average tonnage 786 tons, average crew 93.
(This record does not count the substantial English coastal shipping, mostly of coal.)

were moreover all very much alive: agricultural capital, which in itself constituted half of England's wealth even in 1830; industrial capital, which had been
growing very slowly until its sudden expansion; and a very ancient commercial
capital, smaller in *relative* terms but ready to expand worldwide, creating the
colonialism for which a name and justification would soon have to be found;
finally (if we can lump together the worlds of banking and finance) there was
financial capital which did not wait for the triumph of the City of London to
come into being. For Hilferding,[227] it was the twentieth century, with its profusion of huge corporations and the immense concentration of money in every
form which brought about the advent and the supremacy of finance capitalism
in a sort of unholy trinity in which industrial capitalism was God the Father,
commercial capitalism – a secondary phenomenon – God the Son, and finance
capitalism the Holy Ghost, penetrating everything else.[228]

Rather than take up this perhaps rather questionable image, let us draw the
conclusion that Hilferding rejects the notion of a purely industrial form of
capitalism, that he sees the world of capital as a range of possibilities, within
which the financial variety – a very recent arrival as he sees it – has tended to win
out over the others, penetrating and dominating them from within. It is a view
with which I am very willing to concur, with the proviso that I see the plurality
of capitalism as something going back a long way. Finance capitalism was no
newborn child of the 1900s; I would even argue that in the past – in say Genoa
or Amsterdam – following a wave of growth in commercial capitalism and the
accumulation of capital on a scale beyond the normal channels for investment,[229]
finance capitalism was already in a position to take over and dominate, for a
while at least, all the activities of the business world.

In the English case, it is clear that the range of types of capitalism, including
the rise of 'finance capitalism', already existed well before 1900. Much earlier, in
the wave of revolutions which marked England's tempestuous growth, a financial revolution had even run alongside the country's industrialization; it may not
have launched the latter, but it certainly accompanied it and made it possible. It
is often said that the English banks did not finance industrialization. But recent
studies have shown that both long and short-term credit was available for
industrial enterprise in the eighteenth and even the nineteenth century.[230]

The Bank of England, founded in 1694, was the centre of an entire banking
system. Around it and based on it were the private London banks: 73 of them in
1807, about a hundred during the 1820s.[231] In the provinces, the 'country banks'
which had certainly appeared by the early eighteenth century and which multiplied in the wake of the South Sea Bubble only to collapse with it afterwards,
numbered only a dozen in 1750, but 120 in 1784, 290 in about 1797, 370 in 1800
and at least 650 in about 1810.[232] One author even puts the number at about 900
in the same period, probably counting the branches which several of them
opened. It is true that this spontaneous generation was the triumph of Lilliput
(banks could not have more than six partners)[233] and that their numbers were

created not so much to meet the needs of speculation (which was however by no means a privilege of Londoners), as to meet particular local needs and circumstances. A country bank[234] was often simply an extra counter opened in an already well-established firm where the handling of bills, discounting and credit were no more than good neighbourliness, often carried on quite informally. These improvised bankers came from all kinds of backgrounds. The Fosters of Cambridge were millers and cornmerchants; in Liverpool most of the banks were branches of commercial houses; the Lloyds of Birmingham were originally ironmasters; the Smiths of Nottingham were hosiers; the Gurneys of Norwich were yarn merchants and worsted manufacturers; most Cornish bankers were mine-owners; elsewhere they might be malt or hop merchants, brewers, drapers, mercers or turnpike treasurers.[235]

In short, eighteenth-century banks were the product of local circumstances, rather like the first new industrial undertakings. Provincial England needed credit, it needed facilities for the circulation of bills of exchange, it needed cash, and the private banks fulfilled all these functions since they even had the right to issue bank notes. Indeed this was a major source of profit for them since at least at first, until people had sufficient confidence in them to deposit cash with them, they could only extend their credit by printing money.[236] In theory these banks had gold reserves sufficient to cover their issues, but if there was a crisis accompanied by public panic as in 1745, they were obliged to send in haste to London banks for cash to avoid bankruptcies. These could not always be avoided, during the crises of 1793 and 1816 in particular. And such failures are evidence in themselves that the local banks made large-scale loans, not only in the short but in the long-term.[237]

In general however the system was solid enough, since it was in practice, though not officially, underwritten by the Bank of England, which acted as the 'lender of last resort'.[238] Its own cash reserves were usually adequate to cover unexpected repayments by private banks, in London or the provinces, in times of difficulty. After 1797, when the bank notes of the Bank of England were no longer convertible into gold, they became for local banks the currency into which they undertook in the last resort to change their own notes. A clear sign of general stability was that the private banks became deposit banks, thereby increasing their ability to make loans to farmers or landowners as well as to industrialists, pit-owners or canal builders.[239] The latter took full advantage of the opportunity – the Duke of Bridgewater's loans are a perfect example.

After 1826, when joint stock banks were authorized by law, these made up the new generation of more solidly based banks with greater capital resources than the earlier generation. Were they any more prudent? Not at all since they had to compete with the existing banks for customers, therefore to take more risks. Their numbers grew visibly: there were 70 of them in 1836 but between 1 January and 26 November of that year, no fewer than 42 joint stock banks 'have been set up and are entering into competition with those which already exist'.[240]

The Coal Exchange in London. Engraving by Rowlandson. (Photo Roger-Viollet.)

Soon there would be over a hundred, and with their many branches they would number as many as the country banks which now began to look rather old-fashioned establishments.

London however was for a long time closed to the joint stock banks, but in the end they forced their way in and in 1854 were admitted to the Clearing House of the London banks, that is they could take a full part in the circulation of money and credit of which London was the unique, sophisticated and initiatory centre. The Clearing House, which had been created in 1773 for compensatory payments between banks, was described by the admiring Frenchman Maurice Rubichon in 1811:

> The mechanism for circulation [he writes] is organized in such a way that one could say that in England there is neither money nor paper. Forty London cashiers handle between them almost all the payments and transactions of the kingdom. Meeting every evening, they exchange in the most natural way

the paper they hold respectively so that a thousand-louis [sic] note is often enough to settle the circulation of several million.[241]

Very impressive no doubt – but are these not exactly the terms used by observers in the sixteenth and seventeenth century to describe the mechanisms of the traditional fairs of Lyon or Besançon-Piacenza? The only difference – but an important one – was that clearing meetings were held daily in London, whereas in the great fairs of the past it was four times a year.

On the other hand, banks fulfilled a function that fairs could not. 'In this country', wrote a perspicacious Frenchman, 'no individual, whether in trade or not, keeps his money at home; he keeps it deposited with a banker or rather cashier, on whom he can draw, who keeps his accounts and settles his expenses depending on the state of his credit'.[242] Money accumulated in banks did not lie idle, but became available for risk, since neither banker nor cashier let it moulder in their coffers. As Ricardo put it, the distinctive function of the banker began when he used other people's money.[243] Then there was the money which circulated under pressure, between the Bank of England and the British government, or between the bank as lender of last resort and the other banks and commercial or even industrial firms. And the popular savings banks collected the money saved by the poor – a large amount as a French correspondent writes, for 'the poor man's fortune [in the mass] in England is greater than the rich man's fortune in more than one kingdom'.[244]

To complete the picture, one should mention the establishment in London of a third generation of pseudo-banks – the bill-brokers who founded what were known as discount houses. It should also be pointed out that the private banks in the City of London, which acted as agents and correspondents for regional banks, were able to redistribute credit and to transfer surplus capital from regions like south-east England to the active north-west, a procedure easily grasped, as capital was invested in the best interests of lenders, borrowers and middlemen.

A full account would also examine the Bank of England. The first thing to be said about it is that it was not only a government bank and thereby both blessed with privileges and encumbered with responsibilities; it was also a private bank with its own shareholders and as such a very sound investment: the 'shares ... [originally] created at one hundred pounds sterling stood at £136 in 1803 and are worth £355 today' (6 February 1817).[245] Throughout the eighteenth century they provided fuel for speculation on the Stock Exchanges in both London and Amsterdam. Secondly, the use of Bank of England notes was steadily spreading, reaching the country as a whole and not only the region round the capital to which they had originally been confined. In Lancashire, in Manchester and Liverpool, workers refused to be paid in notes issued by private banks which were often undervalued by shopkeepers.[246] London plus Lancashire was already a large catchment area. But after 1797, the Bank of England bank note became a surrogate form of gold coinage throughout the entire country.

One ought also to look inside the Stock Exchange where new listings were flooding in. In 1825, there were 114 new quotations, 20 in railways, 22 for loans and banks, 17 for foreign mines (especially in Latin America) plus 11 gas-lighting companies. These 114 new quotations alone represented investments of £100 million[247] at least on paper, since funds were not all paid in immediately.

The haemorrhage of English capital towards foreign investment had already begun. It was a movement which had reached fantastic levels by the end of the nineteenth century but was already well under way by 1815,[248] with variable results admittedly, and indeed in 1826 there was a wholesale crisis. Speculation in finance and the Stock Exchange and the export of capital nevertheless continued via the extremely lively money market. By about the 1860s, while industrial output was still growing fast (it had almost doubled in ten years and was to continue expanding at high rates until at least 1880)[249] and when investment *at home* was probably as high as it had ever been in British history,[250] financial investment abroad, which had been rising rapidly since mid-century, was already in some years reaching the same level as the *total* investment on British soil.[251] Moreover the *percentage* accounted for by trade and transport in national income increased steadily, rising from 17.4% in 1801 to 15.9% in 1821, 22% in 1871 and 27.5% in 1907.[252]

How then can one think of 'industrial' capitalism as the only 'true' capitalism, triumphing over commercial capitalism ('false' capitalism?) and finally, reluctantly, making way for ultra-modern finance capitalism? Financial, industrial and commercial capitalism (since capitalism never stopped being connected with trade) coexisted throughout the nineteenth century, as they had before the nineteenth century and would do after it.

What did change constantly over time were the rates and the timing of profits: these could vary from sector to sector, country to country and it was in the light of such variations that the respective volumes of capital investment themselves changed. Between 1830 and 1870 or so, the period of most intense industrialization in Britain, the capital/revenue quotient seems to have reached its highest known level.[253] But is this explained simply by the virtues of industrial capitalism in itself – or by the fact that British industry was able to expand during these years to match the enormous world markets which Britain unquestionably dominated? This seems to be indicated by the contrast with Parisian capitalism which during the same period took the course which it regarded as most profitable and opportune *for itself* and the one from which it could best challenge Britain, and fell back on finance. Paris became quite widely accepted as a centre for movements of capital within Europe.

> Over the last twenty years [wrote the Chevalier Séguier from Paris in September 1818] Paris has become the principal centre for banking operations in Europe, whereas London is not really a banking city. The result is that an English capitalist who wants to effect some banking operation, say a transfer of funds from one country to another, is obliged to turn to one of the European banking

centres and since Paris is the nearest, it is there that most English transactions are handled today.[254]

His remarks might not stand up to scrutiny, but there is no doubt that Paris was carving out a place for itself alongside and in the shadow of London, that it was becoming reasonably competitive, and if Bagehot is right in his history of the Stock Exchange, the pendulum swung against Paris only after 1870. It was after the Franco-Prussian War, he writes, that the English became bankers to the rest of Europe.[255]

How important was the short-term economic climate?

Does this question – the last in the chapter and one which cannot be answered categorically – take us away from our original purpose which was to go beyond the historical context of the industrial revolution? Yes to some extent, because the time-span I have in mind here is the comparatively short-term (nothing longer than a Kondratieff). So it does divert us from the long-term and brings us to vantage points nearer the reality under observation: we shall be looking at certain details in close-up.

The economic fluctuations of varying length which seem to succeed one another like waves rolling in from the sea, are a rule in world history, a rule which has reached down the ages to us and will carry on operating. Like a repeated rhythm – Charles Morazé uses the term 'dynamic structures' – these movements are as if pre-ordained. Focusing on this kind of movement takes us inevitably to the heart of the problems we have been looking at, but by particular paths, namely those of the history of prices, the interpretation of which has been one of the major problems of historiography over the last forty or fifty years. In this field, British historians are by no means overshadowed, indeed they were the first and some of the best collectors of price series. But they do not look at the short-term climate (*la conjuncture*) in the same way as other (notably French) historians.

To oversimplify a complex issue, I would say that British historians do not regard the *conjuncture* as an exogenous force – as the French school does, its point of view having been more or less explicitly formulated by Ernest Labrousse, Pierre Villar, René Baehrel and Jean Meuvret. For these writers, and for me, the *conjuncture* determines the processes which accompany it, it exerts an influence on human existence. For our British colleagues, the *conjuncture* of a given country is determined by national events or processes. For example, French historians see the stagnation and fall of prices between 1778 and 1791 as being explained by the international *intercycle* (short-term cycle) identified by Labrousse; British historians see them as the result of the war with the American colonies (1776–83) and its consequences. I am myself too aware of the mutual benefits of both perspectives not to accept that both views may be valid, and that the explanation ought to take both into account. But depending whether one or the other is preferred, responsibilities, or perhaps I should say efficient causes, might change position and nature.

T.S. Ashton[256] and those who agree with him[257] are clearly right when they list the series of factors which may influence short-term change. Top of the list comes war. No one will disagree with that. More precisely, fluctuations arose from swings between war and peace (the Seven Years' War, 1756-63; the American War of Independence, 1775-83; the French Revolutionary and Napoleonic Wars, 1793-1802, 1803-15). Then there are the fluctuations in the rural economy (which remained Britain's major economic sector, it must be remembered, until about the 1830s): the harvest might be good, average or poor and bad years (1710, 1725, 1773, 1767, 1792-3, 1795-6, 1799-1800) always marked the start of the so-called *ancien régime* crises[258] which affected the whole of economic life. Even in the nineteenth century, the increasingly frequent and massive calls made on foreign wheat had repercussions on the British economy, if only because payment had to be made quickly (and in cash say the correspondents) to ensure the rapid arrival of sacks of grain or barrels of flour.

Another influence on fluctuations in the English economy was the trade cycle, the set of upward and downward swings which had their effect on the general situation. And there was also the money supply, gold and silver coinage on the one hand and notes of every provenance on the other. The London Stock Exchange (which was always 'sensitive', and to which fear was a more frequent visitor than optimism)[259] was a curious seismograph which not only registered all the movements around it but also had the diabolical power of itself triggering off earthquakes: as it did in 1825-6, 1837 and 1847. Every ten years or so, as had already been the case towards the end of the eighteenth century, the summits of economic life would be shaken by a credit crisis, while at the same time traditional *ancien régime* type crises were still possible.[260]

Such are the conclusions of our British colleagues. As for French historians, rightly or wrongly they see the *conjuncture* as a reality in its own right, although it is far from easy to *explain* in its own right. We agree with Léon Dupriez and Wilhelm Abel that prices form some sort of totality. Dupriez has even spoken of a *prices structure*. Prices, according to this view, are related to each other and if they go up and down together it is because their particular variations are combined. Above all, this is not a 'vibration' confined to one economy, however important that country may be. Britain did not create her own price levels, nor the fluctuations in her trade, nor even her own money supply; the other economies in the world – the whole world – all contributed and all economies moved almost in unison. This is what we as historians found most striking when we first began work in this field: for some indication of the surprising results, see René Baehrel's very revealing and persuasive work.

The climate which raised, halted or lowered prices in England was not a climate obeying a time-scale peculiar to England, but one governed by 'world time' (cf. chapter 1). It may very well be the case that this 'world time' was in part dictated by Britain, or even that London was its essential epicentre – but the rest of the world helped to shape and determine a movement which was by no means the private property of the British Isles. The consequences are obvious. The 'sounding-board' for prices was the entire world-economy of which Britain was the core. So the economic movement affecting Britain was in part of external origin, and events outside Britain, notably in nearby Europe, may have something to do with British history. Europe and Britain were contained within the same economic climate – which does not mean to say that their experience was identical. When describing a conjunctural *crisis* in the economy, I have on the contrary stressed that it does not and cannot have the same impact on the strong and the weak (for instance on Italy and Holland in the seventeenth century); consequently that it is the occasion of a redistribution of functions and of international economic relations, usually ending up by making the strong stronger and the weak weaker. This is why I do not agree with the argument used by Peter Mathias[261] to deny the role played, between 1873 and 1896, by the downward curve of a Kondratieff cycle and its responsibility for the 'Great Depression' which affected England during these years. While growth rates in both Germany and America also fell during the same period, he argues, it is clear that the situation was very different in Germany, the United States and Britain, and that the British Isles fell back in *relative* terms, losing their share in the world economy. That is perfectly true: what would become evident to the world in 1929 was casting its shadow before. But the fact remains that growth slowed down *simultaneously* in Germany, the United States, Britain and indeed in France. And it is the way the *graphs* all dip together, whatever the actual price level in each country, which is the surprising but undeniable thing about this crisis.

What was obvious in the nineteenth century and is even more obvious in the world today, namely an economic trend affecting huge areas in a similar way and at very much the same time, can already be detected in the eighteenth century or even earlier. So it is very tempting to compare what was happening in Britain between the 1780s and 1812–17, with what was going on in France, which we can study thanks to Ernest Labrousse's exhaustive study. But we should not assume too much too soon: the French picture will not be directly reflected across the Channel. We have a number of different graphs to consider and they do not all speak the same language. If we could compare price, wage and output trends from country to country according to the same criteria, it would be much easier to spot coincidences and divergences, and the problem of similarity or difference would be quickly resolved. This is not the case. But if we compare the British and French graphs for prices of goods produced and consumed, we can see straight away that the French graph behaves much more dramatically than the British. Perhaps this is only to be expected: the water may boil less fiercely at the centre of the world than elsewhere. It is not very easy, on the British price curve taken from Deane and Cole, to spot an intercycle between 1780 and 1792; rather

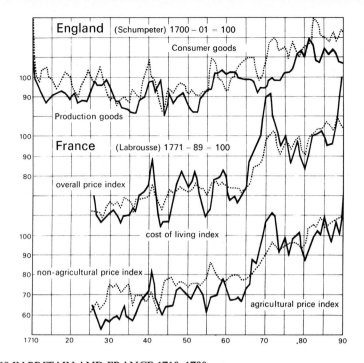

56 PRICES IN BRITAIN AND FRANCE 1710–1790
The Labrousse intercycle shows up clearly on the French graphs, but does it appear in the British figures? (After G. Imbert, *Des Mouvements de longue durée Kondratieff*, 1959, p. 207.)

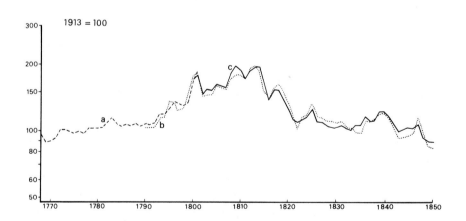

57 LONG-TERM TRENDS IN BRITISH PRICES
In the smoothed-out graph showing long-term change, the 'stability' referred to by Leon Dupriez can easily be detected between 1772 and 1793. The nearest thing to the French intercycle is the plateau of the 1780s. The Kondratieff cycle begins, as in France, in about 1791, reaches its peak in 1810–12 (in France in about 1817) and falls to its lowest point in 1850–1. The three different lines (continuous, dashes and dots) represent different series of calculations. (After P. Deane and W.A. Cole, *British Economic Growth 1688–1959*, 1962.)

prices mark a sort of plateau, a period of 'stability' as Léon Dupriez would call it, arguing that this period of stagnation began in 1773. On the other hand, the graphs quite emphatically concur about the Kondratieff cycle which follows: it begins in 1791, peaks in 1812 and reaches its lowest point in 1851.

We may conclude that the British industrial revolution experienced two movements, roughly between 1781 and 1815, a first and second wind so to speak, the first a rather difficult period, the second easier. In very broad terms, this was also the rhythm experienced by France and the rest of the continent. Louis X V I's France, racked with problems and about to open the door to violent political upheaval, had something in common with George I I I's England, which was also going through a bad patch. In England there would be no political explosion at the end of the road, but the road itself would be a painful one. For about ten years there was a pause in the upward movement which had hitherto blessed the British economy. It would not be true to say that everything began to go wrong, but it was certainly not going as right as in the past. England, like France, was paying the price for the fantastic efforts and money expended on the American war. And the crisis which followed complicated things greatly, redistributing functions and underlining differences between sectors. Trade expanded in spectacular fashion in both France and England, but in both countries the trade balance was upset, running into deficit. Vigorous attempts at recovery were undertaken, but with only limited success. Could not the signature of the Eden Treaty in 1786, a truce between two hostile and mutually distrustful powers, be regarded as an effort to run for cover?

As a rule the result of an abnormally long depression acts as a severe test of business concerns, in which those which adapt and stand up to attack will survive, while those too weak to survive go to the wall. It was England's good fortune to have entered these rough waters just as the 'second generation' of inventions was coming into being: the spinning jenny (1768); the water-powered frame (1769); the powered drill (1775); the rotary steam-engine (1776–81); iron puddling (1784); the first usable threshing machine (1786); the perfected form of the lathe (1794) – cumulatively a huge technical investment paving the way for recovery.

In 1791, the skies cleared: prices rose, business picked up, there was a greater division of labour, resulting in greater productivity. English agriculture benefited from this until Waterloo, and middle-sized farms survived thanks to high food prices. It was indeed the generally favourable situation which made it possible to indulge in the insane expenditure on the Revolutionary and Napoleonic Wars (£1,000 million was spent by England alone).[262] But since this age was not the private property of Britain, the continent also saw the creation of modern industry, though on a smaller scale.

The improving situation however sent prices up faster than wages in Britain. Since the population was also expanding, the result was a drop in living standards as per capita income fell, in current prices, between 1770 and 1820.[263] In 1688, it had been £9.1; in 1770, it was £19.1; in 1798, £15.4; in 1812, £14.2; in 1822, £17.5. Even clearer evidence is provided by the graphs calculated by E.H. Phelps Brown and Sheila Hopkins, showing the wages of English stone-masons between the thirteenth and nineteenth centuries, reproduced with explanations in Figure 58. This is quite a conclusive graph, since it shows over a period of centuries the regular correlation between price rises and the fall in real wages: rising prices seem to produce an increase in output and a rise in population – interrelated phenomena, causally linked – but wages invariably fall; under the conditions of the *ancien régime*, progress was always at the expense of the living standards of the workers. And this rule, which is indeed the unmistakable sign of the *ancien régime*, can still be seen at work, according to the Brown-Hopkins figures, between 1760 and 1810–20, with wages hitting their lowest levels in about the 1800s, just as the graph for the economic situation in general is moving towards its highest point.[264] When the wage situation improved after 1820, as prices fell, it was simply that the old rules were asserting themselves. The real miracle, the real change did not happen until the beginning of the next Kondratieff cycle, after about 1850 (another key date both in Britain and on the continent). This time when prices moved up, wages kept pace; continuous growth had at last appeared.

This brings me to the heart of a debate which too many historians have perhaps cannily avoided; it concerns the price that Britain paid for becoming 'the first industrial nation'. I am inclined to agree with the earliest historians who studied this question, that there was indeed a deterioration in the well-being of the British masses, a decline in real wages, for farm labourers as well as for workers in factories or transport. I tend to think (and I must proceed with caution here, since I am no expert on this period) that the first phase of industrialization between 1760 and 1815 was even more painful than the period which followed Waterloo, although unrest among both workers and peasants was more widespread and more endemic after the British victory that it had been before. But is not unrest itself evidence that things were, if not good, at least improving or reaching sufficient levels to support it? It is however true and this was the *extra* price of industrial growth compared with the other forms of growth which had preceded it) that between 1817 and 1850 the rise in real wages and per capita income registered on the Brown-Hopkins graph was in part cancelled out for the labouring masses by the dramatic impact of over-rapid urbanization – which combined the catastrophic effects of wretched housing, unhealthy and even contaminated food (for lack of sufficient means of transport), with the social upheaval which tore individuals away from their family roots and the resources of the village community. But between 1780 and 1815, with the collapse of real wages (beginning it should be noted in 1760,[265] that is with the sharp rise in output and population which characterized the latter half of the eighteenth century and not only with the outbreak of the American War of Independence) the situation was even more dramatic.

'Two generations were sacrificed to the creation of an industrial base.' This conclusion by present-day historians[266] based on the witness of contemporaries, is certainly borne out if we view England in the period through the eyes of the French commander and *mestre-de-camp* Pillet.[267] Wounded and taken prisoner at Cintra in Portugal in 1807, he lived for many years in England until his release, and if he had no great love for the country (what prisoner ever loves his jailers?) he was a perceptive observer, writing without bitterness and apparently with a natural inclination to impartiality. His memories of England were of very hard times: 'I have seen all her factories without work', he writes, 'her people troubled with famine and crushed by taxation, her paper money discredited'.[268] In 1811, 'the manufacturers being unable to pay their workmen gave them for wages the products of their own manufacture; and in order to buy bread, these unfortunate creatures had to sell them on the spot at two-thirds of their real value'.[269] Another witness, Louis Simond, who was also a lucid observer and an admirer of England, noted at the same date[270] that 'the worker cannot buy with his regular pay the bread, meat and clothes necessary for his upkeep and that of his family'. As for farm labourers, 'their wages lag ... painfully behind the general rate for everything'. In Glasgow in 1812, he observed[271] that 'the wages of the cotton workers ... are no more than a quarter what they were nineteen years ago, although everything has doubled in price in the meantime'. We may query the exact figures he gives, but not the general impoverishment he was condemning.

But Commander Pillet saw further still, it seems to me, in the sense that as a military man he was aware of England's extraordinary military effort. In order to provide men for the army, the English government was recruiting soldiers 'in a much more frightening proportion that any of the appeals made to our population'.[272] The upkeep of the armies was a colossal burden: there were over 200,000 men under the colours (and English soldiers' pay was four times that of the French)[273] and the enormous fleet had to be maintained too. Hence perhaps the inflexible harshness with which soldiers and sailors were treated, as members of the most wretched classes of society, 'the scum of the earth'.[274] Of a younger son who went to the bad and whose family bought him a commission in the army, it was said, 'the rascal is fit to be hanged and good only to become a redcoat'.[275] This was England's true sub-proletariat, supplied with men by the poverty of the actual proletariat, worker, peasant or vagrant. What should we blame? Perhaps not industrialization, nor capitalism which was now storming the commanding heights of wealth, nor even the war itself nor the general economic climate in which everything was bathed – but all of these at once.

Many historians do not wish to face up to this disturbing fact. They simply refuse to admit it. One will argue that there is no precise or satisfactory method of measuring living standards. Another will say that the situation of the working class was worse or at any rate no better, before the first examples of mechanization. A third says he does not believe that prices ever fell between 1790 and 1830. But what prices are we talking about – nominal or real prices? And do the graphs not plainly tell us that prices first rose then fell? And what about wages?

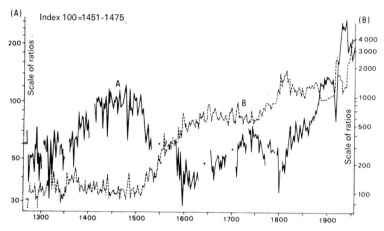

(A) Index 100=1451-1475   (B)

58   THE 'HOUSEWIFE'S SHOPPING BASKET'
This graph, like those calculated by Abel and Fourastie-Grandamy (cf. vol. I, p. 134), shows how historians of the economy have tried to extract from a price-wage relation something like per capita income. The English stonemason was paid a certain wage and consumed a certain number of essential products. A group of such essential products, sometimes described as 'the housewife's shopping basket', has been used as an indicator. The dotted line shows changes in the price of the shopping basket, the continuous line the relation between wages and the contemporary price of the shopping basket (the period 1451-75 was chosen as an index = 100). Comparison of the graphs shows that any period when prices were stable or dropping (1380-1510; 1630-1750) saw an improvement in consumption and well-being. When prices rise there is a fall in living standards; between 1510 and 1630 and again between 1750 and 1820, in the early days of the industrial revolution. After that, wages and prices rise in unison. (After E.H. Phelps-Brown and Sheila Hopkins, in *Essays in Economic History*, ed. E. Carus-Wilson, II, pp. 183 and 186.)

It seems abundantly clear that the English people paid very dearly for their victories, even for the advance in agriculture which enriched only a certain class of farmers, and much more heavily for the machines, the technical triumphs, the commanding lead in trade, the pre-eminence of London, the fortunes of the industrialists and the shareholders in the Bank of England – the price for all these and not merely for the military victories of its armies and navy and the Battle of Waterloo was a high one. It is only fair to add that later, after 1850, the British people as a whole, whatever the inequalities of society, shared in Britain's triumphs on the world stage. It is the destiny of a people which finds itself at the centre of a world-economy to be *in relative terms* the richest and least badly-off. Dutch men and women in the seventeenth century or the 'Americans' of today, whatever their position in society, enjoyed or continue to enjoy the privilege which was possessed by the British in the nineteenth century.

Material progress and living standards

Seen through the lens of the *conjuncture*, the British industrial revolution of the eighteenth and nineteenth centuries appears in rather a new light. This is one more vantage-point from which to view the complicated landscape of growth. The industrial revolution was a collection of problems hard to disentangle, borne along on a wider stream. Its very size forces us to ask questions about the broader history of the world, about the real transformations and motives behind growth, about the beginnings of continuous growth (1850 seems a more appropriate date than 1830-2 which is often suggested as marking the end of the first stage of the industrial revolution). It also urges us to reflect on long-term European growth of which the industrial revolution marks the most spectacular phase, between a past which was long uncertain and a present to which uncertainty seems to be returning.

If we measure growth by the two variables G.N.P. and per capita income (or as I would prefer to say G.N.P. and the real wages of the Brown-Hopkins stonemason), we might follow Wilhelm Abel[276] in observing that these two variables increased side by side in the twelfth and thirteenth centuries – providing an early model of 'sustained growth'. After 1350 and until 1450, G.N.P., the volume of output and the mass of the population declined, but the well-being of survivors increased, they were relieved of the tasks imposed upon them by progress, and benefited from the lull. During the much-vaunted sixteenth century (specialists in the sixteenth century are rather 'nationalist' about their century) and until 1625-50, both population and output rose once more, Europe became more densely settled, but general well-being steadily decreased. Progress always took its toll. After 1650 the 'seventeenth-century crisis', which historians have conscientiously painted in very black colours, lasted until 1720, 1730 or 1750. And the same phenomenon occurred as in the period after 1350: a measure of individual well-being went hand in hand with economic stagnation. René Baehrel is right.[277] Then the process began again in the eighteenth century: a rise in 'prosperity' and a drop in real wages.

From the middle of the nineteenth century, which broke the rhythm of growth established during the *ancien régime*, the world apparently embarked upon a new age: the secular trend was characterized by a simultaneous rise in population, prices, G.N.P., and wages, interrupted by only short cyclical depressions as if 'sustained growth' was here to stay.

But only 120 years have passed between 1850 and 1970. Have the long crises of the secular trend gone for ever with the coming of Modern Times? It is difficult to answer because the truth is that the secret of these secular movements, the key even to their simple correlations is still unknown to us; consequently we lack a substantial element in historical explanation. As a result many historians, and not the least among them, find it easy to be ironic about these historical cycles which can be observed and noted but not explained. Do they really exist?

Is it really possible to believe that human history obeys all-commanding rhythms which ordinary logic cannot explain? I am inclined to answer yes, even though the phenomenon is as puzzling as the climatic cycles, whose existence we are forced to admit, since the evidence stares us in the face, although the experts can still only suggest hypotheses about their origin. I do believe in these tidal movements which seem to govern the physical and economic history of the world, even if the favourable or unfavourable indicators which trigger them off, and which are the product of so many relationships, remain a mystery. I believe in them so firmly that since the beginning of our present difficulties, in 1972–4, I have often asked myself: is this the downward slope of a Kondratieff cycle? Or are we indeed embarking upon a much longer slide, a reversal of the secular trend? If so, are not the day-to-day remedies proposed to meet the crisis completely illusory? For the reversal of the secular trend is a structural crisis which could only be resolved by thorough-going structural demolition and reconstruction.

Only a few years ago, when I outlined these arguments in a lecture, my prognosis of a long-term crisis made my audiences smile. To make forecasts like this in the name of history, and in the name of a long sequence of secular cycles in the past which we can only identify without being able to explain them, is of course a very risky business. But today's economists, armed with all the data about the present experience, also seem to be reduced to hypotheses. Are they not just as incapable as the rest of us of predicting the *length* or even of explaining the nature of the crisis into which we are plunging a little further every day?

By Way of Conclusion: Past and Present

WHAT I HAVE DONE in this book – and it was not so very difficult though it did raise a number of problems – was to introduce the word *capitalism* with its various meanings and ambiguities, into the broad arena of early modern world history. Was I right to welcome it in? To use it as an *essential* model, applicable to several centuries? A model is like a ship: built on land, launched on water. Will it float? Can it sail? If it is seaworthy, perhaps its analytic cargo will be valid too.

Capitalism, as I have understood it, has proved throughout this book to be a good barometer. Taking it as a guide has meant being able to tackle in a direct and useful way the basic problems and realities: the long-term (*la longue durée*); divisions of economic life; world-economies; secular trends and other fluctuations; the complex and complicating tangles of social hierarchies, not to say the class struggle; the ever-present yet varying role played by dominant minorities; even the series of industrial revolutions. What better subject then for these final pages than this explosive topic, the central focus of all the problems and debates raised in the book? But is it really worth recapitulating here, even briefly, all the evidence, arguments and examples the reader has already met in what has gone before and which we should be able to take as read? I am of the view that the classic conclusion, in which a book's central arguments are rehearsed imperturbably for one last time, as if closing the door on everything that has been said, is inappropriate in a work of history, which can never claim to be complete, to have told the truth once and for all.

At the end of such a lengthy undertaking, I feel rather the need to throw open the doors and windows, to give the house a good airing, even to go outside it. Having constructed as I went along my conceptual framework which ought to be applicable to more than the pre-industrial modern period (otherwise it can hardly claim to belong to history in the deepest sense) I should rather like to launch it on the waters and in the setting of another period. And while we are at it, why not take the present day as that period? Why not, that is, take the realities we have ourselves seen and felt? This would take us out of the magic world of retrospective history and into the living landscape which needs no reconstruction, but lies before us in all its richness and confusion.

There is nothing illogical about this: is it not the secret aim and underlying motive of history to seek to explain the present?[1] And today, now that it is in touch with the various social sciences, is history not also becoming a science of a kind, imperfect and approximate as they are, but ready to ask questions as much as to answer them, to be a measure of the present as well as of the past? That at any rate is what encourages me to embark on a venture I consider not only possible and useful but even pleasurable. Let us disregard, without excessive heart-searching, the risks inherent in a comparison which will take little notice of that bogey of the historian, anachronism. As we emerge from our long journey through the past, the present may be a refreshing way of getting our bearings – and even perhaps a test of truth.

It goes without saying that I make no claim to explain the present in the light of history. I would simply like to see how the explanations and expository schemas I have used stand up to the rough waters of today. Is the model I have built on the frame of pre-nineteenth-century capitalism still seaworthy? Can it withstand the violent buffetings it will clearly receive in the twentieth century? I do not believe that the present contradicts the past; on the contrary, it helps to illuminate it and vice versa. There is no shortage of analogies. But such continuity as there is can only apply to the West, to the so-called 'free world', which no longer encompasses the entire globe as it did before 1917. With the dramatic experiments carried out by the socialist countries, capitalism has vanished from large areas of the planet. So today's world is one which contains both continuity and discontinuity, and this contradiction will always remain on the horizon of the problems I shall be considering in the following order: capitalism as a long-term structure; capitalism as part of the social complex; whether capitalism is in a fit condition to survive or not (though if it were to disappear, would all the inequality in our societies vanish overnight? I rather doubt it); and finally capitalism as distinct from the market economy, which is for me the essential message of this long quest.

Capitalism and the long-term (la longue durée)

Throughout this book, I have argued that capitalism has been *potentially* visible since the dawn of history, and that it has developed and perpetuated itself down the ages. On this point I give my vote to Theodor Mommsen,[2] to Michael Rostowtzeff[3] and to Henri Pirenne.[4] Far in advance, there were signs announcing the coming of capitalism: the rise of the towns and of trade, the emergence of a labour market, the increasing density of society, the spread of the use of money, the rise in output, the expansion of long-distance trade or to put it another way the international market. When, in the first century AD, India seized or at any rate penetrated the islands of the East Indies; when Rome held an area even greater than the Mediterranean in her power; when China invented paper money in the ninth century; when the West reconquered the Mediterranean between the eleventh and thirteenth century; when a world market began to take shape in the sixteenth century, the 'biography of capital' was starting to be written in one form or another. Many historians, more cautious than I, refuse to go back any further than the sixteenth or even eighteenth century, identifying capitalism more or less with the cataclysmic explosion of the industrial revolution. But even in this 'short-term' perspective, we are talking about three or five centuries, and therefore about a long-lived structure - which is not the same thing as an absolutely unchanging reality. The long-term is made up of a succession of repeated movements, with variations and revivals, periods of decline, adaptation or stagnation - what sociologists would describe as *structuration, destructuration* and *restructuration*. Sometimes too there are major breaks with the past - and the industrial revolution was certainly one such. But I would maintain, rightly or wrongly, that throughout even this formidable transformation, capitalism remained essentially true to itself. Is it not in the nature of capitalism, a sort of rule of the game, that it thrives on change, drawing strength from it, being ready at any moment to expand or contract itself to the dimensions of the all-enveloping context which, as we have seen, limits in every period the possibilities of the human economy everywhere in the world?

It would however be a mistake to imagine capitalism as something that developed in a series of stages or leaps - from mercantile capitalism to industrial capitalism to finance capitalism, with some kind of regular progression from one phase to the next, with 'true' capitalism appearing only at the late stage when it took over production, and the only permissible term for the early period being mercantile capitalism or even 'pre-capitalism'. In fact as we have seen, the great 'merchants' of the past never specialized: they went in indiscriminately, simultaneously or successively, for trade, banking, finance, speculation on the Stock Exchange, 'industrial' production, whether under the putting-out system or more rarely in manufactories. The whole panoply of forms of capitalism - commercial, industrial, banking - was already deployed in thirteenth-century Florence, in seventeenth-century Amsterdam, in London before the eighteenth century. It is undoubtedly the case that in the early nineteenth century, the coming of machines made industrial production a high-profit sector and capitalism went over to it on a massive scale. But it was by no means confined to this sector. When the first fantastic profits of the cotton boom in Britain fell, in the face of competition, to 2 or 3%, the accumulated capital was diverted to other industries, steel and railways for instance; to an even greater extent though, there was a return to finance capitalism, to banking, to more speculation than ever on the Stock Exchange, to major international trade, to the profits derived from exploitation of the colonies, to government loans etc. And here again, there was little or no specialization: the Wendel family in France were steelmasters, bankers, mill-owners in the Vosges and suppliers of military equipment for the Algiers expedition in 1830.[5]

Secondly, despite everything that has been written about the liberal competitive capitalism of the nineteenth and twentieth centuries, monopoly is by no means a thing of the past. It has simply taken on new forms, a whole range of them, from trusts and holding companies to the famous American multinational firms which in the 1960s tripled the number of their subsidiaries abroad. In 1973, 187 of them, with subsidiary companies in at least five foreign countries, accounted for 'not only three-quarters of US investment abroad, but also for half the total of US exports and one third of total sales of manufactured goods on the US market'. Accused of taking jobs away from workers in their own country by setting up subsidiaries abroad, of contributing to the trade deficit and of playing a disastrous role in the international money markets, including speculation against the dollar, they were the object of inquiries by the American Senate for several years – but seem to be none the worse for it today. The multinationals too have a finger in every pie – in industry of course (since they invest in low-wage countries); in finance inevitably, given the size of their short-term disposable funds ('more than twice the reserves of the central banks and the international monetary institutions', so that a 2% shift in their liquidities would be enough to provoke an acute monetary crisis anywhere in the world, according to a US Senate committee); but they also have commercial interests: it was advanced in defence of the multinationals in 1971 that they were responsible for a majority of American exports (62%) whereas they actually produced only 34% of them.[6]

In short, the chief privilege of capitalism, today as in the past, remains the ability to *choose* – a privilege resulting at once from its dominant social position, from the weight of its capital resources, its borrowing capacity, its communications network, and, no less, from the links which create between the members of a powerful minority – however divided it may be by competition – a series of unwritten rules and personal contacts. Its sphere of action has undoubtedly widened, since all sectors of the economy are now open to it and in particular it has very largely penetrated that of production. But it is also true that just as in the past capitalism did not control the whole of the market economy, so today there are still quite considerable areas of activity with which it does not concern itself, leaving them to a market economy still operating under its own steam, to small business and to the determination of producers and workers in modest enterprises. Capitalism has its own preserves: top-level real estate and Stock Exchange speculation, banking, large-scale industrial production which by virtue of its size, and the strength of its organization, has considerable freedom in price-fixing and in international trade. Sometimes, but only in special circumstances, capitalism concerns itself with agricultural production or even transport – for instance those shipping companies which sail under flags of convenience in order to escape tax and which have made it possible to amass fantastic fortunes. And since it does have the freedom to choose, capitalism can always change horses in mid-stream – the secret of its vitality.

Its capacity to adapt, its versatility and consistent strength do not of course shield capitalism from every risk. In major crises, numbers of capitalists go under, but there are always others who survive or take their place. Creative responses are indeed often made outside capitalist circles, since innovation has more than once come from below. But such solutions almost automatically find their way to the owners of capital and the end result is a revitalized capitalism often even stronger than before, more energetic and efficient than the old. The vicomte d'Avenel was surprised and on the whole pleased to note that with the passage of time wealth changes hands many times, so that on a single estate for instance several different 'races' of owners may succeed one another.[7] He was right, but such takeovers do not in the end eliminate either private wealth or private property. The same is true of capitalism: it may change all the time but it carries on inheriting the succession. What Henry Hope, a leading Amsterdam businessman once said of trade in 1784 after the fourth Anglo-Dutch War, could also be said of capitalism: 'It is often ill but it never dies'.[8]

Capitalism and the social context

The worst error of all is to suppose that capitalism is simply an 'economic system', whereas in fact it lives off the social order, standing almost on a footing with the state, whether as adversary or accomplice: it is and always has been a massive force, filling the horizon. Capitalism also benefits from all the support that culture provides for the solidity of the social edifice, for culture – though unequally distributed and shot through with contradictory currents – does in the end contribute the best of itself to propping up the existing order. And lastly capitalism can count on the dominant classes who, when they defend it, are defending themselves.

Of the various social hierarchies – the hierarchies of wealth, of state power or of culture, that oppose yet support each other – which is the most important? The answer as we have already seen, is that it may depend on the time, the place and who is speaking.

A businessman might reply that at present politics is the most important, that the power of the state is such that neither banking nor industrial capital stand a chance compared to it. And there are certainly serious commentators who have written of the all-powerful state, crushing everything in its path, stifling initiative in the private sector, sapping the beneficial freedom of the 'innovator'. The state, they say, is a mastodon that must be driven back into its cave. But it is of course possible to read the opposite – that capital and economic power are entrenched everywhere, crushing the freedom of the individual. We should not let ourselves be deceived: the truth is of course that both state and capital – a certain kind of capital at any rate, the monopolies and big corporations – coexist very comfortably, today as in the past; capital does not seem to be doing so badly. It has, as it always did, burdened the state with the least remunerative and most expensive tasks: providing the infrastructure of roads and communications, the army, the massive costs of education and research. Capital also lets the state take charge of public health and bear most of the cost of social security. Above all, it shamelessly benefits from all the exemptions, incentives, and generous subsidies granted by the state – which acts as a machine collecting the flow of incoming money and redistributing it, spending more than it receives and therefore obliged to borrow. Capital is never very far away from this providential source of bounty. 'Contrary to the myth of the private sector as the source of initiative whose dynamism is stifled by government action, late [or as some people would say mature] capitalism has found, in the range of activities peculiar to the state, the means of ensuring the survival of the entire system' – the capitalist system needless to say. This reflection comes from a review by the Italian economist Federico Caffe[9] of two books generally in agreement with this position, by C. Offe[10] on contemporary Germany, and James O'Connor[11] on the United States in 1977. Lastly, it is thanks to its friendly relations, indeed symbiosis, with the state – the dispenser of fiscal incentives (to stimulate the great god investment), of lucrative contracts, of measures which make it easier to reach foreign markets – that 'monopoly capitalism', which J. O'Connor contrasts with the 'competitive sector', prospers. Consequently, O'Connor argues, 'the growth of the state sector [including the welfare state] is indispensable for the expansion of private industry and in particular the monopolist industries'. Although 'economic power and political power are formally separate, there is a close network of informal relations between them.'[12] I will not quarrel with that – but collusion between the state and capital is nothing new. It dates back to the beginning of the modern period and is so regular that every time a state falters – whether the state of Castile in 1557 or the French monarchy in 1558 – capitalism visibly misses a beat too.

The relations between capitalism and culture are even more ambiguous because they contain a contradiction: culture is both support and challenge, guard dog and rebel. It is true that a challenge will often wear itself out after its most violent explosions. The protests in Luther's Germany against the monopolies of big firms like the Fuggers and Welsers, in the end came to nothing. Almost invariably, culture becomes a mainstay of the existing order and capitalism derives not a little of its security from it.

We are still being told today that capitalism is if not the best, at any rate the least bad regime, that it is more efficient than socialism while at the same time leaving individual property intact, that it favours individual initiative (shades of Schumpeter's innovator). The arguments in its favour are sprayed like artillery fire over a broad range, sometimes apparently very far from the target. Thus since money for instance is clearly a structure which furthers injustice, every thesis in favour of social inequality is another argument for capitalism. Keynes in 1920[13] pronounced himself unconditionally in favour of 'inequality in the distribution of wealth' which was in his view the best way of swelling the accumulated capital indispensable to the vigour of economic life. Sixty years later, *Le Monde* in August 1979 was telling us that 'inequalities of every kind are a natural phenomenon so what is the point of denying them?'[14]

In a debate like this, any and every authority can be invoked, from Fustel de

Coulanges or Georges Dumezil to Konrad Lorenz[15] or a certain recent critic of Michelet, inveighing against the liberal camp. It is argued that human nature is unchangeable, therefore that society is unchangeable too; that it has always been unjust, unequal, subject to hierarchy. History is thus dragged in to testify. Even the old myth of the 'hidden hand' of the market, adjusting supply and demand better than any human intervention, will not lie down and die. Its message is that by pursuing his own interest, the individual will serve the interest of all – so let battle commence and may the best man win! America has become intoxicated with the myth of the self-made man, who builds up his fortune from scratch, an honour and an example to the nation. There are certainly plenty of rags-to-riches stories in America and elsewhere, but not only is honesty not always their most conspicuous feature, they are less common than is often supposed. Sigmund Diamond[16] has brought relish to the task of discovering how many of the so-called self-made men in the United States actually concealed the headstart they had received from a family fortune built up over several generations, just like the 'bourgeois' fortunes in Europe after the fifteenth century.

What has disappeared however is the euphoria and complacency of early nineteenth-century capitalism; and the new defensive language is in fact a response to the vehemence of socialist attacks, rather as in the sixteenth century the Counter-Reformation was a response to the Reformation. There has been a predictable sequence of blast and counterblast. And since no element in society exists in isolation, the deepening crisis in our present-day economies and societies is indicative of a profound cultural crisis too, as we know from our experience of 1968. Herbert Marcuse[17] who, without wishing to, became the guru of this revolution, was quite justified in saying (23 March 1979) that 'it is stupid to describe 1968 as a defeat'. 1968 shook the foundations of society, broke habits and taboos, even destroyed apathy: the fabric of family and society was sufficiently torn for new life styles to be created at every level of society. It is in this sense that it really was a cultural revolution. After 1968, capitalism, at the heart of much-decried western society, was in a less secure position than before, under attack not only from socialists and orthodox Marxists but from new groups opposed to power in every form, whose rallying-cries include 'Down with the state!'

But time passes; ten or fifteen years are nothing in the slow-moving history of society, but a long interval in the lifetime of an individual. Those active in 1968 have been reabsorbed into a long-suffering society whose patience gives it prodigious powers of resistance and recuperation. Inertia is the feature it lacks the least. So the cultural revolution may not have been a failure – but one would have to think very hard before pronouncing it an outright success. In any case have there ever been any outright successes in cultural matters? The Renaissance and the Reformation were both outstanding and long-lived cultural revolutions, coming one after the other. It was already an explosive enterprise to have reintroduced Greece and Rome to Christian civilization; to tear apart the seamless robe of the Church was even more earth-shaking. Yet in the end the dust settled, everything was absorbed into the existing order and the wounds healed. The Renaissance ended with Machiavelli's *Prince* and the Counter-Reformation. The Reformation loosed upon the world a new dominant Europe, supremely capitalist; in Germany it produced a crew of petty princelings – not a happy result. And did Luther not betray the rebel cause in the Peasant War of 1525?

Can capitalism survive?

Boris Porchnev[18] some years ago gently reproached me and other 'bourgeois' (i.e. western) historians, for talking at length about the origins and early stages of capitalism without ever considering its end. I have at least some excuse – since I have confined my studies to the early modern period it is not my fault if at the end of the nineteenth century, capitalism was still going strong. And while western capitalism is undoubtedly going through a period of uncertainty and crisis, I do not believe that it is on the point of collapse. It no longer, admittedly, excites the admiration which Marx himself could not help feeling for it; nor is it viewed, as it once was by Max Weber or Werner Sombart, as the culminating stage of a long development. But that does not mean that any system which might replace it in some relatively smooth evolution might not turn out to be strikingly similar.

I may be quite wrong, but I do not have the impression that capitalism is likely to collapse of its own accord, in some form of 'endogenous' deterioration; for any collapse to take place, there would have to be some external impact of great violence; and a credible alternative would have to be available. The colossal weight of a whole society and the powers of resistance of an alert ruling minority are not likely to be easily overthrown by ideological speeches and programmes or by momentary electoral success. Wherever socialism has triumphed in the world, it has been as the result of some external pressure and in circumstances of extreme violence – whether the Russian revolution of 1917, the setting up of socialist states in East Europe after the Second World War, the victory of the Chinese revolution in 1949, the triumph of the Cuban guerillas in 1959, or the liberation of Vietnam in 1975. And all these movements were founded on absolute confidence in the socialist future which may be less forthcoming today.

No one will deny that the present crisis, dating from the early 1970s, is a threat to capitalism. It is far more serious than that of 1929 and even large firms will probably be swallowed up in it. But capitalism as a system has every chance of surviving. *Economically* speaking (I do not say *ideologically*) it might even emerge strengthened from the trial.

We have after all seen what role was usually played by crises in pre-industrial Europe: they tended to eliminate the small firm (small that is in capitalist terms), the fragile undertaking created in times of economic euphoria, or the old-fashioned business – that is to say they reduced competition rather than increasing it and usually ended with the bulk of economic activities concentrated in a few hands. In this respect, nothing has changed. At national and international level, there has indeed been a 'new deal' but it has benefited the strongest, and I am inclined to agree with Herbert Marcuse[19] who argued in a recent debate with Jean Elleinstein that 'crises are essential to the development of capitalism; inflation and unemployment etc. [nowadays] encourage the centralization and concentration of capitalism. This is the beginning of a new phase of development but it is by no means the final crisis of capitalism'. Centralization and concentration are indeed the silent demolition and construction workers of our social and economic architecture. Back in 1968, Giovanni Agnelli, the chairman of Fiat, was predicting that 'in twenty years there may be no more than six or seven makes of car in the world'. And today nine companies between them account for 80% of world car production. Secular crises (and as I have said, the present crisis looks suspiciously like one) exact a penalty for the increasing discrepancy between the structures of supply, demand, profit, employment, etc. Breakdowns begin to occur and in the inevitable readjustments, some activities are reduced or even eliminated altogether. But new avenues of profit open up at the same time for the benefit of the survivors.

Major crises also provoke a new deal of a sort in international relations. Here too the weak tend to get weaker and the strong stronger, although world hegemony may change hands and geographical location. The world has profoundly changed, in many ways, in the last few decades. The American economy has shifted towards the south and west (a contributory factor to the decline of New York) – to such an extent that Jacques Attali[20] has even spoken of a shift of the world's centre of gravity from the Atlantic to the Pacific, with a new economic axis running between the United States and Japan. And there has also been a split in the Third World, with the new wealth of the oil-producing countries and the accentuated poverty and distress of the other less developed countries. But these years have also seen the industrialization (effected largely from outside by western nations and in particular by the multinational companies) of the backward countries which were until recently confined to the role of exporters of raw materials. In short, capitalism has had to rethink its policies in those large areas of the world which the western world-economy had for so long dominated – exploitable areas with low living standards, like Latin America, Africa now in theory liberated, or India. It is possible that India has now crossed a critical threshold: having been long accustomed to famine (in 1943, 3 or 4 million people died in Bengal) India has now made such progress in agriculture that with the aid of two or three good harvests she found herself for the first time, in 1978, heavily in surplus – and therefore obliged to think about exporting grain because of the quite unexpected problems of storage, difficult to solve at short notice. This does not however mean that the stage has yet been reached when the mass of Indian villagers will be the buyers of manufactured objects 'made in India'. Poverty remains widespread and the population is still increasing at the rate of

13 million a year.[21] So I think it can be assumed that even faced with a new Third World, capitalism will, for some time to come, be able to reorganize its means of domination or devise new ones, using yet again the formidable strength of acquired position and the weight of the past.

'Tradition and previous generations', Marx wrote, 'weigh like a nightmare on the minds of the living' – and not only on the minds, on the very existence of the living too, one might add. Jean-Paul Sartre may have dreamed of a society from which inequality would have disappeared, where one man would not exploit another. But no society in the world has yet given up tradition and the use of privilege. If this is ever to be achieved, all the social hierarchies will have to be overthrown, not merely those of money or state power, not only social privilege but the uneven weight of the past and of culture. The experience of the socialist countries proves that the disappearance of a single hierarchy – the economic hierarchy – raises scores of new problems and is not enough on its own to establish equality, liberty or even plenty. A clear-sighted revolution, if such a thing is even possible – and if it were, would the paralysing weight of circumstances allow it to remain so for long? – would find it very difficult to demolish what should be demolished, while retaining what should be retained: freedom for ordinary people, cultural independence, a market economy with no loaded dice, and a little fraternity. It is a very tall order – especially since whenever capitalism is challenged, it is invariably during a period of economic difficulty, whereas far-reaching structural reform, which would inevitably be difficult and traumatic, requires a context of abundance or even superabundance. And the present population explosion is likely to do little or nothing to encourage the more equitable distribution of surpluses.

A conclusion to end conclusions: capitalism and the market economy

It is in the end at the political level that the distinction – to my mind beyond doubt – between capitalism in its various guises and 'the market economy' takes on its full significance.

The rise of capitalism in the nineteenth century has been described, even by Marx, even by Lenin, as eminently, indeed healthily competitive. Were such observers influenced by illusions, inherited assumptions, ancient errors of judgment? In the eighteenth century, compared to the unearned privileges of a 'leisured' aristocracy, the privileges of merchants may perhaps have looked like a fair reward for labour; in the nineteenth century, after the age of the big companies with their state monopolies (the Indies companies for instance) the mere freedom of trading may have seemed the equivalent of true competition. And industrial production (which was however only one sector of capitalism) was still quite frequently handled by small firms which did indeed compete on the market and continue to do so today. Hence the classic image of the entrepreneur serving the public interest, which persisted throughout the nineteenth century, while the virtues of laissez-faire and free trade were everywhere cele-brated.

The extraordinary thing is that such images should still be with us today in the language spoken by politicians and journalists, in works of popularization and in the teaching of economics, when doubt long ago entered the minds of the specialists, certainly before 1929. Keynes was already writing about imperfect competition. Today's economists go even further and distinguish between mar-ket prices and monopoly prices, that is they see a two-tier structure, a monopolist sector and a 'competitive sector'. This two-stage model is to be found in J. O'Connor's writing as well as in Galbraith's.[22] Is it therefore wrong to describe as the 'market economy' what some people would call the 'competitive sector'? At the top come the big monopolies, while underneath them competition is confined to small or medium-sized concerns.

The distinction is by no means universal in everyday discussion, but the habit is gradually growing of using 'capitalism' to refer to big business only. Increas-ingly capitalism is being used as a *superlative*. In France for instance, which are the concerns held up to public abuse? The 'trusts', the multinational corporations – that is, public hostility is accurately and rightly directed at the top. The little shop where I buy my daily paper could hardly be called a capitalist enterprise, though if it belongs to a chain of shops, the chain could be said to be part of capitalism. Nor could one describe as capitalist the little firms or independent manufacturing enterprises sometimes known in France as 'the 49s' because they want to keep the total of their employees under the magic number of 50, to avoid the fiscal or union regulations affecting larger concerns. These small businesses are legion. But they are visible in large numbers in the bitter conflicts which now and then put both them and the problem which presently concerns us in the limelight.

Over the twenty years or so before the crisis of the 1970s, New York – at that time the leading industrial city in the world – saw the decline one after another of the little firms, sometimes employing less than thirty people, which made up its commercial and industrial substance – the huge clothing sector, hundreds of small printers, many food industries and small builders – all contributing to a truly 'competitive' world whose little units were both in competition with, yet dependent upon each other. The disorganization of New York was the result of the squeezing out of these thousands of businesses which in the past made it a city where consumers could find in town anything they wanted, produced, stored and sold on the spot. It was the big firms, with their big production units out of town, which ousted the little men. The bread which an old-fashioned bakery used to make for New York schools is now brought in from New Jersey.[23]

Here then is a good example, in the most advanced country in the world, of what a competitive economy could be – an obsolete economy to be sure, employing small numbers and managed on a personal basis. It has now gone for ever, leaving a gap in the heart of New York which will never be filled. But there are still examples of this old-fashioned activity to be seen today. Prato, the big textile centre near Florence, is the best example I can think of, a real hive of thriving small family businesses, with a workforce ready to turn its hand to anything, quick to follow changes in fashion or the markets, with old-world practices sometimes reminiscent of the putting-out system. The big Italian textile firms are all suffering from the crisis at the moment, but there is still full employment in Prato.

But it is not my intention to list examples, simply to point out that there is a sort of lower layer in the economy – it may be small or large, and we may call it what we like, but it exists and is made up of independent units. So we should not be too quick to assume that capitalism embraces the whole of western society, that it accounts for every stitch in the social fabric. Neither the little workshops of Prato nor the small printers of New York can be regarded as examples of true capitalism – that would be completely wrong, both socially and in terms of economic organization.

Finally, it should be said that the competitive sector does not account for everything large-scale capitalism leaves aside or abandons. Today, just as in the eighteenth century, there is quite a sizeable lower floor, a sort of bargain basement, below the other two storeys; some economists estimate it at about 30 to 40% of economic activity in the *industrialized* countries. This surprisingly large figure, for which estimates have only recently appeared, is made up of all the activities outside the market and state controls – fraud, barter of goods and services, moonlighting, housework – that domestic economy which St Thomas Aquinas regarded as the *economia pura* and which still of course exists today. It is still possible then to use the three-tier model whose relevance to the past has already been discussed. It can still be applied to the present. And our statistics which do not find room anywhere for the 'basement' of the economy, give us only an incomplete picture.

This is enough to make one think again before assuming that our societies are organized from top to bottom in a 'capitalist system'. On the contrary, putting it briefly, there is a dialectic still very much alive between capitalism on the one hand, and its antithesis, the 'non-capitalism' of the lower level on the other. It is sometimes said that big business tolerates small firms, although if it really tried it could sweep them aside. How generous! In much the same way, Stendhal thought that in Renaissance Italy, a cruel world if ever there was one, the big cities let the small towns survive out of the goodness of their hearts. I have argued (and I think I am right) that the big cities would not have been able to survive without the smaller ones at their service. As for the big companies of today, Galbraith argues that they only respect small businesses because the latter, being on such a small scale, have much higher unit production costs, which makes it possible for market prices to be fixed at levels providing handsome profits for the larger firms – as if the big companies, if they were left alone in the field, could not perfectly well fix prices and profits at any level they liked! The truth is that they need the smaller firms, first and foremost to carry out the humble tasks indispensable to any society, but which capitalism does not care to handle. Secondly, like the eighteenth-century manufactories which frequently drew on family workshops in the surrounding districts, the big firms farm out certain tasks to sub-contractors, who deliver finished or semi-finished goods. There are small workshops in Savoy today turning out metal parts for faraway factories. Then too there is a need for retailers and middlemen. All these chains of sub-contractors may be directly dependent on capitalism but they are in themselves merely another branch of small business.

Indeed it seems that if the conflict between capitalism and the layer beneath were a strictly economic one – which it is not – both sides would have an interest in peaceful coexistence – the conclusion reached by a recent conference of economists.[24] But government policies may intervene. Since the last war, several European countries have consciously adopted policies designed to eliminate small business on the New York pattern: they are seen as a hangover from the past and a sign of economic backwardness. The state itself creates monopolies – to take just one example, *Électricité de France* (the nationalized French electricity company) is today being accused of being a state within the state, holding up the development of alternative forms of energy. And it is the biggest private firms which receive state aid and subsidy, whereas banks are supposed to restrict credit to small firms – which amounts to condemning them to vegetate or vanish.

There could be no more dangerous policy. This is to repeat in another form the fundamental error committed by the socialist countries. Read what Lenin wrote: 'Small-scale commercial production is, every moment of every day, giving birth *spontaneously* to capitalism and the bourgeoisie . . . Wherever there is small business and freedom of trade, capitalism appears'.[25] He is even supposed to have said: 'capitalism begins in the village market-place'. His conclusion was that in order to get rid of capitalism, its very roots that is, individual production and the freedom of trade had to be dug out. Are Lenin's remarks not in fact a homage to the enormous creative powers of the market, of the lower storey of exchange, of the self-employed artisan or even of individual resourcefulness – creative powers which provide the economy not only with a rich foundation but with something to fall back on in times of crisis, war, or serious economic collapse requiring structural change? The lowest level, not being paralysed by the size of its plant or organization, is the one readiest to adapt; it is the seedbed of inspiration, improvisation and even innovation, although its most brilliant discoveries sooner or later fall into the hands of the holders of capital. It was not the capitalists who brought about the first cotton revolution; all the new ideas came from enterprising small businesses. Are things so very different today? One of the leading representatives of French capital said to me the other day: 'It is never the inventors who make a fortune'; they have to hand over to someone else. But they have the ideas in the first place! A recent report from M.I.T. points out that over the last fifteen years more than half the jobs created in the United

States have been in small firms employing less then 50 workers.

Finally, if we are prepared to make an unequivocal distinction between the market economy and capitalism, might this offer us a way of avoiding that 'all or nothing' which politicians are constantly putting to us, as if it were impossible to retain the market economy without giving the monopolies a free hand, or impossible to get rid of monopolies without nationalizing everything in sight? The programme proposed by the 'Prague spring' – socialism at the top, but freedom and 'spontaneity' at the base – was put forward as a double solution to a double and unsatisfactory reality. But what kind of socialism will be able to maintain the freedom and mobility of the individual enterprise? As long as the solutions put forward amount to replacing the monopoly of capital with the monopoly of the state, compounding the faults of the former with those of the latter, it is hardly surprising that the classic left-wing solutions do not arouse great electoral enthusiasm. If people set about looking for them, seriously and honestly, economic solutions could be found which would extend the area of the market and would put at its disposal the economic advantages so far kept to itself by one dominant group in society. But the problem does not essentially lie there; it is social in nature. Just as a country at the centre of a world-economy can hardly be expected to give up its privileges at international level, how can one hope that the dominant groups who combine capital and state power, and who are assured of international support, will agree to play the game and hand over to someone else?

30 October 1979.

Notes

Translator's note: Wherever possible, when a French edition of an English-language source is quoted in the text, the original has been traced and the page reference in the notes amended. This has not always been possible. References to works originally published in French have been left unaltered, except where there is a recent and easily available English translation.

Abbreviations used in notes:

A.d.S.	Archivio di Stato.
A.E.	Affaires Etrangères (Foreign Affairs), Paris.
A.N.	Archives Nationales, Paris.
B.M.	British Museum (now British Library), London.
B.N.	Bibliothèque Nationale, Paris.
C.S.A.	Central State Archives, Moscow.
P.R.O.	Public Record Office, London.

NOTES TO FOREWORD

1. The expression 'world time', which was used for the French title of this volume, (*Le Temps du Monde*) is borrowed from Wolfram Eberhard, *Conquerors and Rulers. Social Forces in Medieval China*, 2nd edn., 1965, pp. 13 ff., quoted by Immanuel WALLERSTEIN, *The Modern World System*, 1974, *p.* 6.

2. Ashin DAS GUPTA, 'Trade and Politics in 18th Century India', in *Islam and the Trade of Asia*, ed. D. S. RICHARDS, 1970, p. 183.

3. René BOUVIER, *Quevedo 'homme du diable, homme de Dieu'*, 1929, p. 83.

4. Jean IMBERT, *Histoire économique des origines à 1789*, 1965; Hans HAUSHERR, *Wirtschaftsgeschichte der Neuzeit*, 1954; Hubert RICHARDOT and Bernard SCHNAPPER, *Histoire des faits économiques jusqu'à la fin du XVIIIᵉ siècle*, 1963; John HICKS, *A Theory of Economic History*, 1969.

5. *Allgemeine Wirtschaftsgeschichte des Mittelalters und der Neuzeit*, 2 vols., 1958.

6. Friedrich NOVALIS, quoted in *L'Encyclopédie*, 1966, p. 43.

7. René CLEMENS, *Prolégomènes d'une théorie de la structure économique*, 1952, esp. p. 92.

8. Witold KULA, in conversation, many years ago. Cf. *On the Typology of Economic Systems. The Social Sciences. Problems and Orientation*, 1968, pp. 109-27.

9. José GENTIL DA SILVA, exact reference mislaid and untraceable by the author himself when consulted.

10. W. W. ROSTOW, *Politics and the Stages of Growth*, 1971.

11. Article by K. S. KAROL in *Le Monde*, 23 July 1970.

12. Quoted by Cyril S. BELSHAW, *Traditional Exchange and Modern Markets*, 1965. p. 5.

13. Joseph SCHUMPETER, *History of Economic Analysis*, 2nd edn., 1955, I, p. 6.

14. Jean POIRIER, 'Le commerce des hommes', in *Cahiers de l'Institut de*

science économique appliquée, n° 95,
November 1959, p. 5.
15. Marc GUILLAUME, *Le Capital et son double*, 1975, p. 11.
16. Jean-Baptiste SAY, *Cours complet d'économie politique pratique*, I, 1828, p. 7.

17. Fernand BRAUDEL, 'Histoire et sciences sociales: la longue durée', in *Annales E.S.C.*, 1958, pp. 725–53.
18. J. SCHUMPETER, *op. cit.*, ch. 2 passim. (According to Mrs Elizabeth BOODY-SCHUMPETER, a fourth method would have been through sociology.)

NOTES TO CHAPTER I

1. See above, Volume II, chapter 5, on the use of the term 'set'.
2. SIMONE DE SISMONDI, *Nouveaux Principes d'économie politique*, ed. Jean WEILLER, 1971, p. 19.
3. *Ibid.*, p. 105, n. 1.
4. I first found this word used in the special sense employed here in Fritz RÖRIG's book, *Mittelalterliche Weltwirtschaft, Blüte und Ende einer Weltwirtschaftsperiode*, 1933. Hektor AMMANN, in *Wirtschaft und Lebensraum der Mittelalterlichen Kleinstadt*, n.d., p. 4, rightly qualifies this as 'eine Art Weltwirtschaft', 'a sort of world economy'.
5. Léon-H. DUPRIEZ, 'Principes et problèmes d'interprétation', p. 3, in *Diffusion du progrès et convergence des prix. Etudes internationales*, 1966. The ideas expressed in this chapter have much in common with those of I. WALLERSTEIN, *op. cit.*, although I do not always agree with him.
6. Fernand BRAUDEL, *La Mediterranée, . . .*, 1st French edn., 1949, pp. 325, 328 ff.
7. Fernand BRAUDEL, *The Mediterranean and the Mediterranean World in the Age of Philip II*, English trans., 2 vols., 1972–3, I, p. 387 (hereafter referred to as *Medit*; all page references are to the English edition of 1972–3, published by Collins, which is a translation of the second French edition of 1966).
8. A. M. JONES, 'Asian Trade in Antiquity', in *Islam and the Trade of Asia, op. cit.*, p. 5.
9. I have used the expressions 'rules' or 'tendencies', following the example of Georges GURVITCH (*règles tendancielles*) to avoid using the stronger 'laws'.

10. Paul SWEEZY, *Modern Capitalism*, 1974, p. 143.
11. Immanuel Wallerstein's expression.
12. Georg TECTANDER VON DER JABEL, *Iter persicum ou description d'un voyage en Perse entrepris en 1602 . . .*, 1877, pp. 9, 22–4.
13. Pedro CUBERO SEBASTIÁN, *Breve Relación de la peregrinación que ha hecho de la mayor parte del mundo*, 1680, p. 175.
14. Louis-Alexandre FROTIER DE LA MESSELIÈRE, *Voyage à Saint-Pétersbourg ou Nouveaux Mémoires sur la Russie*, 1803, p. 254.
15. *Medit.*, I, p. 282.
16. Philippe de COMMYNES, *Mémoires*, III, 1965 edn., p. 110.
17. René DESCARTES, *Oeuvres*, I, *Correspondance*, 1969, p. 204.
18. Charles de BROSSES, *Lettres familières écrites d'Italie en 1739 et 1740*, 1858, p. 219.
19. Jacques de VILLAMONT, *Les Voyages . . .*, 1607, p. 203.
20. *Ibid.*, p. 209.
21. Meaning of course 'free-thinking'.
22. Brian PULLAN, *Rich and Poor in Renaissance Venice*, 1971, p. 3.
23. *Voyage d'Angleterre, de Hollande et de Flandres*, 1728, Victoria and Albert Museum, 86, NN 2, f° 177. The 'Brownists' referred to are the members of the Protestant sect inspired by the teachings of Robert Browne in the 1580s.
24. *Ibid.*, f°s 178–9.
25. Hugo SOLY, 'The "Betrayal" of the Sixteenth Century Bourgeoisie: a Myth? Some considerations of the Behaviour Pattern of the Merchants of Antwerp in the Sixteenth Century', in *Acta historiae neerlandicae*, 1975, pp. 31–49.

26. Louis COULON, *L'Ulysse françois ou le voyage de France, de Flandre et de Savoie*, 1643, pp. 52-3 and 62-3.
27. Alonso MORGADO, *Historia de Sevilla*, 1587, f° 56.
28. Who was also king of Portugal until 1640.
29. Evaldo CABRAL DE MELLO, *Olinda restaurada. Guerra e Açucar no Nordeste 1630-1654*, 1975, p. 72.
30. *Ibid.*
31. Charles CARRIÈRE, Marcel COURDURIÉ, *L'Espace commercial marseillais aux XVIIe et XVIIIe siècles*, typescript, p. 27.
32. A.N., Marine, B7 463, 11 (1697).
33. Patrick CHORLEY, *Oil, Silk and Enlightenment. Economic Problems in XVIIIth century Naples*, 1965. See also Salvatore CIRIACONO, *Olio ed Ebrei nella Repubblica veneta del Settecento*, 1975, p. 20.
34. See above, Volume II, chapter 4.
35. *Medit.*, I, pp. 125 ff.
36. *Ibid.*, p. 391 and note 177. The reference *is* to oil, not 'wine' as the English edition reads mistakenly. *Mea culpa.* (S.R.)
37. Ernst WAGEMANN, *Economía mundial*, 1952, II, p. 95.
38. Johann Heinrich Von THÜNEN, *Der isolierte Staat in Beziehung auf Landwirtschaft und Nationalökonomie*, 1876, I, p. 1.
39. E. CONDILLAC, *Le Commerce et le gouvernement*, 1776, 1966 edn., pp. 248 ff. for instance describes the economy of an imaginary island.
40. *Siedlungsgeographische Untersuchungen in Niederandalusien*, 1935.
41. See above, Volume II, pp. 36-42.
42. In *The Wealth of Nations*, quoted by Pierre DOCKÈS, *L'Espace dans la pensée économique*, 1969, pp. 408-9.
43. See below, this chapter.
44. H. PIRENNE, *Histoire de Belgique*, III, 1907, p. 259.
45. A. EMMANUEL, *L'Echange inégal*, 1969, p. 43.
46. In a paper given at the Prato conference, April 1978.
47. *Ibid.*
48. Johann BECKMANN, *Beiträge zur Œkonomie . . .*, 1781. III, p. 427. In about 1705, there were 84 trading firms, of which 12 were Spanish, 26 Genoese, 11

French, 10 English, 7 from Hamburg, 18 Dutch or Flemish; François DORNIC, *op. cit.*, p. 85, citing Raimundo de LANTERY, *Memorias*, Part II, pp. 6-7.
49. Jean GEORGELIN, *Venise au Siècle des Lumières*, 1978, p. 671.
50. Tibor WITTMAN, 'Los metales preciosos de América y la estructura agraria de Hungria a los fines del siglo XVI', in *Acta historica*, XXIV, 1967, p. 27.
51. Jacques SAVARY, *Dictionnaire universel de commerce . . .*, 1759-1765, V, col. 669.
52. Jacques DOURNES, *Pötao, une théorie du pouvoir chez les Indochinois Jörai*, 1977, p. 89.
53. Abbé PRÉVOST, *Histoire générale des voyages*, VI, p. 101.
54. J. PAQUET, 'La misère dans un village de l'Oisans en 1809', in *Cahiers d'histoire*, 1966, 3, pp. 249-56.
55. Germaine LEVI-PINARD, *La Vie quotidienne à Vallorcine au XVIIIe siècle*, 2nd edn., 1976.
56. 'Cervières, une communauté rurale des Alpes briançonnaises du XVIIIe siècle à nos jours', in *Bulletin du Centre d'histoire économique et sociale de la région lyonnaise*, 1976, n° 3, pp. 21 ff.
57. Quoted by Isaac de PINTO, *Traité de la circulation et du crédit*, 1771, pp. 23-4.
58. H. C. DARBY, *An Historical Geography of England before A.D. 1800*, 1951, p. 444.
59. E. NARNI-MANCINELLI, Matteo PAONE, Roberto PASCA, 'Inegualanzia regionale e uso del territorio: analisi di un' area depressa della Campania interna', in *Rassegna economica*, 1977.
60. Christiane KLAPISCH-ZUBER, *Les Maîtres du marbre. Carrare 1300-1600*, 1969, pp. 69-76.
61. Moscow, C.S.A., 705/409, f° 12, 1785.
62. *Le Monde*, 27 June 1978.
63 and 64. See above, Volume II, chapter 5, p. 459.
65. T. S. WILLAN, *Studies in Elizabethan Foreign Trade*, 1959, p. v.
66. Pierre BRUNEL, *L'Etat et le Souverain*, 1977, p. 12.
67. The *Dogado* was the name given to the complex of lagoons, islets and estuaries on the north coast of the Adriatic which constituted the approach to Venice. (*Enc. Ital.*, XIII, p. 89).

68. Elena FASANO, *Lo Stato mediceo di Cosimo I*, 1973.
69. Georges LIVET, *L'Équilibre européen de la fin du XVe à la fin du XVIIIe siècle*, 1976.
70. Claude MANCERON, *Les Vingt Ans du roi*, 1972, p. 121.
71. Ragnar NURKSE, *Problems of Capital Formation in Underdeveloped Countries*, 1953, p. 4.
72. P. CHAUNU, *Séville et l'Atlantique*, VIII, 1, 1959, p. 1114.
73. A. EMMANUEL, *op. cit.*, p. 32.
74. David RICARDO, *Principles of Political Economy and Taxation*, Everyman edn., 1955, p. 81.
75. G. TOMASI DI LAMPEDUSA, in *Il Gattopardo* (*The Leopard*), Milan, 1958.
76. Maurice LEVY-LEBOYER, François CROUZET and P. CHAUNU.
77. Until the creation on 24 March 1776 of the *Caisse d'Escompte*.
78. See below, chapter 2.
79. *Op. cit.*, p. 10.
80. I. WALLERSTEIN, *The Modern World System*, part II, chapter 2 (read in typescript).
81. J. GEORGELIN, *Venise au siècle des Lumières*, *op. cit.*, p. 760.
82. *Ibid.*, p. 14 and *passim*.
83. *Medit.*, II, p. 696.
84. Jacques GERNET, *Le Monde chinois*, 1972, p. 429.
85. See below, chapter 5.
86. Quoted by H.R.C. WRIGHT, Proceedings of Leningrad congress, 1970, V, p. 100.
87. W. KIENAST, *Die Anfänge des europäischen Staatensystems im späteren Mittelalter*, 1936.
88. *Geschichte der Kriegskunst . . .*, 1907.
89. I am quoting from memory. The incident is recounted in the papers of Diego Suárez, which used to be in the archives of the Government-General building in Algiers.
90. E. CABRAL DE MELLO, *Olinda restaurada . . .*, *op. cit.*, *passim*.
91. *Ibid.*, p. 246.
92. I have exchanged some correspondence on this subject with Professor CRUZ COSTA of the University of São Paulo.
93. On the introduction of the bayonet, see J.U. NEF, *War and Human Progress*, 1954, pp. 251–4.

94. Quoted by J.U. NEF *War and Human Progress*, p. 156.
95. Pasquale VILLANI, 'La società italiana nei secoli XVI e XVII', in *Ricerche storiche ed economiche in memoria di C. Barbagallo*, 1970, I, p. 255.
96. Philippe Auguste d'ARCQ, *La Noblesse militaire*, 1766, pp. 75–6; my italics.
97. B.G. ZANOBI, in Sergio ANSELMI, *Economia e Società; le Marche tra XV e XX secolo*, 1978, p. 102.
98. Cf. I. WALLERSTEIN, *op. cit.*, p. 87.
99. Federico BRITO FIGUEROA, *Historia económica y social de Venezuela*, I, 1966, *passim*.
100. Sir George STAUNTON, *An authentic account of an Embassy . . . to the Emperor of China . . . from the papers of . . . the Earl of MacCartney*, 1797, page reference to French edn. untraceable in original.
101. Louis-Narcisse BAUDRY DES LOZIÈRES, *Voyage à la Louisiane et sur le continent de l'Amérique septentrionale fait dans les années 1794–1798*, 1802, p. 10.
102. Peter LASLETT, *The World We Have Lost*, 1979 edn., p. 30 ff.
103. *Medit.*, I, p. 468.
104. See above, Volume II, p. 147.
105. *Ibid.*
106. A.d.s. Venice, Senato Zecca, 42, 20 July 1639.
107. Abbé Jean-Bernard LE BLANC, *Lettres d'un François*, 1745, II, p. 42.
108. *Ibid.*, p. 43.
109. *Ibid.*, p. 1.
100. *Ibid.*, III, p. 68.
111. Jacques ACCARIAS DE SERIONNE, *La Richesse de l'Angleterre*, 1771, p. 61.
112. These questions were discussed at the 1978 Prato conference, with contributions from T.C. SMOUT (on Scotland), H. KELLENBENZ and P. BAIROCH.
113. A. DAS GUPTA, art. cit., in *Islam and the Trade of Asia*, ed. D.S. RICHARDS, 1970, p. 206.
114. *Précis de sociologie d'après V. Pareto*, 2nd edn., 1971, p. 172.
115. G. IMBERT, *Des Mouvements de longue durée Kondratieff*, 1959.
116. *Théorie économique du système féodal: pour un modèle de l'économie polonaise*, 1970, p. 48.

117. Cf. the recent discussion of the Kondratieff cycle: W. W. Rostow, 'Kondratieff, Schumpeter and Kuznets: Trend Periods Revisited', in *The Journal of Economic History*, 1975, pp. 719–53.

118. W. Brulez, 'Séville et l'Atlantique: quelques reflexions critiques', in *Revue belge de philologie et d'histoire*, 1964, n° 2, p. 592.

119. P. Chaunu, *Séville et l'Atlantique*, VIII, 1, 1959, p. 30.

120. Dietrich Eberling and Franz Irsigler, *Getreideumsatz, Getreide und Brotpreise in Köhn, 1368–1797*, 1976.

121. F. Braudel and F. Spooner, 'Prices in Europe from 1450 to 1750', in *The Cambridge Economic History of Europe*, IV, 1967, p. 468.

122. P. Chaunu, *op. cit.*, p. 45.

123. *Gazette de France*, p. 489.

124. Pierre Chaunu, *Les Philippines et le Pacifique des Ibériques*, 1960, p. 243, n. 1.

125. L. Dermigny, *La Chine et l'Occident. Le commerce à Canton au XVIIIᵉ siècle, 1719–1833*, I, 1964, p. 101, n. 1.

126. 'En Inde aux XVIᵉ et XVIIᵉ siècles: trésors américains, monnaie d'argent et prix dans l'Empire mogol', in *Annales E.S.C.*, 1969, pp. 835–59.

127. Quoted by Pierre Vilar, Stockholm Congress, 1960, p. 39.

128. Rondo Cameron, 'Economic History, Pure and Applied' in *Journal of Economic History*, March 1976, pp. 3–27.

129. *Il Problema del trend secolare nelle fluttuazioni dei prezzi*, 1935.

130. G. Imbert, *op. cit.*

131. *Ibid.*

132. 'Les implications de l'emballement mondial des prix depuis 1972', in *Recherches économiques de Louvain*, September 1977.

133. In *Annales E.S.C.*, 1961, p. 115.

134. P. Leon, in Stockholm Congress, 1960, p. 167.

135. *La Crise de l'économie française à la fin de l'Ancien Régime et au début de la Révolution*, 1944, pp. viii–ix.

136. *Théorie économique du système féodal...*, *op. cit.*, p. 84.

137. 'Gazettes hollandaises et trésors américains' in *Anuario de historia económica y social*, 1969, p. 333.

138. P. Vilar, *L'Industrialisation en Europe au XIXᵉ siècle*, Colloque de Lyon, 1970, p. 331.

139. Joan Robinson, *Economic Heresies*, 1971, p. 18.

140. P. Beyssade, *La Philosophie première de Descartes*, typescript, p. 111.

141. Earl J. Hamilton, 'American Treasure and the Rise of Capitalism' in *Economica*, November 1929, pp. 355–6.

142. E. H. Phelps Brown, S. V. Hopkins, 'Seven Centuries of Building Wages', in *Economica*, August 1955, pp. 195–206.

143. Charles Seignobos, *Histoire sincère de la nation française*, 1933.

NOTES TO CHAPTER 2

1. The foregoing remarks are based on Paul Adam's typescript, *L'Origine des grandes cités maritimes indépendantes et la nature du premier capitalisme commercial*, p. 13.

2. Paul Grousset, preface to Régine Pernoud, *Les Villes marchandes aux XIVᵉ et XVᵉ siècles*, 1948, p. 18.

3. *Studi di storia economica*, 1955, I, p. 630.

4. 'Income tax' was the term used for the tax levied by Pitt the Younger in 1799.

5. Henri Pirenne, *La Civilisation occidentale au Moyen Age du XIᵉ au milieu du XVᵉ siècle*, in *Histoire générale*, ed., G. Glotz, VIII, 1933, pp. 99–100.

6. *Cours complet d'économie politique pratique*, *op. cit.*, I, p. 234.

7. *Traité de la circulation et du crédit*, *op. cit.*, p. 9.

8. Renée Doehaerd, *Le Haut Moyen Age occidental, économies et sociétés*, 1971, p. 289.

9. P. Adam, *op. cit.*, p. 11.

10. An expression used by Henri Pirenne during a lecture given in Algiers in 1931.

11. 'The Closing of the European Frontier', in *Speculum*, 1958, p. 476.

12. Wilhelm Abel, *Agrarkrisen und Agrarkonjunktur*, 1966, p. 19.

13. Johannès Bühler, *Vida y cultura en la edad media*, 1946, p. 204.
14. B.H. Slicher van Bath, *The Agrarian History of Western Europe, A.D. 500–1850*, 1966, p. 24.
15. Yves Renouard, *Les Villes d'Italie de la fin du Xe au début du XIVe siècle*, 1969, I, p. 15.
16. Karl Bosl, *Die Grundlagen der modernen Gesellschaft in Mittelalter*, 1972, II, p. 290.
17. He has often said this in my hearing. Cf. Armando Sapori, 'Caratteri ed espansione dell'economia comunale italiana', in *Congresso storico internazionale per l'VIII° centenario della prima Lega Lombarda*, Bergamo, 1967, pp. 125–36.
18. 'What accelerated technological progress in the Western Middle Ages?', in *Scientific Change*, ed. Crombie, 1963, p. 277.
19. 'Les bases monétaires d'une suprématie économique: l'or musulman du VIIe au XIe siècle', in *Annales E.S.C.*, 1947, p. 158.
20. *L'Économie rurale et la vie des campagnes dans l'Occident médiéval*, 1962, I, p. 255.
21. *La Nascità dell'Europa, sec. X–XIV*, 1966, pp. 121 ff.
22. 'La civiltà economica nelle sue esplicazioni dalla Versilia alla Maremma secoli X–XVII', in *Atti del 60° Congresso Internazionale della 'Dante Alighieri'*, p. 21.
23. *Wirtschaftsgeschichte Deutschlands von 16. bis 18. Jahrhundert*, 1951, I, p. 327.
24. *Mittelalterliche Weltwirtschaft . . .*, 1933, p. 22.
25. Similar remarks on the influence of Frankfurt-am-Main can be found in Hans Mauersberg, *Wirtschafts- und Sozialgeschichte zentraleuropäischer Städte in neuerer Zeit*, 1960, pp. 238–9.
26. H. Pirenne in *Histoire générale*, ed. G. Glotz, VIII, *op. cit.*, p. 144.
27. *Ibid.*, p. 11.
28. *Ibid.*, p. 90. Henri Laurent, *Un Grand Commerce d'exportation. La draperie des Pays-Bas en France et dans les pays méditerranéens, XIIe–XVe siècles*, 1935, pp. 37–9.
29. H. Pirenne, *op. cit.*, p. 128.
30. They did so eventually on 30 January 1598, by order of Queen Elizabeth; the text is given in Philippe Dollinger, *La Hanse (XIIe–XVIIe siècles)*, 1964, pp. 485–6.
31. Tibor Wittman, *Les Gueux dans les 'bonnes villes' de Flandre (1577–1584)*, 1969, p. 23; Hippolyte Fierens-Gevaert, *Psychologie d'une ville, essai sur Bruges*, 1901, p. 105; E. Lukca, *Die Grosse Zeit der Niederlande*, 1937, p. 37.
32. Datini Archives, Prato, 26 April 1399.
33. H. Pirenne, *op. cit.*, p. 127.
34. J.A. van Houtte, 'Bruges et Anvers, marchés "nationaux" ou "internationaux" du XIVe au XVIe siècle', in *Revue du Nord*, 1952, pp. 89–108.
35. *Brügges Entwicklung zum mittelalterlichen Weltmarkt*, 1908, p. 253.
36. *Op. cit.*, p. 16.
37. On the whole of this paragraph see P. Dollinger, *op. cit.*
38. H. Pirenne, *op. cit.*, pp. 26–7.
39. P. Dollinger, *op. cit.*, p. 42.
40. Witold Hensel, Aleksander Gieysztor, *Les Recherches archéologiques en Pologne*, 1958, pp. 54 ff.
41. P. Dollinger, *op. cit.*, p. 21.
42. Renée Doehaerd, 'A propos du mot "Hanse"', in *Revue du Nord*, January 1951, p. 19.
43. P. Dollinger, *op. cit.*, p. 10.
44. *Medit.*, I, p. 140.
45. P. Dollinger, *op. cit.*, p. 177.
46. *Ibid.*, p. 54.
47. See above, Volume II, p. 359.
48. P. Dollinger, *op. cit.*, p. 39.
49. *Ibid.*, p. 148.
50. *Ibid.*, p. 39.
51. *Ibid.*, p. 59.
52. *Ibid.*, p. 86.
53. Henry Samsonowicz, 'Les liens culturels entre les bourgeois du littoral baltique dans le bas Moyen Age', in *Studia maritima*, I, pp. 10–11.
54. *Ibid.*, p. 12.
55. *Ibid.*
56. *Ibid.*
57. P. Dollinger, *op. cit.*, p. 266.
58. *Ibid.*, p. 55.
59. *Ibid.*, p. 130.

60. *Ibid.*, p. 95.
61. *Ibid.*, pp. 100-101.
62. Marian MALOWIST, *Croissance et regression en Europe, XIVᵉ-XVIIᵉ siècles,* 1972, pp. 93, 98.
63. P. DOLLINGER, *op. cit.*, p. 360.
64. M. MALOWIST, *op. cit.*, p. 133.
65. *Ibid.*, p. 105.
66. Eli F. HECKSCHER, *Mercantilism*, Eng. trans., 1955, I, p. 329.
67. *Histoire des prix et des salaires dans l'Orient médiéval,* 1969, p. 237.
68. Robert-Henri BAUTIER, 'La marine d'Amalfi dans le trafic méditerranéen du XIVᵉ siècle, à propos du transport du sel de Sardaigne' in *Bulletin philologique et historique du Comité des Travaux historiques et scientifiques,* 1959, p. 183.
69. M. del TREPPO, A. LEONE, *Amalfi medioevale,* 1977. This book challenges the traditional history of Amalfi which concentrates exclusively on trade.
70. M. LOMBARD, *art. cit.*, in *Annales E.S.C.,* 1947, pp. 154 ff.
71. Armando CITARELLA, 'Patterns in Medieval Trade: The Commerce of Amalfi before the Crusades', in *Journal of Economic History,* December 1968, p. 533 and n. 6.
72. R.-H. BAUTIER, *art. cit.*, p. 184.
73. R.S. LOPEZ, *op. cit.*, p. 94.
74. Y. RENOUARD, *op. cit.*, p. 25, n. 1.
75. Elena C. SKRZINSKAJA, 'Storia della Tana' in *Studi veneziani,* X, 1968, p. 7. *'In mari constituta, caret totaliter vineis atque campis'.*
76. M. CANARD, 'La Guerre sainte dans le monde islamique', *Actes du IIᵉ Congrès des sociétés savantes d'Afrique du Nord,* Tlemcen, 1936, in II, pp. 605-23.
77. The chrysobull of Alexius Comnenus in May 1082 exempted the Venetians from all payment (H. PIRENNE, *op. cit.*, p. 23).
78. Giuseppe TASSINI, *Curiosità veneziane,* 1887, p. 424.
79. Gino LUZZATTO, *Studi di storia economica veneziana,* 1954, p. 98.
80. Benjamin DAVID, 'The Jewish Mercantile Settlement of the 12th and 13th century in Venice: Reality or Conjecture?', in *A.J.S. Review,* 1977, pp. 201-25.
81. Wolfgang von STROMER, 'Bernardus Tauronicus und die Geschäftsbeziehungen zwischen der deutschen Ostalpen und Venedig vor Grundung des Fondaco dei Tedeschi', in *Grazer Forschungen zur Wirtschafts- und Sozialgeschichte,* III.
82. G. LUZZATO, *op. cit.*, p. 10.
83. *Ibid.*, pp. 37-8.
84. Giorgio GRACCO, *Società e stato nel medioevo veneziano (secoli XII-XIV),* 1967.
85. Heinrich KRETSCHMAYR, *Geschichte von Venedig,* 1964, I, p. 257.
86. W. HEYD, *Histoire du commerce du Levant au Moyen Age,* 1936, p. 173.
87. Not as terrible as all that, according to Donald E. QUELLER Gerald W. DORY, 'Some Arguments in Defense of the Venetians on the Fourth Crusade', in *The American Historical Review,* n° 4, October 1976, pp. 717-37.
88. R.S. LOPEZ, *op. cit.*, pp. 154 ff.
89. Jacques MAS-LATRIE, *Histoire de l'Ile de Chypre sous le règne des princes de la maison de Lusignan,* 1861, I, p. 511.
90. On this point, see above, Volume II, p. 200.
91. Richard HENNIG, *Terrae incognitae,* 1950-1956, III, p. 109 ff.
92. A view rejected by F. BORLANDI , 'Alle origini del libro di Marco Polo', in *Studi in onore di Amintore Fanfani,* 1962, I, p. 135.
93. Elizabeth CHAPIN, *Les Villes de foires de Champagne des origines au début du XIVᵉ siècle,* 1937, p. 107, n. 9.
94. Henri PIRENNE, *op. cit.*, I, p. 295.
95. H. LAURENT, *op. cit.*, I, p. 39.
96. Robert-Henri BAUTIER, 'Les foires de Champagne', in *Recueil Jean Bodin,* V, 1953, p. 12.
97. H. PIRENNE, *op. cit.*, p. 89.
98. Félix BOURQUELOT, *Étude sur les foires de Champagne,* 1865, I, p. 80.
99. Hektor AMMANN, 'Die Anfänge des Activhandels und der Tucheinfuhr aus Nordwesteuropa nach dem Mittelmeergebiet', in *Studi in onore di Armando Sapori,* p. 275.
100. The derivation of this name is unknown - it *may* have been the name of the street in Florence where the *Arte de Calimala* had its warehouses (*Dizionario enciclopedico italiano*).
101. *Medit.*, I, p. 317.

102. *Ibid.*
103. H. LAURENT, *op. cit.*, p. 80.
104. Henri PIGEONNEAU, *Histoire du commerce de la France*, I, 1885, pp. 222-3.
105. *Ibid.*
106. Mario CHIAUDANO, 'I Rothschild del Duecento: la Gran Tavola di Orlando Bonsignori' in *Bulletino senese di storia patria*, VI, 1935.
107. R.-H. BAUTIER, *op. cit.*, p. 47.
108. F. BOURQUELOT, *op. cit.*, I, p. 66.
109. H. LAURENT, *op. cit.*, p. 38.
110. *Ibid.*, pp. 117-18.
111. R.-H. BAUTIER, *op. cit.*, pp. 45-6.
112. Vital CHOMEL, Jean EBERSOLT, *Cinq Siècles de circulation internationale vue de Jougne*, 1951, p. 42.
113. See below, section on Venice.
114. Wolfgang von STROMER, 'Banken und Geldmarkt: die Funktion der Wechsel-stuben in Oberdeutschland und den Rheinlanden', paper given to the *Settimana di Prato*, 18 April 1972, 4th week, F. Datini.
115. Augusto GUZZO, Introduction to the *Secondo Colloquio sull'età dell' Umanesimo e del Rinascimento in Francia*, 1970.
116. Giuseppe TOFFANIN, *Il Secolo senza Roma*, Bologna, 1943.
117. Guy FOURQUIN, *Les Campagnes de la région parisienne à la fin du Moyen Age*, 1964, pp. 161-2.
118. But NB the attempt by Philippe IV de Valois to renew the privileges of the Champagne fairs in 1344-9. Cf. M. de LAURIÈRE, *Ordonnances des rois de France*, 1729, II, pp. 200, 234, 305.
119. *Banca e moneta dalle Crociate alla Rivoluzione francese*, 1949, p. 62.
120. *Ibid.*
121. Raymond de ROOVER, 'Le rôle des Italiens dans la formation de la banque moderne' in *Revue de la banque*, 1952, p. 12.
122. See above, Volume II, p. 124.
123. Carlo CIPOLLA, *Money, Prices and Civilization*, 1956, pp. 33-4.
124. H. KRETSCHMAYR, *op. cit.*, II, p. 234.
125. *Ibid.*, pp. 234-6.
126. *Ibid.*, p. 239.
127. *The Foundations of Capitalism*, 1959, pp. 29 ff.
128. Hannelore GRONEUER, 'Die Seeversicherung in Genua am Ausgang des 14. Jahrhunderts' in *Beiträge zur Wirtschafts- und Sozialgeschichte des Mittelalters*, 1976, pp. 218-60.
129. H. KRETSCHMAYR, *op. cit.*, II, p. 300.
130. Christian BEC, *Les Marchands écrivains à Florence 1375-1434*, 1968, p. 312.
131. *Medit.*, I, p. 339.
132. *Ibid.*
133. *Bilanci generali*, 1912 (ed. Reale commissione per la pubblicazione dei documenti finanziari delle Repubblica di Venezia, 2nd series).
134. See below, chapter 4.
135. *Bilanci generali*, 2nd series, I, 1, Venice, 1912.
136. *Ibid.*, Documenti n° 81, pp. 94-7. Text printed in H. KRETSCHMAYR, *op. cit.*, II, pp. 617-19.
137. *Medit.*, I, p. 498.
138. It is *normally* agreed that the ratio between the annual coinage issued by the mint and the amount of money in circulation was 1 to 20.
139. Pierre-Antoine, Comte DARU, *Histoire de la République de Venise*, 1819, IV, p. 78.
140. Oliver C. COX, *The Foundations of Capitalism*, 1959, p. 69 and n. 18 (following MOLMENTI).
141. See below, this chapter.
142. A.d.S. Venice, Notario del Collegio, 9, f° 26 v°, n° 81, 12 August 1445.
143. *Ibid.*, 14, f° 38 v°, 8 July 1491; Senato Terra, 12, f° 41, 7 February 1494.
144. *Medit.*, II, pp. 894-5.
145. Ad.S. Venice, Senato Terra, 4, f° 107 v°.
146. P. MOLMENTI, *La Storia di Venezia nella vita privata . . .*, 1880, I, pp. 124, 131-2.
147. Piero PIERI, 'Milizie e capitani di ventura in Italia del Medio Evo', in *Atti della Reale Accademia Peloritana*, XL, 1937-8, p. 12.
148. H. KRETSCHMAYR, *op. cit.*, II, p. 386.
149. Girolamo PRIULI, *Diarii*, ed. A. Segre, 1921, I, p. 19.
150. Federico CHABOD, 'Venezia nella politica italiana ed europea del Cinquecento', in *La Civiltà veneziana del Rinascimento*, 1958, p. 29. On the arrival of the ambassadors from Spain and from 'king' Maximilian, Archivio Gonzaga, series E, Venezia 1435, Venice, 2 January 1495.

151. H. HAUSHERR, *op. cit.*, p. 28.
152. *Bilanci*, I, pp. 38-9. Not in 1318, as William McNEILL writes in *Venice, the Hinge of Europe 1081-1797*, 1974, p. 66, but before 1228, cf. *Bilanci* ..., I, pp. 38-9, on the site of the *Fondaco dei Tedeschi*: '*qui tenant fonticum Venetie ubi Teutonici hospitantur*'.
153. J. SCHNEIDER, 'Les villes allemandes au Moyen Age. Les institutions économiques', in *Recueil de la Société Jean Bodin*, VII, *La Ville, institutions économiques et sociales*, 1955, part 2, p. 423.
154. Antonio H. DE OLIVEIRA MARQUES, 'Notas para a historia de Feitoria portuguesa da Flandes no seculo XV', in *Studi in onore di Amintore Fanfani*, 1962, II, pp. 370-476, esp. p. 446. Anselmo BRAACAMP FREIRE, 'A Feitoria da Flandes', in *Archivio historico portuguez*, VI, 1908-1910, p. 322 ff.
155. *Medit.*, I, p. 471.
156. G. LUZZATTO, *op. cit.*, p. 149.
157. *Medit.*, I, p. 302.
158. Alberto TENENTI, Corrado VIVANTI, 'Le film d'un grand système de navigation: les galères marchandes vénitiennes, XIVᵉ-XVIᵉ siècles', in *Annales E.S.C.*, 1961, p. 85.
159. *Op. cit.*, pp. 62 ff.
160. Federigo MELIS, *La Moneta*, typescript, p. 8.
161. Federigo MELIS, 'Origenes de la Banca Moderna', in *Moneda y Credito*, March 1971, pp. 10-11.
162. Federigo MELIS, *Storia della ragioneria, contributo alla conoscenza e interpretazione delle fonti più significative della storia economica*, 1950, pp. 481 ff.
163. Federico MELIS, *Sulle fonti della storia economica*, 1963, p. 152.
164. See above, Volume II, pp. 289 ff.
165. R. HENNIG, *op. cit.*, III, pp. 119 ff and IV, p. 126.
166. G. TASSINI, *op. cit.*, p. 55.
167. E. LATTES, *La Libertà delle banche a Venezia*, 1869, chapter 2.
168. Gino LUZZATTO, *Storia economica di Venezia, dal XIᵉ al XVIᵉ s.*, 1961, p. 101.
169. G LUZZATTO, *op. cit.*, p. 212.
170. G. LUZZATTO, *op. cit.*, p. 78.
171. G. LUZZATTO, *Studi ...*, *op. cit.*, pp. 135-6.
172. *Ibid.*, p. 130.
173. Reinhold C. MUELLER, 'Les prêteurs juifs à Venise', in *Annales E.S.C.*, 1975, p. 1277.
174. G. LUZZATTO, *Studi ...*, *op. cit.*, p. 104.
175. *Ibid.*, p. 104.
176. *Ibid.*, p. 106, n. 67.
177. 'Le rôle du capital dans la vie locale et la commerce extérieur de Venise entre 1050 et 1150', in *Revue belge de philologie et d'histoire*, XIII, 1934, pp. 657-96.
178. 'Aux origines du capitalisme vénitien', review of the preceding article in *Annales E.S.C.*, 1935, p. 96.
179. R. MOROZZO DELLA ROCCA, A. LOMBARDO, *I Documenti del commercio veneziano nei secoli XI-XIII*, 1940, quoted by G. LUZZATTO, *Studi ...*, p. 91, n. 9.
180. G. LUZZATTO, *Storia economica ...*, *op. cit.*, p. 82.
181. *Ibid.*, pp. 79-80.
182. Raymond de ROOVER, 'Le marché monétaire au Moyen Age et au début des temps modernes', in *Revue historique*, July-Sept., 1970, pp. 7 ff.
183. *Medit.*, I, p. 378.
184. *Ibid.*
185. F. MELIS, *La Moneta*, *op. cit.*, p. 8.
186. Frederic C. LANE, *Venice, a maritime republic*, 1973, p. 166.
187. *Ibid.*, p. 104.
188. *Industry and Economic Decline in 17th Century Venice*, 1976, pp. 24 ff.
189. A.d.S. Venice, Senato Terra, 4, fᵒ 71, 18 April 1458.
190. Domenico SELLA, 'Les mouvements longs de l'industrie lainière à Venise aux XVIᵉ et XVIIᵉ siècles', in *Annales E.S.C.*, Jan.-March 1957, p. 41.
191. Brian PULLAN, *Rich and Poor in Renaissance Venice*, 1971, pp. 33 ff; Ruggiero MASCHIO, 'Investimenti edilizi delle scuole grandi a Venezia (XVI-XVII sec.); paper given to Prato conference in April 1977.
192. A.d.S. Venice, Senato Mar, II, fᵒ 126, 21 February 1446.
193. D. SELLA, *art. cit.*, pp. 40-1.
194. Ömer Lutfi BARKAN, 'Essai sur les données

statistiques des régistres de recensement dans l'Empire ottoman aux XVᵉ et XVIᵉ siècles', in *Journal of economic and social history of the Orient*, August 1957, pp. 27 and 34.

195. A Senate decision of 18 February 1453 declares unequivocally the need '*ob reverentiam Dei, bonum christianorum honorem, nostri dominii et pro commodo et utilitate mercatorum et civium nostrorum*', to go to the aid of Constantinople, a city of which it could be said that 'it is considered to be a part of our State and should not fall into the hands of infidels', '*civitas Constantinopolis que dici et reputari potest esse nostri dominii, non deveniat ad manos infidelium*', A.d.S., Venice, Senato Mar, 4, 170.

196. A.d.S. Venice, Senato Secreta, 20, fᵒ 3, 15 January 1454.

197. H. KRETSCHMAYR, *op. cit.*, II, pp. 371 ff.

198. Damião PEREZ, *Historia de Portugal*, 1926-1933, 8 vols.

199. Ralph DAVIS, *The Rise of the Atlantic Economies*, 2nd ed., 1975, p. 1.

200. See in particular the works of Vitorino MAGALHAĒS-GODINHO.

201. R. DAVIS, *op. cit.*, p. 4.

202. Gonzalo de REPARAZ , *La Epoca de los grandes descubrimientos españoles y portugueses*, 1931.

203. Prospero PERAGALLO, *Cenni intorno alla colonia italiana in Portogallo nei secoli XIVᵉ, XVᵉ, XVIᵉ*, 2nd edn., 1907.

204. Virginia RAU, 'A family of Italian merchants in Portugal in the XVth century: the Lomellini', in *Studi in onore di A. Sapori, op. cit.*, pp. 717-726.

205. Robert RICARD, 'Contribution à l'étude du commerce génois au Maroc durant la période portugaise, 1415-1550' in *Annales de l'Inst. d'Etudes orientales*, III, 1937.

206. Duarte PACHECO PEREIRA, *Esmeraldo de situ orbis* . . ., 1892, quoted by R. DAVIS, *op. cit.*, p. 8.

207. *Op. cit.*, p. 11.

208. V. MAGALHAĒS-GODINHO, 'Le repli vénitien et égyptien et la route du Cap, 1496-1533'. in *Éventail de l'histoire vivante*, 1953, II, p. 293.

209. Richard EHRENBERG, *Das Zeitalter der Fugger*, 1922, 2 vols.

210. Hermann VAN DER WEE, *The Growth of the Antwerp Market and the European Economy (14th-16th Centuries)*, 1963, II, p. 127.

211. Henri PIRENNE, *Histoire de Belgique*, 1973, II, p. 58.

212. G.D. RAMSAY, *The City of London*, 1975, p. 12.

213. Émile COORNAERT, 'Anvers a-t-elle eu une flotte marchande?', in *Le Navire et l'économie maritime*, ed. Michel MOLLAT, 1960, pp. 72 ff.

214. *Ibid.*, pp. 71 and 79.

215. G.D. RAMSAY, *op. cit.*, p. 13.

216. H. PIRENNE, *op. cit.*, II, p. 57.

217. G.D. RAMSAY, *op. cit.*, p. 18.

218. Lodovico GUICCIARDINI, *Description de tous les Pays-Bas*, 1568, p. 122.

219. H. VAN DER WEE, *op. cit.*, II, p. 203.

220. E. COORNAERT, 'La genèse du système capitaliste: grand capitalisme et économie traditionelle à Anvers au XVIᵉ siècle', in *Annales d'histoire économique et sociale*, 1936, p. 129.

221. O.C. COX, *op. cit.*, p. 266.

222. Hermann VAN DER WEE, *op. cit.*, 3 vols.

223. *Ibid.*, II, p. 128.

224. *Ibid.*, II, p. 120.

225. J. VAN HOUTTE, *op. cit.*, p. 82.

226. Renée DOEHAERD, *Etudes anversoises*, 1963, I, pp. 37 ff, 62-3.

227. Anselmo BRAACAMP FREIRE, *art. cit.*, pp. 322 ff.

228. H. VAN DER WEE, *op. cit.*, I, Appendix 44/1.

229. *Ibid.*, II, p. 125.

230. *Ibid.*, II, pp. 130-1.

231. *Ibid.*, II, p. 131.

232. *Ibid.*, II, p. 129.

233. *Ibid.*

234. Anselmo BRAACAMP FREIRE, *art. cit.*, p. 407.

235. V. MAGALHAĒS-GODINHO, *L'Economie de l'Empire portugais aux XVᵉ et XVIᵉ siècles*, 1969, p. 471.

236. John U. NEF, 'Silver production in central Europe, 1450-1618', in *The Journal of Political Economy*, 1941, p. 586.

237. *Medit.*, I, p. 545.

238. Richard GASCON, *Grand Commerce et vie urbaine au XVIᵉ siècle, Lyon et ses marchands*, 1971, p. 88.

239. H. VAN DER WEE, *op. cit.*, II, p. 156.
240. Earl J. HAMILTON, 'Monetary inflation in Castile, 1598-1660', in *Economic History*, 6, January 1931, p. 180.
241. 1529, the Paix des Dames; 1535, the occupation of Milan by Charles V.
242. Fernand BRAUDEL, 'Les emprunts de Charles Quint sur la place d'Anvers', in Colloques Internationaux du C.N.R.S., *Charles Quint et son temps*, Paris, 1958, p. 196.
243. H. VAN DER WEE, *op. cit.*, II, p. 178, n. 191.
244. Pierre CHAUNU, *Séville et l'Atlantique*, VI, pp. 114-5.
245. See below, chapter 3.
246. J. VAN HOUTTE, *op. cit.*, p. 91.
247. *Medit.*, I, p. 480.
248. H. VAN DER WEE, *op. cit.*, II, p. 179.
249. Hugo SOLY, *Urbanisme en Kapitalisme te Antwerpen in de 15. de Eeuw*, summary in French, p. 457 ff.
250. T. WITTMAN, *op. cit.*, p. 30.
251. P. DOLLINGER, *op. cit.*, pp. 417-18; cf. the illustration on p. 106.
252. H. VAN DER WEE, *op. cit.*, II, pp. 228-9.
253. *Ibid.*, p. 238.
254. *Ibid.*, II, p. 186.
255. Charles VERLINDEN, Jan CRAEYBECKX, E. SCHOLLIERS, 'Mouvements des prix et des salaires en Belgique au XVIe siècle', in *Annales E.S.C.*, 1955, pp. 184-5.
256. John LOTHROP MOTLEY, *La Revolution des Pays Bas au XVIe siècle*, II, p. 196.
257. *Ibid.*, III, p. 14.
258. *Ibid.*, III, ch. 1.
259. *Medit.*, I, p. 482 and n. 122. For an up-to-date discussion of the question, see William D. PHILLIPS and Carla R. PHILLIPS, 'Spanish wool and Dutch rebels: the Middelburg incident of 1574', in *American Historical Review*, April 1977, pp. 312-30.
260. H. VAN DER WEE, 'Anvers et les innovations de la technique financière aux XVIe et XVIIe siècles', in *Annales E.S.C.*, 1967, p. 1073, and *The Growth of the Antwerp Market . . .*, II.
261. H. VAN DER WEE, in *art. cit. Annales E.S.C.*, 1967, p. 1071.
262. *Ibid*, p. 1073, n. 5.
263. *Ibid.*, p. 1076.
264. Raymond de ROOVER, *L'Evolution de la lettre de change, XVIe-XVIIIe siècles*, 1953, p. 119.
265. *Les Gueux dans les 'bonnes villes' de Flandre, 1577-1584*, Budapest, 1969.
266. B.N., Ms. Fr. 14666, f° 11 v°. Report of 1692.
267. Giovanni BOTERO, *Relationi universali*, 1599, p. 68.
268. *Ibid.*
269. Comtesse de BOIGNE, *Mémoires*, 1971, I, p. 305.
270. Jacques HEERS, *Gênes au XVe siècle*, 1961, p. 532.
271. Jérôme de LA LANDE, *Voyage d'un Français en Italie*, 1769, VIII, pp. 492-3.
272. The unpublished *Voyage* by the Comte d'ESPINCHAL, 1789, Clermont-Ferrand Library.
273. *Ibid.*
274. *Ibid.*
275. Vito VITALE, *Breviario della storia di Genova*, 1955, I, p. 148.
276. *Ibid.*, p. 163.
277. *Medit.*, I, p. 390.
278. V. VITALE, *op. cit.*, I, p. 346.
279. *Ibid.*, p. 349.
280. *Ibid.*, p. 421.
281. Hannelore GRONEUER, *art. cit.*, pp. 218-260.
282. *Ibid.*
283. A.N., K 1355, 21 May 1684.
284. A.N., A.E., B¹ 529, 12 April, 1710.
285. B.N., Ms. Fr., 16073, f° 371.
286. Giuseppe FELLONI, *Gli Investimenti finanziari genovesi in Europa tra il Seicento e la Restaurazione*, 1971, p. 345.
287. Fernand BRAUDEL, 'Endet das "Jahrhundert der Genuesen" im Jahre 1627?', in Festschrift for Wilhelm Abel, p. 455.
288. Roberto S. LOPEZ, *Studi sull'economia genovese nel Medio Evo*, 1936, pp. 142 ff.
289. Roberto S. LOPEZ, frequently referred to this in conversation, and in one of his unpublished lectures.
290. *Medit.*, I, pp. 342-3.
291. As Camelo TRASSELLI has often argued in his lectures.
292. Cf. the text and references in V. VITALE, *op. cit.* (see note 275 above).
293. R.S. LOPEZ, *Genova marinara del Duecento: Benedetto Zaccaria, ammiraglio e mercante*, 1933, p. 154.

294. Carmelo TRASSELLI, 'Genovesi in Sicilia' in *Atti della Società ligure di storia patria*, IX (LXXXIII), fasc. II, p. 158.
295. *Ibid.*, pp. 155-78.
296. *Ibid.*, and *viva voce*.
297. *Ibid.*
298. Carmelo TRASSELLI, 'Sumario duma historia do açucar siciliano', in *Do Tempo e da Historia*, II, 1968, pp. 65-9.
299. See above, Volume II, pp. 420-1.
300. Gerónimo UZTARIZ, *Théorie et pratique du commerce et de la marine*, 1753, p. 52.
301. Renée DOEHAERD, *Les Relations commerciales entre Gênes, la Belgique et l'outremont*, 1941, I, p. 89.
302. R. RICARD, *art. cit.* (see note 205).
303. Ramon CARANDE, 'Sevilla fortaleza y mercado', in *Anuario de historia del derecho español*, II, 1925, pp. 33, 55 ff.
304. Virgina RAU, 'A family of Italian merchants in Portugal in the XVth century: the Lomellini', in *Studi in onore di Armando Sapori*, pp. 717-726.
305. André -E. SAYOUS, 'Le rôle des Génois lors des premiers mouvements réguliers d'affaires entre l'Espagne et le Nouveau Monde', in *C.r. de l'Académie des Inscriptions et Belles-Lettres*, 1930.
306. Felipe RUIZ MARTÍN, *Lettres marchandes* ..., p. xxix.
307. *Ibid.*
308. *Medit.*, I, p. 339.
309. F. BRAUDEL, 'Les emprunts de Charles Quint sur la place d'Anvers', *art. cit.*, p. 192.
310. R. CARANDE, *art. cit.*
311. Henri LAPEYRE, *Simón Ruiz et les asientos de Philippe II*, 1953, pp. 14 ff.
312. *Medit.*, I, 343-4.
313. Felipe RUIZ MARTÍN, *Lettres marchandes* ...., p. xxxviii.
314. Giorgio DORIA, 'Un quadriennio critico: 1575-1578. Contrasti e nuovi orientamenti nella società genovese nel quadro della crisi finanziaria espagnola', in *Mélanges Franco Borlandi*, 1977, p. 382.
315. Giorgio DORIA, paper given at Madrid Conference, 1977.
316. *The International Economy and Monetary Movements in France*, 1972, pp. 23 ff.
317. Felipe RUIZ MARTÍN, *Lettres marchandes* ..., p. xliv.
318. *Ibid.*, p. xxxii.
319. *Ibid.*, pp. xxx-xxxi.
320. *Medit.*, I, p. 503.
321. This ordinance created the *escudo*, or gold crown which replaced the *excellente* of Granada. Cf. *Medit.*, I, p. 472 and note 66.
322. Henri PIRENNE, *Histoire de Belgique*, IV, 1927, p. 78.
323. *Medit.*, I, pp. 504 ff.
324. *Ibid.*, I, pp. 510-11. F. RUIZ MARTÍN. *El Siglo de los Genoveses*, unpublished.
325. Fernand BRAUDEL, 'La vita economica di Venezia nel secolo XVI', in *La Civiltà veneziana del Rinascimento*, p. 101.
326. *Ibid.*
327. *Medit.*, I, p. 322 and n. 232, and p. 503, n. 275.
328. See above, chapter 1, n. 48.
329. F. BRAUDEL, *art. cit.*, 'Endet das "Jahrhundert" ...', pp. 455-68.
330. A.E. FEAVEARYEAR, *The Pound Sterling*, 1931, pp. 90-1.
331. A.E., M et D, Hollande, 122, f° 248 (report from Aitzema, 1647).
332. José GENTIL DA SILVA, *Banque et crédit en Italie au XVIIᵉ siècle*, 1969, I, p. 171.
333. F. BRAUDEL, *art. cit.*, 'Endet das "Jahrhundert" ...', p. 461.
334. Michel MORINEAU, 'Gazettes hollandaises et trésors américains', in *Anuario de Historia economica y social*, 1969, pp. 289-361.
335. J. DE LA LANDE, *Voyage en Italie, op. cit.*, IX, p. 362.
336. *Ibid.*, IX, p. 367.
337. *Gli Investimenti finanziari genovesi in Europa tra il Seicento e la Restaurazione*, 1971.
338. *Ibid.*, p. 472.
339. *Ibid.*, p. 168, note 30.
340. *Ibid.*, p. 249.
341. *Ibid.*, pp. 392, 429, 453.
342. B.N., Ms Fr. 14671, f° 17, 6 March 1743.
343. G. FELLONI, *op. cit.*, p. 477.
344. Since Genoa allowed Protestant merchants to settle in the city, so presumably could handle their competition.
345. Carmelo TRASSELLI.
346. José GENTIL DA SILVA, *op. cit.*, pp. 55-6.

NOTES TO CHAPTER 3

1. Throughout this chapter, the term Holland is frequently used, following the rather unsatisfactory usage of the present day, to refer to the whole of the United Provinces.
2. Violet BARBOUR, *Capitalism in Amsterdam in the Seventeenth Century*, 1963, p. 13.
3. See above, Chapter 2.
4. Richard TILDEN RAPP, 'The Unmaking of the Mediterranean Trade . . .' in *Journal of Economic History*, September 1975.
5. G. de USTARIZ, *op. cit.*, p. 97. The area of the United Provinces, it might be useful to recall, was of the order of 34,000 km².
6. *Oeuvres complètes*, I, p. 455. Turgot had translated into French the work of the English economist Josiah Tucker, (1712–1799) *A Brief Essay on the advantages and disadvantages which respectively attend France and Great Britain with regard to trade.*
7. A.N., K 1349, 132, f° 20.
8. *The Complete English Tradesman . . .*, 1745, II, p. 260. Defoe tells us that he has this on good authority but does not say whose.
9. A.N., Marine, B⁷, 463, f° 30.
10. G. de USTARIZ, *op. cit.*, p. 98.
11. Jean-Baptiste d'ARGENS, *Lettres juives*, 1738, III, p. 192.
12. Jacques ACCARIAS DE SERIONNE, *Les Interêts des nations de l'Europe développés relativement au commerce*, 1766, I, p. 44.
13. Jean-Nicolas de PARIVAL, *Les Délices de la Hollande*, 1662, p. 10.
14. A.E., M. et D. 72, Hollande, November 1755.
17. L. GUICCIARDINI, *op. cit.*, p. 288.
16. GAUDARD DE CHAVANNES, *Voyage de Genève à Londres*, 1760, unpaged.
17. *Viaje fuera de España*, 1947, p. 1852.
18. C. R. BOXER, *The Dutch Seaborne Empire*, 1969, p. 7.
19. J.-N. de PARIVAL, *op. cit.*, p. 76.
20. *Ibid.*, p. 56.
21. *Ibid.*, p. 82.
22. *Ibid.*, p. 13.
23. *Ibid.*, p. 26.
24. *Ibid.*, p. 12.
25. 'The Role of the Rural Sector in the Development of the Dutch Economy, 1500-1700', *Journal of Economic History*, March 1971, p. 267.
26. Jean-Claude FLACHAT, *Observations sur le commerce et sur les arts d'une partie de l'Europe, de l'Asie, de l'Afrique et des Indes orientales*, 1766, II, p. 351.
27. Charles WILSON, *England's Apprenticeship 1603-1763*, 1965, 3rd ed. 1967, p. 71; Immanuel WALLERSTEIN, *The Modern World System*, II, ch. 11.
28. Barry SUPPLE, *Commercial Crisis and Change in England 1600-1642*, 1959, p. 34.
29. Jean-Claude BOYER, 'Le capitalisme hollandais et l'organisation de l'espace dans les Provinces-Unies', *Colloque franco-hollandaise,* typescript, esp. p. 4.
30. J.-N. de PARIVAL, *op. cit.*, p. 83.
31. Jan de VRIES, 'An Inquiry into the Behavior of wages in the Dutch Republic and the Southern Netherlands, 1500-1800', typescript, p. 13.
32. Pieter de LA COURT, *Mémoires de Jean de Witt*, 1709, pp. 43-4. (English trans., attrib. to John de Witt, *The True Interest and Political Maxims of the Republic of Holland and West Friesland*, 1702.)
33. *Op. cit.*, p. 216.
34. Abbé SCAGLIA, in Hubert G.R. READE, *Sidelights on the Thirty Years' War*, London, 1924, III, p. 34, quoted by John U. NEF, *War and Human Progress*, 1950, p. 14.
35. Ivo SCHÖFFER, 'Did Holland's Golden Age co-incide with a Period of Crisis?', *in: Acta historiae neerlandica*, 1966, p. 92.
36. *Journal de Verdun*, November 1751, p. 391.
37. A.N., K 879, 123 and 123 *bis*, n° 18, f° 39.
38. J.L. PRICE, *The Dutch Republic during the 17th Century*, 1974, pp. 58 ff.
39. P. de LA COURT, *op. cit.*, p. 28.
40. J.-N. de PARIVAL, *op. cit.*, p. 104.
41. Johann BECKMANN, *Beiträge zur Œkonomie . . . 1779-1784*, II, p. 549.
42. *Op. cit.*, p. 37.

43. A.N., A.E., B¹ 619, 6 March 1670.
44. J. SAVARY, *op. cit.*, I, p. 84.
45. J.-B. d'ARGENS, *op. cit.*, III, p. 194.
46. *Le Guide d'Amsterdam*, 1701, pp. 2 and 81.
47. *Ibid.*, pp. 82-3.
48. *Gazette d'Amsterdam*, 1669, 14, 21, 28 February and 18 June.
49. *Le Guide d'Amsterdam*, *op. cit.*, p. 1.
50. J. ACCARIAS DE SÉRIONNE, *op. cit.*, I, p. 173.
51. J.L. PRICE, *op. cit.*, p. 33.
52. J.-N. de PARIVAL, *op. cit.*, p. 41.
53. W. TEMPLE, *Observations upon the Provinces of the United Netherlands*, 1720, p. 59 (Cambridge edn., 1932, p. 126).
54. *Le Guide d'Amsterdam*, 1701, pp. 1-2.
55. G.V. MENTINK and A.M. VAN DER WOUDE, *De demografische outwikkeling te Rotterdam en Cool in de 17ᶜ en 18ᶜ eeuw*, 1965.
56. J.-N. de PARIVAL, *op. cit.*, p. 33.
57. Friedrich LÜTGE, *Geschichte der deutschen Agrarverfassung vom frühen Mittelalter bis zum 19. Jahrhundert*, 1967, p. 285. IVO SCHÖFFER, in: *Handbuch der europäischen Geschichte*, ed. Theodor SCHIEDER, IV, 1968, p. 638. (*Hannekemaier* means 'day-labourer' in Dutch, and *peopen* and *moffen* were pejorative colloquial terms used to describe Germans).
58. A.N., Marine, B⁷, 463, fᵒ 39, (1697).
59. More significant than the Jews from Germany, the Sephardic Jews were mostly Portuguese and had their own cemetery at Ouwerkerque (*Le Guide d'Amsterdam*, 1701, p. 38; see also the bibliography in Violet BARBOUR, *op. cit.*, p. 25, n. 42); on Portuguese Jews, see E.M. KOEN's article 'Notarial records relating to the Portuguese Jews in Amsterdam up to 1639', in *Studia Rosenthaliana*, January 1973, pp. 116-27.
60. *Die Juden und das Wirtschaftsleben*, 1911, p. 18; *Medit.* (English translation), I, pp. 629 ff and II, 816.
61. *Medit.*, I, pp. 629 ff.
62. Ernst SCHULIN, *Handelsstaat England*, 1969, p. 195.
63. See above vol. II, pp. 157-9.

64. Léon VAN DER ESSEN, *Alexandre Farnèse, prince de Parme, gouverneur général des Pays-Bas, 1545-1592*, IV, 1935, p. 123.
65. C.R. BOXER, *op. cit.*, p. 19, note 5.
66. *Voyage en Hollande*, in: *Œuvres complètes*, 1969, XI, p. 336, quoted by C. MANCERON, *op cit.*, p. 468.
67. J.-N. de PARIVAL, *op. cit.*, p. 36.
68. J. ALCALA ZAMORA Y QUEIPO DE LLANO, *España, Flandes y el Mar del Norte (1618-1639). La última ofensiva europea de los Austrias madrileños*, 1975, p. 58.
69. W. TEMPLE, *op. cit.*, p. 26.
70. J.-N. de PARIVAL, *op. cit.*, p. 19.
71. A.-N., K 1349, 132, fᵒ 162 vᵒ ff. (1699).
72. A.N., M 662, dos. 5, fᵒ 15 vᵒ.
73. A.N., K 1349, 132, fᵒ 168.
74. Jacques ACCARIAS DE SÉRIONNE, *La Richesse de la Hollande*, 1778, I, p. 68.
75. A.E., C.P. Hollande, 94, fᵒ 59.
76. J. ACCARIAS DE SÉRIONNE, *op. cit.*, I, p. 69.
77. Which went in the end to the big merchants, A.N., M 662, dossier 5, fᵒ 13 vᵒ.
78. A.N. K 1349, 132, fᵒ 174 and vᵒ.
79. For some reason (an unintended omission?) there is no mention of oil.
80. A.N., A.E., B¹, 624.
81. J. ACCARIAS DE SÉRIONNE, *op. cit.*, I, p. 255.
82. *Ibid.*, II, p. 54.
83. C. WILSON, *Anglo-Dutch Commerce and Finance in the Eighteenth Century*, 1941, p. 3.
84. P. de LA COURT, *op. cit.*, p. 28.
85. Quoted by C. WILSON, *Profit and Power. A Study of England and the Dutch Wars*, 1957, p. 3.
86. I. de PINTO, *op. cit.*, p. 263.
87. Jacques ACCARIAS DE SÉRIONNE, *La Richesse de l'Angleterre*, 1771, notably pp. 42 et 44.
88. J.-B. d'ARGENS, *op. cit.*, III, p. 193.
89. A.N., A.E., B¹, 619, Pomponne's correspondence, the Hague, 16 May 1669. The 20,000 ships Colbert speaks of are pure exaggeration. In 1636, the Dutch fleet consisted of 2300 to 2500 vessels, plus the 2000 herring-busses. Cf. J.L. PRICE, *op. cit.*, p. 43. My estimate (600,000 tons) corresponds to W. VOGEL's 'Zur Grösse der Europäischen

Handelsflotten', in *Forschungen und Versuche zur Geschichte des Mittelalters und der Neuzeit*, 1915, p. 319.

90. W. Temple, *op. cit.*, p. 47, (Cambridge edn., 1932, p. 97).

91. J.-B. Tavernier, *Les Six Voyages . . .*, 1676, II, p. 266.

92. A.N., Marine, B⁷, 463, fᵒ 45, 1697.

93. A.N., M 785, dos. 4, fᵒˢ 68–9.

94. *Ibid.*

95. With the hull opened at the after end to accommodate the masts.

96. *Le Guide de l'Amsterdam*, 1701, p. 81.

97. Maltese Archives, 65–26.

98. L. Dermigny, *Le Commerce à Canton . . ., op. cit.*, p. 161, note 4.

99. A.N., G⁷, 1695, fᵒ 52, 15 February 1710.

100. On this expedition, cf. Isaac Dumont de Bostaquet, *Mémoires*, 1968.

101. A.N., K 1349, nᵒ 132, fᵒ 130.

102. Moscow C.S.A., 50/6, 537, 1, 12/23 January 1787.

103. 'Dutch Capitalism and the European World economy', in: *Colloque franco-hollandais*, 1976, typescript, p. 1.

104. 'Les interdépendances économiques dans le champ d'action européen des Hollandais (xviᵉ-xviiiᵉ siècles)', in: *Colloque franco-hollandais*, 1976, typescript, p. 76.

105. Francisco de Sousa Coutinho, *Correspondencia diplomatica... durante a sua embaixada en Holanda*, 1920–1926, II, 227, 2 January 1648: '*que como he de tantas cabeças e de tantos juizos differentes, poucas vezes se acordão todos inda pera aquillo que milhor lhes està*'.

106. A.R.J. Turgot, *op. cit.*, I, p. 373.

107. That is exercising control from above (in theory at least).

108. A.N., K 1349, fᵒ 11.

109. W. Temple, cited by C. Boxer, *The Dutch Seaborne Empire, op. cit.*, p. 13.

110. A.N., K 1349, fᵒ 35 vᵒ. Holland alone provided over 58% of the tax contribution of the United Provinces.

111. I. Schöffer, in: *Handbuch . . ., op. cit.*, p. 654.

112. C. Proisy d'Eppes, *Dictionnaire des girouettes ou nos contemporains d'après eux-mêmes*, 1815.

113. 'The Low Countries', in: *The New Cambridge Modern History*, IV, 1970, p. 365.

114. K.H.D. Haley, *The Dutch in the 17th Century*, 1972, p. 83.

115. A.N., K 1349, fᵒ 7 and 7 vᵒ.

116. B.M. Vlekke, *Evolution of the Dutch Nation*, 1945, pp. 162–6, quoted by C.R. Boxer, *op. cit.*, p. 11, note 4.

117. J.-N. de Parival.

118. A word derived from *calfat*, *calfateur* = caulker, 'Someone of no consequence'.

119. J.-N. de Parival, *op. cit.*, p. 190.

120. *Le Guide d'Amsterdam, op. cit.*, p. 21.

121. *Op. cit.*, p. 39, quoted in C.R. Boxer, *op. cit.*, p. 37.

122. I. de Pinto, *op. cit.*, pp. 334–5.

123. J.L. Price, *op. cit.*, p. 220.

124. *Ibid.*, p. 224, quoted in French: '*Le françois qui est pour les intelligents . . . le flament qui n'est que pour les ignorants*'.

125. A.N., K 849.

126. Marcel Marion, *Dictionnaire des institutions de la France aux XVIIᵉ et XVIIIᵉ siècles*, 1923, p. 521.

127. On the early cultivation of potatoes in the Low Countries, see Chr. Vandenbroeke, 'Cultivation and Consumption of the Potato in the 17th and 18th Century', in: *Acta historiae neerlandica*, V, 1971, pp. 15–40.

128. A.N., K 849, nᵒ 18, fᵒ 20.

129. I. de Pinto, *op. cit.*, p. 152.

130. J.-N. de Parival, *op. cit.*, p. 41.

131. A.N., K 1349, 132, fᵒ 215.

132. A.N., K 849, fᵒˢ 17–18.

133. *Ibid.*

134. *Ibid.*

135. I. de Pinto, *op. cit.*, p. 147.

136. *Journal du commerce*, January 1759.

137. Warsaw, Central Archives, Radziwill Collection, 18 August 1744.

138. I. de Pinto, *op. cit.*, p. 94.

139. The term used, *faire paroli*, comes from gaming, 'to outbid or raise the stakes'.

140. J. de Vries, 'An Inquiry into the Behavior of Wages . . .', *art. cit.*, p. 13.

141. Jules Michelet, *Histoire de France*, XIV, 1877, p. 2.

142. A.E., C.P. Hollande, 35, fᵒ 267 vᵒ, 15 May 1646.

143. The *Vereenigde Oost-Indische Compagnie*, the Dutch East India Company.

144. A.N., K 1349, 50 v°.
145. *Ibid.*
146. *Op. cit.*, p. 53.
147. A.E., C.P. Hollande, 46, f° 309.
148. The 17 directors of the V.O.C.
149. C.R. BOXER, *op. cit.*, p. 46, quoted by G. PAPAGNO, *art. cit.*, pp. 88–9; see below, note 271.
150. A.N., M 785, dos. 4, f°s 16–17.
151. J.G. VAN DILLEN, 'Isaac Le Maire et le commerce des Indes orientales', in: *Revue d'histoire moderne*, 1935, pp. 121–37.
152. A.N., A.E., B¹, 619, 18 June 1665.
153. J. DU MONT, *Corps universel diplomatique du droit des gens, contenant un recueil des traitez . . .*, 1726, IV, p. 274.
154. José Gentil DA SILVA, 'Trafics du Nord, marchés du "Mezzogiorno", finances génoises: recherches et documents sur la conjoncture à la fin du XVIᵉ siècle', in: *Revue du Nord*, avril-juin 1959, p. 146.
155. I. WALLERSTEIN, *The Modern World System*, *op. cit.*, I, p. 211; P. JEANNIN, *art. cit.*, p. 10.
156. *Moeder* in the sense of original, basic.
157. Cited by I. WALLERSTEIN, *op. cit.*, pp. 198–9.
158. *Medit.*, I, p. 140; V. VAZQUEZ DE PRADA, *Lettres marchandes d'Anvers*, 1960, I, p. 48.
159. J.G. DA SILVA, *Banque et crédit en Italie . . .*, I, p. 593, note 183.
160. *Ibid.*
161. Germaine TILLION, *Les Ennemis complémentaires*, 1960.
162. A. GRENFELD PRICE, *The Western Invasions of the Pacific and its Continents*, 1963, p. 29.
163. Simancas, E°-569, f° 84 (nd.); Virginia RAU, 'Rumos e vicissítudes do comércio do sal português nos seculos XIV à XVIII', in: *Revista da Faculdade de Letras* (Lisboa), 1963, n° 7, pp. 5–27.
164. Felipe RUIZ MARTÍN, unpublished study.
165. *Medit.*, I, p. 590.
166. *Medit.*, I, p. 63.
167. *Medit.*, I, p. 638; Jean-Pierre BERTHE, 'Les Flamands à Séville au XVIᵉ siècle', in: *Fremde Kaufleute auf der iberischen Halbinsel*, ed. H. KELLENBENZ, 1970, p. 243.

168. Jacob VAN KLAVEREN, *Europäische Wirtschaftsgeschichte Spaniens im 16. und 17. Jahrhundert*, 1960; *Medit.*, I, pp. 636 ff.
169. J. VAN KLAVEREN, *op. cit.*, pp. 116–17.
170. A.N., K 1349, no 133. Memorandum about the government of the Provinces of the Netherlands, f°s 3 and 4. H. PIRENNE, *op. cit.*, 1973, III, p. 60.
171. 'Gazettes hollandaises et trésors américains', in: *Anuario de Historia económica y social*, 1969, pp. 289–361.
172. Earl J. HAMILTON, *art. cit.*, in: *Economic History*, 1931, pp. 182 *sq.*
173. *Medit.*, I, p. 510.
174. *Medit.*, I, pp. 640–2.
175. *Navigatio ac itinerarium Johannis Hugonis Linscotani in Orientalem sive Lusitanorum Indiam . . .*, 1599.
176. Abbé PRÉVOST, *op. cit.*, VIII, p. 75.
177. *Ibid.*
178. See the useful summary which opens W.H. MORELAND's classic study, *From Akbar to Aurangzeb*, 1922, pp. 1–44.
179. Simancas, Estado Flandes 619, 1601.
180. Abbé PRÉVOST, *op. cit.*, VIII, pp. 75–6.
181. A.N., K 1349, quoted by BOXER, *op. cit.*, p. 23.
182. W.H. MORELAND, *op. cit.*, p. 19, note 1.
183. A.N., K 1349, f° 36.
184. R. DAVIS, *op. cit.*, p. 185.
185. A.d.S. Genoa, Spagna, 15.
186. C.S.P. East Indies, p. 205, Cottington to Salisbury, 18 February 1610.
187. L. DERMIGNY, *op. cit.*, I, p. 107.
188. *Ibid.*, I, p. 106.
189. David MACPHERSON, *Annals of Commerce*, 1805, II, p. 233.
190. L. DERMIGNY, *op. cit.*, I, p. 105, note 1.
191. A.N., Marine, B⁷, 463, f° 145; J. SAVARY, *op. cit.*, V, col. 1196.
192. A.N., K 1349, f° 44.
193. C.G.F. SIMKIN, *The Traditional Trade of Asia*, 1968, p. 188.
194. W.H. MORELAND, *op. cit.*, p. 63.
195. C.G.F. SIMKIN, *op. cit.*, p. 225.
196. C.R. BOXER, *op. cit.*, p. 143.
197. *Ibid.*, p. 196.
198. W.H. MORELAND, *op. cit.*, p. 32.
199. *Ibid.*, p. 38.
200. C.G.F. SIMKIN, *op. cit.*, pp. 199 ff; A.N., K 1349.

201. Constantin RENNEVILLE, *Voyage de S. van Rechteren . . .*, 1703, II, p. 256.
202. D. MACPHERSON, *op. cit.*, II, p. 466.
203. Hermann KELLENBENZ, 'Ferdinand Cron', in: *Lebensbilder aus dem Bayerischen Schwaben*, 9, pp. 194-210.
204. Duarte GÓMES SOLIS, *Mémoires inédits de . . .* (1621) ed. Bourdon, 1955, p. 1; J. CUVELIER, L. JADIN, *L'Ancien Congo d'après les archives romaines, 1518-1640*, 1954, p. 499, 10 April 1632.
205. A.N., K 1349, 132, f° 34.
206. Cf. *The Famous Voyage of Sir Francis Drake*, in J. HARRIS. *Navigantium atque Itinerantium Bibliotheca*, vol. I, 1764.
207. *Medit.*, I, pp. 302 et 305.
208. The capture of Amboyna was followed by the massacre of the English, who were arrested for conspiracy and executed after a sham trial, W.H. MORELAND, *op. cit.*, p. 23.
209. Abbé RAYNAL, *Histoire philosophique et politique des établissements et du commerce des Européens dans les deux Indes*, 1775, III, p. 21.
210. C. RENNEVILLE, *op. cit.*, V, p. 119.
211. Kristof GLAMANN, *Dutch Asiatic Trade, 1620-1740*, 1958, p. 68.
212. *Ibid.*, p. 168.
213. W.H. MORELAND, *op. cit.*, p. 64.
214. K. GLAMANN, *op. cit.*, p. 58.
215. A. LIOUBLINSKAIA, *Lettres et mémoires adressés au chancelier P. Séguier, 1633-1649*, 1966. Letter of Champigny, Aix, October 1647, pp. 321-2.
216. F. de SOUSA COUTINHO, *op. cit.*, II, p. 313. Letter to marquis of Niza, 17 February 1648.
217. K. GLAMANN, *op. cit.*, p. 120.
218. *Ibid.*, p. 131.
219. A.N., Marine, B⁷, 463, f° 253, report of 1687.
220. *Ibid.*
221. K. GLAMANN, *op. cit.*, pp. 91-2.
222. A.N., Marine, B⁷, 463, f°ˢ 177-8.
223. *Ibid.*, f°ˢ 161, ff.
224. *Ibid.*
225. L. DERMIGNY, *op. cit.*, I, p. 281.
226. A.N., Marine, B⁷, 463, f°ˢ 158-60.
227. *Ibid.*
228. François PYRARD DE LAVAL, *Seconde Partie du voyage . . . depuis l'arrivée à Goa jusques à son retour en France*, 1615, II, p. 353.
229. Abbé PRÉVOST, *op. cit.*, VIII, pp. 126-9.
230. Or by throwing 'the superfluous pepper into the sea' (Ernst Ludwig CARL, *Traité de la richesse des princes et de leurs États et des moyens simples et naturels pour y parvenir*, 1722-1723, p. 236).
231. C. RENNEVILLE, *op. cit.*, V, p. 124.
232. A.N., Marine, B⁷, 463, 251-2.
233. C.G.F. SIMKIN, *op. cit.*, p. 197.
234. W.H. MORELAND, *op. cit.*, p. 77.
235. C.G.F. SIMKIN, *op. cit.*, p. 197.
236. K. GLAMANN, *op. cit.*, pp. 19 et 207.
237. *Ibid.*, p. 166.
238. *Ibid.*, p. 265.
239. *Ibid.*, 231.
240. L. DERMIGNY, *op. cit.*, III, p. 1164.
241. *Op. cit.*, p. 265.
242. A.N., G⁷, 1697, f° 117, 21 August 1712.
243. G. de UZTÁRIZ, *op. cit.*, p. 103.
244. K. GLAMANN., *op. cit.*, p. 6; J. SAVARY, *op. cit.*, V, col. 1606 ff.
245. C.G.F. SIMKIN, *op. cit.*, p. 192.
246. A.E., Mémoires, Hollande, 72, 243.
274. K. GLAMANN, *op. cit.*, p. 60.
248. Abbé PRÉVOST, *op. cit.*, IX, p. 55.
249. A.N., Marine, B⁷, 463, f° 205.
250. Warships had much bigger crews: the 11 ships which left Texel with Matelief in 1605 carried a total of 1357 crewmen, or an average of 123 men per ship. So the estimate might be anywhere between 8000 (50 per ship) and 16,000 men (100 per ship). C. RENNEVILLE, *op. cit.*, III, p. 205.
251. A.N., Marine, B⁷, 463, f° 205.
252. J.-P. RICARD, *op. cit.*, p. 376.
253. *Essai politique sur le commerce*, 1735, p. 51.
254. Moscow, C.S.A., 50/6, incomplete reference.
255. By a team led by Ivo SCHÖFFER.
256. C.G.F. SIMKIN, *op. cit.*, p. 182.
257. J. SAVARY, *op. cit.*, V, col. 1610-1612.
258. A.N., A.E., B⁷, 619, The Hague, 25 June 1670.
259. J. SAVARY, *op. cit.*, I, col. 25 and V, col. 1612.
260. K. GLAMANN, *op. cit.*, pp. 244 ff.
261. *Ibid.*, pp. 252 ff.
262. *Ibid.*, p. 248.
263. Moscow, C.S.A., 50/6, 539, 57,

Amsterdam, 25 July–5 August 1788.
264. *Op. cit.*, p. 249.
265. *Ibid.*, p. 265.
266. *Ibid.*, pp. 229–31.
267. *Op. cit.*, I, p. 465.
268. C. BOXER, *The Dutch Seaborne Empire*, *op. cit.*, p. 52; *Les Six Voyages* ..., 1681, II, p. 420.
269. W.H. MORELAND, *op. cit.*, p. 315.
270. A.N., Marine, B⁷, 463, fᵒˢ 245 and 257–8.
271. Giuseppe PAPAGNO, 'Struttura e istituzioni nell' espansione coloniale: Portogallo e Olanda', in: *Dall' Età preindustriale all'età del capitalismo*, ed. G.L. BASINI, 1977, p. 89.
272. Francesco CARLETTI, *Ragionamenti del mio viaggio in torno al mondo*, 1958, pp. 213 ff.
273. K. GLAMANN, *op. cit.*, pp. 33 ff.
274. *Ibid.*, p. 34. Cornelis Bicker, in 1622, was a *bewindhebber* in the West Indies Company, while his brother Jacob was in the East India Company.
275. *Ibid.*, pp. 35–6.
276. W.H. MORELAND, *op. cit.*, p. 61.
277. *Grande Enciclopedia portuguesa brasileira*, III, article 'Baïa'.
278. R. HENNIG, *op. cit.*, p. 8; Victor von KLARWILL, *The Fugger News Letters*, 1924–1926, I, p. 248.
279. In the sense of a charter granted.
280. A.N., K 1349, 132, fᵒ 107 vᵒ.
281. A.d.S. Florence, Correspondence with Genoa, V, 32.
282. J. ACCARIAS DE SÉRIONNE, *Richesse de la Hollande*, *op. cit.*, pp. 137–8.
283. J. CUVELIER, L. JADIN, *op. cit.*, pp. 501–2.
284. K. GLAMANN, *op. cit.*, p. 155.
285. Cf. above, chapter 1.
286. British Museum, Sloane, 1572, fᵒ 65.
287. A.N., K. 1349, 132, fᵒ 117 vᵒ.
288. J. DU MONT, *op. cit.*, VI, p. 215.
289. *Sertão* = (lit.) undergrowth, the bush.
290. *Journal du voyage de deux jeunes Hollandais*, *op. cit.*, p. 377.
291. A.N., Marine, B⁷, 463, fᵒˢ 216–17.
292. B.N., Ms. Portugais, 26, fᵒ 216 and 216 vᵒ, Lisbon, 8 October 1668.
293. P. de LA COURT, *op. cit.*, p. 52.
294. J. DU MONT, *op. cit.*, I, p. 15.
295. Simancas, Estado Flandes, 2043.
296. A.N., K 1349, 132, fᵒ 34 vᵒ.
297. Maltese archives, 6505, early eighteenth century.
298. A.N., K 1349, 132, fᵒ 135.
299. L. GUICCIARDINI, *op. cit.*, p. 108.
300. C. WILSON, *Anglo-Dutch commerce* ..., *op. cit.*, p. 20.
301. 1748, I, pp. 339–40.
302. *Ibid.*
303. A.N., B¹, 619, Pomponne's correspondence, 1669. Konrad Van Beuningen was the ambassador of the United Provinces to the king of France.
304. *Ibid.*, D'Estrades, the Hague, 5 February, 1665.
305. D. DEFOE, *A Plan of the English Commerce*, 1728, p. 192.
306. LE POTTIER DE LA HESTROY, A.N., G⁶, 1687 (1703), fᵒ 67.
307. A.N., B¹, 619, 27 June 1669.
308. *Ibid.*, 30 October 1670.
309. J.-F. MELON, *op. cit.*, Eng. transl. *A Political Essay upon Commerce*, by D. Bindon, 1739, p. 334.
310. *Ibid.*, p. 334.
311. *Ibid.*, p. 335.
312. That is it required a constant supply of liquid currency.
313. Moscow, C.S.A., 50/6, 490, 17 April 1773.
314. J. ACCARIAS DE SÉRIONNE, *Les Intérêts des nations* ..., *op. cit.*, II, p. 200.
315. J. SAVARY, *op. cit.*, I, col. 331 ff.; J. ACCARIAS DE SÉRIONNE, *op. cit.*, I, p. 278.
316. J. ACCARIAS DE SÉRIONNE, *op. cit.*, II, p. 250.
317. *Ibid.*, II, p. 321.
318. *Ibid.*, I, p. 226.
319. *Ibid.*
320. A.N., A.E., B¹, 165. 13 February 1783.
321. J. ACCARIAS DE SÉRIONNE, *op. cit.*, I, p. 278.
322. *Ibid.*
323. *Ibid.*
324. C.P. KINDLEBERGER, *Manias, Bubbles, Panics and Crashes and the Lender of Last Resort*, ch. 2.
325. J. SAVARY, *op. cit.*, I, col. 8.
326. The terms *transport* and *transfer* were both used.
327. J. ACCARIAS DE SÉRIONNE, *op. cit.*, II, pp. 314–15.
328. 'Traites et retraites' – the former meant a withdrawal, the latter a payment.

withdrawal, the latter a payment.

329. Giulio MANDICH, *Le Pacte de Ricorsa et le marché étranger des changes*, 1953.

330. C. WILSON, *Anglo-Dutch Commerce...*, *op. cit.*, p. 167.

331. J. ACCARIAS DE SÉRIONNE, *op. cit.*, I, p. 226.

332. *Ibid.*, II, p. 210.

333. *Ibid.*, I, p. 397.

334. The English gold coins, value one pound sterling, which were first minted in 1489 by Henry VII.

335. A.d.S. Naples, Affari Esteri, 804.

336. The exchange rate at which it became more advantageous to send gold abroad than to pay by banker's draft. (R. BARRAINE, *Nouveau dictionnaire de droit et de sciences économiques*, 1974, p. 234).

337. A.N., Marine, B⁷, 438, Amsterdam, 13, 26 December 1774.

338. In *L'Express*, 28 January 1974.

339. J. ACCARIAS DE SÉRIONNE, *op. cit.*, II, p. 201.

340. A.N. Marine B⁷ 438, f⁰ 6, Amsterdam 17 March 1774, letter from Maillet du Clairon.

341. F. RUIZ MARTÍN, *Lettres marchandes...*, p. xxix.

342. *Medit.*, II, p. 700.

343. Eric J. HOBSBAWM, *The Age of Revolution*, pp. 44-5.

344. C. WILSON, *Anglo-Dutch Commerce...*, *op. cit.*, pp. 88-9.

345. 'Obligations' was sometimes the term used.

346. A.E., C.P. Hollande, 513, f⁰ 360, the Hague, 9 March 1764.

347. Moscow, C.S.A., 480, 50/6.

348. Moscow, C.S.A., 12/23, mars 1784, 50/6, 522, f⁰ 21 v⁰. NB the expression *prime* or bonus. A French document (A.E., C.P., Hollande, 577 f⁰ 358, 12 December 1788) refers simply to the *bénéfice* (profit). The profit on a Russian loan of 3 million florins was 120,000 fl., that is 4%.

349. See above chapter 2.

350. Moscow, C.S.A., 480, 50/6, f⁰ 13, Amsterdam, 2-13 April 1770.

351. *Ibid.*, f⁰ 6, Amsterdam, 29 March-9 April 1770.

352. Moscow, C.S.A., 472, 50/6, f⁰ 3 v⁰-4, Amsterdam, 18-29 March 1763, and 25 March-5 April 1763.

353. Moscow, C.S.A., 539, 50/6, 62, v⁰, 26 August 1788.

354. A.E., C.P., 578, f⁰ 326, 2 June 1789.

355. *Ibid.*, 579, f⁰ 3, 3 July 1789.

356. *Ibid.*, f⁰ˢ 100 v⁰ ff., 18 août 1789.

357. Sweden, 448 000 km², Norrland, 261 500, southern Sweden, 186 500.

358. Maurice ZIMMERMAN, *États scandinaves, régions polaires boréales*, in: P. VIDAL DE LA BLACHE, L. GALLOIS, *Géographie universelle*, III, 1933, p. 143.

359. G.K. Bücher's well-known distinctions between the household economy, the urban economy and the territorial economy.

360. See above, chapter 1.

361. P. DOLLINGER, *La Hanse...*, *op. cit.*, p. 52.

362. Claude NORDMANN, *Grandeur et liberté de la Suède (1660-1792)*, 1971, p. 93.

363. *Ibid.*, p. 17.

364. Counting the land surface only, no more than 3 inhabitants per km².

365. *Op. cit.*, p. 17.

366. A distinction is usually made between Sweden's 'greatness' before 1721 and her 'freedom' in the eighteenth century.

367. *Ibid.*, p. 94.

368. *Ibid.*, p. 45.

369. P. DOLLINGER, *op. cit.*, pp. 527-8.

370. V. BARBOUR, *op. cit.*, p. 102.

371. C. NORDMANN, *op. cit.*, p. 50.

372. *Ibid.*, p. 453.

373. Eli F. HECKSCHER and E.F. SÖDERLUND, *The Rise of Industry*, 1953, pp. 4-5.

374. C. NORDMANN, *op. cit.*, p. 243.

375. J. SAVARY, *op. cit.*, V, col. 1673.

376. Sometimes described as 'masked' ships.

377. C. NORDMANN, *op. cit.*, pp. 63-4.

378. L. DERMIGNY, *op. cit.*, I, pp. 173, *sq.*

379. 'The Economic Relations between Peasants, Merchants and the State in North Eastern Europe, in the 17th and 18th Centuries', paper at Bellagio conference, 1976.

380. See above, Vol. II, pp. 225 ff.

381. The *Bücher von Bauernschulden* which could be used as evidence in court.

382. Pierre JEANNIN, *L'Europe du Nord-Ouest et du Nord aux XVIIᵉ et XVIIIᵉ siècles*, 1969, p. 93.

383. The *hemman* was the hereditary property of the Swedish peasant. The

spelling *heman* is sometimes found, e.g. in A.N., K 1349.

384. C. Nordmann, *op. cit.*, p. 15.

385. Maria Bogucka, 'Le marché monétaire de Gdansk et les problèmes du crédit public au cours de la première moitié du XVIIᵉ siècle', Prato conference, typescript, 1972, p. 5.

386. *Op. cit.*, V, col. 579-80.

387. M. Bogucka, art. cit., p. 3.

388. Walter Achilles, 'Getreidepreise und Getreidehandelsbeziehungen europäischer Räume im 16. und 17. Jahrhundert', in: *Zeitschrift für Agrargeschichte und Agrarsoziologie*, April 1959, p. 46.

389. Marian Malowist, *Croissance et régression en Europe*, 1972, p. 172.

390. Sven-Erik Aström, paper at Bellagio conference, 1976 (quoted note 379 above).

391. As demonstrated by Witold Kula, *Théorie économique du système féodal*, 1970, pp. 93 ff.

392. J. Savary, *op. cit.*, V, col. 578.

393. Le Pottier de La Hestroy, doc. cit., fº. 17.

394. Père Mathias de Saint-Jean (alias Jean Éon), *Le Commerce honorable...*, 1646, pp. 89-90.

395. P. Boissonnade, P. Charliat, *Colbert et la Compagnie de commerce du Nord (1661-1689)*, 1930, pp. 31 ff.

396. Le Pottier de La Hestroy, doc. cit., fº. 18.

397. A.N., A.E., B¹, 619, the Hague, 5 Sept. 1669.

398. A.N. G⁷, 1695, 52.

399. A.N., M 662, nº 5, fº 1 vº.

400. *Ibid.*, fº 98.

401. *Ibid.*, fº 59 vº.

402. *Ibid.*, fº 115.

403. C. Nordmann, *op. cit.*, pp. 54-5.

404. Le Pottier de La Hestroy, doc. cit., fº. 25.

405. Père Mathias de Saint-Jean (alias Jean Éon), *op. cit.*, pp. 30 ff., pp. 87 ff.

406. See Chapter 2.

407. *Anglo Dutch Commerce...*, *op. cit.*, pp. 6-7.

408. *Ibid.*

409. *Ibid.*, p. 10 et note 5.

410. *A Plan of the English commerce*, 1728, p. 163.

411. C. Wilson, *op. cit.*, pp. 7-10.

412. E. Schulin, *op. cit.*, p. 230. 'All our merchants must turn Dutch factors'

413. C. Wilson, *op. cit.*, pp. 16-17.

414. *Ibid.*, p. 11.

415. C. Wilson, *England's Apprenticeship...*, *op. cit.*, p. 322.

416. *La République hollandaise des Provinces-Unies*, 1968, p. 33.

417. *Op. cit.*, pp. 223 ff.

418. Constantin Renneville, *Voiage de Paul van Caerden aux Indes orientales*, 1703, II, p. 133.

419. A company which pre-dated the creation of the V.O.C.

420. C. Renneville, *op. cit.*, pp. 170-3.

421. Jean Meyer, *Les Européens et les autres*, 1975, p. 253.

422. Art. cit., August 1763.

423. C.H.E. de Wit, quoted by J.L. Price, *op. cit.*, p. 220 and note 9.

424. A.N., Marine, B⁷, 435, fº 2.

425. *Gazette de France*. 24 April 1772.

426. *Ibid.*

427. A.N., Marine, B⁷, 434, fº 30; 435, fᵒˢ 1 ff. 'The failure of the house of Clifford and Son has been followed by two or three others of less importance but which have further increased fears and caused a complete loss in confidence.'

428. Moscow, C.S.A., 50/6, 506, fº 49.

429. A contrast remarked upon by C. Carrière, M. Courdurié, *op. cit.*, I, p. 85: 'The agricultural cycle does not exactly fit in with the activity of the great international port' (Marseille in this instance).

430. *Anglo-Dutch Commerce...*, *op. cit.*, p. 176.

431. J. Accarias de Sérionne, *Les Intérêts de l'Europe...*, *op. cit.*, II, p. 205.

432. M.G. Buist, *At Spes non fracta. Hope and Co*, 1770-1815, 1974, pp. 12-13.

433. M. Torcia, *Sbozzo del commercio di Amsterdam*, 1782, p. 9.

434. A.E., C.P. Hollande, 513, fº 64 vº.

435. C. Wilson, *op. cit.*, p. 168.

436. M. Torcia, *op. cit.*, p. 9.

437. A.d.S Venise, Inghilterra 119, fº 92, 92 vº.

438. C. Wilson, *op. cit.*, pp. 167-168.

439. *Gazette de France*, 584, Hamburg, 22 Aug. 1763.

440. *Ibid.*, 624, Copenhagen, 3 September 1763.
441. Moscow, C.S.A., 50/6, 472, fº 50, 12 Aug 1763.
442. *Ibid.*
443. *Ibid.*, fº 51 vº.
444. *Ibid.*
445. 'Disconte' is used for 'escompte' in the original.
446. Moscow, C.S.A., 50/6, 472, fº 44.
447. A.N., A.E., C.P. Hollande, 513, fº 64 vº.
448. *Surchéance = Surséance = sursis*, reprieve.
449. A.d.S. Naples, Affari Esteri 800, the Hague, 2 August 1763.
450. *Ibid.* A report from Berlin had been received.
451. *Gazette de France*, 544, 4 August 1763.
452. A.d.S. Naples, Affari Esteri 800.
453. *Gazette de France*, 296, the Hague, 22 April 1763.
454. M. TORCIA, *op. cit.*, p. 9.
455. Moscow, C.S.A. 50/6, 490, 1/2.
456. *Ibid.*
457. *Ibid.*
458. *Ibid.*
459. *Anglo-Dutch Commerce . . .*, pp. 169 ff.
460. A.N. Marine, B⁷, 435, Amsterdam, 7, 5 April 1773.
461. A.N., Marine, B⁷, 438, Amsterdam, 7, 28 March 1774.
462. A.N., Marine, B⁷, 435, Amsterdam, 3, 4 February 1773.
463. Thursday 24 October 1929. Cf. J.K. GALBRAITH, *The Great Crash, 1929*, 1955.
464. Intercycle, the ten to twelve year cycle.
465. C.E. LABROUSSE, *La Crise de l'économie française . . .*, *op. cit.*, p. XXII.
466. Robert BESNIER, *Histoire des faits économiques jusqu'au XVIIIᵉ siècle*, 1962–1963, p. 249.
467. Moscow, C.S.A., 50/6, 539, fº 47.
468. C.P. THURNBERG, *Voyage en Afrique et en Asie, principalement au Japon, pendant les années 1770-1779*, 1794, p. 30.
469. A.E. C.P. Hollande, 543, Amsterdam, 28 December 1780.
470. Expression from the book by Pieter GEYL, *La Révolution batave (1783-1798)*, 1971.
471. I. SCHÖFFER, *op. cit.*, pp. 656 and 657.
472. Moscow, C.S.A., 50/6, 531, fº 51.
473. *Ibid.*, 534, fº 126 vº.
474. *Ibid.*, 530, fº 62.
475. *Ibid.*, 531, fº 92-3, Amsterdam, 18/29 December 1786.
476. *Ibid.*, 50/6, 531, fº 66.
477. *Ibid.*
478. M.G. BUIST, *op. cit.*, p. 431.
479. That is the stadtholder.
480. A.E. C.P. Hollande, 565, fºˢ 76-83.
481. P. GEYL, *op. cit.*, p. 90.
482. A.E. C.P. Hollande, 575, fº 70.
483. P. GEYL, *op. cit.*, pp. 94, ff.
484. *Ibid.*, p. 95.
485. A.E. C.P. Hollande, 575, fºˢ 253 ff., the Hague, 14 December 1787; cf. also A.E., C.P. Hollande, 578, fº 274, the Hague, 15 May 1789.
486. *Ibid.*
487. A.E., C.P. Hollande, 576, fº 46, 3 April 1788.
488. A.E., C.P. Hollande, 575, fº 154 vº, 25 October 1787.
489. Moscow, C.S.A., 50/6, 533, fº 60.

NOTES TO CHAPTER 4

1. Jean ROMEUF, 1958; Alain COTTA, 1968; H. TEZENAS DU MONTCEL, 1972, and even BOUVIER-AJAM et al., 1975. The term 'domestic market' is perhaps more usual, at least in certain contexts, in English, but for the sake of clarity 'national market' is used throughout for *marché national*. (Tr.)
2. Cf Pierre VILAR, 'Pour une meilleure compréhension entre économistes et historiens. "Histoire quantitative" ou économétrie rétrospective?', in *Revue historique*, 1965, pp. 293-311.
3. Jean MARCZEWSKI, *Introduction à l'histoire quantitative*, 1965; R.W. FOGEL, in particular *The Economics of Slavery*, 1968; among his many articles, 'Historiography and retrospective econometrics' in *History and Theory*, 1970, pp. 245-64; 'The New Economic

History, I, Its findings and methods, in *Economic History Review*, 1966, pp. 642-56.

4. See above, vol. II.

5. Cf. Pierre CHAUNU's article 'La pesée globale en histoire', in *Cahiers Wilfredo Pareto*, 1968.

6. François PERROUX, 'Prises de vue sur la croissance de l'économie française 1780-1950' in *Income and Wealth*, V, 1955, p. 51.

7. W. SOMBART, *Der moderne Kapitalismus*, 1928, II, pp. 188-9, suggests that the primitive local market and the international market both appear earlier than intermediary markets, including the national market.

8. See above, chapter 1.

9. Louis CHEVALIER, *Démographie générale*, 1951, esp. p. 139.

10. 'Etudes sur l'ancienne communauté rurale en Bourgogne. II. La Structure du manse' in *Annales de Bourgogne*, XV, 1943, p. 184.

11. These minuscule units may be very old indeed. Frédéric HAYETTE thinks that the villages of Europe grew up within the framework of settlement patterns of the Roman era and only began to emerge from these in the eighth and ninth centuries. 'The Origins of European Villages', in *The Journal of Economic History*, March 1977, pp. 182-206 and the comments of J. A. RAFTIS, pp. 207-9.

12. Guy FOURQUIN, in Pierre LEON, *Histoire économique et sociale du monde*, 1977, I, p. 179; the area of a *commune* in France could be smaller than 10 km² in rich regions but might be as much as 45 km² in poor regions.

13. LEVI-PINARD, *La Vie quotidienne à Vallorcine*, *op. cit.*, p. 25.

14. Michael WEISSER, 'L'économie des villages ruraux situés aux alentours de Tolède', typescript, 1971, p. 1.

15. *Crises agraires en Europe (XIIᵉ-XXᵉ siècle)*, 1973, p. 15.

16. Cf. Pierre CHEVALIER, *La Monnaie en Lorraine sous le règne de Léopold (1698-1729)*, 1955, p. 126, n. 3 (1711).

17. Lucien GALLOIS, *Paris et ses environs*, n.d. (1914), p. 25.

18. Letter from R. BRUNET, 25 November

1977: 'There seems to be a typical size of 1000 km² which cannot, I think, be a matter of chance'.

19. According to R. BRUNET, these are, in ascending order, Beauvaisis: 800 km² (questionable); the Woëvre: 800 km²; pays d'Auge: 1200 to 1400 km²; Valois: 1000 km²; Othe: 1000 km².

20. Guy CABOURDIN, *Terre et hommes en Lorraine du milieu du XVIe siècle à la guerre de Trente Ans, Toulois et comté de Vaudémont*, 1975, I, p. 18.

21. Jean NICOLAS, *La Savoie au XVIIIe siècle*, 1978, p. 138. Tarentaise: 1693 km², Maurienne: 1917 km²; Chablais: 863 km²; Genevois: 1827 km².

22. Before 1815, from information provided to me by Paul Guichonnet.

23. Marco ANSALDO, *Peste, fame, guerra, cronache di vita valdostana del sec. XVII*, 1976.

24. Emile APPOLIS, *Le Diocèse civil de Lodève*, 1951, pp. v and vi, 1 and 1 n. 2.

25. G. CABOURDIN, *op. cit.*

26. Marzio ROMANI, lecture at Paris, 8 December 1977.

27. Lucien FEBVRE in *Annales E.S.C.*, 1947, p. 205.

28. Armand BRETTE, *Atlas des bailliages ou juridictions assimilées, ayant formé unité électorale en 1789*, n.d., p. viii: 'Out of over 400 *bailliages* which formed electoral constituencies in 1789, probably not one did not have some parishes which were divided in half, uncertain or disputed by neighbouring *bailliages*'.

29. In this long paragraph, the terms province, region, natural region and consequently the terms provincial market and regional market are interchangeable. On these problems see André PIATIER, *Existe-t-il des régions en France?*, 1966; *Les Zones d'attraction de la région Picardie*, 1967; *Les Zones d'attraction de la région Auvergne*, 1968.

30. 'Tableau de la France' in *Histoire de France*, II, 1876, p. 79.

31. 'Ritratti di cose di Francia' in *Opere complete*, 1960, pp. 90-1.

32. J. DHONDT, 'Les solidarités médiévales. Une société en transition: la Flandre en 1127-1128' in *Annales E.S.C.*, 1957, p. 529.

33. P. CHEVALIER, *op. cit.*, p. 35.
34. 1712-1770. Maria Theresa appointed him administrator of the Austrian Netherlands from 1753 till his death.
35. A.d.S. Naples, Affari Esteri 801, the Hague, 2 September 1768. On the facilities granted by the government in Brussels for importing wool to Ostend, cf. *ibid.*, 27 May 1768.
36. *The Opposition to Louis XIV*, 1965, p. 217.
37. P. CHAUNU, in: F. BRAUDEL and E. LABROUSSE. *Histoire économique et sociale de la France*, I, vol. I, p. 28.
38. Joseph CALMETTE, *L'Élaboration du monde moderne*, 1949, pp. 226-7.
39. Ernest GOSSART, *L'Établissement du régime espagnol dans les Pays-Bas et l'insurrection*, 1905, p. 122.
40. Eli F. HECKSCHER, *Mercantilism*, 1955, I, pp. 45 ff.
41. Thorold ROGERS, *History of agriculture and prices in England*, 1886, quoted by HECKSCHER, *op. cit*, I, p. 48
42. *ibid.*
43. Abbé COYER, *Nouvelles Observations sur l'Angleterre par un voyageur*, 1749, pp. 32-3.
44. A.N., Marine, B⁷, 434, *c*. 1776.
45. A. PONZ, *op. cit.*, I, p. 1750.
46. Marcel REINHARD, 'Le voyage de Pétion à Londres (24 novembre-11 décembre 1791)', in: *Revue d'histoire diplomatique*, 1970, pp. 35-6.
47. Otto STOLZ, 'Zur Entwicklungsgeschichte des Zollwesens innerhalb des alten deutschen Reiches', in: *Vierteljahrschrift für Sozial-und Wirtschaftsgeschichte*, 1954, 46, I, pp. 1-41.
48. *Bilanci* . . ., *op cit.*, I, p. CI, 20 December 1794.
49. Ricardo KREBS, *Handbuch der europäischen Geschichte*, ed. Theodor SCHIEDER, 1968, vol. 4. p. 561.
50. E. HECKSCHER, *op cit.*, I, p. 108.
51. Charles CARRIÈRE, *Négociants marseillais au XVIIIᵉ siècle*, 1973, pp. 705 and 710-12. About 1767.
52. A.N., H 2940; L.-A. BOITEUX, *La Fortune de mer*, 1968, p. 31, after Philippe MANTELLIER, *Histoire de la communauté des marchands fréquentant la rivière de Loire*, 1867.
53. J. SAVARY, *op cit.*, I, col. 22-3.
54. A.d.S. Genoa, Lettere Consoli 1/26, 28 (London, 11/12 December 1673).
55. A.N., F 12, 65, f° 41 (1 March 1719).
56. A.N., H 2939 (printed document).
57. *Ibid.*
58. P. DOCKÈS, *op cit.*, p. 182.
59. R. BESNIER, *op cit.*, p. 99.
60. Moscow, C.S.A., 93/6, 439, f° 168. Paris, 20 November-1 December 1786.
61. *Gazette de France*, 3 January 1763 (London 24 December 1762).
62. I. de PINTO, *op cit.*, p. 2.
63. Traian STOIANOVICH, unpublished typescript.
64. Michel MORINEAU, 'Produit brut et finances publiques: analyse factorielle et analyse sectorielle de leurs relations', unpublished paper, Prato conference, 1976.
65. 'Zur Entwicklung des Sozial Produckts in Deutschland im 16. Jahrhundert', in: *Jahrbuch für Nationalökonomie und Statistik*, 1961, pp. 448-89.
66. Art. cit., p. 18.
67. 'L'unite économique des Balkans et la Méditerranée à l'époque moderne', in: *Studia historiae oeconomicae*, Poznan, 1967, 2, p. 35.
68. *La Catalogne dans l'Espagne moderne* . . ., 1962, III, p. 143.
69. B.N., Ms. fr. 21773, f° 31.
70. *Die Entstehung der Volkswirtschaft*, 1911, p. 141.
71. I am using the term anachronistically to refer forward to the future Banks of England, France, etc.
72. C.P. KINDLEBERGER, *Manias, Bubbles, Panics and Crashes and the Lender of Last Resort*.
73. Irfan HABIB, 'Potentialities of capitalist development in the economy of Mughal India', *Journal of Economic History*, 1969, p. 41 and note 30.
I. HABIB, 'Usury in Medieval India', in *Comparative Studies in Society and History*, VI, July 1964.
74. 'Commercial Expansion and the Industrial Revolution', in: *The Journal of European Economic History*, IV, 3, 1975, pp. 613-54.

75. *Cádiz y el Atlántico, 1717-1778*, 1976.
76. P. DOCKÈS, *op. cit.*, p. 157.
77. Emmanuel LE ROY LADURIE, 'The chief defects of Gregory King', in *The Territory of The Historian*, trans. B and S. Reynolds, 1979, pp. 173-91.
78. Pierre de BOISGUILBERT, *Détail de la France*, 1699, ed. I.N.E.D., 1966, II, p. 584.
79. *Op. cit.*, pp. 153 ff.
80. François PERROUX, quoted by Jean LHOMME, in: *Georges GURVITCH, Traité de sociologie*, 3rd ed., 1967, I, p. 352, note 2.
81. Date of the publication of the pioneering study by Arthur Lyon BOWLEY and Josiah C. STAMP, *National Income*.
82. 'Europe's Gross National Product, 1800-1875', in: *The Journal of European Economic History*, 1976, p. 273.
83. *Comptabilité nationale*, 1965, pp. 3, 6, 28, 30. Cf. F. FOURQUET. *Histoire des services collectifs de la comptabilité nationale*, 1976, p. v.
84. The term seems to have been used for the first time by William PETTY in *Political Arithmetick*, 1671-1677.
85. Letter from Louis JEANJEAN, 9 January 1973.
86. See above Vol. II.
87. Simon KUZNETS, *Economic Growth of Nations, Total Output and Production Structure*, 1971, pp. 66 ff.
88. Jacques ATTALI, Marc GUILLAUME, *L'Anti-économique*, 1974, p. 32.
89. As pointed out by F. PERROUX, quoted by C. VIMONT, in: Jean ROMEUF, *Dictionnaire des sciences économiques*, 1958, II, p. 984.
90. *Ibid.*, p. 982.
91. *Dictionnaire économique et financier*, 1975, p. 1014.
92. In: Jean ROMEUF, *op cit.*, p. 985.
93. 'Estimations du revenu national dans les sociétés occidentales pré-industrielles et au XIXᵉ siècle', in: *Revue économique*, March 1977.
94. *Ibid.*
95. *Ibid.*, p. 193.
96. A.d.S. Venice, Senato Mar, 23, f° 36, 36 v°, 29 September 1534.
97. That is the population of Venice plus the Dogado.
98. Based on the annual wage-bill for woollen-workers (20,000 people, 5000 workers, 740,000 ducats) assuming the population of Venice to have been 200,000.
99. P. MANTELLIER, *op. cit.*, p. 388. For Frank Spooner's calculations, cf Figure 31 below.
100. VAUBAN, *Projet d'une dixme royale*, 1707, pp. 91-3.
101. Charles DUTOT, *Réflexions politiques sur les finances et le commerce*, 1738.
102. *Ibid.*, I, pp. 366 ff.
103. J.D. GOULD, *Economic Growth in History*, 1972, p. 4.
104. *Ibid.*, p. 5.
105. See the first version of Vol I of this book (*Capitalism and Material Life 1400-1800*, trans. M. Kochan, Fontana edn., (1974) p. 129.)
106. H. VAN DER WEE, 'Productivité, progrès technique et croissance économique du XIIᵉ au XVIIIᵉ siècle', unpublished paper, Prato conference, 1971.
107. On 'Gross Product and Public Finance, 18th and 19th centuries'.
108. 2nd ed. 1952.
109. J. de VRIES, *The Dutch Rural Economy in the Golden Age, op. cit.*, p. 95.
110. Cf. P. BAIROCH, 'Population urbaine et taille des villes en Europe de 1600 à 1700', in: *Revue d'histoire économique et sociale*, 1976, n° 3, p. 21.
111. M. REINHARDT, 'La population des villes, sa mesure sous la Révolution et l'Empire'. in: *Population*, 1954, p. 287.
112. *Op. cit.*, I, 1952, pp. 61 ff.
113. In 1700, 81% of the world's active population was in the primary sector (agriculture, forestry, fishing etc.) In 1970 the figure was 54.5% cf. Paul BAIROCH, 'Structure de la population active mondiale de 1700 à 1970', in: *Annales E.S.C.*, 1971, p. 965.
114. Pieter de LA COURT, *Mémoires de Jean de Witt*, 1709, pp. 30-1.
115. Gregory KING, *An Estimate of the Comparative Strength of Great Britain and France . . .*, 1696.
116. François QUESNAY, *Tableau oeconomique*, 1758.
117. K. GLAMANN, informative letter of 12 October 1976. Cf Figure 29.

118. *François Quesnay et la physiocratie*, 1958, I, pp. 154 ff.

119. 'Zur Entwicklung des Sozialprodukts . . .,' art. cit., p. 489.

120. Jean MARCZEWSKI, 'Le produit physique de l'économie française de 1789 à 1913', in: *Histoire quantitative de l'économie française, Cahiers de l'I.S.E.A.*, n° 163, July 1965, p. XIV.

121. *Ibid.*

122. *Ibid.*

123. *Medit.*, I, (Eng. trans) pp. 420 ff.

124. Robert E. GALLMAN and E.S. HOWLE, 'The Structure of U.S. Wealth in the Nineteenth Century', Conference of Southern Economic Association; Raymond W. GOLDSMITH, 'The Growth of Reproducible Wealth of the United States of America from 1805 to 1950' in: *Income and Wealth of the United States: Trends and Structure*, II, 1952.

125. *Op. cit.*, p. 66.

126. 'La fortune privée de Pennsylvanie, New Jersey, Delaware (1774)', in: *Annales E.S.C.*, 1969, p. 245.

127. Hubert BROCHIER, Pierre TABATONI, *Économie financière*, 2nd ed., 1963, p. 131.

128. J.H. MARIÉJOL, in: Ernest LAVISSE, *Histoire de France*, 1911, VI, Part I, p. 37.

129. P.G.M. DICKSON, 'Fiscal Need and National Wealth in 18th Century Austria', paper given at Prato conference, 1976.

130. *Op cit.*, see above note 115.

131. VAUBAN, *op cit.*, p. 153.

132. 'Taxation in Britain and France 1715–1810', paper given at Prato, 1976, published in: *The Journal of European Economic History*, 1976, pp. 608-9.

133. Museo Correr, Donà delle Rose Collection, 27.

134. A.N., K 1352.

135. See above, note 98.

136. Lucien FEBVRE, 'Un chapitre d'histoire politique et diplomatique: la réunion de Metz à la France' in: *Revue d'histoire moderne*, 1928, p. 111.

137. Jacques BLOCH-MORHANGE, *Manifeste pour 12 millions de contribuables*, 1977, p. 69; and a suggestive article by two economic journalists, David WARSH and Lawrence MINARD, 'Inflation is now too serious a matter to leave to economists' in: *Forbes*, 15 November 1976, p. 123.

138. In Britain, Nicholas KALDOR, Dudley JACKSON, H.A. TURNER, Frank WILKINSON; in the United States, John HOTSON; in France, J. BLOCH-MORHANGE and cf. the article by David WARSH and Lawrence MINARD.

139. J. ROBINSON, *The Accumulation of Capital*, 1956, p. 19.

140. *An Economic History of Sweden*, 1954, pp. 61, 69, 70, 116.

141. 'Le revenu national en Pologne au XVIᵉ siècle', in: *Annales E.S.C.*, 1971, n° 1, pp. 105-13.

142. 'L'urbanisation de la France au XIXᵉ siècle', in: Conference of French economic historians, 1977.

143. E.A. WRIGLEY, 'The Supply of Raw Materials in the Industrial Revolution', in: *The Economic History Review*, 1962, p. 110.

144. *The International Economy and Monetary Movements in France 1493–1725*, 1972, p. 306.

145. *Op cit.*, II, p. 587.

146. *Staat und Staatsgedanke*, 1935, p. 62.

147. *Le Bourgeois*, 1911, p. 106.

148. Jean BOUVIER, forthcoming article in *Annales, E.S.C.*

149. P. ADAM, *op. cit.*,

150. René GANDILHON, *Politique économique de Louis XI*, 1941, p. 322.

151. In: F. BRAUDEL and E. LABROUSSE, *Histoire économique et sociale de la France*, II, 1970, pp. 166-7.

152. The document is in the personal possession of Paul Guichonnet. There is a photocopy at the Maison des Sciences de l'Homme, Paris.

153. B.N., Ms. fr. 21773, fᵒˢ 133 ff.

154. Régine ROBIN, *La Société française en 1789: Semur-en-Auxois*, 1970, pp. 101-9.

155. B.N., Ms. fr. 21773, fᵒˢ 133 ff.

156. *Ibid.*

157. *Histoire économique de la France*, 1939, p. 232.

158. R. GASCON, in: F. BRAUDEL and E. LABROUSSE, *op. cit.*, I, p. 256.

159. Cardinal François MATHIEU, *L'Ancien Régime en Lorraine et en Barrois*, 1907, p. XIII.

160. René BAEHREL, *Une Croissance: la Basse-Provence rurale (fin du XVIᵉ siècle-1789)*, 1961, *passim*, notably pp. 77 ff.

161. J. ACCARIAS DE SÉRIONNE, *Les Intérêts des nations de l'Europe ...*, *op. cit.*, I, p. 224.

162. J. HUGUETAN, *Voyage d'Italie curieux et nouveau*, 1681, p. 5.

163. A.N., 129, A.P., 1.

164. A.N., 125, A.P., 16 (1687).

165. B.N., Ms. fr. 21773, fᵒˢ 73 to 75 vᵒ.

166. Arthur YOUNG, *Travels in France*, 1892 ed., p. 16.

167. A. PONZ, *op. cit.*, p. 1701.

168. E. LABROUSSE, in: F. BRAUDEL and E. LABROUSSE, *op. cit.*, II, p. 173.

169. A.N., G⁷ 1674, fᵒ 68, Paris, 17 December 1709; A.N., G⁷, 1646, fᵒ 412, Orleans, 26 August 1789.

170. *Ibid.*, fᵒˢ 371, 382; 1647, fᵒ 68, Orleans, 1, 22 April, 17 December 1709.

171. Moscow, C.S.A., 93/6, 394, fᵒ 24 and 24 vᵒ, 30 September 1783.

172. H. RICHARDOT, *op. cit.*, p. 184, quoted by P. DOCKÈS, *op. cit.*, p. 20.

173. In: F. BRAUDEL and E. LABROUSSE, *op. cit.*, I, p. 22.

174. *Ibid.*, I, p. 39.

175. P. DOCKÈS, *op cit.*, p. 156.

176. *Ibid.*, p. 308.

177. *Ibid.*, pp. 23 and 353.

178. Quoted by Marcel ROUFF, *Les Mines de charbon en France au XVIIIᵉ siècle*, 1922, p. 83, note 1.

179. 9 April 1709, quoted by Claude-Frédéric LÉVY, *Capitalistes et pouvoir au siècle des Lumières*, 1969, p. 325.

180. Quoted by P. DOCKÈS, *op. cit.*, p. 298.

181. Raymond COLLIER, *La Vie en Haute-Provence de 1600-1850*, 1973, p. 36.

182. R. GASCON, in: F. BRAUDEL, E. LABROUSSE, *op. cit.*, I, vol. I, p. 328.

183. José Gentil DA SILVA, *Banque et crédit en Italie ...*, *op. cit.*, p. 514.

184. *Ibid.*, pp. 94, 285, 480, 490.

185. M. MORINEAU, 'Lyon l'italienne, Lyon la magnifique', in: *Annales E.S.C..* 1974, p. 1540; F. BAYARD, 'Les Bonvisi, marchands banquiers à Lyon', in: *Annales E.S.C.*, 1971.

186. A.N., G⁷, 1704, 111.

187. R. GASCON, in: F. BRAUDEL, E. LABROUSSE, *op. cit.*, I, p. 288.

188. Frank C. SPOONER, *op. cit*, cf. note 144 above.

189. Denis RICHET, *Une Société commerciale Paris-Lyon dans la deuxième moitié du XVIᵉ siècle*, 1965, lecture given to Paris and Ile-de-France History Society.

190. *Histoire de Marseille*, III, pp. 236-7.

191. D. RICHET, *op. cit.*, p. 19.

192. *Œuvres*, ed. G. SCHELLE, 1913, I, p. 437.

193. P. DOCKÈS, *op. cit.*, p. 247.

194. Jules DELABORDE, *Gaspard de Coligny, amiral de France*, 1892, III, p. 57.

195. *Mémoires de Jean Maillefer, marchand bourgeois de Reims*, 1890, p. 52.

196. E. BRACHENHOFFER, *Voyage en France 1643-1644*, 1925, pp. 110, 113.

197. Lewis ROBERTS, *The Merchants Mapp of Commerce*, 1639, quoted by E. SCHULIN, *op. cit.*, p. 108.

198. B.N., Ms. fr. 21773, fᵒˢ 31 ff.

199. *Ibid.*

200. *Ibid.*

201. André RÉMOND, 'Trois bilans de l'économie française au temps des théories physiocratiques', in: *Revue d'histoire économique et sociale*, 1957, pp. 450-1.

202. Mostly in A.N., G⁷.

203. C.-F. LÉVY, *op. cit.*, p. 332.

204. Jacques SAINT-GERMAIN, *Samuel Bernard, le banquier des rois*, 1960, p. 202.

205. C.-F. LÉVY, *op. cit.*, p. 338.

206. Mathieu VARILLE, *Les Foires de Lyon avant la Révolution*, 1920, p. 44.

207. A.N., KK, 1114, fᵒˢ 176-7. Memorandum by M. d'Herbigny, *intendant* of Lyon, with observations by M. de la Michodière, *intendant* in Lyon in 1762.

208. M. VARILLE, *op. cit.*, p. 45.

209. A.N., G⁷, 359-60.

210. P. de BOISLISLE, *Correspondance des contrôleurs généraux ...*, 1874-1897, II, p. 445.

211. A.N., G⁷, 363, 25 July 1709.

212. *Ibid.* 15 July.

213. *Ibid.* 2 August 1709.

214. M. VARILLE, *op. cit.*, p. 44.

215. Guy ANTONIETTI, *Une Maison de banque à Paris au XVIIIᵉ siècle, Greffulhe, Montz et Cie*, 1789-1793, 1963, p. 66.

216. A.D. Loire-Atlantique, C 694, document pointed out to me by Claude-Frédéric LÉVY.

217. Edgar FAURE, *La Banqueroute de Law*, 1977, p. 55.
218. *Op. cit.*, map n° 1.
219. Henri HAUSER, 'La question des prix et des monnaies en Bourgogne', in: *Annales de Bourgogne*, 1932, p. 18.
220. *The Elizabethans and America*, quoted by I. WALLERSTEIN, *The Modern World System, op. cit.*, p. 266, note 191.
221. Fritz HARTUNG, Roland MOUSNIER, 'Quelques problèmes concernant la Monarchie absolue', in: *International conference of historical sciences Rome*, 1955, vol. IV, p. 45.
222. In: F. BRAUDEL, E. LABROUSSE, *Histoire économique et sociale de la France*, II, p. 525.
223. R. BESNIER, *op cit.*, p. 35.
224. *Beauvais et le Beauvaisis de 1600 à 1730. Contribution à l'histoire sociale de la France du XVIIᵉ siècle*, 1960, pp. 499 ff.
225. Jean DELUMEAU, 'Le commerce extérieur de la France', in: *XVIIᵉ siècle*, 1966, pp. 81-105; by the same author, *L'Alun de Rome*, 1962, pp. 251-4.
226. Emmanuel LE ROY LADURIE, preface to A. d'ANGEVILLE, *Essai sur la statistique de la population française*, 1969, p. xx.
227. Michel MORINEAU, 'Trois contributions au Colloque de Göttingen', in: *Vom Ancien Régime zur französischen Revolution*, ed. Albert CREMER, 1978, p. 405, note 61.
228. *Ibid.*, pp. 404-5.
229. J.C. TOUTAIN, paper given at Edinburgh International Economic History Conference, 1978, typescript.
230. Between 1702 and 1713, French privateers captured 4543 prizes from the enemy, E. LABROUSSE in F. BRAUDEL, E. LABROUSSE. *op. cit.*, II, p. 191.
231. Quoted by Charles FROSTIN, 'Les Pontchartrain et la pénétration commerciale française en Amérique espagnole (1690-1715), in: *Revue historique*, 1971, p. 310.
232. Michel AUGÉ-LARIBÉ, *La Révolution agricole*, 1955, p. 69.
233. Abbé Ferdinando GALIANI, *Dialogues sur le commerce des bleds*, 1949, p. 548.
234. A.N., F¹², 724.
235. M. MORINEAU, 'Produit brut et finances publiques …', art. cit.

236. Edward Fox, *History in a Geographic Perspective, The Other France*, 1971.
237. B.N. Ms. fr. 21773.
238. *Ibid.*, fᵒˢ 127 vᵒ-131.
239. A.N., G⁷, 1685, 67.
240. E. Fox, *op. cit.*, p. 63.
241. *Les Négociants bordelais, l'Europe et les îles au XVIIIᵉ siècle*, 1974, pp. 381 ff.
242. B.N., Ms. fr. 21773, fᵒ 148.
243. A.N., G⁷, 1692, fᵒ 146.
244. Louis TRENHARD, *Histoire des Pays-Bas français*, 1972, p. 330.
245. Art, cit., p. 437.
246. Jean MEYER, *L'Armement nantais de la seconde moitié du XVIIIᵉ siècle*, 1969, p. 62.
247. A.N., G⁷, 1686, fᵒˢ 59 and 60.
248. *Gazette d'Amsterdam*, 1672.
249. A.N., Colonies, F 2A, 16 et F 2A, 15 (4 March 1698).
250. A.N., 94 AQ 1 (8 January 1748).
251. A.N., G⁷, 1698, 224 (19 February 1714).
252. *Ibid.*, 223 (7 February 1714).
253. According to Victor HUGO, *En voyage: Alpes et Pyrénées*, 1890.
254. A *généralité* was an administrative division of which an *intendant* was in charge.
255. François de DAINVILLE, 'Un dénombrement inédit au XVIIIᵉ siècle: l'enquête du contrôleur général Orry, 1745', in: *Population*, 1952, pp. 49 ff.
256. Art. cit., pp. 443 and 446.
257. E. LABROUSSE, in: F. BRAUDEL, E. LABROUSSE, *op. cit.*, II, p. 362.
258. Marcel MARION, *Les Impôts directs sous l'Anrien Régime principalement au XVIIIᵉ siècle*, 1974, pp. 87-112; it was a tax created in 1749, based on the *dixième*; 'it was never much more than a tax on the income from land and fell far below an actual twentieth', M. MARION, *Dictionnaire des Institutions*, p. 556.
259. Jean-Claude PERROT, *L'Age d'or de la statistique régionale française, an IV-1804*, 1977.
260. A.N., F¹², 721 (11 June 1783).
261. *Toulouse et la région Midi-Pyrénées au siècle des Lumières, vers 1670-1789*, 1974, p. 836 and general conclusion.
262. On this problem cf. Anne-Marie COCULA, 'Pour une définition de l'espace aquitain au XVIIIᵉ siècle', in: *Aires et structures du commerce français*, ed.

Pierre LÉON, 1975, pp. 301-9.

263. Philippe de VRIES, 'L'animosité anglo-hollandaise au XVIIᵉ siècle', in: *Annales E.S.C.*, 1950, p. 42.

264. *Letters and Papers, Foreign and Domestic of the Reign of Henry VIII*, ed. BREWER, III/II, 1867, p. 1248, quoted in E. HECKSCHER, *op. cit.*

265. Abbé J.-B. LE BLANC, *op. cit.*, I, p. 137.

266. *Travels in France, op. cit*, p. 5.

267. A.L. ROWSE, 'Tudor Expansion: the Transition from Medieval to Modern History', in: *William and Mary Quarterly*, 1957, p. 312.

268. SULLY, *Mémoires*, III, p. 322.

269. Abbé J.-B. LE BLANC, *op, cit.*, III, p. 273.

270. Jean-Gabriel THOMAS, *Inflation et nouvel ordre monétaire*, 1977, p. 58.

271. J. SAVARY, *op. cit.*, III, col. 632.

272. J.-G. THOMAS, *op. cit.*, pp. 60-1.

273. J.D. GOULD used the term as the title for his book on the subject, *The Great Debasement*, 1970.

274. A penny-weight (dwt.) was one twentieth of an ounce. The silver content of 11 ounces 2 dwt to 12 ounces works out at 222/240 = 37/40.

275. J.D. GOULD, *op. cit.*, table on page 89.

276. Raymond de ROOVER, *Gresham on Foreign Exchange*, 1949, p. 67.

277. *Ibid.*, p. 68.

278. *Ibid.*, pp. 198 ff. and 270 ff.

279. A.E. FEAVEARYEAR, *The Pound Sterling. A History of English Money*, 1963, pp. 82-3.

280. J. Keith HORSEFIELD, *British Monetary Experiments 1650-1710*, 1960, pp. 47-60.

281. Created by Charles II in 1663.

282. A.E., C.P. Angleterre, 173, f⁰ 41.

283. *Ibid.*, f⁰ 132, 8 October 1696.

284. J.K. HORSEFIELD, *op. cit.*, p. 50.

285. Jacques E. MERTENS, *La Naissance et le développement de l'étalon-or, 1696-1922*, 1944, p. 91.

286. J.-G. THOMAS, *op cit.*, pp. 68-9.

287. J.K. HORSEFIELD, *op. cit.*, p. 85.

288. *Op. cit.* p. 80. 'In France all funds are known indiscriminately as "paper" ... This expression is deplorable'.

289. Louis SIMOND, *Voyage d'un Français en Angleterre pendant les années 1810 et 1811*, 1816, II, pp. 228 ff.

290. Maurice RUBICHON, *De l'Angleterre*,

1815-1819, p. 357. 'After 1808, guineas completely vanished from circulation', L. SIMOND, *op. cit.*, I, p. 319 and II, p. 232.

291. L. SIMOND, *op. cit.*, pp. 227-8.

292. Arnold TOYNBEE, in the French edition, *L'Histoire*, 1951, p. 263. (Quotation untraceable in English.)

293. Bartolomé BENNASSAR, *L'Angleterre au XVIIᵉ siècle (1603-1714)*, n.d., p. 21.

294. See above, vol. II., Ch. 1.

295. T.S. WILLAN, *The Inland Trade*, 1976.

296. Daniel DEFOE, *The Complete English Tradesman*, 5th ed. 1745, I, pp. 340-1.

297. *Ibid.*

298. *Ibid.*, I, p. 342.

299. T.S. WILLAN, *River Navigation in England, 1600-1750*, 1964, p. 133.

300. Quoted by Ray Bert WESTERFIELD, *Middlemen in English Business particularly between 1660 and 1760*, 1915, p. 193.

301. T.S. ASHTON, *An Economic History of England: the 18th century*, 1972, pp. 66-7.

302. René-Martin PILLET, *L'Angleterre vue à Londres et dans ses provinces pendant un séjour de dix années*, 1815, p. 23.

303. J.K. HORSEFIELD, *op. cit.*, p. 15.

304. Eric J. HOBSBAWM, *Industry and Empire*, 1968, p. 11, and Sydney POLLARD, David W. CROSSLEY, *The Wealth of Britain, 1085-1966*, 1968, pp. 165-6.

305. J. ACCARIAS DE SÉRIONNE, *Les Intérêts de l'Europe ...*, *op. cit.*, I, p. 46.

306. E. HOBSBAWM, *op, cit.*, p. 253.

307. S.G.E. LYTHE et J. BUTT, *An Economic History of Scotland, 1100-1939*, 1975, pp. 70 ff.

308. T.C. SMOUT, *A History of the Scottish People*, 1969, p. 242.

309. *Ibid.*, pp. 165 ff.

310. T.C. SMOUT, Paper at Prato Conference, 1978.

311. J. ACCARIAS DE SÉRIONNE, *La Richesse de l'Angleterre*, *op. cit.*, p. 52.

312. T.C. SMOUT, *op. cit.*, p. 226.

313. Charles BAERT-DUHOLANT, *Tableau de la Grande-Bretagne, de l'Irlande et des possessions angloises dans les quatre parties du monde*, Paris, an VIII, I, p. 202.

312. The Pale was a 'palisade which moved forward and back depending on the

fortunes of war'. P. Vidal de la Blache, *Etats et nations de l'Europe*, 4th edn., n.d., p. 307.

315. For instance J.H. Plumb in a chapter of his book, *England in the Eighteenth Century*, 1973, pp. 178 ff. under the unexpected title 'The Irish Empire'.

316. Christopher Hill, *Reformation to Industrial Revolution, A social and economic history of Great Britain*, 1967, p. 131.

317. J.H. Plumb, *op. cit.*, p. 179.

318. *Épocas do Portugal económico*, 1929. The cycles refer to the successive cycles of commodity production in Brazil: the dyewood cycle, the sugar cycle, the gold cycle, etc.

319. C. Baert-Duholant, *op. cit.*, I, pp. 320-55.

320. I. de Pinto, *op. cit.*, p. 272.

321. A.N., A.E., B¹, 762, f° 253. My italics.

322. *Ibid.*

323. Moscow, C.S.A., 35/6, 312, f° 162, 9 December 1779, 2 February 1780.

324. A.E., C.P. Angleterre, 533, f° 73, 14 March 1780.

325. J.H. Plumb, *op. cit.*, p. 164.

326. *États et nations de l'Europe*, *op. cit.*, p. 301.

327. Pablo Pebrer, *Histoire financière et statistique générale de l'Empire britannique*, 1834, II, p. 12.

328. Jonathan Swift, *History of the Four Last Years of the Queen*, written in 1713 and published posthumously in 1758, quoted by P.G.M. Dickson, *art. cit*, pp. 17-18.

329. D. Defoe, *op. cit.*, II, p. 234.

330. A.N., 257 AP 10.

331. *Journal du Commerce*, 1759, pp. 105-106; quoted by I. de Pinto, *op. cit.*, p. 122.

332. Quoted by P.G.M. Dickson, *art cit.*, p. 23.

333. A.N., 257 AP 10.

334. L.C.A. Dufresne de Saint-Léon, *Études sur le crédit public*, 1824, p. 128.

335. J.-B. Say, *op. cit.*, VI, 1829, p. 187.

336. I. de Pinto, *op. cit.*, pp. 41-2.

337. P.G.M. Dickson, *op. cit.*, p. 16.

338. *Ibid.*

339. Moscow, C.S.A., n.d., 35/6, 3190, f° 114.

340. Cracow Archives, Czartoryski collection 808, f° 253.

341. Moscow, C.S.A., 3301, f° 11 v°, Simolin, 5-16 April 1782.

342. Museo Correr, P.D., C 903/14.

343. Orville T. Murphy, 'Du Pont de Nemours and the Anglo-French Commercial Treaty of 1786', in: *The Economic History Review*, 1966, p. 574.

344. D. Guérin, *La Lutte des classes sous la Première République, bourgeois et 'bras nus' 1793-1797*, 1946, p. 51.

345. A.N., A.E., B¹, 762, f° 151, 26 June 1787.

346. A.E., M. et D, Angleterre, 10.

347. A.N., A.E., B¹, 762.

348. J. Savary, *op. cit.*, V, col. 744.

349. M. Rubichon, *op. cit.*, II, p. 354.

350. A.N., A.E., B¹, 762, f° 161.

351. *Ibid.*, f° 162.

352. *Ibid.*, f° 255.

353. A.E., M. and D. Angleterre, 10, f°s 96 et 106.

354. *Ibid.*

355. Vorontsov Archives Moscow, 1876, IX, p. 44, London, 4/15 November 1785.

356. J. Van Klaveren, 'Die historische Erscheinung der Korruption', II, in: *Viertel-jahrschrift für Sozial und Wirtschaftsgeschichte*, 1958, p. 455.

357. A.N., A.E., B¹, 762, f° 255, 18 December 1789.

358. R. Besnier, *op. cit.*, p. 38.

359. P. Mathias and P. O'Brien, *art. cit.*, pp. 601-50.

360. T.J. Markovitch, *Histoire des industries françaises: les industries lainières de Colbert à la Révolution*, 1976.

361. A.N., G⁷, 1692, f° 34.

362. Albert Cremer, 'Die Steuersystem in Frankreich und England am Vorabend der französische Revolution', in: *Von Ancien-Régime zur französischen Revolution*, 1978, pp. 43-65.

363. *Op. cit.*, I, pp. 31 and 275.

NOTES TO CHAPTER 5

1. Throughout this chapter I have been guided by two books, Michel Deveze, *L'Europe et le monde à la fin du XVIIIᵉ siècle*, 1970; Giorgio Borsa, *La Nascità del*

mondo moderno in Asia orientale, 1977.

2. This is not the ideal expression since it includes in 'non-Europe' the eastern part of the continent. But can one say 'non-West'? Charles VERLINDEN, in *L'Avènement des temps modernes*, ed. Jean-Claude MARGOLIN, 1977, p. 676, writes of 'L'Europe vraiment européenne', 'truly European Europe'.

3. Giuliano GUOZZI, *Adamo e il Nuovo Mondo. La nascità dell'antropologia come ideologia coloniale: dalle genealogie bibliche alle teorie razziali*, 1977.

4. Edmundo O'GORMAN, *The Invention of America*, 1961; François PERROUX uses the same expression in *L'Europe sans rivage*, 1954, p. 12: 'Europe, which – in many senses of the word – invented the world . . .'.

5. Francisco LÓPEZ DE GÓMARA, *Historia general de las Indias, Primera Parte*, 1852, p.156.

6. Friedrich LÜTGE, *Deutsche Sozial- und Wirtschaftsgeschichte*, 1966, p. 288; H. BECHTEL, *op. cit.*, II, p. 49.

7. *Les Fonctions psychologiques et les œuvres*, 1948.

8. C. MANCERON, *op. cit.*, p. 524.

9. B.N., Ms. fr. 5581, f° 23, 2 December 1717.

10. P. CHAUNU, *Séville et l'Atlantique..., op. cit.*, VIII, p. 48.

11. Alonso de ERCILLA, *La Araucana* (published in 1569), 1910, ch. XXVII, p. 449.

12. Alvaro JARA, *Tierras nuevas, expansión territorial y ocupación del suelo en América (s. XVI-XIX)*, 1969; Pierre MONBEIG, *Pionniers et planteurs de São Paulo*, 1952.

13. François CHEVALIER, *La Formation des grands domaines au Mexique. Terre et société aux XVIe-XVIIe siècles*, 1952, p. 4.

14. Frédéric MAURO, *Le Brésil du XVe à la fin du XVIIIe siècle*, 1977, p. 145.

15. Roland MOUSNIER, in: Maurice CROUZET, *Histoire générale des civilisations*, V, 1953, p. 316.

16. D. PEDRO DE ALMEIDA, *Diario*, p. 207, quoted by Oruno LARA, *De l'Atlantique à l'aire caraïbe; nègres cimarrons et révoltes d'esclaves, XVIe-XVIIe siècles*, n.d., II, p. 349.

17. The *quilombo*, a Brazilian word meaning the place of refuge for runaway slaves.

18. Frédéric MAURO, paper given at Prato, 1978.

19. D. A. BRADING, *Miners and merchants in Bourbon Mexico 1763-1810*, Cambridge, 1971, p. 233.

20. 'Introduction à l'histoire de Guadalajara et de sa région', C.N.R.S. Conference, *Le Rôle des villes dans la formation des régions en Amérique latine*, pp. 3 ff.

21. *Les Mécanismes de la vie économique dans une société coloniale; le Chili (1680-1830)*, 1973, pp. 262 ff.

22. Pedro CALMÓN, *Historia social do Brasil*, 1937, p. 191. The exodus took place in 1871.

23. Georg FRIEDERICI, *El Caracter del Descubrimiento y de la Conquista de América*, 1973, p. 113.

24. D. A. BRADING, *op. cit.*, p. 5

25. *Capitalism and Slavery*, 4th ed., 1975.

26. *Ibid.*, p. 30.

27. Karl MARX, *Capital, I*, quoted by Pierre VILAR, Problems of the formation of capitalism', in: *Past and Present*, 1956, p. 34.

28. Marcel BATAILLON, *Etudes sur Bartolomé dé Las Casas*, 1965, p. 298.

29. M. DEVÈZE, *op. cit.*, p. 358.

30. M. DEVÈZE, *Antilles, Guyanes, la mer des Caraïbes de 1492 à 1789*, 1977, p. 173.

31. Nicolás SÁNCHEZ ALBORNOZ, *La Población de América latina*, 2nd ed., 1977, pp. 62 ff.

32. J. L. PHELAN, *The Millennial Kingdom of the Franciscans in the New World*, 1956, p. 47.

33. Juan A. and Judith E. VILLAMARIN, *Indian Labor in Mainland Colonial Spanish America*, 1975, p. 17.

34. Jean-Pierre BERTHE, 'Aspects de l'esclavage des Indiens en Nouvelle-Espagne pendant la première moitié du XVIe siècle' in; *Journal de la société des américanistes*, LIV-2, p. 204, note 48.

35. Alvaro JARA, paper given at Prato, 1978.

36. Father AJOFRIN, 1763, quoted by D. A.BRADING, *op. cit.*, p. 276.

37. Anibal B. ARCONDO, 'Los precios en una

economia en transición. Cordóba durante el siglo XVIII' in: *Revista de economia y estadística*, 1971, pp. 7-32.

38. According to Daniel DEFOE, *Moll Flanders*, Abbey Classics, edn., quoted by E. WILLIAMS, *op. cit.*, p. 18.

39. M. DEVÈZE, *Antilles, Guyanes ...*, *op. cit.*, p. 185.

40. Édouard FOURNIER, *Variétés historiques et littéraires*, 1855-1863, VII, p. 42, note 3.

41. R. MOUSNIER, *op. cit.*, p. 320.

42. Giorgio SPINI, *Storia dell' età moderna*, 1960, p. 827.

43. E. WILLIAMS, *op. cit.*, p. 19.

44. D. W. BROGAN, introduction to E. WILLIAMS, *op. cit.*, p. viii.

45. In 1860, with the coming of the railways, Cuba developed monster-sized sugar plantations of 11,000 acres, whereas in Jamaica, the largest were barely as much as 2000, E. WILLIAMS, *op. cit.*, pp. 151-2.

46. E. WILLIAMS, *op. cit.*, p. 26.

47. Adam SMITH, *The Wealth of Nations*, 1961 edn, ed. E. CANNAN, II, p. 99.

48. 'Sociedad colonial y sublevaciones populares; el Cuzco, 1780', typescript, p. 8.

49. Émile-G. LÉONARD, *Histoire générale du protestantisme*, III, 1964, pp. 6, 692 ff.; 'L'Église presbytérienne du Brésil et ses expériences ecclésiastiques', in: *Études évangéliques*, 1949.

50. J. LYNCH, *The Spanish American Revolutions, 1803-1826*, 1973, p. 128, quoted by Nicole BOUSQUET, *La Dissolution de l'Empire espagnol au XIXe siècle*, unpub. thesis, 1974, p. 106.

51. François COREAL, *Voyages aux Indes occidentales*, 1736, I, p. 244.

52. P. CHAUNU, *Séville et l'Atlantique ...*, *op. cit.*, t. VIII₁, p. 597.

53. C. FREIRE FONSECA, *Economia natural y colonizacão do Brasil (1534-1843)*, 1974, unpublished thesis.

54. Cf. first edn. of Vol I, *Capitalism and Material Life*, *op. cit.*, p. 60.

55. J. ACCARIAS DE SÉRIONNE. *Les Intérêts des nations de l'Europe ...*, I, 1766, p. 56.

56. F. COREAL, *op. cit.*, I, pp. 220-1.

57. F. MAURO, *Le Brésil ...*, p. 138.

58. J. ACCARIAS DE SÉRIONNE, *op. cit.*, I, p. 85. *Bravos* in this context meant 'savages'.

59. Marcel GIRAUD. *Histoire de la Louisiane française*, 1953, I, pp. 196-7.

60. Quoted by J. M. PRICE, in Virginia B. PLATT and David C. SKAGGS, *Of Mother Country and Plantations*, 1972, p. 7.

61. Charles M. ANDREWS, *The Colonial Period of American History. The Settlements*, I, 1970, pp. 518-19.

62. Enrique FLORESCANO, *Precios del maiz y crisis agricolas en Mexico (1708-1810)*, 1969, p. 314.

63. Russell WOOD, in *Journal of Economic History*, March 1977, p 62, note 7.

64. D. A. BRADING, *op. cit.*, p. 347.

65. German ARCINIEGAS, *Este Pueblo de America*, 1945, p. 49, compares this crisis to a sort of Middle Ages.

66. F. COREAL, *op. cit.*, I, pp. 353-4. Popayan is a province of Colombia, south-east of Bogota.

67. N. BOUSQUET, *op. cit.*, p. 42. Socorro, a town in Colombia in Santander province.

68. François CHEVALIER, 'Signification sociale de la fondation de Puebla de Los Angeles', in; *Revista de historia de América*, 1947, n° 23, p. 127.

69. Reginaldo de LIZARRAGA, 'Descripción del Perú, Tucuman, Río de la Plata y Chile' in: *Historiadores de Indias*, 1909, II, p. 465.

70. D. A. BRADING, *op. cit.*, p. 17.

71. A. N., Marine, B⁷, 461, f° 39. William Pitt the Elder (1708-1778) received the title of Earl of Chatham in 1766.

72. M. DEVÈZE, *L'Europe et le monde ...*, *op. cit.*, p. 331, after M. L. HANSEN, *The Atlantic Migration (1607-1860)*, and H. COWAN, *British Emigration to North America*, 1961.

73. *Ibid.*

74. A.N., A.E., B III, 441. 'Palatines' meant natives of the Palatinate.

75. *Ibid.*

76. I.e. the shipowner's account.

77. *Livres*, paid to the shipowner.

78. A.N., Colonies, C 11 4 11, f°ˢ 205 ff.

79. A.N. Colonies, C 11 4 11.

80. R. MOUSNIER, *op. cit.*, p. 320.

81. A.N., A.E., B. III, 441, 1782.

82. A.N., A.E., C.C.C. Philadelphia, 7, f° 358, New York, 27 October 1810.

83. Fawn BRODIE, *Thomas Jefferson; an*

Intimate History, 1976.

84. A.N., A.E., B III, 441, 1781.

85. *Ibid*.

86. J. F. JAMESON, *The American Revolution considered as a Social Movement*, 1925, pp. 46 ff.

87. *Ibid*., p. 48.

88. *Ibid*., p. 31.

89. P. J. GROSLEY, *Londres*, 1770, p. 232.

90. J. F. JAMESON, *op. cit*., p. 31.

91. Michel FABRE, *Les Noirs américains*, 2nd ed., 1970.

92. A.N., Marine, B⁷, 467, 17 February 1789.

93. Adam. SMITH, *op. cit*., 1961 edn., vol. 2, p. 97.

94. Bernard BAILYN, *The New England Merchants in the 17th Century*, 1955, pp 16 ff.

95. A.N., Marine, B⁷, 458.

96. A.N., A.E., B III, 441.

97. P. J. GROSLEY, *op. cit*., p. 232.

98. J. ACCARIAS DE SÉRIONNE, *Les Intérêts des nations . . ., I*, pp. 211-13.

99. E. WILLIAMS, *op. cit*., p. 147, quoting J. W. FORTESCUE, *A History of the British Army*, 1899-1930, IV, part I, p. 325.

100. R. MOUSNIER, *op. cit*., p. 327.

101. A.d.S.Naples, Affari Esteri, 801, the Hague, 21 October 1768.

102. J. ACCARIAS DE SÉRIONNE, *Les Intérêts des nations . . ., op. cit*., I, p. 73, note a.

103. J. ACCARIAS DE SÉRIONNE, *La Richesse de l'Angleterre, op. cit*., p. 96.

104. A.E., C.P. United States, 53, fᵒˢ 90 ff. Georgetown, founded in 1786 is now a suburb of Washington.

105. The date usually quoted is that of the victory of Sucre at Ayacucho on 9 December 1824. I prefer the date of 1825, that is when London first became excited about investment in South America.

106. Earl Diniz MacCARTHY MOREIRA, 'Espanha e Brasil: problemas de relacionamento (1822-1834)' in: *Estudos ibero-americanos*, July 1977, pp. 7-93.

107. Jacob VAN KLAVEREN, *Europäische Wirtschaftsgeschichte Spaniens . . ., op. cit*., 1960, p. 177.

108. LE POTTIER DE LA HESTROY, *doc. cit*., fᵒ 34.

109. Ernst Ludwig CARL, *op. cit*., II, p. 467.

110. A.E., C.P. (Angleterre), 120, fᵒ 237.

111. Quoted by Lewis HANKE, 'The Portuguese in Spanish America', in: *Revista de historia de América*, 1962, p. 27.

112. British Museum, Add. 28370, fᵒˢ 103-104, El duque de Medina Sidonia to Matheo Vázquez, San Lucar, 17 September 1583.

113. *Ibid*., fᵒ 105.

114. A.N., Marine, B⁷, 232, fᵒ 325, quoted by E. W. DAHLGREN, *Relations commerciales et maritimes entre la France et les côtes de l'océan Pacifique*, 1909, p. 37.

115. Some historians have even spoken of a quota of only 4 per cent at the end of the seventeenth century, which I find hard to believe. A. GARCIA-BAQUERO GONZALEZ, *op. cit*., I, p. 82.

117. F. COREAL, *op. cit*., I, p. 308.

118. CARRIÈRE, *Négociants marseillais . . ., op. cit*., I, p. 101.

119. A.E., M. et D. (Amérique) 6, fᵒˢ 287-91.

120. A.N., F¹², 644, fᵒ 66, March 1722.

121. A.N., A.E., B¹, 625, the Hague, 19 February 1699.

122. N. BOUSQUET, *op. cit*., p. 24; Simon COLLIER, *Ideas and Politics of Chilean Independence, 1808-1833*, 1963, p. 11.

123. Alice CANABRAVA, *O Comércio português no Rio da Prata (1580-1640)*, 1944; Marie HELMER, 'Comércio e contrabando entre Bahia e Potosi no século XVI', in: *Revista de historia*, 1953, pp. 195-212.

124. H. E. S. FISHER, *The Portugal Trade*. 1971, p. 47.

125. J. ACCARIAS DE SÉRIONNE, *Les Intérêts des nations . . ., op. cit*., I, p. 86.

126. Quoted by J. VAN KLAVEREN, 'Die historische Erscheinung der Korruption, in ihrem Zusammenhang mit der Staats- und Gesellschaftsstruktur betrachtet', I, in: *Vierteljahrschrift für Sozial- und Wirtschaftsgeschichte*, December 1957, pp. 305-6, note 26.

127. Gonzalo de REPARAZ, 'Los caminos del contrebando', in: *El Comercio*, Lima, 18 February 1968.

128. A.N., K 1349, fᵒ 124 and 124 vᵒ.

129. A.N., G⁷, 1692, memorandum from Granville-Locquet, fᵒ 206 vᵒ.

130. N. BOUSQUET. *op. cit*., p. 17, after Pierre CHAUNU, 'Interpretación de la

Independencia de América Latina' in: *Perú Problema*, n° 7, 1972, p. 132; J. VICENS VIVES, *An Economic History of Spain*, 1969, p. 406.

131. Claudio SANCHEZ ALBORNOZ agrees that he did write this, but neither of us has been able to find the exact reference.

132. A.E., M. et D. (America) 6, f° 289.

133. The *asiento*, the monopoly of providing black slaves for the Spanish colonies in America, was practised from the sixteenth century. At the beginning of the War of the Spanish Succession (1701) it went to France. In 1713, it took the form of an international treaty when Philip V granted it to England: the agreement signed with the South Sea Company arranged for the annual shipment of 48,000 slaves over a period of 30 years and permitted the Company to send two ships of 500 tons, the *navios de permiso* to the colonial fairs. Although article 16 of the treaty of Aix-la-Chapelle renewed it in 1748 for another 4 years, the English company in fact gave it up in 1750.

134. M. DEVÈZE. *L'Europe et le monde . . .*, pp. 425-6.

135. Decree of 18 May 1756, A. GARCIA-BAQUERO GONZALEZ, *op. cit.*, I, p. 84.

136. N. BOUSQUET, *op. cit.*, p. 8.

137. Ships which in theory sailed individually but whose cargoes had been registered (*registradas*) on departure.

138. A. de Indias, E 146, quoted by G. DESDEVISES DU DEZERT, *L'Espagne de l'Ancien Régime*, III, 1904, p. 147.

139. *Ibid.*, p. 148. The fourteenth port, opened in 1788, was San Sebastian.

140. Moscow, C.S.A., 50/6, 500, 3, Amsterdam, 12/23 January 1778.

141. Oscar CORNBLIT, 'Society and Mass Rebellions in Eighteenth Century Peru and Bolivia', in: *St Antony's Papers*, 1970, pp. 9-44.

142. The chambers of commerce, which arranged and controlled foreign trade and enjoyed considerable privileges.

143. Cf. J. R. FISHER. *Government and Society in Colonial Peru*. 1970, esp. pp. 124 ff.

144. D. A. BRADING, *op. cit.*, pp. 226, 232.

145. Ibid., p. 18; A.E., C.C., Mexico, 1, f°s 2-15.

146. 'Obstacles to Economic Growth in 19th Century Mexico', in *American Historical Review*, February 1978, pp. 80 ff.

147. *Ibid.*, p. 82.

148. A. HANSON JONES, art. cit.

149. J. VICENS VIVES, *Historia social y económica de España y America, op. cit.*, IV, p. 463.

150. According to the calculations, also rather doubtful, of Holden FURBER in *John Company at work*, 1948, p. 309. These calculations do not include contraband.

151. A.E., C.P., (United States) 59, f° 246 v°.

152. Jurgen SCHNEIDER, 'Le commerce français avec l'Amérique latine pendant l'âge de l'indépendance (première moitié du XIXe siècle)' in: *Revista de historia de América*, 1977, pp. 63-87.

153. Nico PERRONE, 'Il manifesto dell'imperialismo americano nelle borse di Londra e Parigi' in *Belphagor*, 1977, pp. 321 ff. There was a flight of capital to Europe; 'most of it was sent to France', a situation referred to in November 1828, A.E., M. et D., (America) 40, 501, f°s 4 ff.

154. A.N., A.E., B. III, 452.

155. 'Feudalismo y capitalismo in América latina', in: *Boletín de estudios latino-americanos y del Caribe*, December 1974, pp. 21-41.

156. For what follows, see A.N., Marine, B⁷, 461, Memorandum on the situation of the United States concerning domestic industry and foreign trade, dated February 1789.

157. *op. cit.*, p. 49.

158. Quoted by B. H. SLICHER VAN BATH, art. cit., p. 25.

159. See above, Vol.II.

160. E. FLORESCANO, *op. cit.*, p. 433.

161. C. GIBSON, *The Aztecs under Spanish Rule*, 1964, p. 34.

162. M. BATAILLON, *op. cit.*, p. xxxi.

163. *Ibid.*, p. xxx.

164. *Der Charakter der Entdeckung und Eroberung Amerikas durch die Europäer*, 1925, I, pp. 453-4.

165. E. WILLIAMS, *op. cit.*, pp. 30 ff and 126.

166. 'Lo zucchero e l'Atlantico', in: *Miscellanea di Studi sardi e del commercio atlantico*, III (1974), pp. 248-77.

167. M. Devèze, *L'Europe et le monde...*, pp. 263 ff.

168. Robert Challes, *Voyage aux Indes d'une escadre française (1690-1691)*, 1933, pp. 85-7.

169. The Contra Costa was the term for the Indian Ocean coast of Southern Africa.

170. W. G. Randles, *L'Empire du Monomotapa du XVᵉ au XVIIIᵉ siècle*, 1975, p. 7.

171. Roland Oliver and G. Matthew, *History of East Africa*, 1966, p. 155.

172. Auguste Toussaint, *L'Océan Indien au XVIIIᵉ siècle*, 1974, p. 64.

173. Moscow C.S.A., 18 October 1774, complete reference mislaid.

174. K. G. Davies, *The Royal African Company*, 1957, pp. 5 and 6.

175. N. Sánchez Albornoz, *op. cit.*, p. 66.

176. W. G. L. Randles, *L'Ancien Royaume du Congo des origines à la fin du XIXᵉ siècle*, 1968; J. Cuvelier and L. Jadin, *op. cit.*; G. Balandier, *La Vie quotidienne au royaume de Kongo du XVIᵉ siècle*, 1965.

177. J. Savary, *op. cit.*, see the article 'manille', III, col. 714.

178. J. Cuvelier and L. Jadin, *op. cit.*, p. 114.

179. Pierre Poivre, *Voyages d'un philosophe, ou Observations sur les mœurs et les arts des peuples de l'Afrique, de l'Asie et de l'Amérique*, 1768, p. 22.

180. *La Cosmographie universelle...*, 1575, fᵒ 67.

181. Philip Curtin, *Economic Change in Precolonial Africa. Senegambia in the Era of the Slave Trade*, 1975, pp. 235, 237-47.

182. Cf. first edn. of Vol I, *Capitalism and Material Life*, p. 23.

183. B. Bailyn, *op. cit.*, p. 16.

184. Père Jean-Baptiste Labat, *Nouvelle Relation de l'Afrique occidentale*, 1728, IV, p. 326, a propos of Gambia.

185. P. Curtin, *op. cit.*, p. xxii.

186. *Ibid.*, p. 4.

187. W. G. L. Randles, *L'Ancien Royaume du Congo...*, *op. cit.*, p. 69.

188. *Ibid.*, p. 87.

189. O. Lara, *op. cit.*, II, pp. 291-2.

190. J. Beraud-Villars, *L'Empire de Gao. Un État soudanais aux XVᵉ et XVIᵉ siècles*, 1942, p. 144.

191. W. G. L. Randles, *L'Ancien Royaume du Congo...*, *op. cit.*, p. 132.

192. *Ibid.*

193. *Ibid.*, p. 135.

194. W. G. L. Randles, *L'Empire du Monomotapa...*, *op. cit.*, p. 18.

195. W. G. L. Randles, *L'Ancien Royaume du Congo...*, *op. cit.*, p. 216.

196. *Konkwistadorzy Portugalscy*, 1976.

197. Paul Milioukov, Charles Seignobos, Louis Eisenmann, *Histoire de Russie*, I, 1932, p. 158, note 1; *Medit.*, p. 191.

198. J.-B. Labat, *op. cit.*, V, p. 10.

199. A term meaning 'adventurers'.

200. W. G. Randles, *L'Ancien Royaume du Congo...*, *op. cit.*, pp. 217 ff.; C. Verlinden, in J. C. Margolin, *op. cit.*, p. 689. The word *pombeiro* may come from *pumbo*, the busy market in what is now Stanley Pool.

201. Gaston Martin, *Nantes au XVIIIᵉ siècle. L'ère des négriers (1714-1774)*, 1931, pp. 46 ff.

202. P. Curtin, *op. cit.*

203. *Ibid.*, pp. 334 ff.

204. Y. Bernard, J.-C. Colli, D. Lewandowski, *Dictionnaire...*, *op. cit.*, p. 1104.

205. M. Devèze, *L'Europe et le monde...*, *op. cit.*, p. 310, and references to C. W. Newbury, Reginald Coupland, C. Lloyd, D. Curtin, H. Brunschwig.

206. A.E., C.C.C. London, 12, fᵒˢ 230 ff., Letter from Séguier, 12 May 1817.

207. *Considérations... sur l'abolition générale de la Traite des Nègres adressées aux Négociateurs qui doivent assister au Congrès de Vienne, par un Portugais*, September 1814, pp. 17-18. (B.N., Paris, LK 9, 668.)

208. This paragraph owes much to Jacqueline Kaufmann-Rochard's book, *Origines d'une bourgeoisie russe, XVIᵉ-XVIIᵉ siècles*, 1969.

209. C. Verlinden, *op. cit.*, see note 2 above, pp. 676 ff.

210. I. Wallerstein, *op. cit.*, p. 320.

211. Walther Kirchner, 'Über den russischen Aussenhandel zu Beginn der Neuzeit', in: *Vierteljahrschrift für Sozial- und Wirtschaftsgeschichte*, 1955.

212. B. H. Summer, *Survey of Russian*

History, 1947, p. 260, quoted by R. M. MATTON, in: *Russian Imperialism from Ivan the Great to the Revolution*, ed. Taras HUNCZAK, 1970, p. 106.

213. George VERNADSKY, *The Tsardom of Moscow, 1547-1682*, V, 1969, p. 166.

214. Artur ATTMAN, *The Russian and Polish Markets in International Trade 1500-1650*, 1973, pp. 135 ff.

215. *Ibid.*, pp. 138-40.

216. The *rijksdaaler* or *rigsdaler* or *rixdollar*, the official thaler of the Netherlands, minted since the Estates-General of 1579.

217. M. V. FECHNER's book (in Russian) on Russian trade with the East, 1952; Leon Poliakoff kindly provided me with a resumé of the whole book and translations of key passages.

218. A. GERSCHENKRON, *Europe in the Russian mirror*, 1970, p. 54.

219. Marian MALOWIST, 'The economic and social Development of the Baltic Countries, xvth-xviith century', in : *Economic History Review*, December 1959, pp. 177-189.

220. A.N., K 1352, f° 73, c. 1720.

221. *Ibid.*

222. Samuel H. BARON, 'The Fate of the Gosti in the reign of Peter the Great', in: *Cahiers du monde russe et soviétique*, October-December 1973, pp. 488-512.

223. J. KAUFMANN-ROCHARD, *op. cit.*, p. 88.

224. *Ibid.*, pp. 87 and 227.

225. *Ibid.*, pp. 227-8.

226. J. KULISCHER, *Wirtschaftsgeschichte Russlands*, I, p. 447.

227. Or *riad*: a gallery of shops.

228. 1 pood = 16.38 kg.

229. J. KULISCHER, *op. cit.*, I pp. 447 ff.

230. On the following, see Jerome BLUM, *Lord and Peasant in Russia from the 9th to the 19th century*, pp. 106 ff.

231. Michael CONFINO, *Systemes agraires et progrès agricole. L'assolement triennal en Russie aux XVIIIᵉ-XIXᵉ siècles*, 1970, p. 99.

232. Frédéric Le PLAY, *L'Ouvrier Européen*, 1877-9, quoted in J. BLUM, *op. cit.*, pp. 316-17.

233. Vorontsov Archives, *op. cit.*, xxiil, p. 327.

234. J. BLUM, *op. cit.*, p. 283. Roger PORTAL, 'Manufactures et classes sociales en Russie au XVIIIᵉ siècle', in *Revue*

historique, April-June 1949, p. 169.

235. Peter Simon PALLAS, *Voyages ... dans plusieurs provinces de l'Empire de Russie et dans l'Asie septentrionale*, Paris, 1794, I, p. 14, note 1.

236. J. BLUM, *op. cit.*, pp. 302-3.

237. *Ibid.*, pp. 293-4.

238. *Ibid.*, pp. 300-1.

239. *Ibid.*, p. 288.

240. *Ibid.*, p. 290.

241. *Ibid.*, p. 473.

242. J. KAUFMANN-ROCHARD, *op. cit.*, p. 191.

243. Louis Alexandre FROTIER DE LA MESSELIÈRE, *Voyage à Saint-Pétersbourg ou Nouveaux Mémoires sur la Russie, op cit.*, p. 116.

244. Auguste JOURDIER, *Des forces productives, destructives et improductives de la Russie*, 1860, p. 118.

245. J. P. KILBURGER, *Kurzer Unterricht von dem russischen Handel*, quoted by J. KULISCHER, *op. cit.*, p. XII, pp. 248 and 329.

246. J. KAUFMANN-ROCHARD, *op. cit.*, p. 46.

247. Adam OLEARIUS, *Voyage en Moscovie, Tartarie et Perse*, 1659, p. 108, quoted by J. KAUFMANN-ROCHARD, *op. cit.*, p. 46.

248. J. KULISCHER, *op. cit.*, p. 338.

249. J. BLUM, *op. cit.*, p. 286.

250. J. KAUFMANN-ROCHARD, *op. cit.*, pp. 39 ff.

251. Vorontsov Archives, *op. cit.*, XXI, p. 333.

252. J. KAUFMANN-ROCHARD, *op. cit.*, p. 65.

253. François BARRÊME, *Le Grand Banquier*, 1685, p. 216.

254. A.N., Marine, B⁷, 457, 1780.

255. A.E., M. et D. (Russia), 7, f° 298, c. 1770.

256. A.E., M. et D. (Russia), 2, f° 176, 1773.

257. P. Philippe AVRIL, *Voyage en divers États d'Europe et d'Asie, entrepris pour découvrir un nouveau chemin à la Chine ...*, 1692, p. 103.

258. Eugenio ALBERI, *Relazioni degli ambasciatori veneti durante il secolo XVI*, 1839-1863, III, 2, Giac. Soranzo, p. 199.

259. A.d.S. Venice, Inghilterra, London, 18-19 June 1703.

260. J. SAVARY, *op. cit.*, V, col. 658 ff.

261. Boris NOLDE, *La Formation de l'Empire russe*, 2 vol., 1952-1953.

262. François-Xavier COQUIN, *La Sibérie, peuplement et immigration paysanne au XIXᵉ siècle*, 1969, pp. 9-10.

263. *Ibid.*

264. p. CAMENA D'ALMEIDA, in: *Géographie universelle*, V, 1932, p. 258.

265. Details from F.-X. COQUIN, *op. cit.*, p. 109.

266. A.E., M. et D. (Russia), 2, fᵒˢ 187 vᵒ-188.

267. F.-X. COQUIN, *op. cit.*, p. 11.

268. *Ibid.*, p. 12.

269. A.E., M et D. (Russia), 7, fᵒˢ 246-9. 'Observations pour l'abbé Raynal'.

270. P. CAMENA D'ALMEIDA, *op. cit.*, p. 217.

271. J. G. GMELIN, *Voyage en Sibérie . . .*, 1767, II, p. 50.

272. *Ibid.*, II. 123.

273. J. KAUFMANN-ROCHARD, *op. cit.*, p. 200.

274. *Gazette de France*, 4 April 1772, p. 359.

275. W. LEXIS, 'Beiträge zur Statistik der Edelmetalle nebst einigen Bemerkungen über die Wertrelation', in: *Jahrbuch für Nationalökonomie und Statistik*, XXXIV, 1908, p. 364.

276. C. M. FOUST, 'Russian Expansion to the East through the 18th Century', in: *Journal of Economic History*, 1961, p. 472.

277. Maurice-Auguste de BENYOWSKY, *Voyages et mémoires . . .*, 1791, p. 63.

278. P. S. PALLAS, *Voyage à travers plusieurs provinces de l'Empire russe*, 1771-1776, III, p. 490.

279. *Ibid.*, p. 487.

280. M.-A. de BENYOWSKY, *op. cit.*, p. 48.

281. A.E., M et D. (Russia), 2, fᵒ 188.

282. James R. GIBSON, *Feeding the Russian Fur Trade: provisionment of the Okhotsk seaboard and the Kamtchatka peninsula, 1689-1856*, 1970.

283. Ernst HOFFMANN, *Reise nach den Goldwäschen Ostsiberiens*, 1847, 1969 ed., pp. 79 ff.

284. In 1728, 1732, 1741, 1746, 1755.—A.E., M. et D. (Russia), 2, fᵒˢ 183-5.

285. *Ibid.*

286. J. SAVARY. *op. cit.*, V, col. 659 ff.

287. C. M. FOUST. art. cit., p. 477.

288. J. G. GMELIN, *op. cit.*, I, p. 49.

289. C. M. FOUST, art. cit., p. 477; A.N., A.E., M. et D. (Russia), 2, fᵒ 182.

290. Vorontsov Archives, *op. cit.*,IX, pp. 32-3.

291. Gino LUZZATTO, *Storia economica dell'età moderna e contemporanea*, II, 1952, p. 16.

292. A.N., A.E., B¹, 485.

293. A.d.S. Naples, Affari Esteri, 800; *Gazette de Cologne*, 23 September 1763. Russian currency could be exchanged in London apparently from 1762.

294. Moscow, C.S.A., Vorontsov Collection, 1261, 4-446.

295. Vorontsov Archives, *op. cit.*, XXI, p. 137.

296. *Ibid.*, p. 315.

297. *Ibid.*, X, p. 201.

298. J. BLUMD, *op. cit.*, p. 293.

299. R. PORTAL, art. cit., pp. 6 ff.

300. J. BLUM, *op. cit.*, p. 294.

301. A.N. Marine, B⁷, 457.

302. A.N., K 1352.

303. Vorontsov Archives, *op. cit.*, VIII, p. 363.

304. Fernand GRENARD, *Grandeur et décadence de l'Asie*, 1939, p. 72.

305. A.E., M. et D. (Turkey), 36, fᵒ 16.

306. G. TONGAS, *Les Relations de la France avec l'Empire ottoman, durant la première moitié du XVIIᵉ siècle*, 1942, p. 141.

307. Giovanni BOTERO, *Relationi universali*, 1599, II, pp. 117-18.

308. C. BOXER, 'The Portuguese in the East, 1500-1800', in: *Portugal and Brazil, an Introduction*, ed. H. V. LIVERMORE, 1953, p. 221.

309. A.d.S. Venice, Relazioni, B 31.

310. François SAVARY DE BRÈVES, *Relation des voyages de . . .*, 1628, p. 242.

311. Maestre MANRIQUE, *Itinerario de las misiones que hizo el Padre F. Sebastian Manrique . . .*, 1649, p. 460.

312. Abbé PRÉVOST, *op. cit.*, IX, 1751, p. 88 (Voyage of A. de Rhodes, 1648).

313. Edward BROWN, *A Brief Account of Some Travels . . .*, 1673, pp. 39-40.

314. T. STOIANOVITCH, typescript, paper to *Conférence de la Commission d'histoire économique de l'Association du Sud-Est européen*, Moscow/Kiev, 1969.

315. W. PLATZHOFF, *Geschichte des europäischen Staatensystems, 1559-1660*, 1928, p. 31.

316. Herbert JANSKY, in: *Handbuch der europäischen Geschichte*, ed. T.

SCHIEDER, *op. cit.*, IV, p. 753.

317. *Ibid.*, p. 761.

318. Jorjo TADIC, 'Le commerce en Dalmatie et à Raguse et la décadence économique de Venise au XVIIᵉsiècle', in: *Aspetti e cause della decadenza economica veneziana nel secolo XVII*, 1961, pp. 235-274.

319. Robert MANTRAN, 'L'Empire ottoman et le commerce asiatique au XVIᵉ et au XVIIᵉ siècle', in: *Islam and the Trade of Asia, ed.* D.S. RICHARDS, *op. cit.*, p. 169. Baghdad was occupied in 1534, Basra in 1535 and again in 1546.

320. Moscow, C.S.A., 276-1-365, fᵒˢ 171-5.

321. A.E., M. et D. (Turkey) 11, fᵒˢ 131-51.

322. *Brouillarts* registers in which transactions were recorded from day-to-day.

323. Pierre BELON, *Les Observations de plusieurs singularitez et choses mémorablestrouvéesenGrèce,Asie,Judée, Égypte, Arabie et autres pays estranges,* 1553, fᵒ 181 vᵒ.

324. Abbé PRÉVOST, *op. cit.*, IX, p. 88.

325. *Gazette d'Amsterdam*, 13 December 1672. Kaminiec, today Kamenec Podolsk in the Ukraine, was in succession Turkish, Tartar, Polish until 1793, then Russian.

326. Paul-Ange de GARDANE, *Journal d'un voyage dans la Turquie d'Asie et la Perse, fait en 1807 et 1808,* 1809, p. 13.

327. Marciana Library, Scritture, Oro e argento, VII, MCCXXVIII, 55.

328. The gold ducat minted by the kings of Hungary, often imitated abroad.

329. Ugo TUCCI, 'Les émissions monétaires de Venise et les mouvements internationaux de l'or', in: *Revue historique*, July 1978, p. 97, note 23.

330. *Ibid.*, p. 109, note 65.

331. F. REBUFFAT, M. COURDURIE, *Marseille et le négoce marseillais international* (1785-1790), 1966, pp. 126 ff.

332. C. SONNINI, *Traité sur le commerce de la mer Noire*, n.d.

333. A.N., A.E., B¹, 436, quoted by T. STOIANOVITCH, typescript, p. 35.

334. In his Paris lectures in 1955.

335. *Medit.*, II, p. 721.

336. *Ibid.*, I, p. 286.

337. Henri MAUNDRELL, *op. cit.*, 4th ed. 1800, p. 14.

338. In a local publication unfortunately mislaid.

339. A.d.S., Naples, Affari Esteri, 800, the Hague, 21 August 1761.

340. Moscow C.S.A., 4113, 158, fᵒ 4, Venice, 4/15 December 1787.

341. A.E., M. et D. (Turkey) 15, fᵒˢ 154-9.

342. *Observations sur l'état actuel de l'Empire ottoman* (written in French and never published in English), ed. Andrew S. EHRENKREUTZ, 1965, pp. 49-50.

343. *Ibid.*, p. 53.

344. *Ibid.*, p. 54.

345. By the treaty of Kučuk Kajnardzi.

346. By the treaty of Constaninople (January 1784) recognizing the cession of Crimea to Russia.

347. See above, Vol. I.

348. K. N. CHAUDHURI, *The Trading World of Asia and the English East India Company, 1660-1760*, 1978, p. 17.

349. A.E., M. et D. (Turkey), 11, fᵒˢ 131-51, 1750.

350. H. FURBER, *op. cit.*, p. 166.

351. A.E., M. et D. (Turkey), 11, fᵒ 162.

352. *Ibid.*, fᵒ 151, 1750.

353. H. FURBER, *op. cit.*, p. 66.

354. A.E., M. et D. (Turkey), 11, fᵒˢ 70 and 70 vᵒ.

355. *Ibid.*, fᵒ 162.

356. Moscow, C.S.A., 35/6, 371, fᵒ 32.

357. *Ibid.*, 93/6, 438, fᵒ 81.

358. Luigi CELLI, Introduction to *Due Trattati inediti di Silvestro Gozzolini da Osimo, Economista e Finanziere del sec. XVI*, 1892, p. 8.

359. Moscow, C.S.A., October 1787, incomplete reference.

360. M.-A. de BENYOWSKY, *Voyages et mémoires . . ., op. cit.*, I, p. 51.

361. 'Agenda for Ottoman History', in: *Review*, 1, 1977, p. 53.

362. Moscow, C.S.A., March 1785, complete reference mislaid.

363. *Handbuch der europäischer Geschichte*, ed. T. SCHIEDER, *op. cit.*, p. 771.

364. A.d.S. Naples, Affari Esteri, 805.

365. Michel MORINEAU, paper at Prato conference, 1977, typescript, p. 7.

366. J. ROUSSET, *Les Intérêts présens des puissances de l'Europe*, 1731, I, p. 161.

367. Ange GOUDAR, *Les Intérêts de la France mal entendus . . .*, 1756, I, p. 5.

368. For this paragraph I have drawn particularly on Giorgio Borsa, *La Nascita del mondo moderno in Asia orientale*, 1977, and Michel Devèze, *L'Europe et le monde, op. cit.*

369. Maurice Lombard, *L'Islam dans sa première grandeur*, 1971, p. 22.

370. Cf. first edn. of Vol. I, pp. 306-7.

371. The Arab name (Zendj = 'black men') for the southern coast of Somalia as far as Mozambique.

372. *Indonesian Trade and Society*, 1955.

373. The Tamil population lives in southern India and Sri Lanka (formerly Ceylon).

374. Archibald R. Lewis, 'Les marchands dans l'océan Indien', in: *Revue d'histoire économique et sociale*, 1976, p. 448.

375. *Ibid.*, p. 455.

376. *Ibid.*, pp. 455-6.

377. Donald F. Lach, *Asia in the Making of Europe*, 1970, I, p. 19.

378. Franco Venturi, *L'Europe des Lumières, recherches sur le XVIIIᵉ siècle*, 1971, pp. 138-9.

379. C.G.F. Simkin, *op. cit.*, p. 182.

380. Giorgio Borsa, *op. cit.*, p. 31.

381. A.N., Colonies, C², 254, f⁰ 15 v⁰.

382. L. Dermigny, *La Chine et l'Occident ..., op. cit.*, II, p. 696.

383. See above, chapter 3.

384. L. Simond, *Voyage d'un Français en Angleterre ..., op. cit.*, II, p. 280.

385. Victor Jacquement, *Voyage dans l'Inde ...*, 1841-1844, p. 17.

386. M. Devèze, *op. cit.*, p. 223.

387. British Museum, Sloane 1005.

388. R. Challis, *Voyage aux Indes ..., op. cit.*, p. 436.

389. A.N., Colonies, C², 105, f⁰ 233.

390. François Martin, (1640-1706) governor general of the French *Compagnie des Indes* from 1701.

391. A. N., Colonies, C² 105, fᵒˢ 256 v⁰ and 257.

392. Maestre Manrique, *op. cit.*, p. 398.

393. K. N. Chaudhuri, *op. cit.*, pp. 447-8.

394. A.N., A.E., B III, 459.

395. A.N., Colonies, C², 75, f⁰ 165.

396. Probably bonds, the short-term Company loans. Saha Panchanam, 'Einige Probleme der kapitalistischen Entwicklung Indiens im 19. Jahrhundert', in *Jahrbuch fur Wirtschaftsgeschichte*, 1970, I, pp. 155-61.

397. V. I. Pavlov, *Historical Premises for India's Transition to Capitalism*, 2nd ed., 1978, pp. 326-32.

398. K. N. Chaudhuri, *op. cit.*, p. 455.

399. *Ibid.*, p. 456.

400. Abbé Prévost, *op. cit.*, I, pp. 35, 48, 49.

401. Carlo M. Cipolla, *Guns and Sails in the early phase of European Expansion*, 1965, p. 138.

402. *Ibid.*

403. *Ibid.*

404. T. T. Chang, *Sino-Portuguese Trade from 1514 to 1644*, 1934, p. 120, quoted by C. M. Cipolla, *op. cit.*, p. 138.

405. *The Embassy of Sir Thomas Roe to the Court of the Great Moghol*, 1899, II, p. 344, quoted by G. Borsa, *op. cit.*, p. 25.

406. C. M. Cipolla, *op. cit.*, p. 139, note 17.

407. K. N. Chaudhuri, *op. cit.*, pp. 457 et 461.

408. I. Bruce Watson, 'The Establishment of English Commerce in North-Western India in the Early Seventeenth Century', in: *Indian Economic and Social History*, XIII, n⁰ 3, pp. 384-5.

409. K. N. Chaudhuri, *op. cit.*, p. 461.

410. A.N., A.E., B III, 459, Memorandum from Bolts, 19 messidor an V.

411. According to which merchants and artisans agreed to deliver goods.

412. I.B. Watson, *art. cit.*, pp. 385-9.

413. A.N., A.E., B III, 459.

414. A.N., Colonies, C², 105, fᵒˢ 218 v⁰-220.

415. A.N., Colonies, C¹¹, 10, 31 December 1750. See Pierre Poivre's quarrel with the commander of *Le Mascarin* in Canton in June 1750.

416. C. Boxer, *The Portuguese Seaborne Empire, 1415-1825*, 1969, p. 57, quoted by I. Wallerstein, *op. cit.*, p. 332.

417. V. I. Pavlov, *op. cit.*, p. 243.

418. E.g. Norman Jacobs, *Modern Capitalism and Eastern Asia*, 1958.

419. B. R. Grover, 'An Integrated Pattern of Commercial Life in the Rural Society of North India during the 17th-18th centuries', in: *India Historical Records Commission*, XXXVII, 1966, pp. 121.

420. L. C. Jain, *Indigenous Banking in India*, 1929, p. 5.

421. For a discussion of the meaning of this

word, see Irfan Habib, *The Agarian System of Mughal India*, 1963, pp. 140 ff.

422. Irfan Habib, 'Potentialities of Capitalistic Development in the Economy of Mughal India', in *Journal of Economic History*, 1969, pp. 32-78, esp. p. 39.

423. Satish Chandra, 'Some Institutional Factors in Providing Capital Inputs for the Improvement and Expansion of Cultivation in Medieval India', in: *Indian Historical Review*, 1976, p. 85.

424. *Ibid.*, p. 89.

425. B. R. Grover, art. cit., p. 130.

426. S. Chandra, art. cit., p. 84.

427. I. Habib, 'Potentialities', art. cit., *Journal of Economic History*, 1969, p. 38.

428. *Ibid.*, p. 46.

429. *Ibid.*, p 35.

430. *Ibid.*, p. 35, note 8.

431. Abbé Prévost, *op. cit.*, XI, pp. 661-2.

432. *Ibid.*, pp. 651-2.

433. *Ibid.*, p. 652.

434. The Bengal maund 34.5 kg, the Surat maund 12.7 kg (K. N. Chaudhuri, *op. cit.*, p. 472).

435. B. R. Grover, art. cit., pp. 129-30.

436. I. Habib, 'Potentialities ...' art. cit., p. 38. W. H. Moreland, *op. cit.*, pp. 99-100, 103-4.

437. I. Habib, 'Usury in Medieval India', art. cit., p. 394.

438. B. R. Grover, art. cit., p. 138.

439. The Indian state of which Bombay is the capital.

440. I. Habib, 'Potentialities ...,' art. cit., pp. 64-5.

441. *Ibid.*, p. 62.

442. Sonnerat, *Voyage aux Indes Orientales et à la Chine*, 1782, I, pp. 103 et 104.

443. *Jahangir's India: the Remonstrantie of Francisco Pelsaert*, 1925, p. 60, quoted in I. Habib, 'Potentialities', art. cit., p. 62.

444. I. Habib, 'Potentialities ..., art. cit., p. 63.

445. *Ibid.*, p. 63.

446. Abbé Prévost, *op. cit.*, X, p. 1.

447. *Ibid.*, X, p. 93.

448. *Ibid.*, X, p. 237.

449. H. Furber, *op. cit.*, p. 10.

450. I. Habib, 'Potentialities ...', art. cit., p. 69.

451. A.N., Marine, B⁷, 443, fº 254.

452. V. I. Pavlov, *op. cit.*, p. 329.

453. H. Furber, *op. cit.*, p. 187.

454. A.N., Colonies, C², 105, fº 291, vº.

455. H. Furber, *op. cit.*, pp. 189-90.

456. V. I. Pavlov, *op. cit.*, p. 233.

457. K. N. Chaudhuri, *op. cit.*, p. 260.

458. *Ibid.*, p. 258.

459. Abbé Prévost, *op. cit.*, X, p. 65.

460. I.e. without signing a contract of compulsory delivery with the artisans.

461. A.N., A.E., B III, 459, April 1814. 'Mémoire sur le commerce de l'Inde, que fesoit l'ancienne compagnie des Indes ...', fᵒˢ 1-32, *passim*. (To translate this list of gallicized names for Indian fabrics, K.N. Chaudhuri's list of fabrics (*op. cit.*, Appendix 4, pp. 501-5) has been consulted.-Trans).

462. *Ibid.*, fº 12.

463. Satish Chandra, 'Some Aspects of the Growth of a Money Economy in India during the Seventeenth Century', in: *The Indian Economic and Social History Review*, 1966, p. 326, and B. R. Grover, art. cit., p. 132.

464. B. R. Grover, art. cit., pp. 128, 129, 131.

465. *Ibid.*, p. 132.

466. The site of the French factory of Pondicherry, which suffered from shortages of food supplies as well as of goods.

467. A.N., Colonies, C², 75, fº 69.

468. Percival Spear, *The Nabobs*, 1963, pp. xiv ff.

469. A.N., C², 286, fº 280.

470. I. Habib, 'Potentialities ...,' art. cit., p. 41.

471. *Ibid.*, p. 55.

472. Abbé Prévost, *op. cit.*, X, p. 232.

473. Roland Mousnier, in: Maurice Crouzet, *Histoire générale des civilisations*, IV, 1954, p. 491.

474. Abbé Prévost, *op. cit.*, X, p. 235.

475. *Trousses*, folded cloaks which were slung behind the saddle.

476. A.N., Colonies, C², 56, fᵒˢ 17 vº ff., 1724. Cloth imports in this period were worth 50,000 *écus* a year.

477. Abbé Prévost, *op. cit.*, X, p. 245.

478. I. Habib, 'Potentialities ..., art. cit., pp. 59 ff.

479. *Ibid.*, pp. 59.

480. Abbé Prévost, *op. cit.*, X, p. 146.

481. François BERNIER, *Voyages ...
contenant la description des États du
Grand Mogol ...*, 1699, I, p. 94.
482. Abbé PRÉVOST, *op. cit.*, X, p. 235.
483. *Ibid.*, X, p. 95.
484. P. SPEAR, *op. cit.*, p. xiii.
485. M. N. PEARSON, 'Shivaji and the Decline
of the Mughal Empire', in : *Journal of
Asian Studies*, 1970, p. 370.
486. A. K. MAJUMDAR, 'L'India nel Medioevo
e al principio dell'età moderna' in:
Propyläen Weltsgeschichte, ... (Italian
translation), VI, 1968, p. 191.
487. *Ibid.*, p. 189.
488. A Hindu sect devoted to Vishnu, founded
in the early sixteenth century. The
Sikhs founded the kingdom of Lahore.
489. H. FURBER, *op. cit.*, p. 303.
490. A. K. MAJUMDAR, *op. cit.*, p. 195.
491. *Medit ...*, I, p. 371.
492. H. FURBER, *op. cit.*, p. 25.
493. Giuseppe PAPAGNO, 'Monopolio e libertà
di commercio nell'Africa orientale
portoghese alla luce di alcuni documenti
settecenteschi', in: *Rivista storica
italiana*, 1974, II, p. 273.
494. A.N., A.E., B III, 459, Memorandium
from Louis Monneron, 1 Prairial An IV.
495. A.N., 8 AQ 349.
496. T. RAYCHAUDHURI, *Readings in Indian
Economy*, 1964, p. 17, quoted by V. I.
PAVLOV, *op. cit.*, p. 87.
497. V. I. PAVLOV, *op. cit.*, pp. 86–8.
498. *Ibid.*, pp. 239 ff.
499. *Ibid.*, pp. 324–35.
500. *Ibid.*, pp. 99 ff.
501. K. N. CHAUDHURI, *op. cit.*, p. 273.
502. V. I. PAVLOV, *op. cit.*, p. 215.
503. *Ibid.*, p. 216.
504. *Ibid.*, p. 217. This was no doubt why, if
the English did import steel to India in
the eighteenth century, in particular for
shipbuilding, it was always Swedish,
never British steel.
505. Armando CORTESÃO, in: *The Suma
Oriental* by Tome PIRES, 1944, II, pp.
278–9; V. MAGALHÃES GODINHO, *op. cit.*,
p. 783.

506. M. A. P. MEILINK-ROELOFSZ, *Asian Trade
and European Influence*, 1962, pp. 13 ff.
507. O. W. WOLTERS, *Early Indonesian
Commerce*, 1967, pp. 45 ff.
508. Abbé PRÉVOST, *op. cit.*, VIII, p. 316.
509. *Ibid.*, VIII, p. 312.
510. *Ibid.*, IX, 74 (1622).
511. *Ibid.*, XI, p. 632.
512. SONNERAT, *op. cit.*, II, p. 100.
513. On these questions see G. COEDES's
classic study 'Les Etats hindouisés
d'Indochine et d'Indonésie', 1948, in
Histoire du monde, ed. M. E.
CAVAIGNAC, vol. VII.
514. M. A. P. MEILINK-ROELOFSZ, in: *Islam
and the Trade of Asia*, ed. D. S.
RICHARDS, *op. cit.*, pp. 137 ff.
515. Luis Filipe F. R. THOMAZ, 'Maluco e
Malaca', in: *A Viagem de Fernão de
Magalhães e a questão das Molucas*, ed. A.
TEIXERA, 1975, pp. 33 ff.
516. *Ibid.*, p. 33.
517. Quoted in PAVLOV, *op. cit.*, p. 221.
518. *Ibid.*
519. Abbé PRÉVOST, *op. cit.*, I, p. 116.
520. *Ibid.*, I, p. 115.
521. M. A. Hedwig FITZLER, 'Der Anteil der
Deutschen an der Kolonialpolitik
Philipps II von Spanien in Asien' in:
*Vierteljahrschrift für Sozial-und
Wirtschaftsgeschichte*, 1935, p. 251.
522. L. F. F. R. THOMAZ, art. cit., p. 36.
523. Abbé PRÉVOST, *op. cit.*, I, p. 336 (1592).
524. *Ibid.*, VI, pp. 62–3.
525. *Ibid.*, VIII, pp. 480 ff.
526. *Op cit*, pp. 160 ff.
527. A.N., Colonies, C^{11}, f^0 10 v^0.
528. *Op. cit.*, p. 174.
529. *Voyage en Inde du comte de Modave,
1773-1776*, ed. J. DELOCHE, 1971,
p. 77.
530. *Ibid.*
531. 'I. Wallerstein et l'Extrême-Orient,
plaidoyer pour un xvie siècle négligé',
Leyden Conference, October 1978,
typescript.
532. 'Littoral et intérieur de l'Inde', Leyden
Conference, October 1978, typescript.

NOTES TO CHAPTER 6

1. Cf. LITTRÉ, *Révolution:* 'Return of a star to
the point it started from'.

2. Hannah ARENDT, *On Revolution*, 1963.
3. Jürgen KUCZYNSKI, 'Friedrich Engels und

die Monopole', in: *Jahrbuch für Wirtschaftsgeschichte*, 1970, 3, pp. 37-40.

4. Adolphe BLANQUI, *Histoire de l'économie politique en Europe depuis les Anciens jusqu'à nos jours*, 1837, II, p. 209. 'Hardly had it sprung from the brains of those two men of genius, Watt and Arkwright, than the Industrial Revolution took possession of England'; cf. R.M. HARTWELL, *The Industrial Revolution and economic growth*, 1971, p. 111; Peter MATHIAS, *The First Industrial Nation. An Economic History of Britain 1700-1914*, 1969, p. 3.

5. Maurice DOBB, *Études sur le développement du capitalisme*, 1969, p. 274, note 3; A. BESANÇON, in: *Quarterly Journal of Economics*, XXXVI, 1921, p. 343.

6. W.W. ROSTOW, *The Stages of Economic Growth*, 1960.

7. Simon KUZNETS, *Economic Growth of Nations*, 1971.

8. Simon KUZNETS, 'Capital formation in Modern Economic Growth', Third International Economic History Conference, Munich, 1965, I, p. 20, note 1.

9. Phyllis DEANE, *The First Industrial Revolution*, 1965, p. 117.

10. 'Encore la révolution anglaise du XVIIIᵉ siècle', in: *Bulletin de la Société d'histoire moderne*, 1961, p. 6.

11. In the preface to the French translation of T.S. ASHTON, *The Industrial Revolution*, 1955.

12. J. HICKS, *A Theory of Economic History*, op. cit., pp. 151-4.

13. J.-B. SAY, *Cours complet d'économie politique*, op. cit., II, p. 170.

14. T.S. ASHTON, 'The Treatment of Capitalism by Historians', in: *Capitalism and the Historians*, ed. F.A. HAYEK, 1954, p. 60.

15. P. Deane, op. cit., pp. 116, 117 and note 1, after W.W. ROSTOW, *The Economics of Take off into Sustained Growth*, 1963.

16. Ignacy SACHS, *Pour une économie politique du développement*, 1977, p. 9.

17. *Ibid.*

18. This quotation from the Chilean economist Oswaldo SUNKEL, is taken from I. SACHS, op. cit., p. 34.

19. Ignancy SACHS, *La Découverte du Tiers Monde*, 1971, pp. 18-30.

20. *Ibid.*

21. A.N., F¹², 1512 C, bundle 5.

22. Lynn WHITE, *Medieval Technology and Social Change*, 1962, p. 80; M. ROSTOVTZEFF, *The Social and Economic History of the Hellenistic World*, 1967, I, p. 365.

23. Stephen Finney MASON, *A History of the Sciences*, 1953, p. 48.

24. A. VIERENDEL, *Esquisse d'une histoire de la technique*, 1921, I, p. 38.

25. Edward Fox, *History in a Geographical Perspective, The Other France*, 1971, *op. cit.*

26. *La Révolution industrielle du Moyen Age*, 1975.

27. *La Crise du féodalisme*, 1976.

28. 'An Industrial Revolution of the thirteenth Century', in: *Economic History Review*, 1941.

29. The expression had earlier been used of Germany, either by G.F. von SCHMOLLER or by F. PHILIPPI.

30. Eleonora M. CARUS WILSON, 'The Woollen Industry' in: *The Cambridge Economic History*, II, 1952, p. 409.

31. *Little Red Book of Bristol*, ed. F.B. BICKLEY, 1900, 58, II, 7.

32. Frederic C. LANE, 'Units of Economic Growth historically considered', in: *Kyklos*, XV, 1962, pp. 95-104.

33. W. ABEL, *Agrarkrisen und Agrarkonjunktur*, op. cit., p. 51.

34. C.M. CIPOLLA, 'The Professions, The Long View', in: *The Journal of European Economic History*, Spring 1973, p. 41.

35. G. BOIS, op. cit., p. 246.

36. Roger BACON, quoted by L. WHITE, *Medieval Technology ...*, op. cit., p. 134.

37. Jacob Cornelius VAN LEUR, *Indonesian Trade and Society*, 1955, p. 20.

38. See above, Vol. II.

39. Herman KELLENBENZ, *Deutsche Wirtschaftsgeschichte*, I, 1977, p. 167.

40. Gemma MIANI, 'L'économie lombarde aux XIVᵉ et XVᵉ siècles', in: *Annales E.S.C.*, June 1964, p. 571.

41. Renato ZANGHERI, 'Agricoltura e sviluppo del capitalismo', In: *Studi storici*, 1968, p. 539.

42. Eric J. HOBSBAWM, 'Il secolo XVII nello sviluppo del capitalismo', in: *Studi storici*, 1959-1960, p. 665.
43. Carlo PONI 'All' origine del Sistema di fabbrica . . .', in: *Rivista storica italiana*, 1976, pp. 444. ff.
44. L. WHITE, *op. cit.*, p. 129.
45. *Ibid.*, p. 28.
46. Gino BARBIERI, *Le Origini del capitalismo lombardo*, 1961; G. MIANI, art. cit.
47. John U. NEF, 'The Progress of Technology and the Growth of Large-Scale Industry in Great Britain, 1540-1640', in: *Economic History Review*, October 1934, p. 23.
48. S. POLLARD and D.W. CROSSLEY, *The Wealth of Britain . . .*, *op. cit.*, 1968.
49. John CLEVELAND, *Poems*, 1650, p. 10.
50. John U. NEF, art. cit., pp. 3-24.
51. S. POLLARD and D.W. CROSSLEY, *op. cit*, p. 85.
52. *Ibid.*, p. 130.
53. *Ibid.*, pp. 84 and 95.
54. Charles HYDE, *Technological Change and the British Iron Industry, 1700-1820*, 1977.
55. See the section on technology, later in this chapter.
56. C. HYDE, *op. cit.*, pp. 42 ff., 144.
57. S. POLLARD et D. W. CROSSLEY, *op. cit.*, pp. 105 and 136-7.
58. *Ibid.*
59. *Ibid.*, pp. 142-3.
60. John U. NEF, *The Conquest of the Material World*, 1964, pp. 141-3.
61. 'The Origins of the Industrial Revolution', in: *Past and Present*, April 1960, pp. 71-81.
62. *L'Industrialisation en Europe au XIXe siècle*, ed. Pierre LÉON, François CROUZET, Richard GASCON, Lyon, 7-10 October 1970, 1972.
63. Pierre VILAR, 'La Catalogne industrielle. Réflexions sur un démarrage et sur un destin', in: *L'Industrialisation en Europe au XIXe siècle*, *op. cit.*, p. 421.
64. Jacques BERTIN, *ibid.*, p. 477.
65. M.W. FLINN, *The Origins of the Industrial Revolution*, 1965, p. 96
66. H.J. HABAKKUK, 'Historical Experience of Economic Development', in: E.A.G. ROBINSON ed., *Problems of Economic Development*, 1955, p. 123.
67. Paul BAIROCH, *Révolution industrielle et sous-dévelopment*, 1974, p. 73.
68. E.L. JONES, 'Le origini agricole dell'industria', in: *Studi storici*, IX, 1968, p. 567. (This article is similar to but not identical with the same writer's 'Agricultural origins of industry', in *Past and Present*, 40, 1968, pp. 58 ff.)
69. Jethro TULL, *The Horse Hoeing Husbandry*, 1733.
70. Jonathan David CHAMBERS and Gordon Edmund MINGAY, *The Agricultural Revolution 1750-1880*, 1966, pp. 2-3.
71. *Ibid.*
72. *Ibid.*
73. *Ibid.*
74. P. BAIROCH, *op. cit.*, tables pp. 222 et 226; P. MATHIAS, *The First Industrial Nation*, *op. cit.*, table, p. 474.
75. Charles-Alexandre de BAERT-DUHOLANT, *Tableau de la Grande-Bretagne . . .*, *op. cit.*, IV, pp. 242-3.
76. E.L. JONES, art. cit., pp. 568 ff. (Cf. art. cit , *Past and Present* 1968, pp. 62 ff.)
77. E.A. WRIGLEY, in: *Past and Present*, 1967, quoted by E.L. JONES, art. cit., p. 569.
78. E.L. JONES, art. cit., p. 570, or *Past and Present* article p. 63
79. *Ibid.*, pp. 572-4.
80. J.D. CHAMBERS and G.E. MINGAY, *op. cit.*, p. 18.
81. *Ibid.*, pp. 199-201.
82. M. RUBICHON, *op. cit.*, II, p. 13.
83. Abbé J.-B. LE BLANC, *Lettres d'un Français*, *op. cit.*, II, pp. 64 and 66-7.
84. M. RUBICHON, *op. cit.*, II, pp. 12-13.
85. *Ibid.*, II, p. 122.
86. P. BAIROCH, *op. cit.*, p. 87.
87. *Ibid.*, p. 215.
88. R. REINHARD, A. ARMENGAUD, J. DUPAQUIER, *Histoire générale de la population mondiale*, 1968, pp. 202 ff.
89. Roland MARX, *La Révolution industrielle en Grande-Bretagne des origines à 1850*, 1970, pp. 57-8.
90. *Ibid.*
91. Alexis de TOQUEVILLE, *Voyages en Angleterre*, 1958, pp. 59 and 78.
92. E. HOBSBAWM, *Industry and Empire*, op. cit., p. 40.
93. In: *L'Industrialisation en Europe au*

XIXe siècle, op. cit., p. 590.

94. P. DEANE, *op. cit.*, p. 34.
95. E. HOBSBAWM, *op. cit.*, p. 42.
96. *A History of Technology*, ed. C. SINGER, E.J. HOLMYARD, A.R. HALL, T.L. WILLIAMS, 1958, IV, pp. 301-3.
97. P. BAIROCH, *op. cit.*, p. 20.
98. *The Trading World of Asia and The English East India Company 1660-1760, op. cit.*, pp. 273 ff.
99. Only 10% by 1791, Ch. HYDE, *Technological Change . . ., op. cit.*, p. 66.
100. P. BAIROCH, *op. cit.*, p. 249.
101. C. HYDE, *op. cit.*, p. 219.
102. *Ibid.*, pp. 47-51.
103. *Ibid.*, pp. 37-40.
104. *Ibid.*, pp. 57 and 79.
105. *Ibid.*, p. 71.
106. *Ibid.*, p. 93.
107. *Ibid.*, pp. 83-94.
108. Francis K. KLINGENDER, *Art and the Industrial Revolution*, 1968, pp. 9-10.
109. *Histoire générale des techniques*, ed. M. DAUMAS, 1962, III, p. 59.
110. *Ibid.*, p. 13.
111. David S. LANDES, *The Unbound Prometheus*, p. 88.
112. Emile LEVASSEUR, *La Population française*, 1889-1892, III, p. 74.
113. E.A. WRIGLEY, 'The Supply of Raw Material in the Industrial Revolution', in: *The Economic History Review*, art. cit., p. 13.
114. J. HICKS, *op. cit.*, 2nd ed., 1973, p. 147.
115. E. LABROUSSE, in: *L'Industrialisation de l'Europe au XIXe siècle, op. cit.*, p. 590.
116. P. DEANE, *op. cit.*, pp. 90-1.
117. E. HOBSBAWM, *Industry and Empire, op. cit.*, p. 51.
118. P. MATHIAS, *op. cit.*, p. 250.
119. E. HOBSBAWM, *The Age of Revolution*, 1973 edn., p. 54 and note.
120. *Ibid.*, p. 52.
121. *Ibid.*, p. 57.
122. *Ibid.*, p. 54.
123. J.H. CLAPHAM, *An Economic History of Modern Britain*, 1926, pp. 441-2.
124. Quoted by E. HOBSBAWM, *Industry and Empire, op. cit.*, p. 40.
125. L. SIMOND, *op. cit.*, I, p. 330. The first bale of American cotton arrived in about 1791.
126. Quoted by P. DEANE, *op. cit.*, p. 87.

127. After 1820 for cotton, after 1850 for wool; S. POLLARD and D.W. CROSSLEY *op. cit.*, p. 197.
128. L. SIMOND, *op. cit.*, II, pp. 102-3.
129. P. MATHIAS, *op. cit.*, p. 270.
130. P. DEANE, *op. cit.*, p. 56.
131. J. ACCARIAS DE SÉRIONNE, *La Richesse de la Hollande, op. cit.*
132. François CROUZET, *L'Economie britannique et le blocus continental 1806-1813*, 1958, I, p. 157.
133. P. DEANE, *op. cit.*, p. 56.
134. M. RUBICHON, *op. cit.*, II, p. 312.
135. Thomas S. ASHTON, *An Economic History of England. The 18th Century*, 1955, pp. 132 ff.
136. F. CROUZET, *op. cit.*, pp. 294 ff.
137. M. RUBICHON, *op. cit.*, II, p. 382, I have replaced the word 'guerrillas' in the original by 'guerilleros'.
138. W.W. ROSTOW, *op. cit.*, p. 560.
139. L. SIMOND, *op. cit.*, II, p. 284.
140. *Ibid.*, p. 282.
141. M. RUBICHON, *op. cit.*, I, p. 575.
142. *On Depreciation*, p. 69.
143. P. DEANE, *op. cit.*, pp. 58 ff.
144. D. MACPHERSON, *op. cit.*, III, p. 340.
145. T.S. ASHTON, *op. cit.*, p. 63.
146. P. MATHIAS, *op. cit.*, p. 466.
147. AMALENDU GUHA, review of P. MATHIAS, *The First Industrial Nation, op. cit.*, in: *The Indian Economic and Social History Review*, vol. 7, September 1970, pp. 428-30.
148. See above, chapter 4.
149. As D. MACPHERSON says, cf. note 144.
150. P. DEANE, W.A. COLE, *British Economic Growth*, 1688-1959, 1962, p. 48.
151. Which was a quite normal percentage, cf. M. RUBICHON, *op. cit.*, I, p. 574.
152. T.S. WILLAN, *The Inland Trade. op. cit.*, ch. 1.
153. R.-M. PILLET, *L'Angleterre vue à Londres et dans ses provinces, op. cit.*; 'Colliers' are of course ships carrying coal.
154. *Historical Geography of England before 1800*, 1951, ed. H.C. DARBY, p. 522.
155. D. DEFOE, *Tour . . .*, I, p. 63, quoted by H.C. DARBY, *op. cit.*, p. 498.
156. T.S. WILLAN, *River Navigation in England . . ., op. cit.*
157. *Ibid.*, p. 94.
158. C. DUPIN, *op. cit.*, p. 163, note.

159. *Ibid.*, p. 171.
160. M. RUBICHON, *op. cit.*, II, p. 111.
161. T.S. WILLAN, *The Inland Trade, op. cit.*
162. J.H. CLAPHAM, *op. cit.*, pp. 381-2.
163. C. DUPIN, *op. cit.*, pp. 148 ff.
164. P. MATHIAS, *op. cit.*, p. 277.
165. C. DUPIN, *op. cit.*, p. 149.
166. *Ibid.*, p. 144.
167. *Ibid.*, p. 157.
168. M. CUCHETET, *Voyage de Manchester à Liverpool par le Rail Way et la voiture à vapeur*, 1833, p. 6.
169. *Ibid.*, p. 11.
170. *Ibid.*, p. 9.
171. *Ibid.*, p. 8.
172. Charles P. KINDLEBERGER, *Economic Development*, 1958, p. 96.
173. J.R. HARRIS, in: *L'Industrialisation de l'Europe au XIXᵉ siècle, op. cit.*, p. 230.
174. M. RUBICHON, *op. cit.*, I, pp. 529-30.
175. See above, section on international trade.
176. *Op. cit.*
177. D. DEFOE, *Tour ..., op. cit.*, 1927 ed., I, p. 2
178. P. ADAM, typescript, p. 92.
179. D.C. NORTH, R.P. THOMAS, *The Rise of the Western World*, 1973, p. 157.
180. John HICKS, *Value and Capital*, 1939, p. 302, quoted by R.M. HARTWELL, *op. cit.*, p. 114.
181. Jean ROMEUF, *Dictionnaire ...*, I, p. 354.
182. My italics; Y. BERNARD, J.-C. COLLI, D. LEWANDOWSKI, *Dictionnaire ... op. cit.*, p. 401.
183. *Op. cit.*, pp. 185 ff.
184. S. KUZNETS, *op. cit.*, *Economic growth of nations.*
185. 'Prise de vues sur la croissance de l'économie française ...', art. cit., pp. 46-7.
186. P. BAIROCH, *op. cit.*, p. 44, table IV.
187. Gaston IMBERT, *Des mouvements de longue durée Kondratieff*, 1959.
188. E.H. PHELPS BROWN, Sheila V. HOPKINS, ' Seven Centuries of Building Wages', in: *Economica*, August 1955, p. 197.
189. R.M. HARTWELL, *op. cit.*, p. XVII.
190. S. KUZNETS, *op. cit.*, pp. 303 ff.
191. Quoted by Raymond ARON, *Les Étapes de la pensée sociologique*, 1967, p. 321.
192. See above, Vol. II.
193. J. HICKS, *op. cit.*, p. 155 ' ... It was casual labour that was the typical condition of the preindustrial proletariat.'
194. See above, Vol II.
195. Neil J. SMELSER, *Social Change in the Industrial Revolution. An application of Theory to the Lancashire Cotton Industry 1770-1840*, 1967, p. 147.
196. P. MATHIAS, *op. cit.*, p. 202.
197. *Ibid.*, p. 203.
198. A.E., C.C. London, fᵒˢ 146-51, 13 March 1817.
199. Neil J. SMELSER, *op. cit.*, pp. 129 ff.
200. *Ibid.*, p. 165.
201. L. SIMOND, *op. cit.*, II, p. 103.
202. E. HOBSBAWM, *Industry and Empire, op. cit.*, p. 51.
203. *Ibid.*, p. 55.
204. P. MATHIAS, *op. cit.*, p. 170.
205. *Ibid.*, p. 151.
206. *Ibid.*, p. 152.
207. *Ibid.*, pp. 152-3.
208. The residue from malt after brewing.
209. L. SIMOND, *op. cit.*, pp. 193-4.
210. P. MATHIAS, *op. cit.*, p. 153.
211. *Ibid.*, p. 154.
212. R.M. HARTWELL, 'The Tertiary Sector in English Economy during the Industrial Revolution', in: *L'Industrialisation de l'Europe ..., op. cit.*, pp. 213-27.
213. P. MATHIAS, *op. cit.*, p. 263.
214. R.-M. PILLET, *op. cit.*
215. Cf. the debates at the Lyon conference, *L'Industrialisation de L'Europe*, esp. p. 228.
216. See above, chapter 4.
217. H.C. DARBY, *op. cit.*
218. Cf among others, the classic studies by A.N. DODD, *The Industrial Revolution in North Wales*, 1933; H. HAMILTON, *The Industrial Revolution in Scotland*, 1932; J.D. CHAMBERS, *Nottinghamshire in the Eighteenth Century*, 1932; W.H.B. COURT, *The Rise of the Midland Industries*, 1938; T.C. SMOUT, *A History of the Scottish People 1560-1830, op. cit.*
219. E.L. JONES, 'The constraints of Economic Growth in Southern England 1660-1840 in Munich Conference of Economic History, 1965.
220. *England in the Reign of Charles II*, 1934.
221. *English Social History*, 1942, p. 298.
222. Albert DEMANGEON, 'Iles Britanniques', in: *Géographie universelle*, I, 1927, p. 219.

223. *Ibid.*, p. 149.
224. G.M. Trevelyan, *op. cit.*, p. 298 et note 1. These figures indicate a per capita income higher in the north than the south (£10 as against £7) which may mean that ordinary people were better off north of Gloucester.
225. A. Demangeon, *op. cit.*, p. 149.
226. T.S. Smout, paper given at Prato, 1978.
227. Rudolf Hilferding, *Das Finanzkapital*, 1910, French edition of 1970.
228. *Ibid.*, pp. 311-12.
229. See above, chapters 2 and 3.
230. R. Hilferding, *op. cit.*, pp. 175-7.
231. François Crouzet, *L'Economie de la Grande-Bretagne victorienne*, 1978, p. 280.
232. P. Mathias, *op. cit.*, p. 169.
233. In 1826 out of 552 banks, 49 had one director, 157 had 2, 108 had 4, 43 had 5, and 26 had 6. A.E. C.C. London, 21, f°s 168-77, 22 March 1826.
234. The French diplomatic reports often translate 'Country Bank' slightly misleadingly as *banque de comté*.
235. P. Mathias, *op. cit.*, p. 170.
236. *Ibid.*, p. 171.
237. *Ibid.*, p. 176.
238. *Ibid.*, pp. 172-3.
239. *Ibid.*, pp. 171-2.
240. A.E., C.C., London, 27, 319-51, 12, 1837.
241. M. Rubichon, *op. cit.*, II, p. 259.
242. Chevalier Séguier, London, 5 August 1818; A.E., C.C. London, 13, f° 274.
243. W. Bagehot, *Lombard Street, a description of the money market*, 1873, p. 21.
244. A.E., C.C., London, 22, f° 275, London, 24 July 1828.
245. A.E., C.C., London, 12, f° 38 v°.
246. T.S. Ashton, 'The Bill of Exchange and Private Banks in Lancashire 1790-1830' in *Papers and English Monetary History*, ed. T.S. Ashton et R.S. Sayers, 1953, pp. 37-49.

247. A.E., C.C. London, 20, f° 29, London, 10 February 1825.
248. T.S. Ashton, *The Industrial Revolution*, 1948, p. 108.
249. P. Deane and W.A. Cole, *op. cit.*, p. 296.
250. *Ibid.*, p. 305.
251. S. Pollard and D.W. Crossley, *Wealth ... op. cit.*, p. 199.
252. P. Deane and W.A. Cole, *op. cit.*, pp. 166 et 175.
253. *Ibid.*, pp. 304-5.
254. A.E., C.C. London, 13, f° 357, 6 September 1818.
255. W. Bagehot, *Lombard Street*, 1873, p. 31.
256. *Economic Fluctuations in England 1700-1800*, 1959.
257. P. Mathias, *op. cit.*, pp. 227 ff.
258. The terminology now familiar to French historians from the work of E. Labrousse.
259. A.E., C.C. London, 101, 14 November 1829.
260. See above, chapter 3.
261. P. Mathias, *op. cit.*, p. 404.
262. *Ibid.*, p. 144.
263. P. Bairoch, *Révolution industrielle, op. cit.*, p. 271, table n° 28.
264. E.H. Phelps Brown and S. Hopkins, art. cit., pp. 195-206.
265. S. Pollard and D.W. Crossley, *op. cit.*, p. 185.
266. *Ibid.*
267. R.-M. Pillet, *op. cit.*
268. *Ibid.*, p. 30.
269. *Ibid.*, p. 24.
270. L. Simond, *op. cit.*, I, p. 223.
271. *Ibid.*, II, p. 285.
272. R.-M. Pillet, *op. cit.*, p. 31.
273. *Ibid.*, p. 350.
274. *Ibid.*, p. 337.
275. *Ibid.*, p. 345.
276. W. Abel, *Agrarkrisen und Agrarkonjunktur op. cit.*
277. R. Baehrel, *Une Croissance: la Basse-Provence rurale (fin du XVIe-1789)*, 1961.

NOTES TO CONCLUSION

1. Émile Callot, *Ambiguïtés et antinomies de l'histoire et de sa philosophie*, 1962, p. 107, quoting Marc Bloch, *Apologie pour l'histoire ou métier d'historien*, 5th ed., 1964, p. 10.
2. Theodor Mommsen, *Römische*

Geschichte, (many times quoted critically by Marx in *Capital*, always referred to as *Herr* i.e. *Mr* Mommsen). Cf. Berlin edn. of *Das Kapital*, 1947-1951, II, p. 175, n. 39; III, p. 359, n. 47 and 857, n. 45. The crucial passage is perhaps the following, from the third volume of *Capital*, Ch. XLVII, 'Introductory Remarks': 'Even in the agricultural societies of antiquity, which show the greatest analogy to capitalist agriculture, namely Carthage and Rome, the similarity with plantation management is greater than with that form which really corresponds to the capitalist mode of exploitation. There existed at one time a formal analogy which however appears as a deception in all essential parts to a man familiar with the capitalist mode of production and who does not, like Mr Mommsen, discover a capitalist mode of production in every monetary economy'.

3. See esp. *Storia economia e sociale dell'impero*, 1933, p. 66, challenged by Paul VEYNE, 'Vie de Trimalchion' in *Annales E.S.C.*, 1961, p. 237.

4. Cf. the position he several times takes up, esp. in *Les Etapes sociales du capitalisme*.

5. Theodore ZELDIN, *France 1848-1945*, 1973, I, p. 75.

6. Jacqueline GRAPIN, in: *Le Monde*, 11-12 November 1973.

7. *Découvertes d'histoire sociale*, 1920, p. 58.

8. Marteng BUIST, *At Spes non fracta*, 1974, p. 431.

9. 'Appunti sull'economia contemporanea: il dibattito attorno all'azione dello Stato nel capitalismo maturo', in: *Rassegna Economica*, 1978, pp. 279-88.

10. C. OFFE, *Lo Stato nel capitalismo maturo*, 1977.

11. James R. O'CONNOR, *The Fiscal Crisis of the State*, 1977.

12. *Op. cit.*, p. 13.

13. Quoted by Paul MATTICK, *Marx et Keynes*, 1972, p. 11.

14. François Richard, *Injustice et inégalité*.

15. René RÉMOND, '"Nouvelle droite" ou droite de toujours', in: *Le Monde*, 20 July 1979.

16. See esp.: *The Reputation of the American Businessman*, 1955, and *The Image of the American Entrepreneur: transformation of a Social Symbol*, 1963.

17. *Paris Match*, 23 March 1979.

18. In private conversation and also in an unpublished typescript, translated from the Russian, in my possession.

19. See note 17.

20. *L'Express*, 9-15 June 1979.

21. Alain VERNHOLES, in *Le Monde*, 21 July 1979, but cf. *ibid.*, September 1979 – famine was already threatening again in Uttar Pradesh.

22. O'CONNOR is quoted in CAFFE *art. cit.*, pp. 285-6; cf. J.K. GALBRAITH, *Economics and the Public Purpose*, 1974, *passim*.

23. Jason ERSTEIN, 'The Last Days of New York', in *New York Review of Books*, 19 February 1976.

24. Conference organized at Paris by the Maison des Sciences de l'Homme and the Bocconi University of Milan, 22-3 February 1979, on 'Small businesses in the European economic system'. The paper referred to was given by Professor Francesco BRAMBILLA.

25. Quoted by Basile KERBLAY, *Les Marchés paysans en URSS*, 1968, pp. 113-14. The quotations from Lenin are from the Russian edition of his collected works, vol. 31, pp. 7-8, and vol. 32, pp. 196, 268, 273.

Index

About the Author

FERNAND BRAUDEL (1902–1985) received a degree in history in 1923 and subsequently taught in Algeria, Paris and São Paulo. He spent five years as a prisoner of war in Germany, during which time he wrote his grand thesis, *The Mediterranean and the Mediterranean World in the Age of Philip II,* which was published in 1949. In 1946 he became a member of the editorial board of *Annales,* the famous journal founded by Marc Bloch and Lucian Febvre, whom he succeeded at the Collège de France in 1949. He was a member of the Ecole Pratique des Hautes Etudes, and from 1962 until his death he was chief administrator of the Maison des Sciences de l'Homme. Professor Braudel held honorary doctorates from universities all over the world.